ROMANS

Paul Barnett

'Paul Barnett's refreshing commentary on the Letter to the Romans is marked by warmth, clarity, careful exegesis of the text, and a fine grasp of the historical circumstances surrounding this letter. Throughout his exposition Dr Barnett sensitively applies the apostle's profound, yet much-needed, message to our own context. I warmly commend this clear exposition of the apostle Paul's gospel.'

Peter O'Brien, Moore College, Sydney

'I am a huge fan of the writing of Paul Barnett and here again he has delivered the goods! He combines a thoroughgoing exegesis which is sane and helpful, as well as lucid and well argued, with a pastor's heart and a good eye for application. This is a brilliant commentary on a key book, which I warmly and wholeheartedly recommend. Every preacher and lay reader should have it and read it!'

Wallace Benn, Bishop of Lewes

'Distinguished New Testament historian and pastor, Paul Barnett, has given us a clearly written commentary on Romans which, while critically conversant with the present debate over the new perspective, is clear and accessible to preachers and Bible teachers. The deft hand of a scholar preacher is everywhere evident in the neat organization, precision, lucid explanative and warmth of this most helpful work.'

**R. Kent Hughes, College Church,
Wheaton, Illinois**

ROMANS

The Revelation of God's Righteousness

Paul Barnett

CHRISTIAN
FOCUS

Paul Barnett is retired Bishop of North Sydney, Visiting Fellow in History at Macquarie University, Senior Fellow in the Ancient History Documentary Research Centre, Macquarie University, Teaching Fellow at Regent College, Vancouver and Faculty Member Moore Theological College Sydney. He was also Head of Robert Menzies College, Macquarie University. He has also written another Focus on the Bible commentary - *1 Corinthians: Holiness and Hope of a Rescued People* (ISBN 978-1-85792-598-2)

ISBN 1-84550-269-8
ISBN 978-1-84550-269-0

© Paul Barnett 2003

10 9 8 7 6 5 4 3 2 1

Published in 2003
Reprinted 2007
in the
Focus on the Bible Commentary Series
by
Christian Focus Publications,
Geanies House, Fearn, Ross-shire,
IV20 1TW, Scotland, UK

www.christianfocus.com

Cover design by Danie Van Straaten

Printed by CPD Wales

Contents

Introduction 7

Part A – Sin

1. The Apostle, the Gospel and the Romans (1:1-17) 21
2. God's Judgement Day Now (1:18–3:20) 41

Part B – Justified by Faith

3. The Righteousness of God (3:21-31) 75
4. Abraham, Man of Faith (4:1-25) 87
5. Justified and Reconciled (5:1-11) 99

Part C – From Plight to Salvation

6. Adam and Christ (5:12-21) 113
7. De-thronement of King Sin (6:1-23) 129
8. Deliverance (7:1–8:4) 153
9. The Spirit of Hope (8:5-39) 175

Part D – The Salvation of Israel

10. More Than a Potter (9:1-33) 207
11. The End of the Law (10:1-21) 225
12. The Triumph of Mercy (11:1-36) 243

Part E – The Law of the Spirit

13. The Appeal (12:1–13:14) 265
14. Welcome the Weak (14:1–15:6) 297

Part F – Missionary Statesman

15. Paul's Apostolic Travel to Rome (15:7-33) 325
16. Christians in Rome (16:1-27) 351

Brief Bibliography 367
Subject Index 369
Scripture Index 381

To Janet Penman Simpson
Missionary, Mother-in-Law, Friend

Introduction

1 Paul's story so far

We know when and where Paul wrote to the Christians in Rome. It was in the year 57 when he spent three months in Corinth as house guest of a wealthy man named Gaius.[1] Paul arranged for the letter to be brought to Rome by Phoebe, a deacon in the nearby church of Cenchreae.[2]

Paul was then in his early fifties.[3] This means he had been a Christian and an apostle for about twenty-five years. His first fifteen years as 'a man in Christ' are called his 'unknown years'. We catch glimpses of him in various places – Damascus, 'Arabia,' Jerusalem and Judaea, Tarsus in Syria-Cilicia and Antioch in Syria. He was still known as Saul. No letter by him has survived from those years.

In the year 47, however, Paul (as he soon became known) set out with a sequence of companions establishing churches westwards from the eastern Mediterranean region. As a Roman citizen Paul appears to have favoured making a Christian base in major cities of Roman provinces, for example, in Antioch in Galatia, in Philippi and Thessalonica in Macedonia, in Corinth in Achaia and in Ephesus in Asia.

As Christ's 'apostle' to the non-Jews ('Gentiles') Paul was keen to preach in Rome, the world capital of the pagan empire. He was frustrated in this ambition by the action of the Roman emperor of the day. In the year 49 Claudius expelled

---

1. Acts 20:2; Romans 16:23.
2. Romans 16:1-2.
3. This conjecture is based on several others, that (1) Stephen's death occurred in 33/34, and (2) that the 'young man' Saul/Paul was about thirty years of age at that time (Acts 7:58).

Jews from Rome and this effectively blocked Paul's way to the imperial capital. Five years later, however, Claudius died and his successor Nero made it possible for Jews to come to Rome.

In the meantime, however, another man – who is unnamed – had laid a 'foundation' in the city so that Paul did not feel free to visit Rome for a sustained ministry. Paul was determined to preach in virgin territory, where Christ's name was not known (15:20-22). Yet Paul believes he may have a contribution to make in Rome, even if not in person. This he will attempt to achieve by writing this letter.

He does plan to come to Rome, but only in transit. He hopes the Roman Christians will receive him for a brief stopover and then 'send him on his way' for missionary work in Spain, the most westerly province of the Empire (15:24).

2. CHRISTIANITY IN ROME

It appears that there were Christians in Rome soon after the resurrection of Jesus. Acts 2:10 indicates that Jews and proselytes from Rome were among the pilgrims in Jerusalem for the Feast of Pentecost who heard Peter's Spirit-inspired preaching of the crucified, risen and ascended Christ. Mention of these Roman Jews implies they were among those who accepted baptism at the hands of the apostles.

We have no certain knowledge of the earliest years of Christianity in Rome. But, based on this Acts reference, it seems likely that the first Christians in Rome were Jews. Although Christian believers, these Jews may have remained members of the numerous synagogues, whatever other Christian associations there may have been.

In the year 49, however, there were serious problems within the large Jewish community in Rome (estimated between 40,000 and 50,000 members). According to the biographer Suetonius, writing in the next century, these 'disturbances' were 'at the instigation of Chrestus'.[4] Riots among the Jews were probably over the claims that Jesus was the long-awaited

---

4. Suetonius, *Claudius* 25:44. Many scholars regard 'Chrestus' as a mis-spelling of 'Christus'.

'Christ', the Messiah-king of Israel. Claudius did not tolerate civil disturbances. His simple remedy was to expel the entire Jewish population. Among those driven out were the Jewish tent-makers Aquila and Priscilla, who were probably also Christians (Acts 18:2-3).

Since the majority of believers in Rome were likely Jewish and therefore forced to emigrate, it follows that those able to remain during Claudius' remaining five years were a relatively small number of Gentiles.

It is likely that when Jews, including Jewish Christians, began returning to Rome in 54 or 55 they were somewhat at a disadvantage, anxious not to provoke further official action against them. It is possible that the Apostle Peter, a Jew, made his way to Rome in the early days of the new emperor, Nero. Earlier Peter had been moving westwards from Palestine and Syria, and then through Corinth (1 Cor. 1:12; 9:5). As an apostle to the 'circumcised' in the land of Israel it was agreed that he should 'go' in further evangelism to fellow-Jews (Gal. 2:7-9). Based on 1 Peter 5:13 ('She who is at Babylon ... sends you greetings') and some hints from the post-apostolic age it appears that Peter did come to Rome. If this conjecture is correct it is likely that Peter's ministry in Rome would have been chiefly directed towards Jews. Was Peter the unnamed 'foundation' layer on whose account Paul will not come to Rome?

We note that Romans is not addressed to 'the Church in Rome', but vaguely to 'all God's beloved in Rome' (1:7). The only reference to a 'church' in Rome is to the 'church' that met in the house of Priscilla and Aquila (16:3). There is no other 'church' in Rome known to us from this Letter. The various greetings in the final chapter draw attention to various persons as having 'households'. Most likely, small house churches gathered in the homes of these named persons.

From chapters 14 and 15 it is evident that Paul saw a need to consolidate and unify the believers in Rome, so as to be 'one heart and mouth' in glorifying the God and Father of our Lord Jesus Christ (15:6). This explains his call to them, whether Jew or Gentile, to 'welcome one another' (15:7; cf. 14:1).

Clearly, then, Paul saw this letter as his 'spiritual gift' in strengthening the Christians in Rome to have a sense of identity as a people of common faith and hope, despite their ethnic differences.

This raises the question how much Paul knew about the precise situation in Rome at the time he wrote, in Nero's early years. By then his friends Priscilla and Aquila had returned to Rome and established a church in their home (16:3-5). It is reasonable to assume that these missionary colleagues told Paul about the fortunes of the faith in the City.

3. IS ROMANS A DOCTRINAL 'COMPENDIUM' OR DOES IT ADDRESS A SPECIFIC SET OF CIRCUMSTANCES?

Scholars are divided on this question. In the Reformation era Melanchthon called Romans 'a compendium of Christian doctrine'. More recently Bornkamm referred to the letter as 'Paul's last will and testament'. Most scholars today, however, think Paul knew about the situation in Rome and wrote the letter to address the concrete circumstances of church life in the Gentile capital.

1. Paul knows of the reputation of the 'faith' (1:8), 'goodness' (15:14) and 'obedience' (16:19) of the Roman Christians.

2. His list of twenty-six friends whom he greets at the end of the letter indicates extensive and up-to-date knowledge of the membership of the community of faith in Rome.

3. Paul is aware of critics, who 'slanderously' claim that he teaches, 'Let us do evil that good may result' (3:8; cf. 6:1). These are probably the same persons who 'cause divisions and put obstacles in your way that are contrary to the teaching you have learned' and who 'deceive the minds of naive people'. Paul warns the Romans, 'Keep away from them' (16:17).

4. Related, perhaps, are the many occasions Paul engages in dialogue with an imaginary person throughout the letter.[5] Paul's questions to this 'person' reflect his awareness of criticism of and opposition to the Pauline gospel. Most of these come from a Jewish quarter, that is, a Jewish Christian quarter.

---

5. 2:1-5, 17-29; 3:27–4:2; 9:19-21; 11:11-24. This kind of imaginary dialogue is known as a 'diatribe' and was common in philosophical schools of the era. It did not imply hostility, however, but was a means of persuasion of others of the writer's point of view.

5. Furthermore, his succession of exhortations beginning with, 'Therefore, let us stop passing judgement on one another' (14:13) and concluding with, 'Welcome one another ...'(15:7) suggests that the writer was aware of the divided nature of the wider community in Rome.

These hints about Paul's knowledge of his readers' situation point to a conclusion that Romans is an 'occasional' letter, written to 'strengthen' (1:11; 16:25) the Romans in areas of perceived weakness.

4. REASONS FOR ROMANS

The reasons Paul wrote Romans are to be found not only in Paul's circumstances at the time but also those of his readers. In regard to Paul himself we must remember that Paul had never visited Rome but intended to do so in the near future. Of all Paul's letters only Romans is directed to a church that he did not found, directly or indirectly. Pre-eminent, therefore, among a cluster of inter-related reasons, was his need to send a letter on ahead of his forthcoming visit.

To that end he supplies a travel itinerary informing them of the details of his travels prior to arriving in Rome (15:23-28). In so doing Paul diplomatically adds that 'many times' he planned to come to them (1:13), something he has 'longed' to do (1:11; 15:22-23). Until now he has been 'prevented' from coming (1:13; 15:22).

Further, not all in Rome will recognize his apostleship. He devotes considerable space to establishing this credential in this letter (e.g. 1:5; 11:13; 15:15-19).

Paul is not planning a visit to a minor city, however, but Rome, the 'Eternal' City, the world capital of the Gentile nations. The saying 'all roads lead to Rome' captures the sense of Rome's unique importance. Given the greatness of Rome it was altogether fitting that this, Paul's *magnum opus*, written on such a grand scale should have been written to the Christians in *Rome*. In a simple sense Romans was Paul's own letter introducing himself, giving his credentials and setting out the broad outlines of his gospel.

What, then, do we learn from the circumstances of the readers as to his reasons for writing? Much of the letter is addressed to matters of special interest to Jews (chs. 2–4, 7, 9–11). It appears that some Jewish believers were attempting to look to Law-keeping (as well as to Christ) for their acceptance by God. Paul must point out that Jews as much as Gentiles need the justifying mercy of God in the death of Christ. Jews as well as Gentiles descend from Adam and inherit his sinfulness and suffer death as a consequence. No one, Jews included, can redeem themselves. Jews need to find the righteousness of God in the only place it can be found, by faith in the Messiah Jesus, crucified and risen. To Jews in particular Paul insists that the gospel of God is Christ-centred, grace-based and Law-free.

At the same time, we detect Paul's concern for Gentile Christians among his readers. Many Gentiles despised Jews at that time. They mocked them for their Sabbath-keeping and for their rules about food. It is possible that Christian Gentiles perpetuated these attitudes towards their Jewish brothers and sisters. Paul refers to Gentile 'arrogance' (11:20) and to the offence caused in the uncaring attitude of the 'strong' (Gentiles) to the 'weak' (Jews) in their scruples about 'days' and 'food' (14:5, 15). Paul warns Gentile believers against such high-mindedness (11:21) and encourages accommodation of Jewish practices, at least when in their company.

Paul's great passion is to establish unity in the one many-membered body (12:3-8), where unhypocritical love is displayed (12:9-13, 16), where there is a spirit of unity in the worship of God with 'one heart and mouth' (15:5-6) based on their reciprocal 'welcome [of] one another' (15:6).

A great goal, may I say *the* great goal of Romans, is for the practical expression of Jews' and Gentiles' unity in Christ displayed in the church. Due to Adam's sin Jews and Gentiles are both culpable before God. Only in Christ do they find the righteousness of God. The only source of that salvation is God himself. He is the God who is 'one', as Jews acknowledged in their daily prayer (Deut 6:4). That 'one' God is the God of the Jew and the God of the Gentile (3:29-30). He sends preachers to speak his word so as to draw the penitent to Christ, but also into the company of other believers who will, in spite of cultural differences, praise the 'one God' with 'one heart and mouth' (15:5-6).

5. Paul's Theology in Romans: A Sketch

Romans is Paul's longest and most closely argued letter. Famous texts like 'the wages of sin is death, but the gift of God is eternal life' (6:23) are much loved and well-known. But for many the Letter as a whole proves daunting.

Are there a small number of leading ideas that would simplify our approach to Romans? Here some statistics prove helpful.[6]

Apart from everyday words like 'and', the word most frequently appearing in Romans is 'God' with more references than any other book in the New Testament. God is 'eternal' (16:26) and 'wise' (16:27), the 'God of hope' (15:13), the 'God of peace' (16:20), and the God who judges justly and without partiality. In this regard, Romans is not so much about who God is as about what God *does*, about God in action, saving men and women from the nations and from his historic nation, Israel.

This saving work God does through Jesus Christ, whose names are the second most frequent occurrences in the letter. Jesus is God's 'Son' (1:3; 5:10), 'his own Son' (8:3, 32), 'the Christ' who is 'God' (9:5), come 'down' among us (10:6), the man without sin (8:3), who in death bore the just condemnation of God for human wickedness (3:25). God raised him from the dead, as 'Son of God in power' as witnessed by the outpoured 'Spirit of holiness' (1:4).

The next most frequent references are to 'Law' and 'sin'. These two words represent the sources of the human predicament that God acts to redeem. 'Sin' originates with the rebellion of Adam, the patriarchal head of the human race and through him, with its penalty 'death', spreads to all (3:9, 23; 5:12, 19).

'Law' (focused on the commandments) came from God, by the hand of Moses. The sinful predisposition from Adam (called 'the flesh') is so deeply ingrained, however, that Law served only to identify unlawful behaviour and, indeed, inflame Law-breaking (5:13, 20). The many references to 'Law'

---

6. See L. Morris, 'The Theme of Romans' in W. Gasque and R. P. Martin (eds) *Apostolic History and the Gospel* (Exeter: Paternoster, 1970), 249-63.

in Romans tell us that Law-keeping was a big issue at the time, most likely from some Jewish Christians who insisted that the old covenant was still in place and that man could be redeemed through the Law (as Jews then believed). But, as Paul tells us in his painful autobiography in chapter 7, Law brought only 'wretchedness' and bewilderment.

That Law-based covenant, however, has been overtaken by a new covenant in the merciful action of God 'sending' and 'not sparing' Christ, 'his own Son.' Through Christ the sinful descendants of Adam find God's just verdict in their favour ('justification') now through the hearing and believing of the word of God, the gospel (1:16-17; 5:18).

As a consequence the Spirit of God is now powerfully at work within believers, strengthening them to live righteously in a manner pleasing to God (7:6; 8:4), in particular to love others (13:8, 10). The age of Law has been replaced by the age of Christ and the Spirit, the preaching of the gospel leading to justification.

Thus Romans is about God in action in Christ saving sinful people from Israel and the nations for his coming kingdom. This he does through the proclamation of the gospel by his apostle Paul (1:5; 15:18-19) and by those men and women who were co-workers in his mission (16:1-7).

6. APPENDIX:
THE NEW PERSPECTIVE ON PAUL IN ROMANS
From the time of the Reformation it was taken for granted that the chief themes of Romans related to the individual, his sinful-ness, salvation and sanctification (chs. 1–8), with some wholesome moral exhortations for the individual (chs. 12–13) and the church (chs. 14–15). Chapters 9–11 were of interest because they raised the vexed issues of predest-ination and election.

A. Historical review
In the latter half of the twentieth century, however, scholars began looking more carefully at the passages relating to relationships between Jews and Gentiles, especially chapters 9–11. The view began to emerge that chapters 1–8

on sin, salvation and sanctification – which had previously been regarded as central – were actually introductory to the main burden of the letter in chapters 9–11 and 14–15. Johannes Munck and others argued that Paul's mission to the Gentiles was undertaken to provoke Jews to turn to Christ and so activate the Second Coming. This interpretation tended to diminish the significance of the salvation of the individual sinner as the central message of Romans.

In 1977 E. P. Sanders published the first of several books that challenged the traditional Reformation interpretation of Romans. According to Sanders God intended the Law to be Israel's godly response to its election and to its covenant God. Sanders calls this 'covenantal nomism', based on *nomos*, the Greek word for Law. According to Sanders *nomos* is not a source of a guilty conscience (as Luther said) but the evidence of God's *grace* towards his people. God gave the people a covenant-Law that was within their capacity to obey.

Sanders said that Luther and the Reformers were wrong in seeing the 'works of the Law' as sinful man's futile attempt to find favour with a holy God. Rather, the correct understanding is that God made his covenant with Israel by grace. Israel's obedience to the Law was a sign of being 'in' the covenant, not of 'getting in' to the covenant. 'Getting in,' argued Sanders, was by God's grace while 'staying in' was by 'works', that is, by Israel's obedience to the Law. Sanders has overturned the traditional reading of Romans as man's failed attempt to find righteousness through 'works' which God has countered by sending Christ so that people might 'believe' in him instead.

Sanders' views have been opposed by some[7] and modified by others, notably Dunn and Wright who have identified 'justification' in positive terms as evidence of 'faith' in Christ and membership in the new covenant by Gentiles.[8]

---

7. E.g. R. H. Gundry, 'Grace, Works and Staying Saved in Paul,' *Biblica* 66 (1985), 1-38; S. Westerholm, *Israel's Law and the Church's Faith* (Grand Rapids: Eerdmans, 1988).

8. J. D. G. Dunn, *The Theology of Paul the Apostle* (Grand Rapids: Eerdmans, 1998), 335-89; N. T. Wright, *The Climax of the Covenant: Christ and the Law in Pauline Theology* (Minneapolis: Fortress, 1991); *What Saint Paul Really Said* (Oxford: Lion, 1997).

B. New Perspective: Points of agreement

(i) Romans is not first and foremost a tract to help people become Christian believers (the so-called 'Roman Road'), though many have found Christ through its key texts.

(ii) Romans is not Paul's reply beforehand to the teaching of medieval Catholicism that a man is justified by his works. True, Paul repeatedly rejects Jewish efforts at self-justification based on 'Law'-keeping and 'works' – doing (e.g. 9:31 – 'Israel ... pursued the righteousness ... based on Law'). But this was not because the Law-keeping of Judaism neatly anticipated medieval Catholicism's preoccupation with religious and moral 'works' for salvation.

Rather, Paul writes against 'Law' and 'works' in Judaism because Jews at that time were rejecting the apostolic preaching that Jesus was the Messiah (9:32 – 'they stumbled over the stumbling stone [the Messiah]'), preferring instead their 'Law' and its 'works'. Jews saw their national identity as defined in various symbols like the Temple, the Law, circumcision, the dietary and purity laws and the religious calendar. These they preferred to Jesus, the crucified but risen Messiah.

C. New Perspective: Points of difference

(i) New Perspective writers tend to see 'justification by faith' as Paul's way of finding a place for Gentiles in the covenant of God. In Romans, however, Paul devotes the greater part of the argument to the need of the *Jews*. So far from fulfilling the 'works of the Law' they demonstrate a practical slavery to the power of sin (3:20). Jews are in as much need of grace-based salvation through Christ's sacrifice as Gentiles. 'All have sinned,' that is, Gentiles and Jews. Only 'in' Christ are Jews as well as Gentiles saved.

(ii) Another difference is the relationship between 'the gospel' and 'justification'. This is illustrated in Tom Wright's popular book, *What Saint Paul Really Said*. 'Justification ... is organically and integrally linked to ... the Gospel' (p. 115). Yet 'justification cannot be put right at the centre since that place is taken by ... Jesus himself ... and the Gospel' (p. 114). While this sounds true, it interposes a number of elements between the announcement of the gospel and the 'justification' of the believer (for example, the work of the Spirit and incorporation into the community of faith by baptism – p. 116). Thus (for Wright) 'justification' is a 'badge of membership' of God's new covenant community, the family of the church (pp. 132-33). Furthermore, (for Wright) 'the doctrine of justification is not what Paul means by "the gospel." It is *implied* by the Gospel ...' In effect, then, Wright separates the 'gospel' from 'justification'. In Paul, however, hearing and believing the gospel *is* the 'power of God for salvation'. It is the end-time moment that immediately brings God's verdict, 'declared righteous' into the present, accompanied by the heavenly gift of the Spirit.

In Romans 10 Paul states that Christ has 'come down' and been 'raised up from the dead' (vs. 6-7) and that the 'word of faith' (v. 8), that is, 'the word of Christ' (v. 17), has been proclaimed. As a direct result they are 'saved' who 'confess with their lips that Jesus is Lord and believe in their hearts that God has raised him from the dead' (v. 9). 'Righteousness' and 'salvation' are their present possession in anticipation of God's end-time verdict in their favour. In short, there is no wedge between Christ and the declaration, 'righteous'. Through 'hearing' the 'word of Christ' and 'believing' in Christ comes 'righteousness from God' *now*.

(iii) A major defect with the New Perspective is that it obscures the believer's assurance of salvation. It is no longer a declaration now of God's future verdict on the penitent sinner. But Paul writes, 'If you confess with your lips that Jesus is Lord and believe in your heart that God raised him from the dead you *will be* saved' (10:9). The impact is intensified when we understand that Paul is speaking about individuals; the verbs '*you* confess ... *you* believe ... *you* will be saved' are *singular*. As I confess Christ, believe in him, I will be saved. The time is foreshortened. It is as if I am in the Kingdom of God now, at this moment, immediately. This is God himself speaking, in his gospel-word.

Part A

SIN
(Romans 1:1–3:20)

Paul sees God bringing his salvation to the nations of the world – the nation of Israel and the Gentile nations. This salvation is necessitated by the 'sin' of both Gentiles and Jews and remedied by the sacrifice of Christ made known in the preaching of the gospel. Paul systematically prosecutes both Gentiles and Jews before the bar of God's judgement where he is found to be entirely just in condemning all. All – both Jews and Greeks – are 'under sin' (3:20) and in dire need of his redemption.

I

The Apostle, the Gospel and the Romans
(Romans 1:1-17)

In this the first part of his letter Paul follows a familiar pattern from his earlier letters, though with some special elements. There is the typical 'writer to receivers, greetings' (vv. 1-7), followed by a thanksgiving and prayer (vv. 8-12), and concluded by his 'narrative' about himself in relation to them (vv. 13-15). The section concludes with a short 'bridge' passage that both 'rounds off' his reference to 'the gospel' (in v. 1) and which also serves as a threshold to the remainder of the Letter (whose subject is the gospel).

1. PAUL TO THE ROMAN CHRISTIANS, GREETING (1:1-7)

In this Paul's most expansive letter we are not surprised to find his most expansive opening section. Two or three verses were sufficient for other letters; but not Romans. Here we find no less than seven verses. They are packed full of critical detail, including the introduction of major teachings that will be developed throughout the letter, two of which are Paul's 'apostleship' and 'the gospel of God', both of which appear in the first verse.

Greek letters of those times had a basic two-part format. A letter began with the name of the sender followed by the names of the receivers with prayers for them. Paul usually adopted that outline, but not in this letter. The novel element in Romans is the lengthy creed-like section about the gospel that comes between the sender and the receivers.

A. The Sender, Paul (v. 1)

Paul alone is the sender; unlike his earlier letters no other name is bracketed with his.[1] This is probably because the letter is to serve as a substitute for his own extended presence in Rome. Because 'another' has 'laid' an apostolic 'foundation' there (possibly Peter) Paul does not feel free to 'build upon' it (15:20). This letter must suffice instead of his own personal ministry. This is something for which subsequent generations, including our own, should be thankful since otherwise this letter would not have been written.

Paul qualifies himself as (1) 'a slave of Christ Jesus,' (2) 'called to be an apostle,' and (3) 'set apart for the gospel of God'.[2] These three are connected and flow from what happened to Paul near Damascus twenty-five years earlier. The risen and glorified Messiah 'called' Saul (as he then was known) to be his 'apostle' (or ambassador), whose whole life as his 'slave' was henceforth 'set apart' to proclaiming 'the gospel of God' to the nations (that is, to the Gentiles or non-Jews). Here Paul describes his 'call' in terms of an Old Testament prophet (cf. Isa. 49:1; Jer. 1:5), though in a sense his vocation was greater since it fulfilled the promises of those and other prophets.

Unlike a 'servant' (*diakonos*) who was free to serve a master, a 'slave' (*doulos*) *belonged* to an *owner*. Paul's 'slavery' was his apostleship,[3] his work for Christ as his 'ambassador' to the nations[4] (2 Cor. 5:20). It was a bondage in which he rejoiced.

Paul was not the only 'apostle of Christ'. We must not forget 'the Twelve' who had accompanied Jesus as disciples, who had witnessed the risen Christ and been commissioned by him (1 Cor. 15:5; Acts 1:12-26). To that number must be added James, the Lord's brother, who, along with Paul, had also seen

---

1. At the end of the letter, however, he sends greetings from Timothy and seven others from Corinth.

2. 'Set apart' (*aphōrismenos*) is (1) perfect tense indicating a singular event in the past which has continuing effects, and is (2) passive voice showing that *God* 'set apart' Paul. By this one word Paul recalls God's Damascus Road dedication of him for this apostolate to the Gentiles.

3. Although the word 'apostle' as applied to Paul is infrequent in Romans (1:1; 11:13), the idea of Paul's 'apostleship' (cf. 1:5) permeates the whole letter (1:8-15; 11:11-13; 15:14-22; 16:25-27).

4. Galatians 1:10; Philippians 1:1; Titus 1:1; 2 Corinthians 5:20.

the risen Jesus (Gal. 1:19; 1 Cor. 9:5; 15:7). The 'apostleship' of these fourteen undergirded the authority and authenticity of the gospel and ultimately of the New Testament canon.

In addition, the term 'apostle', meaning 'missionary' or 'evangelist', was applied in a lesser sense to co-workers of Paul, for example, Barnabas, Timothy and Silas/Silvanus (Acts 14:14; 1 Thess. 2:7). Beyond that, there were 'all the apostles', a wider number of men and women to whom the risen Lord had appeared and who, most likely, engaged in the work of evangelism (1 Cor. 15:6; Rom. 16:7). In a lesser sense, the word 'apostle' is used of envoys or messengers representing a church or churches (Phil. 2:25; 2 Cor. 8:23).

Although there was some fluidity in the application of the term 'apostle' in the New Testament, this office was generally limited to those who had 'seen the Lord' (1 Cor. 9:1),[5] and, therefore, to the generation immediately after Christ.

B. The Gospel (vv. 2-6)

Paul's third qualification to write to them, 'set apart for *the gospel of God*,' is his bridge into a lengthy section about that gospel (1:1-16).

The word 'gospel' and the verb 'gospelling' is critical in the first sixteen verses of the letter. Paul 'serves' God 'in the gospel of his Son' (v. 9) and 'is eager' to 'gospel' the believers in Rome (v. 15) because he is 'not ashamed of the gospel' (v. 16), a statement that brings him to the threshold of the main argument of the letter. Furthermore, 'gospel' and 'gospelling' will reappear in important passages later in the letter (10:15-16; 11:28; 15:15-20).

Furthermore, if we turn to the end of the letter we find a striking similarity between the final paragraph and the one that now follows. Both are about the gospel, (1) that it is in fulfilment of the prophetic writings, (2) that it is focused in Jesus Christ, (3) that it is now proclaimed, and (4) that it is a message to be obeyed (by believing it). In other words, the entire letter is 'framed' with references to 'the gospel',[6]

---

5. Timothy is an exception, as well perhaps as Barnabas and Silas/Silvanus.
6. Technically called an *inclusio*.

indicating that Romans is, first and foremost, about the gospel.

Returning now to our passage in the opening greeting, we note four observations Paul makes about 'the gospel'.

(i) The gospel is 'from God' and 'about God'.
When Paul writes that he was 'set apart for the gospel of God' he could mean either 'the gospel which is *from* God' or 'the gospel that is *about* God'. We do not have to choose. 'The word *from* God' is 'the word *about* God,' his character and his saving acts. And this 'word of God' is the 'gospel of God' spoken by ordinary humans beings.

Other references tell us that some who spoke 'the word of God' were twisting and changing the message (e.g. 2 Cor. 2:17; 4:2). This means that the 'gospel' or 'word of God,' though *spoken*, had a 'given' content that (with appropriate adaptation for the needs of the hearers) must be spoken faithfully and with great care. Paul calls this message 'the *kerygma*' or 'the proclamation' (16:25; 1 Cor. 1:21; 2:4; 15:14). From Paul's letters we are able to reconstruct the items he included when he preached the gospel (e.g. 1 Cor. 15:1-7,11).

The challenge to us is clear. When we preach (or share) the gospel we must remember that this is *God's* word which we must submit to, be true to and not take liberties with so as to make it something we would prefer it to be. Discipline and humility are required.

(ii) God promised the gospel in the Holy Scriptures.
Paul now expands on 'the gospel of God' as that

> which [God] promised beforehand ... in the Holy Scriptures

By 'Holy Scriptures' Paul means the Old Testament Scriptures which he narrows here to the writings of '[God's] prophets'.[7]

---

7. The prophet Isaiah speaks God's 'gospel' to the exiled Israelites of their coming redemption from slavery in Babylon (Isa. 40:9; 52:7; 61:1). Jesus, too, uses this 'gospel' language but refers to deliverance from the cosmic powers of Satan/unclean spirits and sin (cf. Mark 1:14-15).

Those writings were part of the canon of sacred writings used in the synagogues. But they were 'pregnant' with expectation of God's great and final act. They have been likened to an Agatha Christie detective mystery, but without the final chapter where all is revealed based on earlier clues. People in Jesus' day reflected on those clues and looked for a great 'someone' to come. For example, Simeon was 'looking for the consolation of Israel' (Luke 2:25), Anna was 'looking for the redemption of Israel' (Luke 2:38) and Joseph of Arimathea was 'looking for the kingdom of God' (Luke 23:51). Paul is saying, 'Look no more. God has acted. His day has come. He has kept his promises. The mystery is now explained and is to be proclaimed from the roof tops.'

But this means Jesus Christ is no last-minute appearance on the scene. He came by God's appointment as the fulfilment of promises and hopes that went back to the very beginning of the Bible, with the failure of Adam. Thereafter, on page after page of its unfolding story, those Scriptures point onwards to the Coming One. Paul comments, 'For no matter how many promises God has made, they are "Yes" in [Christ]' (2 Cor. 1:20).

(iii) The gospel 'concerns [God's] Son'
God's 'promises' set forth in those prophetic writings were 'concerning his Son'.

    concerning his Son
        who came[8] from   the seed of David
                                according to the flesh
        who was set apart as   the Son of God in power
                                according to the Spirit of holiness
      by his resurrection from the dead
      Jesus Christ our Lord.

Most likely these words originated as a creed about the 'Son of God'. We note (1) two 'legs', each beginning ['the Son of God] who...'; (2) each is qualified by 'according to' but balanced by

---

8. The Greek verb *genomenou* primarily means 'has come' though it is often translated 'was born'.

opposites ('flesh' against 'Spirit'); (3) the former is the *historic* earthly Jesus ('from the seed of David') while the latter that follows chronologically is the *heavenly* 'Son of God,' ('set apart ... in power ... by his resurrection from the dead'). This creed may have originated in the brief period between the resurrection and Paul's conversion.[9]

Important teaching about 'the Son of God'[10] is found in this gospel 'creed'.

1. The 'Son of God' is portrayed in successive modes of existence, first (on earth) as 'who came of the seed of David,' and then (in heaven) as 'who was set apart as the Son of God in power'.

This 'Son of God' who 'came' did not come into being at the time of his birth; he must always have pre-existed and 'come'[11] from another 'state of being'. In short, Paul is teaching that the Son of God was always there, in an absolute and eternal sense. Using his own language Paul is teaching the same 'eternity to eternity' doctrine of Christ as found across the writers of the New Testament, whether John, Peter or the author of Hebrews.[12]

2. This 'Son of God,' who pre-existed eternally before God made his promises through the prophets, 'came' as the man Jesus of Nazareth, God's Messiah.

According to the promise of Nathan the prophet 'great David' was to have 'a greater son,' the Lord's anointed, his Messiah (2 Sam. 7:11-16; cf. Ps. 2). This 'messianic' hope focused on a 'second' David was reiterated generation after generation by the succession of prophets like Isaiah, Jeremiah and Ezekiel[13] to the end of the era of the Old Testament and beyond. It was a hope that burnt in the hearts of Israelites in Jesus' own day.[14]

---

9. We note (1) 'seed of David' suggests a Palestinian rather than a non-Palestinian formulation, and (2) 'Spirit of holiness' is a non-Pauline usage with an archaic ring.

10. In precise terms it is 'God ... [his] Son'.

11. The verb 'came' implies movement from one place to another, that is from pre-existence to incarnate life as the son of David.

12. John 1:1, 14, 43-51; 1 Peter 1:20-21; Hebrews 1:1-3.

13. Isaiah 11:1-5, 10; Jeremiah 23:5-6; 33:14-17; Ezekiel 34:23-24.

Jesus was descended from King David, 'according to the flesh' as the writings of the New Testament make clear.[15] The apostles proclaimed Jesus to be the Messiah, the son of David, according to the flesh.[16]

The man Jesus from Nazareth, was a Jew, a son of Abraham and specifically 'the son of David', as Peter speaking for the Twelve confessed (Mark 8:29) and (ironically) *blind* Bartimaeus 'saw' (Mark 10:48).

In short, Jesus was, by descent from David and in fulfilment of the words of the prophets, the rightful anointed king of Israel. When he rode up to David's city and temple to find due recognition as Messiah he found only rejection. Yet out of Israel's rejection of her king God provided for the salvation of that nation and all peoples and a king for all peoples (see on 15:7-13).

3. Jesus is 'Son of God in power' by his resurrection from the dead.

As resurrected from the dead, he has poured out 'the Spirit of holiness' in demonstration that he has been 'set apart'[17] as 'the Son of God in power'. The Son of God incarnated as the Messiah Jesus of Nazareth was subject to weakness, hunger, thirst, fatigue and the spiritual distress of the 'testing' in the wilderness and at Gethsemane. These sufferings and 'testings' were real, as was his eventual death. But raised from the dead, Christ as 'Son of God in power' suffers no more, nor shall we who belong to him.

At this time there is a 'crisis of Christology' which has two related parts. One is the assertion that Jesus was merely a 'charismatic' kind of man, in the way some politicians, gurus or entertainers have a kind of 'star quality'. In his case, however, Jesus is seen by many as a 'remarkable' prophet or rabbi – but nothing more. His Davidic descent is disputed and

---

14. Mark 12:35; John 7:41-42.

15. Matthew 1:1, 17; 20:30-31; Luke 1:27, 32, 69; 2:4; 3:23-31; 2 Timothy 2:8; Revelation 5:5; 22:16.

16. Acts 2:30; 13:22-23, 32-34; cf. see on Romans 15:12.

17. 'Set apart' is Greek passive voice and indicates reverently that God set his Son apart.

with it his messianic status. The other aspect of this crisis is
the denial of his genuine bodily resurrection and exaltation.
The net result of these two views is that Jesus was, after
all, just another man, whose remains are still decomposing
somewhere in Palestine. Notwithstanding this revisionism of
the Gospels some theologians seek to create a kind of myth
that says, despite Jesus' ordinariness of identity and life, and
his non-vicarious death from which he did not rise again,
we do nonetheless worship him as the 'risen Lord'. But this
is mere projection, nothing more than words, nothing more
substantial than a mirage and a metaphor.

How different Paul's little gospel 'creed' is from this kind
of 'revision' of theology. The One who was always the 'Son
of God,' in fulfilment of the promises of God made through
the prophets, 'came' *historically* as Jesus the Christ and after
'three days' was raised alive *historically* as the powerful Son
of God. Seamlessly, the 'same' eternal Son was born, lived
and died as the historical Jesus and without discontinuity
and was made the risen and exalted Lord (cf. Acts 2:22, 24,
32, 36).

(iv) Paul proclaims this gospel to the Gentiles.
The gospel of God is 'concerning his Son' and it is propagated
by means of Paul's apostleship.

> ... the gospel of God ... concerning his Son ... through whom
> we[18] received grace and apostleship for the obedience of
> faith among all the Gentiles for his name's sake among
> whom are you also the called of Jesus Christ.

Again we hear echoes of the momentous event near
Damascus when, 'through God's Son,' Paul 'received grace
and apostleship,' the 'call to be an apostle' to bring about the
'obedience of faith among all the Gentiles'. In the gospel God
commands the hearers to believe in the Son of God.[19] Along
similar lines Paul told the Galatians that

18. Note that 'Paul' now speaks in the plural, 'we,' which is an 'apostolic' plural
(analogous to the 'royal' we).
19. Romans 15:18; 16:26; cf. 2 Corinthians 9:13.

God ... set me apart from birth and called me by his grace,
was pleased to reveal his Son in me so that I might preach
him among the Gentiles (1:15-16)

Paul's apostleship to the Gentiles was special. To no other
apostle was there so specific or individualized a 'call' to take
the message of Christ to the Nations.

True, the risen Christ sent his disciples to 'make disciples
from among the nations' (Matt. 28:18-20) but there was little
initial inclination to do so, as far as we know. The original
apostles, led by Peter, concentrated on evangelizing the
Jews of Palestine for the first twenty years, with some
contact with Samaritans and God-fearers but little or any
with outright Gentiles. Paul, however, from the time of
his 'Damascus call' began pressing the claims of Christ on
Gentiles, beginning in Damascus, Arabia and Syria-Cilicia.[20]
In the later forties, he and Barnabas intentionally set out
westwards from Antioch in Syria for a series of missionary
tours in which he planted the gospel in the Roman provinces
Galatia, Macedonia, Achaia and Asia. Thus, Paul was a
'special' apostle of Christ planting the gospel among the
Gentiles as no one else did.

Few things speak so powerfully about Paul's conversion
as his complete turnaround regarding the Gentiles. Saul
of Tarsus, the pre-Christian Paul, was a former persecutor
of Stephen and other 'Hellenist' believers of Jerusalem,
a fanatical Jewish 'zealot' who preached circumcision to
block Gentiles entering the ranks of God's people.[21] Now,
however, Paul as Christian and apostle crossed land and sea
to bring salvation to the Gentiles. He vehemently rejected
any requirement that Gentile believers submit to the 'works
of the Law'.

Paul did not see himself as the only preacher of the gospel
to the Gentiles. Among his readers in Rome are Gentile
believers (vv. 5b-6; 11:13; cf. Acts 28:14-15). To our knowledge
these did not become Christians through Paul's ministry.

---

20. Galatians 1:17, 21; Romans 15:15-19, 20; Galatians 1:17, 21.
21. Galatians 5:11.

C. The Receivers of the Letter: Saints in Rome (v. 7)
Paul addressed his letter to

All who are in Rome beloved of God called to be saints.

There is no mention of the receivers as 'church' as in most other letters by Paul (but see Philippians 1:1). Most likely this omission reflects the unusual origins and history to date of Christianity in the Eternal City.

The first believers were probably those Jews who responded to Peter's preaching at the Feast of Pentecost a quarter of a century earlier (cf. Acts 2:10) who, on returning home, would have remained members of the various synagogues. In the year 49 Claudius expelled the Jews from the city because of disturbances among them due to Chrestus (a misspelling of Christus?).[22] Between Claudius' decree in 49 and his death in 54, as well as later, Gentile believers were probably in the majority.

The absence of the word 'church' (*ekklēsia*[23]) here points to the non-existence of a specifically Christian assembly in Rome. Most likely Jews continued to gather with fellow-Jews in the synagogues as well as in distinctly Jewish house groups. Gentile believers appear to have gathered in their house groups. This would explain Paul's address to the Christians in Rome merely as 'beloved' and 'saints'. Paul's teaching about the roles of Jews and Gentiles in the purposes of God (chs. 9–11) and his appeal to both groups to find unity in one assembly (chs. 14–15) may point to a major reason for the writing of this letter, that is, to create a 'church' in Rome.

2. THANKSGIVING AND PRAYER (VV. 8-12)
His greeting finished, Paul, following his usual custom, launches into thanksgiving and prayer for his readers. He was, indeed, a devout man. From no other New Testament

---

22. Suetonius, *Claudius* 25.4. Most likely this means that some Jews began preaching Christ in the synagogues leading to disturbances so that Claudius expelled all the Jews from Rome (cf. Acts 18:2).

23. There was, however, a 'church' in the house of Priscilla and Aquila as mentioned in chapter 16 (v. 5).

writer do we have anything approaching the sense of prayerfulness as we do from Paul. He prays for his readers, many of whom like most of the Roman Christians he had never seen. Reciprocally, he urges his churches repeatedly, 'pray for us' (e.g. 15:30).

Prayer in this passage consists of both 'thanksgiving' and 'intercession'. The two go together. Prayer is no mere ritual or mantra. Paul is praying to a person, his Father, who is there, who hears and will answer prayer. Intercession expresses true and personal faith, while thanksgiving acknowledges the confidence that God has heard and has answered, is answering or will answer our requests. Whether thanksgiving follows or precedes intercession, as here, the two should be kept together.

A. Thanksgiving (v. 8)
We should immediately notice Paul's words, 'I thank *my* God *through* Jesus Christ.' Our access to God is not in our own right, nor is it direct and immediate. It is only 'through' our mediator Jesus Christ, who is Son to God and Lord to us. This is humbling (reminding us of our inherent unworthiness to approach the holy and good God) but also reassuring (reminding us that we will be welcomed and heard in that name). The God of the universe is *our* God, because Jesus his Son is our Lord.

So why does Paul thank God? It is because 'their *faith* is *being* declared (present tense) in the whole world' (v. 8).[24] Paul is deeply grateful for the fact of their faith in Christ but equally that that faith is being made known (presumably in the worldwide network of churches). Clearly, others yet will become believers through this 'proclamation' by Roman Christians.

B. Prayer (vv. 9-12)
Paul now tells them of his prayer for them. He solemnly promises that God is 'witness' to the truth of his words, for which he will answer one day. He adds immediately that

---

24. At the end of the Letter Paul comments that their obedience has gone forth to everyone (16:19).

he 'worships' God 'in the gospel of his Son,' that is, in every 'gospel activity' whether preaching, catechizing new believers or ordering church life. This is the worship of God.

Reference to the 'gospel' picks up the two main themes of the Greeting (vv. 1-7), and therefore of the letter as a whole. These are, first, his divine call to become an apostle (vv. 1, 5), and second, the centrality of 'the gospel' in Paul's ministry (v. 1; cf. vv. 15, 16). As noted earlier 'the Son of God' is the centre of that gospel (vv. 3-4).

Paul's prayer for them is no perfunctory thing, a mere formality, as prayers we find in the pagan letters of that time tended to be. Paul prays for these Romans, most of whom he had never met, 'unceasingly.'

So what is his prayer for them? It arises out of his thanksgiving that their faith is being declared across the world. It is that,

'if somehow at some time in the will of God I may be able to come to you' (v. 10; cf. 15:32).

His words, 'if somehow at some time in the will of God' express uncertainty. He knew from experience that it was one thing to make plans, but another for those plans to be realized.[25] Paul had 'often' attempted to come to them, but without success, as he will soon explain (v. 13; 15:22). He knew that his hoped for 'coming' was neither immediate nor, indeed, assured (see on 15:31).

Even the great apostle must accept 'the will of God'. It was not as if his prayer was for personal pleasure, for example, to see the sights of the Eternal City. Paul had but one goal; he wanted to come for gospel ministry to them. Neither his prayers, nor ours – even our most noble – are always answered in ways that seem best to us. As it happened, Paul did come to Rome, but as a prisoner. In that city he met his death at the decree of the emperor. Not even the greatest of God's servants always find protection in this life. But then neither did the Son of God.

---

25. See e.g. the carefully laid plans set out in 1 Corinthians 16:5-9, none of which were fulfilled as Paul had hoped.

Paul explains why he had 'prayed without ceasing' that God would 'prosper' his plan to come to them in Rome. He had 'longed' to see them 'to share with them some spiritual gift' (v. 11; cf. 15:23 – 'I have *longed* to come to you for many years'). Paul taught the Corinthians that God's 'gifts' (*charismata*) are for 'sharing' with others for their 'up-building' (1 Cor. 12-14).

His hoped-for coming would be, he says, 'to strengthen you' (v. 11). This is the same word (*stērizō*) we find in his final doxology where he declares that '*God* is able (that is, 'powerful') to strengthen you' (16:25).[26] God's 'power' for their 'strengthening' is released as *Paul* 'shares' his 'spiritual gift' with them, that is, his apostolic gospel (see on vv. 1 and 5). Implied here is Paul's sense that there is a deficiency or 'weakness' in Roman Christianity that needs buttressing. Ever the pastoral diplomat, however, Paul does not say this directly. Since he is not able to remain in Rome it is likely that he planned his letter as the way to 'strengthen' the Roman Christians. This letter, Romans, is Paul's gospel, his comprehensive exposition of the Christian faith (cf. 2:16 where he speaks of 'my gospel').

Paul is quick to acknowledge that the 'sharing' of 'spiritual gifts' is a two-way street (v. 12). He 'longs to see them' to give but also to receive. They, too, are people of 'faith'. They will be encouraged by him and he by them. Some preachers and leaders isolate themselves from 'rank and file' Christians so that they often 'give' but seldom 'receive'. Paul's greatness, however, included his humility in learning from and being encouraged by ordinary folk. It did not matter to Paul that their doctrine needed 'strengthening'. He looked for encouragement from them as fellow-believers.

On arrival Paul will only see them in passing, as he is sent on by them for his mission in Spain (15:24). He assures them that he is not coming to 'build upon' the 'foundation' that has been laid by 'another' (15:20). His visit will be too brief for

---

26. Jesus recognized that 'the flesh is weak' and that men and women need 'strengthening' (Mark 14:38; Luke 22:32). Paul, following his Master, is joined by James, Peter and John in praying for and exhorting the 'strengthening' of believers in the churches (see e.g. 1 Thess. 3:2; James 5:8; 1 Pet. 5:10; Rev. 3:2).

that. His letter will be his abiding legacy (his 'spiritual gift') to them (v. 11), to minister to them, by substitution. The brevity of his stay will prevent the 'building up' of the church in Rome by his direct personal contact. The letter would fulfil that purpose and that, indeed, appears to have been Paul's primary objective in writing.

Whatever the case, whether by his personal presence or by his letter, his apostolic authority and teaching will be brought to bear on them (cf. 2 Cor. 10:9, 11; 13:10).

3. NARRATIVE: PAUL LONGS TO COME TO THEM (vv. 13-15)

Based on his practice in other letters (see e.g. 1 Cor. 1:10-17; 2 Cor. 1:8-11), Paul now begins a personal 'narrative' of his recent experiences with some statement of immediate intentions.

Paul's 'I do not wish you to be unaware' (v. 13) usually points to information that is new to his readers. They may not have known that he had 'often planned to come' to them but 'until now' had been 'prevented' (see also 15:22). From the year 47 when James, Peter and John agreed that Paul should 'go' to the Gentiles he set out on a number of missions from Antioch that took him westwards, towards Rome. Any plan to come to the world capital of the Gentiles, however, was frustrated by a far-reaching decree of the Roman emperor Claudius. In 49 Claudius expelled the Jewish community from Rome 'preventing' Paul the Jew from coming there. He must await the death of the emperor five years later to come to the city.

Why had Paul been so keen to come to Rome? It was, he declares, to 'have a harvest (literally, 'some fruit') also among' them just as he has had 'among the rest of the Gentiles'. That remains Paul's hope.

Although earlier he probably expected to lay an apostolic 'foundation' and build a church at the heart of the Gentile world a new development has made that impossible. In the meantime a 'foundation' has been laid already by someone else, possibly Peter (see on 15:20). Paul may now only 'pass through' Rome, helped by them on his way to Spain (15:24). Nonetheless, he still looked for '*some* harvest' in response to his gospelling among the Gentiles in Rome (see on 15:17-19).

Paul's stated aim of preaching 'where Christ has not been named' (15:20) is not contradicted by his hope of seeking some 'harvest' in Rome. These are general statements and not intended in a legalistic sense.

In verse 14 Paul expands on the 'the Gentiles' of the previous verse calling them 'Greeks and barbarians' as representing the totality of the peoples of the nations, apart from the Jews. Centuries earlier when Greeks first heard the stammered guttural speech of foreigners, sounding as it did to them as 'bar bar bar', they called such people *barbaroi*, 'barbarians.' In time, however, because of the spread of Greek philosophy, literature and science among other peoples 'Greek' also came to mean 'wise' or 'cultured' and 'barbarian' to mean the 'ignorant' or 'uneducated'. Because the Romans were 'educated' and 'cultured' they came to be included among 'the Greeks' although Latin was their primary language.

But Paul is no intellectual snob; he will preach to both Greeks (the 'wise') and barbarians (the 'foolish'). Indeed, as he says, 'I am *debtor* to both,' referring to God's commissioning of him on the Damascus Road (see also 1 Cor. 9:16 – 'Necessity compels me'). He is the apostle to the Gentiles, whoever they are, 'Greek' or 'barbarian,' 'educated' or 'uneducated'. Unlike Paul, however, some Christian people feel drawn to minister only to the educated middle and upper classes. But Paul's zeal for 'barbarians' as well as 'Greeks' expresses the mind of God who so loved *all* the peoples of the world that he gave up his only Son for them (cf. John 3:16).

It goes without saying, then, that Paul is 'eager also' to 'gospel' the believers who are in Rome. Of interest is Paul's expressed eagerness to 'evangelize *you*,' a reference to Roman readers who are already Christian (v. 7 – 'beloved of God ... saints'; v. 12 – men and women of 'faith'). Is Paul loosely referring to these believers as belonging to the wider Gentile community of the city of Rome whom he hopes to evangelize when he comes? Or, more probably, by 'evangelize *you*' does he mean a deeper ministry to those who are, indeed, Christians but who need to be 'strengthened' in faith (see on v. 11)? In this case, to 'gospel' (or 'evangelize') means more than initially proclaiming the Christian message, but includes providing solid 'building up' of those who have made an initial response (see on 15:20). This letter is Paul's gospel for the Romans and, more broadly, for the Gentiles.

Paul's eventual arrival will give little opportunity for this 'building up' since he is only 'passing through' Rome. It is likely, therefore, that Paul has written this letter to provide that solid grounding in the gospel which his sustained presence would have afforded but which now is not possible.

4. THE GOSPEL: THE POWER OF GOD (vv. 16-17)

By his words, 'For I am not ashamed of the gospel' Paul is rounding off his references to 'the gospel' and 'gospelling' first introduced in his opening sentence and reintroduced in verses 9 and 15. This makes verses 1-17 a unit (called an *inclusio*) in which the dominant idea is 'the gospel of God,' which he had explained in such detail earlier (see on vv. 2-3).

We are surprised that Paul writes, 'I am not ashamed of that gospel.' Why not say positively, 'I am immensely proud of the gospel'? In effect, Paul does mean just that but he says so obliquely by an ironical understatement (called *litotes*). This letter is Paul's gospel.

Did he deny 'shame' for the gospel because of the pressure he felt to hold back from proclaiming it? Paul may well have shrunk from the gospel just as a man pulls his hand from a naked flame. The gospel had been a source of suffering for him.[27] And the reason? Rejection of Christ's claims meant the rejection of the bringer of the message. Being 'ashamed' of Jesus and the gospel, however, is a serious matter.[28] Paul knew well the consequences of 'being ashamed' of Jesus (1 Cor. 9:16 – 'Woe to me if I do not preach the gospel').

Possibly, too, Paul's denial of 'shame' may be directed to the 'objectors' and 'deceivers' in the Roman house churches who opposed Paul's grace-based, Law-free gospel.

---

27. See 8:18, 35-39; cf. 1 Corinthians 4:9-13; 2 Corinthians 1:8-11; 4:7-12; 6:4-10; 11:23–12:10.

28. The Gospel of Mark quotes Jesus using the same word 'ashamed' when he warned about the eternal cost of failing to identify oneself with him and his words (Mark 8:38).

Paul proceeds to state three closely related positive reasons why he is 'not ashamed of the gospel'.

First, the gospel is 'the power of God for *salvation*'. 'Salvation' (*sōtēria*) in everyday language meant 'rescue from dire peril' or 'recovery of health from life threatening illness'. For the apostles, however, 'salvation' pointed to 'deliverance from the wrath of God at the Judgement Day' (13:11; 1 Pet. 1:5, 9).

That unique deliverance was won by the death and the resurrection of Christ (5:9 – 'We are saved from the wrath of God through *him*'). Therefore, although that 'salvation' properly belongs to the future it is a present reality to those who belong to the Messiah, Jesus, crucified and risen (10:13: 'every one who calls on the name of the lord will be *saved*').

While that 'salvation' is 'through' Jesus Christ at the First Easter, a specific moment in history, it is mediated at other places and other times by 'a word'. That word is 'the gospel of God' or 'word of God,' 'the power of God unto (*eis*) salvation.' That special and unique 'word,' though spoken by ordinary and fallible people, is the 'word' from God that brings those who believe it 'into salvation'.

That 'word' is spoken so as to elicit 'faith' from those who hear it. Its 'power for salvation' becomes effective in and for those who believe, for men and women of faith (see on vv. 8 and 12). 'Faith' is one of the great themes of this letter. It is by faith, not 'works of the Law', that we are 'justified' before God (3:30; 5:1) and 'saved' (10:9: 'if you confess with your mouth Jesus as Lord and believe in your heart that God raised him from the dead you shall be *saved*').

At various times throughout history, however, this 'word of God' has been belittled and disparaged. It is only a 'word,' an invisible thing, and what is that next to a miracle, something you can see? Miracles of themselves do not mediate salvation which is by only one means, the gospel of God. Only 'the word of the cross' is the wisdom and power of God (1 Cor. 1:18).

Second, the gospel reveals 'the righteousness of God' (v. 17). Paul's word, 'righteousness' belongs to a group of words much used by him. The correct way to discover word meaning is to begin with an author's own use of the word. In 2:13, where the context is the judgement of

God, those who are 'righteous with God' are also said to be 'justified', that is, pronounced 'righteous' by God. Similarly, in 1 Corinthians 4:4 the word 'declared righteous' (*dedikaiōmai*) is best understood as 'acquitted' (as translated by RSV). Again, in Philippians 3:9 Paul states that he does not have 'righteousness' of his own 'from law' but 'righteousness from God', a righteousness 'based on faith in Christ'. Paul is saying that the 'righteousness *of* God' is God's gracious verdict, 'righteous' (see Matt. 25:37).

In the chapters that follow Paul will bring the Gentiles and the Jews in turn before the bar of God's judgement where, for different reasons, each will be found guilty and subject to the just condemnation of God. In the gospel, however, God declares his acquittal of the guilty, his gracious recognition of them as 'righteous' in Christ, whether Gentile or Jew, despite their sinfulness.

Of particular interest is the verb, 'is being revealed'. The present tense ('*is being*') and the passive ('reveal*ed*') tell us that through the gospel God is *presently* revealing his just and merciful verdict upon the guilty. Paul uses exactly this word in the next verse where, however, it is 'the wrath of God' that 'is being revealed' by God 'from heaven'.

The revelation of that verdict properly belongs to the Last Day. Many have waited anxiously a 'verdict', whether from a jury, a medical report or a university examination. A period of waiting is usual in those circumstances. With God, however, there is no waiting and no uncertainty. Those who reject him are already guilty and condemned and those who belong to Christ are already acquitted and righteous in his sight. The preaching and hearing of the gospel is an eschatological moment, anticipating the End. The 'salvation' of the future is 'now'. This is the 'Day of salvation' (2 Cor. 6:2). Yet, as we shall see in verse 18, God is also declaring his 'wrath' – his negative judgement – now, ahead of the end-time.

The response of 'believing' the gospel is critical, though there is debate over the words, 'from faith to faith.' One possible way to understand this is that the preacher declares the word of God 'from' his faith 'for' the faith response of the hearer. Involved in God revealing his righteous acquittal is the 'faith' of both the speaker of the gospel and the hearer of the gospel.[29]

Third, the gospel is the means to 'life,' that is, *eternal* life in God's coming age, which is another way of referring to the two previously mentioned blessings from the gospel, 'salvation' and 'righteousness from God'. Paul justifies this teaching about 'life' from Habakkuk 2:4:

> He who is righteous from faith will *live*.

As the gospel is spoken and believed the believing respondent is declared 'righteous' (acquitted and accepted) by God and will 'live' in God's kingdom.

Verses 16-17 'round off' the first part of the letter. At the same time they serve as a 'bridge' into the main part of the letter where Paul will explain his gospel (his exposition of Christianity) to the believers in Rome.

5. APOSTLE AND GOSPEL: THE ROMANS AND US

The apostle Paul operated under a number of restrictions (15:20). He would only proclaim Christ in virgin territory, where Christ was not already 'named'. He would not 'build upon' a 'foundation' laid by 'another'. This meant that his long-awaited visit to Rome must be brief.

At the same time, however, Paul was concerned about the gaps in the understanding of the Roman Christians including the failure of Jewish and Gentile believers to 'welcome one another' (15:7) in a common assembly. Accordingly the letter must serve in place of his sustained residential ministry.

But Paul may not have been well-known in Rome and, indeed, may have been the subject of negative report (from his Judaizing opponents in Palestine). For his letter to be well received he needs to establish his apostleship at the outset. This is one reason he is so careful to do so in the first main section of the Letter.

---

29. There are other possibilities: (1) 'from faith to faith' meaning 'faith from first to last,' or, (2) 'from Christ's faithfulness for our faith response.'

His credentials stated, Paul expands on the gospel in the first part of the letter so as to point to it as the great theme of the letter. By 'gospel' and 'evangelizing' Paul means both the proclaiming of Christ and the 'building up' of his people in Christ. If Paul will not have the opportunity to preach the gospel at length when he comes he will use the letter to do so, in his place, both as to proclaiming Christ and also for 'strengthening' the faith of the Roman Christians.

If the original Roman readers needed to know the gospel based on the authority of the apostle to the Gentiles then so too do we today. Thus the opening section of Romans is vitally important. Our salvation depends on it. For as we read Romans God addresses us by his gospel word, by which, as we believe it, we are saved and brought to spiritual adulthood.

STUDY QUESTIONS

1. Do I know or understand God's call upon my life?

2. Why is it so important to Paul to go to great lengths to uphold Christ? Do I uphold Christ?

3. What does this say about Christ – not eternal life – being the center of the gospel?

4. Paul was dramatically changed by the gospel – a complete turn-around toward the Gentiles. What has the gospel caused in my life to be turned-around?

5. There is a 'now' and 'not-yet' to gospel. What does this mean?

6. Paul accepted the will of God in his life. How am I able to accept the will of God?

2

God's Judgement Day Now
(Romans 1:18–3:20)

According to Romans 1:16-17, the gospel is (1) the 'power of God for *salvation*,' (2) 'the revealing of God's *righteousness*' (his righteous verdict), and (3) the means to '*life*'.

At the same time, however, God is also 'revealing' his wrath from heaven 'upon all who hold down the truth'. Thus there are *two* revelations of God at present before the Last Day, the wrath of God seen in human wickedness but, more particularly, his mercy through the gospel.

In the passage that follows Paul brings the Gentile and Jew in turn to the bar of God's courtroom of the Last Day. He prosecutes each in turn demonstrating each is 'without defence'[1] (1:20; 2:1).

But why does Paul assume the role of prosecutor against his readers? There are two reasons. First, each reader must be faced with the reality of his or her rebellion against God. Each person repeats and endorses and re-enacts the Sin of Adam.

Second, because Gentiles and Jews are both 'without defence' before God neither can feel morally or spiritually superior to the other. Because each is in dire, though differing, need before God, because each is saved only by grace through faith, each is able to 'welcome' the other so that 'together' with 'one heart and mouth they glorify God' (15:6-7). God's prosecutor, Paul, reduces everyone to the same circumstance,

---

1. The Greek term *anapologētos*, although usually translated 'without excuse', is better understood in the law-court context of Romans 2–3 as 'without defence'.

that is, 'under sin' (3:9). Each is able to 'welcome' the other as saved by grace alone, apart from works.

1. GOD'S CASE AGAINST THE GENTILES (vv. 18-32)

Paul begins with God's case against the 'Greeks' (cf. 1:16), that is, the Gentiles, for whom he is Christ's apostle. References to idolatry and 'uncleanness' show that he is speaking about Gentiles and not Jews (vv. 23-24). Gentiles may now be the larger group among the Christians in Rome; they need to be reminded of God's grievance against the members of their race (cf. 11:13).

The wrath of God *is being revealed* from heaven (v. 18).

The 'wrath of God' is based on his 'truth' and 'righteousness' and directed without favouritism or prejudice to those whose 'works' fall short of his standards (see on 2:2, 6-11). We should put aside the stereotypes of 'wrath' as fiercely burning 'fire and brimstone'. 'Wrath' is the negative judgement of God, his just and true condemnation, on those who reject him. God's wrath is all the more awesome in being dispassionate. It is not fitful and angry like sputtering fire in oil-filled eucalyptus branches.

This 'wrath' *will be* revealed then, but it also *is being* revealed *now*, within history. Let us ask *to whom*, *why* and *how* God is revealing his wrath at present.

A. To whom is God revealing his wrath?

The key words in this passage are 'godlessness' and 'wickedness'. The former word (*asebeia*) means a refusal to recognise, worship and serve the Creator (as in v. 25). The latter word (*adikia*) is a consequence of the former. Because Gentiles refuse to worship and serve God their sexual and social behaviour is 'wicked' (see vv. 24-31).

The Gentiles' failure is only secondarily ethical (*adikia*/wickedness). Primarily, this failure is the wilful refusal to acknowledge the Creator. It is worth pausing to reflect on Paul's own attitude to God who, he says, is 'forever blessed' (v. 25). In Romans, a letter devoted to the gospel about Christ, there are many references to 'God' (about 150). Paul repeatedly declares moral qualities to be 'of God', that is, marks of his character. These include 'the kindness and forbearance and patience of God' (2:4), 'the truth of God' (3:7), and 'the love of God' (5:5). As well, Paul speaks of 'the God of' referring to qualities he gives us, for example, 'his patience and encouragement' (15:5) and 'his peace' (15:33). He is 'the only wise God,' the One 'through and for whom' are 'all things' (16:27; 11:36). Paul states that 'we shall all stand before the judgement seat of God' (14:10) since 'the whole world' is 'accountable' to him (3:19). This is the God who reveals his 'wrath' against 'godlessness' and 'wickedness'.

It is encouraging and comforting that Paul wrote such things about God despite his own many sufferings. Paul's was no life of ease and privilege. As a pioneer missionary in hostile cultures he experienced physical, emotional and spiritual pain. Yet he did not doubt God, reject God or deny God, but worshipped and served him to the end. Paul stands as a great example and model for us.

God will reveal his 'wrath' not only on the 'day of his wrath', for he also reveals it now 'upon all godlessness and wickedness of men and women' among the Gentile nations.

B. Why is God revealing his wrath?
Why should God's wrath be directed towards human *asebeia*?

As verse 19 explains, it is because 'the knowledge of God' is 'evident,' in two respects. First, it is 'evident' 'in' them, that is, in their moral sense, reflected in the Gentiles' ethical values and virtues (1:32; 2:14-15). Second, it is 'evident' to them, in the creation, as Paul now explains:

> For the invisible things of [God] from the creation of the world being understood, are clearly seen in the things that are made, that is, his invisible power and deity.

Despite these 'evidences' of God 'in' them and 'to' them the Gentiles 'hold down the truth' (v. 18c). Consequently,[2] they are 'without defence' before God on the Last Day.

---

2. The Greek *eis to einai* could be understood either as (1) purpose ('in order that they are without defence'), or (2) consequence ('with the result that they are

Paul's words, 'from the creation of the world' (v. 20), take us back to the early chapters of Genesis and point to God's initial *act* of creation.[3] Equally, however, Paul's words, 'they did not glorify ... God, did not thank God, became vain in reasoning and darkened their hearts' (v. 21), 'became fools' (v. 22), also refer back to the beginning, when Adam rebelled against God.

That *act* of rebellion continues as an *attitude* of rebellion by the peoples of the world, including us today. The invisible God continues to make himself 'known' 'in' us (in our ethical awareness) and 'to' us (being 'clearly seen' by 'the things he has made'). Yet individuals and societies continues to 'stifle' this truth (v. 18). For this reason the 'wrath of God' is being revealed from heaven.

Human rebellion was and is no passive or casual thing, but wilful and deliberate (v. 23).

They exchanged the glory of the	incorruptible	God
for the image of the likeness of	corruptible	man
and	birds	
and	four-legged creatures	
and	serpents.[4]	

The Gentiles have lowered their eyes from the incorruptible God and directed them instead to man-made images of fellowmen and of animals. Worse, they worship these 'created' objects (v. 23).[5]

---

without defence'). The argument of Romans 2:1-11 that God will judge 'according to truth,' 'according to works' and 'without respect of persons' supports (2).

3. Paul's subtle changes in verb tenses move between the initial acts of God's creation and man's rebellion and man's continuing attitude of rebellion in the face of God's continuing revelation of his 'power and deity'.

4. Paul's contemporary, Seneca, believed in the gods but not in representing them by man-made images:

They consecrate the holy and immortal and inviolable gods
in motionless matter of the vilest kind:
they clothe them with the forms of men, and beasts, and fishes
(Cited in Augustine, *City of God* 6.10)

5. Paul's words here reflect his knowledge of the apocryphal work, *The Wisdom of Solomon* (ch. 13).

[They] have	exchanged the truth of God for a lie
and	worshipped and served the creature
rather than	the Creator
	who is blessed forever,
	amen.

Like a man who wilfully and perversely turns from a beautiful and pure wife to a prostitute, the Gentiles have turned away from the incorruptible Creator to pour their affections into decrepit images of men and beasts.

The consequences of Adam's and his children's rejection of the Creator in favour of idols are spiritual blindness (v. 21 – 'their hearts were darkened') and 'foolishness' (v. 22 – 'professing themselves to be wise they became fools'). Greeks prized 'wisdom' above all things (1 Cor. 1:22), yet they were 'fools' in regard to their Creator.

Paul's words remain true for the present sophisticated world. Despite the rightful concern to preserve the creation (the so-called 'environment'), there is no evidence that such focused interest moves the hearts of modern man to 'glorify or thank' God, the Creator of all things.

We are overhearing echoes of Paul prosecuting his Gentile listeners before the bar of God's judgement. 'You reject the worship of your Creator, yet you worship images of man, birds, animals and snakes. The creation around you tells you the Creator is there, whom you should "glorify and thank". But do you worship this Superior Being? No. You make wooden and stone idols of God's lesser creatures and bow down before them. When finally you stand before God you will be "without defence".'

In brief, then, God continues to tell humankind of his existence and power by the evidence in them and around them. It is a limited revelation (God only reveals his threefold personhood in the gospel). But it is a revelation sufficient to arouse man's desire to search for and find God.[6] It is also

---

6. Is man's knowledge of God through creation, that he rejects, (1) full blown and explicit (a 'natural' theology), or (2) a 'vague, unthematic awareness'? For a discussion that favours (2) see R. A. Young, 'The Knowledge of God in Romans 1:18-23: Exegetical and Theological Reflections,' *Journal of the Evangelical Theological Society* 43/4 (2000), 695-707. The strength of Paul's language noted above, however, is more consistent with (1).

sufficient to condemn Gentile man's failure to do that so that both now and on the Last Day he will be 'without defence'.

C. How is God's wrath 'being revealed'?
The heart of the Gentiles' sin is expressed in their acts of 'holding down' and 'exchanging'. They *'hold down* the truth' (v. 18). They *'exchange'* the glory of God for man-made images (v. 23) and they *'exchange* the truth of God for a lie' (v. 25). For this they will be culpable on the Last Day, just as they are at present. God will condemn them then and he is condemning them now as he reveals his wrath from heaven.

How is God revealing his wrath now, ahead of the Final Day? Because of their *asebeia* (godlessness) God hands them over to *adikia* (wickedness). Three times Paul says that 'God handed them over' (vv. 24, 26, 28). The first and the second relate to 'their bodies' (that is, in sexual deviance – vv. 24-27) and the third to 'their minds' (as expressed in fractured social relationships – v. 28-32).

The first is (v. 24):

God handed them over to the lusts of their hearts
for uncleanness to dishonour their bodies among themselves.

God has created man to know and worship him. God has also created man a sexual being to express that sexuality 'according to nature'. But the latter (sexual expression) depends on the former (right worship of God). Where humankind rejects God, God 'hands them over to ... uncleanness'. Thus God is not passive and inactive in heaven, a mere 'Being who is there', as the Greeks believed. Rather God acts in response as the Gentiles lower their eyes from him to worship instead his creatures by means of idols. God is 'revealing his wrath from heaven' now and he is doing so by 'handing over' humankind to 'uncleanness' and the 'dishonouring of their bodies'. Paul does not supply details, though clearly this behaviour is sexual.

God's second 'handing over' of the Gentiles (vv. 26-27) is explicitly sexual.

God handed them over to dishonourable passions.
Their women exchanged natural behaviour for behaviour
    that is against nature.
Likewise, also the men leaving natural relations with
    women were inflamed in lust for one another –
men with men acting shamelessly –
who are receiving the just reward of their error.

The Gentiles' 'exchange' of the worship of God for idolatry
(v. 23) is now matched by women's 'exchange' of 'natural' sexual
practices for practices 'against nature' (v. 26) and men 'leaving'
natural relations with women for 'shameful behaviour' with
one another. (Paul does not indicate the 'just reward'[7] men
receive for this 'error'.) As the Gentiles 'exchange' the worship
of the Creator-God for the worship of man-made images so,
too, men and women 'exchange' 'natural' sexual practices for
practices that are 'against nature'.[8] Paul implies that the latter
action is as perverse and wilful as the former and that both
attract the divine displeasure.

The Greeks regarded heterosexual relationships as 'natural'
and homosexual acts as 'unnatural'. Aristotle observed
that 'the affection between a man and a woman ... happen
according to nature....'[9] However, this recognition, which was
widely acknowledged, proved to be no barrier to widespread
homosexual practice among the Greeks and Romans.[10] This
is Paul's point throughout. Gentiles and Jews have their
standards, but do not live up to them.

---

7. Greek *antimisqia*. The chief opinions are: (1) eternal punishment, (2) physical
debility following debauchery, (3) venereal disease, and (4) the same-sex practices
themselves (so most commentators).

8. Some argue that Paul is saying that same-sex practices are not sinful but merely
'impure' which, however, is not a problem for Gentiles since they are not subject to
Levitical purity laws. See J. Boswell, *Christianity, Social Tolerance and Homosexuality*
(New Haven: Yale University Press, 1980) and W. Countryman, *Dirt, Greed and Sex*
(Philadelphia: Fortress, 1988). In reply, see T. E. Schmidt, 'Romans 1:26-27 – The
Main Text in Context,' in *Striving for Gender Identity* ed. C. R. Vonholdt (Reichelsheim:
Reichenberg Fellowship, 1996), 36-59. For a comprehensive analysis of the texts
of the Old Testament and New Testament on homosexuality with hermeneutical
discussion see R. A. J. Gagnon, *The Bible and Homosexual Practice* (Nashville:
Abingdon, 2001).

9. *Nicomachean Ethics*, 1162a.

10. For a study of Greek attitudes to sexual practices, including homosexuality,
see B. S. Thorton, *Eros* (Boulder: Westview, 1997).

'Same-sex' activity was common in antiquity. It was part of the behaviour of the Egyptians, from whom the Israelites had come, as it was also of the Canaanites to whom they were going.[11] 'Same-sex' practices were commonplace in the lands around the Mediterranean visited by Paul that had been subject to Greek influence and to Roman conquest. Julius Caesar was a notorious bisexual who was said to be 'every woman's man and every man's woman'.[12] The Emperor Nero had a boy named Sporus castrated, 'married' him with all ceremony and lived with him as a wife. While Paul makes no comment about homosexual inclination he refers to male sexual intercourse[13] among the sins that exclude those involved from the kingdom of God (1 Cor. 6:9-11).

In modern developed societies the rejection of God is manifest. Ours is an age of unbelief. God is now effectively abolished from public discourse. His name is rarely mentioned except in blasphemy. In Graeco-Roman times the rejection of the Creator was expressed as idolatry. Today many reject the Creator in preference for an impersonal process called 'evolution', believing that the creation happened by chance. Belief in 'evolution' is, for some, almost a religious dogma. At the same time, as an alternative to the worship of God as Creator, many turn to 'spirituality' in mystical engagement with their own inner beings. In Paul's day the rejection of the Creator was accompanied by 'dishonourable passions'. Today our practical atheism is expressed in a preoccupation with sexuality, including expressions of sexuality that are 'against nature'.

The invisible God has revealed himself through his visible creation, in the universe around us (so Gen. 1). The Creator of man and woman showed them that they should cleave together sexually and become one flesh, leaving mother and father to live together (so Gen. 2). Jesus endorsed the Creator's intention, adding. 'What God has joined together let not man

---

11. Lev. 18:1-3, 22; 20:13.

12. Suetonius, *Julius Caesar* 52.3.

13. In 1 Corinthians 6:9 he brackets *malakoi* (male 'feminine' sexual partners) with *arsenokoitoi* ('males who engage in sexual intercourse with males' – cf. also 1 Tim. 1:10) so as to suggest sexual *acts* between *malakoi* and *arsenokoitai*.

separate' (Mark 10:6-9). Where God's revelation of himself is rejected, humankind departs from the 'natural' coupling of men and women, in the Creator's polarities of sexual expression, for acts that are 'against nature' (v. 24).

The third 'handing over' (v. 28) is to a 'degenerate mind' that results from the Gentiles' refusal in their 'minds' to acknowledge the Creator as God. Here Paul uses the language of the blacksmith who tests the red-hot steel so as to 'approve' or 'disprove' it for use. On one hand, the Gentiles test but 'disprove' God as revealed in his creation so that, on the other, God 'hands' them 'over' to a 'dis-proved' or 'degenerate mind'. As within their minds they reject 'the knowledge of God', so they are 'handed over' by God to a 'rejected mind'. Consequently their 'rejected mind' behaves so as to distort and destroy God's good order for relationships as originally created by him (literally, 'they behave 'against what fits together').

Paul now gives twenty-one examples of this 'dis-located' (or 'un-fitted') social behaviour:

They are filled with full of	all wickedness, evil, greed, spite envy, murder, strife, guile, suspicion, rumour-mongering, slander, haters of God, arrogant, proud, boastful, inventors of evil, rebellious to parents, mindless, faithless, heartless, ruthless.

Clearly these twenty-one evils are important since Paul refers to them again three times (as 'such things' – v. 32; 2:2, 3).

Paul is not saying that all people, at all times, in all places behave like this in every detail. Nor is Paul denying that men and women can and do act nobly. Rather, he is commenting 'broad brush' that observable behaviour in Gentile society has departed from the Creator's intention for ordered and decent human relationships.

If we look at the items on this list and think about their *opposites* we catch a glimpse of how God intends men and women to behave towards one another in society. For example,

God seeks from us not 'wickedness' but 'goodness,' not 'evil' but 'righteousness,' not 'greed' but 'generosity,' not 'spite' but 'goodwill,' and so on. If they loved God with all their hearts they would, indeed, love their neighbours as themselves. But people in the Gentile societies in Paul's day did not treat one another like that, nor do they today.

Man has moved away from God, and God has moved away from man. Like the prodigal son we Gentiles are in the 'far country,' away from God. In that 'far country' the boy was exploited and cruelly used. The greater the distance from God the greater the 'dis-location' in human relationships. We may think that Paul is unduly pessimistic in his judgement. It's worth noting, however, that Paul's comments echo the social commentators of that era.

Within Graeco-Roman society at that time the majority were slaves, class structure was inflexible, provincial administration corrupt, serial divorce commonplace, exposure of unwanted children routine (or else they were maimed for begging or prostitution), and the chief entertainment was watching men and women gladiators killing one another.[14] True, today we are not so overtly coarse as that. It's worth being reminded, however, that the past century, which began with such a sense of moral progress and such high hopes, has witnessed one hundred million people (mostly civilians) killed in war and by genocide.

In verse 32 Paul concludes God's 'case' against the Gentiles begun at verse 18. He argued that they 'stifle' God's truth and 'exchange' it for a lie (vv. 18, 25), that is, they reject their invisible Creator's 'power and deity' revealed in his visible creation (v. 20), preferring instead their own hand-crafted images of humans, birds, animals and snakes (v. 23). In granting these desires God has 'handed' them 'over' to sexual practices that are 'against nature' (vv. 24-27) and to a degenerate 'mind' from which issue attitudes and behaviour that fracture decent and helpful social relationships (vv. 28-31).

---

14. See, e.g. J. Carcopino, *Daily Life in Ancient Rome* (Harmondsworth: Penguin, 1967).

Thus the opening 'Who' of verse 32 refers to the Gentiles
who dismiss the invisible Creator, so that he has 'handed' them
'over' to destructive sexual practices and to a 'rejected mind'
from which has flowed the antisocial behaviour described in
verses 28-31.

> *Who*, although they know the just decree of God
> that those who practise such things are worthy of death,
> not only do these things
> but even approve of those that do them.

Paul's words, 'worthy of death' do not mean a human death
penalty for the crimes of verses 29-31 but *God's* ultimate
condemnation for such behaviour. In other words, Gentile
men and women know within their moral consciousness that
there is a final reckoning for wickedness.

True, God has handed over ungrateful Gentiles to wickedness
of body and mind, yet they still retain an innate sense of
ultimate judgement, however dimly they may perceive it (see
on 2:14-15). Such is their perversity and fallenness, however,
that though they know of such judgement they do those very
things and even approve of others perpetrating them. In short,
they are condemned because their actions are against what
they know to be true. They know about the Creator from his
creation but reject that revelation, subverting that truth for the
lie of idolatry. Equally, they know about a final judgement on
evil but perversely practise and approve the very things that
will attract God's judgement. Gentile men and women are and
will be, indeed, 'without defence'.

2. GOD'S CASE AGAINST THE JEWS (2:1–3:20)

Paul now argues God's case against his chosen people, the
Jews. Their situation is even worse. Jews know of the long-
suffering and kindness of God, but do not repent. They
have the Law of God, condemn others by that Law, but do
not keep it. Once more, Paul is pointing to the principle that
humans have knowledge of and about God, but act against

that knowledge so as to be culpable in the Great Judgement
of God.

A. *God judges according to Truth (vv. 1-5)*

In verses 1-10 Paul addresses an imaginary 'man' who has
interjected an objection to what Paul has been saying.[15]
We now overhear Paul in cut and thrust argument with
a learned debater concerning the gospel. Most likely, this
is not a hypothetical 'objector'. The 'man' we now meet is
articulating views against Paul's Law-free gospel that were
then current in Rome.

Paul has just declared two kinds of behaviour to be subject
to 'God's righteous decree' and 'worthy of death,' his final
condemnation (see on 1:32): those who (1) 'practise' the evils
he has mentioned (1:29-31), and (2) 'approve' the wickedness
they know God will condemn.

In verse 1 Paul adds a third class of person who faces God's
just condemnation, those who judge others for behaviour that
they know is wrong yet who 'do' the same.

> Wherefore, O man, who judge others,
> you are without excuse.
> Because in the very things in which you judge another,
> you condemn yourself.
> For you who pass judgement do the very same things.

Here once more is Paul prosecuting God's case and pronouncing
yet again, 'You are without defence (see on 1:20 – 'So that
they are without defence'). This critic may comfort himself
that he is above and beyond the judgement of God, but it is
a delusion. Whoever passes judgement betrays an awareness
of moral standards by which he passes that judgement, only
to find that he is self-condemned by his own criteria. Each has
much to say now in self-defence but when God's Day comes
each will be reduced to silence.

But the apostle turns momentarily from peppering his
interlocutor with painfully self-evident truths and questions.

---

15. This form of presentation was then called a 'diatribe'.

In verse 2 he states a principle that must be accepted by everybody as authentic, including the 'man' who sits listening to Paul's words.

> Now we know that the condemnation of God
> is according to truth
> upon those who practise such things.

The 'practice' of 'such things' refers back to the twenty-one evils listed earlier (see on 1:29-31). God is no human jury member, the best and fairest of whom make mistakes, as witnessed by those prisoners on 'death row' now shown to be blameless by DNA tests. God's assessment is perfect, 'according to truth.' Only a fool draws comfort from this. God does not judge us by the behaviour of our fellows, whether the lowest or the highest common denominator. God judges us by his standards, 'according to truth.'

So he faces the 'man' with that reality (v. 3).

> Do you reckon, O man,
> who judges those who do such things and also does them
> that you will escape the condemnation of God?

Once more the words 'such things' refer back to the twenty-one acts and attitudes that 'dis-locate' social relationships (see on 1:29-31). God cannot but condemn wickedness, and this he will do 'according to truth'. The 'man' who wishes to argue with God must know that there is 'no escape'. His situation is desperate. Let him hear and open his mind and heart to the 'good news' of the gospel that God graciously 'justifies' those who believe in his Son (see on 1:16-17).

But who is this 'man'? To this point he has belonged to that class of persons who has 'known' God's standards and judged others by those standards while not fulfilling them. From Paul's question to this 'man' in verse 4 his identity begins to emerge. This 'man' is a Jew. For only to a Jew could Paul point to 'the riches of God's *kindness*' and his 'patient *long-suffering*,' aspects of God's character found in the Scriptures of the Old Testament (e.g. Ps. 34:8; Exod. 34:6).

Paul accuses this *Jewish* 'man' of 'despising' that 'kindness' and 'long-suffering' of God so abundantly revealed in the Bible. And he asks:

Do you not know that the kindness of God
leads you to repentance?

Paul cannot but reflect on twenty-five years preaching to fellow Jews, calling on them to 'repent' on account of God's Messiah recently come among them. So much of that preaching, however, had been greeted by stony rejection. Thus he cries out (v. 5)

By your hardened and impenitent heart
you have stored up for yourself wrath
in the day of wrath
at the revelation of the righteous judgement of God.

The Gentile will be condemned because he has culpably subverted the truth of God revealed in creation and conscience, as expressed by his idolatry, sexual practices and destructive social behaviour. How much more serious, however, is the circumstance of the Jew who knows that God is 'kind' and 'long-suffering' but who has rejected the apostolic call to 'repent'. On that basis, we can only wonder at the grim prospects of the person who knows the full revelation of God in the message of the New Testament, but who continues on his way without repentance.

B. God judges impartially, according to works (vv. 6-11)
A few verses earlier Paul declared that the 'condemnation of God is according to truth' (v. 2). This must mean that God assesses each person by the way he has lived. The imaginary Jewish 'man' Paul is addressing must understand that there will be no special concessions to him because he belongs to the chosen race.

No. God will 'repay each person according to his works' (v. 6). Paul sets up a contrast between two basic approaches to life and their respective outcomes (vv. 7-8).

To those who by patient good works
seek glory, honour and immortality,
eternal life.

But to those who from strife and disobedience
disobey truth and obey wickedness,
wrath and fury.

The second group symmetrically balances the first. Yet there
is something beyond rhetoric here. The words 'strife' and
'disobedience' apply exactly to the objectors and deceivers
who are dividing the Christians in Rome (see 16:17-18). 'Wrath
and fury' awaits them. Hopefully the point will not be lost on
the 'man' who hears these words.

This principle of 'judgement according to truth' will apply
to each and every person regardless of race or creed. Paul
teaches this as the basis of God's judgement that will apply
also to Christian believers (2 Cor. 5:10: 'we must all appear
before the judgement seat of Christ, so that each one may
receive good or evil, according to what he has done in the
body').

The apostle now expands further upon the judgements
of God, unfavourable and favourable, according to works
(vv. 9-10).

Pain and distress
upon everyone who works evil
to the Jews first, but also to the Greek.

But glory, honour and peace
to everyone who works goodness,
to the Jews first, but also to the Greek.

For there is no respect of persons with God.

A Jew, like the 'man' Paul is addressing, would expect
'preferential treatment' as a 'son' of Abraham. Paul's words
would come as a shock and a surprise. But the ground is level
on which all stand to be judged by God. It will not matter
to God whether I am Jew or Gentile, rich or poor, clever or

dull, gifted or ungifted, black or white. God will judge me
for my works according to his truth. Unlike humans, who
give favours to the wealthy and the well-connected, God
the judge is 'no respecter of persons,' as Peter also taught
(1 Pet. 1:17 – '[the] Father ... judges each one impartially[16]
according to his works').[17]

C. God judges law-breakers, whoever they are (vv. 12-16)
Paul continues to face the Jewish 'man' with the reality of
God's impartiality. The Jew may have felt superior since God
had chosen Israel as his people and at a precise moment in
history had given them his Law. Gentiles, however, are not
without some sense of the moral principles of that same Law,
however dimly those principles may have been understood.
A Greek like Aristotle wrote treatises on ethical behaviour and
the Romans were noted for their interest in various aspects
of law that govern society. Although a Jew, Paul's early years
in Tarsus and his travels outside Palestine showed him that
the Jews were not the only persons concerned for righteous
behaviour. What matters to God is how Jews live up to the
Law God gave them and how Gentiles live up to those moral
standards which reflect the Law of God.

Accordingly Paul observes that both Jew and Gentile have
'law' which, however, if not kept will invite the judgement of
God (v. 12):

> As many as sin without Law
> will perish without Law, and
> as many as sin under Law,
> will be judged by Law.

Gentiles do not have the Law of God, but if they sin they
will perish since they will be failing to uphold their own

---

16. Note that Peter's word 'impartial' (*aprosōpolēmptōs*) is similar to Paul's [no]
'respect of persons' (*prosōpolēmpsia*). God is an impartial judge.

17. How do we reconcile (1) God's judgement of all (including Christian believers
– 2 Cor. 5:10; 1 Pet. 1:17) according to *works*, with (2) God's gift of righteousness to
those who *believe* in Christ? On the Last Day God will pass judgement on our works
but also acquit us on the ground that we belong to Christ (cf. Rom. 8:1).

moral standards. Jews do have that Law, but if they sin (by breaking their God-given Law) they will be judged by that Law. Gentiles have moral standards and Jews have the Law of God, but *performance* is what matters to God.

Paul relentlessly drives the point home to the Jewish 'man' (v. 13).

> For it is not the hearers of the Law who are
> righteous with God,
> but the doers of the Law will be declared
> righteous [by God].

The mere *hearing* of the Law in the synagogue is useless, unless followed by the *doing* of the Law, a point made also by James (Jas. 1:22: 'Be doers of the word, not hearers only, deceiving yourselves'). Indeed, Paul observes that the repeated hearing of the Law without heeding its message about the One to whom it pointed actually hardened the minds of the Israelites (2 Cor. 3:14 – 'But their minds were made dull, for to this day the same veil remains when the old covenant is read').

If Gentiles, who are 'without [the] Law [of God] sin,' as they do (cf. v. 12), how and against what or whom do they sin? In verse 14 Paul points out that although 'the Gentiles do not have the Law' they 'do *by nature* the things of the Law', thus revealing that 'they are Law to themselves'. Three centuries before Christ Aristotle distinguished between 'written laws', which could be in error, and the 'general law as more in accordance with justice' and which 'never changes'. He continues, 'This law is not of now or yesterday, but is eternal.'[18] Most likely it is to this principle that Paul now points (vv. 15-16):

> They demonstrate that the work of the Law is written in
> their hearts,
>   their consciences bearing witness within them
> and   their reasoning accusing or excusing themselves

---

18. *Rhetoric* 1.15.3-8. The same applies today in what is termed 'natural justice' and the concept of 'civic virtues' which, though not easily defined, are regularly appealed to. A moral sense undergirds all societies.

on the Day when God judges the secrets of men
through Jesus Christ according to my gospel.

Is Paul saying that by having 'the Law of God written on
their hearts' the Gentiles actually 'keep the Law of God'? Not
at all. He is merely observing that the laws of the Gentiles
reveal a moral consciousness along with the inner ability to
distinguish right from wrong. Furthermore, they have the
capacity to 'accuse or excuse' themselves by the ethical criteria
of their own laws. Only in this remote sense do they have the
Law of God, by pale reflection. Paul is not saying that they
observe the Law of God, even in this lesser understanding.
Indeed, there is every reason to believe that as the Jews fail
to keep that Law (see on vv. 17-24), so the Gentiles also fail
to uphold their 'law'. As noted earlier, they both 'do things
that dis-locate' society (1:28) and 'even approve of those who
practise such things' (1:32).

D. God judges the Jews for double standards (vv. 17-24)

Paul reaches the climax of his case against the Jews begun at
verse 1. The entire passage to this point has been devoted to
the judgement of God on the Last Day, a judgement that will
be based on 'truth' (vv. 1-5), that will be 'according to works'
(vv. 6-11) and that will be directed against sin (vv. 12-16).
Paul re-introduces the word 'Law' (nomos), though now more
formally than in verse 12. This is because Jews pointed to the
Law as assurance of their covenant status with God as his
chosen people, and therefore of their 'righteous standing'
with him.

   Only in verses 4-5, however, does it begin to be clear that
Jews were in Paul's mind; only they could know about the
'long-suffering' and 'kindness' of God. Having now identified
the 'man' he is addressing as a Jew the apostle removes any
hope that the children of Abraham will receive special favours
before God's seat of judgement; each person regardless of
race will be evaluated according to his works (vv. 6-11).
Those under Law who sin will be judged by that Law; God is
concerned with doers of the Law, not those who merely hear
(vv. 12-13).

At last (v. 17) Paul directly addresses this 'man' as a Jew. First he recites key elements of Jewishness that, as he knew well, distinguished members of his race from others. These he had repeatedly heard from Jews as he sought to teach them the gospel of Christ. He declares to this 'man' (vv. 17-19)

> If you call yourself a Jew
> and   rest in the Law
> and   boast in God
> and   know his will
> and   approve what is excellent, being taught from the Law,
>   convinced you are
>   a guide to the blind,
>   a light in the darkness,
>   an instructor of the foolish,
>   a teacher of children
> having in the Law the embodiment of knowledge and truth.

There is no trace of sarcasm in these words. Historically speaking, this is a splendid account of what it meant to be a Jew at that time. The Law was, indeed, their 'resting place' and they did 'boast' of their knowledge of the one true God and of his 'will' in the face of the gods of Greece and Rome.

Furthermore, Jews saw themselves as having a mission to the Gentiles, that is, to welcome the Gentile searcher after God into the portals of the synagogue to hear his sacred Law. Israel, indeed, was to be a 'light in the darkness' among the nations (Isa. 49:6: the LORD said ... 'I will make you a light for the Gentiles'). Many thousands of Gentiles became God-fearers, attending the synagogues and submitting to instruction by their rabbis.[19]

From childhood Jewish boys went to the synagogues for careful nurture in the Law of Moses. Sabbath by Sabbath the millions of Jews of the Mediterranean world assembled for instruction and edification in that sacred Law. Philo, a Jewish scholar and a contemporary of Paul, wrote that

---

19. That is not to say, however, that large numbers took the final step of male circumcision. Circumcision for adult males was painful, medically dangerous and irrevocably burnt the bridges back to being a Gentile.

every seventh day there stand wide open in every city thousands of schools of good sense, temperance, courage, justice and other virtues in which the scholars sit in order quietly with ears alert and with full attention, so much do they thirst for that draught which the teacher's words apply (*Special Laws* 2.60-64).

Philo praises his fellow-Jews for their 'virtues'; Paul will now pass a very different verdict.[20]

Paul asks five penetrating questions of this Jewish 'man'.

You then who teach another, will you not teach yourself?
You who preach, 'Do not steal,' do you steal?
You who say, 'Do not commit adultery,' do you commit adultery?
You who hate idols, do you rob temples?
You who boast in the Law, do you dishonour God by breaking the Law?

Paul is accusing the Jews of confusing having the Law with keeping the Law.[21] He says, quoting Isaiah 52:5, 'The name of God is blasphemed among the Gentiles because of you.' Evidently many Gentiles dismissed Israel as a 'light' to them on account of double standards. References to Jews 'stealing' and 'committing adultery' while teaching the Law of God forbidding such practices need no further explanation. 'Robbing temples,' however, is obscure to us and may refer to some notorious events in Paul's day of which we are unaware.

Paul's 'case' against the Jews is the same in principle as he mounted against the Gentiles. Each has a true, though differing, knowledge of God from which, however, each shrinks and is thereby self-condemned as 'without defence' in the day of God's judgement. Gentiles worship, but not the invisible, powerful God known to them in his visible creation,

---

20. No doubt the pre-Christian Paul's verdict on his fellow-Jews would have been affirmative like Philo's. The Damascus Road revelation of Christ may have brought with it a deep conviction of Sin, his own and his people's.

21. The author of 2 Baruch, a Jew and an approximate contemporary of Paul, wrote much the same thing: 'In you [God] we have put our trust because, behold, your Law is with us, and we know we do not fall as long as we keep your statutes.'

but hand-made mute objects. Gentiles do not uphold the 'law' underlying their statutes but engage in practices that fracture and destroy the fabric of society. God's condemnation expressed by Paul against the chosen race is even more trenchant. The Jew has the Law of God, condemns the Gentiles by that Law, but himself does not practice that Law. His plight is desperate; God judges impartially, and condemns on the basis of truth, according to works.

Paul is not saying that every individual Gentile or Jew behaves wickedly. Rather, he is prosecuting God's case against characteristics that mark the various races, that they will be 'without excuse' on the Last Day. Day by day each person's attitudes and actions betray a 'God'-sense and a moral sense which none lives up to and which is the basis of criticism of others. All of us – Gentiles or Jews – are self-condemned.

E. The True 'Jew' (vv. 25-29)
From the time of the Patriarchs the people of Israel held that male circumcision (on the eighth day) was the necessary mark of membership in the covenant of God. By New Testament times, while some thought circumcision might be no more than a metaphor for righteous living, the accepted view isisted that circumcision was indispensable to the covenant. Gentiles were regarded as sexually promiscuous precisely because they were uncircumcised, so that circumcision was held to be obligatory for their conversion to Judaism. Philo, the Jewish scholar from Alexandria and contemporary with Paul, urged that the truest part of the male was his mind which, however, was weakened in its godly resolve by the 'pleasure and impulse' of the sexual organ, hence the necessity for cutting away its foreskin.[22]

On the other hand, the Old Testament teaches that it was possible to be circumcised in the foreskin but not in the heart. Deuteronomy directs the readers to 'circumcise ... the foreskin of your heart' (10:16) and Jeremiah laments that 'the whole house of Israel is uncircumcised in heart' (9:25-26).

---

22. Philo, *Questions and Answers on Genesis III*, 52.

Paul's radical conversion can be measured by his changed attitude to circumcision. Saul the pre-Christian zealot appears to have 'preached circumcision' to bar a too easy access of Gentiles to God's covenant people (Gal. 5:11). By contrast, Paul the Christian preaches a circumcision-free gospel to the Gentiles (Gal. 5:2 – 'If you receive circumcision Christ will be of no value to you').

Equally radical are his words in this passage about circumcision, addressed to Jews. 'Circumcision is profitable,' he teaches (v. 25), 'if you observe the Law. But if you transgress the Law, your circumcision has become uncircumcision.' In other words, failure to keep the Law renders the Jew *un*circumcised.

Worse, the uncircumcised Gentile who keeps (his version of) the Law is to be regarded as 'circumcised' and the circumcised who does not keep the Law will be condemned by the uncircumcised man who does keep the Law (vv. 26-27).

> If an uncircumcised man keeps the just requirements of the Law
> will not his uncircumcision be reckoned [by God] as circumcision.
>
> And he who is by nature uncircumcised and keeps the Law
> will condemn you who has the letter of the Law
> and is circumcised but transgresses the Law.

Most likely, these shocking views were without parallel among Jews of that era. In effect, Paul is redefining the covenant of God, no less. Jews believed that Gentiles *might* possibly be admitted to God's holy people, Israel, depending on the fulfilment of certain conditions, chief among which was circumcision. But it probably did not occur to them to consider that Jews themselves might no longer be in the covenant. (Although John the Baptist came close to this when he said, 'God is able from these stones to raise up children to Abraham' – Matt. 3:9). Yet Paul is now preparing his Jewish reader for that very idea! In fact, Paul is saying that a 'Jew' is not at all defined by circumcision, nor by keeping the 'letter' of the Law', but by something else (v. 28-29).

> For he is no Jew who is one outwardly,
> neither is circumcision in the outward flesh.
> But he is a Jew who is one inwardly,
> and circumcision is of the heart,
>> in   the spirit
>> not   the letter,
> whose praise is not from man but from God.

In speaking of 'circumcision ... of the heart' Paul is echoing the words of the prophets before him who complained that through her disobedience to the Law of God given at Mt. Sinai Israel's 'heart' was 'uncircumcised' (Deut. 10:16; 30:6), 'hard' (Ezek. 3:7) and 'stone'-like , that is, 'dead' (Ezek. 11:19; 36:27). (The 'heart' in the Bible is the place of thinking, feeling and willing.) The prophets' words about the 'heart', though different from Paul's, amount to the same thing; from the time the Lord gave Israel his Law she had turned her back on him.

At the same time the prophets Jeremiah and Ezekiel looked forward to a *new* covenant in which God would give the people a *new* 'heart'. Jeremiah promised 'a new covenant' in which God would 'write his Law on the hearts' of the people (31:31, 33). Ezekiel promised that God would replace' their heart of stone' with 'a heart of flesh' and to 'give [his] Spirit' to them (11:19-20; 36:26).

In verses 28-29 Paul sees God's promises made by his prophets as now fulfilled. The hearts of believers are 'circumcised' by means of 'the Spirit' of God not 'by the letter (that is, the Law)'. In 2 Corinthians 3, again echoing Jeremiah and Ezekiel, Paul uses different language to make the same point. The 'letter' of the Law had 'killed' the people by 'condemning' them (v. 6) but under the 'new covenant' God's 'Spirit' has 'given' them 'life' and is now 'written' in their 'hearts', replacing the 'heart of stone' with 'a heart of flesh' (v. 3).

Paul's radical point must not be missed. The 'true Jew' is no longer defined by blood descent from Abraham, by male circumcision and keeping 'the letter' given through Moses. The coming of Christ and his death and resurrection fulfilled the promises of God through the prophets. God has now 'abolished' his covenant with his particular people, the nation Israel.[23] There is now a new covenant based on (1) the forgiveness of sins through the death and resurrection of Christ, and (2) the inner working of the Spirit of God changing the 'heart' and inclining it voluntarily and spontaneously to keep the Law. This covenant, this new 'circumcision', applies only to those who acknowledge Jesus as Messiah and Lord, regardless of whether they are Jews or Gentiles. The temporary era of Law has passed, superseded by the now permanent era of Christ and the Spirit (see on 7:6; 8:3-4). At the same time, God will honour his promises to the Patriarch Abraham in saving many from his historic people Israel (see on 11:12, 15, 25-29).

F. Answers to the Jewish Objector (3:1-10)

In the passages just completed Paul passed a number of judgements about the Jews, which are the more extraordinary because Paul is a distinguished member of that race (9:3-4a; 11:1-2; Gal. 1:14). True, the Jews 'have' the Law of God, but the 'doing' of it, not merely the 'having' and 'hearing' of it, is the important thing (2:13-14). This they have failed to 'do' despite their pretension to Law-based righteousness. In consequence they have lost their vocation. They are called to be 'a light in the darkness' among 'the Gentiles,' but their transgressions of the Law actually point the Gentiles *away* from the God who gave them the Law (2:19, 23-24). Israel as a nation is not that light, but Paul the apostle to the nations brings that light in the message of Christ (Acts 26:17-18).

Now that the new covenant has come, fulfilling God's promises made through the prophets, 'Jewishness' is radically re-defined. Being a Jew is no longer 'outward,' by the circumcision of the male's foreskin. Being a Jew is not defined

---

23. In 2 Corinthians 3:7, 11, 13, 14 Paul declares that 'in Christ' the old covenant is 'abolished'. This is the true meaning of the verb *katargein*, correctly translated by nrsv as 'set aside' (but incorrectly by rsv and niv as 'fading'.)

by keeping 'the letter,' that is, the Law. No. Being a 'Jew' is now 'inward', true only of one whose *heart* is 'circumcised' and written upon by the Spirit of God (2:28-29). And, this 'Jew' could be a Jew or a Gentile. It no longer matters because the old covenant with Israel is now 'abolished,' 'set aside' (so 2 Cor. 3:7, 11, 13, 14).

But this means that a Jew's race and inherited religion cannot save him. Jews asked one question, 'By what means, if any, can a Gentile be saved?' The answer Jews typically gave was, 'By circumcision and keeping the Law of Moses' (cf. Acts 15:1). Paul, however, asked *two* questions: How can the Gentile be saved *and* how can the Jew be saved? For, as he will soon conclude, *both* are 'under sin' (v. 9).

Both have the same need before God: sin rules both and God will judge and condemn both. Equally, however, God has provided the same deliverance for both in his grace-motivated sending of his Son, the messianic king, crucified and risen, by whom God dedicates to himself a new, forgiven people. But this is to run on ahead.

So outrageous are these assertions that Paul must now echo to himself a number of the objector's questions, three of which he will answer; the final two, however, he does not answer since the answers are self-evident.

First, he asks (v. 1), 'what is the advantage of the Jew' and 'what is the profit of circumcision'? If the uncircumcised man without God's Law 'does' the Law and the circumcised who has the Law 'transgresses' it, how is the Jew better and how is the covenant sign circumcision of value?

There are many advantages, answers Paul (v. 2), the chief of which is that God entrusted his 'words' (*logia*) to the Jews. God chose that race, giving them circumcision as the covenant 'sign' and entrusting to them his 'words' (the writings of the Law and the Prophets). Those 'words' point to the promised Messiah (1:2-3; 15:8-12).

Paul's answer prompts a second question (v. 3). If 'some' of the Jews 'disbelieve' these 'words of God' regarding the One who was to come, what then? Does their 'disbelief' nullify the faithfulness of God to his 'words' of promise? Paul replies solemnly, 'God forbid. Let God be true and every man a liar'

(v. 4). The fundamental truth stands: God is 'faithful' and 'true' to his 'words' regardless of the failure of most Jews to recognize the fulfilment of those 'words'. Paul buttresses his oath-like assurance by an allusion to Psalm 50.[24]

> That you (God) may be　　justified by your words, and
> 　　　　　　　　　　　　prevail when you are judged.

When God is 'judged' by the Jews he will be declared 'justified' by the fulfilment of his 'words' in the coming of Christ.

Paul's third question (v. 5) re-introduces the keywords of the Letter, 'righteousness of God' (see on 1:17). Paul asks, 'If our (Jewish) wickedness shows forth the righteousness of God, what shall we say?' But what does he mean? How was God 'judging the wicked' (Israelites) at that time? Most likely it is God's judging the Israelites for rejecting their Messiah was allowing the Gentiles an opportunity to be saved. The apostle is probably anticipating his teaching when he will write about the many in Israel who refused to accept God's 'righteousness' in Christ (9:30–10:4, 16-21).[25]

Paul's answer (v. 6) is again begun by 'God forbid', followed by the rhetorical question, 'How else will God judge the world?' True, Israel is God's chosen people. But God the just judge cannot make exceptions on that basis. He is a righteous judge who judges righteously and impartially, regardless of race or religion. Those Jews who have rejected the Messiah will be judged no differently from anybody else, by their works.

Paul's fourth question (v. 7) is difficult to grasp. His question is: 'If because of my falsehood God's truth overflows to his glory, why am I still judged as sinful?' 'God's truth' is his promise made to Abraham for the blessing of the Gentiles, which was 'overflowing' to them at that time due to Israel's rejection of Christ. The 'falsehood' was the spiritual blindness of the pre-Christian Paul currently replicated by the Jewish

---

24. The precise words of Psalm 50:6 are: 'And the heavens proclaim his righteousness, for God himself is judge.'

25. Note that 'righteousness of God' is used here, not as God's acquittal, but negatively, in his 'righteous judgement'.

nation, that refuses the Messiah and permits the blessing of God to overflow to the Gentiles.

The objectors seem to be arguing that, according to Paul, God would be acting opportunistically, thus relieving them of responsibility for rejecting Christ. Paul does not answer his question since the answer is self-evident. If, by whatever means, God is fulfilling his promise to the patriarchs to bring his blessing to the Gentiles,[26] this does not relieve the Jews of responsibility to welcome the Messiah who fulfils the promises of God to them.

Paul's fifth question (v. 8) echoes the Jewish objector's accusation that Paul is teaching that a 'good' thing (Gentiles' salvation) results from 'evil' (Jewish rejection of the gospel). But that would mean that 'Jews should do more evil that more good may come to the Gentiles'. This is what some are saying that Paul teaches. But this is blasphemous. God is no callous opportunist but the just judge. Paul leaves the objector's question hanging, adding only, 'Whose condemnation is just.' If Jews disbelieve God's promises to them God is not unjust in extending his mercy to the Gentiles. But this is no justification to do evil.

In verse 9 Paul rounds off his argument by returning to verse 1. 'Are we (Jews) better?' Answers Paul, 'Not at all,' adding dramatically, 'for we previously charged both Jews and Greeks to be *under* sin.' Paul is referring to the 'charge' against Jews and Greeks (Gentiles) that he has been making as from 1:18 ('the wrath of God is being revealed from heaven against all godlessness and wickedness').

Thus verse 9 goes back beyond the sins of Jews (2:1–3:8) to the sins of the Gentiles (1:18-32). He concludes that Jews and Greeks are both 'under,' that is, 'ruled by sin,' 'under the heel of sin' and 'slaves of sin' as he will say later (see on 6:17, 20). Paul will justify this verdict by a series of Old Testament Scriptures.

For a moment, however, let me pause to summarize Paul's teaching in verses 1-9 as it relates to the Jews.

---

26. See on 1:2-3; 15:8, 12.

First, God has given his 'words' to his historic people (v. 2) and God is 'faithful' (v. 3) and 'true' (vv. 4 and 7) to those promises.

Second, God's integrity is not 'set aside' because of the unbelief of (some of) the Jews regarding those 'words' (v. 3), or their 'wickedness' (v. 5) and 'falsehood' (vv. 4 and 7).

Third, God will judge the Jews righteously and impartially, according to their works.

Fourth, if the failure of (some) Jews to engage the 'words' of God meant that the saving righteousness of God has come to others (vv. 5, 7), this does not relieve the Jews of their failure to honour Christ. Nor must opportunistic motives be attributed to God, as if a good end arose from a lack of faithfulness by God to his people Israel.

Fifth, Paul is not, therefore, 'blasphemously' saying – as some claim – that it is good to do evil since God will bring good from it.

G. No one is righteous (3:10-18)

Paul's verdict that 'Jews and Greeks [are] all under sin' is not merely his (human) opinion. Paul writes as an apostle, who bears the authority of the risen Christ (see on 1:1, 5). His apostolic judgement is underpinned by passages from the sacred Scriptures as introduced by, 'Even as it is written' (v. 10).[27] Paul the apostle is echoing the voice of God about all people.

The first text (v. 10 – 'there is not even one righteous person') paraphrases Ecclesiastes 7:19-20:

> Wisdom makes one wise man
> more powerful than ten rulers in a city.
> *There is not a righteous man on earth*
> who does what is right and never sins.

The second (v. 11 – 'no one understands, no one seeks God') quotes Psalm 14:3[28] which, however, begins, 'The fool says in his heart, "There is no God." ' Thus Paul seems to be tapping into

---

27. Paul's Greek word 'written' (*gegraptai*) is perfect tense, passive voice and means a scripture (1) written *by God*, and (2) one that is still 'speaking'.

the 'wisdom' tradition where the 'wise' '*fear* God' and the 'fools'
do not. This may be confirmed by Paul's final text (Ps. 36:1)
which says, 'There is *no fear* of God before their eyes' (v. 18).
From these Old Testament texts God is saying that all people,
Jews included, are 'fools' because they do not 'fear God'.

Paul introduces other Old Testament texts that point to
human wickedness in speech[29] and violent behaviour.[30] It is
a sorry picture, which human history and experience confirms. 'All have turned aside' and have not acted out of genuine
'kindness' but have behaved deceitfully, cruelly and violently.
In other words, they are 'fools' who have said in their hearts
'there is no God' and whose wicked behaviour has expressed
their unbelief.

Earlier, Paul observed that intellectual Gentile idolaters
'professed themselves wise but were fools' (1:22). But it is the
same with the Jews, despite being God's chosen people bearing
his covenant sign (circumcision) and covenant agreement (the
Law) and, above all, having his 'words' of promise (3:2). They,
too, are 'fools'.

H. The Law speaks (3:19-20)
With these two sentences Paul concludes and summarizes the
entire section begun at 1:18.

His opening words, 'We know', appeal to his readers'
knowledge of gospel teaching they received at their baptism
(see 6:17: 'you...have become obedient from the heart to the
pattern of *teaching* to which you were committed'). That is,
Paul is pointing them now to truths they 'know' well.

We know that
    everything   the Law   says
                 it   speaks
    to those who are in the Law.

---

28. Paul quotes the Greek version of the Psalm (13), not the Hebrew on which
our English translations depend, thus explaining the difference in wording.
29. Verses 13-14 quoting Psalms 5, 139 and 10 (with differing words, from the
Septuagint).
30. Verses 14-17 quoting Isaiah 59, Proverbs 1 (with differing words, from the
Septuagint).

But what does Paul mean by 'the Law'? Clearly, he is using the one word 'Law' (*nomos*) in two senses. The first points to the texts from the Old Testament quoted above (vv. 10-18). 'Law' here means the Old Testament. The second reference is to God's 'Law' given at Mt. Sinai, as the basis and standard for Israel's covenant-obedience to God. So, Paul is saying that the Bible 'speaks' to, that is, passes a *verdict* on those who live by the Law God gave to Israel. That verdict is that on the Last Day, 'every mouth will be shut and the whole world will be under the righteous judgement of God' (v. 19b). In other words, God's word written in the Scriptures finds that his covenant-Law condemns the people as Law-breakers. (Paul is speaking directly to Jews though indirectly the same holds true to the Gentiles who have that 'law' in their consciences.)

Paul's wordplay must not be missed, as it easily is in translation. 'Law' demonstrates that 'all are under (*hupo*) sin' (3:9) and that the 'whole world ... is under judgement (*hupo-dikos*) to God'. All without exception are *'under* sin' and *under* judgement'. Without exception all people – Jews and Gentiles – lie defeated 'under Sin,' with Sin's foot on the throat. There is nothing but extreme discomfort in these words.

So Paul concludes.

> Wherefore from the works of the Law
> no flesh will be justified before God
> for through the Law comes the knowledge of sin.

'Do not look to "law" for salvation,' Paul is saying, in particular to the Jew who would have done that very thing. But the same principle applies to the Gentile. No one, Jew or Gentile, fulfils any standard, God-given or man-made. The breaches of the 'works of the law' are the outer symptoms of an inner corruption, that our lives are ruled by Sin. Later, Paul will teach that such Sin is cosmic and ineradicable, derived from Adam, patriarch of the human race at its beginning (5:12-21).

It is wrong to caricature Paul's teaching about sin. Such a caricature would say that 'dismal Paul' is accusing everybody of being steeped in criminal wickedness and evil. In that case the 'good living' citizen who pays his tax smiles to himself as he dismisses the apostle as out of touch and irrelevant to modern and educated people. But Paul is not saying that. No doubt Paul met many decent Jews and Gentiles, relatively speaking. Rather, Paul's irresistible accusation against himself and every human being is that everybody approves of some kind of 'law' but does not practise what he knows to be true. 'Law,' therefore, condemns and cannot save.

Paul's argument begun in 1:18 is straightforward. Regardless of whether we are Gentiles or Jews we fail to do what we know is true. Gentiles stare at creation while their inner sense of morality approves right and condemns wrong. Jews have the unambiguous written 'Law' of God, which they 'hear' but which they do not 'do'. They have had entrusted to them the 'words' of God, especially the promises of the One who was to come, but these they have rejected. In other words, both Gentiles and Jews are 'under sin' and 'under judgement'. By our works each of us in those racial groups prove ourselves, first, to be incapable of achieving God's 'righteousness' and, second, to be unwilling to do so. Only God can impute that righteousness as his gift, as Paul now will proceed to say.

A Note on the 'New Perspective' and the Jews

Broadly speaking, the leading 'New Perspectivists' (Sanders, Dunn and Wright) limit the thrust of Paul's theology to Gentiles. Paul was Christ's apostle to the Gentiles, evangelizing them and devising 'justification by faith' to give *them* access to the covenant of God, rather than by Jewish 'works of the Law', since this would have been impossible. This assumed that the covenant of Abraham was still current and the people of Israel were not required to acknowledge Jesus as Messiah but merely required to 'stay in' the covenant by faithfully observing the 'works of the Law' (circumcision, Sabbath-keeping, calendar, food laws, commandments).

In Romans 2:1–3:9, however, Paul teaches (a) that Jews were as culpable before God as the Gentiles and accordingly as much in need of redemption in Christ as the Gentiles, and

(b) that the old covenant was now 'abolished,' supplanted by the new covenant so that a true 'Jew' might be either a Jew or a Gentile; it all depended on the 'heart' not the fact (or otherwise) of circumcision.

Paul clinches his case in chapter 4 when he teaches that, based on Genesis 15:6, Abraham the fountainhead of Israel was 'justified by faith' and not 'works' (4:1-8). There is only one route to the righteousness of God that is open to humans, whether Jew or Gentile, and that route is Christ crucified and risen, by 'faith' in him.

STUDY QUESTIONS

1. Is there a difference in saying that one is without excuse or without defense?

2. How is God displaying His wrath now?

3. In what ways has God revealed Himself?

4. Where in our culture today do I see God's 'handing over'?

5. How does God want me as a believer to behave in society?

6. Is God unjust or unfair in handing man over to himself?

7. Does man today really believe that he is under judgment, without a defense?

8. How would you compare the Jesus that Paul mentions with the modern day church goer?

9. Where today in our culture do I see the practice of evil and the approving of such wickedness?

10. Since the Gentiles are not 'under the law' how then are they without a defense? How does this apply to modern man? How does it apply to me?

11. Just as the Gentiles blasphemed God based on what the Jews did or did not do, is there such a response against the church today? Why or why not?

PART B

JUSTIFIED BY FAITH
(Romans 3:21–5:11)

Christ's sacrifice is the source of God's verdict 'righteous' which he graciously bestows on sinners who are otherwise subject to God's wrath. God's justifying act is directed to those who believe in Christ and his sacrificial death for them. Paul points to Abraham, the fountainhead of Israel, who prior to his circumcision believed in God and was declared 'righteous'. Thus Abraham as 'believer' is the 'father' of all God's people, Jew and Gentile. Peace with God (reconciliation) is found in and through Christ; such is God's love towards his enemies.

3

The Righteousness of God
(Romans 3:21-31)

A critical point in the letter is now reached. Paul has concluded that on account of Law 'all – Jews and Gentiles – are under sin' (3:9) and 'the whole world is under judgement' (3:20). This brings Paul to speak of the 'righteous' work of God for the salvation of *all*, Jews and Gentiles.

1. THE REVELATION OF THE RIGHTEOUSNESS OF GOD (vv. 21-26)
Paul now re-introduces 'the righteousness of God'. His first reference was to God's *saving* activity through teaching the gospel (see on 1:17) and his second to God's *judging* activity as (many) Jews reject that message (see on 3:5). Which meaning does Paul have in mind in this passage where 'the righteousness of God' is the dominant idea? Clearly it is the first. Paul is speaking about God's *saving* work in the world.

A. The righteousness of God is now revealed (v. 21a)
The greatest moment in history has now come. Paul can scarcely contain his excitement.

> But now
> apart from Law
> the righteousness of God is being displayed...

As Paul has shown, Law did not enable man to live righteously (1:18–3:20). Rather, Law (though in itself 'holy, just and good' – 7:12) has exposed and provoked wrongdoing, the tenacious power of sin in human hearts, both Gentile and Jews. The people of Israel, above all, should know this. At Mt. Sinai God gave them his Law to fulfill as the people he had chosen and saved.[1] From the beginning, however, they broke his Law. Moses pleaded with God to overlook the 'stubbornness,' 'wickedness' and 'sin' of the people (Deut. 9:7-21), and Jeremiah simply says, 'they broke my covenant' (Jer. 31:32).

Paul's words, 'But now', point back to the coming a few years earlier of the Son of God who was born of David's line, whom God raised from the dead (see on 1:3-4). 'But now' signals the end of the former era of 'Law', so that 'from *now on*' a new age has come in which the 'righteousness of God is being displayed' under a 'new covenant' (2 Cor. 3:6, 8, 9).

But how is the 'righteousness of God' *now* 'being displayed? It is by means of the gospel, as the earlier and similar reference in 1:17 made clear.

> I am not ashamed of the gospel ...
> for *in it* the righteousness of God is being revealed.[2]

Attempting to fulfill 'the works of the Law' (3:20) did not issue in righteous living but the opposite. The gospel, however, is *now* displaying 'the righteousness of God', that is, his righteous verdict of acquittal and acceptance of those who have turned in faith to Jesus, the Son of God. Thus, as earlier he dramatically understated it, he is 'not ashamed of' its message.

B. The righteousness of God was witnessed to by the law and prophets (v. 21b)

By 'law' Paul now means the first five books of the Bible in which the covenant Law given by God at Mt. Sinai is reported.

---

1. The word 'law' (*nomos*) appears almost fifty times in Romans. The core meaning is the covenant response God expected in commandment-keeping and ceremonial-observation as given at Mt. Sinai. By extension 'Law' also means the written text of the Old Testament (3:19-20). Sometimes Paul uses 'Law' in a wordplay, but meaning a 'principle' or 'rule' of human behaviour (3:27; 7:21, 23; 8:2).

2. The verbs are different (1:17: *apokaluptetai* / 'is revealed'; 3:21: *pephanerōtai* / 'is displaying') but the meanings are similar. The former is present passive, pointing to God's ongoing activity. The latter is perfect passive and suggests an action of God which he began and continues to do. Both refer to the preaching of the gospel in which God makes known his righteous verdict to those who by faith now belong to Christ crucified and risen.

'The law and the prophets' is Paul's way of referring to the *whole* of the Old Testament (see also on 1:2). In other words, he is pointing out that those scriptures foretold both the saving work of the Messiah and its announcement in the gospel bringing that salvation to the nations.[3] Thus 'the law and the prophets' are *Christian*[4] scriptures and deserve to be read publicly in the churches since they are God's 'witness' beforehand to the coming of Christ and the proclamation of the gospel.

C. The righteousness of God is for all who believe (v. 22)

The righteousness of God is God's saving activity now being revealed in the world (v. 21) through the message about Christ. But to whom is it being revealed? Verse 22 expands on verse 21. God's 'righteousness' is being revealed to those who believe his message.

> ... the righteousness of God is being revealed
> ... to all who believe ...

These words match exactly those given earlier, 'I am not ashamed of the gospel, for it is the power of God for salvation to *all who believe*' (see on 1:16). Clearly believing is the critical human response to God's saving act and his saving word.

Paul's words, 'the righteousness of God through faith *of* (literally) Jesus Christ', have inspired discussion. There is word-play[5] but also ambiguity. Does 'the faith *of* Jesus Christ' mean (1) the *faithfulness of* Christ in doing the will of God for us, or (2) *our* faith directed *towards* Christ? Both views have their advocates.[6]

Perhaps, though, we don't have to decide. Paul may have been making two points by one 'shorthand' statement: that *Christ's*

---

3. See also 2 Corinthians 1:19-20 where Paul also connects the fulfilment of the 'promises of God' in Christ with the apostolic preaching of Christ ('... the Son of God whom we preached ... all the promises of God find their "Yes" in him ...').

4. To be questioned is the current practice of referring to the Old Testament as the *Jewish* Scriptures as if to distinguish them from the Christian Scriptures of the New Testament. Since both Testaments point to Christ, both are Christian Scriptures.

5. English translation of the words 'faith ... believe' masks their close relationship in Greek (*pistis ... pisteuō*).

6. For argument for 'faith in Christ' based on a review of alternative views, see T. R. Schreiner, *Romans* 181-86.

faithfulness towards God and *our* faith in Christ are inseparable and basic to the revelation of God's righteousness in the world.

Christ's faithfulness towards God expressed obediently as, 'Not my will but yours be done' (Mark 14:36), brought him to Jerusalem and ultimately to Golgotha for our salvation. There his enemies mocked his faithfulness to God: 'He trusts in God; let God deliver him now...' (Matt. 27:43). The salvation won for us by Christ's 'faithfulness' is ours as we direct our faith towards him.

The words 'all who *believe*' (v. 22b), are important. It is not that the Jews will be saved by 'doing' the 'works of the Law' and the Gentiles by 'believing' the gospel (see on v. 30). There are not two ways of salvation, one for Jews another for Gentiles.[7] 'For,' as he immediately adds, 'there is no distinction; *all* have sinned and fall short of the glory of God.' That 'all' includes 'all' the descendants of Adam, both Jews and Gentiles, as the previous chapters have shown. God's 'righteous' work of saving people only applies to those Jews and Gentiles who give themselves in faith to the Son of God.

> for there is no distinction;
> all have sinned
> and are falling short of the glory of God.

But why does Paul say 'all *have* sinned' rather than 'all *are* sinning'? The latter option is true, but our present sins and our present 'falling short' flow from the 'original sin' of the first man, the fountainhead of the race, who set all his descendants on a pathway of rebellion against God (see on 5:12).[8] Paul was thinking of Adam when he wrote that we have 'borne the image of the man of dust' (1 Cor. 15:49). When Adam sinned, God's image in him was marred, as it has been since for all his descendants, Jews and Gentiles. This is another way of saying that humankind then lost access to the tree of life and gained death in its place (Gen. 3:23-24; see on 5:12).

---

7. Some 'New Perspectivists' say there are two covenants in parallel, one for Jews another for Christians.

8. For a learned defence of the doctrine of 'original sin', see H. Blocher, *Original Sin* (Leicester: pollos, 1997).

D. All are justified freely, by his grace (v. 24a)

'Justified' is a legal term meaning that an accused person is 'acquitted' or 'deemed innocent' by a judge (see on 2:13 and 1 Cor. 4:4). God, who is just and who judges 'according to truth', passes his favourable verdict 'as a gift' and 'by his grace'. God 'sets us right' with himself as an act of mercy on his part. Sin's presence and power within us all is such that we are incapable of attaining righteousness by our own effort, by 'the works of the Law' (see on 5:12-21; 7:21-25). Apart from God's mercy we are lost.

English translations do not always bring out the close connection between the word 'justified' and 'righteousness'. The verb 'justified' (*dikaioumenoi*) is related to the noun 'righteousness' (*dikaiosunē*) and might be better understood as 'declared right'.[9] The 'righteous' or saving work of God in the proclamation of the gospel is that he declares those who believe in Christ as 'justified' or 'declared to be in the right' with him.

The verb tenses are important. 'All have sinned' (completed action) but '[all] are being justified' (present tense). All were (somehow) present 'in' Adam when he sinned, but all *are being justified* as the gospel is being taught and believed. God's saving activity is an ongoing activity.

E. All are justified through God's propitiatory act of redemption in the death of Christ (vv. 24b-25a)

In another letter Paul wrote, 'One died for all' (2 Cor. 5:14). Here Paul has powerfully spelt out the details in evocative language. God expressed his saving activity in the death of Christ. It was a 'propitiatory' death,[10] that is, it was a sacrifice

---

9. The passive voice here used reverently means that God is the subject of the verb; *God* justifies the sinner, that is, God declares him to be 'in the right'.

10. Scholars debate the meaning of the Greek word *hilastērion* along three main lines.

(1) It means 'mercy seat,' the lid of the ark of the covenant upon which the blood of the sacrificial animal was sprinkled on the Day of Atonement. 'Mercy Seat' was a place of reconciliation between the Lord and his people. Although favoured by Luther and Calvin the problem with this suggestion is that it makes Jesus both the 'lid' and the 'blood' poured on it. Also, some have questioned whether Jesus in his sacrifice should be connected with something so impersonal as a piece of furniture.

that exhausted the righteous displeasure ('wrath') of God upon human wickedness (see on 1:18; 2:5, 8; 3:5). Elsewhere the apostle said that Christ 'became a curse for us' and that 'God made him sin, who knew no sin' (Gal. 3:13; 2 Cor. 5:21). Christ died 'for our sakes,' that is, 'in our places', so that God would declare his righteous verdict to the unrighteous who belong by faith to his Son.

In consequence, Christ's death was a redemptive one. Whereas the word 'propitiatory' captures the language of Leviticus in relation to the sacrifices of the Temple[11], the word 'redemptive' portrays the desperate slave prisoners escaping from Egypt to the freedom of the Promised Land. By Christ's death God liberates the captives from the prospect of an adverse verdict that, like the sword of Damocles, hangs precariously by a thread above our heads. By God's righteous activity on our behalf the 'slavery to fear' has been removed (see on 8:15). Like the fleeing Israelites we are both 'saved' and 'redeemed'.

F. God's saving activity: two consequences (vv. 25-26)
God set forth Christ in his death as a 'propitiation' and as a 'redemption'. This, says Paul, was 'to demonstrate' two realities.

First, the propitiatory and redemptive death of Christ 'demonstrates' God's 'righteous activity' in 'passing over' sins 'previously committed' in the 'patience of God'. Paul is thinking about sins committed in the aeons prior to the death of Christ. He is saying that Christ's death somehow stayed the hand of God's wrath beforehand. In other words, Christ's

---

(2) It means 'expiation,' the covering over of the sin from the sight of God. The RSV translates as 'expiation', and this translation was advocated by C. H. Dodd, who likened 'expiation' to disinfectant eliminating germs.

(3) It means exhausting the just wrath of God on sins. This is no impersonal or crass placating of a vengeful God. God himself 'presents' his very own Son whom he sent as a sacrifice. In other words, God directed the wrath against himself in the person of his Son.

Option (3) best fits the evidence (see Stott, 113-16; Schreiner, 191-93).

11. See Leviticus 16:2,13-15 where *hilastērion* with the definite article means *the* 'mercy seat', that is, the lid of the ark on which the blood of sacrifices were sprinkled. The absence of the article in Romans 3:25 points away from Christ crucified as the 'mercy seat'. Perhaps the 'mercy seat' could be thought of as an Old Testament 'type' anticipating the cross where the Son of God offered himself as a sacrifice to God.

death was effective, to a degree, ahead of Good Friday. Paul is not saying that these sinners were thereby saved, but rather that God's hand of final wrath in the judgement of the world was held back in anticipation of the death of Christ.

Second, that death ended a former aeon and inaugurated the final age, 'the now time' as Paul calls it (see v. 21, 'But *now* ...). In the former aeon God merely 'passed over' sins, held back the flood of his wrath. But 'now' God is 'righteous' and 'declares righteous' the person 'who believes in Jesus'. That is, subsequent to that death God not merely 'passes over' sins in a general sense but thoroughly saves individual believers from his judgement on the Last Day. This is redemption, the truest of freedoms.

At the same time, because Christ's death was 'propitiatory,' satisfying God's implacable reaction against wrongdoing, God remains 'righteous' in himself while extending his righteous salvation to the unrighteous through the preaching of the gospel.

2. THE PLACE OF PRIDE (vv. 27-31)

To the Jew, including the Jew who has some knowledge of the gospel, this was radical teaching. Questions would have leaped to the minds of Jewish readers, some of which Paul now anticipates.

The structure of this short passage should be noted.

First question:	*Where is boasting?*
Observation:	A man is justified by faith apart from works.
Second question:	*Is God the God only of the Jews?*
Observation:	God is One, justifying Jews and Gentiles by faith.
Third Question:	*Do we abolish Law through faith?*
Answer:	We uphold the Law.

So, first, Paul asks, 'Where, then, is boasting?' The next sentence shows that 'boasting' occurs where a person believes he is 'justified ... by works', that is, by Law-keeping. Earlier

Paul noted that Jews 'rest in the Law' (2:17). Paul himself had felt 'confident in the flesh' in that he was 'as to righteousness under the Law, blameless' (Phil. 3:6). But so far as genuine Law-keeping is concerned this is a delusion, writes Paul. Law serves only to expose Law-breaking; it even provokes Law-breaking (see on 5:20).

In Jewish culture, Law-keeping created an élite class of religious scholars separate from and 'superior to' the ordinary people. Worst of all, it encouraged spiritual pride such as that of the Pharisee in the Temple who boasted to God about his fasting and tithing as he measured himself off against the tax collector (Luke 18:9-14). Clearly 'boasting' was part and parcel of first-century Jewish culture.

So to the question, 'Where, then, is boasting?' Paul replies, 'It is excluded' (literally, 'shut out'). In another wordplay he continues, 'Boasting is excluded, is it? By what "law"? By the "law" of works? No, by the "law" of faith.' This is daring stuff! Paul the former Pharisee throws the 'law' back at his imaginary objector. The 'law' (or 'principle') of 'faith' spells the end of the 'law' of 'works' and the 'boasting' that went with it.

Then he adds this powerful observation (v. 28):

> For we reckon that a man is justified ('declared right with God') by faith apart from the works of the Law.

This is one of Paul's 'great' texts that settled forever the way to salvation for Martin Luther. It is rather abbreviated. Paul means us to understand 'justified by faith' as meaning 'justified by faith in *Christ*' (see 5:9 where he says that we are 'justified by his blood').

Paul is not saying that we are to have 'faith in faith', as opposed to, and an improvement on, faith in the works of the Law! Rather, he declares that God's 'righteous' activity is fulfilled in us upon hearing the gospel as we direct our faith away from our religious achievements ('works of the Law') to the Son of God, crucified and risen.

The second question (v. 29) has only to be asked to be answered, 'Is he God only of the Jews and not also of the

Gentiles?' Paul's Jewish objector, conscious of 'chosen race' status, may have harboured secret beliefs that God was God only of the Jews. But his own Scriptures did not teach him this. The Lord who chose, redeemed, instructed and sent prophets to Israel is the God of the universe, the master of history who, significantly, made many promises for the blessing of the Gentile nations.[12] So to the question, 'Is he not God also of the Gentiles?' Paul answers, 'Yes, he is God also of the Gentiles.'

Paul now makes a further observation (v. 30):

Since God is One
he justifies   the circumcision   by faith, and
               the uncircumcision   through faith.

Paul confronts the Jewish objector with the creed he recites daily, 'Hear O Israel, the LORD our God is *One*' (Deut. 6:4). Fundamental to that creed and to the First Commandment of the Law is that there is and can only be 'One' God. But he is God of, God to and God for both Jews and Gentiles, as in Paul's reply to the question of the previous verse. Furthermore, he does not discriminate between the 'circumcision' and the 'uncircumcision' as to the way to the righteousness of God. Since both Jew and Gentile are 'under sin' and 'under judgement' there is only one way for both to find salvation, by faith, that is, by faith in the Messiah of Israel and not by means of 'works of the Law'.

The twin realities that God is One and there is one way to righteousness for both Jews and Gentiles relates directly to a pastoral concern of this letter. At that time, apparently, Jewish and Gentile believers were meeting separately. Paul's passion, however, was that each welcome the other and that 'together' they may 'with *one* voice glorify the God and Father of the Lord Jesus Christ' (15:1, 6). Note that there is 'one' God who is to be glorified by all races with 'one' voice.

The last question Paul raises is, 'Are we, therefore, abolishing the Law through faith?' (v. 31). This is a heartfelt question. God's covenant with Israel and her sense of identity as his 'chosen'

---

12. See e.g. Isaiah 66:18-21.

people was at stake in Paul's answer. His interjection, literally, 'Let it not be,' conveys something of the utter seriousness of the question, but also of his answer. He replies:

On the contrary, we are upholding the Law.

To the question, 'are you *abolishing* ...?' Paul's reply is exactly the opposite, 'we are *upholding* ...'. By this he means at least two things.

First, he is 'upholding' the principle of the Law as given by God. Initially the Lord chose, then saved, Israel. Only then did he give the Law. This, too, was as much a matter of 'grace' as his choice and deliverance of the people had been. The people received the Law as their side of God's covenant, which they undertook to fulfil. But 'now' once more God has graciously saved the people, this time in the Messiah, a salvation to be received by faith. Again there are covenant obligations to be fulfilled in willing response to God's gracious salvation, as Paul will spell out in chapters 12–15. Paul is establishing the principles of the Law under a new covenant.

Second, Paul (following Jesus) actually deepens the truest intent of the Commandments ('Law'), that is, to evoke in us love for God and love for our neighbour. The Law as originally given and as amplified in the ethical teaching of Jesus and the apostles spells out in concrete detail what it means to love God and our fellowman (see e.g. on 13:8-10). 'Upholding the Law,' then, means having right attitudes of the heart that are expressed in the right actions of the hand. Both are necessary. If only the heart is involved, the Law remains merely a matter of sentiment. What use is it to love the hungry neighbour but not feed him? But if only the hand is involved, with no inner concern of the heart, the Law degenerates into empty legalism with its accompanying boasting.

3. CONCLUSION

Paul began this section with the words, '... apart from Law' as if law is no more but he ends with the words, '... we uphold the Law.' How has Paul moved from one to the other?

The answer is that God's hour has struck. In the coming of the Messiah, his death and resurrection, and in the spreading of the gospel, God has acted in saving righteousness for both Jews and Gentiles, who alike are Law-breakers. That death had the retroactive effect of staying the hand of God's final wrath on humankind. More particularly that death, being 'propitiatory' and 'redemptive,' makes God both 'just and justifier' of sinners who believe in the Son of God.

Where is boasting? It must not be. Works of the Law contribute nothing to righteousness. Faith alone is the way to receive it.

Where is Israel's special place in the divine plan? Does Israel have God to herself? On the contrary, the One God justifies both Jews and Gentiles in one and the same way, without discrimination, in Christ, by faith in him.

Where is Law? Is it abolished? By no means. Through God's righteous and saving activity Law has come fully into its own, in its true and practical meaning, that is, faith working through love, honouring God and doing good to others (see chapters 12–13; 14:1–15:6).

STUDY QUESTIONS

1. How is the righteousness of God now being displayed?

2. In what ways do I see God's righteousness being displayed today?

3. How are propitiation and redemption linked?

4. Do I see myself as a 'law-breaker'?

5. How are the 'the law' and 'the heart' suppose to be connected? What extremes am I suppose to avoid?

4

Abraham, Man of Faith
(Romans 4:1-25)

This chapter, which is devoted to Abraham, should be understood against the background of the Jewish theology of the day. Jews, including many Christian Jews, held that Abraham's actions, recorded in the book of Genesis, defined members of the true people of God. They pointed to Abraham's circumcision (Gen. 17) and to his obedient willingness to sacrifice Isaac (Gen. 22). To these actions of Abraham – his circumcision and his spirit of obedience – Jewish theologians then added the keeping of the Law given under Moses as non-negotiable for those who truly belonged to God in the End-times.

Paul, the pre-Christian Jew, doubtless subscribed to this theology. All that changed, however, when the risen and ascended Christ confronted Paul on the road to Damascus. Now Paul began to understand that salvation was only to be found 'in Christ' crucified, risen and returning. Belonging to Christ by faith in him was the thing, and nothing else.

For Paul another passage in Genesis was now held to be determinative, that is Genesis 15:6: 'Abraham *believed* God and it was reckoned to him as righteousness.' Romans 4 is Paul's exposition of that great reality. Like Romans as a whole, however, this chapter is not teaching without a real and precise historical context. Paul is responding to the typical Jewish objector who appears to have been opposing Paul's Christ-centred, Law-free gospel. Most likely this kind of objector was to be found in the constituent house churches in Rome. Paul is seeking to address and resolve such objections in the letter before he arrives in person.

1. ABRAHAM (vv. 1-8)

In the previous passage Paul said that God was God of both Jews and Gentiles and that he declared both righteous in exactly the same way, that is, by faith apart from works of the Law (3:28-30). There was an important corollary, namely, that 'boasting' (based on one's works) was therefore 'shut out' (3:27).

In verse 1 Paul applies this principle to the most important of persons, Abraham, the forefather of the Jewish race. We must make the important observation that Paul calls Abraham '*our* forefather'. Paul is speaking as a Jew to fellow-Jews. Indeed, the whole chapter is a conversation between Paul the Jew and fellow-Jews answering their objections and questions. And the subject? The contribution (or otherwise) of 'works of the Law' to 'righteousness' with God.

Working backwards from Paul's words about Abraham it is evident that Jewish theology then held that Abraham 'found' God's approval on account of his works. Most likely they pointed to the patriarch's obedience in leaving Ur of the Chaldees, to submitting to circumcision and in being prepared to sacrifice his son Isaac.

In verse 2 Paul even agrees for 'argument's sake' that if Abraham had been 'justified by works' he would have been able to boast. But then Paul makes the telling addition, 'but not before God', making it clear that it is not possible to be 'justified by works'. Clearly Paul is correcting current Jewish theology, including probably the beliefs of some of his Jewish Christian readers in Rome. For them, apparently, being righteous with God depended on 'works of the Law' and as proof of this they pointed (wrongly) to Abraham's works.

In verse 3 Paul cites the critical text Genesis 15:6 that clinches the matter once and for all:

Abraham believed God
and it was reckoned to him for righteousness.[1]

---

1. Evidently Genesis 15:6 was an exegetical battleground between Jews and Paul at the time, since it is also discussed in Galatians 3:6-14 and James 2:18-26.

In verses 4-5 the apostle applies this text to the proposition momentarily considered in verse 2, 'If Abraham had been justified by works'. So Paul contrasts the one who *works* for 'righteousness with God' with the one who *believes*.

To him who works
his reward is   not reckoned   according to grace
             but [reckoned]   according to debt.
To him who does not work
but [who] believes in him   who justifies the ungodly
   his faith   is reckoned   for righteousness.

Work for righteousness with God, says Paul, and you work yourself hopelessly into an overdraft with God that is unpayable. Believe in God on the basis of his grace, Paul counters, and God will regard you as righteous. It's as simple as that!

Paul, however, is not scoring points in this rather sophisticated theological debate. His citation of Genesis 15:6 and his exposition of it has pastoral intent. He cares deeply about the plight of his fellow-Jew in Rome who bases his relationship with God on human effort, on 'works of the Law'. Because that person is not righteous with God on the basis of faith, he or she does not enjoy inner peace with God and the sense of being loved as a child of God (see on 5:15). In short, Paul longs that men and women enjoy the 'blessing' of God.

In verses 6 to 8 Paul quotes and comments on Psalm 32:1:

David pronounces blessing on the man to whom God reckons righteousness apart from works. 'Blessed are they whose transgressions are forgiven and whose sins are covered. Blessed is the man to whom the Lord will not reckon sin.'

David declared 'blessed' the man or woman who has been forgiven by God. This is the other side of the coin; to be forgiven by God is to be 'reckoned righteous' by him. Whether rich or poor or somewhere in between this is where God's truest blessing is to be found. Let the reader pause for a moment to thank God for this greatest of his blessings.

2. ABRAHAM, FATHER OF BELIEVERS (vv. 9-12)

Paul now anticipates questions from his Jewish objector.

He asks rhetorically in verse 9, was this blessing (forgiven/ reckoned righteous by God) pronounced upon the circumcised (which a Jew would not doubt), or was it also pronounced upon the uncircumcised (which a Jew would doubt very much)? Paul's way of framing the question tells his objector that God is absolutely even-handed in blessing both Jews and Gentiles.

Paul points once more to his key text, Genesis 15:6, and to God's declaration of Abraham's righteousness.

> For we (Jews) say,
> 'Abraham's faith was reckoned to him as righteousness.'

Paul pursues his objector relentlessly (v. 10): 'How then was [righteousness] reckoned to [Abraham]?' 'Was it when he was circumcised or uncircumcised'? The answer is: 'Not in circumcision but in uncircumcision.' In other words, God reckoned the patriarch of the Jews righteous *before* he was circumcised, that is, when Abraham was in effect a *Gentile*! How shocking!

Verse 11 implies the objector's next question: 'if Abraham was declared righteous before his circumcision, why then was he circumcised at all?' Paul's answer reaffirms his key text, Genesis 15:6.

> [Abraham] received circumcision
> as a sign, a seal of the righteousness of faith
> which he had in uncircumcision.

In other words, circumcision contributed nothing to God's gift of righteousness to Abraham. Only the patriarch's faith in God invited that pronouncement. Circumcision was merely an outer 'sign' or 'seal' to Abraham of the inner reality of faith that brought salvation to him.

This was no ad hoc thing in the purposes of God. It was calculated and deliberate in the divine counsels. God gave his righteousness to Abraham the believer when still uncircumcised with a clear intention.

that [Abraham] might be the father of all who believe
even though uncircumcised
so that righteousness might be reckoned to them also.

Paul is saying that God's declaration of righteousness to
uncircumcised Abraham back then at the dawn of salvation
history opened the way to God's declaration of righteousness
to uncircumcised Gentiles now, provided they are believers,
as Abraham was.

What then of the circumcised, his fellow-Jews? Paul turns
to them in verse 12

that [Abraham] might also be the father of the circumcised,
but not only to the circumcised,
but also to those who walk in the steps
of the faith of our father Abraham
when he was uncircumcised.

So believing Abraham is 'father' also to Jews (who believe
in the Messiah). We are surprised, however, that Paul makes
such a glancing reference to his fellow-Jews. He immediately
returns to Abraham the *un*circumcised who was a man of
faith and to those Gentiles who 'walk in his steps' as believers.
Clearly it is Abraham's faith in God rather than circumcision
that is dominant in Paul's mind (see on 2:25-29). Let the Jewish
objector grasp this radical truth. For not until then will he
understand that only 'in Christ' and by faith in him is God's
righteousness to be found.

3. NOT BY THE LAW (vv. 13-15)

For the Jew, including the Jewish hearer of this letter who
sat in the Christian house meeting in Rome, the purposes
of God were focused on Moses and the Law that God gave
at Mt. Sinai. Not so, says the Apostle Paul (v. 13), once more
echoing the words 'the righteousness of faith' from his key
scripture in Genesis 15:6:

The promise to Abraham (and to his seed)
to be the heir of the world
did not come through Law
but through the righteousness of faith.

God's 'promise' to Abraham (and his descendants) to 'inherit the world' gathers up the many promises to Abraham – numberless progeny,[2] possession of the land of Canaan,[3] all nations being blessed in Abraham and his 'seed'.[4] The first man, Adam, by his apostasy from God, forfeited the promise of a people owning his name and a land to live in. God, however, promised to restore both a people and a land to faithful Abraham and to his 'seed', that is, Jesus Christ.[5] Thus Paul can assure the (mostly Gentile) Corinthian Christians, 'all things are yours ... things to come' (1 Cor. 3:21, 23). God's many promises to Abraham will be fulfilled in those who by faith in him belong to Jesus the Messiah, Abraham's 'seed'.

In verse 14, Paul again appears to be correcting the Jewish objector. Current Jewish theology said that God's promises of blessing were for those who keep the Law of God given at Mt. Sinai. In reply, Paul points out that God made no such promises when he gave the Law. His promises about inheriting the world were made to Abraham four centuries beforehand.[6] Besides, 'promise' and 'Law' are mutually exclusive. God's 'promise' can only be met with 'faith' for its fulfilment. Law, based as it is on human effort, nullifies both 'promise' and 'faith'.

Furthermore, Law has the effect of engendering wrath, that is, the wrath of God (v. 15). In Abraham's day the Law had not been given. To be sure, sin was a present reality, as from the time of Adam (as the sinful actions of the patriarchs show), but it was not explicitly recognised as sin (see 3:20: 'through the Law is the knowledge of sin'; 5:13: 'sin was in the world before the Law was given, but sin is not counted where is no Law'). Once the Law came in the time of Moses, however, sin was identified with its wrathful consequences and – as Paul will say later – the imposition of Law tended to provoke further sin (see on 7:7-12). In short, it is clear that

Law did not attract the saving promises of God nor, therefore, inspire faith in God through those promises. Law only served to show up human shortcomings and stir them up further.

4. ABRAHAM, OUR FATHER (vv. 16-22)

In verse 16 Paul draws an important conclusion based on the previous verses 13-15.

> For this reason it is by faith
> that the promise is received
> according to grace
> and confirmed to all Abraham's seed
> not only to the adherents of law
> but also to those who hold the faith of Abraham
> who is the father of us all.

Here Paul is redefining the true people of God, the people of the End-time. Who are they? They are believers, both Jews ('the adherents of the Law') and Gentiles ('those who hold the faith of Abraham'). By what principle are they the people of God? By the principle of 'grace', that is, not by the principle of 'works' of Law-keeping. God has given his word of promise and those who have *believed* him are his people.

There is consistency in God's purposes from beginning to end. At the beginning of salvation history Abraham, the 'father of us all,' was a believer. So shall all the people of the End-time be believers. This is God's way to his righteousness, to acceptance with him as his children.

In verse 17 Paul establishes this from Scripture (Gen. 17:5) where God says:

> A father of many nations I have appointed you.

In regard to God, Paul adds:

> In the presence of God
> Abraham believed in him who gives life to the dead
> and calls things that are not as though they were.

Abraham and Sarah were elderly and beyond child-bearing when God promised that many nations would descend from them. Yet Abraham heard God's promise and drew near into his presence and believed that promise. He did so on account of 'who' God is – the One who created the universe from nothing and the One who also *re*-creates, that is, 'who raises the dead.'[7] This God, the God of infinite power and goodness, promised old Abraham many descendants and Abraham believed him.

Since God's promise to Abraham was for generations of descendants it meant that his faith was future-looking, that is, that it was trust in God laden with *hope*. So Paul observes that Abraham 'hoping against hope believed' (v. 18). What did the patriarch believe and hope for? Abraham 'had been told' by God to look to the stars in heaven, and had been promised, 'So shall your seed be' (Gen. 15:5). Thus Abraham believed that by the power of God the Almighty 'he would become the father of many nations'.

Now this was a great act of faith and hope for the centenarian since, as Paul observes of him (vv. 19-21), his body was 'as good as dead' and the womb of Sarah was barren. In spite of these inescapable physical realities, Abraham's faith did not flag nor did distrust in God deflect him from the divine promise. Rather, his faith in God became more powerful as he became fully convinced that what God had promised he was able to do.

Paul concludes (v. 22), reflectively returning to the key text (Gen. 15:6) introduced back in verse 3: 'Wherefore it was reckoned to [Abraham] for righteousness.' The antecedent of 'it' is the patriarch's belief in God which has been mentioned directly or indirectly in every verse in this passage (vv. 16-22). That belief was not vague and diffuse but directed specifically to God's promise to the old man. Further, despite the apparent impossibility of progeny Abraham's faith actually increased as time went by, such was his confidence in God's veracity, goodness and power. In short, Abraham's faith was not merely a formal faith or a list of items to be assented to as in a creed

---

7. See 2 Corinthians 1:9.

(important as that might be). Rather, Abraham's faith related specifically to God's promises *to him and Sarah* in their own circumstances. God's promise to Abraham would hold true or it would fail. Abraham believed that the promise would become a reality and, as a matter of history, it came to pass. That is what he believed and set his hope towards and for that reason God declared Abraham to be 'righteous' in his sight.

5. RIGHTEOUSNESS NOW (vv. 23-25)
Now comes the application of Genesis 15:6 to which Paul has been pointing since verse 3.

Abraham is 'father' to the believers in Rome to whom Paul is writing. His fatherhood or ancestry, however, is not like a bearded great-grandfather in a faded photograph whose blood runs in our veins. Our relationship with our forefather Abraham is different. It is not about his genes living in us. Rather, it is our imitation of Abraham's faith in God's promise that makes us his 'children' and part of the great family of God. In this regard we must set Abraham alongside Adam, the first man who was, indeed, the biological forefather of all people everywhere. The contrast could not be more stark. Adam was a rebel with a closed fist in the face of God. Abraham, however, was a believer who expressed his trust in God in active and sacrificial obedience.

Thus, in verses 22-23 Paul tells the the Roman Christians and us that Genesis 15:6 ('righteousness was reckoned to him') was not written only for Abraham but also for us today.

> Righteousness will be reckoned
> to those who believe in him
> who raised Jesus our Lord from the dead.

Do we see what Paul is saying? God's ways have not changed. As Paul said in verse 17 Abraham believed in God 'who gives life to the dead' and for that God reckoned him as righteous before him. For Paul's readers today, the issue remains the same: do we believe in God who raises the dead? Specifically do *we* believe that God raised Jesus our Lord from the dead? Such a belief then made Abraham our father and today makes us his children.

Christ's resurrection was real, not merely token or symbolic. Christ was truly dead and truly buried but no less truly raised bodily to life on the third day. This is history. But it is unseen to us, just as God's promise was unseen to Abraham. Yet he believed notwithstanding God's invisibility, and so do we.

Paul concludes this chapter-long exposition of Genesis 15:6 with a beautifully balanced aphorism about the death and resurrection of Jesus (referred to in the previous verse – '[God] who raised Jesus ... from the dead'.) Most likely these words were originally composed (by Paul?) as a teaching 'tradition' or faith formula for catechetical purposes.[8]

> [Our Lord Jesus]
>   was handed over   for our transgressions
> and   raised   for our justification.

Let us consider Paul's words, beginning with 'handed over' (one word in the original Greek – *paredothē*). History and prophecy underlie 'handed over'. As a matter of history Paul's word 'handed over' echoes the Gospels. Jesus was 'handed over' – from Judas to Caiaphas, from Caiaphas to Pilate, from Pilate to the execution squad (see Mark 14 and 15). Paul also quotes the early tradition about the night Jesus was 'handed over' (1 Cor. 11:23). By whom was Jesus 'handed over'? Jews or Gentiles or both? The answer is both; Caiaphas the Jew and Pilate the Gentile were equally culpable. Ultimately, however, it was God who 'handed over' his Son into the hands of wicked men who killed him. Yet by that unjust death has come our salvation.

As a matter of prophecy we see Paul here recalling the words of Isaiah who prophesied that the Lord's Servant would be 'handed over for our sins' (Isa. 53:12). Here the meaning of the preposition 'for' (Greek: *dia*) is critical. In both Isaiah 53 and Paul's allusion to it the word 'for' does not express purpose but *cause*. It was *because* of our sins that Jesus was 'handed over'. Our transgressions brought about his death.

In the second leg of the verse Paul uses two more words that bear further reflection. One is the word 'raised,' that is, Jesus

---

8. Other examples of such traditions in Romans include 1:1-4; 10:9.

was 'raised *by God*,'[9] as the women were told at the mouth of the empty tomb on Easter morning (Mark 16:6). Jesus 'raised (by God)' is firmly embedded in the early tradition 'received' by Paul (in Damascus?) which he 'handed over' as foundational for the churches (1 Cor. 15:4).

The other significant word is 'justification' (Greek: *dikaiōsis*) a close relative of 'righteousness' (Greek: *dikaiosunē*) the keyword of the chapter. God's raising of Jesus was not a bare event, but laden with meaning. 'He was raised *for our justification*,' that is, for God's approval of us as 'right' with him.

As in the first leg, the preposition 'for' (Greek: *dia*) is *causal*. The raising of Christ *caused* our 'justification'. On account of his resurrection of Jesus, God graciously recognises as 'righteous' those very ones whose transgressions *caused* the death of his Son. God reckons (or imputes) his righteousness to those who believe in him as the resurrector of Jesus our Lord.

6. CONCLUSION

Jews then believed that biological descent from Abraham and keeping the Law of Moses made them God's special people and assured them of membership in his coming kingdom.

Paul has demonstrated that, on the contrary, all people, Jews included, are 'under sin' and therefore like the rest of the world 'under judgement' by God (see on 3:9 and 5:19). As things stand all people are condemned because of sin.

The great news, however, is that God has provided the means of acquittal in the sacrificial death of his Son, the Messiah Jesus, descendant of David whom he raised from the dead. Based on Christ's death and resurrection God offers his gift of righteousness to those who believe in him.

This righteousness, however, is found only in Christ and not in human religious self-effort. This cuts across the Jewish theology that was held among many Jewish Christians, including apparently those who attended Christian groups in Rome. These Jews pointed to the works of obedience of Abraham and the works required by God in his Law given to Moses.

---

9. This is the implication of the divine passive (*ēgerthē*) but is stated directly in the previous verse and also by Peter to Cornelius in Acts 10:40 ('*God* raised him ...').

In this chapter Paul has responded to these Jewish objections to his Law-free gospel. His great controlling text is Genesis 15:6 where God reckons Abraham righteous on account of his faith in the divine promises. Abraham exercised that faith before he was circumcised, that is, when he was in effect still a Gentile! It is Abraham's faith as imitated by Jews and Gentiles that makes him 'our father,' 'the father of us all'.

STUDY QUESTIONS

1. Do I see my salvation as truly a 'blessing' from God?

2. Do I rest on my baptism for salvation as the Jew rested on his circumcision?

3. How has God's law affected me in how I look at my sin?

4. Is my 'right standing' before God something that I can experience now or do I have to wait until the future?

5

Justified and Reconciled
(Romans 5:1-11)

In writing to the scattered house churches in Rome Paul has one eye on the Jewish objector to his Law-free gospel and the other on the genuine believer, whether Jewish or Gentile. In the previous chapter the apostle has been occupied with the former but he now turns to the latter.

Few pages of Paul's writings so eloquently set out the blessings of Christian belief as this. Through Christ the believer is now justified, reconciled and at peace with God, given a gracious standing in the presence of God and assured of salvation for the Last Day. At the same time, however, Paul by no means plays down the dire circumstances of some of his readers, then and now. They were and remain morally powerless, godless, sinners, enemies of God and destined for his wrath.

Is there a keyword in this passage, which is so familiar and so much loved? Most likely it is the word 'exult'[1] (vv. 2, 3 and 11). Also important are the time-words 'now' (*nun* – vv. 9 and 11), 'still' (*eti* – vv. 6 and 8) and 'right time' (*kairos* – v. 6).

In his pre-Christian days Paul the Jew had believed that God would reveal all things at the End, in particular who was and who was not 'righteous' before him. That revelation was thought to depend entirely on God's evaluation of, and reward for, self-effort in good works. The Last Day was thought of like the day exam results are posted on a noticeboard revealing who had passed and who had failed.

---

1. The Greek term is *kauchaomai*, 'I boast' ('I rejoice' – RSV, NIV).

The radical teaching of the Apostle Paul is that God's verdict 'righteous' can be revealed 'now' before the End while this present age 'still' continues. That verdict, moreover, does not and cannot depend on self-effort or works, but only on Christ and whether or not one belongs to him. If one does, indeed, belong to him he is deemed 'righteous' 'now', even though he is 'still' ungodly. The Day of Judgement has been brought forward into the present and God's verdict is known, and that verdict is good to those who believe.

As a result of God's saving activity in Christ that secures their ultimate futures, Paul and his fellow believers 'boast,' that is, 'exult in,' their sure hope of sharing God's glory and even of the sufferings that strengthen that hope (vv. 2 and 3). Furthermore, they 'exult in' God himself (v. 11).

But is there a pastoral issue that Paul is addressing here? In the previous chapter it was the theological misunderstanding of the Jewish objector. Is there something we can identify as prompting Paul's exposition in these verses? Most likely Paul is concerned for sufferings, both his own and his readers'. True, the believer will be safe in the Last Day on account of Christ's 'blood' and his risen 'life' (vv. 9 and 10). But what of the present time with its 'afflictions'? The Jews among the Roman Christians had been expelled from Rome under Claudius in AD 49 and had only been able to return in the past two or three years. They were not strangers to suffering. Paul's appeals later in the letter – 'Bless those who persecute you... Repay no one evil for evil... Never avenge yourselves' and the observation that 'rulers ... do not bear the sword in vain' – give dark hints of pain for all who confessed Christ in Rome at that time.[2] By way of ministry Paul encourages them that 'affliction' ultimately strengthens 'hope', and hope, that is, *what* is hoped, will 'not disappoint' when finally it is revealed (vv. 3-5).

1. Peace with God and Access to Grace (vv. 1-5)
Paul is saying that because we are 'justified' by faith we enjoy two blessings 'through Jesus Christ our Lord': peace with

2. Romans 12:14, 19; 13:4.

God and access to a gracious standing with God. As a result
we 'exult' inwardly in our future hope, even in sufferings
in the meantime. Hope, when it is finally realized, will not
disappoint, as in the meantime we are reassured by our love
for God inspired by the Holy Spirit.

The opening words in verse 1, 'Therefore being justified by
faith,' pick up earlier similar references, for example, 'no flesh
shall be justified by works of the Law,' 'being justified freely
by his grace,' and 'we reckon that a man is justified by faith'.[3]
Nothing could be clearer than that individuals and the church
are 'justified' or 'deemed righteous' by God only on the basis
of faith.[4]

It is clear from the previous chapter, where Paul is responding to a Jewish objector, that under contemporary Judaism
man was thought to be 'right with God' based on 'works of the
Law'. It seems, too, that people in general instinctively think
that salvation depends on human goodness and self-effort.
If so, then the New Testament teaching that 'righteousness'
from God depends on his grace, arising from faith not works,
is God's great surprise.

Because God has declared us to be 'right' with him 'we
have peace with God',[5] or as he will say shortly, 'we have been
reconciled to God ... we have received the reconciliation' (vv. 10
and 11). Prior to God's justification of us we were his enemies
(v. 10) and a 'state of war' existed between God and us. Is it not
true that in our unregenerate state we distrust and resent God?
But now there is peace, but not a passive peace, a mere absence
of conflict, but positive, harmonious and loving relationships
with God that he himself has initiated 'through Jesus Christ our
Lord'. Because we have 'peace *with* God' we also begin to know
the inner 'peace *of* God that passes all understanding' (Phil. 4:7).

There is also an objective 'peace' that is ours 'through Jesus
Christ our Lord'. The prophets promised the blessing of 'peace

---

3. 3:20, 24, 28.
4. The very grammatical form of the word 'justified' (*dikaiōthentes*) tells us this.
The Greek aorist tense and the passive voice (divine passive) point to a completed
act done by God.
5. Ancient manuscripts leave open whether the reading should be 'we have
peace' or 'let us have peace'. On balance I have opted for the former; God's act of
justification has established peace as an accomplished fact.

with God' or his *shalom* as a picture of the End-Time. This 'peace' was to be mediated by the long awaited king-messiah from the line of David under whom righteousness, justice and freedom will be universal and eternal.

> Of the increase of his government and *peace*
> there will be no end.
> He will reign on David's throne
> and over his kingdom,
> establishing and upholding it
> with justice and righteousness
> from that time on and forever   (Isa. 9:7).

> ... out of you [Bethlehem] will come for me
> one who will be the ruler of Israel....
> He will stand and shepherd his flock
> in the strength of the Lord....
> And they will live securely,
> for then his greatness
> will reach to the ends of the earth.
> And he will be their *peace*   (Micah 5:2, 4-5).

From our position on God's time-line these promises have already been fulfilled in principle 'through' the coming, death and resurrection-ascension of Jesus, Messiah and Lord. Yet the concrete realization of this 'peace' lies in the future, at his coming. On this future 'peace' we set our hope.

In verse 2 Paul speaks of a further blessing 'through Jesus Christ our Lord' as a consequence of being 'justified by faith':

> ... through him also we have access
> into this grace in which we stand.[6]

'Access' (*prosagōgē*) was an 'audience' with a king, a right of entry into the presence of a monarch. We might think, therefore, that Paul is suggesting 'access' to God as Father 'through Jesus Christ'. This, indeed, is true but it may not be

---

6. The verbs 'have' *[eschēkamen]* and 'stand' (*hestēkamen*) are both in the Greek perfect tense signifying a past act that is now continuing. As similar sounding words Paul may have intended a 'wordplay' or pun.

his point here. More likely the apostle means that 'through Christ' we are now 'under grace' and not 'under Law' (6:14). Our 'natural' way of thinking tells us that we must 'work, work, work' to win God's favour. Even when we grasp the unexpected truth that God saves us by grace and deals with us by grace we keep returning to the grudging 'work' attitude of a resentful slave. We must constantly remind ourselves that we are not under Law but under grace as beloved children of our dear heavenly Father (6:24; 8:15-16).

The latter part of verse 2, 'we boast at the hope of the glory of God,' picks up and balances 'we have peace with God' of the previous verse. Because 'we have peace', also 'we boast'. 'Boast' (*kauchaomai*) can have an ugly or an exalted meaning, depending on its object. Here, because it is directed to the hope of the glory of God, it is exalted and means 'exult in'. Most likely Paul is contrasting the doubtful Jewish practice of 'boasting' in one's 'works' (cf. 3:27 – 'What then becomes of our boasting? It is excluded'). 'Being justified by faith,' however, we 'exult' in the prospect of God's glorious future for his children.

Paul's next words are dark and deep. In verse 3 he says that we also exult in our 'afflictions'. Paul often uses this word (*thlipsis*, meaning 'downward pressure' upon oneself) for sufferings arising from Christian confession and ministry (see e.g. 2 Cor. 1:3-11). It is not that Paul is a masochist enjoying pain for its own sake.

'Afflictions' are not an end in themselves, for they nurture something further, namely, 'patience'. This word *hupomonē*, which literally means 'remaining under', suggests the necessity of submitting to circumstances that we cannot change. As active people who automatically seek to 'fix' things, this 'patience' does not come easily! Yet, like 'afflictions' the experience of learning 'patience' also nurtures something else, 'tested-ness' (*dokimē*). This is a favourite word of Paul's from the world of the blacksmith where it was used for the hammering of the red hot horse-shoe or plough, shaping and testing it on the anvil. This 'shaping and testing' engenders 'hope', that is, hope of 'the glory of God'.

Paul is reflecting on the Christian life overall. That 'life' begins with faith in Christ that attracts God's gracious declaration of 'righteousness'. When we set out on the Christian life, however, we may be quite immature and shallow. In time the unfolding circumstances of life bring their 'afflictions', which stubbornly remain to teach us 'patience'. 'Patience' in turn brings a deepened character that is 'tried and tested', causing our eyes to look in hope beyond this world to God's kingdom where there will be justice and no more crying or pain. All of this says Paul 'we know', a technical term for knowledge arising from Christian catechising.

Paul's word 'hope' (*elpis*) is both the act of hoping and its content. It is quite different from our word 'wish', which is merely our 'desire' with no certainty of fulfilment. 'Hope,' however, is directed towards God's promise and is certain even though its realization lies in the future. Thus, Paul assures us (v. 5), 'hope does not disappoint' or 'make us ashamed'. When God makes 'hope' reality it will exceed all our expectations, beyond our wildest dreams. Paul told the Corinthians that eye had not seen, nor ear heard, nor had the heart imagined the good things God has prepared for those who love him (1 Cor. 2:9; 2 Cor. 4:16-18). In John's splendid visions, including a new heaven and a new earth, a beautiful bride and a massive and magnificent city, each speak of the wonders of God's kingdom (Rev. 21:1-8).

Nor has God left us only with words of promise, adequate though they are. He has poured and continues to pour (*ekkechutai*)[7] his love into our hearts through the Holy Spirit that he gave us. Two meanings are intended by this – our sense of God's love for us (replacing the previous slave's fear of God[8]) and our love for God, our dear Father.

God's declaration of his 'righteousness', following upon our faith in Christ, is objective. But it is matched by the subjective inner reality of his Spirit now present within us. God's 'righteousness' and God's 'Spirit' go together, two sides of the one coin, as it were.[9] Both come from the gospel and both anticipate the Last Day. Then and there God will welcome

7. This is the force of the Greek perfect tense.
8. '... you did not receive the spirit of slavery to fall back into fear but you have received the Spirit of Sonship' (8:15).
9. See Galatians 3:2; 2 Corinthians 3:8-9.

us his children, righteous through his merciful gift, sinners though we were. Moreover, the Spirit will then be present in all his fullness. The word of the gospel and the presence of the Spirit tell us now that we have not hoped in vain.

2. The Matchless Love of God (vv. 6-8)

In verse 8 Paul carries forward his teaching about 'the love of God' through the Holy Spirit poured into our hearts (v. 5). The brightness of God's love is set against the darkness of human sin now sketched in verses 6-8.

Here Paul returns to the theme of human godlessness and wickedness that dominated the lengthy passage in 1:18–3:20. Nothing could be clearer from the Bible than that this age is 'fallen', shot through with deceit and injustice. Humans continue to break the commandments of God. True, the tide comes in with some matters (e.g. awareness of the needs of disabled people) but the tide goes out with others (e.g. tax fraud). There is progress and regress but no ultimate advance in goodness.

Humankind is as fatally flawed now as when Paul wrote to the Romans. Three times Paul writes, 'still' – 'still feeble ... still godless ... still sinners.'[10] 'Feeble' means morally debilitated, 'godless' means literally just that (God-less, without God), and 'sinner' means to be way wide of the moral mark set by God's commandments. These are the marks of Adam and his race.

God did not await the moral improvement of Adam's race before acting for its salvation. Indeed, God knew that no such renovation was in prospect or possible. After all, the prophets had come and gone to Israel without noticeable overall repentance. The Gentile nations had not been without their ethical teachers, again without real change for the better. It was in the midst of history, while we were still far off from him, that God intervened in mercy for the redemption of humankind.

Nonetheless, this intervention was 'at the right time'. Not all moments of time are the same. Some are infused with

---

10. There is sonorous repetition – *eti asthenōn ... eti asebōn ... eti hamartōlōn.*

meaning, for example, the moment a marriage proposal is offered and accepted and the engagement ring is worn for the first time. God has such moments in the broader sweep of history, in particular the appearance of his Son in Israel in fulfilment of the Law and the Prophets. This was God's 'right time'.[11]

At that 'right time' God showed his matchless love for the 'feeble,' the 'godless,' and the 'sinners'. Paul teaches this by four statements, the first and fourth of which declare that Christ died for us as ungodly/sinners.

> Christ died for the ungodly.
> Scarcely for a righteous man someone would die.
> Perhaps for a good man someone might be bold enough to die. Christ died for us while we were still sinners.

In the second and third statements Paul appeals to common human attitudes. Who would be prepared to give his or her life to save another person? You would be unlikely to dash into a burning house laying down your own life for a 'righteous' man. Perhaps you might dive into a boiling sea losing your own life for a 'good' and generous woman.[12] But who would lose his life to save a brutal killer like Adolph Hitler, Joseph Stalin or Idi Amin? Most would express regret at the death of such a person, yet decide that their own lives were worth more.

But such is God's overwhelming love for us that Christ – his own Son (v. 10) – died for us, not for us as 'righteous' or 'good', but as the morally feeble, godless sinners that we are.[13] Here the infinitely worthy One has died for the infinitely unworthy ones who deserve only the just judgement of God.

---

11. The general word in the New Testament for time is *chronos* and the particular word for the 'right time' is *kairos*.

12. Scholars debate whether 'righteous' and 'good' are roughly the same or quite different. The evidence seems to support the interpretation of the two as different, that is, one would conceivably die for a 'good' person but scarcely for one who was merely upright or 'righteous'.

13. In the New Testament the love of God/Christ is repeatedly connected with the atoning death of Christ (see e.g. John 3:16; Galatians 2:20; Revelation 1:5). The classical study of this theme is J. Denney, *The Death of Christ* (London: Tyndale, 1960).

Have we grasped the stark truth that we, the people for whom
Christ died, are not marginally feeble, marginally godless and
marginally sinners, but comprehensively so? Only then can
we begin to plumb the depths of God's love for us and the
extent of the sacrifice Christ underwent for us.

3. Saved from the Wrath of God (vv. 9-11)
In this short section Paul twice uses the words, 'how much
more' (vv. 9 and 10). The style of argument springs from the
'major to the minor', from the 'harder to the easier'.[14] Here
God has done the 'harder' thing, justifying the godless and
reconciling his enemies through the blood of Christ/the death
of his Son. Let there be no doubt that he will save them from
his wrath on the Last Day.

In verse 9 Paul returns to his opening words '[we] being
justified' (v. 1). Here, though, there is a striking alteration.

[We] being justified by faith
[We] being justified by his blood

'By his blood' means 'by his sacrificial death' and reminds
us that our 'faith' is not the instrument of our 'righteousness'
before God, as if we humans are the sources of our own
salvation. We are not justified by faith as if faith were just
another 'work'. Not at all. We are saved by Christ, that is, by
Christ's blood. 'Faith' is merely the hand of the moral beggar
receiving this gift from the hand of God.

What then of the 'wrath' of the Day of Judgement? Will
Christ's blood prevail for us then? Indeed, yes, says Paul: 'We
will be saved through Christ from the wrath.'

In verses 10 and 11 Paul introduces the words 'reconcile' and
'reconciliation'. This is the first time Paul has used these terms,
though not the last (see 2 Cor. 5:18-20 for his classic statement).
'Reconciliation' is the action of making enemies into friends
and where the former hostility is replaced by peace (see on
v. 1), harmony and good will. Although the word is not used

---

14. This is the reverse of the usual rabbinic pattern (called *qal wahomer*) that
argues from the 'lighter to the heavier' (as employed by Paul, e.g. in 2 Cor. 3:7-9).

in Jesus' parable we see the father of the prodigal 'reconciling' the returning boy to himself by fully restoring him as his son (and not merely giving him a job on the farm).

This reconciliation is necessary because we are 'enemies', that is, of God. The enmity comes from our side and is directed towards him, our Creator, to whom we owe everything and who we should thank but do not. It is our nature and instinct to resent and distrust God and to rebel against his laws. The hostility is ours. It is we who are – because we need to be – 'reconciled' to God. The passive voice shows that *God* does the reconciling. God reconciles his enemies 'to himself' (as 2 Cor. 5:19 also specifically says). Grammatically God is both the subject and the indirect object. God picks us up, turns us round, and places us down facing him, now as his friends at peace with him.

This God does 'through the death of his Son'. In that death God deals with his own just wrath towards our sins and declares those who believe in Christ to be 'righteous'. At the same time through his Spirit God removes from our hearts the former hostility, distrust, thanklessness and rebellion we felt towards him, for we are now his children.

What is the relationship between 'justification' and 'reconciliation'? The former word is a Law-court term and the latter word is a relational term. While many scholars regard 'reconciliation' as the core idea associated with the atonement, the reality appears to be otherwise. The former term, 'justification'/'righteousness,' occurs frequently in Paul's writings, the latter term only infrequently. Careful study of this passage and 2 Corinthians 5:18-20 indicates that the counting of sinners 'righteous' before him in Christ lies at the centre of Pauline thought, with reconciliation consequential to it.

So, says Paul (getting back to the argument of the chapter), since God has done this incomparably hard thing (reconciling his enemies to himself through the death of his Son), do not doubt that he will do the easier. When we stand before God as judge, 'having been reconciled', we will be saved by Christ's risen life. Most likely this refers to the risen and ascended Christ pleading his righteous cause for us at that time (see 8:34: 'Christ Jesus ... is at the right hand of God, who indeed intercedes for us'). Because he has died for us he will stand with us and for us in that dreaded hour (cf. 1 John 2:1-2).

Paul now concludes this whole passage (v. 11). The force of his opening words, 'Not only so', is debated. Most likely Paul is going back to the opening words of the chapter rather than continuing to reflect on being saved from the wrath of the Last Day. Certainly the words 'exult in' and 'through our Lord Jesus Christ' take us back to verses 1 and 2. As well, 'reconciliation' exactly corresponds with 'peace with God' in verse 1.

> We exult in God
> through our Lord Jesus Christ
> through whom
> we have now received the reconciliation.

'Reconciliation' – God restoring all things harmoniously to himself – will happen at the End (cf. Rom. 11:15). But, says Paul, 'reconciliation' has happened 'now' (*nun*) before the End, through the death of the Son of God (v. 10). The centre of gravity of God's salvation history is not the future but the past, in the appearing, death and resurrection of the Son of God. This is the *nun*/ the 'now,' the significance laden *kairos* /'moment' of God's salvation. As a result we may know that we are 'righteous' *now* and 'reconciled' to God *now*.

Consequently, Paul says, we 'exult in God'. Formerly, Paul the Jew of the tribe of Benjamin, Pharisee of the Pharisees and persecutor of the heretical Christian sect, 'exulted in his works' but not in his God. But no more. 'Now,' because he is justified by Christ's blood, reconciled through the death of God's Son and at peace with God, he 'exults in God' himself, into and under whose grace he has now been granted access.

STUDY QUESTIONS

1. Can I really say that I boast in my afflictions?

2. How does my justification help me endure affliction?

3. How has having peace with God affected my relationships with others?

4. What does access to the Father truly give me?

5. What then, is the purpose of affliction?

6. What is the true hope that I have for eternity?

7. Do I really understand what my sin cost?

8. Do I exalt in God for my salvation or in my own works?

PART C

FROM PLIGHT TO SALVATION
(Romans 5:12–8:39)

In the first part of the letter, Paul demonstrated that God would be entirely justified in condemning the people of the Gentiles and Jews respectively. Yet his mercy prevailed over his justice, in salvation of both Gentiles and Jews in Christ, through the preaching of the gospel.

All members of those peoples stand in need of salvation since all are descended from Adam. Each person sinned and died in him, patriarchal head of us all. For those united with Christ crucified, buried and risen through the gospel and their baptism, there is the assurance that both Sin and Death stand defeated.

Contrary to Jewish belief at the time, the Law and Commandments do nothing to mitigate Sin or Death. Only attachment to Christ achieves this freedom. This is to have the mind of the Spirit, to walk in the Spirit and to be led out by the Spirit, the evidence of which is the cry, 'Abba, Father.'

The Christian must negotiate many perils along the way, including the birth-death cycles as well as persecution. Yet because of his invincible determination, God will not be stopped in his declared intention in saving and glorifying those whom he has chosen.

6

Adam and Christ
(Romans 5:12-21)

In the previous section (5:1-11), Paul addressed his readers pastorally, encouraging their patience in the face of present afflictions and instilling certain hope against the coming judgement, based on the justifying and reconciling work of Christ.

Now, however, Paul paints a broader canvas, encompassing all people, the world and human history going back to Adam, no less. Yet these words are not penned in a historical vacuum. There was a particular circumstance in Rome to provoke Paul to write in this way. Most likely Paul is once more thinking of the Jewish objectors in the house churches in Rome who reject his Law-free theology. For this group Law was all important, both for them-selves as Jews in their continuing loyalty to the Covenant Lord and also – as they saw it – for those Gentiles who sought to be 'included' by God in the New Israel.

But, argues Paul, Sin and its accompaniment Death entered the human race with Adam the first man[1] long before Moses

---

1. There can be no doubt that Paul regards Adam as a genuinely historical figure. In more recent times questions have been raised regarding Adam's historicity by (1) modern scientific studies about the origin of the species, and (2) by the use of non-literal, symbolic language in the early chapters of Genesis (e.g. the word 'Adam' means 'man' and is derived from 'adamah' meaning dust). For a spirited and scholarly defence of 'the historical Adam' see H. Blocher, *Original Sin*, New Studies in Biblical Theology 5 (Leicester: IVP, 1997), 37-62. Blocher points out (1) that the book of Genesis presents Adam historically as the primeval patriarch of the whole human race, and (2) that the account of the era from Adam to Abraham may well have encompassed tens of thousands of years so as to approximate to many anthropological opinions as to the first appearance of *homo sapiens*.

and the giving of the Law. We Jews should know this, implies Paul. Moses' first book, Genesis, tells us about Sin and Death in its opening chapters!

Romans 5:12-21 addresses two human crises, Sin and Death, about which some comment must be made before we address the text of this passage. First, we must notice that Sin (*hamartia*) is uniformly used in the singular. Paul is not speaking of individual sins but of Adam's great Sin, his act of rebellion against God in which all his descendants participated. Hence the word 'Sin' is capitalised throughout. Second, it is likely that by 'death' Paul means more than biological death. The contrastive bracketing of 'death' with 'eternal life' (5:21; 6:23) suggests that Paul means his readers to understand by 'death,' *'eternal* death'[2] (which he calls, 'the Last Enemy' – 1 Cor. 15:26). Thus Adam's and our Sin brings both biological death and eternal death. (The latter is Paul's way of speaking about 'hell', a word that is not found in his letters.[3])

These twin crises of Sin and Death were created by the first man (long before Law was given), but those crises were resolved by another man, Jesus Christ (long after Law was given). While the commandments in the Law defined Sin, and even provoked Sin, the fact is that Law served only to condemn Sin – Adam's and ours. Law did nothing positive or redemptive. Where Adam was disobedient, however, Christ was obedient. Whereas Adam's trespass brought condemnation to all, Christ's saving act brought justification for all who believe in him.

Accordingly, the immediate intention of this passage is to address those Jews who wished to reinstate Law as a non-negotiable part of the gospel of God. Paul will have none of this. Significantly the language of 'righteousness' and 'justification' is prominent in this passage. Law served only to reveal man's *'unrighteousness'*, but the true and Law-free gospel centred in Jesus and his death brings God's verdict of 'righteous' to all true believers.

---

2. Paul's idioms 'life to life' and 'death to death' (2 Cor. 2:16) suggest, on one hand, 'biological life to eternal life' and, on the other, 'biological death to eternal death.'

3. The keywords translated 'hell' (Gehenna and Hades) are not found in Paul's writings.

Paul is not merely debating Jewish objectors, neatly meeting their points with his, as it were. Rather Paul exults in the triumph of the grace of God in the face of human wickedness. Ungrateful and disobedient Adam rebelled against his God, but God responded with his greater grace in the free gift of righteousness and life in Jesus Christ. One man brought Death to all but God with overflowing grace sent another man, whom he raised from the dead, to give life in place of Death to the children of Adam.

1. IN ADAM ALL SINNED, ALL DIED (V. 12)

Paul's opening 'therefore' (v. 12) picks up the preceding passage (5:6-11) where he spoke of our moral weakness, our godlessness and Sin, and our hostility towards God and the inevitability of his wrath against us all. Put briefly Paul is now saying, 'Therefore ... all sinned.' But how, and under which circumstances and with what consequences have '*all* sinned'?

Therefore,			
just as		sin	came into the world through one man
and	through sin		
	death		
so also	death	came to	all men
because[4]			all sinned.

Paul is reiterating earlier observations about universal sinfulness (3:9 – '*all* are under sin'; 3:23 – '*all* have sinned ...'). Here, however, Paul explains that Sin entered the human race 'through one man'. Later he amplifies this as 'through the disobedience of one man the many were constituted sinners' (see v. 19).

The Apostle is basing this on the narrative of the early chapters of Genesis. God placed Adam (and Eve) under him as stewards in the 'garden of God', promising his blessing provided they 'knew their place' honouring their Creator in his Lordship over them. This, however, they did not do.

---

4. Augustine, who was Latin-speaking, wrongly translated Paul's Greek *eph'hō* as 'in whom,' that is, 'in Adam.' Most probably Paul's words mean, 'Inasmuch as, because....' The meaning is unaffected despite Augustine's error.

Rather, the first man disobeyed the Lord and disbelieved his warning that death would surely follow. Adam's reckless attempt to seize the place of the kindly Creator is a woeful story of ingratitude and stupidity.

Excluded from Eden the consequences were immediate. Their firstborn Cain murdered his brother Abel. More evil was to follow, as narrated in the early chapters of Genesis. The outcome of Adam's rebellion is nothing less than humanity's alienation from God, the coming of dark forces into the human psyche, and the dislocation of the social order. War, exploitation and injustice are the all too easily observable results of that Sin. Adam's revolt against God was a matter of deep distress. Some decades before the coming of Christ a devout Jew reflected on Adam's 'fall'.

> O Adam, what have you done?
> When you sinned,
> your fall occurred not only for you,
> but for us your descendants   (4 Ezra 7:118).

Another Jewish writer commented that Adam's Sin brought Death to all his progeny.

> For when Adam first sinned
> [he] brought an untimely death over all ...

Paul says much the same to the Corinthians, '... all have died' (2 Cor. 5:14), by which we infer he means that '... all have died *in Adam*'.

Clearly, then, Paul is teaching that all people sinned 'in Adam' and all people died 'in Adam'. It's not merely that Adam introduced a virus called 'sin' that his descendants 'catch' so that they too sin and die. Rather, we actually sinned when he sinned and we died when he died. Paul is saying that all humankind were there acting in and with Adam.[5]

---

5. Blocher, *Original Sin*, 63-81, reviews two competing views on Romans 5:12: (1) that sin followed by death is a disease that spread from Adam, and (2) Augustine's view that we were all present in Adam when he sinned and was condemned to die. Blocher rejects (1) and affirms (2). Blocher, however, explains this is in more biblical terms than Augustine. Adam was our 'racial head' and all humanity belongs to the covenant people of the first man who sinned against God.

Two questions leap from the page. One is that this teaching seems to us strange and, indeed, unfair. Why should I be condemned to die because of the wicked action of my distant ancestor Adam? We ask, 'where's the justice in that?' Paul, however, does not address our question. Most likely this was not a question that would have occurred to him. He probably regarded our 'connected-ness' with the 'first man' as a given. Paul's mindset was Hebraic and corporate, ours is more typically Greek and individualistic.

Most likely the explanation goes along the following lines. Each of us is what we are on account of those who have gone before, going back ultimately to Adam. I am an Australian due to a decision to migrate there, made by an Irishman I never knew. I had no say in that and there is nothing I can (or want to) do to make me, for example, an Englishman or a Croatian. The poet John Donne observed that 'no man is an island'. I cannot extricate myself from the action taken by my Irish ancestor, whose blood flows in my veins. I am what I am because of his choices, and the choices of others long ago, going back ultimately to the choices of the First Man. I may question the morality of my accountability for Adam's action but I cannot doubt the practical reality that Adam constituted me a law-breaker whose condemnation I and others will share.

This explanation is not altogether satisfactory. I may feel unhappy at the (apparent) injustice under which I am condemned for the actions of someone millennia ago. True. But ask yourself, 'Am I different from Adam? Do I seek to honour and thank God daily? Do I willingly and gladly live under his rule as a good steward of his creation? Do I love God and care for others in love?' The grim reality is that I do not, and that day by day I endorse and confirm Adam's Sin. The fact is, I rather admire Adam.

The fact of universal sinfulness, including our own, and of death can scarcely be denied. Nor can any serious or honest person claim to be free from a God-denying self-centredness nor can he deny that the out-flowing wrongdoing has been done freely by us. It is sobering to think back over our lives reflecting on our sins, both active and passive. Each of us knows that in the final judgement by God the blame will be ours and no one else's, and that his negative assessment of us will be fair and reasonable, as Paul pointed out in chapters 2–3. It is that 'fairness,' however, that should most inspire fear within us, in prospect of that moment.

A second question occurs. How was Adam's Sin transmitted to his descendants, ultimately down to us? Some early Christian theologians, notably Augustine of Hippo, taught that the sexual excitement of the procreative act was the source of sinfulness in the next generation. This, however, has no basis in biblical exegesis.[6] Others have likened the spread of sinfulness to the spread of a virus like HIV from parent to child. This, too, is without scriptural warrant and in any case minimizes our own responsibility for our sins. The plain fact is that specific texts in the Bible give but little help as to how Adam's Sin and Adam's Death were passed on to us.[7]

2. FROM ADAM TO MOSES (vv. 13-14)

In asserting that 'Sin was in the world until [the giving of] the Law' Paul is evidently correcting a false understanding, but whose? Most likely, Paul is addressing those Jewish objectors in the Roman house churches who claimed that the giving and the keeping of the Law was God's answer to Adam's Sin. Shortly before Paul's time a Jewish writer expressed just that belief.

> We have nothing now besides the Almighty *and his Law*.
> If we prepare our hearts and make ourselves ready,
> in this way we shall again acquire everything
> which we have lost and much better things than we had lost...
> (2 Baruch 85:3-4).

---

6. Augustine's view was based on David's words in Psalm 51:5 ('in iniquity was I born...') which, however, according to a truer understanding of Hebrew idiom means only that David's own life was shot through with sin from beginning to end. For discussion, see Blocher, *Original Sin*, 27-29.

7. See further Blocher, *Original Sin*, especially chapter 5. Blocher notes that since so much of what we are – as to temperament and physical constitution – *is* hereditary we must allow the possibility that our sinfulness was genetically transmitted – ultimately deriving from Adam. We all belong to the one human race whose 'head' was the first man. He 'constituted' us what we are – both as to the image of God and to the marring, through his Sin, of that image. Our nobility (such as it is) is from Adam and our fallen-ness (such as it is) is also from Adam. On account of that fallenness we his children are likewise fallen and on account of his death we too die.

This passage teaches that the Law is potentially redemptive. At that time Jewish theologians looked to the Law and the keeping of Law as the remedy for Adam's Sin and the recovery of Eden. Neither anticipated God's merciful dispatch of 'the last Adam' to repair the damage of the 'first man, Adam'.[8]

Doubtless the pre-Christian Paul shared this view. Now, however, with truer insight, based on the risen Christ's encounter with him and his own sober realization of the power of Sin (see on Rom. 7), he pointed out the limitations of Law. Law identifies Sin so as to condemn Sin but also to increase sins. Moreover, Law is impotent to deal with the scourge of Death.

> Sin was in the world before Law.
> Indeed, sin is not reckoned without Law.
> But death reigned from Adam until Moses,
> even over those who did not sin like Adam

Paul's response is measured, but strong. First, he states the fact of Sin's long history ('Sin was in the world before Law'). Second, he concedes – to a point – a role for Law ('Sin is not reckoned without Law'). Nevertheless, third, he points to the dominance of death as irrefutable proof of the presence of Sin ('But, on the contrary, death reigned from Adam to Moses'). Fourth, death ruled even over those whose Sin differed from Adam's ('Death reigned ... even over those who did not Sin like Adam'). All things considered, says Paul, Law is no restorer of innocence, no means to recapturing what was lost by Adam.

3. ADAM AS A 'TYPE' OF CHRIST (vv. 15-17)

In the latter part of verse 14 Paul contrasted Christ – 'the one who was to come' – with Adam. Paul uses two current

---

8. To use Paul's language in 1 Corinthians 15:45. Paul's Adam/Christ contrast in 1 Corinthians 15:20-28, 42-50, written a few years before Romans, shows that Paul's thinking was well developed by the fifties at least, but most likely much earlier. In 1 Corinthians 15 Paul is emphasizing Adam as the 'man of dust', the *psychikos* ('soulish') man who introduced death to humanity, making it impossible for his descendants un-transformed to enter the kingdom of God. Christ, however, is the 'man of heaven' who by his resurrection has been victor over death and who gives the Spirit to those who belong to him.

Jewish ways to makes this contrast: (1) by referring to Adam as a 'type' of Christ, and (2) by employing the so-called 'light to heavy' idiom where he says, 'if *a* is true by how much more is *b* true.'

Paul's reference to Adam as a 'type' (*tupos*) or 'pattern' of the one who was to come calls for explanation. In calling Adam a 'type' Paul is regarding Adam as pre-figuring Christ, Adam's 'antitype'.[9] The New Testament 'antitype' fulfills the Old Testament 'type', but in the case of Christ in a deeply contrastive manner, as the two 'light to heavy' comparisons make clear.

The first 'light to heavy' contrast (vv. 15 and 16) is between the consequences of Adam's 'trespass' that brought 'condemnation' (*katakrima*) to many and the grace of God (*charis*) in Jesus Christ that overflowed to many for 'justification' (*dikaiōma*).

> But the gift is not like the trespass.
> For if by the trespass of   one man the   many sinned
>   how much more did   the grace of God
>   and the free gift by grace
>   in   one man Jesus Christ
>   overflow to the many.
> The free gift is not like the sin of the one man.
> For the judgement from one man   was for condemnation
> but the gift   from many trespasses was for justification.

This rather jumbled translation reflects Paul's evident excitement where his words tumble over one another. True, in Adam's 'trespass' (*paraptōma*, literally, 'fall') and 'sin', 'the many sinned' with 'many trespasses' in consequence of Adam's wickedness. Adam's 'fall,' therefore, evoked 'judgement ... for condemnation' (*krima ... eis katakrima*) for 'the many,' that is, 'all men' (v. 12).

Now, of course, God would have been perfectly just to let things stand as they were, with his judgement falling on Adam and his Law-breaking descendants as a matter of course. Paul,

---

9. See e.g. 1 Corinthians 10:6 ('these things were *types* for us') and 1 Peter 3:21 ('baptism an *antitype* [to the water of the flood]').

however, is utterly overwhelmed by God's actual reaction to Adam's rebellion. Instead of the wrath that would have been entirely warranted, Paul speaks instead of 'the grace of God' and his 'free gift' embodied in the man Jesus Christ that overflowed to 'the many' for 'justification'.

Thus we are presented with two groups of men and women each called, 'the many.' One group, humanity as a whole, is attached by birth to Adam and faces death and condemnation due to trespasses – his and ours in him. The other group is attached by the Word of God to Jesus Christ and, notwithstanding their solidarity in Sin with Adam, enjoys the sure promise of righteousness from God.

Paul's second 'light to heavy' contrast (v. 17) is between 'Death' that previously 'reigned as king' over Adam's descendants and 'Life' that now 'reigns as king' over Death for those who receive the grace of God in Jesus Christ.

> For
> if by the trespass of one man
>   death reigned through the one
> how much more
> will those who receive the   overflowing grace
>   and   free gift of righteousness
>   reign in life through the one man
>   Jesus Christ.

Paul is picking up earlier references to death – 'through' Adam's sin 'death came to all men' and 'death reigned from Adam...' (vv. 12 and 14). He is also anticipating the promises of 'eternal life' that he is about to make (vv. 18 and 21; cf. 6:4, 22-23).

We must not miss the connection between the 'righteousness' God deems believers to have and his gift to them of 'eternal life'. Those who are already 'righteous' by faith already have 'eternal life' in the presence of God. Judgement and condemnation have been overturned and Death cast from his throne. God's 'overflowing grace' and his 'free gift of righteousness' have placed Life-laden believers on the throne with Death under their feet. Adam lit the fire, but Christ extinguished the blaze and rebuilt the ruined city.

The Jewish objector who wishes to reinstate Law into the purposes of God is tragically blind to the immeasurable greatness of the 'grace' of God in the face of Adam's and our Sin which warranted only God's punishment. The same, however, must be said of those contemporary theologians and teachers who dismiss justification by faith as God's way to Eternal Life and who insist, instead, on some form of works righteousness.

4. IN ADAM CONDEMNATION, IN CHRIST JUSTIFICATION (vv. 18-19)
On the observation of the previous verses Paul draws a strong conclusion, 'So then ...' (*ara oun*),[10] in which he sets side by side Adam and Christ and the consequences of their respective actions.

```
So then
as         through the trespass       of one
                        condemnation came      for all
so too     through the righteous act   of one
                        righteousness of life came for all.
For
just as    through the disobedience   of one man
                        the many were constituted sinners
so also    through the obedience      of one man
                        the many were constituted righteous.
```

Each verse explains and amplifies the other. On one hand, through the 'trespass' or 'disobedience' of one man 'the many were constituted sinners' so that 'condemnation came to all'. On the other hand, through the 'righteous act' in 'obedience' of one man in his death, 'the many were constituted righteous' so that 'righteousness of life came for all'. Paul exults in the 'righteous act' of Christ in dying for others.

5. JESUS, SUFFERING SERVANT, SON OF MAN, MESSIAH
Paul's reference to the 'obedience of one' and the 'righteous act of one' for the sake of 'many' appears to be echoing Jesus'

---

10. This is the first, but not the last occasion Paul will use this strong inferential *ara* in Romans (see 7:3, 25; 8:12; 9:16, 18; 14:12, 19.

words, 'the Son of Man came ... to serve and to give his life a ransom for *many*' (Mark 10:45).

Here Jesus sees himself fulfilling prophecies of Isaiah and Daniel. Isaiah prophesied the coming of the Servant of God who was to suffer for the sins of his people, 'justifying *many*' (Isa. 53:11-12). Daniel saw a vision of 'one like a son of man' (that is, a *man*) who was to rule over all peoples and be worshipped by them (Dan. 7:13-14). In other words, through Daniel, God was promising a 'new Adam', a human person who would be Lord of all, a divine figure.

Jesus combines the prophecies of Isaiah's 'suffering servant' and Daniel's 'son of man' as fulfilled in his own person. In the following statement Jesus implies that he is both the 'new Adam' ('son of man') and the 'servant' (he 'came ... to serve') who will suffer for the salvation of 'many'.

	For even the Son of Man	
	came not	to be served
but		to serve
and		to give his life a ransom for many
		(Mark 10:45).

In this present passage Paul's repeated mention of Jesus as 'the one' (vv. 15, 17, 18, 19) picks up and interprets Jesus' reference to himself as 'son of man'. In Jesus' day, the title 'son of man' was a term for the Messiah.[11] According to Jesus he is that 'One', the new Adam, the son of man/the Messiah, who will offer up his life (in death) for the release ('ransom') of 'many'. Paul's words, 'through the obedience of one man the many were constituted righteous,' depend upon and arise from the words of the Lord Jesus quoted above, which in turn fulfil the prophecies of Isaiah and Daniel.

6. SUPERABUNDANT GRACE (vv. 20-21)

Paul now returns to address the concerns of the Jewish objectors who reject Paul's Law-free gospel and who seek to reinstate the keeping of Law for justification, both for Jews

---

11. Mark 8:30-31; 14:61-62.

and Gentiles. True, the Law was given at a point in history. Law, however, did not solve the problem of universal Sin introduced by Adam. Law provided the means of defining and identifying Sin, but did nothing to reverse its accompaniment, Death (vv. 13-14).

Now, adds Paul, Law entered for two God-given, closely connected purposes. The first (set out in v. 20) was for the Law 'to increase' or multiply[12] the trespass. Significantly, 'Trespass' and 'Sin' are synonyms and both are singular. Thus Law did not stir up a greater number of individual breaches of the commandments so much as intensify and reinforce the underlying attitude of rebellion to the kindly will of the Creator.

But this intensification of Sin, he said, was to reveal the infinitely greater outpouring of God's grace in the face of such wickedness. 'Thus,' he continues, 'where Sin increased, grace more abundantly overflowed.'[13] In other words, God did not merely meet Law-inspired Sin with grace equal to that Sin. Rather, his grace was immeasurably greater than that Sin, such is his love for sinners. We cannot but be reminded of his Son, the Lord Jesus Christ, who 'ate with sinners' and was called 'the friend of sinners'. In Jesus' life and death, as recorded in the Gospels, we catch glimpses of the 'super-abounding' grace of God.

God had a second and connected purpose in the Law increasing Sin (v. 21) which in turn super-abundantly increased the grace of God.

> Just as
> sin   reigned in death
> so too
> grace might   reign   through righteousness unto eternal life
>   through Jesus Christ our Lord.

Paul depicts two kings reigning – King Sin and King Grace. From the time of Adam, King Sin exercises his reign in the Death of those he rules, that is, Adam's descendants in the

---

12. The verb *pleonazō* appears in Romans only in 5:20 and 6:1.

13. The verb *perisseuein* means to overflow. Paul, however, has intensified this by attaching the preposition *hyper*, 'over' to the verb; *hyper-perisseuein* means 'superabundant outpouring'.

human race. The outcome and end point of Sin's reign is our physical death and our Eternal Death. From Christ, however, King Grace exercises his reign through the gospel which gives 'righteousness' and its companion 'eternal life' to believers.

In brief, then, Paul is correcting those who seek to reinstate Law as a remedy for Sin and as the way of salvation. Nothing could be further from the truth, says Paul. Law serves only to entrench Sin. But Sin, thus deepened in its resolve and now seen for what it is, shows up the length and breadth and depth of the love of God for those caught in Sin's trap. That love issued in the ultimate remedy for Sin, which is the gift of 'righteousness' to believers, and, with that 'justification,' 'eternal life.'

7. CONTEMPORARY APPLICATION
Several points of application speak to us from these pages of Paul the Apostle.

First, all human beings as descendants of Adam are 'under sin' and 'under' God's just condemnation. Adam's 'fall' both constituted his descendants rebels against God and also predisposed them to sinful behaviour.

Each of us is centre of our respective universes, usurping the place that only God should occupy. More than one person has observed that the letter 'I' is the centre of the word 'sin'. This 'I'– centredness is both Adam's great Sin and ours. We knowingly, freely and willingly usurp God's place and, resolve as we might from time to time, we prove to be unwilling to remove ourselves from the centre. In the final analysis, self is unwilling to step down from the throne and put God in his rightful place. Particular sins, which vary from person to person, flow from that great Sin. When we face God as judge it will not be possible to blame Adam or our more immediate parents for this. The only way to 'righteousness' and 'eternal life' is 'in Christ', by the grace of God.

Second, while the precise circumstance that provoked Paul to write verses 12-21 has long since passed, Paul's rejection of Law as remedy for Sin has continuing implications. The appeal to Law-keeping as the way to securing God's favourable verdict 'justified' is not confined to Jews such as those Roman

Jews who objected to Paul's grace-based teaching. Within Christendom the unreformed churches continue to teach that religious duties and good works contribute, along with faith, to God's acceptance of us. Furthermore, enquiry of the typical non-Christian as to his or her understanding of the way to salvation will invariably bring the answer, 'By my goodness and good deeds'. Self-effort as the way to God appears to be lodged deep in the sinful human psyche. A righteousness of God, understood as his gift flowing from grace based on faith in Christ, proves to be surprising and, for many, offensive. In short, while history and culture have moved on from Paul's time and the writing of Romans, the issues raised by the objectors and Paul's response remain sharply relevant for every generation since, including today.

Third, Paul's exposition of our solidarity and connection with Adam rules out the 'humanistic' view of Pelagius[14] and others who argue that human beings unaided can fulfil the Law of God and so please God. Pelagius' teaching[15] that 'man can live without sin' continues in the optimism about human goodness expressed since the Enlightenment, including within contemporary Liberal Theology. Such views, however, are at odds with human experience of moral failure and as expressed by Paul in Romans 7. In addition, since this viewpoint implies man has the capacity to satisfy God's standards, it means that Christ's redeeming death and resurrection for sinners were unnecessary.

Fourth, society's present denial of human sinfulness has dire consequences. The daily news should tell us that Sin is real and pervasive. That we need locks on our doors, bars on our windows and alarm systems for our homes should

---

14. Pelagius was a learned monk who came from England and taught in Rome c. AD 400. His views were criticized by Augustine. Pelagianism was condemned at the Third Ecumenical Council (held in Ephesus, AD 431).

15. It appears that the Jewish objectors in Rome anticipated Pelagius' teaching. As Jews they were most likely influenced by the Pharisees, guardians of Jewish orthodoxy. Josephus, Paul's near contemporary, wrote that the Pharisees held that 'to act rightly or otherwise rests, indeed, for the most part with men, but that in each action fate [i.e. God's providence] cooperates' (*Jewish War* ii. 163). Another approximate contemporary, Rabbi Akiba, said, 'All is foreseen, but freedom of choice is given' (Mishnah, *Aboth*, iii.16). Free will and belief in the Law as redemptive seem to have been the twin doctrines Paul is opposing.

tell us something about human nature. Post-enlightenment humanism continues to believe in the myth of fundamental human goodness in spite of daily evidence to the contrary, including within our own lives. We expect more than we should from one another and yet never seem surprised by the depths of evil around us.

Of course we must acknowledge the remnant of the divine image in us, which explains a certain continuing nobility. Yet it is a fatal error to engage in, for example, psychology-based therapy on the assumption of fundamental goodness rather than on the assumption of fundamental sinfulness. Likewise parents are dangerously naive if their upbringing of children does not assume an inherent self-centredness in the child. Unless modified by nurture and firm discipline and ultimately by regeneration, the 'funny' selfishness of the child becomes tragically unfunny in the emerging adult.

STUDY QUESTIONS

1. What is the sin of Adam that Paul is addressing?

2. What is the purpose of the Law?

3. Why does Paul go to such great lengths to make a case for the universalness ('all') of Adam's sin and its affects?

4. If one clings so tenaciously to the law is he able to recognize his own sin?

5. How does the law reveal sin?

7

De-thronement of King Sin
(Romans 6:1-23)

Romans 6 has been very important in the history of piety among Protestant Christians. This chapter has been the principal quarry for teachings about the 'victory life' and the possibility of spiritual and moral 'perfection'.[1] This is understandable since this passage is principally concerned with 'death to Sin' and 'living to God'. Yet it is unlikely that Paul penned these words to be a basis of the 'higher life' or the 'second blessing'[2] teaching that so captivated earlier generations of Christians through the great convention gatherings of the past.

Before looking at Paul's text in more detail it is worth noticing four features of this chapter.

First, Paul organizes this chapter around two questions, one at the beginning ('What, therefore, shall we say?') and the other – more briefly – in verse 15 ('What, therefore?').[3]

---

1. Three 'holiness' catch-cries from Romans are 'justified' (ch. 5), 'sanctified' (ch. 6) and 'glorified' (ch. 8).

2. The so-called 'second blessing' was based on a kind of two-stage approach to the message and challenge of the gospel. First, one believed in Jesus for salvation. But then later one committed one's all to him as Lord and so entered into the 'second blessing' when the Spirit was believed to come. It is true that God blesses us whenever we commit everything to Jesus as Master. This commitment and re-commitment tends to repeat throughout the years of our pilgrimage. Yet from the viewpoint of biblical theology there is no two-stage message. Christ is at once Saviour and Lord and our single response is to believe in him as Saviour and to submit to him as Lord.

3. Throughout the letter, Paul appears to be responding to criticisms and questions from a Jewish quarter, most likely from Jewish Christians in Rome. See comments on 2:1, 3, 17-24; 4:1; 9:1-3, 6, 14, 19, 30; 11:1, 11. Above all, throughout this letter Paul is defending his Law-free gospel to the (Christian) Jews who appear to have taken such exception to it.

Each question is followed by a further question that takes the Roman Christians back to the time of their baptism. Thus he asks: 'Are you *unaware?*' in verse 3 and 'Do you *not know...?*' in verse 16.

Paul then gives a reminder of teaching they would have received at that time. In the first case (vv. 4-14), Paul picks up and drives home the necessity of death to Sin symbolized by their descent into the baptismal water. In the second case (vv. 17-23), Paul calls for their 'slavery' to righteous behaviour, based on the catechetical teaching they received at their baptism. Freed from Sin they are to be slaves to righteousness. In other words, Paul is taking the Roman Christians back to the fundamentals of the faith they were taught at their baptism.

Second, this passage (6:1-23) addresses the same two crises (Sin and Death) as its predecessor (5:12-21). Sin (*hamartia*) is used in the singular, as if personified, so that Paul is not speaking of our individual or particular sins but of Adam's great Sin, his rebellion against his Creator (in which we participated and which we continue to endorse). Furthermore, by 'death' Paul means 'eternal death' (Death) and not merely 'biological death' as is clear by his contrastive bracketing of 'death' with 'eternal life' (6:23; cf. 5:21).

Third, the imagery of the passage is important. The picture of the 'kingly rule' of Sin and Death continues from the previous chapter (5:14, 17, 21) into this chapter (6:12: 'Do not let Sin rule as king'). The Christian is to reject Sin's 'kingly rule'. Then, however, Paul changes the image to 'Lord' and 'slave', an image that dominates the remainder of the chapter. The believer has been 'set free' from slavery to Sin to be the obedient slave of the 'Lord' in righteousness.

Fourth, Romans 6 is a window into the practices of the early Christians in regard to 'initiation' into the faith. First, this passage reveals that baptism was accompanied by instruction. Paul speaks of the 'pattern of teaching (*tupos didachēs*) to which [believers] were handed over' (v. 17). At the end of the letter he warns the Romans to note those who oppose 'the teaching' (*didachē*) which they have 'learned'.[4] This is

---

4. The word 'disciple' (*mathētēs*) is derived from the verb, 'learn' (*manthanō*), used in Romans 16:17.

consistent with extensive evidence in the New Testament that new believers were carefully instructed at the time of baptism.[5] Such formulated instruction before baptism must have been widespread since Paul merely assumes the practice in Rome. Second, this passage gives strong hints that believers went 'down into' and arose 'up from' the baptismal water.[6]

1. WITH CHRIST IN DEATH, BURIAL AND RESURRECTION (vv. 1-14)

A. Misinformation corrected (vv. 1-3)
Paul's opening question, 'What, therefore, shall we say?' (vv. 1), signals a further interaction with his Jewish critics in the Roman house churches (cf. the shorter version in verse 15 – 'What, therefore?'[7]). They are saying that Paul teaches antinomianism (literally that he is 'against Law'). These critics seem to be quoting Paul as preaching, 'It's good to continue in Sin that grace may increase.' Paul's earlier heated retort, 'Why are we blasphemed as saying by some, "Let us do evil that good may come"?' (see on 3:8), is responding to the same distorted version of his teaching. Evidently Paul's critics parodied his Law-free gospel as his permission not only 'to continue in Sin' but to do so 'in order to multiply God's grace'.

In rejecting this misrepresentation of his gospel Paul points to the death and resurrection of Christ as the pattern for the metaphorical 'death and resurrection' of Christians, that is, of those who belong by faith to the Messiah crucified and raised.

'Sin' is deeply personal, even *personified* as an evil king who now rules Adam's descendants. This powerful notion of Sin will become extremely important in this and the following chapter. In this chapter Paul resumes references to Sin introduced earlier:

---

5. The Book of Acts refers to the apostles' 'teaching' (*didachē* – 2:42; 5:28) and other New Testament writings refer to 'teaching' (*didachē* – 2 John 9) or 'doctrine' (*didaskalia* – Rom. 12:7; 15:4) and 'the confession' (*homologia* – Heb. 3:1; 10:23). In time these teaching 'outlines' assumed a 'trinitarian' shape from which early versions of the 'Apostles' and 'Nicene' creeds developed, both of which were originally used at baptismal services and only later became church creeds.

6. His language of 'death'/'burial' and 'being raised' appears to support a New Testament practice of immersion rather than effusion (pouring).

7. See 2:1, 3, 17-24; 3:8; 4:1; 9:1-3, 6, 14, 19, 30; 11:1, 11.

all are under Sin	3:9
through one man Sin entered the world	5:12
Sin reigned in death	5:21

His Jewish Christian critics seem to think that their efforts at keeping the Law can actually defeat Sin. Paul, however, insists that not only Gentiles but Jews are equally 'under Sin', that is, the Sin that entered the stream of human history with Adam. Sin's unbreakable hold is demonstrated in the eventual death of all Adam's children. Law is powerless to deliver sinners from sinful ways; Law merely reveals the presence and extent of Sin's hold over human hearts.

Thus Paul is doing no more than pointing to the impotence of Law to redeem man from Sin. But his opponents twist this to say that Paul advocates continuance in Sin to attract even more grace from God.

Paul will have none of this and replies, 'By no means'[8] (v. 2), adding a further question to affirm what he really believed.

> We who have died to Sin
> how will we still live in it?

His very framing of the question shows that he is convinced believers have 'died to Sin'. How can they 'still live in' Sin?

In verse 3 Paul supports this rebuttal by an appeal to the teaching the Roman Christians would have received at their baptism (see on v. 17: 'You were obedient from the heart to the pattern of teaching to which you were handed over'). So he must now remind them of that basic baptismal instruction.

> Surely you are not unaware that
> as many as were baptized into Christ Jesus
> were baptized into his death?

Clearly, as baptized persons in Rome they were not 'unaware' of this since baptism depended upon being carefully

---

8. The Greek (*mē genoito*, literally, 'may it never be') is Paul's very strong denial of the proposition in a presenting question. This form is common in Romans where Paul frequently asks and answers questions.

catechized. To this 'knowledge' Paul makes his appeal, as he does throughout the chapter. His critics should know that baptism into Christ meant being joined by faith with him in death (and resurrection). That death was a death 'to Sin' as a way of life, as Paul proceeds to teach.

B. Into and up from the waters of baptism (vv. 4-11)

The initial 'therefore' of verse 4 springs from the assertion of the previous verse that 'we (that is, all Christians) were baptized into Christ's *death*'. If they were 'with' him in death, it follows that they were 'with' him in *burial*.[9] This death and burial 'with' Christ is not an end in itself but is for a purpose that, raised 'with' Christ, 'we might walk in newness of life'. That is, our baptism into Christ is entirely positive in its intended outcome.

> Therefore
>   we were buried with Christ
>   through baptism into his death
>   in order that
>   just as   Christ was raised from the dead
>   through the glory of the Father
>   so too   we might walk in newness of life.

This (most likely) is Paul's commentary on a baptismal catechism and it is one of his most finely crafted statements. Notice, first, his allusion to the *death, burial* and *resurrection* of Christ, which are fundamental not only to the narratives of the four Gospels but also to the apostolic preaching of the gospel (see 1 Cor. 15:3-4). Then, second, we have his strong statement of purpose signalled by 'in order that ... just as ... so too'. That purpose is expressed as 'walking in newness of life' and is amplified in verses 21-22. In other words, this catechetical teaching about Christ is not 'out there', remote, distant and at 'arm's length' as it were, merely a matter for the intellect. Rather (as Paul will say in the next verse), believers

---

9. Throughout Paul uses the language of entombment, that is in a vault in the rock face rather than in a grave dug into the ground.

are actually 'united with' Christ in his burial, death and resurrection.

How are Christians 'united with' Christ? Paul teaches that 'through baptism' as a sign of genuine faith believers are 'crucified with' Christ (*sunestaurōthē* – v. 6) and 'buried with' (*sunetaphēme*) him, and so are 'united with' him. Paul expresses confidence that those so 'united with' Christ through baptism into his death and burial will also 'live with' him in his future Kingdom (v. 8). Their 'unity with' Christ is and will be total.

In passing, we note how easily Paul refers to the historical facts of Jesus' death, burial and resurrection. His *death* is specifically said to be by crucifixion (v. 6). His *burial* (v. 4) is also found in the earliest pre-formed gospel tradition,[10] echoing the Gospel narratives.[11] His resurrection, expressed as 'he was raised' (vv. 4 and 9), is also found in the earliest pre-formed Gospel tradition.[12] In other words, Paul's references to the critical events of the first Easter, though adapted to the current pastoral needs in Rome, are cast in language that is consistent with earliest oral tradition going back to the historical events of the death, burial and resurrection of Jesus of Nazareth. Paul does not argue for the historicity of these events; they are assumed to be true.

Returning to our text, two possible misunderstandings about baptism need to be anticipated. First, baptism is no empty sacramental act. In baptism, a person is publicly testifying to the inner reality of trust in Christ crucified, buried and raised. If clear and firmly directed faith is absent, baptism is an empty sign, devoid of meaning. Christians have sometimes placed confidence in outward signs, independent of genuine faith. In the museum near Ephesus there is a marble statue of the head of the Roman emperor Augustus. Into Augustus' forehead

---

10. 1 Corinthians 15:4 (*etaphē*); Romans 6:4 (*etaphēmen*).

11. It is possible that the Gospel of Mark (or a precursor) predated Paul's letter to the Romans (see on 12:7) and that Paul may have derived this burial information from that source. Paul is probably depending verbally as well on Peter, the disciple of Jesus and a 'witness to' his sufferings (1 Pet. 5:1), with whom Paul stayed' for several weeks (Gal. 1:18-20).

12. 1 Corinthians 15:4 has exactly the same verb in the same configuration (*ēgerthē*) as in Romans 6:4, 9 and Mark 16:6.

some Christians of a later era have chiseled a cross, thinking somehow to make that pagan a Christian by this outward act. There must be true and lively faith, otherwise outward signs, baptism included, are meaningless.

Second, baptism into Christ demands a correspondingly radical change of life. Christ's death *for* Sin is to become the believer's death *to* Sin; his burial is to become the believer's burial to the old way of life; and his resurrection from the dead is to become henceforth a pattern for the believer's new way of life. In short, the Christian's life is to be 'shaped' by Christ crucified, buried and raised.

All this was deeply personal to Paul. The risen Christ appeared to and spoke to him on the road to Damascus. At his baptism Paul would have 'received' instruction about the death, burial and resurrection of Christ (see 1 Cor. 15:1-4). Paul was then baptized to mark the 'death' of his old life and the 'resurrection' of his new life. Thus Paul speaks personally but also inclusively for his Roman readers. His experience is their experience.

In verse 5 he confirms and summarizes the previous verse.

For if we are   united with him   in the likeness[13] of his death
    we shall be [united with him]   in   his resurrection

Once more Paul echoes the great events of Good Friday and Easter Day. At Golgotha the Messiah was crucified late on the eve of the Sabbath, but by the morning of the First Day the tomb was empty because the Lord had 'risen indeed'. Once again we emphasize that Paul does not put Christ at arm's length from believers. On the contrary, Christians are 'united with'[14] him, joined to him, by baptism. The relationship could not be closer.

This is the language of certain hope. Paul is saying that in baptism believers are joined to Christ's death, burial and resurrection and will one day themselves be raised bodily. How

---

13. The unusual words, 'in the likeness of his death', most likely refer to Christian baptism as being a 'death' 'like' Christ's death.

14. The adjective *sumphutos* occurs only here in the New Testament. Originally an agricultural word, it is probably to be understood in the generalized sense of 'united with'.

can Paul be so confident? For one reason only. It is because Christ has truly died, been buried and raised alive, therefore those who belong to him can look forward to their resurrection.

Earlier Paul asked, 'Are you unaware?' Now (v. 6) he appeals to them in positive terms.

> *Knowing* this
> that   our old man was crucified with him
>   in order that   our body of sin might be abolished
>   that   we might no longer be enslaved to Sin.

Paul identifies our 'old man' (*palaios* ... *anthrōpos*) with our 'body of sin'. What does he mean? Most likely he is thinking once more about Adam 'in whom we all sinned' and through whose sin Death entered the human race (see on 5:12). Paul speaks of Sin in the singular and in personal terms, as if it were a malevolent king. 'Sin ruled in Death,' he wrote (5:21). In other words, Sin dominates our lives and motivates and gives direction to everything we do, including even our most apparently self-less acts. The miseries of the human race result from the accumulation and multiplication of Sin's rule over individuals.

But, says Paul, 'knowing this *that*...' This is his routine way of appealing to 'knowledge' based on the catechetical teaching his Christian readers had been given. Paul is reminding them that Sin's kingly rule begun under Adam and came to an end when Christ, the Last Adam, was crucified. In addition to dying *for* the sins of believers he also died *to* terminate Sin's domination in their lives. As Paul will say soon, 'Sin will not rule you' (v. 14). For the moment, however, we must wait for the Apostle to tell us precisely *how* this will happen (see vv. 11-14).

In the meantime (v. 7) Paul will make an important observation about death. 'For,' he says, 'he who has died is justified from Sin.' What does this unusual statement mean? This is Paul's compressed way of saying that one who died in Christ [in baptism] to Sin, is justified from Sin. This is the same as saying, 'he who believes is justified from Sin.' What is baptism except the public confession of 'belief' in Christ? In this one short sentence Paul eliminates 'cheap grace' and 'easy believism' where faith in Christ is shallow, self-serving and not accompanied by 'death' to old ways.

In verses 4-7 Paul's focus was on baptism into the death and burial of Christ. In verses 8-10, however, he turns to reflect on being united in baptism with Christ in his resurrection. Verses 8-10 symmetrically balance verses 4-7. The one plunged into the waters of baptism does not remain there but rises to the surface and emerges up from the water. He died and was buried but is now alive, never to die again.

Paul signals this in verse 8 with the observation, 'But if we died with Christ we believe that we shall live with him.' Our 'death' and 'burial' in baptism was with a view to our immediate 'resurrection' from the waters and the beginning of our risen life 'in Christ'. Thus our baptism marks the end of Sin's tyrannical rule over us and the beginning of the Father's rule in our lives. Baptism into Christ is the beginning of the Future.

With the words, 'Knowing that' (v. 9), Paul once again recalls their initial grounding in Christian teaching. That teaching relates to the fact that Christ was raised from the dead, never to die again.[15] On the island of Patmos Christ said to John, 'Fear not ... I died and behold I am alive for evermore' (Rev. 1:18). Truly he died, so that for a brief three days death was Lord over him. But because his resurrection is absolute and final Death now lies defeated and broken beneath his feet, as Paul told the Corinthians (1 Cor. 15:26-27), death will never again 'lord it' (*kurieuō*) over him.

Paul immediately justifies this statement (v. 10) as signalled by the opening word, 'For.'

---

15. Why is Paul emphatic that 'Christ being raised from the dead will *never* die again'? In his day, the pagan mystery cults provided for a religious catharsis based on washings and various religious ceremonies to mark a new 'spiritual' beginning. This belief, however, was based on myth; no one thought historical reality underlay the myth. See e.g. Lucius Apuleius, *The Golden Ass*, 'Metamorphoses' 11.21.24 (written AD 125). Paul, however, insists that Christ's death, burial and resurrection, which happened once as an authentic historical event, is the basis for Christian conversion that is likewise real and historical. In the mystery cults the new beginning was entirely emotional and religious; no behavioural change was expected. For Paul, however, baptism into Christ is to mark a new beginning that is entirely ethical and moral, the end of Sin's dominance in one's life, no less.

For

        the death   he died   he died to Sin once and for ever
but   the life   he lives   he lives to God.

Christ died for our sins (4:25), that is, for our justification by God. Equally, Christ died to end Sin's dominion 'once and for all' (*ephapax*).[16] Death is the 'last enemy,' but Christ has defeated him.

Alive from the dead, Christ 'lives to God,' that is, the Man Christ Jesus is freed forever from Sin's potential mastery over him in death. Henceforth, he is subject only to the rule of God. Never again will he contemplate the rule of Death, as he did in the Garden of Gethsemane. For never again must he die for our sins. His work for us is 'finished' (John 19:30). But the same now holds true for those who are united to the risen Christ by faith/baptism. By his resurrection for us Christ has destroyed Death. The new David has slain this evil Goliath who now lies at his feet. The children of wicked Adam shout for joy; they are now free of his curse.

Paul's initial 'Likewise' in verse 11 focuses our minds once more on our unity with Christ in his historical death and resurrection through faith/baptism. Because we are 'with him' in his death and resurrection, what is true for him is and will be true for us. Christ is now 'dead' to the lordship of Sin that was previously demonstrated (briefly) in his death and burial. The risen Christ is now and forever 'alive to God'. But so, too, are we.

Thus Paul exhorts the original hearers, and every Christian reader since, to 'reckon' or 'work out' that, similar to Christ, they are now free from Sin's lordship demonstrated in death, both biological and eternal. Rather, Christians must understand that they are even now 'alive in Christ Jesus to God'.

This verse has been misunderstood to mean that by mentally 'reckoning ourselves to be dead to Sin' we become morally

---

16. This *ephapax* and its close relative *hapax* mean 'once and for all time' and speak of God's absolute and final, never to be repeated, saving intervention in Christ in history (Rom. 6:10; 1 Cor. 15:6; Heb. 6:4; 7:27; 9:7, 12, 26, 27, 28; 10:2, 10; 1 Pet. 3:18; Jude 3). For the classic study see Oscar Cullmann, *Christ and Time* (London: SCM, 1962 ET).

perfect, or at least by this means enter into a 'higher life' and 'victory' over Sin. Paul, however, is speaking of our 'victory' in Christ over the prospect of Death. Sin reigns in Death, but since Death is now defeated by Christ crucified and risen, the lordship of Sin in Death has been defeated for the believer. It is this Paul encourages us to 'count on' or 'reckon'. This has consequences for our struggle with 'continuing sin', as he will now explain. But that struggle and hoped for victory does not involve convincing ourselves that we are or can somehow be immune from temptation or sinful behaviour.

C. Verses 12-14.

Paul's introductory 'Therefore' (v. 12) is a bridge between the theological (vv. 4-11) and the practical (vv. 12-13). Through baptism into Christ crucified, buried and raised, believers are now dead to the kingship of Sin exercised in death. So, with this in mind, what is the believer to *do*?

> Therefore
> do not let Sin rule as a king in your mortal body
> so that you obey its passions.

This is Paul's command to the will, based on the understanding of the mind he encouraged in verse 11. Sin's reign in Death has been ended by Christ's resurrection. No longer is Death going to have the last say with believers. Beyond biological death they look forward to the resurrection of the Last Day. Because Death has been de-throned by the resurrection of Jesus, the Christian must not allow Sin to sit on the throne any longer. Because Sin has been de-throned, it follows that in the meantime the believer must not yield to the 'passions' (or, 'lusts') of the body. What does Paul mean? He elaborates further in the verses following.

In verse 12 Paul amplifies in specific terms his more general exhortation in the previous verse. He is addressing those who, as it were, have freshly come up from the waters of baptism. This he does in two parts, negative and positive. Notice his words.

Neither present your members as instruments of wickedness to Sin
but   present yourselves   to God
as if alive from the dead
and   your members as instruments of righteousness to God.

Here is the answer to the question prompted by the previous
verse, that is, how does one reject Sin's rule in the body? The
baptized believer, as delivered from Death by the resurrection
of Christ, is to make critical decisions about his or her
'members', that is, the 'members' of the body. Such 'members'
are capable of being 'instruments'[17] either of 'wickedness' or
'righteousness'. Clearly, since in Christ-resurrected I am now
(in principle) resurrected, 'alive from the dead', I will not
hand over my limbs and organs for wicked behaviour but for
godly and righteous behaviour.

It is by this exercise of the will based on the informed
mind that I repudiate Sin's practical rule in my life. Pastorally
speaking, it is recognised that such teaching is not always
easy to fulfil. The new Christian often brings to the Christian
life an accumulation of unhelpful attitudes and practices. But
there is forgiveness for failure, and there is strength from God
to move forward. In Charles Wesley's words, 'He breaks the
power of cancelled sin. He sets the prisoner free.' Not least in
the church there are the resources of fellowship, advice and
help that should be sought in circumstances of special need.

In verse 14 Paul concludes this section with words of
promise which, however, take us back to the immediate
difficulty. This entire chapter was written (so it seems) to
rebut the Jewish Christians in Rome who wished to reinstate
the Law as a fundamental of the Christian life, both for Jews
and Gentiles. Thus Paul promises, comfortingly, 'For Sin will
not Lord it over you.' How can he say this? It is 'because you
are not under Law but under grace'. Whoever Paul intends by
his words, '*You* are not under Law,' whether Jews or Gentiles,
each needs to understand that being 'under Law' is not an
option. The Jewish Christian is no longer under Law and the
Gentile Christian must not be brought under Law.

---

17. The Greek word *hopla* literally means military weapons. The 'hoplites' were
heavily armed Greek soldiers.

As we noted in the previous section (5:12-21), Law revealed Sin and inflamed Sin but proved impotent to diminish its power. God's grace or kindness, however, underlies the coming, death and resurrection of the messianic Saviour. He has borne the penalty for our breaches of the Law and in his death and resurrection made possible our death to Sin and our resurrection to new life. Not because we have to (Law) but because we want to (grace), we now willingly offer our total selves to God as his slaves, and so find deliverance. Law makes us its slaves, but grace sets us free.

The introduction of the word 'Lord' (v. 14) signals a change in imagery from kingship of Sin (and rejection thereof) to freedom from slavery to 'Lord Sin', a theme which dominates the remainder of the chapter.

2. YOU WERE SLAVES BUT YOU ARE NOW FREE (vv. 15-23)

A. Set free by the Baptismal Teaching (vv. 15-17)
The second question in the chapter ('What, therefore?' – v. 15) is an abbreviated form of the first ('What, therefore, shall we say?' – v. 1). Most likely, in both Paul is responding to the Jewish Christians in the house-based churches in the Eternal City who object to Paul's Law-free preaching. Paul's second question, ('Shall we sin because we are not under Law but under grace?'), while prompted by the preceding verse, also resembles the question at the beginning of the chapter ('Shall we continue in Sin that grace may increase?'). Paul's emphatic reply, 'By no means', is identical with his reply to the first question (see on v. 2).

In verse 16 Paul once more follows the pattern in the first verses of the chapter. Once more he appeals ('Do you not know?') to their initial grounding in the gospel.

Do you not know that
to whom you present yourselves as slaves to obey
slaves you are to the one you obey
whether   of Sin   for death
or   of obedience   for righteousness.

The imagery of slavery, although merely metaphorical to us, was basic to the culture and economy of Paul's world. His point is simple. The one to whom a slave offers himself becomes the 'lord' and owner of the slave. So, asks Paul, who will that 'lord' be – 'Sin' or 'obedience [to God]'? If the 'lord' is 'Sin', the result will be 'death'. If, however, the 'lord' is 'obedience', the result will be 'righteousness', the practical 'righteousness' of a godly life as the outcome of 'obedience'.

The 'obedience' in question is explained in verse 17. This is one of Paul's brief (as opposed to lengthy) 'thanksgivings'.[18] Paul's 'Thanks be to God' reminds us how devout a man he was, ever ready to raise his voice in recognition of God's goodness. On this occasion his God-directed gratitude is on account of the conversion of his Roman readers.

> You were slaves of Sin
> but you became obedient from the heart
> to the pattern of teaching
> to which you were handed over.

There is much to note in this important statement.

First, as the word 'were'[19] implies, the readers had been long- term 'slaves' of Sin. Regardless of whether they had been Jews or Gentiles, they had lived by and in conformity to the ways of fallen Adam.

Second, the contrasting verb tense used for *'became obedient'*[20] implies a specific point when they ceased being slaves of Sin and 'became obedient from the heart', that is, genuinely and sincerely.[21]

Third, it was their obedience to the 'pattern of teaching' which they came to obey that liberated them from slavery to Sin. Through their obedience to the teaching of the Word of God they became obedient to God himself.

---

18. See. e.g. 7:25; 1 Corinthians 15:57; 2 Corinthians 2:14; 8:16; 9:15.

19. The Greek imperfect tense, implying habitual behaviour.

20. The Greek aorist tense, implying a change of behaviour.

21. Paul makes a similar 'before and after' contrast for the Corinthians. Some had been habitually immoral, but subsequent to Paul's preaching in the city they came to be washed, justified and sanctified and, as a result, had changed their ways (1 Cor. 6:11).

Fourth, reference to 'pattern of teaching' (*tupon didachēs*) implies a fixed format of teaching at their baptism, as mentioned earlier (vv. 3-4). Although Paul did not lay the foundation of Christianity in Rome, nonetheless he assumes that these believers have been instructed in a 'pattern of teaching' at the time they were baptized. It is clear from verses 3-6 that such a grounding in the faith included basic teaching about the identity of Jesus as Christ and Lord, his death for sins and resurrection for new life, and also the expectation that those who confessed faith in him at baptism were expected now to 'walk in newness of life'.

Fifth, to our surprise Paul speaks of the baptized in Rome being 'handed over' to this 'pattern of teaching'. From other passages we know that apostles and evangelists 'handed over' set forms of teaching to new converts.[22] This occurred also in Rome, since these readers were 'obedient from the heart' to it. Here, however, the emphasis is subtly different; these converts are said to have been 'handed over' to the teaching, a telling reminder to them of its importance. This 'obedience' to the 'pattern of teaching' had been the means to 'righteous' living, as it will continue to be into the future.

B Set free for slavery (vv. 18-20)
In verse 18 Paul reminds the Romans of the results of their obedience to the 'pattern of teaching'. They were, he tells them, 'set free from their Sin.' The grammatical form of the word is familiar as this comparison shows.

5:1	*Being justified*	by faith...
5:9	*Being justified*	by his blood...
6:18	*Being set free*	from Sin...

The verbs ('being justified' and 'being set free') are expressed in a tense and mood[23] that says that God is the author of the action and we are the recipients. *God* has justified us; *God* has set us free from Sin.

There is a second leg to verse 18.

22. See e.g. 1 Corinthians 11:2; 15:1-3; Colossians 2:6-7.
23. Aorist tense, passive voice.

Being set free from Sin you became enslaved to righteousness.

This antinomy (use of apparent opposites) aptly describes the Christian life. Paul reminds his readers that becoming a Christian involved being set free from Sin *for* slavery to righteousness, as his grammar subtly shows.[24] Freedom from the lordship of Sin (in Death) is not an end in itself. The Christian has been 'set free' from one 'lord' (Sin) for 'slavery' to another 'lord' ('righteousness'). In this case (as in v. 16) 'righteousness' is not God's gift of imputed righteousness but man's actual righteousness, though the former is the source of the latter.

Paul's emphasis on 'slavery to righteousness' is understandable in view of the accusations against him, that is, he is opposed to Law (see on 3:8; 6:1). True, subservience to Law is not part of Paul's gospel, whether for Jews or Gentiles (vv. 14-15). Indeed not. But Paul is no libertine. On the contrary, as we see here, Paul is deeply concerned that Christians are 'captured' by and 'enslaved to' righteous behaviour. Yet that life of 'righteousness' does not arise from self-justification, as it would from a Law-based theology. Rather, actual righteousness is to spring from and be inspired by God's gracious gift of righteousness to those who by baptism are united with Christ crucified, buried and raised.

In verse 19 Paul apologizes that he is speaking of 'freedom' and 'slavery' by way of illustration. As we have already noted, such language is somewhat remote to us now but at that time must have been extraordinarily powerful. A majority of the population in the Graeco-Roman world were slaves. Thus Paul's insistence that the Christians become 'slaves' makes his point clearly.

He sets up a stark contrast between their former, pre-Christian way of life and their present post-baptismal way of life.

---

24. It is freedom 'from' (*apo*) Sin 'with a view to' righteousness (*tē dikaiosunē*).

For
just as   you presented   your members
             as slaves   to uncleanness
             and   to ever greater lawlessness
so now   present   your members
             as slaves   to righteousness
                          for sanctification.

The former lifestyle marked by 'uncleanness' and 'lawlessness' identifies these converts as Gentiles, as confirmed by an earlier reference to Gentiles' (sexual) 'uncleanness' (1:24). In our view, after the death of Emperor Claudius in AD 54, Gentiles would have been in the majority and Jews in relatively depleted numbers in the Roman house groups. Nonetheless, Paul is able to assure such Jews disaffected by his Law-free gospel that Gentiles have been profoundly rehabilitated morally by that very gospel.

His words, then, are directed to these Gentile believers reminding them about the evils they have left behind and reinforcing the need to 'present' their limbs and organs to righteous living issuing in 'sanctification' (hagiasmos). This word can mean both (1) one's 'position' in Christ with God in a state of holiness,[25] and also, depending on that, (2) one's 'progress' in Christ in holiness. Option (2) is probably to be preferred here[26] since 'captivity' to true 'righteousness' will mean 'bearing fruit' which implies 'change' and 'spiritual progress'.[27]

From verse 19, we should note that though this 'presenting' of oneself and one's constituent parts occurs at the time of baptism, it does not end then. By no means! Rather, involved here is a practical and periodically detailed audit of the genuineness of one's 'consecration' of the parts and the whole in the service of God.

---

25. As in 1 Corinthians 1:30; 2 Thessalonians 2:13.

26. Option (1) also occurs, e.g. 1 Thessalonians 4:3 – '... this is the will of God, your sanctification.'

27. Some have argued that whereas Romans 3–5 is about 'justification' chapters 6–8 concern 'sanctification' (meaning 'progress' or 'transformation,' as above). This is to be doubted. True, the word 'sanctification' (hagiasmos) occurs twice in Romans 6 (see also v. 22; though nowhere else in the letter). For this word to determine the subject matter of the chapter and the two following we would expect a greater linguistic concentration (e.g. 'justification' occurs many times in chs 3–5).

Many and inspiring are the great hymns of self-dedication, but none are more moving than Frances Havergal's simple poem written in 1874:

Take my life and let it be
Consecrated Lord, to thee;
Take my moments and my days,
Let them flow in ceaseless praise.

Take my hands and let them move
At the impulse of thy love;
Take my feet, and let them be
Swift and beautiful for thee.

Take my voice and let me sing
Always only for my king;
Take my lips and let them be,
Filled with messages from thee.

In verse 20, as also in verse 18, Paul again uses the 'slave' and 'free' antinomy to point up the contrast between pre- and post-baptismal living. Here, however, the order is reversed. And the words are a painful reminder of that past life.

When you were slaves of Sin
you were free in respect of righteousness.

Before the word of God came, he reminds them, they were subject to the 'lordship' of Sin and therefore of Death. That was their 'slavery'. At that time, let them be reminded, their minds and hearts did not turn to righteous behaviour so as to please God. They were not captivated by or captured for righteousness; they were 'free' from it.

C. 'Fruit' Then and Now (vv. 21-22)

Paul continues the contrast between the pre- and post-baptismal living of these Gentiles in Rome. Now, however, he leaves behind the 'slave' and 'free' imagery, preferring instead the language of 'fruit' (*karpos*). In the New Testament, 'fruit' is used for visible and concrete actions, both positive (Gal. 5:22: 'The fruit of the Spirit ...') and negative (Matt. 7:16-20: 'By their fruit you shall know them'). By 'fruit' the New Testament writers mean outward behaviour which reveals the true state of the heart.

So Paul urges them to remember who and what they were.

> Therefore what fruit did you have   then
> of which you are ashamed   now?
> For the end of those things is death.

The contrast in the words 'then' (*tote*) and 'now' (*nun*) points to the radical change between their former and present lives. In this verse, however, the emphasis is on the former life. As sons and daughters of Adam, they had been governed by Sin and faced the consequence, Death. In retrospect they will surely agree that their 'fruit' was shameful, evidence in advance of eternal Death, to which each day brought them closer. (We are justified in thinking Paul means 'eternal Death' as opposed to physical death, since in the next verse he speaks of 'eternal life'.)

In verse 22, however, the apostle directs them to think about their present lives.

> But now   having been set   free   from Sin
>   having been made   slaves   to God
>   you are having your fruit for sanctification.
>   And the end is eternal life.

In mind here is their obedience to the 'pattern of teaching' and their confession at baptism. In consequence God both set them free from Sin and made them slaves to himself, as is implied by the passive voice in both verbs. Now they have 'fruit', outward behaviour as evidence of true inner change of heart and mind, that is, of sanctification. Now the total direction of life is reversed. Previously they were headed in the direction of eternal Death, their shameful deeds confirming that awful path along the way. Now, however, God has re-directed them toward eternal life, with their worthy fruit as evidence of where they are now headed.

Paul's words are not merely descriptive of the 'miracle' of their conversion in Christ through the gospel. Additionally they are of contemporary pastoral importance. Quite clearly Paul seeks to encourage and confirm their ongoing growth as Christians, with greater and greater evidence of the 'fruit' of righteousness.

The challenge to us modern readers is to continue to 'bear fruit' more and more. It is easy, in the midst of a busy life, to be distracted from godly living, to be sound in orthodoxy but with a heart that is dead towards God. The spiritual excitement of the newly baptized is to be renewed again and again within our lives. Otherwise we may become like the fruitless lemon tree in my garden. It has luxuriant foliage but just one or two lemons per year, a miserable crop. This is not what we look for in a lemon tree, and it is not what God looks for in us.

D. Wages and Gift (v. 23)

The preceding passage (vv. 15-22) is rich in contrasts.

(i) In verses 16-19, Paul contrasts two slaveries, one to Sin (following Adam), the other to God (by obeying from the heart 'the pattern of teaching'.)

Slavery to Sin	>uncleanness	>lawlessness	>Death
Slavery to God	>righteousness	>sanctification	>Eternal Life

(ii) In verses 21-22, he contrasts two 'fruits' of these 'slaveries', the evils of 'uncleanness' and 'wickedness' on one hand, and (progress in) 'holiness,' on the other.

(iii) In verses 21-22, using the word *telos*, the apostle contrasts two 'ends' or 'finishing' points to the human journey, Death on one hand, Eternal Life on the other.

In verse 23 Paul draws together these contrasts into one splendid, justly famous summary.

For	the wages	of Sin	is Death
but	the gift	of God	is Eternal Life
	in Jesus Christ our Lord.		

King Sin pays his slaves a 'wage'[28] and that wage is Eternal
Death. Adam and his sons and daughters, without exception,
discrimination or favouritism, receive that payment at life's end.
That is all that they have to look forward to. God, however, does
not pay wages (see on 4:4-5) but only makes gifts. God's 'gift'
or 'gratuity' (*charisma*) to Adam's descendants is another man,
'our Lord Jesus Christ.' By his death for Sin and resurrection
from the dead, Christ defeated Death, the 'Last Enemy', and
made available in its place Eternal Life. Death-bound children
of Adam who believe in Christ through the gospel now have
from the hand of God his entirely free gift of Eternal Life. The
apostle John wrote: 'He that has the Son has life' (1 John 5:12).

The so-called 'Roman road' explaining the 'way of salvation'
links 3:23 ('all have sinned') with 6:23 ('the wages of sin is
death, but the free gift of God is eternal life, in Jesus Christ').
It is safe to say that millions have found the mercy of God in
a personal sense of salvation and peace with God from these
great Pauline texts.

It must not be forgotten, however, that (most likely) Paul
was writing this letter and these chapters to correct a dangerous
distortion of the gospel through the insistence on the role of
Law demanded by some in the Roman assemblies. Twice in this
chapter Paul repudiates such a notion. In one place he says, 'You
are *not* under Law *but* under grace' (v. 14) and in another, 'we
are *not* under Law *but* under grace' (v. 15). The 'not ... but' format
leaves no doubt. Here we must not fail to notice a connection
Paul makes. His twofold assertion, 'you/we ... are under *grace*
(*charis*)' is matched by 'the gift (*charisma*) of God is eternal life'.

Paul's defence of the 'grace of God' to his Roman critics is
not finished. Paul must turn his attention towards those who
advocate the Law of God as the basis for the Christian life.
As Paul will say, speaking autobiographically, such a man is
indeed 'wretched'.

3. Theological Reflection

If it is granted that Paul in Romans 6 is responding to Jewish
Christians who were seeking to reinstate Law for believers,

---

28. The Greek *opsōnia* implies a soldier's paltry rations.

we may ask: how is this chapter relevant? The 'Judaizing' crisis is long passed, as it had by the end of Paul's life. So: if no one is pressing Christians to submit to the Old Testament Law of God as a means to gain God's approval (as they appear to have urged in Paul's day), how does this chapter assist us today?

Here we must understand that the theology of the Pharisees informed mainstream Jewish thought and practice in Paul's day. Significantly, Pharisaism taught that the will of man was assisted by God to make it able to please God. Josephus, a former Pharisee, wrote that the Pharisees 'do not deprive the human will of the pursuit of what is in man's power'. He added, 'it was God's will that there should be a fusion and that the will of man with his virtue and vice should be admitted to the council chamber of fate [i.e. Providence].'[29] In other words, the most influential Jewish theologians of the era taught that man, with God's help, was capable of pleasing God by self-effort. Most likely, those Roman Jews (who were also Christians) who opposed Paul's Law-free gospel were Pharisee-influenced, convinced that man can (and must?) win the help of God by observing 'the works of the Law', that is by their own efforts.

A Christian parallel with this Jewish theology is found in the theology of Pelagius, who taught that man freely took the first step God-wards.[30] Formerly as a Pharisee Paul most likely held similar views about human freedom. Now, however, as a man in Christ he has come to see Sin's dominion as absolute in human experience, broken only through the gospel joining Adam's children to Christ crucified and risen. This and only this is God's way of bringing Sin's dominion exercised in Death to an end.

STUDY QUESTIONS

1. How is this idea of 'more sin, more grace' still prevalent today?

---

29. *Jewish Antiquities* xviii.13.
30. Pelagius, a British monk who taught early in the fifth century, held that the will of man was entirely free and that men and women can please God in their own strength.

2. How are you united with Christ?

3. What is the true significance of baptism?

4. How does baptism unite us with Christ in his death, burial and resurrection?

5. How does your knowledge of the truth of Christ's death, burial and resurrection help you have victory over sin in your life?

6. How am I able to reject sin's rule in my body?

7. What must I do to exercise my will so that I do not fall prey to temptation?

8. Have you moved from being a slave to sin to being a slave to righteousness?

9. Are others able to see you bearing the fruit of righteousness?

8

Deliverance
(Romans 7:1–8:4)

In the previous chapter Paul has been defending his Law-free gospel (as it appears) to Jewish critics in the house churches in Rome. Their objection is that a Law-free gospel leads to lawlessness. He has responded to this by letting his Jewish hearers overhear his words to Gentile believers, reminding them of the life-changing impact of the gospel and of their baptism into Christ crucified and risen. Previously these Gentiles had led lives of 'uncleanness' of which they are now ashamed. Now, however, they are bearing the righteous fruits of sanctification and they are doing so in Christ, *without* Law.

In Romans 7:1–8:4 Paul continues his defence of his gospel of grace. Now, however, he is addressing his Jewish critics directly, as the following references to Law indicate.

I am speaking to those who know the Law	verse 1
You have been put to death to Law	verse 4
Now you are discharged from the Law	verse 6
[Law] which held us captive	verse 6
[Slaves] in oldness of letter [of the Law]	verse 6
the Law is holy	verse 12
the Law is spiritual	verse 14
the Law is good	verse 16
the Law of God	verse 22
the Law of God	verse 25
the Law of Sin and Death Chapter 8,	verse 2

If further proof were needed we might note that Paul uses the word 'commandment' (as a synonym to Law) no less than six times in this passage.

Basically, then, in this chapter Paul seeks to drive home to Jewish believers that the Law has failed to rescue Jewish people like them from the power of Sin, both prior to but also subsequent to baptism into Christ.

There is a deeper point, however, that Paul is making here beyond the immediate pastoral needs of his Roman readers. Two texts, in particular, establish this.

> 7:6 But now we are discharged from the Law,
>   having died to that in which we were held captive,
>   so that we might serve   in newness of the Spirit
>   and not   in oldness of the Letter.

> 8:2 For   the law of the Spirit of life in Christ Jesus
>   has set you free
>   from   the Law of sin and death.

By 'Letter' Paul means the Law given through Moses as the basis of the old covenant. Due to sin, however, Israel did not and could not fulfil that Law. The era of Law is now ended, abolished and superseded by Christ's justifying work as applied to the believer by the Holy Spirit. God relates with man and man with God 'in Christ' and 'by grace' and 'in the Spirit'.

In Romans 7:1–8:4 Paul teaches this great theology of fulfilment by Christ and the Spirit by telling his own story of moral failure as a man under Law.[1] In chapter 7 is Paul's spiritual autobiography.[2]

---

1. Paul is continuing a theme begun at 5:12-21 where he taught about the kingship of Sin in the Death of Adam and all his descendants. Through the entire passage, 5:12–8:4, Paul only refers to 'Sin' (singular) and not 'sins' (plural). In 5:12-21 Law did nothing to rescue God's people from Sin and Death; only Christ has done that in his death and resurrection. In chapter 6 he reminded them that Christ has delivered Gentiles from past shameful and unclean behaviour by their baptism into Christ crucified and risen (and not by Law).

2. According to D. Moo, *The Wycliffe Exegetical Commentary. Romans 1–8* (Chicago: Moody Press, 1991), 448-56 there are four possible ways of identifying the 'wretched man': (1) Paul, writing autobiographically, (2) Paul writing as Adam,

This passage is a scholars' and preachers' battleground.[3] 'Forget the message of Romans overall,' people often say. 'Just tell us *who* is the "wretched man" in chapter 7!' Is he Paul before conversion? Is he the 'carnal' Christian prior to the 'victory' of the 'higher life'? Or, is he just the ordinary Christian struggling with 'continuing' sin?

I suggest that the third option is closest to Paul's intention, but with a difference. Paul is first and foremost speaking as a Jew, that is, as a man who had been 'under Law'. Gentile believers can have little appreciation what this meant. In this passage Paul is autobiographically pointing up the futility of relating to God by Law. Is there an application to Gentiles, to those who have never been 'under Law'? The answer is 'yes' and that answer is that any attempt to approach God other than 'by grace' brings the same sense of futility, even to those who have never been subject to the Mosaic Law.

Paul's immediate pastoral concern was twofold. He did not want Jewish believers to attempt to relate to God through Law and he did not want Gentile believers to be brought under Law. Let both Jew and Gentile understand that knowing God depended on believing in Christ crucified and risen for one's righteousness before God. This – and only this – brings the strong Spirit of God to enliven and empower men and women to know and please God.

Paul's experience under Law falls into two parts: (a) when he came under Law as an adolescent Jew (vv. 7-14), and (b) in the period since, when he lived under Law as an adult, both as a Jew but also as a Christian (vv. 15-25). This would perhaps explain why he speaks in the past tense for the earlier period and in the present tense for the later period.

---

(3) Paul personifying Israel under Law, (4) Paul writing existentially, as if everyman. Moo favours (3), incorrectly in my view. Most likely, Paul is writing autobiographically, though with some allusions to Israel's story as well.

3. For a helpful review of the various attempts to identify the 'wretched man', see J. I. Packer, 'The "Wretched Man" Re-visited: Another Look at Romans 7:14-25,' in *Romans and the People of God*, eds. S. K. Soderlund and N. T. Wright (Grand Rapids: Eerdmans, 1999), 70-81.

1. JEWISH BELIEVERS DISCHARGED FROM LAW (vv. 1-6)

Verse 1 is a question addressed to Jews ('I speak to those who know the Law').

A. A Question to Jewish Readers (v. 1)

> Or, are you unaware...
> that the Law is Lord over a man
> as long as he is alive.

The words, 'Or, are you unaware...' (found also in 6:3), are rather reproachful. Paul thinks Jewish Christians should know what he is about to say. References to 'Law' and 'Lord' are hints that Paul is continuing to discuss matters raised earlier; he spoke about 'Law' in 5:12-21 and to 'Lord' and to 'as long as he is alive' in 6:1-23. In other words, what follows is not free-standing, but part of a longer exposition.

B. Analogy of a Married Woman (vv. 2-3)

In verses 2-3 Paul now illustrates his point by reference to a wife's obligations under Law to a husband.

> A married woman is bound by Law
> to her husband while he is alive.
> But if the husband dies
> she is discharged from the Law
> that bound her to her husband.
>
> So then she will be known as an adulteress
> if while her husband is alive
> she belongs to another man.
> But if her husband dies
> she is free from the law
> so that she is not an adulteress
> if she belongs to another man.

Law binds a wife to her husband while he is alive. If during his lifetime she lives with another man she is an adulteress, but if the husband dies and she remarries she is not an adulteress. The power of Law is ended by death.

C. Application to Jewish Readers (vv. 4-6)

The initial 'Likewise' of verse 4 directs the force of Paul's analogy to his fellow Jewish Christians. At the same time it picks up the incredulous 'Or, are you unaware' from verse 1.

> Likewise, my brothers,
> you also have been put to death to the Law
> through the body of Christ
> so that you may belong to another
> to him who has been raised from the dead
> that you may bear fruit to God.

Since they 'have been put to death to Law' the natural inference is that these readers are Jews. Previously they had been 'alive' to Law and, as it were, 'married' to Law.

Like the Gentile believers in their baptism (6:5-6), these Jewish believers have also 'been put to death' 'through the body of Christ,' that is, 'through' his death by crucifixion. Like the Gentile believers they too have been raised again to life. But theirs hasn't been the only death; Law has also died. There is a double death. Like the widow in the analogy the Jewish Christian is now set free to marry again. Because Law is now dead to her, this 'widow' is free to re-marry, and her new 'husband' is Christ who has been raised from the dead. 'Married' now to the risen Christ, the Jewish believer will bear fruit to God.

In short, Paul is telling these Jews that as Christian believers the Law is dead to them and they are dead to Law, so that they are now free to belong exclusively to the risen Christ. Then, just as the believing Gentiles are doing (see on 6:22), the Jewish believers will also bear the fruit of ever-increasing righteousness to God.

The point of the analogy as applied to the readers then and now is straightforward. It is that we bear fruit in the Christian life through being joined by faith and trust to our risen Lord. Looking to Law will bear no fruit, but looking to the living Lord will. As we turn to him we are indwelt by the Spirit and begin to bear good fruit pleasing to God.

In verse 5 Paul appeals to his fellow-Jews to remember the
days of the 'flesh', that is, of the time before he and they were
united with Christ by faith and baptism.[4] 'Let's be honest,'
says Paul the Jew to fellow-Jews. 'To all appearances we
were devout Law-keeping Jews. The reality was otherwise.
Our sinful passions worked in our members and bore fruit
for death.' In other words, Paul is saying to fellow-Jews that
having Law did not make a scrap of difference to their 'sinful
passions' and the reality of Death. Adam sinned and died, and
so too do all his descendants, whether Gentiles or Jews. Sin
was and is King over all, reigning in Death, regardless of the
adherence to Law (see on 5:13-14). In this Jews were and are
no different from Gentiles; the sins of both are a matter for
shame (see on 6:21; cf. 2:17-29; 3:23).

All that has changed, says Paul in verse 6. His opening
words, 'But now' point to the great moment when he and other
Jews were baptised into Christ and died and were buried to
the old life and raised alive to the new.

But now
discharged from the Law
having died to that which held us captive
so that we   are slaves   in the newness   of the Spirit
and   not   in the oldness   of the letter.

Formerly, pre-Christ and pre-baptism into Christ, he and his
fellow-Jews were slaves to the Law, that is, to 'the oldness of
the Letter (that is, the Law)'. As he says elsewhere, that 'letter'
killed (2 Cor. 3:6). But now the (Christian) Jew is 'discharged'
from 'dead Law' to be 'joined' to the risen Christ in order to
be 'slaves' in the new life by the Spirit of God. Here Paul is
anticipating the teaching of 8:1-4 where the just requirement
of the Law (love – 13:8, 10) is fulfilled in those who walk by
the Spirit.

Paul is declaring that the temporary era of Law and
Commandments is now passed, abolished and superseded by

---

4. 'Flesh' is Paul's word for our 'fallen' nature as progeny of Adam. The word will
become important later in chapter 7, continuing into chapter 8.

the death of the Messiah bringing the gift of righteousness and the gift of the Spirit, making the children of Adam the children of God (see 8:15).

No longer are believing Jews like Paul in bondage to rules, regulations and rituals to please God, based on their own self-effort. No longer must he and they be anxious whether their efforts will be sufficient to please God, knowing that his standards are absolute. Now in Christ they are forgiven everything. Now they are free from the otherwise inevitable kingship of Sin reigning in Death over them. God is no longer their judge in a hearing whose outcome they fear. Rather, God is their Father because Christ is their Saviour and Lord. The judgement of God has been passed and it has been passed on Christ, in their place. They are now free, 'discharged' from that prison of fear.

Subjection to the Law is for Paul and for them in the past – or should be. But this appears to be the very reason Paul is writing. Some Jews among the believers in Rome appear to want to be under Law and, most likely, to subject Gentiles also to the Law. Paul, too, as a lifelong Jew may also have found himself drifting back into old ways of thinking.

2. Law is not Sin (vv. 7-12)

Paul has made the bold statement that as a Jew who is in Christ he is 'discharged from the Law' (v. 6), a statement he knows may rankle some fellow-Jews among the Christians in Rome. So, in verse 7, he articulates their anticipated objection, namely – 'So, Paul, you are saying that the Law is Sin.'[5]

This pointed reply, 'By no means' is his answer. 'The Law is not Sin, indeed not, but...' Yes, there is a 'but'.

verse 7	*But* I did not know Sin except through Law. I had not known coveting except that the Law had said, 'You shall not covet.'

---

5. In reply Paul follows a format he used earlier (see 6:1-2, 15) – (a) his question: 'What shall we say?' with their objection, and (b) his conclusive reply 'By no means'.

verse 8   But Sin taking advantage of me
             through the commandment
             worked all manner of covetousness in me,
             for apart from Law Sin was dead.

verse 9   At one time I was alive apart from Law
             but when the commandment came
             Sin came to life and I died.

verse 10   The commandment that was to give life
             gave only death.

verse 11   For Sin taking advantage of me
             through the commandment
             deceived me and killed me.

verse 12   So then
             the Law is holy
             and the commandment is holy
             and righteous and good.

This is the language of personal experience. We ask, who is the speaker? Clearly it is Paul, and Paul is writing as a Christian. But *about whom* is he writing? There are two main options. (1) Paul the *Jew* prior to his baptism in Christ, or (2) the post-baptismal *Christian* Paul?

Most likely, in my view, option 1 is to be preferred. This is Paul as a Christian looking back on his life as a Jew, a man under Law. The passage above appears to reflect his life as a Jewish boy and adolescent who is coming to understand the impact of Law in his conscience. Later he continues that story as an adult (see on vv. 15-20).

As a child and young teenager Paul was nurtured in a strict Jewish family in Tarsus. His reference to the 'commandment' probably refers to the time when as a thirteen-year-old he was instructed in the commandments so as to be publicly initiated as a 'son of commandment' (*bar mitzvah*). These words speak of the effects in his conscience of the new awareness of the Law as an emerging adult. The commandment revealed

Sin and inflamed Sin, so that Paul 'died' in the sense of lost innocence.

Why does Paul tell this story to Jewish readers? It is so that they will not turn back to Law, nor seek to bring Gentiles under Law. Law is a way to death. Only in Christ and the Spirit is the life of God to be found.

One thing is clear. Paul was then speaking to a situation in the first century. Paul is not speaking initially to Gentile Christians. True, in chapter 6 he reminded Gentiles of the impact on them of their baptism into Christ and its ongoing moral challenge. But in chapter 7:1–8:4 he is speaking as a Jew to Jews. Gentile converts had not been subject to Law; his words would not make sense to them.

3. INDWELLING, REMAINING SIN (vv. 13-20)

A. How Good kills (vv. 13-14)
Yet another question answered strongly, 'By no means' signals that once more Paul is anticipating Jewish objections (see on 6:1, 15; 7:7). Paul has just said that Sin brought death through the commandment. 'So Paul are you saying that the good commandment brings death?' His reply, 'By no means' is once more followed by 'But ...'

But	Sin – that it might be revealed to be Sin –	
	worked death	through the good
that	Sin might	be revealed as exceedingly sinful
		through the commandment.

There is a decorative vine with pretty flowers which, however, prove lethal if eaten. It is aptly called 'deadly night shade'. The commandment which is good nonetheless proves fatal when introduced to the human species suffering under the contagion known as Sin. The commandment itself is good, but when administered to the sick patient brings spiritual death.

In verse 14 Paul uses the word 'fleshly' to portray the human condition into which we welcome or introduce Law at our peril.

> For we know that the Law is spiritual
> but I am fleshly, sold under Sin.

The contrast is clear. Law is 'spiritual' but I am 'fleshly'. The related word 'flesh' (*sarx*) appeared in verse 5 and will become dominant at 7:18–8:13. 'Flesh' describes the spiritually 'fallen' condition of Adam and his tribe. This condition of 'flesh' is no light thing. Speaking representatively for all – Jews and Gentiles – Paul declares himself to be 'sold under Sin'. Here the imagery of slavery 'under' Sin accords with previous references (cf. 3:9 – 'all are under sin'; 5:12 – 'all sinned'; 5:21 – 'Sin reigned in death').

B. Mystifying Behaviour (vv. 15-20)

Paul's account of moral failure and baffling behaviour in these verses is justly famous.

verse 15	That which I do I do not understand. For I do not do what I wish, but what I hate, that I do.
verse 16	But if I do what I do not want, I affirm that the Law is good.
verse 17	So then it is no longer I that do it but Sin that lives within me.
verse 18	For I know that in me, that is in my flesh, no good lives.
verse 19	For the good I desire I do not but the evil I do not desire I do
verse 20	But if what I do not desire I do it is no longer I that do it but Sin living in me.

If in verses 7-14 Paul is reflecting on his distant past then in verses 15-20 he appears to be speaking in the present. Many have pointed out that the verb tense changes to the present tense at verse 15 onwards, suggesting that those verses express Paul's current situation. The question to resolve is this. In verses 15-20, is Paul referring to himself retrospectively as a Jew under Law, or currently as a Christian coming again under Law? Perhaps we do not have to decide. It is quite possible Paul has both situations in mind. What is clear is that, given the presence of Sin in mortal flesh, the introduction of Law as a basis of righteousness is devastating. Let Jewish Christians in Rome reject any idea of a return to Law-keeping, either for themselves or for the Gentiles.

In other words, as a Jew in Christ, Paul acknowledges past and present moral failure, despite knowing better. He looks on this as mystifying behaviour, sensing the good God wanted him to do, but instead doing the evil he did not approve. As he now understands, that failure was due to just one reason, Adam's Sin lived on in him.

4. THE LAW OF WRETCHEDNESS (vv. 21-25)
In these the concluding verses of chapter 7 Paul refers many times to 'Law'. Not every case, however, is a reference to the Law of God, in the commandments. By skilful word-play Paul also uses the word for other purposes.

In verse 21, Paul tells the readers what he now sees to have been his experience.

> I find, then, the law
> that when I want to do good
> evil is close by.

Throughout this chapter Paul has dismissed and rejected the role of Law in the life of the Jewish believer. Here Paul uses the word 'law' in another sense, as a dynamic principle whereby inevitably and invariably whenever someone seeks to do good, evil is crouching nearby.[6] It is a 'law', in this case a 'law' of fallen nature, that desire to do good (i.e. keep the commandments) is accompanied by the presence of evil.

---

6. Possibly in Paul's mind were the Lord's words to Cain, '... sin is crouching at your door; it desires to have you' (Gen. 4:7).

Verses 21-22 substantiate this by the introductory 'For'.

> For I rejoice in the Law of God in my innermost being,
> but I see another law in my members
> warring against the law of my mind
> and taking me captive to the law of Sin
> that lives in my members.

Paul is contrasting (1) his 'innermost being' (mind) with his 'members' (organs and limbs), and (2) the 'Law of God' with the 'law of Sin'. Using vivid battle language he sees Sin as an aggressor laying siege to his 'innermost being' (which shelters the Law of God) and taking him captive. Yes, his mind agrees with the Law of God but Sin easily has his way; Paul is his prisoner. His 'innermost being' is at the whim of a body captured by a foreign invader.

Thus in verse 24 the apostle who exclaims, 'Wretched man, I ...' is Paul the Jew for whom – as he now understands – Law has been a source of pain throughout his life, whether as an adolescent or adult, whether before or after his baptism into Christ. Because of the power of Adam's Sin living in him he experiences a fundamental dislocation between his mind (which approves of Law) and his body (subject to Sin). Paul's life (his body) was and is like a defective motor car with 'a mind of its own' that will not go where he steered it or travel at the speed he decided or stop when he applied the brakes.

It would be a mistake, however, to infer from the above that Paul is a tortured soul wrestling unsuccessfully with deep and dark sins. Rather, he is as coolly analytical as ever but chooses an 'I'-based method of teaching, as he does on other occasions (e.g. 1 Cor. 13:11: 'When I was a child, I spoke as a child, I thought as a child...'). Now as a man 'in Christ' who has been sensitised by the Spirit to indwelling Sin he sees the forces that had been and still were at work in him.

At the same time Paul is not implying that he was morally reprobate and corrupt in every way. Significantly, in the section 5:12–7:25 he only ever speaks of Sin (singular) but not of sins (plural). Paul does not say that his life is as full of sins as a rat is full of fleas. His only point throughout is that Sin ruled in his fallen flesh and that Law only made things worse, both before and after baptism into Christ.

Who, then, is the 'Wretched man, I' who asks, 'Who will rescue me from this body of death?'

The answer that makes best sense of this passage is that Paul under Law was the 'wretched man'. Thus Paul is clinching the case he began to make back in 5:12. Pure and simple his point is, that he and all people sinned in Adam and have died in Adam, including Jews like himself. Law does nothing to mitigate Sin or rescue its adherents from Death. But Paul is teaching this so that people understand that the age of grace has come, expressed in the death of Christ and empowered by the inner presence of the Spirit.

So Paul concludes the chapter.

Thanks be to God, through Jesus Christ our Lord.
So then   with the mind I serve   the Law of God
but   with the flesh   the law of Sin.

This is extraordinarily frank and quite unromantic. Yes, Jesus Christ our Lord will rescue from 'this body of death' that is under the rule of Sin. Indeed, he alone is the rescuer, not Law. But it is an *eventual* rescue, not an immediate rescue. It is the rescue that faith and hope look forward to. But it will not occur in this life ahead of Christ's return. In the meantime, Paul[7] as a Jew served with his mind the Law of God (which he approved of) but equally the 'law of Sin' (which was destructively active in his body).

So what has Paul been teaching in 5:12–7:25? In brief, it is that Sin and Death entered history in and with Adam with devastating effect to all his descendants. To (Christian) Jews among his original hearers Paul is saying that Law cannot rescue man from Sin and Death, but that only Jesus

---

7. The emphatic pronouns *autos egō* leave no doubt that Paul is speaking for himself. Yet his rhetorical technique throughout the chapter has been to tell his story in this highly personalised way as a teaching device. Let the Jewish Christian readers agree that what was true of him would be true also of them if they were to go back to Law. Law cannot rescue from Sin and death.

Christ crucified but risen does that – but in an ultimate, not immediate, sense.

5. DELIVERANCE (CH. 8 VV. 1-4)

Earlier (7:7-25) it was clear from his deeply personal references that Paul was telling his own story as a Jewish man under Law, first as an adolescent 'son of the commandment' and then an adult both before and after he was a man 'in Christ'. Paul recognised that the Sin of Adam lived on in him. Because of Sin in his body of flesh he acknowledges that Law was and is unable to rescue him in the last day, but only Christ (7:25) can do that.

In this present section Paul continues to speak personally, but not in terms of wretchedness under Law but of deliverance in Christ by grace. He now knows clearly what he may have only dimly perceived before the Damascus Road encounter, that is, the Law of God had brought a sense of failure and defeat. As a man in Christ he understands that Adam's Sin continued (and continues) in him and that whenever he was under Law or comes under Law he is defeated and destroyed. In a word, he is a 'wretched' man. He tells his story to deter his fellow-Jewish Christians from returning to Law-keeping.

Romans 8:1 is one of Paul's great texts and much loved by Christians, but the conjunction 'then' calls for explanation.

There is, then, now no condemnation
to those who are in Christ Jesus.

Most likely Paul's 'then' (*ara*) picks up his question ('Who will rescue me from the body of death?) and his answer ('I thank God, through Jesus Christ our Lord' – 7:24-25). Christ *will* rescue Paul and other believers from their Sin-controlled flesh, their bodies of death, that is, in the Last Day.

This future rescue, in turn, depends on God's saving act in the past, in the death and resurrection of Christ. In this regard we remember Paul's words, 'Being justified by his blood we will be saved from the wrath to come through him' (5:9). In other words, by Christ's 'blood' which was shed in the past we have been saved for the future from God's condemnation on the Last Day. This act of salvation occurred at the first Good Friday, at Golgotha. Then and there God passed judgement on and condemned his innocent Son in the place of culpable Law-breakers. That first Good Friday was the mid-point in world history. Human history has been punctuated, bisected so that 'now', that is, from *now on*, 'there is no condemnation.'

But for *whom* is there no condemnation? Paul is clear. It is those who are 'in Christ Jesus', that is, people who have taken refuge in Christ Jesus crucified in their place. The apostle has in mind those who have heard and believed the gospel and who have entrusted themselves to Christ and demonstrated that inner commitment publicly, at baptism.

By their faith/baptism they are 'in Christ,' joined to him in his death, burial and resurrection. In Christ's death they die to the penalty of Sin (condemnation) and the power of Sin (Death). They rise from the waters washed clean, assured that 'in Christ' they too are resurrected, alive to God forever, able to face the Last Day at peace with God (see on 5:1).

In verse 2 Paul once more uses the word 'Law' in several senses (as he had earlier in 7:21, 22, 23, 25). This he does to contrast two destinies – the destiny of those who belong to Adam (Sin and Death) with the destiny of those who belong to Christ (no condemnation/the Spirit and Life).

For	the Law of the	Spirit of	Life in Christ Jesus
has set me[8] free			
from	the Law of	Sin and	Death.

Paul speaks of 'Law' in the sense of respective outcomes of belonging to Adam or Christ. These outcomes are absolute,

---

8. Based on variations in early manuscripts there is debate whether the correct reading should be 'you,' 'us' or 'me'. Though 'us' in verse 4 supports the 'us' in verse 2, the singular 'me' better fits the general context from chapter 7, and is to be preferred. While 'you' is the 'harder reading', and is supported by textual scholars for that reason, it doesn't make good sense.

inevitable and unavoidable. 'The Law of Sin and death' is the Law of God in the commandments given at Mt. Sinai, a Law that spells Death to Adam and his tribe due to Sin. In starkest contrast is another 'Law' that supersedes it. This 'Law' is no less absolute, namely, that those 'in Christ Jesus' are not condemned but given the Spirit and therefore 'Life' in place of Death.[9] Descend from Adam and Eternal Death will follow due to Sin. Belong by faith/baptism to Christ, and Eternal Life will follow due to the Spirit. The transient age of Law has passed and the abiding Age of Christ and the Spirit has come.[10]

Verse 3 explains this (beginning with 'For').

> *For* what   the Law could not do
>   because it was debilitated through the flesh
>   God [did]
>   sending his own Son
>   in the likeness of sinful flesh
>   and for Sin
>   condemned Sin in the flesh.

Here is another majestic Pauline statement. It is, however, a little elusive, as is apparent in this fairly literal translation. The contrast is between the failure of Law and the achievement of God. Because of 'the flesh', that is, the fallen condition of Adam's race it was impossible for Law to deliver from 'condemnation' due to Sin.

What was 'impossible' (*adunaton*) for Law to do in humans, however, God actually *did* for them in a man, the man Christ Jesus. God condemned their Sin in the person of his Son. Paul's words, which originally may have been a creed or confession, are among his most important statements about God, his *own* Son and the Spirit.

---

9. Put another way, as Paul said earlier, 'The wages of Sin is Death but the gratuity of God is Eternal Life' (6:23).

10. As Paul also teaches in 2 Corinthians 3:6-11.

First, we learn that God is *Father* since it was his 'very own'[11] Son whom he sent (see also 8:15: '"abba," Father'; 15:6: 'the God and Father of our Lord Jesus Christ').

Second, God *sent* his Son into the world (cf. Gal. 4:4: 'God sent forth his Son'), echoing Jesus' own words. In the Gospel of John Jesus often says that the Father has 'sent' him, using the same verb (*pempō*) as Paul does in Romans 8:3 (e.g. John 5:23: 'He that does not honour the Son does not honour the Father who sent him'). In his First Letter, but using a different verb (*apostellō*), John writes, 'The Father has *sent* his Son as the saviour of the world' (4:14).

Third, the Son of God was truly a man though without sins, as in the words 'in the *likeness* of sinful flesh'. Adam's rescuer from Sin and its penalty (condemnation) and power (Death) must be qualified in two respects: he must be genuinely human (like Adam) and he must be sinless (unlike Adam). In an earlier letter Paul wrote, 'Him who knew no sin God made sin for us, that we might become the righteousness of God in him' (2 Cor. 5:21).[12]

Fourth, the mission God sent his Son to accomplish was 'in regard to Sin'. Specifically, God 'condemned Sin,' that is, the Sin of Adam, in the flesh of the sinless Son of God. For this reason Paul was able to say a few verses earlier, 'There is now no condemnation for those who are in Christ Jesus' (v. 1).

Fifth, we find an understated but real affirmation of God's triune character and activity in these words. *God* (that is, the Father) sent his *own Son* that we might walk according to the *Spirit*. God sends; the Son is sent; the Spirit of God/of Christ imparts the Spirit of sonship strengthening believers for holiness.

---

11. Literally, 'God sent his *of himself* (*heautou*) Son.' A unique and intimate relationship is implied; Christ is not one Son of God among other sons of God. Christ's pre-existence is presupposed by these words. Jesus' words about his Father as 'Abba' (Mark 14:36) and himself as 'beloved' (Mark 12:6) and 'only begotten' (John 3:16) most likely are the source of Paul's view of Christ as 'God's very own Son'.

12. Many New Testament writers affirm the sinlessness of Christ. For example, both Peter and the writer to the Hebrews speak of him as 'without blemish' (1 Pet. 1:19; Heb. 9:14).

True, the Father sent his Son to teach God's truth and be a pattern for others. Yet Christ's primary task was to bear in his own innocent body the penalty of Adam's and our Sin. This is Paul's striking way of describing and interpreting the death of Jesus at Golgotha a few years earlier.

In verse 4 Paul states God's purpose in sending his Son and condemning Sin in his flesh. It was, he says

> that the just requirement of the Law
> might be fulfilled in us
> who do not live   according to the flesh
> but   according to the Spirit.

To live 'according to the flesh' is to live the way Adam did, in rebellion against God. That powerful instinct continues to indwell believers and to pull them away from God and back to live the way they used to live. But this way to live is not an option for those who belong to Christ. There is only one way now, that is, 'according to the Spirit.' Paul will expand on this in the next section. In brief, the way of the Spirit is to live to God through *Christ*, that is, based on the grace of God not on our self-effort.

Does this mean an amoral and ethically irresponsible way of life is permissible for those who 'in Christ' face 'no condemnation'? This, indeed, appears to be precisely the criticism Paul's Jewish objectors in Rome are voicing against him. 'His Law-free gospel leads to lawlessness', they complain.

'Quite the reverse,' is Paul's response. Rather, he insists, 'the just requirement of the Law is to be fulfilled' in those who live by faith in Christ. 'And what is that?' we imagine them asking. As he will soon explain, 'the just requirement of the Law' is 'love', that is, love for God and love for others. This is clear from his words, 'Owe no one anything, except to love one another ... love is the fulfilling of the Law' (13:8, 10).

Then are the commandments (the Law) irrelevant? Not at all. The commandments, though stated negatively as 'not to commit adultery,' 'not to steal,' 'not to covet', teach us behaviour that is *un*loving towards our neighbour. At the same time, as Paul teaches throughout his letters, genuine love means reversing the negatives in the commandments as full-orbed positive behaviour. For example, the Christian is not to steal but to work hard so as to give to people in need (Eph. 4:28). The 'just requirement of the Law' is not merely not to steal, but additionally to work hard so as to have resources to give to those in need.

Thus the Christian life is an ethical life, positive not merely negative, full-orbed not minimal, generous not miserly, glad not grudging. Yet the doing of good in these 'just requirements of the Law' is not to gain the approval of God. Because of unremoved and continuing Sin we can never achieve God's standard of righteousness by Law-keeping. Because of Sin any attempt to win God's verdict 'righteous' through Law-keeping must fail. On that account, God condemned our Sin in the dying body of his Son to set us free from Law-keeping. Yet, having done that God directs us to live by the Law of love to and for others, strengthened by the Spirit of God. So far from being irrelevant, the commandments point the way to the areas of behaviour where loving behaviour will be fulfilled (e.g. not stealing, but working to give to others).

In brief, then, man cannot come into the presence of God through Law-keeping, but only 'in Christ' through faith in him. Thus the Christian life is 'faith [in Christ] working through love' as Paul told the Galatians (Gal. 5:6). The direction that 'love' takes, while informed by the Law, is empowered by the Spirit of God.

Romans 7:6–8:4 tells Paul's story as a Jew from a Christian's perspective. Previously it was life ruled by Law, as it is still, potentially. Yet life under Law is fruitless due to Sin in the body of flesh/death. The only way to live is as a man in Christ delivered from Law in order to love God and his neighbour. Paul's purpose in telling his story is to deflect Jewish Christians from reinstating Law and from bringing Gentiles under Law.

How do Paul's words apply today in our world, which is very different from his? First, they continue to be authoritative to Jewish Christians. The 'works of the Law' relating to ceremonies like Passover, while unproblematic as a cultural expression of Jewishness, must not be regarded as obligatory for acceptance with God. Only in Christ is salvation to be found.

Second, Gentile Christians, for whom Law is part of the Old Testament and therefore within the canon of Holy Scripture, must not allow themselves to be made subservient to Law as a way to know God. There is but one such way for all people, whether Jew or Gentile, that is, Christ crucified and risen.

Christians of whatever background should note an ever-present subtle tendency to reintroduce religious legalism and an apparent readiness to depend on such 'works'. This may include church-going as a perceived obligation, or devotional 'quiet times' or the necessity to share the faith, or even details of dress. Doubtless some are important enough. But if Christian practices assume the place of 'Law', as they easily can do, then Paul's teaching in Romans 7:1–8:4 becomes applicable.

For us today the message of Romans 7:1–8:4 is straight-forward. Because of Sin we are only 'righteous' before God in Christ by whose death we are set free from condemnation in order to live a life of love.

STUDY QUESTIONS

1. Do you understand the implications of being set free from the law of sin and death?

2. What do you do when you have this struggle of righteousness and unrighteousness in your life?

3. If Christ has freed you from the law of sin and death, why then do you still have this struggle between obeying God and not obeying God?

4. Where do you see legalism creeping into your life? Into the church?

5. What are some positive ways of expressing the Law in showing love?

9

The Spirit of Hope
(Romans 8:5-39)

The lengthy passage regarding Adam's Sin, begun at 5:12, is now concluded. Through the gospel men and women 'in Adam' are now men and women 'in Christ' who have the Spirit. For them the kingly rule of Sin exercised in death is now ended and the kingly rule of God has begun. Also 'ended' is the dispensation of Law as the means of knowing God, a dispensation that failed on account of Sin. Paul teaches this by means of his own spiritual autobiography narrated in the previous passage (7:1–8:4). Paul, mindful of the inner struggle with 'indwelling Sin', now moves on to discuss the believer's life 'in the Spirit'.

In the first major section Paul discusses the coming of the Spirit to believers, a thread he picks up from verse 4.[1] Believers live in and through the Spirit, who demonstrates their present sonship and gives to them assurance of their inheritance of the kingdom of God (vv. 5-17). Yet before that destiny is realised, they must pass through the sufferings of this present time that arise from the birth-death cycle and from persecution (vv. 18-27, 35-38). This they will successfully negotiate because of the 'invincible determination of God'

---

1. Paul made earlier references to the Spirit. The Spirit's historic coming is evidence that Jesus Christ is the Son of God 'in power' (1:4). The 'letter' (i.e. the Law) is Paul's abbreviated way of referring to the now-superseded Old Covenant; the Spirit is the mark of the New Covenant (2:29). The Spirit, given by God at the time of justification, brings an awareness of the love of God (5:5). Delivered from Law, believers now serve God in 'newness of Spirit' (7:6).

arising from his 'foreknowledge' of them prior to creation (vv. 28-38). Because of his determination no force can prevail against them, no charge can be sustained against them, and no power will be strong enough to separate them from his love.

1. THE SPIRIT AND THE FLESH (vv. 5-17)

Note that Paul is not primarily contrasting defeated ('carnal' or 'fleshly') Christians with victorious ('spiritual') Christians.[2] He is not engaging in 'higher life' or 'victory' teaching. Rather, he is contrasting the believer's former way of life when he was an unbeliever (which he calls 'flesh') with his present way of life as a believer (which he calls 'Spirit'). Nonetheless, the power of Sin (the 'flesh') continues, dragging the believer down from God and back towards the 'old' (pre-Christian) life.

Who, then, was Paul addressing in Rome, and why? The reference to 'Law' (v. 7) tells us that the theme of the previous passage in 7:1–8:4 is being continued. Jews who seek to reinstate Law for salvation and who seek to subject Gentiles to Law need to know that the Commandments were not able to be fulfilled in Adam's descendants, Jews included. This is because – to anticipate – they and all Adam's children are 'flesh' not 'Spirit'.

A. Two 'Minds' – Flesh and Spirit (vv. 5-8)

In these verses Paul continues to contrast those who are 'in Christ' and the rest of humankind, who are 'in Adam' (as from 5:12). He characterises those who are 'in Adam' as 'flesh' and those 'in Christ' as 'Spirit'.

In the previous verse Paul used the Old Testament imagery of 'walking' (that is, how one 'lives,' practically speaking). Now in verse 5 he pursues further the idea of 'walking' but connects it with the 'mind' (phronēma). The 'mind' directs the 'walking' feet, telling them which way to go. Those 'in Adam' and those 'in Christ' 'walk' separate ways, each according to their respective 'minds'.

---

2. In 1 Corinthians 3:1-4 Paul is making just that comparison, but he is not doing so in Romans 8:5-17.

Those 'separate ways' Paul describes as 'the things of' either 'the flesh' or 'the Spirit'. 'The things of the flesh' are (1) the sins of the Gentiles (1:18-32: idolatry, 'unclean' sexual practices, socially destructive behaviour), and (2) the sins of the Jews (2:12-29 – hearing but not doing the Law, though pretending to). By 'the things of the Spirit,' however, Paul has in mind the fruits of righteous living and growth in holiness evident in those who have been set free from slavery to Sin (6:18-22).

In verse 6 he contrasts the two 'minds'.

For
> the mind of the flesh is death
but   the mind of the Spirit is life and peace.

What does the 'mind' think about? The future, says Paul. The 'mind' of those who are 'in Adam' (who are 'flesh') knows that 'death' is all that the future holds for them. On the other hand, the 'mind' of those who are 'in Christ' (who have 'the Spirit') knows that 'life and peace' await them. Thus the 'mind' of Adam's descendants is despair but the mind of those who are in Christ is joy and hope (14:17: 'the kingdom of God ... is righteousness, peace and joy in the Holy Spirit').

By 'life' Paul means 'eternal life' (as in 5:21; 6:22, 23) and by 'peace' he is thinking of 'peace with God' (reconciliation) based on the atonement made by Christ (as in 5:1, 10-11). In referring to 'death' as the opposite of 'life and peace', Paul means not only biological death but, more profoundly, 'eternal death,' capital D death, the dreaded final separation from God.

But this provokes the question, 'Why should this be?' which he answers in verse 7.

Because
> the mind of the flesh is at enmity with God.
>> It   is not subject to the Law of God
for   it   is not able [to be].

This is a severe rebuff to the apologists for Law-keeping as a way of knowing God and for fulfilling his covenant. Those who are 'in Adam', who 'walk' according to the 'mind of the flesh' are incapable of being subject to the Law of God. Adam's 'mind' and the 'minds' of his people are hostile to God. Pointedly Paul is saying that this 'enmity' against God is as true for Jews who purport to be 'under Law' as it is for the 'law-less' Gentiles.

Here Paul is referring back to the sad testimony of his experience as a man under Law, whether as an adolescent 'son of commandment' (7:7-14) or as an adult (7:15-24). Whether before or after conversion, there is only 'wretchedness' and bewilderment for man under the Law of God (7:15-24a). Delight in the Law in his mind as he did, Paul speaks only of failure to submit to that Law due to indwelling Sin in his 'members', his 'flesh', his 'body of Death'. In other words, he is telling those apologists for Law-keeping that their hopes and outlook are futile. Only in Christ crucified and risen is there victory over moral failure that enables the believer to fulfil the Law. It is the victory of forgiveness.

So Paul pointedly concludes (v. 8), 'Those who are in the flesh are not able to please God,' that is, through Law-keeping. The aim to 'please God' sums up well our whole purpose in living (see 2 Cor. 5:9: 'we make it our aim to please him'; also Gen. 6:9: '"righteous" Noah pleased God').

Could there be a higher aim than to 'please God'? If not by Law-keeping, then by what means? Later in the letter Paul writes that to 'present our bodies as a living sacrifice' is 'well-pleasing to God' (12:1). In similar vein he says that the kingdom of God is not food and drink (to be abstained from, according to some) but righteousness, joy and peace in the Holy Spirit. This, he says, is 'well-pleasing to God' (14:17-18). In other words, voluntary self-dedication to God is what pleases him and not keeping of commandments or dietary regulations as a way to acceptance with him.

B. *Put to death the deeds of the flesh (vv. 9-13)*
In verse 9 Paul turns directly to address his readers as those 'in Christ' who have left behind their life 'in Adam'.

You, however, are not in the flesh
but in the Spirit.

Paul is emphatic at this point; his readers are 'in the Spirit'.[3] But who are the 'you' (plural pronoun) he now addresses so directly? Are they Jewish believers as in the immediately prior reference to 'you' (7:4) or, more likely, are they believers in general, both Jews and Gentiles, who have been 'called' through the gospel and who are now 'dead' in Christ to the penalty of Sin (6:11)?

Paul speaks about the Spirit in a variety of ways – as 'the Spirit' (vv. 4, 5, 6, 9a, 10, 13, 16), 'the Spirit of God' (vv. 9b, 14; cf. v. 11c), 'the Spirit of Christ' (v. 9c), 'Christ in you' (v. 10), or 'the Spirit of [God] who raises the dead' (v. 11). Those who have opened their hearts to the gospel and have publicly identified with Christ in baptism are not 'in the flesh' but 'in the Spirit'. By 'in the flesh' Paul means their former life as unbelievers and by 'in the Spirit' he means their present life as baptised believers. This is Paul's 'broad-brush' assurance to his readers that they are, indeed, Christian believers.[4]

Paul, however, makes a qualification (v. 9b), begun with 'if indeed'.

You ... are ... in the Spirit,
if, indeed, the Spirit of God dwells in you.

Paul's readers in Rome were mixed, including those Jews who were urging a return to Law-keeping. He must remind them, and all readers since, that mere attendance at a Christian gathering does not guarantee the presence of the Spirit. If the Spirit is truly present it is due only to belief in the saving message of Christ and not by the works of the Law, as Paul told the Galatians (3:1-5).

What test might the readers apply to themselves to determine if 'the Spirit of God' was now dwelling in them? Paul's simple test is to ask: do they pray to God as 'abba, dear Father' with the simple faith of a small child in a trusted 'papa' (see on v. 15)?

But all might not pass that test. So he pauses to add this warning, introduced with a telling 'if' (v. 9c).

---

3. As reflected in the position of the free-standing pronoun 'you' at the head of the sentence and in his use of the strongest contrastive word for 'but'.

4. As in 1:8; 16:19.

If anyone	does not have the Spirit of	Christ
he	has no part	in him.

If the reader has the Spirit of Christ he belongs to Christ, both for now but also for the endless ages of the kingdom of God. But if the reader does not have Christ's Spirit he does not belong to him.

Having duly exhorted and warned his readers, Paul makes two positive and closely connected statements about those who have the Spirit.

First (v. 10), the presence of the indwelling Christ makes their 'spirits' alive. This is evidence of 'righteousness' before God (i.e. 'justification').

	If Christ is in you		
	the body	is dead	on account of sin
but	the spirit	is life	on account of righteousness.

Because of Adam's Sin death came to all his tribe, without exception. Every child of Adam – unbeliever as well as believer – is dying biologically. But the gospel declares that Christ is 'in' those who 'belong to him' (v. 9), that is, those who are 'righteous' before God through faith in Christ. Their 'spirits'[5] are alive. By this Paul means their inner selves are 'alive' to God as their 'abba, their dear heavenly Father' (v. 15). They will not face Eternal Death since they are 'alive' in Christ forever, as he now explains.

Second (v. 11), he promises that God will raise up dead bodies by his Spirit (fulfilling the prophecy of Ezekiel 37:1-14).

If the Spirit			
of him who	raised Jesus	from the dead	lives in you
he who	raised Christ	from the dead	
will also			
make alive		your mortal bodies	
		through his Spirit who lives in you.	

---

5. The translations render Paul's word *pneuma* as 'your spirit' or 'spirits' and not as God's Spirit. It can hardly be otherwise since the word balances, and is opposite to, 'body'. The 'body' is dead but [your] 'spirit' is alive. This is confirmed in verse 16 where Paul also refers to 'our spirits'.

Paul says much in this neatly balanced sentence, beginning and ending as it does with 'the Spirit': (1) God *has* raised Jesus from the dead, (2) he *will* also raise believers from the dead, and (3) he *will* do so through his Spirit who indwells them. True, the body is indeed 'mortal' (dying) due to Sin (see v. 10), but God will raise the body from the dead by his indwelling Spirit.

Based on these sure promises of God Paul drives home his appeal to the readers in verses 12 and 13.

So then, brothers and sisters,		
we are debtors		
not to the flesh,	to live according	to the flesh
[but to the Spirit,	to live according	to the Spirit].
For if	you live according	to the flesh
		you will die.
But if by the Spirit		
	you kill the practices	of the flesh
		you will live.

The strong opening connectors, 'So then' (*ara oun*), tie Paul's words back to the promise of verses 10 and 11. Because Christ is in me my dying body will be raised alive, just as Christ was raised alive. 'So then,' says Paul, we owe the flesh (Sin) nothing since it is the source of death. Rather, we owe the indwelling Spirit everything since he is the source of life.

Paul is taking his readers back to their pre-conversion behaviour, to the days of 'the flesh' before 'the Spirit' began to indwell them. If they revert to their former practices as men and women 'in Adam', they will, indeed, die. Based on earlier references he is thinking of the Gentiles' idolatry and sexual immorality and the Jews' hypocrisy. It is easy to regard the Gentiles' gross indecency as 'works of the flesh', but the more subtle evils of the Jews are no less so.

At the same time, however, believers are now those who live in two worlds. They are 'in Adam' as his descendants and they are 'in Christ' through the gospel and their baptism into him. Thus at the same time they are 'in the flesh' and 'in the Spirit'. The Christian's own person is a battleground between the 'flesh' (continuing Sin) that would drag him down (and back to the former life) and the 'Spirit' who would raise him up.

Previously, before the gospel and the coming of the Spirit, men and women 'in Adam' were 'slaves to Sin'. But now the slaves have been liberated to become, instead, slaves to God bearing righteous fruits of holiness (see on 6:22). This, however, does not occur automatically or passively as they limply 'let go and let God', as some have said. On the contrary, they are called upon actively to 'put to death the deeds of the body [of Sin]'.

This calls for clarification.

(i) 'Death to flesh' is a metaphor for intentional rejection of the old ways. This may not happen overnight, but may involve a struggle for many years. Self-awareness to avoid circumstances of recurring temptation is called for. It is easy enough to be trapped in the evil webs of internet pornography, for example, the more so since these can be accessed in secrecy.

(ii) Yet it would be a mistake to think Paul is only referring to sexual sins, though they are included. The self-tortured monks who flogged themselves in monastery cells or sat for lifetimes alone on poles testify to their well-meant struggle for mastery over sexual temptation. The less overt 'spiritual' sins of pride, arrogance, envy, bitterness and hypocrisy of the apparently mature Christian are equally dangerous since they are less obvious.

(iii) Our sinfulness in 'the flesh' tends to be expressed differently throughout our lives. The sexual temptations of the younger adult are often replaced unnoticed with the passing years by greed, obsession about financial security, lust for power and a desire to make a name for ourselves, come what may.

(iv) We are not to struggle alone; we put these things to death by the Spirit. God himself comes to our aid. We enlist the help of God's strong Spirit to fight against and to defeat the flesh.

(v) Our struggle against 'the flesh' is life-long, and it is a struggle in which there will never be complete victory. At the same time there is always forgiveness from God for us, his children. Martin Luther said that the believer is 'always a sinner' yet 'always forgiven' and 'always penitent'. God mercifully ties us to himself by the fact of our continuing sinfulness. How great would be our spiritual arrogance if we were not dependent on God for his forgiveness!

(vi) If there is a 'psychological' dimension to our sins (e.g. some form of addiction) we should seek help from those who are both Christian and professionally qualified. In short, we should seek help and be honest about the problem.

C. Children of God (vv. 14-17)

In the previous verses Paul has been telling his readers about the work of the Spirit. At the time they were joined to Christ, the Spirit gave them his 'mind', a mind of 'life and peace', to direct their feet to walk in his paths and so to 'please God' (vv. 5-8). Those who have the Spirit 'belong to' Christ, both now and forever (v. 9). By the Spirit God will 'raise from the dead' those in whom the Spirit lives (vv. 10-11). Believers are to 'live by the Spirit' and 'put to death' the works of the flesh (vv. 12-13).

In verse 14 Paul sums up all this by the words, 'For as many as are being led by the Spirit.' The word 'being led' (*agontai* – present tense) points to 'being impelled' out of the old life into the kingdom of God. Such a decisive event is clear from the verb tense used in the next verse where Paul twice writes, 'you...received the Spirit.' Clearly, this refers to that 'moment' when through the gospel they believed in Christ and 'received the Spirit'. As a consequence they are now continually 'being impelled forward by' the Spirit.

Paul speaks of such Spirit-'impelled' people as 'sons [and daughters] of God'. This term has both a future, but also a present meaning. The sons and daughters of God are the 'people-kingdom' whom God will rule in the new age. They are also the people to whom God is 'Father' at this present time. Having the Spirit is God's demonstration to them that they 'belong to Christ' (v. 9). Because they belong to Christ they too, like him, are children of God.

In verse 15 Paul contrasts the 'Spirit of slavery' with the 'Spirit of sonship'. As noted above, his twofold reference to 'received' points to that decisive moment when they turned to Christ after hearing the gospel.

> You did not   receive the Spirit of slavery   again for fear
> but you   received the Spirit of sonship
>   in which we cry, 'abba, Father.'

Slavery meant being owned by a 'lord' (who may be cruel) and having no rights. The 'lord' had absolute power to do with the slave whatever he pleased. Being a slave implied having a servile spirit and living out an existence of insecurity and terror. How different, by contrast, it was to be a son, in this case of a good and caring father. Their ways of life and their inner attitudes were quite different.

Paul's reference to 'the spirit of slavery again for fear' most likely points to Law and Law-keeping which, it appears, some of the Jews among the Roman Christians sought either to introduce or to reinstate. The word 'again' supports the notion that Paul is thinking here of Jews and God-fearers. But a return to Law would be retrograde since 'under Law' there was only 'slavery for fear'. Law-keeping was an insidious bondage. Who could know if one's good works outweighed the bad? The Pharisees multiplied rules and regulations to guard the Law and despised the people for their ignorance of the Law (John 7:49: 'This mob that does not know the Law is accursed'). Peter called Law-keeping slavery (Acts 15:10: 'Now, therefore, why tempt God to lay a yoke on the neck of the disciples that neither our fathers nor we are able to bear').

But the 'Spirit you received' was not one of 'slavery ... for fear'. Quite to the contrary, Paul tells them that they received the Spirit that makes them sons and daughters of God, so that they, and all Christians, call him, 'abba, Father.' With this Aramaic word 'abba' embedded in the Greek of Paul's letter we hear the voice of Jesus in prayer (Mark 14:36: 'abba, Father, all things are possible to you'). He also taught his disciples to approach God as 'abba, Father'. So far from having a distant reverence for the Almighty, Jesus spoke to God as a toddler would first speak to his father, 'papa.' The rabbis were outraged that Jesus should take such liberties (John 5:18: 'he called God his own Father, making himself equal with God'). Yet nothing in the Bible is more important than Jesus' revelation that the Creator of the universe is 'dear Father'. Through faith in Jesus ('his own Son') and through receiving the Spirit the children of Adam become the children of God.

Paul appeals to experience, the Romans' and ours (v. 16).

> The Spirit himself is bearing witness with our spirit
> that we are the children of God.

Each person has a 'spirit' (see on v.10), an 'inner self.' The inner self is conscious of being son or daughter of a parent. Few things in life run so deep as one's 'spirit's' awareness of this. The sense that one is a child of God is not only communicated by the word of God to the mind, but equally it is communicated by the Spirit of God to the 'spirit' or inner self. Christ was God's own Son by nature; this was something he 'knew' from earliest years (Luke 2:49: 'Do you not know that I must be in my father's house?'). For Adam's children to know that they are God's children, and that God is not their judge but their 'Father', is his wonderful and entirely undeserved gift.

In verse 17, Paul extends the idea of being a child of a parent to being an heir of the parent's estate. By this Paul is moving the Romans' thinking on from the present (work of the Spirit) to the future (life in the kingdom of God).

If	we are	children,	
then	we are	heirs of God	
		co-heirs	with Christ
if indeed	we suffer		with him
that	we might also	be glorified	with him.

The practice of bequeathing possession to one's children is an ancient one. Paul appeals to this proverbially to make a point about his role as an apostle-father (2 Cor. 12:14: 'parents ought to lay up treasure for their children'). It was unlikely that a slave would be written into the owner's will to inherit the estate. But this was precisely the expectation of the children. They are named in the will as heirs of their father. It is his duty, but also his pleasure.

Christ, the Son of God, is the sole natural heir of God's kingdom. As adopted children of God we are 'heirs' by grace, just as we are 'children' of God by grace. This points up the futility of a Law-based approach to God currently being urged by some in Rome. Only by grace do we take our place alongside Christ as a rightful heir of the kingdom of God. There is, however, an 'if' – 'if indeed we suffer with him.' It is the recognition that the children of God are 'aliens and sojourners' in this age, as also Christ was. His witness was rejected, in his case in an ultimate sense, leading to his death. We, too, must be prepared for the same rejection.

Paul will expand on these sufferings later in the chapter (see vv. 18-25, 34-38). Suffice it for the moment to observe that Paul's audience, whether Jews, Greeks or Romans, found his message of the Lordship of Christ and his call for repentance from sins to be uncongenial. The various floggings and stonings that he suffered were on account of a message that was alien and objectionable. Paul's converts in the churches suffered as well, because they confessed Christ as Lord. But this was something Christ expected and required. To be ashamed of him meant that one was no longer a disciple and faced his shame at the Last Day (Mark 8:38: 'whoever is ashamed of me ... of him will the Son of Man also be ashamed'). But to be identified with him by confession and witness will mean to be glorified with him.

2. SUFFERINGS NOW, GLORY THEN (VV. 17-27)

A. Saved by Hope (vv. 17-25)

In the previous passage (vv. 5-17) Paul wrote about the work of the Spirit whom we 'received' in the *past* (giving us the mind of the Spirit) and whom we continue to receive in the *present* (making us conscious that we are children of God, crying 'abba, Father'). The Spirit also has a *future* role for us, one that is implicit in our 'being led' or 'being impelled' forward out of the prison of this present age toward the freedom of the kingdom of God. Indeed, one of the marks of the kingdom will be the 'fullness of the Spirit'. In anticipation of that 'fullness' we receive the 'down payment' (*arrabōn* – a commercial word, meaning 'deposit') of the Spirit.[6]

There were several hints in verses 16-17 that pointed to the future. One was the reference to 'sons of God,' 'sonship' and 'children of God'. God's end-time kingdom is not a continent or a geographical space but a people in whose hearts he will rule and whose rule is willingly accepted in the hearts of his sons and daughters. Another hint was Paul's promise that the children of God are 'inheritors ... of God' (v. 17).

The ground having been prepared, Paul directs his readers to the future (v. 18).

> For I reckon that
> > the sufferings of the present time
> are not worth comparing with
> > the coming glory that will be revealed to us

In Romans 8 these 'sufferings' are threefold.

First, there is the suffering of 'emptiness' (v. 20). Because God is 'not there' and deemed irrelevant, a sense of 'futility' or 'despair' in inevitable. This is more pronounced in 'eras of unbelief,' such as the one in which we live. That 'emptiness' is seen in art, music and literature that is chaotic and anarchic. Equally it is seen in the 'lost' youth generations, often expressed in substance abuse and suicide.

Christian people are not insulated from emptiness, depression and despair. Some of the great heroes of Christianity suffered from depression and other disorders (e.g. Bunyan, Cowper, Lord Shaftesbury).[7] Many church members and church ministers suffer profoundly.

Second, there is the 'fallen' and 'corrupt' state of the creation's death cycle about which Paul will soon say more (vv. 20-23).

Third, there are the sufferings of Paul and other believers that arise from their identification with Christ, the rejected One (vv. 35-36). All people, believers included, participate in

---

6. 2 Corinthians 1:22; 5:5; Ephesians 1:14.
7. See Gaius Davies, *Genius, Grief and Grace* (Fearn: Christian Focus Publications, 2001).

the first and second, but only to believers do the third type of sufferings apply. Nonetheless, these 'sufferings' – from both sources – are as nothing compared to the glory that will be revealed to believers. Elsewhere Paul spoke of that 'glory' as being 'of eternal weight beyond comparison' (2 Cor. 4:17). There can be no doubt, Paul's 'heart' was in the future and not in the present.[8]

In verses 19ff, Paul depicts 'the creation' as 'forward looking', anticipating God's coming revelation of the future.

> For the eager anticipation of the creation
> awaits the revelation of the sons of God.

To the eye of the biologist, nature is cyclical. The seasons come and go and come again. Animals and plants are born, give birth, then die. On and on and round and round. But, to the eye of faith and hope, history is not cyclical but linear and full of hope. Paul likens the creation to the woman who welcomes the birth contractions as the sign that the long-awaited birth is near. Nature is not going round and round in an impersonal, meaningless and endless cycle, says Paul, but is 'almost human,' straining forward to see the sons of God revealed. It is not nature's curiosity to see who, after all, will prove to be the 'real thing', as it were. Rather, the creation understands that when those sons of God appear, this will signal the restoration of nature as a New Eden. That 'new creation' will be re-inhabited by the former sons and daughters of Adam who, by the Word and the Spirit, are now the sons and daughters of God.

How did creation come to have this eager expectation? In verse 20 Paul explains that Adam's rebellion against God also dragged the creation down with him in death.

> For   the creation was subject to futility
>   not willingly
>   but through the One who subjected it,
>   in hope.

---

8. See e.g. 1 Corinthians 7:29-31.

Most likely Paul is thinking about the 'futility' or 'emptiness' of death. Adam's Sin brought death, not only to himself but also to the created world.[9] This was the Creator's just determination, not a 'willing' decision of the animals and trees. Eden itself became subject to death, so that the whole of creation was trapped in an apparently endless birth-death cycle. The death of men, women and children most clearly shows up the futility and emptiness of creation, calling into question everything we do and are. Every relationship is ended by death, every good work left unfinished. How much more would Mozart, for example, have contributed to the world's enjoyment had he not died at thirty five years of age? Yet that very 'futility' cries out for redemption, for hope. In other words, in the mind of God creation is not a merry-go-round of birth and death, going nowhere. Rather, God gave creation the sense that it has a future. Somehow it knows that its Maker will abolish the 'last enemy', death. He will restore the creation, and the creation knows this and strains forward for that glad day.

Here two correctives are necessary. First, we must reject the idea of a non-material 'heaven'. From early times in Christian history believers began thinking that 'heaven' was 'up there', inhabited by disembodied souls in white gowns seated on clouds playing harps. This vision owes more to Greek philosophy than to the Bible's vision of the kingdom of God. That kingdom is ahead of us at the end of history, not above us in the clouds. It is not dis-embodied but re-embodied.

Second, this present creation is not going to be replaced but redeemed, renewed and restored. True, there are references to a fiery end to the earth (2 Pet. 3:10: 'the earth ... will be

---

9. Paul's teaching is interesting to compare with a contemporary view of God's judgement on Adam's Sin: 'But when Adam transgressed my commandments, the creation was judged: but then the ways of the aeon became narrow, sad and laborious, miserable and bad, full of danger and great impending miseries; but the ways of the great aeon are wide and sure and they bear the fruit of life. If those who are alive thus did not enter into these difficulties and vanities they could not obtain what is stored up for them' (4 Ezra 7:10-13). Like Paul, 4 Ezra envisages a present aeon and a coming aeon. Unlike Paul, 4 Ezra sees this present aeon as a kind of necessary purgation based on human effort. For Paul, God – not man – is the agent of salvation from this age to the next.

burned up'). But this probably refers to God's purging of evil from the earth rather than his total destruction of the cosmos. At the Last Day, believers, alive or 'asleep', will be 'changed' (1 Cor. 15:52). So, too, the creation will be 'changed', which explains why it strains forward 'in hope'.

It is important to be clear about this. In late antiquity, civilization was crumbling due to the barbarian invasions of the Roman Empire. At the same time, society was morally corrupt and cruel. Thousands of Christian men and women withdrew from cities and towns to monastic communities in the deserts and other isolated places. Many held a negative view of their own bodies (because of fevered sexual temptation) and of creation, which they saw as 'evil' (and in no way 'good') and fit only to be 'torched' in the end. It is unwise to pass judgement on the actions of others from this safe distance. Yet the withdrawal of monks and nuns from society during late antiquity and in the medieval period proved to be 'a vote of no confidence' in marriage and family life and in the work men and women do in sustaining and improving society. At the time of the Reformation these attitudes were reversed to the blessing and progress of many new nations. A 'replacement' view of the end-times results in a negative view of 'involvement' in creation and society whereas a 'restoration' view encourages both sensible 'engagement' with creation and commitment to society.

In verse 21 Paul gives the grounds for the 'hope' the creation eagerly awaits.

Because the creation itself
will also be set free
from   the slavery to   corruption
for   the liberty   of the glory
                        of the children of God.

From these words we understand that the 'revelation of the sons of God' (as in v. 19) will be their deliverance from slavery to corruption and death and their visible appearance as 'children of God'. The doors of the dark dungeon will be thrown open and prisoners will burst forth into the light, free at last as the sons and daughters of God in his kingdom. As well, however, Paul declares that the creation itself will be liberated from its prison, its birth-death cycle. Creation 'fell' when Adam sinned but it will be liberated when the children of God are set free.

Paul bases these observations on what 'we know' (v. 22).

> For we know that the whole creation
> is groaning together and in birth pain together
> until now.

Paul's words, 'we know' appeal to existing teaching that the readers already 'know'. Most likely in referring to the elements of creation as 'in birth pain together' (*sunōdinei*) Paul is pointing back to Jesus' teaching about the 'pre-birth contractions' that signal an imminent birth (Mark 13:8: 'this is the beginning of birth pangs' – *archē hōdinōn*), the arrival of the kingdom of God. Jesus' teaching on present difficulties signalling the coming of the Son of Man most likely became known in the early churches, including in Rome.

Once more we see the new creation as in some sense continuous with the former creation, not totally replacing it. The sufferings of the present creation are called 'birth pangs', foreshadowing the arrival of a newly-born new creation. This is in line with the 'hope' felt by the creation in the midst of its pain (see on v. 20). In other words, death – though tragic and an 'enemy' – is also a sign of hope, the 'birth' of the new creation.

This great future hope for the creation prompts Paul to refer once more to the great future hope of the believer, since the two are locked together. In turn this leads Paul, in verse 23, to reintroduce the subject of the Holy Spirit, which was broken off at verse 17.

> But not only the creation
> but   also we ourselves who have the first-fruits of the Spirit
> also   we ourselves groan within ourselves
> awaiting   our adoption as sons
>   the redemption of our body.

This rather literal translation highlights the connection between the creation and the children of God which the repetition of the emphatic 'also we ourselves' establishes. The creation awaits its redemption but so 'also we ourselves' await redemption, that is, of our body. Redemption in both creation and humanity is not 'spiritual' but physical, as 'the redemption of our body' shows.

At the same time, however, the coming of the kingdom will mean the 'fullness of the Spirit of God'. In this present age believers have been given the Spirit, but only as 'firstfruits' and not yet in his 'fullness'. ('Firstfruits' were the first reapings of a crop dedicated to God.) The Spirit, whom believers 'received' when they believed in Christ through the gospel, prompts 'groaning within ourselves', a longing both for the coming liberation from the cycle of birth-and-death (as in verse 21) but also, positively, for the 'adoption as sons' (*huiothesia* – as in verse 15). True, believers are 'children of God' now but they will not enjoy that relationship with God in its 'fullness' until the kingdom of God becomes a reality. In this age his children disappoint God their Father by disobedience and lack of trust in him. But soon it will be otherwise.

In verses 24-25, Paul returns to the theme of 'hope', which was introduced in verse 20, and so draws this short passage to a conclusion.

> For we are saved by hope.
> Hope that is seen is not hope.
> For who hopes for what he sees?
> But if we hope for what we do not see,
> we await it with patience.

By 'saved' Paul is reminding his readers that the most fundamental aspect of 'salvation' or 'being saved' is future. 'Salvation' is but one of several ways by which the future life in the kingdom of God is described; other descriptions include 'eternal life,' 'righteousness'/'justification,' 'redemption' and 'reconciliation'. Paul's word 'hope' (noun and verb) means 'what is hoped for', that is, being 'saved'. Since this belongs to the coming age it is not yet seen, though the 'first-fruits of the Spirit' give an inner foretaste of that hope.

This hoped-for-salvation, however, is not uncertain because it is not yet seen. Its eventual fulfilment rests on God's sure promises so that believers 'await it with patience'. This patient waiting is connected with the work of the Spirit assuring them that God's promises are true and that they are not waiting in vain (cf. 5:5: 'Hope does not make us ashamed because the love of God has been poured into our hearts by the Holy Spirit who has been given to us').

B. The Spirit comes to our aid (vv. 26-27)

'Hope' for the blessings of the kingdom of God cannot be separated from the activity of the Spirit of God. On one hand, the children of God, like the unredeemed children of Adam, are caught in the birth-death coils of this age. Children of God suffer and die, as well as others. On the other hand, however, because they have 'the Spirit of sonship' (that cries, 'abba, Father') they know that their final destination is not *here* in the present age but *there* in the coming age.

For this reason Paul begins verse 26 with 'Likewise, the Spirit also.' The Spirit inspired 'hope' in the hearts of the children of God. So what will he 'also' do?

> Likewise the Spirit also helps us in our weakness.
> For we do not know how to pray as we ought,
> but the Spirit himself pleads for us with unutterable[10] groans.

Note that the Spirit's prayer to God is for us; it is not his prayer for others which we do not pray because of our 'weakness'. Indeed, 'our weakness' is not our defects in prayer but our fallen-ness, our solidarity with others in a fallen world. It is the 'weakness' of children of Adam caught in the web of sickness, dying and death and all the other human physical and moral frailties of this 'present evil age' (Gal. 1:4).

---

10. Gordon D. Fee, *God's Empowering Presence* (Peabody: Hendrickson, 1994), pp. 579-86, takes this to refer to private tongues-speaking. In my view, however, there is not enough evidence to be sure what the words 'unutterable groans' mean.

Even as children of God we are blinded by Sin so that we do not know how or what to pray for ourselves according to the will of God. God would have our prayers for ourselves fall in with his great plan of calling to himself those he had previously chosen (see on vv. 28-30). Since our prayers only imperfectly grasp that plan we do not pray as we ought. Yet the Spirit knows precisely how we should pray. Paul did not write these words to relieve us of our obligation to pray for ourselves or for others. But they do bring comfort since often we do not know what to pray.

According to verse 27 God himself, the searcher of our hearts, who knows the mind of the Spirit, knows that the Spirit prays for the saints according to the will of God. So we are greatly comforted that the Spirit is praying good things for us, though we are quite unaware of his intercessions on our behalf.

3. God's end-time family (vv. 28-30)

This justly famous passage is often considered on its own, free-standing, as it were, as the key proof text for the Calvinistic doctrine of predestination. True as that doctrine may be, and indeed, truly found in these verses, it must be read in its particular context of deliverance from suffering and not treated in isolation, as abstract theology, as it were.

On one hand, these verses follow hard on the preceding passage about suffering in this present age and the sure hope of the deliverance of the children of God. On the other hand, they anticipate the agonies, mentioned in verses 35 and 38, that would separate God's children from his love were it not for the strength of that love (v. 38).

Hence in verse 28 the 'all things' that 'work together for good' are precisely those sufferings of this present evil age that, despite their negative character, nonetheless 'co-operate' together for the ultimate 'good' of the children of God in the coming age.

Paul's words, 'we know,' point to a well-known apostolic teaching in the churches.

We know that
   to those who love God
      everything is working together towards good
   to those who are called according to his purpose.

This is the call to true faith of those who are already 'children of God' and who live in the painful intermediate time between their baptism into Christ and the arrival of the coming age. Like others in this age, 'those who love God' suffer within the birth-death cycle that enslaves humanity. Unlike others, however, they suffer the additional pain in sharing the rejection of their Lord. Yet Christians may find it difficult to see through their tears any vestige of God's great ultimate plan from which their 'sonship' will one day be revealed. How can this terrible thing (of the moment) be for my 'good' or anyone's 'good'? Yet the eye of faith and hope sees through the pain and says just that.

Confidence in the sovereignty of God in dire circumstances is one of the fundamentals of the faith. It is one thing – and very necessary – to assent to the great historical facts of the gospel as touching the birth of Christ, his miracles, atoning death, resurrection from the dead and return in glory. But, I submit, confidence in God's sovereign goodness in the midst of a baffling and painful providence is equally important, if not more so. Yet as we actively trust him in those circumstances we share in his kingly rule during the 'not yet' times ahead of the Last Day.

But why can Paul make the bold assertion that 'all things work together for good for those who love God'? Verse 29 is his answer.

Because
those whom he foreknew
   he also pre-identified[11]
   to be conformed to the image of his Son
   that he might be the first-born
      among many brothers.

This passage expands upon its predecessor (vv. 18-23). There the apostle wrote of the glory yet to be disclosed, namely, the

---

11. Usually translated 'predestined' the word (*proōrizō*) derives from *pro*, 'before' and *horizō*, 'I mark out' (our word 'horizon' stems from it). Literally speaking, it means 'horizoned beforehand'. The word 'predestined' carries a lot of freight which I have sought to avoid by using the word 'pre-identified'.

revelation of the sons of God, liberated from their bondage to decay and death. Now Paul elaborates about the children of God, that they are a family of brothers and sisters clustered around the elder brother Christ, in whose 'image' they have now all been 'conformed'. This is a magnificent vision of God's great future for his sons and daughters.

God 'foreknew' these 'children of God', that is, he knew who they were and he knew about them in the ages before the creation. 'Knowing' them in advance, he also 'marked them out' ('pre-identified' them) in advance. His intention (as we see in the next verse) was effectively to identify them beforehand so as to save them from the ravages of the present evil age and finally to gather them safely into his great family.

These 'foreknown' ones, however, are not barely saved from this age for the next. In the midst of their sufferings they are actually being changed, 'conformed to the image of the Son of God.'

How does this process of 'conformity' occur? Later Paul tells them it is 'by the renewal of your mind' (12:2), that is, by their continuing welcome of the word and the Spirit. In another letter Paul declares that as we 'behold' Christ (in faith and hope) we are being 'transformed into his image' by the Spirit (2 Cor. 3:18). In Adam and his tribe the divine image was defaced due to Sin. In Christ, however, the divine image has reappeared, but greater and more brilliant than it had been as the image of God in Adam. The work of repair occurring in believers does not merely restore what Adam lost. Rather, they are being remade into the greater image of Christ.

And the purpose? It is, says Paul, that Christ 'might be the first-born among many brothers and sisters'. While the unusual word *prōtotokos* literally means 'first-born', it is better to take it as meaning 'pre-eminent'. Thus understood, Christ will be 'head and shoulders' above, a prince over his brothers and sisters in his 'tribe,' the family of God.

In verse 30, Paul repeats 'those ... he pre-identified' from the previous verse but adds other deeds of God that bring about their 'conformity to the Son of God'.

and	those	he 'pre-identified'	
	these		he also called
and	those	he called	
	these		he also justified
and	those	he justified	
	these		he also glorified.

Here we see the 'invincible determination of God' to see his plan through to the end. Nothing will stop him or separate from his love those whom he foreknew (see on vv. 35-38). Through the gospel God effectively 'calls' and 'justifies' within this present age those he 'foreknew' and 'pre-identified' before history began. These he will 'glorify' in the ages to come, that is, 'conform [them] to the image of his Son'. The doctrine of the 'perseverance of the saints,' while true to the Bible, may be misnamed. It may be better called the 'determination of God,' that is, the determination of God to glorify those whom he foreknew despite their sufferings in this age.

It is understandable that verses 28-30 have been a centre of interest. Many have questioned the fairness of God 'foreknowing' and saving some but not others. Yet in light of the Sin of Adam and his tribe no one has any claim on God's mercy, as chapters 2 and 3 have shown. The reasons why events in history unfold remain a mystery to us. Equally, we have no way of knowing why God saves some and not others. Ultimately that is God's business, not ours. In this passage Paul is saying no more than that God is God and that God will have his way in his world with and for his people (see on 9:19-21). The point of the present passage is that, despite the evils of the age through which the children of God make their way, God will not be deflected from his good purposes for them.

Pastorally, some doubt that they are among these chosen ones. There is a way of reassurance. Approaching God in prayer as 'abba, Father' is only possible to those who are truly children of God. This is evidence of the indwelling Christ and thus of God's foreknowledge. God's children need to know that they are and will be safe in his hands, come what may. They may fail him, not least in the midst of the sufferings and persecutions described in this chapter, but God will not fail them.

4. GOD IS FOR US (vv. 31-39)

In these verses Paul expands upon the 'determination of God' to glorify those he has 'foreknown', as set out in the previous section (vv. 28-30). He asks, 'What shall we say about these things?' – referring to God's 'foreknowledge'. He then confronts this teaching with three difficult questions, which he then answers.

It is likely that Paul's readers in Rome had become demoralised under persecution. Oppression and rejection bring doubt and spiritual insecurity. 'Perhaps unconquerable spiritual forces are against us. Perhaps God himself has it in for us and is against us.' Paul's words here are powerfully reassuring and they point us to Christ as the pledge of God's goodness and care, and also to his resolute determination to glorify those he 'foreknew'.

A. Who is against us? (vv. 31-32)

Paul knows that there is much 'against' the children of God, the birth-death cycle with its sense of 'futility' on the one hand (vv. 18-22) and persecution (vv. 35, 38) on the other. In the midst of these the believer may easily feel overwhelmed by the forces 'against' him.

But Paul assures them that 'God is for us'. That was evident in God's 'foreknowledge' and 'pre-identification' of his children before the ages (vv. 28-30). But the visible demonstration of God's favour towards them is that he 'did not spare his own Son but handed him over for us all'.

Here we are reminded of God's request that Abraham 'hand over' his son Isaac for sacrifice (see Gen. 22:12, 16). In that case God eventually allowed Abraham to 'spare' his son. It was otherwise with God's 'own Son' whom he did 'not spare but handed over for us all,' such is the Father's love for us. God provided Abraham with a substitute, a ram. For God himself no such substitute was at hand. He actually 'handed over' his own Son for us.

Jesus was not one among other sons of God, as many say. The word 'his *own* Son' matches an earlier reference to 'his *very own* Son' (see on 8:3) and establishes the uniqueness of Jesus as the *only* Son of his Father.[12] Paul does not explain here the

---

12. Compare *tou idiou huiou* (8:32) with *ho theos ton heautou huion* (8:3).

words, 'handed him over for us all.'[13] His classical statement occurs earlier where he taught that 'God set forth' his Son as 'a propitiation' who in his death bore the just penalty of God against our sins (see on 3:25). In the deepest of mysteries God favoured us against his Son, whom he 'sent' (8:3) and 'handed over' to sacrificial death, a death that was beyond description in its 'physical' and in its 'spiritual' sufferings.

So, says Paul, we must not doubt that God is 'for us,' echoing David's confidence in God (Ps. 23:4: 'I will fear no evil; for you are with me'; Ps. 56:9: 'this I know, that God is for me'; Ps. 56:11: 'In God I have put my trust, I will not be afraid; what can man do unto me?'). The opening word, 'If,' does not imply doubt but reinforces our confidence, carrying the sense, '*Since* God is for us, *who* can be against us? In other words, Paul is restating the invincible determination of God to save those he 'foreknew'. God is on the side of his children so that nothing can prevail against them. Many have a streak of paranoia, some more than others. Believers need to be confident: God is 'for' them; he is not against them.

Faith in God easily wavers in face of reversals and disappointments. Doubt quickly wells up in times of distress and difficulty. 'Turn your eyes to the cross of Christ,' says Paul. 'Look at what God has done for you at the supreme cost of his own Son. That is the measure of his love for you. God is for you. Nothing – including this present painful crisis (whatever it is) – can prevail against you. God will give you every other (and lesser) thing you need to sustain you for the salvation he has planned for you.'

B. Who shall accuse God's chosen ones? (vv. 33-34)
God's 'chosen ones' ('elect'[14] – RSV) are those whom he 'foreknew' and 'pre-identified' to be the children he will glorify (vv. 29-30). The vestiges of Adam's Sin remain, as the struggle of 'the Spirit' against 'the flesh' within us reminds us (see on vv. 10-13). Perhaps, then, God will accuse us for our continuing sins?

---

13. Paul echoes the Greek text of Isaiah 53:6: 'the Lord gave him up to our sins.'
14. Despite the impression the letter has much to say about the 'elect' and 'election', the Greek word *eklektos* occurs in Romans only here and in 16:13 ('Greet Rufus elect – or eminent – in the Lord').

When God 'justified' us, that is, declared his verdict 'acquitted' in our favour based on the death of Christ, it was not only retrospective but also prospective. That great act of 'justification' was in regard to not only our past but also to our future sins. Once more this picks up words from the previous section, 'those he foreknew ... these he also justified' (v. 30).

Paul asks, 'Who shall accuse?', knowing that God himself is the great accuser in the final judgement (see on 2:16). But since God has 'justified' his chosen ones he will not 'accuse' them.

Paul's next rhetorical question 'Who will condemn?' at first seems unnecessary. In the Last Judgement God the just judge both 'accuses' and 'condemns'. Since he will not accuse, how would he condemn?' Nonetheless, Paul does ask that question, perhaps to drive home the point that God neither 'accuses' nor, therefore, 'condemns' those he has 'justified' in Christ. His answer (v. 34) is a creed-like statement about Christ, which stands as one of the most noble in the New Testament.

| It is rather, | Christ Jesus | who has died, who has been raised who is at God's right hand who also intercedes for us. |

How remarkable that Paul should point so powerfully to Christ – as God's own Son, whom he did not spare, whom he raised up to his right hand – in order to allay our fears about forces that might be 'against us'. Christ himself is our assurance of God's goodness and favour 'for us'.

We cannot but notice the rising crescendo – Christ died, was raised, is at God's right hand, intercedes for us. The emphasis falls on the peak of the crescendo, that Christ 'who is at God's right hand ... also intercedes for us'. The words 'at God's right hand ... interceding ...' combine Psalm 110:1 (the Messiah ruling at 'God's right hand') and Isaiah 53:12 (the sin-bearing Servant 'interceding' on his behalf 'for transgressors').

So far from the very possibility that God might 'condemn' us Paul points out that the Christ who died for us now reigns in authority for us, arguing *his* case on our behalf, as it were, in the courts of heaven (see also 1 John 2:1: 'If any one sins we have an advocate with the Father, Jesus Christ the righteous'; Hebrews 7:25: '[Christ] is able for all time to save those who draw near to God through him since he ever lives to make intercession for them'). Members of Adam's tribe have no case. Christ the sinless, sin-bearing Son of God argues his perfect case on behalf of those who belong to him. It is a case he always wins.[15]

In other words, Paul is saying that God's determination to save 'those he foreknew' cannot and will not be thwarted. In verses 31-34, Paul is teaching us not to be afraid of the baffling circumstances that touch our lives and which easily produce fear, doubt and insecurity. This is Paul the pastor bringing words of comfort to his readers then and now. God has not spared but given up his own Son, no less, for us. He is for us and therefore nothing can be against us, God himself least of all. God our Father will provide whatever else we need along the way to our salvation. Furthermore, the Son who died for us, has been raised to God's right hand as Lord and Messiah, where he advocates his righteousness for us.

C. Who shall separate us from the love of Christ? (vv. 35-39)
In verse 35 Paul lists seven sufferings arising from persecution. Each has touched Paul's own life and echoes the pain of ministry found in earlier letters.[16] Yet the congregations were at one with the apostle in feeling the hot blast of opposition and rejection from that society and culture. So the Romans will know Paul's meaning in his words: pressure, being trapped, persecution, hunger, nakedness, danger, and sword. Remarkably, his words were prophetic of the fury that Nero would unleash upon Christians in Rome, including Paul, less than a decade later.

Such pain, however, is not new but has always been the lot of God's people, as Paul reminds them in verse 36, quoting Psalm 44:22:

---

15. The notion that the saints and the mother of Jesus intercede for believers demeans the dignity and office of Christ and robs them of the confidence that is rightfully theirs in Christ.

16. 1 Corinthians 4:9-13; 15:30-32; 16:9; 2 Corinthians 1:8-11; 4:7-12; 6:3-10; 11:23–12:10.

For your sake
we are being put to death day long
we are reckoned as sheep for slaughter.

Other New Testament authors express the same reality. The
author of Hebrews refers to those who were tortured, mocked,
scourged, imprisoned, stoned, sawn in two, put to the sword,
made destitute, afflicted, ill-treated, wandering over deserts
and mountains (Heb. 11:35-38). John declares, 'If anyone is to
be taken captive, to captivity he goes; if any one is to be slain
with the sword, with the sword he must be slain' (Rev. 13:10).
These sufferings have continued to fall upon God's faithful
ones since the era of the New Testament to the present time.

Against this, however, in verse 37 Paul utters a defiant 'but'
(*alla*).

But we conquer in all these things
through him who loved us.

Paul coins a word 'hyper-conquer' (*hupernikō*) to express
the comprehensive victory over 'all these things', that is, the
persecutions listed above. But that victory is 'through him who
loved us'. It is not at all our strength or inner resources that
enable perseverance in the face of these things. This conquering
is a further demonstration of the absolute, implacable and
invincible determination of God to glorify those he foreknew
before the creation of the cosmos (vv. 28-30).

So (vv. 38-39) Paul brings this section to its passionate
end:

For I am persuaded that
    neither death   nor life
    neither angels   nor principalities
    neither things present   nor things to come
    neither powers
    neither heights   nor depths
                       nor any other created thing
will be able to separate us from the love of God
that is in Christ Jesus our Lord.

The keywords here are 'any other created thing'. The things listed above are each 'created', that is, created by God. Some are 'supernatural' ('angels,' 'principalities,' 'powers,' 'heights,' 'depths') while others are identifiably 'natural' ('death,' 'life,' 'things present,' 'things to come'); yet either way, they are 'created' by God and therefore subject to his rule. These natural and supernatural forces may be marshalled against us in persecution. Yet they will not prevail. God's 'rule' is exercised over these elements in the world and within history for the sake of those who have been 'marked out' as his children.

Let demoralised, persecuted believers understand that their sufferings do not speak of God's rejection or of the greater power of the demons. Rather, even these hostile forces are ultimately under God's sovereign control for our 'good' (as Paul stated earlier in v. 28). God will save his people, come what may. His love is greater.

STUDY QUESTIONS

1. Do I seek to be 'well pleasing' to God?

2. What actions do I need to take in order to put to death the deeds of the flesh?

3. How am I to rely on the Holy Spirit's help for victory?

4. How can I be sure that I have the Spirit of sonship?

5. What do I receive as an 'heir of God?'

6. In what ways has creation been affected by sin?

7. What comfort is there in suffering for Christ?

8. How has God demonstrated that 'He is for us?'

Part D

The Salvation of Israel
(Romans 9–11)

In these chapters Paul addresses the problem of Israel's rejection of her Messiah.

From a Jewish quarter – perhaps articulated by Jewish members of the house churches (prompted by unbelieving synagogue friends?) – comes the shrewd accusation that Paul's ministry to Gentiles assumes that Israel is no longer God's covenant people and that Paul himself is a renegade Jew.

Such an idea is unthinkable, responds Paul, otherwise God himself would have failed to keep his promises to his people. Nor does this mean, as the accusation really implies, that Paul's gospel is fatally flawed. Through chapters 9–11 Paul rejects both propositions; throughout Israel's history only a remnant had ever been responsive to God.

True, at this time Israel as a whole is unresponsive, even hostile. Yet the divine promises to the patriarchs still stand. There will be a future ingathering of Israel.

A related matter is the arrogance of some Gentile believers in Rome towards Israel into whom they have been 'grafted'. Paul warns Gentile believers that they may be removed from the 'olive tree' and the 'natural branches' re-grafted in.

Paul concludes these chapters in an outburst of praise to God for his wisdom and mercy towards humankind, Jews and Gentiles.

10

More Than a Potter
(Romans 9:1-33)

Paul raises and answers an accusation and also many questions in this chapter. Most likely these arose from Jews, including Christian Jews in Rome. The accusation was that Paul cared little for his fellow-Jews, that he had even abandoned the faith of his fathers. Following his assurances that he remains a Jew, Paul peppers himself with questions that he had doubtless heard many times before from fellow-Jews.

1. PAUL, ISRAELITE (9:1-5)
Paul begins by making a solemn assurance (v. 1):

> I am speaking the truth,
> I am not lying.

Jesus forbade oath-taking since, like swearing today, oaths had corrupted speech (Matt. 5:34: 'I say to you, "Do not swear at all"'). Paul's words, while not an oath, nonetheless, are uttered in the power of the Holy Spirit, because he knows that God will be his judge. His conscience tells him this.

What is this 'truth'? It is that he feels profound grief and unceasing sorrow for his brother Jews, his kinsmen (v. 2). That grief is, of course, that the Jews *as a nation* have not responded to their rightful king, the Messiah Jesus (see on vv. 32-33).

But why must Paul promise his truthfulness in such absolute terms? Most likely because numbers of his Jewish readers in Rome did, in fact, suspect him of lying. They may have believed that since Paul was the apostle to the Gentiles he was of necessity against the chosen people. In short, it appears that many Jews regarded Paul as a liar.[1] To this day some Jewish people hold Paul to be an apostate against his fellow-Jews, a renegade and an enemy against the people and religion of his birth. Nothing could be further from the truth. True, he was Christ's apostle to the Gentiles. Yet he always preached 'to the Jews first' and, as he will soon say, his ultimate reason for preaching to Gentiles was to win his fellow-Jews for their Messiah (11:11-15).

Indeed, such was his love for his people that, as he says, 'I could pray that I myself am accursed from Christ for my brothers, my kinsmen according to the flesh' (v. 3). 'Accursed' (*anathema*) picks up the language of the book of Joshua where the defeated, godless city of Jericho was 'handed over to God' for destruction (cf. Josh. 6:17: 'The city and all that is in it shall be devoted to the LORD for destruction'). By Paul's time, however, 'devoted to the Lord for destruction' meant nothing less than 'consigned to hell'. Easily missed are the prepositions 'from (*apo* – 'away from') and 'for' (*huper* – 'on behalf of'). Paul would prefer to be *anathema*, separated 'away from Christ' 'on behalf of' his people. Prompted by the example of Jesus himself, Paul would prefer to be eternally lost 'from Christ' and his Kingdom 'in place of' his fellow-Jews if only they would find salvation in their Messiah.

Paul's reference to his 'brothers ... kinsmen according to the flesh' leads him to list the blessings God historically had bestowed on 'the Israelites' (v. 4).

> To them belong
> > the adoption as sons
> > the glory
> > the covenants

---

1. Paul's solemn assurances that he is not lying probably mean that he was so accused (cf. 2 Corinthians 11:31: 'The God and Father of the Lord Jesus ... knows that I do not lie'; Galatians 1:20: 'In what I am writing to you, before God, I am not lying'; 1 Timothy 2:7: 'For this I was appointed a preacher and an apostle. I am telling the truth. I am not lying').

the giving of the Law
the worship
the promises, and
the fathers.

By 'Israelites' Paul is thinking of God's unique relationship with that 'people' whom he chose, saved and instructed. In the course of two millennia this people benefited from God's mercy in many tangible ways, some of which Paul now lists.

(i) God was Father to them and they were his 'sons' by *adoption* (cf. Exod. 4:22: 'This is what the LORD says: "Israel is my firstborn son"'; Hosea 11:1: 'When Israel was a child, I loved him and out of Egypt I called my son').

(ii) To them God showed himself visibly not in bodily form but in 'brightness' or *glory*, for example, at Mt. Sinai (Exod.24:16: 'and the glory of the LORD settled on Mt. Sinai').

(iii) With them God made *covenants*, chiefly with the patriarch Abraham and with the rescued people at Mt. Sinai (Gen. 15:17-21; Exod. 19:5-6).

(iv) At Mt. Sinai God gave them *the Law*, his 'ten words', together with amplifying instructions for them to fulfill as their 'side' of God's covenant (Exod. 20–24).

(v) Also at Mt. Sinai the Lord gave them *the worship*, that is, his instructions for approaching him in Tabernacle and Temple, as set out in the book of Leviticus.

(vi) To the Israelites God made many *promises* for the future, in particular as noted in Romans, (a) to Abraham (4:13: 'Abraham and his offspring received the promise that he would be heir of the world'), and (b) regarding David (1:2: 'the gospel he promised beforehand ... regarding his Son, who ... was a descendant of David').

(vii) Finally, 'belonging to the Israelites' by God's gift were *the fathers*, Abraham, Isaac and Jacob and his sons, the twelve patriarchs from whom Israel's tribes came.

These tangible evidences of God's blessings on his chosen people were in the distant past. The last and greatest of those blessings lay in the immediate past in the historic ministry of Jesus and, since his resurrection from the dead, in the present.

> ... who are the Israelites ...
> of whom is the Christ according to the flesh,
>   who is over all,
>   God blessed forever.[2]

Here it is not the name 'Christ', but his title, '*the* Christ' (or, in Hebrew, 'the Messiah'), that is, the long-awaited 'son' of David (cf. 1:2; 15:7-12). We learn that the Christ (1) is an Israelite man, (2) is 'over all,' that is, as the risen and exalted Lord of all, and (3) astonishingly, is called 'God'[3] and 'blessed forever' (as in standard benedictions of God, for example in 2 Cor. 1:3: 'Blessed be the God and Father of our Lord Jesus Christ'). This is one of a small number of passages in the New Testament where Jesus is directly called 'God' (see, for example, Hebrews 1:8: 'But about the Son he says, "your throne O *God* will last forever'; John 1:1: 'The Word was *God*'). There are many passages, however, where indirect deity claims are made, whether by Jesus (Mark 2:10: 'The Son of Man has authority on earth to forgive sins') or about Jesus (1 Cor. 16:22: 'If anyone does not love the Lord [Jesus], let him be anathema'; cf. Deut. 6:5: 'Love the Lord your God').

In short, in verses 1-5 Paul has (1) by his list of tangible evidences reaffirmed that the Israelites are God's elect people, but (2) as a fellow-Israelite assured them he is heartbroken that as a race they have not embraced their Messiah. Such is his love for his own people that he even prayed to be cursed by God eternally if that would mean their salvation.

2. Has the Word of God failed? (9:6-13)

But if Israel is God's elect people and God made promises to them, how is it that they have not embraced those promises and acknowledged their Messiah? Has the word of God failed? This is not a piece of aimless musing on Paul's part. Rather, he

---

2. Another translation is possible, that is, 'who is God over all, blessed forever'. Either way Paul declares 'the Christ' to be 'God'.

3. For discussion and review of opinions, see Schreiner, pp. 486-89.

is probably responding to a sustained polemic against him formulated by Jews resistant to his message to them. He raised this issue briefly earlier in the letter (see on 3:3). Now he must discuss it at greater length.

Most likely such people were found among his readers in Rome. Their argument would have been that Israel was God's chosen nation *and* that God's promises do not fail, in particular his 'word' to Abraham promising descendants as numerous as the stars in the heavens (Gen. 15:5). If Jews *en bloc* accepted Paul's message this would be evidence of its genuineness. But the rejection by most Jews of his message is proof in itself that Paul's message is not from God, that he is no messenger of God. Clearly the failure of the greater number of Jews to receive Jesus as Messiah is being cast up at Paul. How will he answer these charges?

Briefly, Paul will point out that God's election of Israel had never been absolute and global. There had always been an elect 'core' within an elect nation. In principle, a limited response by Jews to the word of God was nothing new.

Accordingly Paul asserts at the outset that 'the word of God has not fallen' (v. 6). This picks up his reference to 'the promises' (v. 4) and, much earlier, to 'the gospel he promised beforehand through his prophets in the holy scriptures' (1:2) and to 'the words of God' entrusted to Israel (3:2). Clearly, the notion of 'the words of God'/'the promises'/'the word of God' is critical to Paul; his message is that these 'words' have now, indeed, been fulfilled.

Paul substantiates this assertion (v. 7 beginning, 'For ...') with the following observations based on Israel's sacred history:

For		
not	all who are of Israel	are Israel
nor are	Abraham's descendants	all children
but		

'It is in Isaac that your descendants will be reckoned.'

There was an 'Israel' within 'Israel', an elect group within the elect people. Abraham had 'descendants', but not all were 'children'. Quoting Genesis 21:12 Paul reminds the readers that God's chosen line would be 'in' or 'through' the *promised* child Isaac. Another son, Ishmael born to Abraham and Hagar, was a 'descendant' but he was not a 'child' in the sense of God's purposes of election (see Gen. 16:1-16).

Paul explains further, contrasting the children of flesh (Ishmael) with the children born as by the promise of God (Isaac).

The children of flesh	are not	children of God, but
the children of promise	are reckoned as	descendants.

Thus the two boys Isaac and Ishmael immediately illustrate Paul's point. Physical descent from the primal and elect patriarch, Abraham, does not constitute Isaac and Ishmael as both 'elect'. Clearly Ishmael was rejected.

Paul continues with the example of Rebecca (v. 10). Abraham bore children (elect and non-elect) by several women. Isaac, however (v. 11), had one wife, Rebecca, and from one act of sexual intercourse, and from one emission of his semen were born the twins Esau and Jacob, one elect, the other non-elect.

God's election of one and not the other was evident before Esau and Jacob were born, before either had opportunity to do good works or evil works. That Jacob was chosen and Esau was not depended entirely upon God's choice, though both were twin boys of the one father and the one mother. Everything rested on God 'who calls' (v. 12).

Neither the author of Genesis nor Paul the apostle give an explanation as to the 'why' of God's election. It is the deepest of deep mysteries. Paul merely quotes two biblical texts. In the first (Gen. 25:23) Rebecca was told, 'The older [Esau] shall serve the younger [Jacob].' In the second Paul refers to the prophet Malachi, 'Jacob have I loved and Esau have I hated' (Mal. 1:2-3). It would be unhelpful to press these words into a comprehensive theological statement, as some have, concluding that God 'hates' those he has not chosen. Rather, Paul cites Malachi to illustrate his point that God chose one but rejected the other. The Edomites, who descended from Esau, treated the fleeing Israelites badly, demonstrating that

God's judgement will not be based on non-election, but on works.

3. Is God unjust? (9:14-18)

'If, as you say, God chose Isaac, but not Ishmael, Jacob but not Esau, this can only mean that God is *unrighteous*.' Here Paul has anticipated the next question from his imagined interrogators. The barb in the question is the word, 'unrighteous' (*adikia*), which – they infer – Paul must be saying about God's choice of one but not another. We remember that in Paul's gospel the 'righteousness' (*dikaiosunē*) of God is given to those who believe in Christ (see on 1:17). Clearly they are laying a verbal trap for him. He preaches 'righteousness' but is saying, in effect, that God is 'unrighteous'.

But he dismisses this proposition in verse 15 by a quotation from Exodus 33:19: 'God said to Moses, *I* will be merciful to whoever *I* show mercy and be compassionate to whoever *I* show compassion.' That is, God shows mercy as he chooses to. It does not depend on man's will or exertion (v. 16).

Pharaoh in the Exodus narrative is a case in point (v. 17, quoting Exod. 9:16).

> For this very purpose I have raised you up,
> that I might demonstrate my power in you,
> that my name might be proclaimed in all the earth.

There is more here, however, than meets the eye, as signalled by Paul's word expressing purpose, 'that.' God raised Pharaoh up and demonstrated his power over him in Israel's 'exodus' so *that* God's name be proclaimed everywhere. Based on the example of Pharaoh Paul concludes, 'So then God has mercy on whoever he wills and whoever he wills he hardens.'

Two comments must be made. First, Paul has introduced the example of God's dealings with Pharaoh to prepare the way for God's more recent dealings with Israel herself. As God 'demonstrated his power' in Pharaoh so that the name of God might be made known through Israel among the Gentile nations, so God has 'made known his power' in wrath upon Israel so that the salvation of God might come to the Gentiles.

Disobedient Pharaoh is a paradigm for disobedient Israel, both of whom, however, have been so appointed by God for his greater glory.

Second, while God *being God* has the right to raise up a Pharaoh and a nation for his purposes, this does not relieve either Pharaoh or Israel from their moral responsibility. Pharaoh behaved wickedly despite many opportunities to act rightly. Israel has acted wilfully in her rejection of her king, the Messiah Jesus. Both will be judged by their 'works' (see on 2:6-11).

But this does not end the questioning.

4. How, then, can God judge justly? (9:19-21)

Again, Paul anticipates the follow-up question (v. 19). If God decides to whom he will show mercy and whom he will harden, how, then can he judge people based on moral considerations? Since he is God, and thus almighty and irresistible, how can he still 'find fault' with man? We cannot but admire Paul for courageously articulating these questions. How will he answer?

Paul's reply is categorical (v. 20): 'O man, who are you to answer back to God?' Paul is saying, in effect, 'Man, know your place. God is God, eternal and almighty, the Maker of all. Man is made by God and utterly dependent upon him.' He illustrates this by an example from the potter's craft, one that must have been familiar to those who lived at that time.

> Will a moulded object say to its moulder,
> 'Why have you made me like this?'
> Surely the potter has the right over the unformed clay
> to make one vessel of beauty and another for menial use.

In other words, God must be seen as free to be God, to have ultimate authority in human affairs, for whatever his ultimate purposes might be.

We need, however, to keep to Paul's perspective here. Paul is answering questions about the unbelief of God's historic people in relationship with his sovereign election, on the one hand, and his probity as a just judge, on the other. Paul is not,

for example, addressing the vexed question of the evils of war
or asking why the innocent suffer. These are different issues
calling for a 'wider angle' discussion and a pastorally nuanced
response.

5. More than a Potter (9:22-24)
Paul now returns more directly to the critical question of
Jewish unbelief in contrast to the more positive response of the
Gentiles. He picks up the example of Pharaoh and continues
the 'potter' image into verses 22-23, but with three important
refinements (signalled by the opening, 'But what if ...').

> *But what if* God,
> wishing to demonstrate his wrath and to make known his
>   power,
> bore with much patience a vessel of wrath made for destruct-
>   ion,
> in order to make known the riches of his glory upon a vessel
>   of mercy
> which he prepared beforehand for glory?

What are these refinements to the 'potter' metaphor?
   First, it is true that, like the potter, God is powerful and
has the right to make of clay various 'vessels'. 'But' unlike
the potter who would merely cast an unsuitable vessel to one
side, God shows 'much patience' towards such a 'vessel'.
   Second, even more to the point, God displays such great
patience to the rejected vessel *in order to* shower 'the riches of
his glory upon a vessel of mercy'. Clearly, then, the 'vessels'
are 'humans' about whom God, the compassionate 'potter,'
cares deeply.
   Third, Paul's words are hypothetical, expressing a 'what
if,' rather than a categorical assertion. He does not say that
God has condemned Israel forever. Indeed, as Paul will soon
make clear, he expects a (significant?) restoration of Israel
(11:12 – 'their fullness'; 11:15 – 'their acceptance'; 11:26a
– 'all Israel will be saved') following the 'salvation of the
Gentiles' (11:11) ahead of the 'coming of the deliverer from
Zion' (11:26b).

But *who* are these 'vessels'? In verse 24 Paul makes clear who is the latter 'vessel'. The 'vessel of mercy' is the church of Jesus the Messiah, Jewish and Gentile believers:

Even *us whom he has called,*
not only from the Jews
but also from the Gentiles.

Who, then, are the former, the 'vessel of wrath'? It is composed of unresponsive Jews, 'a vessel ... made for destruction' whom, however, God continues to bear 'with much patience'. This is not to say that God's patience with unbelieving Israel has come to an end. Indeed, not. How could anyone be so sure of God's purposes to say that? Indeed, as noted above, Paul foresees the ultimate salvation of Israel.

But that 'patience' was and is extended to provide opportunity for God, through gospel preaching, to call to himself a new people drawn from the Jews and from the Gentiles. Paul provides biblical substantiation for the inclusion first of the Gentiles, then of the Jews.

6. GOD'S MERCY ON THE GENTILES (9:25-26)
In verse 25, Paul quotes Hosea 2:23 to show that God foresaw the salvation of Gentile people:

I will call	those who were	not my people,	'my people'
	she who was	not loved,	'my beloved.'

To this Paul adds immediately some words from Hosea 1:10:

And in the place where it was said to them,
'You are not my people,'
they will be called,
'Sons of the living God.'

In short, Paul is saying that the Gentiles whom God has called are his *people*, his *beloved*, his *Sons*.

7. God's Mercy on a Remnant of Israel (9:27-29)

But are there many from Israel who will be shown the divine mercy in Paul's times? At present Paul does not envisage a vast harvest from among the elect nation, as quotations from Isaiah show.

> Although the number of the sons of Israel be as the sand
> of the sea,
> only a remnant will be saved.
> For the Lord will execute his sentence on the earth
> with rigour and speed.   Isaiah 10:22-23

> If the Lord of hosts had not left us descendants
> we would have been like Sodom and Gomorrah.
>   Isaiah 1:9

Clearly, then, Paul sees only a 'remnant' of Israel, a few survivors who are currently finding the salvation of God.

8. Explanation at a Human Level (9:30-31)

But how does Paul account for the respective levels of response of Jews and Gentiles to the message of the gospel, in particular the minimal response of the Jews? Earlier, Paul placed his emphasis on the divine will in determining in advance the call of God. Now, however, he approaches the question from the viewpoint of human attitudes and behaviour, first of the Gentiles, then of the Jews (vv. 30-31).

> Gentiles did not pursue righteousness but they received
> righteousness,
> that is, however, the righteousness that is by faith.
> On the other hand, although Israel pursued the Law to
> attain righteousness
> she did not attain [righteousness] in respect of Law.[4]

The Gentile nations were not known for their pursuit of righteousness. Indeed, their unrighteousness was a scandal

---

4. Paul's original text is abbreviated and needs 'righteousness' from the previous verse to be understood.

to Jews. To them the words 'Gentile' and 'sinner' were synonymous (cf. Gal. 2:15: 'we ... are Jews by birth and not Gentile sinners'). Yet, ironically, Gentiles have proved open to the gospel of Christ crucified and risen. Many have believed and been reckoned 'righteous' by God. By contrast, Jews have been preoccupied with Law which, however, they have failed to keep (see on 2:17-24). Furthermore, 'righteousness' has eluded them. They have spurned God's gracious gift. 'Why?' asks Paul. His answer (v. 32) in the original is extremely terse; the words in square brackets have been added to make sense.

Because	[the righteousness that comes] from faith [they did] not [pursue]
but	[the righteousness that comes] from works [they did pursue].

Paul is saying that the Israelites' focus on 'Law' (v. 31), that is, on 'works' (v. 32), excluded their focus on 'faith', or as he will now say, on the *object* of faith. The 'object' he refers to is 'the Stone'.

Paul's reference to the Christ as the 'Stone' (v. 32) depends on a number of passages from Isaiah that mention the 'stone,' passages that had been collected from early times.[5] It is evident that the 'stone' is a metaphor for a man. Paul sees these oracles about the man-'stone' as fulfilled in the coming of the Messiah and the varying attitudes – negative and positive – of the people to him. The people of Israel do one of two things to the messianic 'Stone' God sets among them. They 'stumble' on, that is, they reject the 'Stone' or they 'believe on' the 'Stone'.[6]

They have *stumbled over* the stumbling stone. Isaiah 8:14

Behold I lay in Zion a stone of stumbling and a rock of offence,
and he who *believes* on him will not be put to shame.
                                                    Isaiah 28:16

---

5. Most likely following Jesus' own reference to himself as '*the stone* the builders rejected' (Mark 12:10, quoting Psalm 118:22).

6. The First Letter of Peter also quotes these texts, with Ps. 118:22, though not for the response of Israel to the 'Stone,' but for people in general as they have 'believed' or 'disbelieved' the preached gospel (1 Pet. 2:4-8).

Here Paul is reflecting on recent events, initially the historic ministry of Jesus of Nazareth, then the apostles' mission work among Jews. Paul knew that Jews in Israel preferred their 'Law' and its 'works' – sabbath-keeping, fasting, washings, the temple cultus – to the Messiah who had come among them in fulfilment of the Law and the Prophets. The disputes between Jesus and the Pharisees in Galilee, described in the early chapters of Mark, and between Jesus and the Temple hierarchy, described in the latter chapters of the same Gospel, remind us that the people of Israel preferred 'Law' to Jesus and his kingdom. The 'guardians' of that 'Law' and its 'works', that is, the leading Pharisees and the Temple hierarchy, were Jesus' fiercest opponents, who finally secured his death at Roman hands. The religious outcasts like tax collectors and prostitutes, however, heard him gladly. Their acceptance of Jesus' welcome anticipated the welcome Gentiles gave to Paul's proclamation of God's 'righteousness' to those who belonged by 'faith' to the Messiah crucified and risen, independent of Law-keeping and circumcision. The opposition suffered by Jesus at the hands of 'religious' Jews was replicated in the experience of Paul. Paul, too, suffered at the hands of Jewish guardians of the Law and advocates of circumcision, including even those Jews who professed allegiance to Jesus,[7] the so-called 'Judaizers'.[8]

At heart the Jewish problem was *Christology*, the messianic 'Stone,' Jesus. So focused were they on religious patriotism expressed in 'Law' and its various 'works' that they failed to identify Jesus as the 'Stone' God had set among them. The same trajectory of unbelief continued on from Jesus into the apostolic age, including in the ministry of Paul to them. There were exceptions, however. Jesus' immediate disciples who became the college of the Twelve, numerous believers and church members in Judaea and Galilee, the former persecutor Saul/Paul, were each Israelites. God's word of promise had not failed altogether (see on 11:1-6).

---

7. Acts 15:1, 5. See 2 Corinthians 11:26: 'danger from ... my own people ... from false brothers.'

8. To 'Judaize' strictly means to 'live as a Jew' (so Gal. 2:14), and not to proselytize with Jewish legalism, as in popular understanding.

'Faith' and 'works', then, are not theological abstractions. 'Faith' is the dynamic recognition that Jesus is the Christ, the 'Stone' God set among his people to whom they are to 'come' and in whom they are to 'believe' for 'righteousness'. By contrast, 'works' of the 'Law' are the manifold expressions of Judaism – ritual, ceremony, laws and ethics – upon which Jews depended for their acceptance as 'righteous' with God.

9. Review of Paul's Argument

In answering his questions Paul has travelled some distance from the opening lines of the chapter. Yes, Paul is a Jew who cares about his people Israel, the historic elect people of God, as is evident in the many overt pledges to them (vv. 1-5). But there had always been an elect core within the wider elect nation. Thus God's word of promise to his people has not failed, though it had often fallen on deaf ears, as is still the case (vv. 6-13). But this does not mean God is 'unrighteous'; he *is* God, freely showing mercy on whoever *he* wills (vv. 14-18). Man can no more 'answer back' to God than a pot can call upon the potter to account for the way it is made (vv. 19-21). Yet God is no mere potter nor are men and women mere lifeless lumps of clay. God is 'patient' with one set of human vessels in order to 'show mercy' on another (vv. 22-23). Those 'others' turn out to be responsive Gentiles as well as believing Jews (vv. 24-26). Paul cannot but note that a mere 'remnant' of Israel is responding (vv. 27-29). This poor response is because they 'stumble' over the messianic 'Stone,' Jesus, preferring to seek 'righteousness' from God by the 'works' of the 'Law' (vv. 30-33).

10. Theological Observations

This review reminds us that Paul has offered a tight-knit argument throughout this chapter, using many buttressing texts from the Old Testament. That argument was made in a specific context concerning Jewish unbelief about which Paul wrote to the Roman Christians in the mid to late fifties. Are there theological teachings here that are timeless, and one hopes, timely?

(i) Paul's list of God's overt pledges to his people (vv. 5-6a) remind us that God's 'salvation history' is written in *two* chapters of which the Old Testament relating to Israel is the first. The Old Covenant is pregnant with those promises of God that he has fulfilled in the coming of Christ and the Spirit.

(ii) Human children are born of 'flesh' by the usual biological process. God's children, however, are born of his 'word' of 'promise' (9:8). Esau was an example of the former, Jacob of the latter. God continues to make men and women his 'children' but only by his 'word,' that is, the gospel.

(iii) Salvation, therefore, is all 'of God,' by his sovereign 'call' and cannot be earned by our 'works' (9:12).

(iv) Since God shows mercy to whom he wills (9:15), the recipients of that mercy should be very grateful to God. It is inappropriate for humans to argue with God about those who are or appear to be non-elect (9:20). God is like a potter in his absolute right to make whatever vessels he chooses. Yet, unlike a potter, he shows patience and mercy towards human vessels.

(v) Notwithstanding God's apparent non-call of the nation Israel at this time, God continues to show 'great patience' towards them (9:22). In the meantime God calls to himself people composed of both Gentiles and Jews.

(vi) The non-elect are judged by God according to their works, not by his non-election of them. God is not unrighteous.

(vii) Faithful to his 'word' (9:6), a remnant of Israel is being saved. God is active in the world by his Word and Spirit. Paul foresees the ultimate restoration of Israel (11:26a).

11. A NOTE ON THE 'NEW PERSPECTIVE' ON PAUL IN ROMANS 9
In recent times the 'New Perspective' on Paul has rightly insisted that we should not view Paul's teachings through the eyes of Luther's 'faith' versus 'works' dispute with the medieval Roman church. It is agreed that we must read Romans in its own right and in its own times. Paul was not, in fact, arguing for 'faith' versus 'works' (in general) as a means to the 'righteousness of God'.

The issue between Paul and his Jewish opponents, evident in the above passage in Romans, was *Christology* versus 'works of the Law'. By 'works of the Law' Paul meant specifically God's ethical and ritual requirements that Israel was to fulfil under the Old Covenant. By 'Christology' I mean not only the 'identity' of Jesus as the Davidic Christ and Son of God (see on 1:2-3; 8:3, 32) but also his 'work' as put to death for sins and raised to bestow righteousness to those who believe in him (see on 3:21-26).

Paul's complaint about Israel was that she rejected 'righteousness from God' based on the Messiah Jesus, preferring 'works of the Law'. Thus Israel 'stumbled' over the messianic 'Stone,' Jesus, and thereby insisted that the Old Covenant remained current. Paul, however, stated that the Old Covenant had been 'terminated' in Christ (10:4; 'abolished' – 2 Cor. 3:7, 11, 13, 14).

Some 'New Perspectivists' imply that the Old Covenant remains current for Jews and that the New Covenant, along with 'justification by faith,' is God's provision for Gentiles.[9] Paul, however, insists that Jews, as well as Gentiles, are 'in Adam' and 'under sin' (3:20). For both there is but one means to the 'righteousness of God,' that is, by faith in Christ crucified and risen. Based on the above passage Paul would not countenance the notion of two parallel, equally valid covenants, one for Israel the other for the Gentiles.

STUDY QUESTIONS

1. Have I ever had to prove to someone that I am a Christian like Paul had to prove that he was a Jew?

2. Do you believe God to be 'unjust' in His dealings with Jacob and Esau in Paul's example?

3. How does Paul answer the critic who may think that God is unjust in His dealings with Israel?

---

9. For discussion and rejection of the 'two covenant' theology, see C. A. Blaising, 'The Future of Israel as a Theological Question,' *Journal of the Evangelical Theological Society* (44/3, 2001), pp 435-50.

4. Who is the Stone that Paul refers to? Why do you think that he uses *this* imagery?

5. How does God continue to show patience toward Israel today?

11

The End of the Law
(Romans 10:1-21)

Paul begins and ends this chapter by lamenting Israel's rejection of the gospel of Christ that would have brought to them 'the righteousness of God' (10:1-4; 18-21). Between those extremities is Paul's majestic account of the coming of Christ, the sending forth of preachers of the 'word of Christ and the 'hearing' and 'believing' of that word for righteousness.

Of all the great and eloquent passages in the writings of Paul the apostle none is greater than this. There is music written by J. S. Bach and individual landscapes painted by John Constable which, if these men had contributed nothing else, would have won them a place in history. By analogy, this text is among those of the apostle which secure his place as the writer of words that are both 'inspired' by God but also 'inspiring' to the reader.

1. ISRAEL REJECTS THE RIGHTEOUSNESS OF GOD (vv. 1-3)

In the last sections of the previous chapter Paul noted with sadness that a mere 'remnant' of his nation had found salvation (9:27-29). Why is this? It was, he said, because Israel sought a Law-based righteousness while 'stumbling' over Jesus the messianic 'Stone' God had set in the land for the people to 'believe' in (9:30-33).

Paul continues in this vein. He begins by expressing his passionate grief for his people, as he had at the beginning of chapter 9. His words are addressed to the Gentile readers, though doubtless he knew his fellow-Jews would also hear.

Brothers, my heart's desire and prayer to God for them is
their salvation.

What hindered the Jews finding 'salvation'? Remarkably it
was, Paul says, 'zeal for God.' But it was 'zeal' (*zēlos*) 'not
according to knowledge' (v. 2). There is more to these words
than is commonly understood. Paul does not simply mean
that their eagerness exceeded their common sense, a failing we
associate with the immature. Rather, 'zeal' was a technical term
belonging to the religious culture of the Jews from the time of
Judas Maccabeus' uprising against the Graeco-Syrian attempt
to subvert Judaism two hundred years earlier. 'Zealot' was the
name given to the Jew who had a 'life and death' devotion to
Yahweh, and who practised the symbols of his covenant such
as the rite of circumcision, the Torah, the religious calendar,
the dietary laws and the sanctity of the Temple. The 'zealot'
was prepared to kill and be killed for the honour of the Lord
if any of these symbols was violated.

None knew better than Paul the dangers of 'zeal'. The pre-
Christian Paul had been just that, a 'zealot' for God (Phil. 3:6: 'as
to *zeal*, a persecutor of the church'). Saul of Tarsus had, in effect,
killed Stephen and other followers of Jesus, the dangerous
pseudo-messiah, as Paul then regarded him. Stephen's offence
in Paul's eyes was his attack on the Temple and his alleged
criticism of the Law of Moses (see Acts 6:11-14).

But their patriotic 'zeal' for the symbols of the covenant
was not informed by 'knowledge', that is, of the crucified
and risen Messiah, Jesus. By 'knowledge' Paul is referring to
'knowing' the 'righteousness that comes from God' (v. 3).

For, not knowing	the righteousness	that comes from God
and seeking to establish		
their own	[righteousness]	
they did not submit to	the righteousness	that comes from God.

Paul's words 'the righteousness of God'[1] have a double intent
here. First and foremost, Paul means that 'righteousness'

---

1. See on 1:16-17.

which belongs to God and is a mark of his character. As well, however, it is a 'righteousness' God shares with humans, by acquitting them of sins. They can only come by this 'righteousness' on God's terms, not their own. God's way of sharing his 'righteousness' is unexpected. It is only by his grace to those who by believing in Christ are 'in' him, that is, belong to him. But the Jews of whom Paul now speaks know better than God. They seek to establish their own 'righteousness' with God, based on 'works' of the 'Law' (see on 9:31-32).

It is puzzling that Paul does not directly address his Jewish readers. Rather he is speaking to Gentiles and referring to the Jews indirectly as 'they ... them'. Why is this? Surely Paul would pitch his appeal to them? But no. Yet this cannot imply any lack of compassion or care for them (see on 9:1-5; 10:1). Perhaps the explanation is that Paul hoped they would the better hear his encouragement to them if it came indirectly. Whatever the case, it seems clear that Jewish response then was minimal and that Paul saw no immediate prospect of an improved response.

2. RIGHTEOUSNESS FOR THOSE WHO BELIEVE (V. 4)
Paul's words are the more potent for their brevity.

> *For* Christ is the 'end' of the Law
> for righteousness
> for all who believe.

The introductory 'For' ties verse 4 back into the preceding passage (9:30–10:3) and summarizes that passage. Paul describes Israel's futile attempt to establish 'righteousness' based on Law.

9:31   Israel pursued the Law to attain righteousness ...
9:32   [Israel] pursued righteousness based on works ...
10:3   They seek to establish their own righteousness ...

Israel pursued Law for righteousness based on works. But Christ is 'the end' of 'the Law'.

What does Paul intend us to understand by 'end', 'righteousness' and 'believe'?

By his word 'end' (*telos*) Paul has in mind several layers of meaning. First, 'end' means 'end point' or 'goal'. In this sense Christ is the 'fulfilment' of all the hopes, promises and 'visions' of the 'Law', that is, the entire corpus of the Old Testament. But 'end' also means 'that which terminates'. Understood like this, Christ crucified and risen brings Law to an 'end'. In this second layer of meaning, 'Law' is the covenant God gave the people through Moses at Mt. Sinai. As promised by the prophets, however, God established a 'new covenant' based not on Law, but on the promised Christ who died for sins, and on the Spirit who changes the hearts.[2] But this way of 'righteousness' Israel has rejected.

'Righteousness,' the keyword of the entire letter (see on 1:17), was reintroduced in the previous chapter (see on 9:30-31). By 'righteousness' Paul means God's own 'righteousness' that he shares with sinful man (as in v. 3). But on what terms does God give his 'righteousness' to man?

The answer is provided in the words, 'to all who *believe*' (see on 1:16-17; 3:22–5:1), which in context can mean only one thing, namely, 'all who believe' in 'Christ' who is 'the end of the Law'. 'Christ' has fulfilled the 'promises' of the Law and the Prophets as the Davidic Messiah Jesus, crucified and risen. Thus 'Christ' is the One in whom man is to believe, whether Jew or Gentile, to enjoy the gift of God's righteousness.

Earlier Paul had demonstrated that no one – Jew or Gentile – is capable of achieving his own 'righteousness' (see on 1:18-3:20). This teaching is rejected by most Jews who seek to attain the 'righteousness of God' by the 'works' of the 'Law'. Thus throughout Romans Paul sets 'Christ' against 'works' and 'Law' as the means to the 'righteousness of God'. Paul is insisting that only God can declare sinful people 'righteous,' which he does by way of 'gift' or 'donation' to those who

---

2. See, for example, Jeremiah 31:31-35 ('I will make a new covenant ... I will forgive their wickedness') and Ezekiel 36:26 ('I will give you a new heart and put a new spirit within you; I will remove from you your heart of stone and give you a heart of flesh'). See further 2 Corinthians 3:3, 18 ('you are a letter from Christ ... written ... with the Spirit of the living God...on tablets of human hearts'; 'we all ... are being changed ... from ... the Spirit').

'believe' in Jesus, the son of David and the Son of God, crucified and raised.

'All who believe' has a precise meaning. It is not a vague 'believing', a misty religiosity but a personal trust informed by the apostolic gospel that is intentionally directed towards the Son of God and away from any kind of self-effort hoping for acceptance by God.

3. RIGHTEOUSNESS OF LAW AND RIGHTEOUSNESS OF FAITH (vv. 5-7)

In this passage Paul is contrasting two 'words': the 'word' that 'Moses writes', that is, 'a righteousness based on Law' (v. 5), with the 'word' of 'righteousness based on faith' (vv. 6-7). This continues Paul's contrast between 'Law' and 'faith' begun at 9:30.

First, Paul lets 'righteousness based on Law' speak (v. 5).

> For Moses writes concerning the righteousness that is based on Law, 'The man who does these things will live by them.'

Paul is quoting Leviticus 18:5 where Moses is speaking to the people at Mt. Sinai, setting before them the requirements of the covenant of their rescuer-Lord. That covenant with its requirements was a gift of the Lord. It is untrue to claim that the Old Testament is 'works-based' and the New Testament is 'grace-based'. God's initiative in making both the old covenant and the new covenant was 'grace'. Nonetheless, as the unfolding history of the Old Testament shows, Israel failed to 'live by' the Lord's covenantal requirements, just and holy though they were. As Jeremiah observed, 'they broke my covenant' (Jer. 31:32).

Paul's point from the quotation from Leviticus is straightforward.[3] The old covenant required the people to 'live by' its terms. Since they did not do so, that covenant became a 'letter' that 'kills' because it 'condemns' (2 Cor. 3:6, 9).

---

3. Paul also quotes Leviticus 18:5 in Galatians 3:12, to the same end, that is, under that covenant the people were bound to achieve its terms. According to Galatians 3:13, failure to do so meant that the 'Law' brought a curse from God (cf. Gal. 3:10, quoting Deut. 27:26). Evidently Leviticus 18:5 was a text Paul used in his debates with Jews over Law-based righteousness.

Second, Paul turns to the voice of 'righteousness based on faith' to ask two questions (vv. 6-7). Significantly, both questions focus exclusively on 'Christ,' driving home the truth that 'righteousness-based faith' is directed to the Messiah.

But the righteousness based on faith says this:
'Do not say in your heart,
"Who will go up to heaven?"
(that is, to bring Christ down).'

Or,

'[Do not say in your heart,]
"Who will go down to the abyss?"
(that is, to bring Christ up from the dead).'

These words are closely based on, yet in contrast with, Moses' exhortation in Moab to the people of Israel, as they neared the Promised Land (Deut. 30:11-14).

Now what I am commanding you today is not too difficult
    for you
or beyond your reach.

It is not up in heaven, so that you have to ask,
'Who will ascend into heaven to get it and proclaim it to us
so we may obey it?'

Nor is it beyond the sea, so that you have to ask,
'Who will cross the sea to get it and proclaim it to us
so we may obey it?'

No, the word is very near you;
it is in your mouth and in your heart
so you may obey it.

Moses is referring to the Law God has given the people as his side of the covenant. Moses is assuring the Israelites that the Law is 'not difficult ... nor beyond reach ... up in heaven ... nor ... beyond the sea.' Rather, he says, 'the word is near you ... in your mouth and heart'. Historically, however, that 'word' *did* prove to be 'difficult'. And the reason? This 'word' was to be 'obeyed', as Moses declares three times. This the people failed to do, as Paul explained earlier (see on 2:17-24; 3:3-9). Thus Paul is pointedly contrasting Moses' 'word' of the Law that was to be *obeyed* with the apostles' 'word' about Christ that is to be *believed*.

Paul's calculated adaptation of Moses' words is striking in its affirmation about Christ. In the dispensation of the new covenant there are new terms from God's side. Christ, who is to be *believed*, has replaced Law that is to be *obeyed*. The new covenant is personal and relational in character. The old covenant was national and 'works' based.

Christ, however, is not merely a descendant of David, a merely recycled Davidic king. The 'Christ' who has 'come down from heaven' is the pre-existent Son of God incarnate in Jesus of Nazareth, who lived among his people as the Gospels tell us.[4] Furthermore, Christ has been 'brought up from the dead,'[5] that is, from the 'abyss'.[6] Paul is speaking here about *historical* truths regarding Christ incarnate and resurrected that lie at the heart of the apostolic gospel.

4. THE 'WORD' OF 'FAITH' IN 'HEART' AND 'MOUTH' (VV. 8-11)

Paul's rhetorical expression is worth noting in each of these verses.

In verse 8 he again uses 'says' (from verse 6), buttressed with 'But ...' introducing a question ('But what does it say?').

> But what does [the righteousness based on faith] say?
> The word is near,
> in your mouth and in your heart,
> the word of faith which we preach.

Paul's answer is that the 'word' about Christ's incarnation and resurrection must be found in the 'heart' and 'mouth' of

---

4. See earlier on 1:3; 8:3, 32.

5. See on 1:4; 4:25; 6:4-9.

6. Where Moses speaks of 'the sea' Paul speaks of the 'abyss'. The two were connected in Old Testament thought (cf. Ps. 107:25-26).

believers, just as the 'word' of the Law was to be found in the 'heart' and 'mouth' of the Israelites (alluding to Deut. 30:14, quoted above). Now, however, Paul introduces a critical point, the role of the preacher. How, by what means, is the 'word' about Christ incarnate and risen now 'near', in the 'mouth' and 'heart' of the Christian believer? That 'word' is there for one reason, because of 'the word of faith which we *proclaim* (*kērussomen*).'

This anticipates his powerful statement beginning in verse 14 and reaching its climax in verse 17 that 'Faith comes from what is heard and what is heard comes from the word of Christ'. Thus verses 8 and 17 tell us there is the 'word (*rhēma* – 'spoken word') of faith' and the 'word (*rhēma* – 'spoken word') of Christ'. The two words are the same; the word about Christ elicits faith in him.

In verse 9 Paul explains further what he means (introduced by 'Because ...'):

Because if you confess with your mouth Jesus as Lord
and believe in your heart that God raised him from the dead
you will be saved.

By the 'word' about Christ being in the 'mouth' Paul means the public confession by the individual in the church (at baptism) and by the gathered assembly that 'Jesus is Lord'. In turn, however, this confession must issue forth from what the 'heart' 'believes'. Not to be missed is the connection between 'the word of faith' about Christ that Paul 'proclaims' and the congregational 'confession' of the Lordship of Jesus Christ. Confession of Christ depends on proclamation of Christ.

Several comments must be made.

First, the Christ who 'came down ... from heaven' has been 'raised from the dead' as 'Lord'. The confession, 'Jesus is Lord,' is a primitive one, going back to the Day of Pentecost and it arises from Jesus' identification of himself as 'Lord' based on Psalm 110:1.[7] By speaking of himself as 'Lord' Jesus is applying to himself the identity of the Old Testament

---

7. Acts 2:36; Mark 12:35-37; cf. 1 Corinthians 12:3; 16:22; 2 Corinthians 4:5.

Yahweh-Lord. It is a claim to deity made by Jesus and for him by the apostles.

Second, the 'confession' of the *mouth* follows upon the 'belief' of the *heart* (or, mind). Mouth follows mind. Such is the force of this confession that it issues in end-time salvation from wrath (cf. 5:9: 'we shall be saved by him from the wrath of God').

Third, 'righteousness' – the key word of the letter and of this passage – is equated with 'salvation'. Both are blessings of the end-time, appropriated now by 'faith' in the Messiah, Jesus.

Fourth, easily missed in translation, we note that the pronouns in verses 5-10 are singular ('*thy* heart ... *thy* mouth'). The New Perspective on Paul helpfully points to the corporate nature of salvation and sanctification. Yet, these singular pronouns remind us that all ecclesiology begins with the *individual* heart's belief and mouth's confession. Besides, believers mostly live out their last days in isolation or in nursing homes, away from the church. Corporate 'righteousness' is important, but it must not be made more important than the individual's relationship with the Lord.

Once more (v. 10), Paul begins with a word linking a new sentence with its predecessor, on this occasion the explanatory, 'For ...' His is a closely argued case.

For one believes	with the heart	for righteousness
and one confesses	with the mouth	for salvation.

The confessor of Jesus as Lord 'will be saved' (v. 9) prompting Paul now to speak of 'salvation' preceded by its synonym 'righteousness', the keyword of Romans. Note the relationship between 'proclaiming,' 'believing' and 'confessing'. The apostle 'proclaims' Christ, and a hearer 'believing' in his heart that God has raised Christ from the dead 'confesses' him to be 'Lord'. Confession issues from belief which in turn issues from proclamation.

Once more Paul begins a new verse with the linking word 'For' (v. 11). This is to carry forward 'righteousness'/'salvation' from the previous verse, which Paul will now connect with 'not put to shame'. He does this by reintroducing a partial quote of Isaiah 28:16 (cited more fully in 9:33). Clearly Paul placed great importance on this text which spoke of the Messiah-'Stone' God had laid in Zion.

> For the Scripture says,
> 'all who believe on him will not be put to shame.'

In this briefer adaptation of Isaiah's text Paul is emphasizing three things.

First, while the base Old Testament text spoke of the individual ('*he* who believes'), Paul's citation is global ('*all* who believe'), preparing us for God's provision of *universal* salvation in the next two verses.

Second, 'believe' is directed to 'him' (the Messiah-'Stone'); the act of 'believing' cannot be separated from its object, Christ. 'Believing' is never undirected.

Third, since 'shame' is an end-time reference to God's rejection of the unworthy, the negative 'not be put to shame' is synonymous with the positives, God's declaration of 'righteousness' to believers and his gift of 'salvation' to them (v. 10).

5. CHRIST IS 'LORD OF ALL' (vv. 12-13)

Yet again Paul commences with the linking word, 'For' (v. 12). On this occasion he is carrying forward the '*all* who believe' from verse 11. That 'all' encompasses the human race, represented by its two categories, 'Jew' and 'Greek'. The former are the covenant people Israel; the latter are the Gentiles, the people of the nations.

> For there is no distinction between Jew and Greek.
> For the same Lord [is Lord] of all,
> [bestowing] riches towards all who call upon him.

Implicit here is Paul's earlier verdict that 'all are under sin,' regardless of whether they are Jews or Greeks (see on 3:9). This was a bitter pill for Jews to swallow. Many Jews patronizingly looked for the inclusion of the Gentiles in the covenant people, provided various conditions were fulfilled (notably circumcision). Their assumption, however, was the absolute security of their own special place in God's purposes. It would not have occurred to them to doubt their own 'inclusion'. Yet Paul argues that very thing, as John the Baptist and Jesus had declared beforehand.[8]

Explicit is the Lordship of Christ – incarnate, risen, ascended – over *both* peoples, Jews and Greeks. 'For he is Lord of all.' What are the 'riches' he grants to those who 'call upon him'? The context makes clear that such 'riches' are the end-time blessings realised now, God's removal of 'shame' and his gifts of 'righteousness' and 'salvation'. What does it mean to 'call upon him'? Quite simply, it means to speak to him in prayer as Lord, asking him for deliverance from the human condition (mortality and sin), as well as other pressing needs.

The apostle now wraps up the passage, begun at verse 5. Yet once more he ties the new sentence back to its predecessor by the link word, 'For'. Apart from 'For', the words that follow are an exact quotation from Joel 2:32, though Paul himself gives no hint of this.

For 'everyone who calls on the name of the Lord will be saved'.

The 'Lord' in Joel's text is Yahweh, the God of the Old Testament. 'Call on Yahweh, and you will be saved,' Joel is saying. Yet the context shows that Paul is referring to the 'Lord' who is 'Christ ... raised from the dead' (v. 7). Remarkably, therefore, Paul is identifying Christ with Yahweh.[9] Earlier we noted that Paul referred to Christ as 'God over all, blessed forever' (see on 9:5). Given Paul's strict Jewishness which insisted on the uniqueness of Yahweh (cf. Deut. 6:4: 'Hear O Israel, the LORD our God, the LORD is one'), his confession of *Jesus* as 'Lord' is, indeed, astonishing. Such a conviction flowed from the risen and exalted Christ's encounter with Paul on the Damascus Road, when the young persecutor himself 'called on the name of the Lord [Jesus]'. From that moment of divine intervention

---

8. Matthew 3:10 (John: 'the axe is already laid at the root of the trees'); Mark 12:9 (Jesus: 'the owner of the vineyard ... will ... give the vineyard to others').

9. For other examples see Isaiah 45:23; Philippians 2:11; Isaiah 40:13; 1 Corinthians 2:16. See further Richard Bauckham, *God Crucified* (Grand Rapids: Eerdmans, 1998).

Paul was convinced that Jesus was the Davidic Christ and the Son of God, crucified, risen and exalted.

6. PROCLAIMING, HEARING AND BELIEVING (vv. 14-15)

Paul's highly rhetorical exposition of 'righteousness based on faith' continues (as from v. 4). Verses 14-15 link back to verses 12 and 13 (by the opening, 'Therefore ...') and pick up 'call on him/his name'. A powerful dramatic effect is established by four questions beginning, 'How ...?', and by the carry over of the keywords 'believe', 'hear' and 'proclaim' into the next question. Finally, the passage is rounded off by a moving biblical citation.

Therefore		
how will they call	on him whom they	have not believed?
But how will they believe	on him whom they	have not heard?
But how will they hear	without a preacher?	
But how will they proclaim	unless they are sent?	

Even as it is written,
'How beautiful the feet of those who proclaim good news.'

These words are a matchless account of God's way of bringing 'salvation' to man. God sends a preacher of the Gospel focused on Christ. Those who 'hear' then 'believe' that 'word' and 'call' on Christ the Lord for salvation. Put another way, *calling* on the Lord depends on *believing, believing* depends on *hearing, hearing* depends on *proclaiming, proclaiming* depends on *being sent* (by God).

Here Paul the apostle presents himself as a prophet of liberation. The words 'the word of faith which we preach' and 'How can they preach unless they are sent?' repeat the words 'preach' and 'sent' the prophet Isaiah uses of himself (Isa. 61:1: 'the LORD has anointed me to *preach* good news to the poor. He has *sent* me to bind up the broken hearted').[10]

---

10. Perhaps Paul knew that Jesus applied Isaiah 61:1 to himself in the sermon in Nazareth (Luke 4:18). If so, did this influence Paul in applying Isaiah 61:1 to apostolic ministry?

Paul's buttressing citation, 'How beautiful are the feet of those who *bring good news*' also springs from Isaiah (Isa. 52:7). In this text Isaiah speaks originally of those like himself who tell the good news to Israel in exile in Babylon that her God reigns and that at last she is to be liberated and restored to her homeland. Paul sees Isaiah's prophecy fulfilled in God's sending forth of evangelists (like himself), who proclaim the 'word of Christ' that liberates captives from prison.

Paul's words are timeless and unbounded by race or ethnicity. Will people away from 'Christian' countries 'believe'? Then God must send preachers so that people can call on the Lord? Will people in moribund churches 'believe'? Again, it will be as a preacher comes who will teach the gospel.

7. NOT ALL OBEY THE GOSPEL (vv. 16-17)
Now, however, Paul casts a shadow over his bright account about God sending evangelists.

> But not all obey the gospel.
> For Isaiah says,
> 'Lord, who has believed what he has heard from us?'

In Greek the words 'hear' (*akouō*) and 'obey' (*hupakouō*) are similar so that Paul intends a 'wordplay' between 'How will they *hear* without a preacher?' (v. 14) and 'But not all *obey* the gospel'. How does one 'obey' the gospel? Paul answered that question in advance when he wrote of 'the obedience *of faith*' (see on 1:5). God speaks the gospel (through evangelists) summoning the hearers to obey him, that is, by directing faith towards Christ. 'Obeying' the gospel, however, is not the same as 'obeying' the Law (see on vv. 6 and 7 above). The former calls us into a grace-based relationship of personal trust in Christ who has come, died and been raised for our salvation. The latter, however, while initiated by grace, required Israelites to fulfil the code of Law given by God at Mt. Sinai which, on account of sin, the people failed to do (see on 7:7-25; cf. 2 Cor. 3:6-11).

But to return to Paul's observation, it is evident from the book of Acts, as well as from experience, that not all who *hear* the gospel *obey* its message directing their faith Christ-wards. While this is a general truth Paul appears to be referring to something specific, that is, by and large Israel has failed to obey the gospel. Paul bases this sad observation on his knowledge of Peter's mission to Israel, as well as his own evangelism among his own people.[11] On the other hand, the Gentiles have responded much more positively. To this double-sided phenomenon – Israel's rejection of Christ and the Gentiles' acceptance of Christ – Paul will soon turn (see on vv. 18-21).

In verse 17 Paul rounds off the section that began in verse 4, beginning with a summarizing link word, 'So then.'

> *So then* faith comes from
> what is heard, and
> what is heard
> is through the word of Christ.

The divine sequence is the proclamation of 'the word of Christ' which is 'heard' then 'believed'. Put Paul's way, 'faith' comes from 'what is heard' and 'what is heard' comes 'through the word of Christ'. Most probably by 'word of Christ' Paul means both 'the word *about* Christ' (his incarnation and resurrection – see on verses 6 and 7) and also 'the word that comes *from* Christ' (through evangelists).

This entire passage, beginning in verse 4, but beyond that earlier in 9:30, is about 'righteousness based on faith' as the only means of salvation from God, of 'not being ashamed' in the end-time. Equally, it is crystal clear that such 'faith' or 'believing' is not *undirected* but Christ-centred and Christ-focused. Further, this Christ-directed faith can only arise from 'the word about Christ' (incarnate and risen). At bedrock, therefore, we must underscore the importance of proclamation of the gospel for faith-in-Christ that attracts God's verdict, 'righteous'.

---

11. Peter as the first missioner to Israel (Gal. 2:7-9; Acts 2–12 *passim*); Paul, too, evangelised Jews in Palestine (see on Romans 15:19: 'from Jerusalem in an arc round to Illyricum I have fulfilled the gospel'; cf. Acts 9:26; 26:20: 'First to those in Damascus, then to those in Jerusalem and in all Judaea ... I preached ...').

8. Israel has heard but not obeyed (vv. 18-21)

Paul now resumes his wrestle with Israel's failure (as a nation) to embrace the gospel, picking up this theme from verses 1-3 and 9:1-5. They have 'not obeyed' the gospel (v. 16). Is this because they have 'not heard' the gospel (v. 18)? This would excuse them, perhaps. But no. They have, 'indeed,' heard[12] (v. 18b). Paul buttresses this assertion by quoting Psalm 19:4

Their voice   has gone out into all   the earth
Their words   to the ends of   the inhabited world.

Whether in Palestine or in the Jewish diaspora, whether by Peter, apostle to the circumcised, by Paul or by others, the 'voice' and the 'words' of evangelists has 'gone forth' every-where.

Again Paul asks plaintively, 'Surely Israel did not understand' (v. 19). His inference, however, is that Israel did 'understand'[13] just as she had, indeed, 'heard.' Once more Paul supports his observation by a biblical text, on this occasion quoting Moses in Deuteronomy 32:21.

I will make you jealous
by those who are not a nation,
by a nation that is foolish
I will make you angry.

Israel will be 'jealous' and 'angry' on account of the 'voice' of preachers going out everywhere and being 'heard' and 'believed' by Gentiles. Paul clinches his sad observation about Israel by two further texts, Isaiah 65 verses 1 and 2 respectively.

Isaiah is so bold as to say,
'I was found by those who did not seek me
I have revealed myself to those who did not ask for me.'

and

---

12. English translation cannot bring out the subtlety of Paul's expression. His question, 'Have they not heard?' is so framed as to suggest that the Jews have not heard, thus releasing them from blame. But this escape is short-lived since he adds immediately, 'Indeed [they have!]' (*menounge*).

13. But cf. verse 3: '*not* knowing the righteousness that comes from God.'

Of Israel he says,
'All day long I have held out my hands
to a disobedient and perverse people.'

Despite God's 'great patience' with Israel (see on 9:22) they have proved to be 'disobedient and perverse'. Consequently, God has revealed himself to the Gentiles who had 'not sought' for him thus making the people of Israel 'angry'. Paul is probably hinting at the anger of many Jews directed at him for his mission to the Gentiles and their encouraging response to his preaching of Christ.

But this prompts the painful question, 'Has God rejected his people?' To this he now turns.

9. REVIEW OF PAUL'S ARGUMENT

In this chapter Paul has given a passionate account narrating how Christ 'came' and was 'raised from the dead' (vv. 6-7) and how God 'sent' evangelists to Israel. The 'word' they preached was to be 'obeyed', that is, by 'believing' in Christ, 'calling on' him and confessing him as 'Lord'. Tragically, however, the people of Israel have, by and large, refused to 'believe' in Christ for 'righteousness', instead they have sought to establish their own by 'works' of the 'Law'. That word has now gone forth to the nations where many have received it, to the anger of many in Israel.

10. THEOLOGICAL OBSERVATIONS

Paul's argument is close-knit, with each statement depending on its predecessor joined by link-words and, very frequently, reinforced by a scriptural citation. Clearly Paul is addressing a pastoral situation known to him and, of course, to his readers. We, however, can only make an educated guess why Paul makes the points he does. Whatever the actual circumstances of his readers were, Paul's words are both timeless and timely.

(i) God's purposes are continuous and his ways consistent. God makes men and women his children through his 'word' of promise based on his will in showing mercy to whom he will. True, the temporary dispensation of Law is ended, replaced by God's permanent 'new' covenant centred in Christ and the Spirit. Yet the centrality of the 'word of God' remains. This is the gospel-word that God gives his righteousness to those who, by faith, belong to his Son.

(ii) The 'New Perspective' on Paul is correct in reminding us that Romans, including chapter 10, was directed to a dispute between Paul and the Jews over a Law-based righteousness. Most likely those Jews included Christian Israelites, as well as those who were hostile to Jesus the Christ, as Paul himself had been.

This does not mean, however, that Romans 10 is irrelevant to later disputes over righteousness/justification between Luther and the papacy. Throughout its history Christianity has revealed a tendency to 'works'-based 'righteousness' as tenacious as that displayed by the Jews (as reflected in Romans). Christian ritual is different from that found in Judaism, as are the moral requirements. Nonetheless, fallen human nature is determined to find 'righteousness' from God based on self-effort. Thus while the letter must always be understood in its historical context by a thorough reading from the 'inside', its message centred in 'righteousness' as God's gift is timeless and permanently timely.

(iii) Romans 10 is powerfully centred on Christ as the 'end of the Law,' who 'came from heaven' as the 'Stone' God 'laid in Zion' and who was 'raised from the dead'. The temporary dispensation of Law is 'ended,' replaced by the permanent dispensation of Christ and the Spirit.

(iv) The apostle offers the readers a splendid account of the process by which God brings 'righteousness'/'salvation' to man. 'Faith' that attracts the 'righteousness of God' comes by 'hearing' the 'word of faith' (v. 8), that is, the 'word of Christ' (v. 17) coming from the mouth of a preacher who has been 'sent' by God.

(v) Modernity and globalisation have to a degree destroyed the distinction between Christian and non-Christian countries. Only in a relative way can any nation today be called 'Christian'. How will that be changed? By preachers being 'sent' who 'preach' Christ so that, by the grace of God, their hearers then call on his name.

(vi) Paul's sense of tragedy at Israel's rejection of Christ is appropriately felt whenever any person or group becomes closed off from Christ. Sadly this is as true of many churches as it was of Israel in Paul's day. Corrosive liberalism and a preoccupation with ritual are the chief culprits.

STUDY QUESTIONS

1. How has 'zeal' become such a negative word today?

2. How is promise different from law?

3. What can God's righteousness do for me that the law cannot do? Why then do so many cling to law or works?

4. How was the Old Testament Law grace-based?

5. How can I be sure that I have a grace-based faith and not a works-based faith?

6. With such joy in our salvation, why are so many believers reluctant to confess Christ and proclaim Him? Why is it seemingly left up the 'professionals' such as ministers and evangelists?

7. What connection is Paul making with the Old Testament by declaring that Christ is Lord of all?

8. How does obeying the gospel and obeying the law differ?

9. Does this understanding of a 'preacher being sent' increase my vision for global missions?

12

The Triumph of Mercy
(Romans 11:1-36)

God has not rejected his historic people Israel, though many Israelites are 'hardened' to the message about their Messiah, Jesus. Nonetheless, since God must keep his promises to the patriarchs he will save them at some time in the future. This will follow the ingathering of the Gentiles. Meanwhile, the Gentile believers must not be high-minded but remember the tree into which they have been grafted. God's salvation of Jews and Gentiles speaks of God's mercy.

1. GOD HAS NOT REJECTED HIS PEOPLE (vv. 1-6)
Once more Paul reflects aloud about Israel's rejection of her Messiah when he came among them (9:32: 'they have stumbled over the stumbling stone'). Furthermore, they have 'not believed ... the word of Christ' (10:16-17) that preachers have echoed again and again in their synagogues, both in Palestine and the Diaspora (10:18).

Why is Paul continuing to address this concern with the Romans? As we have noted throughout this commentary, out there in Rome were Jewish critics to whom Paul must respond. Are we able to identify their questions to Paul? Most probably, yes. Earlier Paul's insistence that 'the word of God has not failed' (9:6) was his answer to these Jewish critics. Cleverly they pointed to Israel's non-acceptance of Jesus and to Paul's mission to the Gentiles. They challenged him to admit that God's promises to Israel had 'failed'. Such a thing is unthinkable, they imply; God must be true. The only ominous conclusion was that it was Paul, therefore, who was untrue and in error in his preaching of Christ.

Now Paul begins once more to engage his critics, but on a slightly different tack. Paul puts these words in the mouth of a Jewish critic. 'If, as you claim, God's word of promise has not failed, then God must have rejected his people. How else can you explain the pitifully small number of Jews who acknowledge Jesus as Messiah?'

In reply, twice (vv. 1 and 2) Paul exclaims, God has not rejected his people,' adding in the second instance, 'his people *whom he foreknew.*' He repeats the theme of 'foreknowledge' in verse 5 ('*chosen* by grace').

Paul justifies his confidence in God's ongoing dealings with Israel by referring to himself (v. 1b).

> I myself am an Israelite,
> from the seed of Abraham,
> from the tribe of Benjamin.

Paul must remind them that he, too, is a member of the house of Israel, a descendant of Saul her first king, no less.[1] And he Paul, a Jew, has recognized Jesus as the messianic son of David, the 'Stone' God has laid in Zion (9:32-33).

In verses 2-4 Paul goes on to quote the prophet Elijah who even 'appealed to God *against* Israel' (1 Kings 19:18):

> Lord, your prophets *they* have killed
>   your altars *they* have torn down.
> I only am left and *they* seek my life.

Note the repeated 'they,' referring to God's people, Israel, who have even attempted to kill the *only remaining* prophet of God! Elijah thought that God's light in the darkness in Israel was a mere flickering candle, about to be extinguished. Paul's life, like Elijah's, was 'sought' by his own people (2 Cor. 11:26).

---

1. For other references by Paul to his Jewishness, see 2 Corinthians 11:22; Philippians 3:5-6; Galatians 1:13-14.

But now Paul reminds his readers of God's reply to his prophet.

'I have kept for myself seven thousand men
who have not bowed the knee to Baal.'

God is faithful and God is powerful. Elijah needed to know, as did Paul's Jewish critics, as today we also need to remember, that *God* had 'kept' for himself thousands who were faithful to him. When things look bleak in the churches and church leaders disappoint, as they sometimes do, we easily adopt the 'Elijah' attitude ('I only am left'). But we must not leave God out of our reckoning.

In verse 5 Paul draws his conclusions from Elijah's example:

Thus, at this present time also,
there is a remnant
according to election by grace.

Let the Jewish critics grasp that, as in the time of Elijah, there *is* (and there *will be*[2]) a 'remnant' (*leimma*; cf. 9:27, *hupo-leimma*) of Jewish believers. There was but a tiny group of Jewish Christians in apostolic times. There continues to be a 'remnant' of Jewish Christians, whether in Israel or elsewhere. According to the meaning of Paul's words, there will always be at least some Christian believers among the Jews. This, surely, is an encouragement to press on with ministry among the Jews.

Paul rounds off the passage with a reminder that the saving faith of this remnant of Jews is 'by grace' (so, verse 5: 'according to election by grace'). But this means it is not 'by works'.

If it is by grace, it is no longer by works.
Otherwise grace is no longer grace.

Once more Paul insists that 'grace ... no[t] ... works' is the only basis for Jews acknowledging Christ. God's 'election'

---

2. Based on *gegonen*, which is a perfect tense indicating a past event and an ongoing reality.

(v. 5) demands that his 'grace' is the only route to knowing Jesus as the Messiah. If that way was by means of 'works', it could not be 'by grace'. The one must cancel out the other. But this is precisely why Jewish response to Christ has been so minimal. When confronted with Jesus of Nazareth and the apostles' preaching of Christ, Jews rejected the reality of his identity and his saving work, insisting instead on securing 'righteousness' with God based on 'works of the Law' (see on 9:31–10:3). The symbols of their covenant – the Temple, the Law, the religious calendar, the dietary laws and circumcision – were more important to them than the One who had so recently come among them.

2. THE HARDENING (vv. 7-10)

Paul begins with a rhetorical question, 'What then?', as he continues to reflect on Christ's catalytic impact upon Israel. So he declares:

> What Israel was seeking, this she did not find.

But we are curious as to the meaning. We ask, 'what' was Israel 'seeking' that 'she did not find'? The answer is found by reference to 9:31–10:2. The coming of Christ to Israel gave the nation the opportunity to accept or reject the messianic 'Stone' prophesied by Isaiah. The Gospels narrate the tragic story of disputes between Israel's religious leaders and her Messiah. The Pharisees in Galilee rejected Jesus in favour of their sabbaths, fastings and washings and the Temple leaders had him killed because of his teachings about their Holy Place. In short, they preferred their 'Law' to the Lord's Anointed One, the Messiah.

In rejecting her king and his 'righteousness', Israel *de facto* was seeking to establish her own 'right standing' with God. This she did by 'works of the Law', that is, by the religious practices of Judaism rather than 'by faith', which would have been seen in their turning to the One who had come. By Christ's presence among them, Israel's beliefs, values and relationship with God were revealed as based on self-effort.

Paul is overstating things a little in saying 'What *Israel* was seeking ...' Some, that is, 'the elect' among Israel did, indeed, find 'righteousness' from God. Paul is doubtless thinking of the disciples of Jesus and others like himself who have come to recognize Jesus as the 'One who was to come'. By grace, and through the preaching of Christ, the elect found 'righteousness', though by faith not works. What, then, of 'the rest' who did not?

But the rest were hardened.

While the Greek word 'hardened' differs from that used earlier in relationship to Pharaoh (9:18: 'God ... hardens the hearts of whomever he wills'), there can be no doubt that Paul intends the readers to make a connection between the 'hardening' of Pharaoh and the 'hardening' of Israel.

The passive voice 'were hardened' indicates that *God* 'hardened the rest'. This is the antinomy, or apparent contradiction, between two principles. On the one hand, *Israel* hardened her heart and chose to reject Christ (cf. 10:16: '*they have not all obeyed the gospel*'), just as Pharaoh rejected God's word that Moses spoke to him. Yet, on the other hand, it must be recognized that God, being God, is the ultimate source of all actions. Thus, *God* hardened the rest. It is impossible to reconcile these polarities by human logic, though it is important we accept both elements. Unlike Pharaoh, who kept hardening his heart and was finally destroyed, the passages following shows that Paul held out hope for Israel's ultimate deliverance. But there is a solemn warning for us. Disobedience to God and unbelief do not leave us unaffected. Disobedience progressively hardens us to the Word of God so that we may reach a point when we do not hear him speaking to us.

In verses 8-9 Paul undergirds his statement with several texts from the Old Testament, each of which emphasizes God's role in 'hardening' the disobedient.

Verse 8

> Even as it is written,
> God gave them a spirit of drowsiness,[3]
> eyes that do not see and ears that do not hear.

---

3. The Greek word *katanuxis* is an intensification of *nux*, 'night', and captures the idea of torpor or extreme sleepiness.

Paul has combined two significant passages from the Greek Old Testament. In the first, from Deuteronomy 29:4, the Israelites have 'seen' the miracle of their escape through the Red Sea but the Lord has 'not given them a heart to know, and eyes to see and ears to hear' until forty years later. In the second, from Isaiah 29:10, the Lord has given the disobedient people a 'spirit of deep sleep' so that the words of Isaiah will be to them like 'the words of a sealed book'. Most likely Paul chose these passages pointedly. The Israelites have seen, but yet have not 'seen,' the miracle of the Exodus or the miracles of Jesus. The Israelites have heard but not 'heard' the words of Isaiah or the words of Paul; God gave in both instances 'a spirit of drowsiness'.

To this (v. 9) Paul adds:

> David says,
> Let their table be as a snare and a trap for them
> and as a stumbling block and retribution for them.
> Let their eyes be darkened so that they not be able to see
> and bend their backs forever.

Paul has taken these words verbatim from Psalm 69:22 (from the Greek Old Testament). Strikingly, the whole psalm speaks of David's sufferings at the hands of persecutors among his own people. Metaphorically speaking, these persons have put gall in David's food and vinegar in his drink. David is praying that the 'table' God places before them will likewise be bitter. Most likely Paul has chosen this text because of his kinship with David in sufferings from his own people (cf. Ps. 69:8: 'I am a stranger to my brothers, an alien to my own mother's sons'). Paul's testimony to Jesus has brought him much pain from fellow Israelites. Paul suffered greatly at Jewish hands (1 Thess. 2:14-15: 'the Jews ... drove us out'; 2 Cor. 11:24: 'five times I have received at the hands of the Jews the forty lashes less one'; 11:26: 'danger from my own countrymen'). Nonetheless, while David prayed for God permanently to punish the fractious Israelites, Paul, for his part, looked for the ultimate salvation of his people. To this we now turn.

3. The Salvation of Israel (vv. 11-16)

The following passage is full of hope for the ultimate salvation of Israel. To that point the nation had resisted the claims of the Messiah Jesus, preferring to secure her own 'righteousness' based on Law.

From 10:18 Paul is concluding his personal explanation ('I say ...') regarding God's dealings with Israel, which he began at 9:1:

10:18	'But I say ...'
11:1	'Therefore I say ...'
11:11	'Therefore I say ...'
11:13	'But I say to you Gentiles ...'

Here is Paul, minister of God and apostle of Christ, declaring the word of the Lord about the future salvation of Israel. It is helpful to reproduce verses 11-16 since the whole of Paul's thinking needs to be before us.

11 Have they stumbled so as to fall? In no way!
    But by their transgression salvation has come to the Gentiles,
    so as to make Israel jealous.

12 But if their transgression has meant riches for the world,
    and their failure riches for the Gentiles,
    how much more will their full inclusion mean?

13 But I say to you Gentiles
    to the degree that I am the apostle to the Gentiles
    I glorify my ministry

14 if somehow I may make jealous my fellow countrymen.

15 For if their rejection means the reconciliation of the world,
    what will their acceptance be except life from the dead?

16 For if the first-fruits are holy, so also the whole lump,
    and if the roots are holy, so also the branches.

So what is Paul saying? Clearly while Israel has 'stumbled' over Christ the 'Stone' (see on 9:33), she has not fallen to the ground; there is still hope. But how? Paul has enormous confidence in the goodness and faithfulness of God. God's great cosmic plan for the world is being worked out as Paul and others preach the gospel to the Gentiles (v. 13).

(i) True, Israel's 'trespass'[4] and 'failure' in rejecting Christ has meant the riches of the gospel have been brought to the Gentiles by Paul and others (vv. 11-12).

(ii) The influx of Gentiles into the kingdom of God and the Abrahamic covenant will stir the Jews to jealousy (v. 11; cf. Deut. 32:21b: 'I will make them envious by those who are not a people'). When Jews see Gentiles streaming in, they will be stirred to enter themselves. Possibly this had been Paul's own experience as he ministered to Gentiles in Syria-Cilicia, encouraging him to engage more fully in his westward mission work among Gentiles.

(iii) But the absence of Israel from the centre of God's purposes must be temporary. Jews expected an ingathering of the Gentiles, but attached to Israel (Zech. 8:23: 'In those days ten men from all languages and nations will take hold of one Jew ... and say, "Let us go with you, because ... God is with you."'). Paul speaks of 'their full inclusion' (v. 12) and 'their acceptance' (v. 15), that is, their acceptance of God and God's acceptance of them.

(iv) Paul reasoned that 'their rejection' (their rejection of Christ and God's rejection of them) meant the reconciliation of the world (that is, the gospel coming to Gentiles). How much more will 'their acceptance' (their acceptance of Christ and God's acceptance of them) mean? Nothing short of 'life from the dead', that is, 'the resurrection of the dead.' In other words, Israel's acceptance of Christ will mean the climax of the ages, the onset of the kingdom of God following the universal resurrection.

(v) Paul's analogies in verse 16 relate to the 'elect' within Israel who, like Paul, acknowledge Jesus as Messiah. He is making a simple point. If the 'first-fruits' of sacrificed cake is

---

4. The Greek term *paraptōma* is translated 'fall', as for Adam (5:15).

'holy', so is the whole batch (see Num. 15:17-21). If the 'roots' are 'holy', so are the leaves. These refer to the 'remnant', those small numbers of believing Israelites (see on v. 5). Since they are 'holy', so too will the fully included Israel be 'holy'.

The 'full inclusion' of Israel relates to the people of that nation calling on the name of the Lord Jesus. Since God through Paul makes these splendid promises about Israel how important will it be to press ahead with ministry to the Jewish people.

Paul gives no time frame for these hopes. Nor should we. Nonetheless, such is the intensity of his hope that it can scarcely be doubted. Clearly, too, this is an implied mandate for concerted ministry to Jews.

4. A WARNING TO GENTILES (vv. 17-24)

Paul continues the imagery of 'roots ... branches' for Israel set out in the previous verse. He is imagining the 'tree' of historic Israel growing up from the 'roots' planted by God. Based on this (v. 17), he portrays some branches of the cultivated tree broken off and 'wild' branches grafted in. These 'wild' branches are Gentile believers.

Modern English, unlike Paul's Greek, does not distinguish between 'you' singular and 'you' plural. Throughout this passage the singular forms are used, making it deeply personal and emotionally powerful. Whenever we read 'you', it is helpful to remember Paul is exhorting individual Gentile readers.

> And you, a wild olive, are grafted in among them
> and are participants in the rich root of the olive tree.

The original 'tree' is a cultivated olive. The grafted branches have no place there since they are a different species, a wild olive. This is a rather unusual word picture. Understandably various attempts have been made to explain the horticultural impossibility of grafting one species on to an entirely different species. Most likely, Paul was no authority on horticulture. He is making one simple but very important point. It is by grace alone that the Gentiles are included, grafted in to the tree of historic Israel.

So Paul warns in verse 18, 'Do not boast over the branches.' This does not mean, 'Boast over *yourselves* as branches' but 'do not despise *the branches that were broken off* to make way for you'. These Gentile Christians need to remember that, historically, 'the root supports the branch'; 'the branch does not support the root.' Paul is saying, 'Never forget the "root" and the "tree" into which you were grafted.'

A little reading between the lines leads us to detect in Paul's words a degree of pride on the part of some Gentile believers in Rome, and with it perhaps some haughtiness in regard to their predecessors in Israel. Arrogance towards predecessors is not uncommon as it is easy to regard those who have gone before us, whether in our churches or in the broader society, as inferior. We easily think we know better or do better than them.

In verses 19-20, Paul offers sober advice in his dialogue with individual Gentile Christians. First, he instructs the Gentile believer to remind himself that he is only 'grafted in' because others have been 'broken off.' Then Paul adds an explanatory comment based on a wordplay 'un-faith ... faith,'[5] followed by an exhortation to humility.

> Say [to yourself],
>   'Branches were broken off that I might be grafted in.'
>
> [Paul adds],
>   'True.
>   They were broken off by [their] *un-faith*.
>   But by *faith* you stand.
>   Do not be high minded, but fear.'

Paul is speaking to a unique historical context long since passed. Nonetheless, I should take note that I, too, am 'grafted in' to God's people only by God's kindness. But this calls for ongoing faith, humility before God and holy fear. Thus Paul warns, in verse 21, 'If God did not spare the natural branches, he will not spare you.'

---

5. The Greek reads *apistia ... pistis.*

Paul is writing these chapters as a historian and theologian. As a historian employing the 'allegory of the olive', he narrates the story of many in Israel refusing to acknowledge Jesus, her messianic king, and the Gentiles' unexpected welcome of him. As a theologian Paul explains and interprets these events. So he invites the Gentile reader to stand back from these events and 'take in' the grandeur of God's handiwork in history (v. 22).

Behold the kindness and severity of God.
Upon those who fall, severity.
Upon you, kindness – if you remain in his kindness.
Otherwise you, too, will fall.

Remember that Paul is using singular forms of speech. He is addressing the individual Gentile Christian, imploring him to 'remain in' the kindness of God. Otherwise, he too will fall, as a majority of Jews have.

Paul, however, wishes to point up the 'kindness' of God above his 'severity'. In verse 23, he continues to hold out hope for Jews who have thus far rejected the Messiah:

But even these will be re-grafted into the tree
if they do not continue in unbelief.
For God is able to re-graft them.

This, however, is not only about God's 'kindness'. This is also Paul's quiet way of focusing the mind of the Gentile Christian who is taking his salvation for granted and proudly boasting against the Jews who have been 'broken off.' 'Take care,' Paul is saying. 'You may fall away and your place could once again be taken by a Jew.'

So in verse 24 Paul concludes his allegory of the olive tree. He is warning Gentile Christians against complacency and arrogance.

For if you were cut from a wild olive
and grafted against nature into a cultivated olive,
how much more will these natural branches
be grafted into their own olive tree?

At least three contemporary lessons should be drawn from these words.

First, a general comment. God is master in his universe, including within the apparently autonomous human will. Believers should not become great in their own eyes. The mercy of God is all. He made faith possible.

Second, and more specifically, Paul's gracious tones towards his fellow-Jews should find an echo in all Gentile hearts. In generations after the New Testament, Gentiles were to treat Jews as messiah-murderers. Holocaust and genocide occurred against the sustained background of anti-Semitism in Christian Europe. Paul, however, never sounds that note.

Third, also specifically, Paul words about the re-gathering of Jews are an implicit goad to ongoing mission ministry among Jews.

5. 'All Israel will be saved' (vv. 25-27)

Paul speaks about 'this mystery'. By this he means a secret plan or intention previously not understood but now made clear. Unseen to the naked eye God had been working away, preparing for the moment of 'revelation' Paul is speaking about. In the gospel the 'mystery' is revealed (cf. 16:25) and Paul does not want the Roman Christians to be 'uninformed about it' (v. 25).

What is this 'mystery'?

> A hardening in part has befallen Israel
> until the fullness of the Gentiles comes in.

The words 'a hardening in part' makes the same point as the 'allegory of the olive' where some branches were broken from the tree. In consequence, the 'fullness of the Gentiles' will come in, that is, making up the whole.

The 'fullness of the Gentiles' coming in will precipitate in turn the 'fullness' (*plērōma*) of the Jews (see on v. 12), that is, their 'acceptance' (*proslēmpsis* – v. 15) that Jesus is the Christ. In turn this will mean nothing short of 'life from the dead', the resurrection of the dead at the Last Day. The 'mystery' of God revealed by the gospel is that the 'hardening in part of Israel' provides for the entry of the 'fullness of the Gentiles', which will be followed by the salvation of Israel. Thus he makes this statement, full of hope:

Thus all Israel will be saved.

The word 'thus' (*houtōs*) denotes 'process' or 'mode' – 'in this manner all Israel will be saved.'[6] Part of Israel is hardened opening the way to the inclusion of the 'fullness' of the Gentiles hastening the entry of the 'fullness of the Jews' (v. 12).

What, then, does Paul mean by 'all Israel'? Broadly, three answers have been given.[7]

First, 'all Israel' refers to *all the elect, both Jews and Gentiles* (Calvin, N. T. Wright). The difficulty with this view is that Paul goes on immediately referring to Jews; Gentiles are not under discussion at this point.

Second, 'all Israel' refers to *the ethnic nation as a whole on earth at the end-time* (Moo). Here the problem is that God's purposes had not been co-extensive with the whole nation under the old covenant, but only with elect individuals within Israel (see on 9:6-13).

Third, 'all Israel' refers to the elect from Israel throughout history (Hoffius). This is the best answer and is consistent with God's choice and salvation of a remnant of his people (see on 11:1-10).

But how will 'all Israel' – so understood – be saved? Paul gives the answer by the citation together of a number of Old Testament prophecies (Isa. 59:20-21; 27:9) that point to the future salvation of Israel:

Even as it is written,
'A deliverer will come forth from Zion
and turn ungodliness from Jacob.
And this will be my covenant with them
when I take away their sins.'

---

6. It is less likely that *houtōs* refers to (1) a *temporal* understanding ('and *then* all Israel will be saved'), or (2) a *logical* understanding ('and *in consequence of this process* all Israel will be saved').

7. See B. L. Merkle, 'Romans 11 and the Future of Ethnic Israel,' *Journal of the Evangelical Theological Society*, 43/4 (2000), pp. 709-21, who argues for option (3) above.

'All Israel' will be saved by 'a deliverer' who 'will come forth from Zion,' that is, from heaven. Most likely, this refers to the *parousia*[8] or 'second coming' of Jesus the Christ for his people (cf. 13:11: 'our salvation is nearer to us now than when we first believed').

Some have taken this to mean that at Christ's appearing Israel will then repent ('be turned from ungodliness') and find forgiveness ('I will take away their sins').[9] It would be unwise to derive such a conclusion based on citations of Old Testament texts. Such texts are not 'freestanding' but cited to buttress statements Paul is making.

In our view, therefore, this passage lends no weight to the idea that Israel will turn to Christ at his appearing. The future salvation of elect 'Israelites' will not be different from God's present provision for the salvation of Gentiles. Any notion of a future salvation of Jews apart from the redemption of individuals through the usual processes of gospel ministry is excluded. The gospel is what it is and it will not become something else for the coming deliverance of God's elect from his historic people.[10]

6. THE TRIUMPH OF MERCY (vv. 28-32)
Paul continues to address the Gentile believers in Rome. In verse 28 he makes this carefully 'balanced' statement.

| According to the gospel | they are | enemies on your account. |
| According to election | they are | beloved on account of the fathers. |

Questions arise. What is 'gospel'? How are the Jews to be thought of as 'enemies for the sake of you' Gentiles? By 'gospel' Paul probably means the message that, in Christ, God is now reaching out to Gentiles as well as Jews with his salvation.

8.. The term *parousia*, meaning 'coming' or 'presence', does not occur in Romans.

9. For a discussion with rebuttal of this suggestion, see M.G. Vanlaningham, 'Should the Church Evangelize Israel ? A Response to Franz Mussner and other *Sonderweg* Proponents,' *Trinity Journal* (22 NS, 2001), pp. 197-217.

10. Paul's vision for the salvation of Israel relates to the descendants of Jacob, both in Palestine and in the diaspora. It does not relate to the State of Israel, a political entity.

The Jews have proved to be 'enemies' of God and subject to his wrath because they have both rejected Christ (9:30-10:4, 16-21) and the idea that God's salvation should come to the nations.

Further, as Paul has been saying, this 'enmity' has been 'for you' Gentiles. The 'hardening' of Israel has provided the opportunity for the ingathering of Gentiles (through evangelism – cf. 15:18-19). But the first leg of verse 28 is true only of the interim period ahead of Israel's ultimate 'acceptance' of Christ (see on v. 11). The second leg of the verse, however, sets out the absolute and long-term view. Based on 'election', the people of Israel are 'beloved' of God on account of the promises made to the patriarchs (cf. 15:8: 'Christ became a servant of the circumcised, in order to confirm the promises made to the patriarchs').

By his 'For' introducing verse 29, Paul explains this 'long-term' and absolute statement in the previous verse:

For the gifts and the calling of God are unchangeable.

By using 'gifts ... of God', Paul picks up his words at the beginning of the entire Jew-Gentile passage comprising chapters 9–11 (9:4: 'the Israelites ... whose is the adoption, the glory, the covenants, the giving of the Law, the worship, the promises, the fathers and from whom is the Christ ...'). Along with these 'gifts' Paul adds 'the calling' (echoing 'election' from v. 28). Paul insists that these 'gifts' and this 'calling' are 'unchangeable' (*ametamelēta* – RSV, 'irrevocable'). In other words, God's election of Israel and his promises to the patriarchs were no passing thing; rather they established a permanently stated divine will for this people. The fulfilment of that 'will' still lies in the future with the 'salvation of Israel' at the 'coming of a deliverer' (see on v. 26).

Two implications flow from this. One is that God expresses his will across the whole Bible, beginning in the old covenant and worked out in the new covenant. True, the new covenant fulfils and 'ends' the old covenant (10:4). Yet God's pledges and promises to the 'fathers' of that nation stand for all time.

We must not read the New Testament apart from the Old Testament, as if the promises to the patriarchs have not been made by God. The other implication is the ongoing call of God to bring the 'word of Christ' to Israelites, whether in Palestine or the diaspora. God will save 'all Israel' (v. 26), but he will do so by the gospel.

Yet in verses 30-31, Paul tells the Gentiles how the 'mystery' of the salvation of 'all Israel' will be worked out:

> For just as you were once disobedient to God
> but now have received mercy by their disobedience
> so now they have been disobedient,
> that by the mercy shown to you
> they all may receive mercy.

Before the advent of Christ and the proclamation of the gospel of Christ the Gentiles were 'disobedient to God'. Following the disobedience of Israel (the 'hardening' – vv. 7, 25), the divine mercy came to the Gentiles. By the 'mercy' of God in the coming of the gospel to the Gentiles the Jews, too, will receive mercy (see on vv. 11-16).

Paul insists on the triumph of God's mercy over his wrath upon the disobedient. In verse 32 he concludes:

> God has confined all unto disobedience
> that he may show mercy to all.

By 'all', Paul means 'all' in the sense of 'both' Jews and Gentiles. In distinctive ways, the members of each people group has been disobedient to the revelation of God: the Gentiles had been disobedient to the revelation of God in the created world around them, the Jews had been disobedient to the Messiah God sent among them. Yet through the gospel God is showing mercy, and he will show mercy to the members of each, both Gentiles and Jews. God is entirely justified in showing wrath to Gentiles and Jews on the Last Day, as argued in the first three chapters of Romans. But the gospel of Christ brings the 'righteousness' of the end time to those who cleave by faith to Jesus the Messiah, crucified and risen. In his mysterious purposes God is showing his mercy to Gentiles through the hardening of the greater number of Israelites which will result ultimately in the salvation of Israel, in accord with the promises to the patriarchs. Thus revealed are God's dominant characteristics, his faithfulness to his promise, but also his mercy to the disobedient. 'Mercy' is a keyword in this letter.[11]

It is not too much to say that, in preaching the gospel to Jews and Gentiles, Paul the apostle was an instrument bringing the mercy of God to these peoples.

7. DOXOLOGY (vv. 33-36)
Paul concludes this chapter and, indeed, the entire exposition of the 'mystery' of God's mercy to all people in chapters 9–11 with a powerful doxology (see also 16:25-27).

O the depth of the riches and wisdom and knowledge of God.
How unsearchable are his judgements and inscrutable his ways.
For who has known the mind of the Lord?
Or who has been his counsellor?
Who has given to him that he might be repaid?
Because from him and through him and for him are all things.
To him be glory forever. Amen.

We note the structure: (1) Paul begins by declaring God's riches, wisdom and knowledge and the inscrutability of his plans. Then (2) he poses three rhetorical questions to drive home the greatness and the mystery of God. Next (3) he ascribes to God mastery over history as its source, means and destination. Finally (4), he ascribes eternal glory to God.

Under the impulse of the Spirit of God Paul has given us one of his most inspiring utterances. How comforting to know that the God of the universe is such a Being as this. God is all-knowing, all-powerful *and* merciful.

But we ask, what has stirred Paul to write in this way about God? The answer, clearly, must be found in the context of the doxology. Here three matters stand out.

---

11. 'Mercy' the noun (*eleos* – 9:23; 11:31; 15:9); God 'showing mercy,' the verb (*eleeō* – 9:15, 16, 18; 11:30, 31, 32; 12:8). Also, 'mercies' (*oiktirmos* – 12:1).

One is the triumph of God's mercy over his wrath at the disobedience of Jew and Gentile. This is confirmed by his opening words in the next section, 'I exhort you, brothers and sisters, by the *mercies* of God ...' God is rich in kindness, patience and longsuffering (see on 2:4). Each Jew and Gentile may be disobedient and rightly an object of divine wrath, yet God's mercy, shown in Christ crucified and risen, and in the preaching of the gospel, will prevail. The need for that mercy and its application was explained in earlier passages, chapters 3–8 in particular.

Second, Paul himself is an Israelite, a descendant of Abraham and from the tribe of Benjamin (v. 1). He loves his people and would be prepared to relinquish his own salvation for the sake of his fellow-Jews (9:1-3). More importantly, he knows that God is committed by his word of promise through the patriarchs to the nation Israel (see on 9:6, 9). God's election and calling to Israel is irrevocable. Rejection of Christ by part of Israel was heartbreaking for Paul. Yet he grasped that a better thing lay ahead – ultimately, their 'acceptance' of Christ. Assured of God's fidelity to his Word and to his people, Paul bursts into this paean of praise.

Third, Paul discerns the loving purposes encompassing Adam's race, overturning his Sin which has brought the scourge of death to all people. In Christ, Jews and Gentiles, though sinners, find saving grace in the gospel. The apostle envisages a great family of Jews and Gentiles gathered in the presence of their king, the Messiah Jesus.

8. Review of Paul's arguments in chapters 9-11

(i) Against shrewd Jewish criticism that Paul implies that God has rejected his people, Paul insists that he has not rejected them (11:1-6). Even in Old Testament times there was only ever a remnant of the faithful. Paul himself is an Israelite who remains true to God's revealed purposes. This assertion closely relates to his earlier insistence that the word of God has not failed (9:6-13).

(ii) The sad reality, however, is that the majority of Israel are now 'hardened' against the Messiah, Jesus (vv. 7-10), as Pharaoh was 'hardened' towards the word of God spoken by Moses.

(iii) Yet Paul sees the 'hardening' of Israel as making way for the 'full measure' of the Gentiles to be gathered in by evangelism (10:11-16). Provoked by this, the 'full measure' of Israelites in turn will 'come' in, though we do not know when this will be. In this way 'all Israel will be saved' (vv. 25-27). A 'deliverer will come' to Israel and turn the people from their sins. Paul sees this as the outworking of promises made to the patriarchs, which are irrevocable.

(iv) Using the allegory of the wild olive grafted into the cultivated olive, Paul warns the Gentile Christian not to be arrogant or high-minded (vv. 17-24). As 'natural' branches from Israel were broken off to make way for Gentiles, so they too will be broken off and the 'natural' branches re-grafted.

(v) Paul glorifies God not only for his covenant faithfulness to his historic people, but equally that in the 'mystery' revealed in the gospel he has shown mercy to both Jews and Gentiles, notwithstanding the characteristic disobedience of both (vv. 28-32). The end-point is the gathering of the church of God, made up of believing Jews and Gentiles.

9. THEOLOGICAL OBSERVATIONS

(i) We must conclude from this chapter that God is working his purposes out in mercy for the salvation of the 'full measure' of Gentiles and the 'full measure' of Israelites. We are all confronted by the issues of the personal and the immediate, as well as by crises in the wider world. But seeing the world through Paul's eyes of faith and hope we grasp that God is showing his mercy in salvation, not least ultimately to his historic people.

(ii) Fundamental to the outworking of those great and global plans is the proclamation of the gospel to both Jews and Gentiles. The twentieth century began with high hopes for the evangelization of the world. Those hopes were dashed by two devastating global wars and the loss of theological nerve due to the spread of theological liberalism. Fervently we look to God to move his people worldwide to rise up and proclaim Christ for 'righteousness' by faith.

(iii) Paul's various warnings – to Jews that God has a 'remnant' and to Gentile believers against high-mindedness

– remain pertinent. No matter how bleak the circumstances of the Christian churches, God will always have some people at least to keep alight the gospel message. The Elijah attitude ('only I am left') is to be avoided since it says God is impotent. Further, no matter how excellent my understanding of the gospel or my service to Christ, I do well to be appreciative of those on whose shoulders I stand. Arrogance blinds me to the very nature of that 'faith' that brings me the gift of God's righteousness.

STUDY QUESTIONS

1. If the Jews of Paul's day rejected Christ in favor of their religious works, what religious works do modern men seek in rejecting Christ?

2. How do you know that the Jews have only 'stumbled' on the Stone (Jesus) and not completely fallen?

3. What should my attitude toward the Jews be in light of my own engrafting in this root?

4. Historically, how have the Gentile believers misunderstood Paul's teaching on the Jews and Christ as the Messiah?

5. Does God have a separate way for the Jews to be saved? How then are they saved?

6. How has God displayed His mercy to both Jew and Gentile despite their disobedience?

7. Paul gives an ascription of praise – a doxology – for what God has done. What, in your relationship with Christ, causes you to sound out a doxology?

PART E

The Law of the Spirit
(Romans 12:1–15:6)

Paul's 'appeal' for 'transformed' behaviour is grounded in the 'mercies of God' shown to 'all,' both Jews and Greeks, since 'all are under sin' (3:9).

Based on grace, and independent of the 'works of the Law', God 'justifies' both Jews and Gentiles who, through the gospel, believe in Christ crucified and risen.

Although most Israelites are currently rejecting their Messiah, nonetheless, at a future moment, God will gather in many from his historic people (11:25-32). Therefore, let Gentile believers not be arrogant lest God remove them from his 'olive tree' to re-graft in the Israelites (11:17-24).

Transformed living, then, is not Law-based but Christ-centred, Christ-shaped, Spirit-empowered and expressed in unhypocritical love both to fellow-believers as well as to those outside. Mindful that the 'one' God has 'justified' people from both Jews and Gentiles (3:30), Paul places particular emphasis upon unity in the 'one' body of believers composed of both races, whose members serve one another, 'welcome one another' and with 'one mouth' glorify their God and Father.

13

The Appeal
(Romans 12:1–13:14)

The 'ethical' section of Romans now begins, as signalled by the opening words, 'I appeal to you, therefore,...'

THE NATURE OF THE 'APPEAL'

Due to the complexity and seeming irrelevance of chapters 9-11, many readers pass over those chapters to see Paul's 'appeal' springing from his assurance in chapter 8 that 'no one can accuse or condemn' the believer and nothing 'separate' him from the love of God.

True as those 'mercies' are, it is worth asking how the details of ethical 'appeal' (12:3–15:6) relate to the immediately preceding section in chapters 9–11.

So what does Paul 'appeal' to the Roman Christians to do? For the most part, he encourages them in their relationships towards one another. They are 'one body', so let them serve one another (12:3-8), love one another unhypocritically (12:9-21) and 'welcome one another' (15:7), so that united in Christ the 'strong' and the 'weak' may 'glorify God' with 'one mouth' (15:6). Since the 'strong' and 'weak' most likely refer respectively to Gentile and Jewish Christians we find an immediate link to the two grafted together in the one 'olive tree' (11:17-24). In turn, his appeal to unity in worship (15:6) is connected to serving one another in the 'one body' (12:3-9).

We conclude, therefore, that the core element of the ethical 'appeal' is the unity, love and mutual service of the people of God, who through the gospel are the people of the Messiah, composed of Jews and Gentiles.

Paul's Appeal and the Law

Throughout Romans Paul has been arguing the case to Jews and Gentiles in Rome that they are not 'righteous before God' by the 'works of the Law' but only through their faith in Christ crucified and risen.[1] By 'works of the Law' Paul means both (1) the Commandments given at Mt. Sinai,[2] and (2) ritual practices such as Sabbath-keeping and dietary laws.[3] In the famous chapter 7 Paul told his own story of 'wretchedness' and bewilderment as a man who sought to commend himself to God through Law-keeping.

Paul's point is that the transient era of 'the letter' (i.e. Law) has now passed, abolished by the now-permanent era of Christ and the Spirit. As he observed earlier, 'The Law of the Spirit of life in Christ Jesus has set me free from the Law of sin and death' (8:2; also 2:29; 7:6).[4]

Does this mean, then, that the Law of God has no place under the new covenant of Christ and the Spirit? In the case of 'ritual' observance it is clear that Christ has made these unnecessary by his atoning death. As a matter of discretion, Jewish people are free to observe these in order to identify culturally with people of their race but for Gentile converts these practices are irrelevant.

In regard to the Commandments – the moral and ethical aspects of the Law – Paul affirms these to be 'holy,' 'just,' 'good' and 'spiritual' (7:12, 14). Yet, because of the 'Sin' of Adam continuing in our 'flesh,' we his descendants are unwilling and incapable of fulfilling the Law of God. This is as true in principle for Jews as it is for Gentiles. Law, then, is no way to acceptance with God. Due to Sin, Adamic man cannot rise to the Law's demands.

---

1. See e.g. 3:20, 27-28; 4:2, 6, 25; 5:1; 9:11, 31-33; 11:6.
2. See e.g. 7:8-13.
3. See e.g. 14:17-18.
4. Paul's most comprehensive discussion is 2 Corinthians 3:3-18.

Except, that is, the sinless man Jesus the Messiah whom God 'sent' and in whose own 'flesh' God condemned the Sin of Adam (see on 8:1-4). God now sends his Spirit to those who belong to Christ to enable them to fulfil the 'just requirement of the Law'. That requirement which fulfils the Law is 'love', love of God and love of one's fellowmen. It is by means of Spirit-inspired loving behaviour that the Law is 'established' for the new covenant (see on 3:31).

Such 'love,' however, is not vague and undefined. Nor is it unrelated to Law. The Commandments inform 'love' about what is unloving behaviour, for example, stealing and bearing false witness. Further, Jesus endorsed and indeed deepened the impact of the Commandments (Matt. 5:17-48). He taught, for example, that 'lust' is as serious in the eyes of God as 'adultery', and 'hate' is as serious to God as 'murder'. By so teaching Jesus secured the ongoing role of the Commandments but also their deeper intent (which the pharisaic legalism of the time often ignored). Above all, the New Testament writers have in mind Jesus' own example to inform their understanding of loving behaviour.

We may say, then, that Christ and not Law is the only way to know God and the only way to be 'justified' by him. That said, however, the person justified in Christ is to give concrete expression of that relationship with God by loving behaviour towards others, behaviour that Law defines and helps us understand. For this reason the apostles speak about 'being under the law of Christ' (1 Cor. 9:21) and 'the royal law' (James 2:8).

In Romans chapters 12–13 we find Paul's exposition of 'love' as the expression of a 'transformed life,' that is, of men and women 'justified' before God 'in Christ' and blessed with the presence and the power of the Spirit of God.

PAUL'S ETHICAL 'APPEAL' AND THE TEACHING OF JESUS

It is no coincidence that so much from these chapters resonates with the teaching of Jesus, that is, teaching based on Law that is saturated by his 'love'. The following table helps us see the silhouette of Jesus and his teaching behind the text of Paul in Romans.[5]

---

5. What was the source of these teachings of Jesus that Paul alludes to or echoes, but never quotes exactly or fully, in Romans 12–13? We know Paul wrote

Paul	*Jesus*
Bless those who persecute you; bless and do not curse (12:14).	Bless those who curse you (Luke 6:28).
Live at peace with everyone (12:18).	Be at peace with each other (Mark 9:50).
If your enemy is hungry, feed him (12:20).	Love your enemies, do good to those who hate you (Luke 6:27).
Render to all of them their dues, taxes to whom taxes are due (13:7).	Render to Caesar what is Caesar's ... (Mark 12:17).
He who loves his fellow-man has fulfilled the Law (13:8).	Love the Lord your God .... Love your neighbour as yourself. All the Law and the prophets depend on these two commandments (Matt. 22:37-40).
The commandments ... are summed up in this one rule, 'Love your neighbour as yourself' (13:9).	Do to others what you would have them do to you, for this sums up the Law and the Prophets (Matt. 7:12).
Understanding this present time,	How is it you don't understand this present time? (Luke 12:56)
rise up from your sleep, because	Do not let him find you sleeping (Mark 13:36).
salvation is nearer now (13:11).	Your redemption is drawing near (Luke 21:28).

'Be transformed,' urges Paul. In the passages following, he applies this appeal to relationships with insiders and outsiders, including persecutors and governing authorities (12:3–13:7).

Romans c. 57 but there is no agreement as to the dates of the three Gospels echoed here by Paul. In the case of Romans 13:7/Mark 12:17 the appearance of the exact word 'render' (*apodote*) suggests that a version of Mark may have been extant by the time Romans was written (cf. Rom. 12:18/Mark 9:50). The other texts probably existed in collections of sayings of Jesus circulating at that time and which were later incorporated in the Gospels of Matthew and Luke.

In a word, 'love' is the fulfilment of the Law (13:8-10). Paul concludes with a call to moral vigilance in view of the nearness of our salvation (13:11-14).

1. THE CALL TO TRANSFORMED LIVING (12:1-2)

Paul often uses a 'technical' word in his letters to 'appeal to' or 'encourage'[6] his churches to have distinctly Christian attitudes and behaviour. This is the first[7] occasion the word appears in Romans, signalling the beginning of a passage devoted to 'encouragement'.

a. Paul's Appeal: Its Basis

This 'appeal' rests on his words, '... therefore ... through the mercies of God,' and clearly springs from all he has taught to this point. God's 'mercies' are the many examples of his kindness and patience already mentioned. These include the 'mercy' of God to the peoples of the Gentiles and Jews upon whom his just condemnation rests (1:18–5:11), and to the descendants of Adam whose Sin warrants only their Death. (5:12–8:17). As well, Paul is reflecting on the 'invincible determination of God' to rescue his children from their sufferings to glorify them in the coming age (8:18-39). In the immediately prior passage Paul wrote about the surprising directions the 'mercy of God' has taken in saving both Israelites and Gentiles (11:7-36).

We must note very carefully that Paul's 'appeal' is not to reinstate the Law or its 'works' or any form of legalism as a ground for salvation. Rather, he is appealing to those already saved to 'live out' that salvation as people being transformed by the Word and the Spirit.

b. Paul's Appeal: Its Threefold Content

Paul makes a threefold appeal to his readers.

(i) Present your bodies (to God) as a living sacrifice.

Here we are reminded of his earlier exhortation where he uses the same verb[8] (6:19: 'present your members as slaves

---

6. The Greek word *parakalō,* means 'I encourage, appeal to.'
7. But not the last, see 15:30; 16:17.
8. The Greek word *paristēmi* means 'I present, I yield up.'

to righteousness for sanctification'). In both cases it is the 'members' and the 'body' that believers are to 'present' to God.

This is practical in its outworking, since generally by our 'bodies' we either serve ourselves to the disadvantage of others or we serve God for the benefit of others. Furthermore, God will resurrect our 'bodies' at the Last Day and pass judgement on us according to the deeds of the body (2 Cor. 5:10).

Not long after the era of the apostles, 'Gnosticism' taught that 'mystical' knowledge was all that mattered. Because the 'soul' was secure, one could do as one pleased with the 'body', immersing it in all manner of evil. But no matter. The soul was like a gold bar whose 'gold-ness' could not be corrupted by the filth and mire that clung to it. Paul, however, viewed the body very differently, because the whole of life is expressed in its members.

Paul's metaphorical appeal to 'present' the 'body' as a 'sacrifice' was inspired by the priestly culture of the Temple in Jerusalem. Paul lived in the Holy City from his teen years to his conversion and doubtless witnessed the sacrifice of many animals and observed the smoke of these offerings ascending to the clouds. He was familiar with the priests' scrupulous examination of the fitness of the sheep, goats and cattle for sacrifice and of the priests officiating in the Temple, the High Priest in particular.

These bloody sacrifices of animals by *bona fide* priests are now superseded by the sacrifice of Jesus the Messiah, the true 'Lamb of God'. Matching his 'once-for-all' sacrifice is the ongoing 'sacrifice' of his people. It is the bloodless 'sacrifice' of believers in the self-offering of their 'bodies' (their total beings) in grateful service to their merciful God.

This 'sacrifice' of themselves to God is to have a threefold character:

- It is to be a 'living sacrifice', that is, self-giving, 'vital' and 'alive', not passive and half-hearted with anything held back.
- It is to be a 'holy sacrifice' that is, with bodies given in serving God in moral purity.
- It is to be a 'sacrifice pleasing to God,' not in the Levitical sense of the exact attention to ritual detail, but in the sense of their utter sincerity and integrity before God.

Paul describes this 'sacrifice' as 'logical worship'. It is 'logical' in the sense of its consistency. God saved men and women through a man, his Son, Jesus the Messiah. The saving mediator was both God and man. What can 'saved' men and women offer to God, except their very own selves, that is, their bodies? God does not look for 'silver or gold', least of all animals slain on an altar. God expects only one thing from us, that is, ourselves. But this is not to secure our salvation but to express thankfulness for his gift of salvation.

This 'sacrifice' is also our 'worship'. Gone now are times when special people (priests) offered sacrifices (animals) in a special place (the Temple) at special times (e.g. the Day of Atonement). Christ's sacrifice was for all people at all times in all places. Because Christ 'sanctified' all times and places it follows that now all times and places are alike 'holy' to God and to us. In other words, wherever and whenever ordinary people offer themselves as 'sacrifices to God' is to be considered 'worship', whether in the family, at work or in leisure. Of course, this does not exclude gathering together to pray and to hear the Word of God. This, too, is worship, but 'worship' does not cease when the people walk out through the church door on Sunday mornings.

(ii) Do not be shaped by this age.
This is Paul's second 'appeal'. Most Bible translations urge, 'do not to be conformed to this world.' This implies the 'world' is 'evil' in contradiction of the repeated assertion in Genesis 1 that the creation is 'good'. In any case, the Greek word is *aiōn*, a temporal word from which we derive our English word, 'eon' (an expanse of time). In fact, then, Paul's 'appeal' is, 'do not be "shaped" by this "age".' By 'this age' Paul means that period of time begun with the 'fall' of Adam and ended with the 'revelation of the sons of God' (8:19). In short, 'this age' is the 'age of Adam', the rebel against God, the 'age' where 'Sin rules in Death' (5:21).

This 'age' does, indeed, 'shape' its people. It does not matter which culture or whether the time is ancient, medieval or modern, the Sin of Adam reigns supreme, shaping people after the likeness of Adam's rejection of the kindly Creator.

Earlier in the letter Paul pointed to the gross behaviour of the Gentiles in their idolatry, their 'unclean' sexual activities and their exploitation of one another. The historic people of God were equally in revolt against God, although it was expressed more subtly in hypocrisy and double standards. They are the more culpable because they had greater 'light' from God through the Law and the Prophets.

(iii) But be transformed by the renewal of your mind.
'Do not be "shaped" by Adam and his descendants,' says Paul. 'On the contrary, the word of God has been brought to you and you have been "handed over" to that gospel (6:17). You have been baptised into "Christ" – Christ crucified buried and risen, spelling the end of Adam's way and the beginning of Christ's kingship over us (6:3-4). You have "received the Spirit", you have the "mind of the Spirit" and you are being "impelled forward" by the Spirit. God who "foreknew" you will, by his invincible determination, redeem and glorify you. By his Word and Spirit God has renewed your mind and made you a "new creation" in Christ. He continues to renew your mind as you continue to acknowledge Jesus as Lord and Saviour.'

That continuing renewal will mean continuing trans-formation of life expressed in loving service of others. The onset of the new age will mean the final transformation in which the children of Adam will be glorified as the children of God. But that 'new age' has begun already, dragged back into 'this age' by the preaching and hearing of the gospel and by God's gift of his Spirit to the children of Adam, making them 'new' and beginning in them the process of 'transformation'. That 'transformation' is no impersonal thing, however, but deeply personal. It is the transformation of the children of Adam, 'conformed into the likeness' of Jesus Christ, the Son of God (see on 8:29). It is growth in 'Christ-likeness' and 'Christ-shaped' living, no less.

c. Paul's Appeal: Its Expected Outcome
If we may briefly recapitulate, Paul's 'appeal' is for his readers (1) to offer their bodies as a sacrifice to God in holy living, (2) to reject being 'shaped by' the Sin and Death of the 'age'

of Adam, and (3) to be 'transformed' by minds made new by God's Word and Spirit.

From this Paul expects a good outcome, to 'approve' attitudes and actions that accord with the 'will of God'.

This is quite pointed; Jews looked to the Law to lead to such behaviour. Paul's whole argument against the Jewish advocates of Law in Rome has been that Law leaves its adherents 'wretched' and bewildered and woefully short of the standards God expects. The Sin of Adam continued in his children, including the children of Israel to whom he gave the Law. What the Law was powerless to do, however, Christ has done, sent by God as the sacrifice for sin and the source of his life-giving and life-changing Spirit. Only the gospel of Christ proclaimed and believed is capable of bringing the re-creative Spirit into the lives of Adam's children.

Paul describes the 'will of God' as 'good, pleasing and perfect'. His word 'perfect' is the clue to the meaning. By 'perfect' (*teleion*) Paul is thinking of the 'perfection' of the new age of the kingdom of God (cf. 1 Cor. 13:10: 'when the perfect comes'). In other words, Paul is thinking of the 'will of God' as behaviour fit for the future kingdom of God, which, however, the children of God are to exemplify and express *now*.

This 'transformed living' with discernible outcomes Paul expects to see in the lives of his readers then and now – in a united church and in the members' relationships with one another and the wider community.

2. Transformed Living: In a United Church (vv. 3-8)

We cannot read Romans as if written in a historical vacuum. Those who sat in house churches hearing the letter read knew well that Paul was making a particular point to them. These Roman readers were not a single church, but a series of loosely connected or even disconnected households. Some were Jewish, others Gentile, and held apart by their history and, apparently, by their ethnicity.

At the beginning of the letter, there is no greeting to 'the church in Rome' in a focused sense but only to 'God's beloved ones, called to be saints'. At the end of the letter, Paul expresses his greetings no less than thirteen times, most likely indicating at least thirteen discrete clusters of believers.

Apparently, then, one of the purposes of this great letter is to consolidate these scattered and ethnically diverse groups into one Christian 'body'. This emerges from his exhortations in 14:1–15:7, culminating with his appeal that 'together with one mouth they glorify God' and that they 'welcome one another' (15:6-7).

But Paul anticipates this 'appeal' in verses 3-8 of chapter 12. He begins, in verse 3, with a challenge to their high-mindedness:

> For I say through the grace given me
> to everyone among you
> not to think of yourselves   more highly than you should
> but to think   soberly
> as God has assigned to each his measure of faith.

Paul models humility intentionally to those who pride themselves on their understanding of God's ways. He speaks as an apostle only by that 'grace' God has 'given' to him (cf. 15:15); it does not arise from within him. Paul connects this 'grace given' with that 'measure of faith' which does not come from us, but comes only by the gift of God. He is not thinking here of basic 'saving faith' which we direct towards Christ upon hearing the gospel. Rather, there are degrees of 'faith', to be understood as 'prophetic discernment' of the will and the ways of God. Paul as apostle has received this but he is humble about it as he exhorts the Romans (and us) to be. There can be no unity in the church without humility!

In verses 4-5 Paul introduces the imagery of the human body, that is, of one entity that has many 'members'.

> For
> even as   we have many members in one body
> and   all the members do not have the same function
>
> so too   the many   are one body in Christ
> and   one by one   are members of one another.

Scholars have pondered the origin of this brilliant imagery for the Christian congregation that Paul employed also in First Corinthians (12:12-31). Some suggest the political theories of the day that called the state a body were Paul's inspiration. Others wonder if the practice of making plaster casts of ailing body parts for offering to the god Asklepios for healing may have given the idea to Paul. Since the apostle doesn't tell us, we may do no more than guess!

Whatever the source of the image it remains powerful. Let the reader consider his or her body. Yes, it is one entity. And yes, that entity is composed of numerous members and organs. Think of the medical experts who specialize in the hand, or the foot or the brain as indicative of the complexity of just one human body and its parts.

The Christian congregation is to be like this in two ways.

First, like the human body, the 'many members' who individually belong to Christ are to become 'one body', united in their common praise of God through Jesus Christ in the power of the Spirit. The present situation in Rome where there are numerous diverse and unconnected groups who are kept apart by high-mindedness and misunderstanding is inappropriate.

The same could be said about many a suburb and town where people of true faith in Christ are kept apart for historical reasons long since forgotten and most likely quite unimportant. Often, meagre human and financial resources are dissipated which, if combined, would lead to strengthened local witness to Christ. The inroads of secularism and the challenge of multiculturalism may force healthy consolidation upon many small congregations.[9]

Second, Paul reminds them that each belongs to the other. As in a biological body, where the members and organs are inter-connected and inter-dependent, so too the individual

---

9. Two hundred years after Paul wrote Romans, Eusebius the historian wrote of 'an immense and countless laity' in the church of Rome who supported no less than 1500 widows and persons in distress, served by forty-six presbyters, seven deacons, seven sub-deacons and fifty-two exorcists (Eusebius, *History of the Church*, VI. 43.11-12). This is a spectacular reversal of the broken and scattered communities Paul wrote to in his Letter to the Romans.

believers are to see themselves connected to and belonging to one another. Spiritual pride is the enemy of true unity in Christ, the attitude that says, 'I am a better Christian because I know my Bible better than you, or because I have converted more people than you, or because I have been in the church longer than you.' But humility says, 'I need you and you need me because we belong to one another in Christ. We are family and we are members-together.'

In verses 6-8 Paul expands upon his observation in verse 4b that 'all the members do not have the same function'.

Having differing gifts according to the grace given us
    whether prophecy,   according to the analogy of faith;
    whether ministry,   in our ministering;
    whether teaching,   in our teaching;
    whether encouraging, in our encouragement.

Let him who shares   do so   generously.
Let him who leads   do so   eagerly
Let him who shows mercy do so   cheerfully.

It is noticeable that Paul is silent here about 'church order'. The words 'presbyter' or 'deacon' do not appear in this list of activities. Such 'offices' were known at the time; Phoebe, the bearer of Paul's letter to Rome, was a 'deacon' in the Church of Cenchreae (16:1-2). Yet Paul does not see 'church order' as such to be the key to a healthy and united church; rather what is needed is humble recognision that 'gifts' are just that – 'gifts' from God.

Paul is saying that in a united 'body' the members will 'just get on with it', sharing what they have in recognition that it is from the Lord, and so serving others. Paul is merely giving some examples, so the list is not to be regarded as comprehensive. Although seven functions are mentioned, it is likely that there are three main activities, with the others being sub-sets of these.

(i) 'Prophesying' meant brief 'revelations' of the end-times, with warnings but also encouragement (1 Cor. 14:3, 24-25, 31). We note that 'encouraging' is listed in verse 8a. Most likely this is an expression of 'prophesying'. After apostleship, 'prophesying' was the highest and most useful 'gift' to the church (1 Cor. 12:28; Eph. 4:11).

(ii) 'Ministering' meant giving practical assistance to others, as the seven young Hellenistic Jews of Jerusalem did, led by Stephen (Acts 6:1-6). The three examples begun with the words, 'Let him who ...' are probably expressions of 'ministering'. That is, wealthier members engaged in 'sharing' generously, capable administrators in 'leading' eagerly, and (perhaps) the 'hands on' helpers, who distributed alms[10] to the needy, did so cheerfully. We have an impression of Spirit-filled people humbly but actively helping one another.

(iii) 'Teaching' meant the sustained and systematic instruction in the pre-formed oral traditions and in written texts like the Greek Old Testament and such apostolic writings then in existence. The 'teaching presbyter' in these early churches approximated to the role of the rabbi in the synagogue. His work centred on the 'public reading' of the Scriptures as well as 'instructing' and 'exhorting' from those texts (1 Tim. 4:13). This person was to be supported finan-cially (Gal. 6:6; 1 Tim. 5:17-18) and he became the centre of the emerging 'order' in the early churches and the source of their stability.

It is no coincidence that involved service in the 'one body in Christ' is the first item in Paul's practical expression of 'transformed living'. Just as the human family is God's ideal 'nursery' for nurture and growth, so the 'body of Christ' is the place of giving and receiving of ministry, whether prophesying with its encouragement, or ministering with its relief of need, or teaching with its reinforcement of the truth of the gospel.

We cannot but notice the mix of both verbal and concrete activities. The 'verbal' is fundamental; Christianity is a religion of the Word, spoken and heard. We begin and continue as believers by the hearing and believing the Word of God. Yet we live in a fallen world to which one way or another we fall prey. Sooner or later, we need help. Thus churches which are 'only verbal', and which offer no assistance to members in need, fail to understand passages like this one.

---

10. The English words 'alms' derives from the Greek *eleō* ('I show mercy') as used here by Paul.

3. TRANSFORMED LIVING: LOVING INSIDERS AND OUTSIDERS (vv. 9-21)

In these verses we find a series of staccato imperatives similar to those in other letters by Paul (e.g. 1 Thess. 5:14-22; 2 Cor. 13:11-12) as well as in other writers in the New Testament (e.g. Heb. 13:1-17).

These imperatives appear scatter-gun in their rapidity and also in their apparently random character. A closer look, however, suggests coherence of subject matter throughout. This coherence is centred on the first exhortation relating to 'love' (v. 9a). In turn, this 'core' idea appears to be directed on one hand to insiders and on the other to outsiders.

Let love be unhypocritical.

This is not the only occasion a New Testament writer calls for 'love' to be 'unhypocritical' (*anupokritos* – see 2 Cor. 6:6; 1 Pet. 1:22). The word 'hypocrite' derives from Greek culture and meant an 'actor', someone 'playing a part'. Jesus repeatedly condemned the Pharisees for their 'hypocrisy', for living behind a mask of religious sincerity.

It is no coincidence that an appeal to 'unhypocritical love' appears in a letter by a converted Pharisee who is fighting a rearguard action by Jewish Christians who seek to reinstate Law as a basis for belonging to God's covenant and for membership of his covenant people. It is plain from the Gospels that for the Pharisees Law-keeping meant legalism, and legalism meant hypocrisy. It is safe to say that 'legalism', being right with God based on what *I* do, will usually be accompanied by 'pretence,' 'hypocrisy.'

When the notion of 'hypocrisy' is applied to 'love', it is easy to act 'as if' loving someone by flattery or by showing interest that is not genuine. But this 'playing the part' love is really 'self-love', not 'others-love'. It is self-serving. Those who engage in 'hypocritical love' should stop. Most people aren't fooled for long. In the end no one believes them about anything. Not least, those who 'pretend' to love tend to lose touch with reality about themselves since they are only 'actors' always 'playing a part' and not real people.

The two exhortations that follow immediately take their character from 'love' that is utterly genuine. Paul's call to 'hate evil and cling to the good' (v. 9b,c) is in line with his rejection of the 'hypocritical'. Hypocrisy pretends to be good while being something else; if not evil, then at least having less than decent intentions. 'Un-hypocrisy' does, indeed, 'hate evil and cling to the good.' Taken together, the three exhortations in verse 9 call for 'transparent' living, for genuineness in loving others, and a firm rejection of evil and a commitment to goodness.

a. Loving the Insider (vv. 10-13, 15-16)
In verse 10 the keyword is 'one another', which points to the close mutual relationship that should characterize Christian faith but which appears to have been lacking in Rome.

> Love one another with brotherly affection.
> Outdo one another in showing honour.

Earlier Paul appealed for this, using the imagery of the 'body'. Now he appeals to the notion of 'family' (cf. 1 Tim 5:1-2: 'Do not rebuke an older man but exhort him as you would a father; treat younger men like brothers, older women like mothers, younger women like sisters'). Paul's word for 'love' (*philostorgoi*) means 'loving dearly' which he reinforces by 'in brotherly love' (*philadelphia*, cf. 1 Pet. 1:22: '...for unhypocritical brotherly love, love one another fervently from the heart'). Jesus created this kind of community among his disciples, a fellowship that continued into the church in Jerusalem, and beyond there into the mission churches of the New Testament. So far from the 'high-mindedness' Paul warns against in verse 3, the Romans are to excel in honouring others (cf. Phil. 2:3: 'count others better than yourselves').

In verses 11-12 Paul directs their minds to the quality of their ministry to one another in the 'body' of the congregation, picking up earlier comments in verses 6 to 8.

> Do not slacken in your zeal,
> being fervent in the Spirit,
> serving the Lord,

rejoicing in hope,
being patient in hardship,
being devoted to prayer.

Here is a 'window' into the impact of the gospel and the Spirit of God on those who were members of the early churches. They have been 'handed over to the pattern of teaching' (6:17), they have been publicly baptised into Christ crucified, buried and risen (6:3-4), and they have 'received' the Spirit by whom they were being 'impelled forward' towards their salvation (8:17).

'Now,' says Paul, 'do not be idle in zeal,' that is, the 'zeal' of Christian conversion arising from the Word and the Spirit. Most likely, this leading injunction is now applied to five subsidiary expressions of the Christian life. The first two are connected. 'Be fervent[11] in the Holy Spirit,' says Paul, insisting that dramatic spiritual change comes only from the presence and the power of the indwelling Spirit. 'Being fervent in the Spirit' is not mere religious excitement but rather a focused 'serving[12] the Lord,' that is, the ascended Lord Jesus Christ (1 Thess. 1:9; Eph. 6:7; Col. 3:23). Such 'serving' is total, being expressed in Jesus-centred attitudes, speech and action, both to insiders and outsiders.

The next three expressions are likewise connected, but they also flow on from the previous two. 'Rejoice in hope,' that is, the hope to be with 'the Lord' whom we 'serve' is due to the Spirit who inspires this 'hope'. Such 'hope' is intensified because of the 'hardship' (*thlipsis* is suffering due to persecution) on account of which Paul appeals for 'patience'. Finally, 'devotion in prayer' derives from the Spirit, is directed to the Lord and is conditioned by the grim reality of 'hardship' on the one hand and bright 'hope' on the other.

In modern affluent societies it is easy to slip into a spiritual 'comfort zone' and merely drift along in the Christian life. The problem for Paul's Roman readers, however, was not affluence but persecution. It is clear from other passages in the New Testament that fear of religious oppression powerfully

---

11. Literally, 'boiling' or 'seething' in the Spirit.
12. Literally, 'being enslaved to.'

weakens Christian witness and dulls spiritual zeal (Heb. 6:12; 10:32-39; 12:4-13).

In verse 13 Paul gives two concrete examples of 'unhypo-critical love' and warm 'family affection' (vv. 9 and 10).

> Share together for the needs of the saints.
> Concentrate your efforts on hospitality.

In pre-welfare societies, the 'needs' of widows, orphans and disabled folk were extreme. It is evident that the practical love of Jesus for the needy of Galilee and Judaea continued in the Jerusalem church and the mission churches with the care of widows and orphans (cf. 1 Tim. 5:3-16; James 1:27). These needs may have been met by 'hospitality' (*philoxenia* – 'love of strangers'), that is by taking in such needy folk as lodgers in an era that had not yet established hostels and hospitals.

Travelling ministers arriving in strange cities and towns were also deemed worthy of 'hospitality'. Apart from financial considerations, the inns of those times were notorious for their sexual immorality. Phoebe the deacon from Cenchreae was to be 'welcomed' and 'helped' on arrival in Rome as befitting one who had 'helped' others, Paul included (16:2). Paul, too, expected a similar welcome and assistance when he passed through Rome on his way to Spain (15:24).

Paul's final words about loving the 'insiders' are found in verses 15-16:

> Rejoice with those who rejoice.
> Weep with those who weep.
> Think the same thoughts one with the other.
> Do not be high minded,
> But associate with the lowly.

Such 'love' goes beyond material help (v. 13) to close emotional commitment and attachment. Such is the closeness of this spiritual family that each shares the joys and the sorrows of the other. Such is the depth of their love that they understand and sympathize with the 'thoughts' of the other. This doesn't mean unquestioning agreement in all things but at the very least it includes a respect for the opinions of others.

Paul's warning about 'high-mindedness' picks up a similar idea in verse 3 and suggests this may have been a problem with some in Rome. The 'high-minded' tend to associate only with those they see as their equals. But this is blind to the very humility of God as revealed in the incarnation and death of Jesus (2 Cor. 8:9; Phil. 2:1-18). For his part, Paul was passionately committed to the 'weak' (2 Cor. 11:7, 29) and the poor (1 Cor. 11:22).

From Romans 12 we are able to envisage the pattern of church life Paul thought important.

1. Official positions like 'pastor' or 'rector' or 'bishop' do not figure in Paul's exhortations. We gather from the New Testament that Christianity was at that time essentially a 'lay' movement. True, while clerical leadership is now a 'given' (as it was then), it may be questioned whether its present over-shadowing dominance is consistent with our vision of New Testament Christianity as seen through windows like this.

2. Paul's exhortations are directed to 'function' and not to 'office'. Indeed, 'office' is invisible in Romans, as it is in most of Paul's letters written earlier than the Pastoral Epistles. Those 'functions' are described as both 'activities' (prophesying, ministering, teaching) and 'relationships' (loving, honouring, empathizing), all within the context of 'zeal' (fervour in the Spirit, serving the Lord, rejoicing in hope, being patient under suffering, being devoted to prayer). It is impossible to determine whether or not 'official' persons engaged in these functions.

3. Paul's goal is for a church that is united ('one body in Christ') in the essentials of the faith ('praising the Father with one voice'). He sees spiritual pride ('high-mindedness') as the barrier to that unity.

4. LOVING THE OUTSIDER (vv. 14, 17-21)

From these references it is clear that believers were suffering persecution, though details are lacking about such problems in Rome at the time. From the book of Acts, as well as from his own letters, we know that Paul experienced rejection, scorn, imprisonment, flogging and stoning wherever he went (see on 8:35-36). The strong religious cultures of those times disliked intensely the message of the crucified and risen Messiah. Ordinary believers in the churches also 'shared the same sufferings' as the apostolic leaders (2 Cor. 1:7).

Paul's advice, like that of Peter (1 Pet. 2:21-23; 3:9-17), derived ultimately from Jesus' 'turn the other cheek' teaching, which he embodied in his own trial and execution. Jesus' ethic and example of forgiveness instead of vengeance permeates the entire New Testament and has contributed values that changed the course of history.

Paul commences his exhortations about relating to 'outsiders' with words about persecutors (v. 14).

> Bless those who persecute you.
> Bless   and curse not.

These words and Peter's (1 Pet. 3:9: 'do not return evil for evil ... but on the contrary bless') clearly echo Jesus' teaching in Luke 6:27 and 28: 'Love your enemies ... bless those who curse you.'

In verses 17-19 Paul expands on the Jesus-ethic of forgiveness in place of vengeance.

> Do not   in any way return evil for evil,
> But   take thought how to do good in the sight of all.

> If possible   so far as it depends on you
>   Live at peace with all men and women.

> Do not   avenge yourselves, beloved,
> But   give wrath to God,
> For it is written,
> > *Vengeance is mine,*
> > *I will repay, says the Lord.*

The felt need to 'pay back' is deep-seated in the human psyche. It is evident on the football field, in the schoolyard, in our civil courts and between tribes and even nations. Often the injustice is 'nursed' and remembered for decades, even centuries. There has been an endless cycle of payback violence in Northern Ireland, in the Balkans and in the Middle East. The instinct to take revenge is especially strong when the pain inflicted is unjust, unfair or plain wrong. Innocent suffering is, indeed, an outrage. Jesus suffered despite his innocence of any wrongdoing and so, too, Christians everywhere were suffering although innocent of any crime.

Revenge occurs in two stages. First, there is the festering wound with plans for 'getting back' at the 'enemy'. Then there is the actual execution of the planned revenge. Paul urges against both stages. 'Do not "take thought" for it and do not do it,' is his admonition. Rather, he says, think ahead how you can do good, and indeed, be known for doing good. At times of felt injustice, plan to do good in some way and reject the instinct to take revenge.

Undergirding this non-retaliatory attitude is the knowledge that God is the judge of all, including those who have treated us unjustly. 'Vengeance' for wrongdoing is God's prerogative, not man's, as Paul declares, quoting Deuteronomy 32:35. Thus Paul says, 'Leave wrath to God,' that is, 'give it over to him.' That is excellent advice, because it is both true and helpful. If we allow ourselves to become embittered by unjust treatment, we destroy ourselves and merely compound the damage and add to the hurt.

The original context was persecution, though the application is much wider than that. So, too, is his injunction, 'so far as it depends on you, live at peace with all men and women.' This is not the 'peace at any price' attitude where we compromise with evil for the sake of a quiet life. Christians should seek peaceful relationships, even with enemies and persecutors, as far as possible.

In verses 20-21 Paul goes beyond the reactive to the proactive. Not only are Christians to repudiate 'payback', they are also to seek opportunities to do good. Here Paul quotes from Proverbs 25:21-22:

But   if your enemy is hungry, feed him
            if he is thirsty,   give him something to drink
For doing this you heap coals of fire on his head.

Do not be conquered by evil
But   conquer evil with good.

Providing food and drink is not to be narrowly interpreted. Rather, food and drink symbolize 'doing good' in every way. Thus so far from revenge the Christian will endeavour to do whatever good he can do, even for the one who has proved to be the enemy. The unusual words about 'heaping coals of fire' are much debated, and probably mean that doing good to enemies ultimately shames them to acknowledge the good that has been done to them.

Paul concludes his admonitions about unjust suffering with the powerful exhortation not to be overcome by evil but to overcome evil with good. We are 'conquered' by evil when we engage in counter-punching, in 'giving back' what has been meted out to us. We 'conquer' evil by overcoming our vengeful instincts and doing good to our enemies instead. This is stark and overwhelming. Surely it is beyond us! We must read these words alongside Paul's earlier promise that we 'more than conquer' enemies natural and supernatural 'through him who loved us' (8:37). Most likely, however, our own sinful instincts are more difficult to 'conquer' than the external forces ranged against us. Yet even here we 'more than conquer through him who loved us'.

4. Submission to the State (13:1-7)

In the previous section calling for non-vengeance towards outsiders, the Jesus-ethic and the Jesus-example were the source and inspiration for Paul's admonitions. No less is this true in regard to Paul's teaching about the Christian's submission to the state. Here, too, in the word of Jesus, 'Render to Caesar', and in the example of Jesus in his own submission to Caesar's 'deputy' Pilate, do we find the fountainhead for the apostle's instruction for Christians on this subject.

In this teaching Paul is joined by Peter who also calls for subjection to emperor and governors according to the example of Jesus (1 Pet. 2:13-14, 22-23; cf. Titus 3:1). Most likely both apostles are drawing on a common storehouse of pastoral teaching that went back to Jesus himself, both his teaching and his example.

From the subsequent passage it is evident that the early Christians, following their Messiah, were not political subversives calling for the overthrow of government. This is the more striking since Roman government in both the capital and the provinces was notoriously corrupt and exploitative. The apostles, following Jesus, strongly asserted the fact of the coming end-times and the just judgement of God bringing both blessing to the righteous and condemnation to the wicked. At the same time, however, the Lord's word, 'Render to Caesar,'[13] endorsed the role of the state in the interim era before the onset of the end-times.

The previous section and the present one must be read together. There (12:14, 17-21), the emphasis is on the end-time judgement of God insisting that Christians do not pre-empt the judgement of God by wreaking vengeance for unjust treatment. Here (vv. 1-7), the emphasis is on the role of the state to govern God's world in the interim period and for believers and others to be respectful of and subject to that governance since it is the instrument of God.

In verses 1-2 Paul exhorts the believers to 'be subject' to rulers warning of the consequences of opposition.

> Let every person be subject to
>   the ruling authorities.

For there is no	authority	except	by God
and	authorities	that are there	
		have been appointed	by God
so that he who opposes			
the authority			
resists			
[the authority]		appointed	by God
and those who resist		will be judged.	

The keyword is the repeated word 'authority' (*exousia*) which means 'delegated' authority. This was a political term applied to a Roman governor, such as Pontius Pilate who ruled Judaea in place of the Emperor and by his 'authority'. Paul is teaching

---

13. This may have surprised many Jews of 'zealot' sympathies who would have expected Jesus to be cast in the mould of the violent revolutionary Judas the Galilean. Judas preached that the payment of the new head tax to Rome in AD 6 symbolized the slavery of the covenant people to the sovereignty of the godless Gentiles.

that the emperor and his governors and other rulers exercised their 'authority' by God's appointment. Remember Jesus' words to Pilate, 'You would have no power (*exousia*) over me unless it had been *given* you from above' (John 19:11).

Jesus did not subvert Pilate's God-given 'authority', rather he subjected himself to it despite the injustice of the charge against him. Paul's admonition is similar, doubtless influenced by Jesus' 'render to Caesar' teaching and his example before Pilate.

In that sense Jesus was a 'conscientious objector'. He was responsible to God's 'higher authority' in all that he did, including arriving as messianic king to David's City and clearing the traders from the Temple. In taking the inevitable consequences of these actions, however, Jesus did not advocate overthrowing Roman rule. Where believers see the state as acting against God's will they must be free 'conscientiously' to oppose it, but without overturning the state, prepared to face the consequences, as Jesus was.

Does this mean the authority of the state is absolute, never to be overturned? Not according to the great German scholar and preacher Helmut Thielicke who argued that where a state has become de facto 'criminal' led by a wicked gang, as Nazi Germany had become, then its citizens had a duty to work for its downfall. But apart from such extreme 'criminality' the responsibility of the Christian citizen is to support the state and to seek its improvement and reform. Difficult as it is to accept – as a general statement – tyranny is preferable to anarchy.

In verses 3-4 Paul expands on the role of the ruler.

For rulers are not a terror   to those who do good
                                     but to those who do evil.

Do you wish to have no fear of the [one in] authority?
Then do good and you will have his approval.
For he is a minister of God for your good.
But if you do wrong, be afraid.
For he does not bear the sword in vain.
For he is a minister of God to execute wrath to the wrongdoer.

'Rulers' hold their 'authority' 'under God' and are 'ministers of God'; God's 'deacons' (*diakonoi*) we might say. Their chief role is to punish those who do evil and reward those who do good. Since Peter teaches the same (1 Pet. 2:14), we conclude this to be an apostolic teaching most likely derived from Jesus himself. Reference to 'bearing a sword' is metaphorical. It means the ruler has the means of punishing the wrongdoer.

The Romans, like the Greeks before them, were interested in law-making and in legal process. This may explain Paul's comments that the Gentiles had 'law written on their hearts' (2:15). Furthermore, the Romans imposed 'law' on the world in New Testament times, whether by subjugating rebel tribes, eradicating piracy and banditry, or demanding orderly behaviour in the cities and towns of the empire. Remember the concern of the town clerk of Ephesus that the tradesmen unhappy with Paul take their complaints to the courts rather than stir up civil unrest (Acts 19:38-40). True, Roman rule was erratic and repressive, and its officials were frequently corrupt. Yet, unsatisfactory as it was, it was preferable to the anarchy of civil war, which the Mediterranean world suffered for many years before Augustus emerged in 31 BC as virtual dictator and tyrant.

The point is that Paul regarded such 'authorities' as 'ministers of God' administering justice in the world for him, as his 'deputies,' in the interim period ahead of the Last Day when God himself will finally punish wrongdoers and reward the righteous.

It is likely that Paul's words had special point to his Jewish readers at that time. In AD 49, that is, less than a decade earlier, Claudius the emperor exiled all Jews from Rome on account of their riotous behaviour in the synagogues which erupted because of Christian preaching. This was a harsh action and brought great suffering to the Jews. Only since the death of Claudius three years earlier (in AD 54) had it been possible to return to their city. Jews, including those who belonged to the house churches in Rome, had good reason to resent Roman rule. As well, at that time Jews in Palestine were being badly treated by a sequence of inept, corrupt and cruel governors. The Palestinian Jews had come to the brink of war with Rome.

Indeed, that war broke just a few years later, in AD 66. Paul had good reason at that time to appeal to Jews to be subject to the civil authorities.

In verse 5 Paul imposes this principle of 'civil obedience' on his Roman readers.

> Therefore it is necessary to be subject
> not only because of his wrath
> but also because of your conscience.

Submission to rulers is not an option but 'a necessity' (*anagkē*) and that for two reasons. Failure to do so would incur their wrath against you. As a wrongdoer you will face punishment. The ruler does not carry a sword for no reason! More important by far is 'your conscience'. This is not so much an innate sense of right and wrong with accompanying feelings of guilt or relief. Rather, 'conscience' is one's theological understanding, what one has been taught from the gospel. In this case, 'conscience' means knowing that the state and its rulers are 'ministers of God' and appointed 'by God' to govern in his place ahead of the coming age of the kingdom of God. 'Conscience' knows that to reject these authorities is to reject the means God has ordained for his good government of the world.

Paul concludes this section (vv. 6-7) with specific application of these principles:

> For this reason you also pay taxes.
> Because they are servants of God,
> attending to this very thing.

Render	to everyone	what	is owed
tax	to whom	tax	is due
custom	to whom	custom	is due
respect	to whom	respect	is due
honour	to whom	honour	is due.

Paul has several ways of referring to these 'ruling authorities appointed by God' (v. 1). They are 'rulers' (v. 3) and 'ministers of God' (v. 4). Their chief role in verses 3-5 is to maintain 'law and order'.

In verse 6, however, he also calls them 'servants of God' whose role is the collection of various kinds of taxes, both direct and indirect.[14] Presumably this included the expenditure of taxes on public works and services. These activities were well organized in the cities and towns of the empire. In short, Paul is endorsing the principle of the structures of government from the leader of the nation to the humblest clerk.

Paul's word for 'servant' (*leitourgos*) was used in the Old Testament for those who served in the Temple (Ezra 7:24). By speaking of these secular officers as 'ministers of God' and 'servants of God', Paul is bestowing great honour on such people. Thus he calls for 'respect' and 'honour' to be shown to those who hold such 'offices' (see 1 Pet. 2:13-17).

This teaching is derived from Jesus who, when pressed about paying tax to Rome, said, 'Render to Caesar the things that are Caesar's,' that is, taxes. It is no coincidence that Paul's word 'render' (*apodote*) is the very word used in Mark 12:17, which records the teaching of Jesus. Civil obedience as taught by the apostles Paul and Peter (1 Pet. 2:13-17) flows directly from the teaching of Jesus and the example of Jesus.

Three points of application emerge from this passage.

First, consistent with this, we must pray for those who rule and govern,[15] as we are called upon to do in 1 Timothy 2:1-2.

Second, Christians need to remind 'secular' governors that, whether they know it or not, they are 'ministers of God' and 'servants of God' who hold their 'authority' 'under God', that is by his permission. This carries onerous responsibility for hard work, honesty, justice and even-handedness.

Third, Christians with abilities appropriate to the tasks should consider 'public service' in democratic societies as service of God for the good government of his world in this interim period before the coming of the kingdom.

---

14. Paul's words 'tax' and 'custom' imply direct and indirect forms of taxation. Evidence from Roman writers Tacitus (*Annals* 13.50-51) and Suetonius (*Nero* 10.1) refers to high levels of taxation and to shameless extortion by tax collectors.

15. This teaching was deep rooted in the Jewish tradition before New Testament times (e.g. 1 Maccabees 7:33) and became part of Christian practice in the post apostolic era (e.g. Tertullian *Apology* 30).

5. FULFILLING THE LAW (13:8-10)

Verse 8 carries forward words used earlier. 'Let *love* be unhypocritical' (12:9) continues as 'he who loves' and 'render to everyone what is *owed*' (13:7) as 'owe no one anything'. The real emphasis of this short passage is that 'love fulfils the Law', an observation that occurs in both verses 8 and 10.

> Owe no one anything except to love one another,
> For he who loves his fellow-man has fulfilled the Law.

'Love' towards the 'fellow-man' (*heteron*) echoes God's command, 'Love thy neighbour (*plēsion*) as yourself' (Lev. 19:18), words that reappear in verses 9 and 10. Paul's choice of the word 'fellow-man' instead of 'neighbour' in verse 8 is significant. He is not directing 'love' to 'neighbour' (i.e. the fellow-Jew) but to 'Everyman' (i.e. all people, including Jews, Gentiles, even enemies – 12:14, 17-21). God commended his own love to the morally weak, the godless, the sinners and those hostile to him (5:6-10). Christian believers, like God, are to direct their love beyond their immediate covenantal brothers and sisters to everybody, even their persecutors.

Paul's words remind us of Jesus' answer to the scribe who questioned him about the greatest commandment. The rabbis scoured the Old Testament and identified 613 laws (248 commands + 365 prohibitions) and debated which of these was the greatest. Jesus answered that the first is to love God (based on Deut. 6:4-5) and the second is to love one's neighbour as oneself (based on Lev. 19:18). In Jesus' famous parable, the 'good' Samaritan's 'love for his neighbour' extended beyond his immediate race. Under Jesus' reinterpretaion of the Law the 'neighbour' was one's 'fellowman', regardless of race, religion or circumstances.

Jesus' answer that 'love' transcended the 613 commandments is picked up and enriched by Paul in saying that love of 'fellow-man' 'fulfils the Law'. In a striking way Paul says that our sole 'debt' to our 'fellow-man' is to 'love' him.

Paul's declaration is not made merely for something to say, as it were. It must be remembered that throughout the letter Paul is rebutting those Jewish objectors in the house churches in Rome who urge the reinstatement of the Law and the 'works of the Law' as the *sine qua non* of covenantal membership. In 5:12–8:4 Paul explained that despite Jewish optimism the Law did not prove able to rescue humanity from Adam's Sin and its accompaniment, Death. In fact, Law only served to inflame Sin and to leave an earnest Jew like Paul 'wretched' and bewildered.

The obligation God lays on us is not impersonal Law-keeping but relational loving of others, both inside and outside the church.

In verse 9 Paul justifies this assertion.

The commandments,   'You shall not kill,'
                      'You shall not commit adultery,'
                      'You shall not steal,'
                      'You shall not covet,'
And any other commandment
is gathered up in this word,
'You shall love your neighbour as yourself.

Clearly Paul is superseding the original commandments. First, he consolidates the original commandments of the 'first table' of the Law into one 'new commandment' ('love'). Their function is now limited to identifying unloving behaviour (theft, adultery, etc.). Second, the 'new commandment' is infinitely demanding as well as positive: 'You shall love your neighbour *as yourself.*'

In verse 10 Paul clinches his argument for 'love' over against Law:

Love does not work evil to the neighbour.
Therefore love is the fulfilment of the Law.

The commandments 'not' to 'work evil to the neighbour' (in adultery, theft, etc.) are summed up in one word, 'love.' 'Love,' therefore, fulfils the Law, that is, renders its 'works' redundant.

This short passage, beginning and ending as it does, with the assertion that love 'fulfils' Law picks up Paul's earlier statement that 'the just requirement of the Law is *fulfilled*' in those who 'walk ... according to the Spirit' (8:4). God 'sent' his own Son, condemning man's Sin in his blameless person, so that Adam's children (1) might be free from God's just condemnation and (2) might be blessed with the presence and power of his now-indwelling Spirit (8:14-15). These 'sons of God' did not receive 'a spirit of slavery' to more Law-based 'fear'; rather they are set free to be the 'children' of their 'dear Father'. Not for them, therefore, the slaves' life of Law-keeping but the Spirit-borne 'unhypocritical love' for 'fellowman', whether a fellow-Christian or even a persecutor.

6. No Return to the Flesh (13:11-14)

The opening words, 'And this', while picking up the immediately prior appeal to 'love', most likely also catch up and conclude the entire hortatory section begun at 12:1 ('I appeal to you, therefore, brothers and sisters ...'). Verses 11-14 demonstrate that the various exhortations in chapters 12 and 13 are not merely humanistic but spring from a sense of nearness of the End when God will judge all people.

> And this, knowing the time
> that the hour has already come to be raised up from sleep,
> for our salvation is nearer than when we first believed.
> The night is far gone, the day is near.

In verses 11-12a, Paul is portraying the 'age' begun with Adam's Sin as a 'dark night', in which his children engage in 'works of darkness' (v. 12). Perhaps Paul is adapting Jesus' teaching about wakeful watchfulness throughout the night (Mark 13:35-37). With the dawning of the 'day' will come God's salvation (the reappearance of Christ).[16] 'The night is nearly over,' says Paul, 'the daylight is near.' While 'salvation is nearer than when we first believed', Paul is not sensationalizing the Second Coming, but rather urging the behaviour of the 'light' rather than the 'darkness'. His teaching about 'rulers' exercising God's 'authority' in the world (13:1-7) shows that he did not think the return of Christ was certainly imminent.

---

16. Portrayal of this age as the 'night' appears also in 1 Thessalonians 5:1-11 and Ephesians 5:8-20.

Rather, Paul is saying that with the first coming of Christ the dawning of the day of salvation is 'in principle' imminent, not that it was 'of necessity' imminent in the next few minutes. Paul asserts this 'in principle' imminence of 'salvation' to sharpen the demands for holy living set out in verses 12b-14.

Therefore
let us cast off the works of darkness;
let us put on the armour of light.

Let us walk becomingly as in the day
                not in carousing and drunkenness
                not in sexual acts and licentiouness
                not in quarrelling and jealousy.

But put on the Lord Jesus Christ
and take no forethought for the flesh
how to fulfill its passions.

Paul is directing these exhortations to Gentile believers, some of whom knew from first-hand experience the drinking binges, sexual orgies and quarrelling Paul refers to. These occurred both in high-class banquets and low-class bordellos. The New Testament writers frequently refer to such activities implying their currency in contemporary society (see e.g. Eph.4:17-5:20; Titus 3:3; 1 Pet. 1:14, 18; 4:3-5). These shameful activities are 'dark' since they usually occur at 'night' behind closed doors under the 'cloak of darkness'. Such behaviour has the appearance of 'having a good time' but really speaks of boredom and despair, the sense that life is rapidly slipping away, and equally that death is rapidly approaching.

Paul is appealing to his readers' memory of their baptism when, having heard and obeyed the gospel they were 'united' to Christ crucified, buried and raised (see 6:3-4). At that time they 'put off' the ragged garments of the former life as Adam's child and 'put on' the 'new' life of God's child Jesus Christ, the white garment of holiness. In short, they are to live as Christ lived, in imitation of him, Christ-shaped, as it were. Here Paul is exhorting them to continue as they began in the face of the temptations surrounding them. Their eyes are to be cast forward towards their 'salvation', with no thought for the former life of 'flesh' and its 'passions' when they lived as Adam's children.

Paul's words have been made famous through their impact on a man who read them in AD 386.[17] Brought up as a Christian, this native of Thagaste in North Africa became a professor of rhetoric, first in Rome and then in Milan. He had long since abandoned any vestige of Christian living, and immersed himself in ways of life that typified the godlessness of that time. In Milan he re-entered the Christian circle, though as yet without repentance from sexual promiscuity and without accompanying peace of heart. One day in deep sadness, seated in the garden of a Christian friend, he heard a child singing, 'Take up and read.' Coming inside the house, he opened at random a volume of Paul's letters and read the words, 'not in carousing and drunkenness, not in sexual acts and licentiouness ... but put on the Lord Jesus Christ.' This proved to be a life-changing moment for Augustine, who later became Bishop of Hippo in North Africa and the greatest theologian of the early Christian centuries.

STUDY QUESTIONS

1. Why is love the concrete expression of a true relationship with God?

2. How does 'love' truly fulfill the law?

3. How does renewing my mind, as Paul states, truly transform me?

4. Why does humility foster 'oneness' in the body of Christ? (Not *how* but *why*)

5. Where does hypocrisy seem to rear its head the most in the church today?

---

17. Augustine, *Confessions* viii.28-30.

6. What harm does our vengeance produce to the honor of Christ?

7. How can you pray for brothers and sisters who live in countries where the government is corrupt? What can you pray for concerning that government?

8. What safeguards do you need to put in place in order to not fulfill your fleshly desires?

14

Welcome the Weak
(Romans 14:1–15:6)

The letter to this point has been preparing for this important passage, which reaches its climax in 15:5 and 6 ('May ... God ... give you the same way of thinking ... that with one accord and with one voice you glorify ... God').

Two groups of people are in Paul's mind, the 'weak' and (by inference) the 'strong' (see 15:1). Who are these? Clearly they are Christian believers; Paul refers to them as 'brothers'. Their respective attitudes to food and 'days' identified them as Jews and Gentiles. Almost certainly, then, the 'weak' are Jewish Christians and the 'strong' are Gentile believers. Both belong to the scattered house-based churches in Rome.

But why does Paul call them 'weak' and 'strong'? Two reasons are suggested. First, Paul did not want to intensify existing ethnic differences, so he used other identifying terms. Thus he called Jewish Christians 'weak' because they felt bound to observe practices relating to 'meat' (things one can and cannot eat) and 'days' (setting aside special calendar observances). The 'strong' felt no religious obligation regarding 'meat' or 'days'. Perhaps, too, Paul used the 'weak'/ 'strong' terminology to underscore the obligation of the 'strong' to 'welcome' the 'weak,' in line with Jesus' well-known teachings.

The observance or non-observance of 'meat' and 'days' was and remains deeply divisive. Paul's Spirit-inspired genius was to encourage mutual respect and to urge each to recognize a loyalty higher than to food and time, thus making fellowship possible. That higher loyalty is to Christ who is Lord and judge to each person, regardless of whether 'weak' or 'strong'.

Paul teaches that the important thing is not whether one is 'weak' or 'strong'. The fundamental truth is that each is the 'servant of another', that is, the risen Lord Jesus. Thus let the 'strong' not despise the 'weak' for observing 'meat' and 'days', nor should the 'weak' condemn the 'strong' for not doing so. Yet the burden of the passage is not addressed to the 'weak' but to the 'strong'. The 'strong' are to 'welcome' the 'weak', not causing offence to the 'weak'. Let the 'strong' be prepared to make considerable cultural concessions to the 'weak' for the sake of incorporating them into the 'one body in Christ'.

This passage begins, 'Welcome him who is weak in the faith' and the next passage begins, 'Welcome one another, therefore, as Christ has welcomed you' (15:7). Clearly 'welcoming ' is important and arguably the climax of the entire letter, in particular, the Gentile believers' 'welcome' of the Jewish brothers and sisters.

1. MEAT (vv. 1-4)

At this point in the letter (v. 1) Paul calls on his ('strong') readers, 'Welcome him who is weak in the faith.' The references following to 'meat' and 'days' identify the 'weak' as Jews, that is, those who are by upbringing and culture unable to conduct their lives apart from religious observances connected with *food* and special periods of *time*. For them, 'holiness' and 'purity' meant abstaining from food that defiled and from working on the Sabbath. They are, however, 'weak in *the* faith', that is, in the fundamental *doctrines* of the Christian faith. Most likely, Paul is referring to their shaky grasp on faith in Christ as the means of 'righteousness' in the sight of God on account of which the greater part of this letter has been addressed (chs. 2–7, 9–11). They seek to arrive at their own 'righteousness' based on 'works of the Law' (9:30–10:4). The truth is that only those who by faith belong to Christ are 'righteous' before God.

Clearly the 'strong' are Gentile Christians, that is, people not subject to the same religious scruples as Jews regarding 'meat' and 'days'. Later, Paul calls on people from both groups to 'welcome one another' (15:7). Why, then, in verse 1 does he begin his appeal to *Gentiles*? The answer appears to be that Gentile Christians were now in the ascendancy in Rome. Jews, including Christian Jews, had been expelled from Rome by Emperor Claudius in AD 49.[1] In AD 54, when Nero succeeded Claudius, Jews were allowed to return. I assume that Jews, including Christian Jews, may have been rather slow to make their way back to Rome. Prior to AD 49 Jewish Christians appear to have been predominant; the situation may have been reversed after AD 54. In this case Paul is displaying tender care of his fellow-Israelites in calling upon Gentile believers to incorporate them into the body of Christ.

How are 'strong' (Gentile) Christians to do this? Each is to 'welcome' the one who is 'weak' in the faith. Paul's word 'welcome' (*proslambanō*) means not merely 'receive,' but 'thoroughly receive,' 'warmly welcome.' Luke records that when he and Paul were shipwrecked on Malta, 'the natives showed us unusual kindness for they kindled a fire and *welcomed* us all' (Acts 28:2). Paul is appealing to Gentile believers to extend the hand of friendship and to embrace the Jewish believers into the common fellowship (see on 15:5-6).

Such a 'welcome' must be the universal hallmark of genuinely Christian congregations. Church members need to look out for the outsider, the newcomer and the visitor, in order to extend a warm welcome to such. Sadly this is not always the case. Some come to church searching after God but, finding no friendly greeting, turn away.

But, to return to the situation in Rome that Paul is addressing, the Gentile must not 'welcome' the Jew in order to engage in 'quarrels about opinions' (*diakriseis dialogismōn*). This 'welcome' is not with the intention of debate and dispute. In court houses prosecutors cross-examine defendants and in parliaments party 'opposes' party. The tone and culture of those bodies is *adversarial* which, in broad terms, serves the community well enough. But these Gentile Christians are not

---

1. See Introduction, page 7.

to embrace their Jewish brothers and sisters in order to debate their practices regarding 'meat' and 'days'.

In verse 2 Paul makes a simple observation about the table practices of the Gentile and the Jew. The former 'believes'[2] he may eat everything and anything. It does not occur to the Gentile that eating or not eating has anything to do with 'righteousness' before God; it is part of his cultural heritage. But this will be uppermost in the Jew's mind. Based on his Law, the Jew will eat only vegetables.[3]

Paul was uniquely equipped to make this statement. Raised in a strictly Jewish family in Tarsus and educated in Jerusalem, he knew well the lengths to which fellow-Israelites went in fulfilling the 'works of the Law' in dietary matters. On the other hand, however, through his new calling he now understood what happened at meal tables in Gentile homes. Few knew as Paul did how deeply entrenched eating habits were with both Jews and Gentiles and, therefore, how deep a source division it was between them. For a practical unity to occur among Christians in Rome this issue must be resolved.

Verse 3 addresses the 'strong' and 'weak' in turn. Each will tend to have settled attitudes. The 'strong' will despise the 'weak' for his scruples in not eating this food or that. At that time Gentiles did despise Jews. Tacitus reflects this hostility in his reference to Jews. They 'regard the rest of mankind with all the hatred of enemies. They sit apart at meals' (*History* 5.5). For their part Jews were notoriously censorious, judging and condemning 'Gentile sinners' (Gal. 2:15; cf. Acts 10:28: 'it is unlawful...for a Jew to associate with or visit any one of another nation'). Paul, however, calls upon the 'strong' not to 'despise the weak' and the 'weak' not to 'condemn the strong'. To the 'strong' Paul gives this reason: 'for God has

---

2. We must not miss Paul's wordplay where 'believe' (*pisteuō*) echoes the noun 'the faith' (*pistis*) from verse 1.

3. Philo, a Jew contemporary with Paul, wrote: 'it was not necessary that man the creature most akin to wisdom should be impelled to feast upon [various kinds of fishes, birds and land animals] and so change himself into the savagery of wild beasts. And therefore, to this day, those who have thought for self-restraint abstain from every one of them and take green *vegetables* and the fruits of trees as a relish to their bread' (*On Providence* 2.69-70).

welcomed him.' *God's* 'welcome' of the 'weak'/ the Jew (in Christ – cf. 15:7) is the basis for the 'strong' welcoming the 'weak'.

Paul's question (v. 4), 'Who are you to condemn the servant of another?', suggests that each group was 'judging' and 'condemning' the other. But men do not judge men; the risen Lord will be the judge of all. 'It is,' he says, 'before his *own* Lord that he stands or falls.' I do not judge you and you do not judge me; the Lord judges me (see on vv. 12-13, 22). Paul then adds, to the great encouragement of his readers then and now, 'and he shall be made to stand for the Lord is able (*dunatai* – 'he is powerful') to make him stand.' The Lord Jesus, who has saved us by his death and resurrection, is powerful in enabling us to stand before him with our salvation intact on the last day (cf. 5:10: ' now that we are reconciled [by his death], we shall be saved by his life').

2. Days (vv. 5-9)
Paul continues to refer to Jews and Gentiles, though not explicitly. Perhaps Paul sought to minimize tensions between the two groups by omitting precise ethnic identification? Earlier he addressed the issue of foods abstained from by Jews but freely eaten by Gentiles (vv. 2-3). Now, in verse 5, he turns to the observance or non-observance of 'days'.

> One man judges one day above another.
> The other judges every day the same.

Gentiles did identify days of the week with the gods, e.g. Monday is Old English for the 'moon's day' which in turn corresponded to the Latin *lunae dies* and the Greek *hēmera selēnēs*. The religious ceremonies and festivals of the Gentiles occurred on special days, but the Gentiles were relatively light-hearted about them because they were times of feasting and merriment. Not so with the Jews, especially in regard to their Sabbath. Any work on that day brought defilement in the sight of the Lord.

To our surprise Paul does not come down on one side or the other. What is important, ultimately, is neither the 'day' observed or ignored nor the food eaten or uneaten, but the individual's subjection to the risen Lord Jesus exercised in a spirit of thankfulness.

Let each be fully persuaded in his own mind.

He who observes the day,	observes it	to the Lord.
and he who eats,	eats	to the Lord,
	for he gives thanks	to the Lord

and he who does not eat		
	does not eat	to the Lord
	and he gives thanks	to God.

So long as the focus is on 'meat' or 'days', there will be no possibility of true unity between Jews and Gentiles. But when the believer's eye is directed to the Lord and he acts out of thanksgiving to God, the Gentile will 'welcome' the Jew and together they will with one voice glorify God (15:6). Otherwise, their very coming together will be an occasion for 'quarrels about opinions' on these matters (see on v. 1).

Paul is not merely calling for the spirit of toleration that is much-loved in 'politically correct' societies. Rather, he encourages each party to discern their truest priority, which must not be an item of food or a unit of time, but the Lord Jesus himself. This is the only basis for unity between these culturally disparate groups.

Paul's words are strange to our ears. The 'welcome' by believing Gentiles of their Jewish brothers and sisters was then within reach. Why else would Paul be making this appeal? We long for the day when such fellowship may again be possible. Clearly this was close to Paul's heart and therefore to the heart of the risen Lord Jesus Christ.

The big issues of human existence are 'living' and 'dying'; the matters relating to food and time are negligible in comparison. Christ came to give 'life' to the 'dying' and to deliver from its bondage those who regard 'meat' and 'days' as the meaning of life. Even in the churches, there are many for whom the peripheral are central (e.g. the special 'robes' ministers wear) for whom Christ and the gospel is peripheral. But this is to make central the peripheral and to bring the peripheral to the centre.

In verses 7 and 8 Paul focuses on 'life' and 'death' issues.

> For no one lives to himself
> and no one dies to himself.
> But if we live, we live to the Lord.
> And if we die, we die to the Lord.
> Whether we live,
> whether we die,
> we are the Lord's.

Paul is saying that for the believer the focus of existence is the Lord Jesus Christ, both in 'life' and 'death'. This is because at the very heart of Christ's intentions was his concern for the 'life' and 'death' of those who by their faith in him belong to him. So Paul makes this grand statement in verse 9:

> For to this end Christ died and lived
> that he might rule as Lord
> over the dead and the living.

Are we struck by the sequence, 'Christ died and lived'? Remarkably Paul says nothing here about Christ's 'life' in his three-year ministry (but see 15:3). The reason is that in Christ's 'death and life' is the core of the gospel. He passes over Christ's incarnate ministry, focusing all attention on his sacrifice and resurrection. For by these, the sinful 'lost' find the 'righteousness of God' ahead of the Last Day. In the events of the first Easter God has 'dragged' the judgement and deliverance of the End-time back into a historical 'moment' when the gospel is heard and believed. Thus for 'living' people Christ is Lord. So too is he Lord even to those who die. For in death the formerly lost are not separated from the Lord of their life. Rather, they are 'with' him (cf. 2 Cor. 5:8: 'at home, with the Lord'), ruled over as Lord by him even in death. What are 'meat' and 'days' compared with this?

3. DO NOT CONDEMN, DO NOT DESPISE (vv. 10-13)

Based on the centrality of Christ as regards 'life' and 'death' matters Paul now admonishes the Romans, both Jews and Gentiles. He peppers each in turn with questions along the lines of their respective and characteristic failing, the Jew in 'judging' and the Gentile in 'despising'. But the striking thing here is that Paul calls on each to regard the other as a 'brother'. Paul addresses his readers throughout the Letter as 'brothers' (inclusive for 'brothers' *and* 'sisters' – e.g. 1:13; 11:25; 12:1; 15:14). Now, however, for the first time in the letter he refers each to the other as 'brother'. In the kingdom of God Christ will be 'firstborn among many *brothers*' (8:29). Let them treat one another in 'brotherly' ways now as regards the problem of the moment, namely, that Jews are 'judging' Gentiles and Gentiles are 'despising' Jews over issues Paul regards as peripheral (see on 14:3-4).

| But | you, | why do you | judge | your brother? |
| And | you, | why do you | despise | your brother? |

Paul is not appealing to the 'toleration' demanded in modern pluralistic societies according to the canons of political correctness. No. The apostle is pointing to ultimate reality, that is, each and every person must face *God* as judge, as Paul goes on to state in verses 10c-12.

For all will stand at the judgment seat of God.
For it is written,
'As I live, says the Lord,
before me every knee will bow
and every tongue confess to God.'
Therefore each of us will give an answer about himself to God.

Here Paul is borrowing the language of Roman courts. 'Stand' was a technical term for 'stand *accused*'. A 'judgement seat' (*bēma*) was a 'bench' on which a Roman magistrate sat to

---

4. Paul uses similar language about the universal judgement in 2 Corinthians 5:10 where, however, the judge is not God but Christ. Jesus stood before Pilate who sat upon his 'judgement seat' hearing the accusations (Matt. 27:19; John 19:13). At that time Christ handed himself over to God, the just judge (1 Pet. 2:23).

decide the guilt or innocence of an accused person.[4] To support his assertion Paul quotes Isaiah 45:23 along with some other texts. The mind-focusing reality of life is that at death we all stand before God our judge and each of us will make our answer about how we have lived. What are peripheral matters next to this? How carefully, if at all, should we 'judge' another fellow-human? If God is my judge, how dare I judge another person?

So Paul concludes in verse 13a: 'Therefore, let us not judge one another.' Of course, Paul's words are directed to the Roman Christians, the Jews in particular. But they are relevant for all people at all times. As members of the human race, we judge one another repeatedly, often in ignorance of the circumstances. The fact is that we are children of Adam who must face God as our judge. We are only able to stand 'righteous' in his presence on account of our Lord and Saviour Jesus Christ. So we should think hard before we judge others or pass on our judgements about them to other people.

With these words, Paul rounds off the passage begun at verse 1. In the latter part of this verse (v. 13b) Paul will begin to move his readers on to further and related attitudes to others in the 'mixed' but united assembly Paul expects will result from his letter.

4. GENTILES: 'WALK IN LOVE' (vv. 13b-18)

These words are addressed to the Gentile believers in Rome, as were the opening words of this chapter. Again, this would make sense in the post- AD 54 situation if, as seems likely, the Gentile Christians were in the majority with Jewish believers in the minority. Earlier Paul commented that the 'weak' do not eat meat, but only vegetables (v. 2), a reference to Jewish dietary scruples. The Gentile must not 'despise' the Jew for his weakness (v. 3). But now Paul goes beyond that. He will urge the Gentile to forgo meat-eating (v. 15), at least – so it seems – when in the company of the Jewish brother in Christ.

But first (v. 13b) Paul calls on the Gentile Christians to 'make a judgement'. Here there is a wordplay, a rhetorical device much loved by Paul. First, he said in verse 13a, 'Let us not judge (*krinōmen*) one another,' but then he says, 'but rather judge (*krinate*) ...'. That second 'judgement' or 'decision' is: 'not to place a stumbling block or barrier before a brother' (v. 13c).

The eating of various (but not all) kinds of meat was forbidden to Jews but not to Gentiles (see on v. 2). Jewish abstinence from pork was a classic example and inspired Gentiles to mock and deride Jews. Eating meat and abstaining from meat was a badge, respectively, of Gentiles and Jews. How, then, would a Jewish Christian feel about a Gentile Christian freely eating forbidden meat? Putting ourselves in the shoes of such Jews, we would probably feel outraged by such behaviour. Hence Paul tells the Gentile brother not to place this 'stumbling block' in front of the Jewish believer.

But it is vital that the Gentile understand Paul's reasons. Paul is not requiring the Gentile to come under Jewish food laws. In verse 14 he states in the strongest terms possible his rejection of the proposition that food can bring 'defilement'.

> For I know and am persuaded in the Lord
> that nothing is defiled (*koinos*) in itself.

Later Paul will put it another way, that is, 'Everything is pure' (*kathara* – v. 20). Almost certainly Paul is echoing a teaching of Jesus on the subject of defilement.[5] The Pharisees taught that 'defilement' could be 'caught' by contact with utensils used by a Gentile so that such vessels must be purified by 'washings'. Jesus, however, taught that we are 'defiled' by the evils that issue from our hearts, and not from what we touch or eat (see Mark 7:15-23). In an instant the Jewish people were free in principle from dietary restrictions and from the barrier that hindered them from eating with Gentiles. Nonetheless, for Peter it took the vision at Joppa and the descent of the Spirit on Gentiles at Caesarea Maritima to convince him of the new freedom instituted by Jesus (see Acts 10:9-16).

---

5. Paul's almost certain reference in Romans, a letter written *c.* AD 56/7, to a teaching of Jesus requires that such teaching was extant by that time, whether in an already completed version of Mark or an earlier edition of that Gospel. In short, Romans 14:14 is evidence of the early existence and circulation of Mark or of source material underlying Mark.

Jesus taught that the source of 'defilement' was personal and ethical not impersonal and ritualistic. This not only put him at odds with the Pharisees but also with the common understanding of 'religion'. Millions flock to the wash in the Ganges to find purity, something that fits exactly the western media's stereotypes of religious people. The Pharisees failed to understand Jesus then, just as people generally fail to understand him now. Yet his recognition that defilement originates from within is true to life's experience. We are defiled and destroyed spiritually from within. Knowing this, Jesus anticipated the sacrifice he was soon to make to liberate us from the penalty and grasp of inner evil.

But to return to verse 14, Paul states that 'nothing' of itself 'defiles'. Yet, as he now adds, we may nonetheless *feel* defiled. Conscience controlled by a powerful religious culture may tell me that I am defiled by eating a forbidden food, notwithstanding the Lord's declaration that 'all foods are clean'. It may take a time to be free to eat what was previously forbidden, as Paul recognises in this passage.

> ... nothing is defiled in itself
> except to the one who reckons something is defiled.
> To him it is defiled.

Here we see not only Paul's grasp of the workings of the human heart, but also his big-hearted compassion for those Jews who would suffer through a Gentile's insensitivity. We are reminded of his concern for the 'weak brother', that is, the former idolater who is now a believer who would be destroyed by a mature Christian's exercise of freedom to eat sacrificed meat in an idol's temple (1 Cor. 8:7-13). The details differ. In First Corinthians the 'weak brother' is a Gentile but in Romans the 'weak' are Jews. Yet Paul is pastorally concerned for both Jew and Gentile who are 'weak', that is vulnerable and fragile in their relationship with the Lord.

Paul speaks quite directly to the Gentiles in verse 15:

For if through meat (*brōma*[6]) your brother is made to suffer
you are no longer walking in love.

By 'made to suffer' Paul is thinking of spiritual confusion and
discouragement that will lead to this Jewish believer falling
away from his relationship with the Lord Jesus Christ. Thus
Paul says to the 'strong' in verse 15c: 'Do not let your meat
ruin the one for whom Christ died.'

Paul knew better than most the negative impact of a Gentile
eating meat in the presence of a Jew. Once more, then, Paul
is calling on the Gentile to make practical concessions and to
accommodate his behaviour to the Jewish scruple (see on v. 1).
For the Gentile believer not to do so would be to fail to show
love to his Jewish brother for whom Christ had died. Such
'love' (*agapē*) is the hallmark of the Christian. God's 'love' is
poured into our hearts by the Holy Spirit (5:5) and is to be
shown towards our fellowmen. This is the truest fulfilment
of the Law of God (13:8-10). That love is most chiefly shown
in actions taken or not taken to seek and protect the salvation
of others. Though he does not spell out what he means, most
likely Paul's words mean that the Gentile will forgo eating
meat when in the company of Jews.

At the same time Paul is concerned that Gentiles are not
brought under some kind of new Law in the matter of eating.
Not only does meat of itself not defile; Paul actually calls the
Gentile freedom to eat a 'good' thing (v. 16). Paul is no legalist.
But he understands that the Gentile believer's freedom in
Christ will easily be misunderstood, 'blasphemed' no less,
by Jewish observers. It is his 'blaspheming' of the Gentile
Christian that will cause the Jewish believer to 'stumble'
(v. 13), to 'suffer' (v. 15a) and finally bring about spiritual
'ruin' (v. 15c). So Paul exhorts the Gentile, 'Let not your good
be badly spoken of.'

Paul sums up his thinking (v. 17) in this splendid
declaration.

---

6. More generally *brōma* means 'food'; the context arising from Romans 14:2
suggests the more specific meaning, 'meat.'

```
For the kingdom of God
        is not      meat and drink
but                 righteousness and peace
                    and joy in the Holy Spirit.
```

God's governance of his people (his 'kingdom') as expressed in history ahead of the End, says Paul, is not expressed in what they eat or abstain from. Eating and drinking are not unimportant but they are secondary, that is, they are peripheral. Rather God's kingdom here and now is the enjoyment of his gift of 'righteousness' in Christ crucified and risen, with its accompanying 'peace' with God (5:1) and the 'joy' of heart brought by the Holy Spirit (5:3, 5). But this means that the Gentile believer will gladly forgo meat, rare luxury though it was in antiquity, for the sake of loving the brother Jew coming as he did from a different ethnic and religious background.

Paul rounds off this section with an appeal (v. 18).

```
He who serves Christ in this
        is      pleasing        to God
and             approved        by men.
```

Notice that 'serving Christ' is by serving the brother believer. Christian service as stated here is not vague and unfocused but practical and 'down to earth'. The prophets dismissed merely 'vertical' Temple-based 'worship'. Their concern was that the worship of God be expressed in hearty justice shown 'horizontally' towards the fellow Israelite.

In serving the risen Christ, Paul was concerned above all for the welfare of the fellow-Christian, in this case the *spiritual* welfare of the marginalized Jewish believer. This 'service,' says Paul, is 'pleasing to God' (*euarestos tō theō*), a term originating in a temple sacrifice 'acceptable' to the Lord but used in the New Testament for living acceptably in the presence of God ahead of his end-time judgement (cf. 12:2: 'present your bodies a living sacrifice, *acceptable to God*'; cf. 2 Cor. 5:9; Eph. 5:10; Heb. 13:21). At the same time this 'service' is 'approved by men,' that is, it 'passes the test' (*dokimos*), a blacksmith's term for ironwork that is 'tried and tested'.

Paul sensed that Gentile believers were prone to arrogance regarding Jewish believers (11:20) and showed, as reflected here, a degree of insensitivity. These verses are about safeguarding the Jewish Christian's salvation. They drive the Gentile reader sensitively to consider the impact of his behaviour on Jews in so mundane a matter as the food eaten. This is not a question of providing food for the hungry, an issue that also concerned Paul (see his comments later in 15:25-26). Rather, in this passage Paul is tenderly concerned for his fellow-Israelite's relationship with the Lord Jesus Christ. This has been the burden of Romans throughout. Let the Gentile Christian 'walk in love'.

5. GENTILES: PURSUE PEACE AND UP-BUILDING (vv. 19-21)

These verses build on their immediate predecessors and are the most pointed on the subject of Gentile Christians eating and drinking and the negative impact on Jewish believers. Such behaviour will cause the Jew to 'stumble' (vv. 20c, 21), picking up an earlier reference (v. 13: 'decide ... not to put a *stumbling block* before a brother'). At the same time Paul introduces a new image, 'up-building' and 'demolishing'.

Verse 19 begins with a very strong 'So then' (*ara oun*). All that has been said before is now gathered up in a strong concluding appeal.

So then let us pursue
     the things that make for peace
and the things that make for up-building towards one another.

Paul thought of a church as having a 'foundation' and a 'super-structure'. The 'foundation' had been laid in Rome by 'another man', that is, not by Paul (15:20). Paul is only 'passing through' (15:24) so that this letter must achieve what he will not attempt by his sustained personal presence.

We are now close to the heart of this letter, Paul's concern for the 'superstructure' of Roman Christianity. Paul's passion is to incorporate in 'one body' Gentile and Jewish Christians. He knew that where their respective focus was on 'meat' and 'days', contention must follow. Rather, he directed both to the risen

Lord. Let them find their unity in the knowledge that the Lord was uppermost to each. In particular, let the Gentile believer make concessions regarding meat and drink and so safeguard the salvation of Israelite believers. This is the meaning of 'the things that make for peace ... and up-building'.

On the other hand, however, it will be all too easy to 'demolish' rather than 'up-build' the 'work of God,' that is, the superstructure.

> Do not for the sake of meat pull down the work of God.

Paul fears the ruination of the 'work of God' in Rome through the failure of Gentile believers discerning the effects of meat-eating with Jews.

Before reaching his powerful conclusion once more he asserts that abstinence from meat is not a new law being introduced by him. 'Everything, indeed, is pure' (*kathara*), he insists (v. 20b), echoing his earlier words, 'nothing is defiled (*koinon*) in itself' (v. 14). 'Meat is "pure," it does not "defile" you,' he assures the Gentiles. But your eating of it may destroy your Jewish brothers and sisters.'

So he states his abiding principle in verses 20c-21:

It is wrong	through what you eat to make a man stumble.
It is good	not to eat meat or drink wine
	lest in this your brother stumbles.

Paul speaks of the 'wrong' (*kakos*) and the 'good' (*kalos*) these Gentiles can do their Jewish Christian brothers and sisters. The greatest 'wrong' we can do is to deflect another person from finding eternal salvation in Christ. Likewise, the greatest 'good' we can render is to facilitate another's salvation. 'Eating meat' and 'drinking wine' in themselves are not the issue; both are 'pure' and neither is 'defiled'. The only question is: what will be the effect of this eating and drinking on the Jewish believer's place in the body of Christ in Rome. Paul is in no doubt. For the sake of the Jew's salvation the Gentiles need to make concessions and to accommodate their practices to Jewish scruples.

6. Faith and Judgement (vv. 22-23)

These verses are difficult, as reflected in a lack of consensus among the commentators. Each of the two verses contains pithy maxims or aphorisms. The keywords in both verses are 'faith' and 'condemn'. The 'judging' or 'condemning' is self-directed. Thus the verses are about the individual believer's inner life of 'faith' and self-judgement.

But who is Paul addressing, the 'strong' (Gentile believer), the 'weak' (Jewish believer) or each in turn? In view of the general drift of the text from 14:13 to 15:6, it seems likely that Paul is continuing to address the 'strong' (Gentile believer). Paul has encouraged the 'strong' to abstain from eating meat for the sake of the 'weak'. But does this present problems for the Gentile Christian? Most likely it does necessitate Paul's assurances.

> The faith you have,
> have to yourself in the presence of God.
> Blessed is he who does not condemn himself
> in what he approves.

This is deeply personal; the pronouns are singular. Christian faith is personal, between the believer and God. I am 'saved' as an individual who has heard and believed the gospel of Christ. I will stand before God as an individual and give my own answer for the life I have lived and the service to others that I have rendered. Paul is reinforcing the intense sense of the individual Gentile's accountability to God his judge (vv. 4, 7, 8-12). So Paul is saying, 'Live your life now in God's presence.' To this he adds God's blessing upon a clear conscience in the matter of meat and drink, as well as of 'days'.

True, Paul has urged the 'strong' to abstain from such food for the sake of the 'weak' and his salvation (vv. 13, 15, 20-21). Yet that abstinence is not for the sake of the Gentile abstainer but for the sake of the Jewish brother. Paul does not want the Gentile believer's conscience to be clouded or compromised. Let him be clear. In abstaining from meat for the Jew he is not to condemn himself. It is right in principle to 'approve' the eating. In short, Paul is protecting the abstaining Gentile Christian's conscience in the presence of his God.

Paul continues, in verse 23, by pointing to the dangers of eating without clear understanding:

> But he who has doubts, if he eats,
> is condemned because he did not eat from faith.

This is hypothetical, signalled by 'if he eats'. We are curious. Paul has discouraged the Gentile eating meat, which I assume means in company with Jews. So what does he mean by, 'if he eats'? One answer would be that he is eating meat *in his own home* with only Gentiles present.[7] But what if he eats with lingering doubts planted there perhaps by the scrupulous Jewish brother? Let him understand that his freedom to eat is one of the blessings of the gospel of Christ. Christ's teaching about defilement has liberated the human race from laws restricting the eating of meats (Mark 7:15-23). His death and resurrection have swept away all cultic restrictions touching 'meat' and 'days'. So, 'Yes, Gentile you may eat, but with a free conscience because of Christ, on account of "faith".'

Paul concludes with an aphorism (v. 23b) which, again, reinforces the accountability of the individual to the God who has saved him and who will judge him.

> But everything that is not of faith is sin.

It is sometimes argued that Paul is using 'faith' here in a different way, that 'faith' in this context is not 'saving faith' but a broader kind of assurance about the rightness of action. More likely, however, is the proposal that 'faith' means the same as elsewhere in Romans. That is, Paul has in mind that personal 'trust' in Christ, based on the gospel, that brings God's verdict 'righteous' to the sinner. It is Christ and this 'faith' in

---

7. Paul sees no problem for a believer in eating temple-sacrificed food at home (1 Cor. 10:25, 29-30) though he opposes eating such food in public (8:9-13; 10:14-22). Does this principle carry over into his advice for Gentiles in their eating patterns with Jews, namely, that they are free to eat the meat offending to Jews at home, but not in the company of Jews?

him that sweeps away the plethora of cultic restrictions that defined foods and times as either 'defiled' or 'pure'. Let the Gentile eat if he so chooses, but be clear in his own mind that Christ has set him free to do so.

7. ONE MIND AND ONE VOICE (15:1-6)

Paul concludes his appeal to the 'strong' (Gentile believer) begun at the commencement of this section (14:1). Though a Jew, Paul identifies himself with the 'strong' in caring for the 'weak', that is, his fellow-Israelite believers. For his part, however, Paul had worked through the issues of food and Christian liberty (cf. 1 Cor. 9:21: 'To those outside the Law I became as one outside the Law'). Paul was 'free' in ways that fellow-Jews were not.

Throughout Romans Paul displays his passion for the salvation of his fellow-Jews (10:1; cf. 9:1-5; 11:1). He devotes chapters 2–7 to ensuring they grasp that the 'righteousness' of God is 'in Christ' and is not by 'works of the Law'. In chapters 9–11 he encouraged them that God has a future for Israel, his historic people, in Christ. He longs to see Jewish believers united with Gentile believers in the 'one body' of Christ (9:1-5; 12:4-5), glorifying God their Father with 'one voice' (v. 6).

To that end (v. 1) he calls on the 'strong' in Rome to accommodate themselves to the 'weak'.

> We who are strong
>   ought   to bear the shortcomings[8] of the weak
>   and   not   to please ourselves.

For the first and only time Paul refers specifically to the 'strong' (*dunatoi*); that 'name' was only inferred earlier by reference to their counterpart, the 'weak' (14:1). It is striking that Paul begins with his appeal to the 'strong' and makes greater demands on them throughout this whole passage. The 'strong' are to 'welcome' the weak (14:1), by 'not despising'

---

8. *asthenēmata* is difficult to translate; literally it means 'sicknesses' or 'feeble-ness.'

them (14:3, 10) and, in particular, by abstaining from eating meat in their presence (14:13-23).

Not only in Rome then but equally here and now the great principle remains: the strong 'ought' to bear the shortcomings of the 'weak'. That is their 'obligation' (what they 'ought' to do) and their 'gift'. They are not to 'please themselves' in eating meat alongside Jewish Christians.

This is a fundamental emphasis of the gospel of Christ, though the details may change according to time and place. In the kingdom of the End-time, all existing values, that is, of power and wealth will be overturned. The crucifixion of the Messiah symbolizes the end of the power-plays of this world. His resurrection points on in hope to a new heaven and a new earth. Thus the 'meek' will inherit the earth and the mighty will be cast down from their seats. Therefore Christ called to himself the heavily burdened, the sinners, the lost, the poor, the broken, the marginalized and the 'little' to show the ways of God into his future. Consistently with his Master, and the prophets before him, Paul expresses tender concern for the 'weak' (2 Cor. 11:29: 'Who is weak and I am not weak? Who is made to fall and I am not indignant?'; cf. 1 Cor. 8:13) and for the 'have nots' (1 Cor. 11:22). In this age the strong and the rich sit on top with the pyramid of humanity under them. In the kingdom of God that pyramid will be up-ended and it is to be up-ended now, in the churches. In the church of the crucified but risen Messiah the 'strong' are to support the 'weak' and not vice versa as in the kingdoms of this world.

In verse 2 Paul amplifies the 'obligation' of the 'strong' towards the 'weak' in the church.

> Let each of us please his neighbour   for his good
>   for his up-building.

Here Paul reintroduces his keyword 'up-building' (*oikodomē*). A church community consists of its 'foundation' (Jesus Christ – 1 Cor. 3:11) and its 'building' (people who believe in and act like Jesus Christ). The overriding purpose of all church gatherings is the 'up-building' of its individual members as well as of its corporate life. Critical to this is that 'each' member does not 'please himself' (v. 1) but seeks to 'please his neighbour for his good', that is, his and the church's 'up-building'. This principle applies to all members, though in this passage Paul is specifically urging the 'strong' to 'please' his 'weak' brother in Christ.

By 'up-building' Paul is not speaking about a growth in church membership. Rather, his concern is the development of Christian 'character' as one group of members sensitively and unselfishly 'pleases' those who are 'weak' and disadvantaged. Growth in numbers is desirable, but must not be at the expense of the growth in spiritual maturity that accompanies sacrificial engagement with those who are culturally and temperamentally different from us. A family is a community where people have to 'get on with' others and who grow up in the ups and downs of life together. A church is to be like that. Preoccupation with a church's 'size' may indicate an unawareness of the fundamental nature of true 'church growth' which is the 'up-building' of Christ-centred faith and Christ-like behaviour. There is no reason to believe that God is glorified by the 'size' factor, though we know he is honoured when people behave like Jesus.

The great model of the 'strong' unselfishly ministering to the 'weak' is Jesus Christ himself, as Paul now states in verse 3:

For even the Christ did not please himself.

Paul's opening words, 'For *even* the Christ[9], are quite remarkable. 'The Christ' is not merely a name but Jesus' title as God's anointed king, from the line of David (cf. 1:3: 'God's Son descended from David according to the flesh'; see on 15:12). Yet 'even' this king, the 'strongest of the strong', did not 'please himself' but bore the infirmities of the weak. His unselfishness and humility can be seen at every point, in his coming, his life and in his sacrificial death. In birth he laid aside his filial majesty at the Father's side to become poor in order to make others rich (2 Cor. 8:9). In life and ministry

9. *Kai gar ho Christos ...*

he came among the people 'as one who serves' (Luke 22:27). Most likely Paul's words here echo Jesus' own,[10] 'For *even* the Son of man came not to be ministered to but to minister' (Mark 10:45).[11] Yet 'even' this Great One came as a servant and poured himself out in life and death for others. If 'even' our King did not 'please himself,' then, clearly, neither should we who are his people.

Paul quotes Psalm 69:9 as a biblical foundation for Christ's unselfish service.

> But even as it is written,
> The reproaches of those who reproached you
> fall on me.

David, God's anointed king, was the author of Psalm 69. He speaks of suffering at the hands of his own family as well as his subjects in his 'zeal' for God and for God's 'house' (at that time, the tabernacle).

After the first Easter, however, when the disciples reflected on Jesus' expulsion of the traders from the Temple, the Spirit brought to their memories words that immediately precede Paul's words, 'Zeal for your house consumes me' (John 2:17). Now God's 'house' is his people, that is, those who belong to his anointed King. Clearly, then, this Psalm became important as prophetic for Jesus' zealous but sacrificial care of God's 'house', his church.

The church will always and all too easily take on the character of the world and its values of cleverness and power. The church must always be reshaping itself according to the template of Christ, its King. Not least this will mean that in the church the 'strong' do not 'please themselves' but their neighbours, bearing the infirmities of the 'weak'.

Paul's reference to Psalm 69 prompts him to make a general comment about all the scriptures in verse 4:

---

10. *Kai gar ho huios tou anthrōpou ...*

11. 'Son of man' was an alternative title for 'the Christ' (so Mark 8:29, 31; 14:61-62).

For everything written beforehand
was written for our instruction
that   through the endurance
and   through the encouragement
from the scriptures
we might have hope.

The Scriptures of the Old and New Testament are no ordin-ary writings, but the very 'breath of God' (2 Tim. 3:16: 'all scripture is *God-breathed*'). Written by men 'moved by' the Spirit of God (2 Pet. 1:21), the Scriptures uniquely provide for 'instruction' (*didaskalia*) and also by their message of 'endurance' and 'encouragement' give 'hope' for the people of God. Life in the world is tough going for most Christians, as it was for Paul and the early believers. It was not always easy for him or them then, or us now, to see the hand of God in the circumstances of life. Not least, it must have been extremely hard for Paul to see how God was going to keep his promises to the patriarchs in regard to his elect people, Israel. At the time of writing Israel has turned her back on her Messiah (10:18-21). Nonetheless, Paul 'endured' in his ministry, 'encouraged' to 'hope' in the outworking of God's good promises for the ultimate salvation of Israel. This he did by reading about the long-term fidelity of God to his word (3:2; 9:6), as recorded in the Scriptures' narrative of the history of Israel.

Paul, however, did not find 'hope' through 'endurance' and 'encouragement' by merely reading the Scriptures as if they were merely a human chronicle of the history of his nation. Historical, such writings were. Yet these texts have a focal figure, the Messiah, 'great David's greater son.' The Law and the Prophets eagerly anticipate this Coming One and the Gospels and Letters proclaim him as the Saviour of the world. As the Scriptures of the Old and New Testament are read through the eyes of Christian faith they come to life, by the Spirit of God. Otherwise they are 'dry as dust' texts from the remote past.

Furthermore, these texts have a unique God-breathed character, as noted above, so that God himself 'speaks' through them. The Scriptures impart 'endurance' and 'encouragement' because, as Paul now says (v. 5), God *himself* is 'the God of endurance and encouragement'. And they impart 'hope' because, as Paul says later, God is *'the God of hope'* (15:13). In short, God imparts his own character of 'endurance,' 'encouragement' and 'hope' through the reading of the sacred Scriptures which he has caused to be written for our instruction.

One of Thomas Cranmer's greatest prayers was based on verses 4 and 5.

> Blessed Lord you have caused all holy scriptures to be written for our learning: grant us so to hear them, read, mark, learn and inwardly digest them, that encouraged and supported by your Word, we may embrace and ever hold fast the joyful hope of everlasting life, which you have given us in our Saviour Jesus Christ (Prayer for the Second Sunday in Advent, in *An Australian Prayer Book,* 1978).

In verses 5-6 Paul concludes with a prayer the section he began in 14 :1:

> May the God of endurance and encouragement
> give you the same way of thinking
> according to Christ Jesus
> so that with one accord and with one voice
> you glorify the God and Father of our Lord Jesus Christ.

These words may well express the 'core' message of Paul's letter to the Roman Christians. From chapter 9 onwards Paul has expressed heart-felt concern for the salvation of fellow-Israelites, including believers among them. They are now (apparently) in a minority in Rome in the post-AD 54 era of Nero, marginalized and most likely prone to re-absorption back into fully fledged synagogue membership. At the same time there is evidence of arrogance towards them on the part of Gentile believers (the 'strong' – cf. 11:20). Clearly Paul sees the positive 'welcome' by the 'strong' (Gentile believers) expressed by practical sensitivity and concessions regarding 'meat' and 'days' as critical to the incorporation of Jews in the 'one body in Christ' (12:5). The apostle's great vision is for Jews and Gentiles gathered together serving one another by the pattern of Christ's service and raising 'one voice' in praise of God his Father.

8. REVIEW OF PAUL'S ARGUMENTS

The goal of Paul's appeal is that the 'strong' and the 'weak' in Rome should be united in mind and voice worshipping God (15:5-6). The burden of responsibility lies with the 'strong' to 'welcome' the 'weak' and to make cultural concessions to them to incorporate them into 'one body in Christ' (14:1, 13; 15:1-2; cf. 12:3-7). To that end Paul provides a number of arguments.

(i) The cultural and religious scruples regarding 'meat' and 'days' (by the 'weak') or the absence of such scruples (among the 'strong') are not to be the primary focus of these groups (14:1-12). That would be to perpetuate disputes between the 'weak' and the 'strong'.

(ii) Rather, let each individual recognize that he and others have a higher loyalty beyond 'meat' and 'days' to the risen Lord Jesus Christ. Accordingly, let no one 'condemn' or 'despise' another whose practices are different since he is a servant of this Lord. God, not man, is and is to be the judge (14:10-13)

(iii) The risen Lord has dealt with the issues of 'life and death' which are more critical than 'meat' and 'days' (14:7-9).

(iv) The 'strong' are not to cause the 'weak' to stumble but rather are to contribute to their 'up-building' (14:13, 19). Most likely this means that Gentile believers are to forgo eating meat when assembled with Jewish Christians (14:20-21).

(v) Yet the 'strong' must not see this as a new Law but rather as their concession to 'up-build' the church. The meat is 'pure' and not of itself 'defiled' (14:14, 20). Where Gentile believers do eat meat (e.g. at home), let them do so without self-condemnation (14:22-23). Let Christian freedom in 'meat' and 'days' be exercised with clarity of understanding in good faith.

(vi) Thus, let the 'strong' not please themselves but their neighbours, bearing their shortcomings (15:1-2). Christ is the great model in this (15:3-4).

(vii) The overriding message from God in the Scriptures is 'hope,' that is, in the accomplishment of his purposes of unifying Jews and Gentiles as one people praising him (15:4-6).

9. Theological Observations

(i) The primary emphasis of chapters 9–11 and 14:1–15:6 is upon Jews and Gentiles. Since Paul anticipated the eventual 'salvation' of Israel in Christ (11:25-32) we must continue to hope, pray and work towards that end. Mission work among God's historic people should be a priority for Christians.

(ii) As in 14:1–15:6, the burden of responsibility lies with Gentile believers (the 'strong') in welcoming and accommodating themselves to the scruples and practices of Jewish brothers and sisters (the 'weak'). A united assembly of Jews and Gentiles worshipping the one who is Father to them all is Paul's great hope.

(iii) Beyond the issues relating to Jews and Gentiles there are a number of abiding issues for Christian fellowship:

(a) Matters of culture ('meat' and 'days'), while important to the individual and are matters for his discretion, are nonetheless secondary and if regarded as primary will divide believers.

(b) In his death and resurrection the Lord has dealt with 'life and death' issues.

(c) Unity is possible and to be sought after because each believer is *his* servant and we are all brothers and sisters with the same 'Father'.

(d) Freedom relating to 'meat' and 'days' is to be exercised with clear understanding of the benefits of 'faith' in Christ. Through him nothing is defiled of itself.

(e) Common and united worship in the one body of the crucified but risen Christ, notwithstanding the differences that otherwise would divide, is Paul's great goal for believers, as it should continue to be.

(f) The 'strong' always have the responsibility to bear the shortcomings of the 'weak,' whatever the circumstances.

STUDY QUESTIONS

1. In what areas do you find yourself judging those who you believe to be 'weak?' Observation of holidays, such as Christmas and Easter? Observing the Sabbath?

2. What other 'peripheral' things divide believers today?

3. Knowing that you will be judged by God, does this affect how you are to treat brothers with whom you differ?

4. How can you as a believer accommodate non-believers without compromising the gospel? How can you accommodate immature believers without causing them stumble over freedoms you may participate in?

5. Have there been certain 'freedoms' that you have participated in that have left you feeling uncomfortable afterwards? Why do you think that you felt uncomfortable?

6. How are you able to encourage and strengthen the weak in your church without appearing to be a 'know-it-all' or 'holier-than-thou'?

PART F

MISSIONARY STATESMAN
(Romans 15:7–16:27)

Paul is apostle to the Gentiles but no less concerned for the salvation of Israel.

Now he is coming to Rome, but in transit (to Spain) since another has laid a foundation in the capital. Yet he is deeply concerned for the effective unity in the church, especially that Jews and Gentiles welcome one another 'in Christ'.

After explaining why he is first going to Jerusalem he seeks the prayers of the Roman Christians for an ultimate safe arrival in Rome.

Finally, he pointedly commends Phoebe and calls for greetings to twenty-six named persons, while warning of 'deceivers' who are unnamed.

After sending greetings from friends in Corinth he concludes with a doxology that revisits teachings introduced at the beginning of the letter.

15

Paul's Apostolic Travel to Rome
(Romans 15:7-33)

We learn from the previous passage (14:1–15:6) that Paul called on Gentile Christians to 'welcome' their Jewish brothers and sisters so as to glorify God with 'one voice'. Now, however, Paul calls on both groups to 'welcome one another'. And the reason? It is because Christ the king has 'welcomed' both Jews and Gentiles (vv. 7-13). Paul has a special role in gathering the Gentiles to Christ for this 'welcome'. He himself is Christ's powerful instrument of ministry to these Gentiles, between Jerusalem to Illyricum, where he has 'fulfilled the gospel' (vv. 14-21) with 'no more room' in this region (v. 23). Thus he plans now at last to visit Rome, but only to 'pass through', as he is 'sent' by them onwards for ministry in Spain (vv. 22-24). First, however, he must go to Jerusalem and therefore he urges the Romans to pray for his 'deliverance' from unbelievers in Jerusalem and also that the gifts of the Gentiles which he will deliver will be 'acceptable' to the 'saints' there (vv. 25-33).

1. RECEIVE ONE ANOTHER (vv. 7-13)
Although Christians had been in Rome for a quarter of a century there does not appear to have been a single and unified 'church' gathering that included both Jews and Gentiles. The first believers in Rome were probably Jews returning from the Feast of Pentecost in Jerusalem who most likely continued belonging to the various synagogues in the city. Gentile Christians may have been few in those early years. In AD 49, however, Claudius

expelled the Jews from Rome so that even after his death in
AD 54 they may not have regained the numerical ascendancy
of the earlier years. Christians of both groups in more recent
times appear to have been scattered across a number of house
groups, as suggested by the greetings at the end of the letter
(16:3-16). As well as the absence of a common meeting place,
there were also cultural barriers between Jews and Gentiles.
Jews condemned Gentiles, and Gentiles mocked Jews.
Christian conversion alone did not sweep away the prejudices
these races felt towards each other.

God's plan, however, was to unite Gentiles with Jews under
their common king, the Messiah/Christ. That plan must find
a practical expression in a common gathering which to that
moment had not been realized in Rome (see on 15:5-6). One
of Paul's purposes in writing Romans was to bring together
in 'one body' these hitherto separated and alienated groups.
This, however, was no 'add on' to the gospel but fundamental
to it. For the gospel message about Christ was in fulfilment of
promises and prophecies from the age of the patriarchs that
looked forward to the blessing of all the families of the world
(see e.g. Gen. 12:1-3).

For this reason Paul admonishes Jewish and Gentile believers, 'Welcome one another' (v. 7) in the common gathering as
both groups with 'one voice glorify the God and Father of our
Lord Jesus Christ' (v. 6). The basis for this reciprocated 'welcome' is, 'Even as Christ has also welcomed *you* (that is, both
Jews and Gentiles), to the glory of God.' God's plan for the
reconciliation of the nations began with his election and salvation of a chosen people. But it did not terminate with them;
they were to be the means of joining others to themselves under Christ.

Typically we speak of persons 'welcoming' the gospel or
'receiving' Christ. So we ask, when did Christ 'welcome' these
Jews and Gentiles? A hint is given earlier when it is said that
God 'welcomes' the person who is the 'servant' of Christ, for
whom the Lord died (14:3-4, 8, 15). We conclude, therefore,
that Christ 'welcomes' that person – Jew or Gentile – who
acknowledges him as Lord and turns to him as Saviour. How
encouraging that our Lord 'welcomes' us.

Mention of Christ as the 'welcomer' of Jews and Gentiles prompts Paul to make a statement about Christ that is as grand as it is unnoticed and neglected (v. 8-9a).

For I say
   Christ was made[1] a minister (*diakonos*) of the circumcision
   for the sake of the truth of God
   to confirm the promises to the fathers
   that the Gentiles might glorify God for his mercy.

Here we make two observations. First, Paul's words echo those of Isaiah where the prophet spoke of God's Spirit-anointed 'servant' who will bring 'justice to the nations' and who will be 'light for the Gentiles to open eyes that are blind' (Isa. 42:1-7). Clearly, Christ is that 'servant,' yet with an important qualification. Christ's own 'ministry' began and ended with Israel. It fell to others like Paul to extend the ministry of Christ to the Gentiles (see on vv. 16-19). In this sense Paul is an adjunct 'servant' depending on Christ carrying his light to the nations and so fulfilling Isaiah's prophecy. Paul himself recruited co-workers in his mission to the nations. Paul as God's missionary 'servant' was not alone. Nor did his work end in his generation, but carries on to this day. Thus we see that the vocation of God's 'servant' bringing his light to the Gentiles continues in the missionary work of Christians in the world.

Second, Christ's ministry was 'for the sake of the truth of God', that is, 'to confirm God's promises to the patriarchs.' Chief among such 'promises' was that made to Abraham about his descendants (e.g. Gen. 12:3: 'all peoples on earth will be blessed through you'). Abraham's great descendant was the Christ who was at the same time God's 'servant' to bring his light to the nations.

Paul now buttresses this affirmation about Christ by quoting no less than four Old Testament texts, each of which mentions 'the Gentiles'.

---

1. The tense of the verb 'made' (*gegenesthai*) means that Christ became and remains the minister to the Jewish people. Christ's continuing 'ministry' to Jews occurred first as his apostles, including Paul, preached to Jewish people in Palestine and in the Diaspora. Since Christ remains minister to the Jewish people, it follows that there should be a continuing ministry to them.

For this reason, I will	praise you among the *Gentiles*,
and	sing hymns to your name
	Ps. 18:49/2 Sam. 22:50[2]

Rejoice, *Gentiles*, with his people   Deut. 32:43

Praise the Lord, all you *Gentiles*,
and let all the peoples praise him   Ps. 117:1

The root of Jesse will spring up
one who will arise to rule the *Gentiles*,
in him the Gentiles will hope   Isa. 11:10

When we look at the original contexts of these passages we notice that these Scriptures were really prophesying Christ's rule over the Gentiles.

The first and the fourth Scriptures open up what Paul is really saying. In the first text King David sings praises to God rejoicing that the 'nations' (Gentiles) have been put under God's rule (Ps. 18:47/2 Sam. 22:48). In the fourth text, King David is that 'root of Jesse' who 'will arise' to 'rule the Gentiles'.[3] These texts focused on David connect back to the *credo* in the opening greeting where the Son of God 'came from the seed of David' (1:3). From texts two and three we hear the encouragement to both Israel and the Gentiles to rejoice in God.

From these four texts we learn: (1) 'Great David's greater son,' the Christ, will rule not only his own people Israel but also the Gentile nations; (2) this Christ will praise God that he rules over the Gentiles; (3) the Gentiles in turn will rejoice and praise Christ for his rule over them. In other words, these four passages points to the long-awaited joyful rule of God's Christ, the son of David, over the peoples of the Jews and the Gentiles.

In verse 13, the apostle rounds off this passage with warm words of encouragement to his Jewish and Gentile readers (addressed jointly as, 'you'):

---

2. Much of Psalm 18 is reproduced from 2 Samuel 22.
3. Also 2 Samuel 23:1.

The God of hope
fill *you* with all joy and peace in believing
that *you* overflow in hope
in the power of the Holy Spirit.

In Jesus, the son of David, God's anointed servant-king, the promises made to Abraham that all peoples – Jews and Gentiles – would be blessed, have been fulfilled. Through the gospel God is gathering one people from all the peoples of the world for his own possession. For this reason Paul calls him, 'The God of *hope*' who is powerfully and purposefully bringing his plan to concrete reality. Let the readers have 'hope' and translate this hope into practical experience in Rome.

Their efforts at meeting together across the racial divide though fumbled are, nonetheless, a sign of better things to come. The Day will dawn when King Christ will visibly rule over a great community of Jews and Gentiles, which their poor assembly would only pitifully anticipate. Let them hope now in that 'greater thing' and in the meantime 'welcome one another' in a gathered and unified 'church' of believers, Jew and Gentile (15:5-7).

2. PAUL'S MINISTRY TO THE GENTILES (vv. 14-21)
Paul now returns to the theme of his 'apostleship to the Gentiles' he introduced in the opening section of the Letter (1:1-17). Such ministry is, as he said earlier, a 'grace' from God 'given' to him (v. 15; cf. 1:5; 12:3). But he sees that ministry in 'priestly' terms as fulfilling Isaiah's prophecy as a messenger 'sent' to the nations to bring them to the 'New Jerusalem' as an 'offering' to God (v. 16). He is careful to insist, however, that his gospel ministry to the Gentiles – supernaturally empowered as it was – was fully achieved through the risen Christ working in Paul in a vast sweep of territories (vv. 17-21). Yet he will only preach the gospel in regions where Christ is not yet named, so as not to build on another's foundation (vv. 20-21).

a. A Reminder of his Apostleship (vv. 14-15)
The apostle is a discerning pastor who understood the value of positive encouragement. Perhaps his exhortations about unity

question their ability to achieve it. But no. He is confident in them, in three related areas (v. 14).

> I myself too am fully convinced about you, my brothers, that
>
> you are   full of goodness,
>   filled with all knowledge,
>   able to admonish one another.

'Goodness' is listed elsewhere as a virtue (Gal. 5:22; Eph. 5:9) meaning 'uprightness'. 'Knowledge' is one's grasp of the Gospel issuing in a living 'knowing' of God (the word 'knowing' is sometimes also used of sexual intimacy). 'Able (literally, 'powerful') to admonish' (*nouthetein*) is that strength to teach, encourage and challenge others so as to change patterns of behaviour.

Part of Paul's pastoral skill is subtly to strengthen in others the very qualities about which he expresses confidence. Today's readers of Romans should take note of Paul's words. Perhaps out of misplaced politeness we fail to address our fellow Christians about glaring breaches of behaviour. We, like the Romans, need to be 'full of goodness,' 'filled with all knowledge' and sufficiently morally strong to 'admonish' our fellow-Christians as needed.

With just a hint of apology Paul admits to a degree of 'boldness' in writing to his Jewish and Gentile readers 'by way of reminder' (v. 15), that is, to 'welcome one another' in the common gathering of the church (v. 7). This 'reminder' is 'by the grace (*charis*) given' to him 'by God'. This in turn echoes the opening Greeting of the Letter (1:1-6) where Paul identified himself as 'an apostle' (1:1) and where 'through Jesus Christ' he had 'received *grace* and apostleship for the obedience of faith among all the Gentiles' (1:6; cf. 12:3). Clearly Paul is now picking up and amplifying his earlier references to his God-given 'grace' to be 'the apostle' to the Gentiles.

b. Paul's Priestly 'Offering' of the Gentiles (v. 16)

That amplification, however, is expressed in an unusual way. What immediately strikes us is the language of Temple and sacrifice in verse 16. Paul speaks of himself as a 'priest' (*leitourgos*) engaged in a 'priestly duty' (*hiergein*) offering a 'sacrifice' (*prosphora*) that is 'acceptable' to God (*euprosdektos*) and 'sanctified (*hēgiasmenē*) by the Holy Spirit'. By this metaphor Paul portrays himself as a 'priest' who is 'serving' in the Temple of God, and is 'offering' up to God an 'acceptable' sacrifice. In Paul's ministry around the eastern Mediterranean he has, in a sense, been 'offering' up his Gentile converts to God.

We the readers are puzzled that Paul should speak of his ministry like this. The explanation appears to be that, once again, Paul sees in what he is doing a fulfilment of Old Testament prophecy. Earlier he quoted four separate Old Testament texts that were now being fulfilled (see on vv. 9-12). Here, however, he is echoing but not quoting from one passage, Isaiah 66:18-20. In its context God has promised to gather the Gentiles to the New Jerusalem to see his glory. But not all have yet come there. God will send 'messengers' to the 'nations' (Gentiles), to those who have not heard the name of the Lord, to bring them back.

> I will send [messengers] forth ... to the nations ...
> to those who have not heard my name, nor seen my glory,
> and they shall declare my glory among the Gentiles.
> And they shall bring your brothers from all the nations
> as a gift for the Lord
> ... as though the children of Israel
> should bring their sacrifices to me.[4]

Paul saw himself as an apostle, 'sent' to 'the nations,' where he has been declaring God's 'glory' in preaching the gospel to the Gentiles. His 'brother' Gentiles from the nations are Paul's 'gift for the Lord,' his 'sacrifice' brought to Jerusalem. Those Gentiles (and their money) which were ordinarily seen as 'unclean' by Jews have been, in fact, 'sanctified by the Holy Spirit.' It is likely that Paul saw the collection of money from

---

4. Isaiah 66:18-20, translated from the Greek Old Testament (known as the Septuagint or LXX), the Bible Paul used.

the Gentile churches brought by Gentile converts to Jerusalem (see on vv. 25-28) as evidence that the Lord was fulfilling Isaiah's prophecy. But it is not a final sign; Paul's task is not yet complete. He is coming to Rome and proceeding beyond there to Spain, the western extremity of the Gentile world, to 'offer' to God even more people from the nations.

Paul's task remains incomplete. As a man of his times he could not know the vast extent of the people groups on this planet. Yet the 'obligation' Paul felt to preach to 'Greeks and barbarians' remains unfulfilled (see on 1:14). Christ's Damascus Road commission bestowed on Paul a special status as 'apostle to the Gentiles' and Christ's 'adjunct servant'.

Paul, however, knew he was but one among many others who were involved in the work of ministry, for instance, his own special co-workers (e.g. Timothy and Titus), locally based pastors and teachers, regional evangelists (e.g., Epaphras) and also various travelling preaching 'apostles' (e.g. Andronicus and Junia). In addition, there were ordinary believers who shared the gospel wherever they travelled (e.g. Priscilla and Aquila). In short, the work Paul began, and in which he involved other ministers and believers, will continue until the Second Coming of the Lord Jesus. All Christians today, regardless of their gifts, age, or circumstances must feel the same sense of compulsion that drove Paul onwards in preaching the gospel to the nations and play their part whatever it is, whether going, giving or praying to win the nations for Christ.

c. Paul's Confidence towards God (vv. 17-19a)

Why 'therefore' does Paul 'boast in Christ in the things pertaining to God' (v. 17)? Most likely 'the things pertaining to God' summed up the totality of his ministry to the Gentiles as it fulfilled the promises of God to the nations, as spoken through the prophets (see on v. 16). This is not 'boasting' based on pride of achievement. Boasting was commonplace in that era and culturally acceptable. Rather, Paul exulted before God in the privilege he enjoyed in bearing God's glad tidings to the nations. Paul's was a quiet boasting arising from a profound and humble gratitude to God.

In any case, such 'boasting' was 'in Christ' because, as Paul now proceeds to say (vv. 18, 19), it was *Christ* who worked in and energized Paul for the work he was doing.

> For I will not dare to speak of anything
> except what Christ has accomplished through me
> for the obedience of the Gentiles,
> by word and work,
> by the power of signs and wonders
> by the power of the Spirit of God.

Two observations may be made.

(i) God's Two-Phase Plan

Here we must connect verse 18a back to verse 8 to grasp the respective roles of Christ and Paul in God's plan in reaching first the Jews and then the Gentiles.

> *Christ* was made a minister of the circumcision
> ... that the Gentiles might glorify God for his mercy   (v. 8)

> what Christ has accomplished *through me*
> for the obedience of the Gentiles   (v. 18a)

There were two steps in the divine plan for Jews and Gentiles. Step 1 was Jesus' ministry to the *Jews* in Palestine (v. 8). Step 2 was the risen Christ's ministry *through Paul* to win the 'obedience of the *Gentiles*' (v. 18a). If Christ was the 'servant' of God Paul was his 'adjunct' bringing his Lord's 'light' to the nations (see Isa. 42:1-7). Paul points to the uniqueness and centrality of Christ, God's anointed king over his people, composed of Jews first, but also of Gentiles. Paul's was a special role as the humble pioneer minister of Christ to the Gentile peoples bringing the gospel to them and securing 'the obedience[5] of faith' from them.

---

5. Paul the apostle proclaims the gospel to summons the Gentiles to 'obedience' (15:18) or the 'obedience of faith' (1:5; 16:26) which means both (1) obeying God by putting faith in Christ, and (2) the faith that is expressed in obedience.

(ii) Holy Spirit empowered apostleship

The risen and exalted Christ 'worked through' his 'slave' Paul (1:1), securing that 'obedience' from Gentiles by both 'word' (the proclaimed gospel) and 'deed' ('signs and wonders'). Paul appears to be connecting (1) 'by word' with 'by the power of the Holy Spirit,' and (2) 'by deed' with 'by the power of signs and wonders'. [6]

> by word
> by deed
> by the power of signs and wonders
> by the power of the Holy Spirit.

Paul preached (and wrote) that 'word ... by the power of the Holy Spirit'. He regarded the preaching of the gospel and the believing of it by the hearers as nothing less than the 'power of God' (1:16; 1 Cor. 1:18, 23-24) and the 'demonstration of the Spirit and of power' from heaven (1 Cor. 2:4).

God also blessed Paul's ministry with 'signs and wonders' (see also 2 Cor. 12:12). He was uniquely called as the pioneer apostle to the nations. Such 'signs and wonders' were worked through Paul by the glorified Christ along with his life-changing gospel preaching. But these 'signs and wonders' were to mark the turning of the ages in which the Gentiles were now, for the first time, being included in the saving purposes of God. That new age having begun, being signalled so dramatically from on high, the 'signs and wonders' ceased with the passing of the apostles.[7] There is a parallel here with Moses and the Exodus. Moses spoke the word of God to Pharaoh along with 'signs and wonders' (the plagues, followed by the 'exodus' through the sea – Exod. 7:3; Deut. 4:34). But while miracles occur within the Old Testament, the clustered pattern of 'word' + 'signs and wonders' does not continue after the Exodus into the narrative of the Old Testament.

---

6. Based on the so-called chiastic or 'cross over' structure where the first element connects with the fourth and the second with the third.

7. Miracles, however, were not unknown in the early churches (Gal. 3:1-5; 1 Cor. 12:10, 28).

Yet although Christ's servant witnessed the astonishing power of the Holy Spirit 'by word and by deed' to win the obedience of the Gentiles he also suffered profoundly in the course of his ministry (8:36: 'we face death all day long, we are considered as sheep to be slaughtered'). There was 'power' but also 'weakness'. He proclaimed the resurrection but also the cross of Christ and experienced both 'crucifixion' and 'deliverance' in the course of his apostleship. He spoke on the one hand of 'the word of truth and the power of God' but on the other hand he spoke of 'afflictions and hardships' (2 Cor. 6:7, 4). Nor were Paul's supplications to God always answered according to his hopes. He urged the Romans to pray that God would rescue him from unbelievers in Judaea and that he would come to Rome with joy (15:31-32). But that 'rescue' was through imprisonment and that coming was in humiliation, in chains.

d. Paul has 'fulfilled' the gospel of Christ (v. 19b)
As a consequence of Christ's work in and through Paul by the power of God he can say in verse 19b:

So that I have fulfilled the gospel of Christ
in an arc (*kuklō*) from Jerusalem to Illyricum.

Remarkably Paul does not say, 'I have fully *proclaimed* the gospel of Christ' as the NIV translates it. The verb is 'fulfil' (literally, 'fill up') not 'proclaim' or 'preach'. What does he mean by *'fulfilled* the gospel' (a phrase similar to Col.1:25: 'to *fulfil* the word of God')?
     The probable answer is to be found in verses 20-21 where the initial 'Thus' connects those verses back to verse 19a. 'I have fulfilled the gospel of Christ, *thus* making it my aim to evangelize where Christ is not named.' For that would be to 'build upon another's foundation', which he will not do.[8]

---

8. But is Paul saying (1) that he will not 're-lay a foundation' on an existing foundation (that is, win converts where they have already been won), or (2) that he will not 'build a superstructure' on an existing foundation (that is, build a continuing ministry upon a brand new one)? Tipping the balance in favour of (2) is (a) Paul's

'Fulfilling the gospel,' then, implies two connected ministries. The first is 'laying the foundation' by preaching Christ in virgin territory ('where Christ is not named'[9]) and so winning converts. The second is 'building' upon that 'foundation' a superstructure of mature believers through *further* gospel ministry. Paul was concerned lest the 'foundation' he laid in Corinth (the preaching of Christ crucified and risen) was being superimposed by a 'structure' of different teaching by teachers who came after him (1 Cor. 3:10-12). Because the 'foundation' is Christ, the 'building' erected upon it must also be Christ – the worship of Christ, the confession of Christ, the proclamation of Christ and Christ-like behaviour. 'Fulfilling the gospel of Christ' is nothing less than (1) founding a church *on* Christ, and (2) raising it up to spiritual adulthood *in* Christ.

This understanding of 'fulfilling the gospel' is confirmed by our observation of Paul's ministry in his letters and in the book of Acts. Here we see Paul 'laying a foundation' by proclaiming Christ for the obedience of faith of his hearers. But then we see him 'building upon' that foundation by discipling his converts through teaching and personal example. This included settling them into a Christ-centred congregation furnished with patterns of behaviour and church life led by carefully chosen local leaders. Paul also encouraged believers to seek the salvation of 'those outside' (1 Cor. 10:33–11:1) and he inspired local preachers to take the gospel to their locality (like Clement, Euodia and Syntyche in Philippi[10]) and to regions beyond (like Epaphras to the Colossians in the Lycus valley[11]). Paul wanted the faith of the churches to 'echo forth' from his churches into whole provinces, as it did in Macedonia and Achaia from the church in Thessalonica (1 Thess. 1:8). For Paul to 'fulfil the gospel', it required that he lay a 'foundation'

---

failure to use the word 'lay ... again' (as in Heb. 6:1), and (b) his words 'build ... upon' suggest a superstructure 'built ... upon' a foundation. Paul will not erect a superstructure on another's foundation. But he will build a superstructure upon a foundation that he has laid.

9. In Isaiah 66:18 it is Yahweh's name that not been heard by the nations (see on v. 16 above). Paul, however, in echoing Isaiah substitutes Christ's name for Yahweh's.

10. Philippians 4:2-3.

11. Colossians 1:7.

of converted people and erect on it a 'building' made up of a solidly constructed, gospel-sharing congregation.

Even when absent Paul provided for the ongoing work of 'building upon' the foundation that had been laid. He maintained close pastoral contact with his churches through envoys like Timothy and Titus.[12] Above all, however, it was by his carefully-crafted letters, which were read aloud repeatedly to the gathered congregations, that even *in absentia* he continued to 'build upon' the initial foundation. Through this letter Paul was 'gospelling' the Roman Christians towards maturity, even although he did not lay the foundation there (see on 1:11, 15).

This two-stage concept of 'gospelling' may explain how Paul can claim to have 'fulfilled the gospel in an arc from Jerusalem to Illyricum'. For Jews, Jerusalem was the 'navel' of the world, the centre of the universe, towards which the nations would return one day. The Roman province Illyricum (modern 'former' Yugoslavia) was the dividing line between the western and eastern halves of the Roman Empire. So Paul had 'fulfilled the gospel' to Gentiles in Nabataea and Damascus (the region of Jerusalem), in Syria-Cilicia, in Galatia, in Macedonia, in Achaia, in Asia and 'into' (*mechri*) Illyricum. To be sure, he has not evangelized every individual nor even every settlement. As a Roman citizen he has strategically targeted Roman provinces through ministry in leading Roman cities where he could expect a measure of protection from provincial authorities. But from the churches in those nodal points the gospel has spread throughout localities and whole provinces. For example, though Paul was based in Ephesus the whole province of Asia heard the word of the Lord (Acts 19:10). As he reminded the Colossians, 'all over the world this gospel is bearing fruit and growing' (Col 1:6).

Paul, however, is not content with having 'fulfilled the gospel of Christ from Jerusalem to Illyricum'. He will continue that arc-like outreach by moving on from Rome to Spain, to the extremity of the western part of the Roman Empire. Furthermore, though he will not do more than 'pass through'

---

12. Cf. 2 Corinthians 12:28.

Rome (see on v. 24), this very letter to Roman believers testifies to his passion to 'strengthen' the work of the gospel in that city (see on 1:11).

e. 'Other' Places (vv. 20-21)

But since Christ is already 'named' (that is, confessed as 'Lord') in Rome Paul will now bypass this city and region. 'Another' has laid a 'foundation' and Paul will not come to reside in Rome to erect a 'building' upon it. In other words, Paul will share his 'spiritual gift' of apostleship by 'strengthening' (1:11) believers in the city for a brief period but he will not attempt to 'fulfil the gospel' there by erecting a building on that foundation. His great letter, however, will contribute to that purpose in place of his sustained presence.

This passing reference helpfully reminds us that Paul was by no means the only person engaging in the work of Christian ministry. So seriously did Paul view the work of this 'other' person, he must regrettably shelve his long-held plans to come for long-term ministry in Rome. He deeply regrets that others have not observed the same scruples in Corinth (2 Cor. 10:13-16).

But who is this 'other' person who has 'laid a foundation' in the Eternal City? It is unlikely to have been those converted Jews on their return from pilgrimage to Jerusalem for the Feast of Pentecost (cf. Acts 2:10). 'Another foundation' sounds rather too formal for the rather *ad hoc* beginnings associated with those Jews who probably remained members of the various synagogues in Rome during those early years. The best guess is that the unnamed 'foundation' layer is the Apostle Peter.

After the Jerusalem Council in *c.* AD 49 Peter visited Corinth with his wife in *c.* AD 54 (1 Cor. 9:5; cf. 1:12; 3:22). Presumably the focus of Peter's ministry in the Achaian capital was to Jews; previously Peter had been apostle to the circumcised in the Land of Israel (Gal. 2:7-8). It is possible Paul has Peter in mind when alluding negatively to 'another' person who has been working in his 'field' of missionary labours in Corinth (2 Cor. 10:16). According to early church evidence Peter made his way to Rome,[13] arriving perhaps by the mid-fifties (that is after the death of Claudius in AD 54 when Jews were again allowed to reside in Rome). In this case it is most likely that Peter concentrated his ministry on Jews and Jewish believers. If so, Peter's ministry would not have advanced the integration of Jewish with Gentile believers so dear to Paul. By the hypothesis that Peter was the apostolic 'foundation' layer Paul would have two reasons not to reside in Rome. First, he was committed to evangelizing where Christ was not named, which was not possible in Rome. Second, to labour alongside Peter in the same city, where his ministry was to Jews and Paul's was to Gentiles, may have actually deepened the divisions and deferred indefinitely the consolidation of the Jews and Gentiles into one common body (see on 15:5-7).

Paul's passion to bring the gospel 'where Christ is not named' is expressed in a quotation adapted from Isaiah 52:15 which he sees as fulfilled in his ministry.

| Those who have not been told | *about him* | will see, and |
| those who have not heard | *of him* | will understand. |

Significantly these words belong to Isaiah's prophecy about the Servant of the Lord who will suffer and die in place of his chosen people, for their sins (Isa. 52:13–53:12). The Gentile nations and their kings, however, will be astonished when they hear about this Servant. They 'will see' and 'understand,' however, not through Christ directly but indirectly, through Paul's pioneer preaching to them. Paul, therefore, 'extends' *the* Servant's ministry to the Gentiles and is himself, in a derived sense, a 'servant of the Lord' (see on v. 8). This, however, is true of all genuine missionaries. They are servants of the Servant, extending his saving ministry very often at high cost to themselves. That, certainly, was true of Paul (cf. 8:36: 'for thy sake we are being killed all the day long').

3. PAUL'S ONWARD TRAVEL PLANS (vv. 22-24)

A few verses earlier Paul located himself somewhere between 'Jerusalem' and 'Illyricum' (v. 19). More precisely Paul is writing to the Romans from Corinth near the end of seven-

---

13. 1 Clement v-vi.

year ministry to the churches in Macedonia, Achaia and Asia. So now Paul outlines his plans for the future, especially as they relate to the believers in Rome.

First, he will travel to Jerusalem with the collection from the churches of the Gentiles. That accomplished, he will come at last to Rome, though only for a brief visit. One of the purposes of the letter is to request hospitality for that sojourn and provisioning for his onward journey to Spain.

So why has the apostle to the Gentiles not come sooner to Rome, the world capital of the Gentiles? It is because someone else (another apostolic leader, presumably) has already arrived so that Christ is already being 'named' in Rome. That 'foundation' has now been laid and Paul will neither re-lay that foundation nor personally erect his superstructure upon it. Paul is called to be a pioneer apostle preaching Christ to those who have not previously heard of him.

The existence of an already laid 'foundation' is the 'reason' he has been hindered[14] for so long, in fact 'for many years,' in coming to them (vv. 22, 23; cf. Acts 19:21). So how is he able 'now' to come to them? It is, he says, 'because I no longer have any room to work in these regions' (v. 23). 'These regions' are, of course, those that lie 'in an arc between Jerusalem and Illyricum' in which he has already 'fulfilled the gospel' (see on v. 19b); Christ is now everywhere 'named' in that geographic sweep as a result of Paul's apostleship.

Paul, however, is coming to Rome 'on his way to Spain' and he 'hopes to see' them as he 'passes through' (v. 24; cf. v. 28). Understandably Paul is rather cautious in speaking of his hopes in coming to Rome, for two reasons. Christianity in Rome was not of his creation but 'work in progress' begun by others, by one 'foundation' layer in particular (possibly Peter, see comments on vv. 20-21). As well, Paul had critics and opponents among the Jews (both Christian and non-Christian). Indeed, the greater part of Romans is devoted to winning Jews for faith in Christ apart from the law (2:1–8:4), to assuring them

---

14. The Greek word *enekoptomēn* is an imperfect passive (of *enkoptein*, 'to hinder') suggesting that *God* had been blocking Paul's Rome-wards journeying, most likely because of Claudius' decree in AD 49 barring Jews from Rome, but presumably including the prior arrival of the unnamed foundation-layer.

that God's promises to Israel had not failed (chs. 9–11), and to securing their place in the congregation in Rome (14:1–15:7).

Allowing for a certain diplomatic tone, we discern two objectives underlying this brief visit, which we note not only from verse 24 but also from the beginning of the letter (1:11-13, 15).

First, Paul expected (briefly) to 'gospel' them (1:15-17), thus 'sharing' his apostolic 'gift' with them for their 'strengthening' (1:15, 5, 11; 16:25). Since this letter must serve in place of his extended visit, its contents and teaching give us a good sense of the thrust of the apostolic ministry he hoped to fulfil while in Rome. Perhaps Paul planned to expound and apply his own letter as his 'gospel' ministry in Rome.

Second, Paul looked forward 'first' to enjoying the company of the Roman believers but then to be 'sent on his way'[15] by them to Spain. In short, Paul did not plan to settle to tent-making to support himself in Rome but he hoped to be provided with somewhere to stay for his brief visit and then to be furnished with some money and other necessities for his onward journey.

It is to overstate the matter to propose, as some scholars have, that Paul's chief aim in writing Romans was to secure Rome as a launching platform for his mission to Spain. At most, his expectation would have been for modest hospitality and provisioning. He was after all a tent-maker of independent attitude who supported himself in long-term missionary situations, as he expected Spain to be. Rather, his letter was to serve a purpose not possible in his short-term visit, that is, the grounding of the Roman Christians securely in the gospel and uniting in one body the disparate Jewish and Gentile elements.

Scholars have questioned why Paul planned to go to Spain. Was it because a Jewish community there would provide Paul the opportunity to preach 'first' to the Jews (1:16)? But evidence is lacking for a Jewish presence in the Iberian peninsula at that time. Did Paul equate Spain with the 'Tarshish' of Isaiah 66:19 as among places that had not seen God's glory and to which

---

15. The verb 'send on' (*propempō*) is used in the New Testament for temporary hospitality and short-term provisions for the missionary who is 'passing through' (Acts 15:3; 20:38; 21:5; 1 Cor. 16:6, 11; 2 Cor. 1:16; Titus 3:13; 3 John 6).

the Lord would 'send' his messengers? Quite possibly. There is, however, an adjunct to this view that is problematic. Some propose that Paul believed that Christ would return when converts from 'Tarshish' were won and brought with their 'collection' of money to Jerusalem as an 'offering' to the Lord. Evidence that Paul thought this way is lacking.

In fact, there were many nations of the Gentiles still to be won for Christ by his pioneer apostle, for example, Germany, Gaul, Britain, Egypt and Parthia. Perhaps Paul was systematically 'fulfilling the gospel of Christ' in the nations surrounding the Mediterranean, beginning with the north-eastern quadrant (Jerusalem to Illyricum) so that the north-western sector was the logical next step. Paul's reason for going to Spain may have been as simple as that. Since Rome would not be home for his ministry, the believers there could at least 'send him on his way' by short-term hospitality and provisions for his onward journey.

There is no evidence that Paul ever reached Spain. He arrived in Rome in the early sixties for a period of imprisonment. After a brief period of release, during which he appears to have revisited the Aegean region, he was returned to Rome where he was martyred in the middle sixties during Nero's assault on the church.

4. BUT FIRST PAUL WILL GO TO JERUSALEM (vv. 25-28)

Paul is writing to the Romans from Corinth where the authorized representatives of the churches will soon converge bringing their gifts from the members of the churches (see 1 Cor. 16:1-3; Acts 20:2-4). For some time Paul had been securing these financial contributions from the believers of the provinces of Galatia, Asia, Macedonia and Achaia for the sake of the 'poor saints of Jerusalem'.

Several reasons inspired Paul in arranging this major task.

First, when James, Peter and John agreed that Paul should 'go' to the Gentiles Paul agreed to 'remember the poor', that is, the poor in Judaea (Gal. 2:7-9). A famine began in c. AD 46/47 with effects lasting for many years. Jewish believers who were already suffering from the famine were also persecuted by other Jews, adding to their distress. Paul's 'collection' of money for Jews in Palestine from the Gentile Christians was a practical expression of relief within the world-wide new covenant people of God (cf. 2 Cor. 8:13-15; 9:12-15).

Second, as Paul will now say (v. 27), the Gentile believers owe a 'spiritual debt' to the Jerusalem Church, from which the gospel had come to the Gentiles. Paul is teaching that Jewish and Gentile believers are 'one people', so the Gentiles have an 'obligation to share' their 'material' blessings with Jerusalem in response to the mother church's readiness to share their 'spiritual' blessings. Jews of the Diaspora annually sent their gifts for the upkeep of the Temple in Jerusalem as a symbol and expression of their solidarity with David's City. In a sense, Paul's collection from the Gentiles so far evangelized (from Jerusalem to Illyricum) symbolized and expressed the reality that they really were part of the Messiah's people, although they were Gentiles and not the historic covenant people, Israel.

Third, Paul saw his ministry to the Gentile nations as fulfilment of prophecy, in particular Isaiah 66:18-20 (see on v. 16). God, through his prophet, promised to 'send' messengers to the nations where his 'name was not yet heard'. These messengers, among whom Paul included himself, would bring back 'brothers from all the nations as a gift to the Lord'. Paul would point to the Gentiles and their money brought by him to Jerusalem as a 'gift to the Lord' that he prayed would be 'acceptable' to the believers (see on v. 31b).

We must note that Paul is not merely sharing travel details with his Roman readers, but making a point. There is now one people, not two, who are saved by and ruled by Christ their king. Jewish and Gentile ethnicity and culture are secondary to this new reality. Paul's brief reference to the collection, with the reciprocal obligations of both Gentile and Jewish believers, drives home the need for Roman Christians, whether Jewish or Gentile, to 'welcome one another' and to 'glorify God with one voice' (15:7, 6).

Here we see a glimpse of the apostle as a great statesman and diplomat who worked hard to unite the two wings of Christianity, Jewish and Gentile. Not that Paul believed in unity at any price. No one defended the great doctrines of salvation more vigorously than Paul, as reading Galatians, 2 Corinthians, Philippians or Romans shows. Yet some matters were merely cultural practices and not 'core' beliefs. These secondary issues included foods eaten or not eaten, days observed or not, as discussed by Paul in his fourteenth chapter of this letter. How would Paul have acted today in the face of the fragmented and scattered nature of modern denominations? Based on his love of unity in truth we may be confident that Paul would have sought and promoted unity in the truth of Christ at every opportunity.

Paul speaks of 'completing' his Jerusalem visit and 'sealing for them this harvest'. What does he mean? This 'harvest' is part of the metaphorical language of sacrifice used earlier. In verse 16 Paul called 'the Gentiles' (embodied in their representatives as bearers of the Gentiles' money) an 'offering' by him as a 'priestly minister' which, he prayed, would be 'acceptable [to God]'. A few verses later he will pray that his 'ministry to the saints in Jerusalem' will be 'acceptable' to them (v. 31). The problem for Paul was that not all the 'saints' appear to have understood his ministry in these prophetic terms. He must 'seal' this understanding with the believers in Jerusalem.

That mission in Jerusalem accomplished, however, Paul will travel from Jerusalem to Rome (a hazardous sea journey taking up to three months). On arrival in Rome he will enjoy fellowship for a period before being sent on to Spain (v. 28). But that visit to Jerusalem weighs heavily on his heart and so he urges the Roman believers to pray for him there.

5. PRAY FOR PAUL IN HIS TRAVELS (vv. 29-33)
Nonetheless, Paul 'knows' that he will come 'in the fullness of the blessings of Christ' (v. 29). He does not mean by this a sure confidence of a trouble free journey and safe arrival in Rome. Paul knew better than most about the dangers of travel and of the danger to him by those who opposed his preaching, especially in Jerusalem (see 2 Cor. 11:25-26). The next two verses call for prayer against the problems that Paul anticipated in Jerusalem. Rather, Paul knew that his coming to

Rome for ministry among the believers would be the occasion of 'the blessings of Christ' when he would be 'refreshed' with them (v. 32). Earlier Paul had expressed similar confidence about the mutual benefits each would enjoy through his coming (see on 1:11).

A realist about the difficulties he faced in Jerusalem, Paul now appeals to the Romans to pray for him (v. 30). He couches his moving appeal in *trinitarian* terms, a reminder of the three persons in the divine Godhead.

> I appeal to you, brothers and sisters,
> through *our Lord Jesus Christ,*
>
> and through the love of *the Spirit*
>
> to ... pray for me
>
> *to God ....*

He makes his appeal based (1) on Jesus Christ's Lordship over both them and him, about which so much of this letter has been devoted, and (2) their common possession of the Spirit of God who blesses them with 'love' for God and for each other (see on 5:5). Their prayer is directed (3) to 'God', which here as elsewhere in Paul's letters means 'God, the Father' of the Lord Jesus and of believers.

The Romans' prayer is to be a matter of discipline, energy and perseverance, as indicated by 'strive together in ... your prayers' (RSV). Our word 'agony' derives from the verb Paul uses (*sunagonizomai*), which was used for 'wrestling' in athletic contests, and which Paul elsewhere associates with prayer (Col. 4:12). Perhaps Paul has in mind Jacob's all-night wrestle with the angel (Gen. 32:22-32). Prayer to God is no mere ritual or empty repetition for Paul, but a determined struggle urging God to hear and answer.

That struggle in prayer was directed to Paul's forthcoming visit to Jerusalem, for the two groups about whom Paul was deeply concerned, the 'disobedient'[16] and 'the saints'. Whether an Israelite was 'disobedient' or 'saint' depended entirely on his attitude to Jesus as Messiah.

---

16. Paul's word is *apeithountes*, 'disobedient ones.' Less precisely RSV and NIV have 'unbelievers' as, for example, in 1 Corinthians 6:6 (*apistoi*).

'The disobedient in Judaea' captures Paul's sense of tragedy that Israel was 'a disobedient people' who have rejected their Messiah (10:21; cf. 11:31). Judaea was a place of danger for Paul as we know from his own pen (1 Thess. 2:14-15: 'the Jews killed the Lord Jesus ... and drove us out') as well as from the book of Acts (9:23, 29). So let the Romans pray that he will be 'delivered' from 'the disobedient' in Judaea.

By the grace of God, however, there were also 'saints' (*hagioi*, 'holy ones') among God's historic people in Judaea. These originated as the first Galilean followers of Jesus of Nazareth who after his resurrection became the church of Jerusalem led at first by Peter (and John) but later by James the Lord's brother. Over a period of time the influx of priests and Pharisees (Acts 6:7; 15:5) and the rise of Jewish nationalism tended to make the 'saints in Jerusalem' more conservatively Jewish and somewhat resistant to Paul's ministry to the Gentiles.

But Paul is now bringing Gentile converts with their gifts to Jerusalem and he hopes to 'seal' this 'harvest' to the 'saints' in Jerusalem (see on v. 28). So let the Romans pray that these Jewish believers will find Paul's 'ministry' (*diakonia*) 'acceptable' (*euprosdektos* – as in v. 16) to them. In short, Paul is concerned that the Church of Jerusalem will share his conviction that the prophecy of Isaiah 66:18-20 is being fulfilled as the apostle brings Gentiles from the nations (with their gifts) to Jerusalem as a sign that Isaiah's oracle is being fulfilled in Paul's ministry (see on v. 16).

Paul sees the positive answer to these two prayers as 'through the will of God' (v. 32). If that proves to be the case, as he hopes, he will, indeed, 'come to them' in Rome 'in joy'. But that coming is no sightseeing excursion to a magnificent city. Paul is coming to find 'mutual refreshment' with this group of Christian believers, as earlier he had looked forward to 'mutual encouragement' with them (see on 1:11-12). He knows that he has much to give, but also much to receive, even from ordinary and unexceptional folk.

God answered Paul's prayers for 'deliverance' from 'the disobedient' in Judea, though it meant imprisonment for several years. The book of Acts, however, is silent about the 'saints' acceptance or otherwise of Paul's 'gift' of the Gentiles. Presumably they accepted Paul's collection, though whether graciously or ungraciously we do not know. But it was the will of God for Paul to come to Rome, though he did so in chains. God's answer to our prayers is not always in the terms in which we have prayed!

6. Paul's Prayer for Peace (v. 33)

Before Paul introduces Phoebe from Cenchreae, the bearer of the letter, and gives his greeting to his many friends in Rome he will pronounce his blessing of peace upon the Roman believers. Such a prayer is common near the conclusion of Paul's letters.[17] This 'peace' comes from 'the God of peace' (1 Cor. 14:33). There is the individual's 'peace with God' arising from Christ's death for sinners (as in 5:1). But Paul is thinking more here of peace between people, that is, between Jewish and Gentile believers who lacked practical unity (see on 15:5-6). So he prays rather pointedly, 'peace be with you *all*.' Let the Roman Christians – Jews and Gentiles – fulfill the apostle's prayer by their attitudes and behaviour.

7. Application of Romans 15 to Today

In Romans 15 Paul is teaching that Jesus the Messiah ministered to the Jews as a first step towards reaching the Gentiles. To that point God had restricted his saving purposes to Israel, the people descended from Abraham. Christ's second step began with his interception of Paul near Damascus that changed the life direction of the young persecutor. In his own words he declared, 'Through Christ I received grace and apostleship for the obedience of faith among all the nations' (1:5). Henceforth Paul saw himself as 'set apart for the gospel of God' (1:1) and a 'debtor to both Greek and barbarian' (1:14). After almost a quarter of a century as an apostle he is able to say that from 'Jerusalem to Illyricum' he has 'fulfilled the gospel of Christ' as a pioneer, 'foundation' laying missionary (15:19-20).

---

17. For example, 2 Corinthians 13:11; Philippians 4:9; 1 Thessalonians 5:23; 2 Thessalonians 3:16.

Paul's ministry to Gentiles was no *ad hoc* thing. He understood that many Scriptures foresaw the messianic king rejoicing that he ruled both his historic people Israel and the nations (15:8-12). Isaiah prophesied that God's messengers would bring the Gentiles to Jerusalem as a 'gift' to God and Paul saw himself as a servant of the Servant fulfilling that oracle in the Gentiles and their gifts that he brought to the Holy City (15:16, 28, 31).

So the question is: has Paul done it all? Is God's mission to the Gentiles fulfilled in Paul, his messenger to the nations? How should we understand Romans 15 today? Does Romans 15 have any application to us now? What is Christian ministry *after* Paul?

(a) Paul was, indeed, the apostle to the nations in the generation in which the messianic king, Jesus, appeared. If Christ was the 'servant' of God bringing his light to the nations, the actual implementation of this 'servanthood' was achieved through his apostle. Paul was the first apostle intentionally to 'go' to the Gentiles. Based on the 'finished' work of Christ alone Paul pressed his fellow-Jewish believers for the inclusion of the Gentiles in the covenant of God on the same basis as Jews, namely, 'the obedience of faith' in the Messiah crucified and risen. Thus as the pioneer missionary to the Gentiles and as insightful theologian Paul has made possible the continuing mission to the nations of the world. That task remains incomplete and will only cease with the return of Christ.

(b) Even in his own day Paul was not the sole apostle to the nations. In his Great Commission Christ sent his original followers to 'make disciples from the nations' (Matt. 28:18-20). Paul himself indicates that someone else had brought Christ's 'name' to Rome before him and had laid a 'foundation' there 'upon' which he would not build. Paul was a special apostle, but he was not the only apostle nor the only minister. The door lies open for others in subsequent generations to take the gospel to the nations. Indeed, Paul could not have known how an immense task that is and continues to be. Through his dedication and personal sacrifice Paul made a valiant beginning to a work that is yet to be completed and into which others must enter.

(c) Paul saw gospel ministry in two steps: (1) 'foundation laying' (winning converts through initial proclamation of Christ), and (2) 'building' a superstructure 'upon' it (raising those converts to maturity in Christ). Both 'steps' remain critical. There continues to be a need for 'foundation' layers who proclaim Christ and win converts. Equally, those who belong to congregations need to see themselves as part of a 'body' that is being 'built up' in dedication to Christ and whose members seek the salvation of the lost. In short, every Christian without exception has a vital role to play.

STUDY QUESTIONS

1. Many churches say that they are friendly. What then makes for a 'welcoming' church?

2. Since Christ is Lord over all how should this affect our missionary zeal? Weaken it or strengthen it?

3. Is our 'fulfilling the gospel' and different today than in Paul's day? Why was Paul so motivated to fulfill the gospel? What was his compulsion?

4. How can Paul's request for pray in his journeys propel your praying for missionaries and world missions?

5. Do you find prayer to be a 'wrestling' at times? What do you do to persevere in prayer?

16

Christians in Rome
(Romans 16:1-27)

Paul brings his letter to the Romans to its conclusion. As in some other letters Paul deals with matters relating to people in his final pages.

There are five sections:

(i)   Commendation of Phoebe (vv. 1-2);
(ii) Greetings to people and groups in Rome (vv. 3-16);
(iii) An 'appeal' warning against 'deceivers' (vv. 17-20);
(iv) Greetings from various friends in Corinth (vv. 21-23);
(v)   Concluding doxology (vv. 25-27).

1. PAUL'S COMMENDATION OF PHOEBE (vv. 1-2)

Paul's words, 'I commend', are of a technical nature, and were used in a letter of introduction to 'commend' a person known to the writer but not to the readers.

It is likely that Phoebe acted as the trusted bearer of Paul's letter to the Romans; no other person is named in Romans in this regard. Phoebe would have collected the scroll from Paul at the house of Gaius in Corinth, and then embarked at the port of Lechaion in order to travel to a port on the western coast of Italy, from where she would make her way by road to a contact address in Rome, most likely the home of Prisca and Aquila. The journey would have taken about two weeks. Phoebe is unlikely to have travelled alone. On her arrival, presumably Prisca and Aquila would have invited all the known believers in Rome to gather for the reading of the letter.

It is likely that Phoebe acted as Paul's 'envoy' to the Romans, bringing news from Paul and the sending church. It is likely, too, that the envoy-letter bearer would read and explain Paul's words to the gathered groups. Other envoys who brought letters seem to have had this role, for example, Timothy and Titus to the Corinthians (1 Cor. 4:17; 16:10; 2 Cor. 8:16-18; 12:18), Tychicus to the 'Ephesian' and Colossian congregations (Eph. 6:21-22; Col. 4:7-8), Epaphroditus to the Philippians (Phil. 2:25-30), and Silvanus to the congregations in Asia Minor (1 Pet. 5:12).

In addition to introducing Phoebe as a trusted person, the intent of Paul's 'commendation' of her was that the Roman Christians should 'welcome' and 'help [her] in whatever she may need'. In other words, they are being asked to provide her with lodgings and provisions during her stay in Rome.

In this brief reference we learn that Phoebe was (1) 'our sister,' that is, a fellow-Christian (most likely a Gentile[1]), (2) a 'deacon' (*diakonos*) of the church in Cenchreae (Corinth's port to the Aegean), and (3) a 'helper' of many, Paul included. The latter word (*prostatis*) meant 'patronness' and 'benefactress', and suggests that Phoebe was a woman of means who, among other acts of 'service,' provided lodgings and provisions for travelling Christian workers. Indeed, Paul is requesting that the Romans minister to Phoebe in the very way she has 'helped' many (including him?).

These verses are a small window through which we see several aspects of life in the mission churches in the fifties. First, there was a church in Cenchreae, a 'daughter' to the church in Corinth. Second, the 'order' of 'deacon' was by then operative, and a woman was engaged in that ministry. Third, we see Christian workers travelling from church to church and being given hospitality on arrival.

2. GREETING TO PEOPLE AND GROUPS IN ROME (vv. 3-16)

Paul's greeting of so many prompts the question as to how Paul knew their names and circumstances. Were they people Paul had known previously in other churches but who have

---

1. The name Phoebe was prominent in pagan mythology and was not a name that would have been given to a Jewish girl.

now settled in Rome? True, Paul knew particular people like Prisca and Aquila, but it seems unlikely that he knew everyone he names. More likely is the suggestion that Paul had recently received news from Rome telling him of the current situation including the names of key members.

Whatever the case, Paul now exhorts the Roman Christians to 'greet' various named people, beginning with his close friends and former hosts Prisca and Aquila[2] and concluding with a general encouragement to 'greet one another with a holy kiss' (v. 16).

In other letters Paul encourages the members to 'greet one another' (1 Thess. 5:26; 2 Cor. 13:12; Phil. 4:21; cf. Heb. 13:24). Here, however, there is a striking difference. In urging these 'greetings' Paul provides both the names and information about those to be 'greeted'. This he does in no other letter, suggesting that these persons do not know one another and that, in effect, Paul is introducing them to one another. In other words, the people named had previously met in separate groups and were perhaps meeting together for the first time, gathered – as it were – to hear the apostle's letter read to them.

At the same time, the nature of the information Paul gives is warmly commendatory and serves to legitimize those persons.[3] Thus these detailed 'greetings' are analogous to Paul's technical 'introduction' to and commendation of Phoebe (vv. 1-2). Most likely there were many other Roman Christians beyond the persons named, their families, and others 'with' them who belonged to various groups and meetings in Rome. But Paul singles out twenty-six for his imprimatur, his seal of theological approval. 'Take note of these people,' Paul is saying. 'I am confident in their grasp of the gospel and in their personal integrity.'[4]

Further, his silence about the names of others is highly suggestive.[5] By inference these are not to be looked to for example

---

2. Acts 18:1-3.

3. This is more likely in our opinion than that Paul mentions only those he knew or knew of, whereas in other churches he knew most people.

4. See 1 Corinthians 4:16-19; 16:15-18.

5. Paul's letters assume the presence of critics and opponents in the churches but it is not Paul's practice to mention their names. Perhaps to do so would both enhance their opposition to Paul while also unhelpfully shaming those named.

and leadership. Furthermore, the contrast must be noted between the named persons Paul is endorsing (vv. 3-16) and the passage immediately following where Paul urges the Romans to 'take note of those who create dissensions and erect stumbling-blocks against the teaching you learned' (vv. 17-20). The Letter to the Romans in large measure has been directed to correcting the influential but erroneous beliefs of these 'dissenters'.

Instead of commenting on these verses individually it may be helpful to analyse the passage topically, as follows.

(i) There are at least three house church groups:

verse 5a   'the church in the house [of Prisca and Aquila]'
verse 14   'the brothers with [Asyncritus et al]'
verse 15   'the saints with [Philologus and Julia et al]'

It is possible, however, that a dozen other 'clusters' are implied by the individuals, couples or groups named by Paul. Beyond that there may have been synagogue-linked groups to which Paul's main opponents belonged.

Of the twenty-six persons named at least eight are or appear to be Jews:

verse 3	Prisca and Aquila	(so Acts 18:1)
verse 6	Mary	(a Jewish name)
verse 7	Andronicus and Junia	(relatives of Paul)
verse 10	Aristobulus	(a Jewish name)
verse 11	Herodion	(a Jewish name; relative of Paul)
verse 13	Rufus and his mother	(also Paul's 'mother')

As many as six Jewish-led house-groups are implied. These Jewish names confirm that some Jews re-entered Rome after the death of Claudius in AD 54 when his decree of AD 49 expelling Jews from Rome would have lapsed.

(ii) The list can be divided between those who are directly connected with Paul's mission and others he merely names.

a. *Paul's mission associates*

Prisca and Aquila,	('risked their lives' for Paul)
Mary,	('who worked hard for you')
Andronicus and Junia,	('noted apostles')
Urbanus,	('fellow-worker')
Tryphaena and Tryphosa,	('workers in the Lord')
Persis, the beloved	('worked hard in the Lord')

b. *Paul's friends*

Epaenetus	('my beloved'; 'first fruits in Asia')
Ampliatus,	('my beloved in the Lord')
Stachys	('my beloved')
Apelles,	
Aristobulus[6] and his family,	
Herodion,	('my kinsman')
Narcissus and his family	('who are in the Lord')[7]
Rufus and his mother,	('also my "mother"')
Asyncritus,	}
Phlegon,	}
Hermes,	} and the brothers with them
Patrobas,	}
Hermas	}
Philologus and Julia	}
Nereus	}
His sister	} and all the saints with them
Olympas	}

The lines of distinction between the two groups is blurred.[8] For example, Epaenetus may have belonged in the first group.

---

6. Scholars debate whether this Aristobulus may have been grandson of Herod the Great and brother of King Agrippa 1. Arguably Paul would have hinted accordingly if this were the case.

7. It is possible that the family and slaves of Narcissus were 'in the Lord' but not Narcissus himself. Aristobulus also may not have been a believer but only his household.

8. The division between 'clergy' and 'lay' was not yet clear-cut, though it would be emerging by the time the Pastoral Letters were written (cf. 1 Timothy .3:1).

(iii) More detailed comment is appropriate for Prisca and Aquila (vv. 3-5a) and Andronicus and Junia (v. 7)

Prisca and Aquila (vv. 3-5a)

Prisca (also known as Priscilla) and Aquila were Jews from Pontus, who plied the same tent-making trade as Paul (Acts 18:1-3), and who may have been travelling traders on account of their successive location in Rome, Corinth, Ephesus, Rome and Ephesus. The details of their 'risks' taken for Paul are not known. Prisca's name usually comes before her husband's and implies greater wealth or status, or perhaps a more prominent role in Paul's circle of mission associates. Prisca and Aquila appear to have been among Paul's closest supporters and friends. They played a critical role in teaching the gifted Alexandrian Jew, Apollos (Acts 18:26).

Andronicus and Junia[9] (v. 7)

Andronicus and Junia are, most likely, husband and wife. They were 'in Christ' before Paul, suggesting they had been among the disciples of Jesus. Although Jews ('kinsmen' of Paul), their names are Greek, suggesting they had come originally from the Diaspora rather than from Palestine (cf. Acts 6:1). Paul's description of them as 'apostles' suggests that they were among 'all the apostles' to whom the resurrected Jesus 'appeared' (1 Cor. 15:7) and who subsequently became itinerant missionaries. In this regard they were 'eminent'. As 'kinsmen' or relatives[10] of Paul it is possible they may have shared their faith with the pre-Christian Paul. Their presence in Rome implies strong involvement is missionary work there.

Finally, five observations may be made about those to be 'greeted'.

First, we are struck by the repetition of reference to various persons as 'beloved' or being 'in Christ' or 'serving the Lord'. The common linkage of these persons to Christ is striking. Deep Christian commitment is implied by these references.

---

9. Junia is most likely a woman's name, unless the spelling is Junias.

10. We know of the 'son of Paul's sister' who warned him of a plot against him (Acts 23:16). Does this suggest there were networks of relatives of Paul in Jerusalem?

Second, Paul's lengthiest 'greetings' are reserved for Prisca and Aquila and Andronicus and Junia, and they are singled out on account of their (likely) involvement in the Pauline mission. This is consistent with Paul's method of securing theological stability in churches by identifying trusted and reputable leaders (cf. 1 Cor. 16:15-18: 'Stephanas ... Fortunatus and Achaicus ... deserve recognition'). At the same time it is evident that Paul's mission was no solo effort, but that many were involved, in varying ways and different levels.

Third, apart from the commendation and introduction of Phoebe 'the deacon of the church in Cenchreae', there is no mention of any office-bearer in this chapter, including among the Roman Christians. For all practical purposes, then, Christianity was a lay movement at that time. This would change towards the end of the New Testament period into the era of the so-called 'apostolic fathers'.

Fourth, we are struck by the references to women involved in various forms of ministry. Phoebe is the honoured bearer of the letter, and perhaps its expositor (vv. 1-2). Prisca's name appears before her husband Aquila's, suggesting some kind of practical pre-eminence. Junia, with her husband Andronicus, was an 'eminent apostle', or missionary. Along with Phoebe, Prisca and Junia we also note Mary ('who worked hard among you'), Tryphosa (who, with her husband – or brother, Tryphaena, were 'workers in the Lord'), Persis the sister ('who worked hard in the Lord') and Rufus' mother (who cared for Paul). In an age when most women were uneducated and barred from religious leadership, the prominence of women in the mission to the Gentiles must have been striking.

Fifth, the twenty-six names reflect Greek, Roman and Jewish origin. The general impression is one of relative aff-luence. Some of these are most likely traders (e.g. Prisca and Aquila). Others have aristocratic (Jewish) names (e.g. Aristo-bulus, Herodion). All are directly or indirectly addressed in terms of 'households'. The presence in Rome of Prisca and Aquila and Andronicus and Junia speak of people travelling throughout the Empire. Clearly these arrivals contributed significantly to the shape and direction of the new movement in Rome.[11]

3. Paul's warning against 'deceivers' (vv. 17-20b)

This severe warning appears unexpected at the end of the letter. The warm commendation of Phoebe and the affectionate greeting to the several dozen named believers in Rome contrasts most markedly with the coldness towards these unnamed persons.

> I appeal to you, brothers,
> to watch out for
> those   who   cause dissension
> and   who   place stumbling-blocks
> against the teaching that you learnt.
> Keep away from them.

> For such men do not serve   the Lord Christ
>   But   their own belly,
> And through smooth speech and flattery
>   they   deceive the hearts of the innocent.

Paul warns against the roadblocks these men place in the way of true teaching. He is thinking of the 'pattern of teaching' to which the Romans were committed at their baptism (6:3-4, 17). The consequences of deflecting believers from the truth are (1) the deception of less well-informed members, and (2) the creation of divisions among believers in Rome.

Who are these men,[12] these agents of Satan (v. 20) who are 'deceiving' the Roman Christians? As discussed in the Introduction these men most likely are the 'objectors' we have encountered throughout the letter. It is not too far from the truth to say that one of Paul's reasons for writing this, his *magnum opus*, is to respond to the objections and criticisms of this group.[13]

It is scarcely conceivable that Paul would introduce such dangerous enemies to the gospel in the last sentences of the letter without some prior warning. But this he has done (in

---

11. Romans is written in Greek and not in Latin, which suggests that the readers named and unnamed originated in the east where Greek was the common language.

12. Paul's Greek makes masculine gender likely.

13. It is fair to say, however, that few commentators see a connection between these men and earlier references in Romans.

my opinion) in the extended references to the objections and criticisms dotted throughout the Letter.

The following observations may be made about these 'objectors' as we have encountered them throughout Romans.

(1) They are Jews who, against Paul's Law-free gospel, seek to reinstate the 'works of the Law' (including male circumcision) as a basis for Gentiles' 'righteousness' with God and their acceptance by God in his covenant. In effect, they are attacking 'justification by faith alone, apart from works of the Law'.

(2) They regard Paul as a renegade Jew who is disloyal to his people and who dismisses God's covenant promises to Israel (9:1-5). In effect, they charge Paul with saying that God is finished with his historic people and is only concerned with the Gentiles.

These observations from the earlier sections of the letter are consistent with his present brief comment that they 'serve their belly' (*koilia*), that is, Jewish scruples to do with eating (see on 14:1-23), rather than 'the Lord Christ'.

They are, indeed, dangerous, says Paul. First, they purport to be Christians, for why would Paul say they 'do not serve the Lord Christ' unless it appeared that they did? Were they Jews and nothing else, Paul would scarcely have spoken about them like this. Second, they are bent on persuading others to their views, using 'kind words' and 'flattery'. The source of such fatally seductive speech and its original exemplar is 'Satan' (v. 20), who deceived the first man and woman. Paul regards the activities of these 'deceivers' in Rome as 'satanic'.

Paul, however, concludes on a positive and optimistic note (v. 19). The report of the Roman Christians' 'obedience'[14] has gone out to everyone, so that Paul 'rejoices' about them. Yet he is concerned for them. He wishes them to be 'wise' for what is 'good' and 'innocent' about 'evil'. Paul may be echoing Jesus' words: 'be *wise* as serpents and *innocent* as doves' (Matt. 10:16).

---

14. Significantly Paul wrote earlier that their 'faith' was proclaimed universally (1:8). Paul sees 'faith' and 'obedience' as inextricably connected. True 'faith' is 'obedient' to Christ.

Paul assures them that 'the God of peace' will quickly 'trample down' Satan 'beneath their feet' (v. 20), which prompts us to remember God's promise that Eve's 'offspring' will crush the serpent's heel (Gen. 3:15). The present lack of 'peace', through the divisions among believers in Rome, is Satan's doing but it will be put right by the 'God of peace'.

By way of application we should note that false teaching and the undermining of apostolic truth is, indeed, 'satanic.' Further, it is dangerous because it deflects the 'weak' and 'new' Christian from the gospel of Christ. Let those who open their mouths as teachers of the Word of God take great care to teach only the truth of the gospel, neither more nor less. At the same time, the 'God of peace' will ultimately prevail and triumph. God will always somehow preserve the truth of his gospel in the world.

4. PRAYER AND GREETINGS (vv. 20c-23)
His warning ended, Paul prays that 'the grace of our Lord Jesus Christ be with' the hearers of this letter, whether in Rome or wherever it would be read.[15]

The 'grace' of Christ springs both from the 'grace' he manifested in his incarnation and in his death and resurrection. Paul expanded on that 'grace' as revealing Christ's incredible generosity and humility in the words, 'though he was rich, yet for your sakes he became poor, that you through his poverty might be rich' (2 Cor. 8:9). To hearers tempted, perhaps, to approach God based on the self-effort of 'works', this prayer is pointed. From first to last, our salvation is 'by grace'.

Paul also expanded on this 'grace' in his famous trinitarian prayer: 'The grace of the Lord Jesus Christ, the love of God and the fellowship of the Holy Spirit be with you all' (2 Cor. 3:14).

The apostle sends greetings from a number of people who most likely were close by when he wrote the letter.

Timothy, his 'fellow-worker', greets them. Timothy was not entrusted with bringing Paul's second letter to Corinth but was dispatched from Ephesus to Macedonia. Now, however,

---

15. See also 1 Corinthians 16:23; Galatians 6:18; Philippians 4:23; 1 Thessalonians 5:28; 2 Thessalonians 3:18; Philemon 25.

Timothy is once again in Corinth, in a church he co-founded with Paul almost a decade earlier (2 Cor. 1:19). As an honoured associate of Paul's, his name appears first.

Next come greetings from Paul's fellow-Jews (*sungeneis*), Loukios (not 'Luke,' which is spelt differently), Jason and Sosipater.

Tertius, the 'writer of the letter', adds his own signature greeting ('I, Tertius ... greet you'). Paul often used a scribe in writing his letters (1 Cor. 16:21; Gal. 6:11; Col. 4:18; 2 Thess. 3:17). While in other letters the amanuensis may have had some freedom of expression, in so important a letter as this it is likely that Paul carefully dictated every word.

Gaius also sends his greetings. Probably this is the 'Gaius' of 1 Corinthians 1:14, whose complete Roman name was Gaius Titius Justus, the God-fearer who attended the synagogue in Corinth and whose house was next door to the synagogue. This Gaius was evidently a man of means since he provided hospitality not only to Paul, but also to the 'whole church'. It appears that Paul wrote his Letter to the Romans in Gaius' home.

Another significant person to send greetings to Rome was Erastus, who Paul refers to as the 'treasurer' (*oikonomos*) of Corinth. Some uncertainty surrounds the precise office Erastus held, though he was certainly a well-known city leader. An inscription bearing the name Erastus, 'public works commissioner' was discovered near the theatre in Corinth. It is not certain if this is the same 'Erastus'.

Finally, Paul sends greetings from Quartus, 'the brother' Christian who is, however, otherwise unknown.

These 'greetings' from Corinth, like those exhortations to 'greet' Roman Christians, tell their own story of the affection between these believers, distant geographically from one another though they were.

5. Doxology (vv. 25-27)

These verses have a liturgical ring to them and form a fitting conclusion to the letter. We can imagine the appointed reader in the congregation drawing breath to utter these words of direct praise to God.

> To him who is powerful...
> to the only wise God...
> be glory forever,
> amen.

There are several other 'doxologies'[16] to God in the New Testament, for example, Hebrews 13:20-21. Some doxologies are quite brief, for example, Romans 11:36; Galatians 1:5; Philippians 4:20; 1 Timothy 1:17. Along with this one, two others begin with the identical words, 'to him who is powerful'[17] (Eph. 3:20; Jude 24).

God is 'powerful' and 'wise', to which we may add that he is also 'good' (Ps. 100:5). Life's experience is often marred by injustice, tragedy and disappointment but day by day believers press on with faith and hope to their salvation knowing that they are in the hands of a Father who is 'powerful,' 'wise' and 'good'.

a. By his gospel God 'strengthens' his people.

In the precise context of our passage God is 'powerful' to 'strengthen' the Roman Christians. This picks up exactly Paul's 'longing' expressed at the beginning of the Letter, that by his coming he may impart some spiritual gift to 'strengthen' them (1:11). At the same time, the immediate context spoke of dangerous 'deceivers' and 'dividers' of the Roman Christians. God will 'strengthen' the people in the face of these problems.

In everyday use this word (*sterizō*) meant 'securing firmly', for example, a loose floor board. Luke used this word for Jesus when he 'fixed his face' to go towards Jerusalem (Luke 9:51). The writers of the New Testament repeatedly pray for and encourage the 'strengthening' of individuals and churches in their faith in the face of adversity, for example, in 1 Thessalonians 3:2, James 5:8, 1 Peter 5:10 and Revelation 3:2.

---

16. A 'doxology', from the Greek word *doxa* ('glory'), ascribes praise to God in terms of his 'brightness' of character.

17. The Greek is *tō..dunamenō*, 'to him who is *powerful*.' The usual English translation, 'to him who is able,' masks the force of Paul's original word.

How does Paul know that God 'strengthens' his people? It is, he says

according to   my gospel   and
                    my proclamation[18]

The 'gospel' that Paul *proclaimed* was, as he wrote earlier, 'the power of God for salvation to all who believe' (1:16). God brings people to 'believe' in him through that gospel and he 'strengthens' people in their faith through that ministry. God's supernatural 'power' in raising alive his dead 'Son' continues to be revealed in the lives of those who hear and believe by the divine 'power' of the 'gospel of God'.

b. The gospel is a 'mystery' that was 'long hidden'.
'Mystery' (*mustērion*) is one of Paul's keywords, though it is not easy for us modern readers to understand its meaning. As used by Paul, it means 'a plan of God that was previously hidden but which is now revealed'. That 'hidden plan' was that 'all the Gentiles' were to be summoned to obey the Word of God by believing in his Son, Jesus Christ.

Of course, there were strong hints beforehand in 'the prophetic writings' that it was 'the command of the eternal God' that peoples of all nations be gathered into his kingdom. The Lord promised Abraham that '*all peoples* on earth will be blessed through you' (Gen. 12:3). Through Isaiah God promised to make his Servant (that is, Christ) 'a light to the Gentiles' to 'bring his salvation to the ends of the earth' (Isa. 49:6).

These intimations, however, were for the most part unnoticed by members of God's historic people. Indeed, Jonah, one of God's prophets to Israel, strongly resisted going to preach to the Gentile people of Nineveh. By New Testament times it was clear that Israel's attitude to Gentiles was negative and defensive. For centuries the nation had been occupied

---

18. Paul's original readers were familiar with 'gospel' (*euangelion*) and 'proclamation' (*kērupsgma* – see on 1:1), which are similar in meaning. They were used of a Roman emperor announcing important news throughout the Empire that a great military victory had been won. Such news would, of course, 'strengthen' the confidence of the people in the military capacity of their emperor.

militarily in turn by Persians, Greeks and Romans. The Greeks in particular threatened to corrupt Israel's religious purity with the imported evils of idolatry and sexual permissiveness.

The Pharisees defended the covenant of God by 'hedging' the Law with numerous subsidiary rules and by provisions for purity by ritual washings. Not least, Jews were not permitted to eat with Gentiles. The effect of the Pharisees' influence was to widen the gap between Jews and Gentiles and to make the inclusion of Gentiles more difficult. The insistence on male circumcision was calculated to deter Gentiles from a too-easy access to the people of God.

c. Paul's gospel reveals that 'mystery'.
But God's decisive hour has struck, signalled by the critical word, 'now' (*nun*).

> the mystery hidden[19] for long ages
> but is *now* made manifest
> and by the command of the eternal God
> is   made known

This 'revelation' of the 'long-hidden mystery' has now occurred, but by a two-stage process, the first involving Christ alone and the second involving Christ working through his apostle, Paul. Earlier Paul referred to Christ as 'minister of the Jews' and to himself, Paul, as 'minister *of Christ* to the Gentiles' (15:8, 16).[20] In this two-step programme God brought salvation to his historic people the Jews through his 'minister' Christ and then to the Gentiles through 'Christ's minister' Paul. By God's gracious calling of him, Paul saw himself as having a special place in that plan, an extension of Christ's own ministry, no less (15:18). Thus Paul enjoyed a special revelation of the long-hidden 'mystery' of God mercifully to gather in the peoples of the Gentiles into his kingdom (see on 11:11-15; cf. Eph. 3:1-9).

---

19. Literally, a 'mystery' that had been '*long silent*' (*sesigemenou*).
20. The risen Christ sent forth his apostles to the Gentiles (Matt. 28:19; Luke 24:47). His gospel must be preached to all the nations of the world (Mark 13:10; 14:9). Yet, in the purposes of God, that task fell not to those originally commissioned, but to Paul.

d. The gospel is the main theme of this letter.
If we compare the final three verses of Romans with the first six verses in the letter we see that common to both passages is Paul's discussion of the gospel. The gospel that was prophesied (as 'a mystery') in the prophetic writings is now made known in the proclamation of Jesus Christ. By it God summons the Gentiles to obey it by believing in Christ. These common elements are not accidental, but deliberate. They intentionally 'round off' the letter, by a rhetorical device called an *inclusio*. Paul's point is to enclose the whole letter with these references to the gospel at the beginning and the end.

By this he sends to his readers, then and now, an unmistakable signal. The 'message' of Romans overall is 'the gospel of God, what Paul here calls 'my gospel, the proclamation of Jesus Christ ... for the obedience of faith for all the Gentiles'. Yet, at the same time, as we know from chapters 9–11, Paul was no less passionate about the salvation of his fellow-Israelites. Indeed, the burden of the letter as a whole is Paul's articulation of God's concern for the salvation of 'all,' both Jew and Gentile, in the 'one' body praising God with 'one mouth'.

STUDY QUESTIONS

1. Paul commends many fellow workers. How can you commend those believers who work with you or on your behalf such as pastors, elders, deacons, Sunday School teachers, etc.?

2. What does Paul warn us about concerning those who seek to deceive believers?

3. How does God strengthen His people with the gospel?

4. What is the mystery that has now been revealed that Paul refers to?

5. What are the two key themes of the book of Romans?

Bibliography

C.E.B. Cranfield, Romans ICC (Edinburgh: T&T Clark, 1979)

D. Moo [details soon]

T. R. Schreiner, Romans (Grand rapids: Baker, 1998).

P. Stuhlmacher, [details soon]

J.R.W. Stott, Romans (Downers Grove: IVP/US, 1994).

Subject Index

Abel 116
Abraham 87-98, 198
   God's promises to 64, 66-7, 91-5,
    .... 211-12, 327, 329
   justified by faith 72, 88-9, 90-1
Achaia 7, 29, 336, 337, 338, 342
Adam
   age of sin and death in Adam 271
   apostasy of 92
   contrasted with Abraham 95
   contrasted with Christ ... 114, 119-22
   God's image in 78
   human solidarity in 115-17, 126
   introduction of sin and death
      through 113-16
     see also original sin
   mind of the flesh, 'in Adam' ... 176-8
   the 'old man' and 136
   as a 'type' of Christ 119-22
adoption 186
   of Israel 209
afflictions 103-4, 335
   see also sufferings
Ampliatus 355
Andronicus 332, 355, 356-7
Anna 25
antinomianism, rebuttal of 131-3, 141-9
Antioch (Syria) 7, 29, 34
Apelles 355
Apollos 356
Apostles' Creed 131n5
apostleship 22-3
   Paul as apostle to the Gentiles 29,
      .... 34-6, 329-39, 340-9
   Paul's apostolic authority and
      teaching 33-4, 334-5, 336-7
apostolic fathers 357
Aquila 9, 10, 332, 355, 356, 357
Aristobulus 354, 355, 357

Aristotle 47, 56, 57
Asia 29, 337, 340, 342
Asia Minor 352
Asklepios 275
assurance
   of being a child of God 179, 183-6
   New Perspective's obscuring of ... 17
   that God is for us 198-201
Asyncritus 354, 355
atonement 108, 177
   Day of Atonement 79n10, 271
    see also propitiation
Augustine of Hippo 118, 295
Augustus, Octavianus 134-5, 288
authority of the state 285-9

Babylon 237
baptism 132-9
   implications for Christian life ....
      .... 139-49, 294-5
barbarians 35, 190, 332, 347
Barnabas 23, 29
Bartimaeus 27
Baruch, second book of 118
belief *see* faith
Bible *see* Scripture
blindness, spiritual 45, 66-7
boasting
   exultation *see* exultation
   in the Law 81-4
bodily presentation 269-71
bodily resurrection 180-1, 189-93, 270
body of Christ 274-7
   see also Church
body of sin 136
   see also flesh
Bornkamm, Günther 10
burial, with Christ 133-5

Caesar, (Gaius) Julius.....................48
Caesarea Maritima 306
Caiaphas...96
Cain...116
calling of God 197
  see also election
Calvin, John............................ 79n10, 255
Cenchreae...352
  church in................................7, 276
ceremonial observance 301-3
charismata see spiritual gifts
children of flesh..................................212
children of God............................ 196-203
  assurance of...................... 179, 183-6
  children of promise 211-12, 221,
  ....7, 243-5
Chrestus..8, 30
Christian life
  as a battleground between the flesh
    and the Spirit 180-1
    see also sanctification
  caring for the weak 297-321
  fulfilling the Law through love.......
    ....170-2, 267-9, 291-3
  with no return to the flesh 293-5
  under persecution..................... 282-5
    see also persecution
  in the Spirit.............................. 170-2
  submission to the state 285-90
  transformation in a united church...
    ....273-7, 310-11, 325-9
  transformation through love ..267-73,
    ....278-85, 291-3
  up-building one another 310-11,
   315-17
  of victory over sin 139-48
  of victory over sufferings........ 201-3
  walking in love 305-10
Christology.. 25-8
  versus works of the law 219, 222,
   227-31
Church
  church order...............................276
  collection for the Jerusalem church
    ....331-2, 342-4, 347
  foundation-laying 8, 310, 336-7,
    ....340, 349
  Gentile Christians to welcome 'weak'
    Jewish Christians 297-321
  Jews and Gentiles to receive one
    another............................... 325-9
  leadership............................282, 357

love in the church................. 279-82
  in Rome....................9-10, 30-6, 352-7
  superstructure ...310-11, 335n8, 336,
    ....340, 349
  transformed living in a united
    church 273-7, 310-11, 325-9
  unity in Christ see unity in Christ
  up-building of............310-11, 315-17
  warnings against deceivers... 358-60
circumcision.......................................61-4
  of Abraham 90-1
  and the covenant people... 61-5, 234-5
  and Gentile God-fearers.........59n19
  of the heart 61, 63, 65
  not required by Gentile believers... 29
  preached by Saul of Tarsus before
    his conversion...................29, 62
  as a sign of faith..........................90-1
Claudius I..................... 7-8, 9, 30, 34, 299
Clement..336
collection of money......331-2, 342-4, 347
condemnation
  in Adam..................................122
  forbidden............................... 304-5
  through the Law.....................63, 229
  no condemnation for those in Christ
   167-72
  as penalty of sin............................167
confession of faith 231-4
conscience......... 54, 207, 289, 307, 312-13
consecration (self-dedication) 145-6,
    .... 178, 269-71
Corinth.....................7, 336, 338, 342, 361
Corinthians...............................33, 92, 104
covenant of God
  circumcision and the covenant
    people 61-5, 234-5
  God's covenants with Israel........209
    see also gospel; Law; promises
      of God
'covenantal nomism'...........................15
Cranmer, Thomas................................319
creation 48-9
  futility and hope of 188-92
culture
  Jewish 82, 226, 270, 298-9, 307
  as of secondary importance..321, 343

Damascus 29, 337
Daniel..123
David, king.................................89, 248, 328
Day of Atonement................. 79n10, 271

days, celebratory keeping of......... 301-3
deacons 352
    rulers as God's 'deacons' 288
    see also Phoebe
death
    from Adam to Moses 119
    baptism into Christ's death..... 133-9
    Christ's breaking of the rule of
        death 137-8, 149
    creation's death cycle............... 188-9
    deliverance from the Law of sin and
        death 166-72
    eternal 114, 125, 147, 177
    to the flesh 178-83
    God's love and the death of Christ..
        106-7
    handing over of Jesus to...............96
    propitiatory death of Christ ... 79-81
    as result of Adam's sin..... 78, 113-16
    as result of reign of sin ... 124-5, 132,
       147
    to sin.. 132-9
    and spiritual life 180
defilement..................................307, 313
deliverance .. 37, 65, 141, 153-72, 190, 235
    see also salvation
depression 187
despising 304-5
disobedience
    of Adam........................... 114-16, 122
        see also original sin
    hardening of the heart through........
        .... 247-8, 258
    judgment on..................................55
    and the mystery of salvation .. 258-9
    'the disobedient in Judaea'...... 345-6
Donne, John 117
doxologies 33, 259, 361-2, 361-5
Dunn, J. D. G. 15, 71

Earth.................................... 189-90
Eden 189
Edomites............................... 212-13
election
    of 'all Israel'............................255, 258
    the gospel and the election of Israel
        256-9
    by grace 245-6
    of Israel 211-13, 255, 256-9
    of those God foreknew 197, 244
Elijah... 244-5
    attitude of 262

emptiness.................................187, 189
encouragement 33, 276, 277, 318-19
end times 188-93
    God's end-time family 194-7
        see also Last Day
endurance 318-19
enemies
    of God 99, 101, 108, 256-7
    love of 283, 291
    reconciliation of 101, 107-8
    treatment of............................. 284-5
envoys..................................23, 337, 352
Epaenetus 355
Epaphras..332, 336
Epaphroditus 352
Ephesus...............................7, 288, 337
Erastus 361
Esau 212, 221
eschatology see end times
eternal life.................. 39, 121, 148-9, 177
ethics
    in Christian life see Christian life
    defilement as a matter of.............307
    of forgiveness......................... 283-5
    the place of the Law in 266-7
    and the teaching of Jesus ..267-9, 283
Eudia...336
evangelism 236-8, 261
    hospitality for travelling ministers
       352
    of Jews..................................238, 321
    proclaiming the gospel to the
        Gentiles............28-9, 34-6, 236-7,
        .... 261, 332-42
    two steps of gospel ministry......333,
        ....349, 364
Eve..115
evolutionary theory 48
expiation.....................................80n10(2)
exultation.......... 100, 101, 103, 109, 332-3
Ezra, fourth book of.........................116

Faith
    of Abraham 88-95, 98
    amidst sufferings.........................195
    Christological faith versus works of
        the Law 219, 222, 227-31
    confession of 231-4
    as dynamic recognition of Christ ...220
    from hearing the gospel
        proclamation......................... 236-8
    justification by
        see justification by faith

meat-eating and.......298-301, 312-14
obedience of *see* obedience
observance of special days and...301-3
received through hearing the gospel
....37
relationship to the Law 83-5
righteousness received by........ 38-9,
....77-8, 88-91
see also justification by faith
strengthening of 362-3
tests of 103-4
thanksgiving for 31
that God is for us................. 198-201
unity with Christ through....... 133-9
working through love.............. 170-2
faithfulness
of Christ...................................... 77-8
Jewish disbelief and the faithfulness
of God 65-6, 68
false teaching 358-60
family of God
the church as the vessel of mercy...216
in the end-times....................... 194-7
Jesus' pre-eminence in.................196
fear of God 68-9
festival observance 301-3
flesh 161-5, 168, 170
no return to the flesh 293-5
Spirit and 176-83
foolishness.................................... 45, 68-9
foreknowledge of God............ 195-8, 244
forgiveness 283
freedom
Christian freedom and respect for
weaker brothers............. 297-321
of Jewish believers from the Law ....
.... 156-9
the Law-free gospel *see* gospel
liberation of creation.............. 188-93
from sin, for righteousness 130,
.... 139-49
fruit of obedience 147-8
fruit of sin 147

Gaius 7, 361
Galatia...337, 342
Gentiles
admission to the covenant people
.............................62-4, 216, 249-50
Christian debt to the Jerusalem
church 343
Christ's rule over 328

exhorted to pursue peace and up-
building 310-11, 315-17
the 'fulness of the Gentiles'..... 254-5
Gentile Christians to welcome 'weak'
Jewish Christians.............297-321
to glorify God together with the
Jews 83, 302, 319-20, 343
God's acceptance of............... 215-16
God's mercy on............................216
gospel light brought to 64
gospel proclamation to....28-9, 34-6,
..........................236-7, 261, 332-42
grafted in to the tree of historic
Israel................................. 251-3
as 'Greeks and barbarians'...35, 332,
....347
Israel's hardening as warning to......
.... 251-4
Israel's jealousy of Gentile believers
....250
and Jews to receive one another ......
.... 325-9
as law-breakers........................... 56-8
openness to the gospel 217-18
Paul as apostle to the Gentiles.. 28-9,
........................34-6, 329-39, 340-9
Paul's concern for Gentile believers
....12
revelation of God's wrath to ... 42-51
true circumcision and.............. 62-4
warnings to Gentile Christians
against Jewish deceivers 358-60
and the works of darkness.........294
Gethsemane...................................27, 138
glory of God 103, 188, 331
shown to Israel 209
Gnosticism..270
God
as author and subject of the gospel..24
blessings of God on Israel..... 208-10
certainty that God is for us . 198-201
family of *see* family of God
foreknowledge of 195-8, 244
gospel as power of 36-9
the Holy Spirit *see* Holy Spirit
humility of....................................282
known as Father 168
as potter 214-16
promises of *see* promises of God
as reconciler 107-9
'right time' of 105-6
Romans' focus on God's action ...13,
.... 143, 168-9

Romans' focus on God's character
....43, 53-4
sending of the Son........................169
Son of God
see Jesus Christ; Son of God
sovereign goodness of..... 195, 202-3
universal sovereignty of.... 83, 202-3
word of *see* word of God
godlessness........... 42-3, 46, 105, 115, 295
goodness.......................................330
belief in human goodness....... 126-7
of God 195, 202-3
gospel
as display of the righteousness of
God..76
election of Israel and............... 256-9
as end of boasting in the Law... 81-4
as an eschatological event.............38
fulfilling the gospel.................. 335-8
Gentile openness to................ 217-18
as God's means of strengthening his
people 362-3
the Law-free gospel 114-15
as main theme of Romans...23-8, 365
as a mystery 254, 258-9, 363-4
obedience to the gospel...237-40, 333
as only way of salvation for Jew and
Gentile 78, 81-4, 222, 256
as the power of God................... 36-9
proclamation to the Gentiles ... 28-9,
...............34-6, 236-7, 261, 332-42
Romans as Paul's gospel 33, 36
two steps of gospel ministry......333,
....349, 364
grace
as base of old and new covenants..229
as basis of justification...................79
as basis of membership of God's
people 93-5
denial of cheap grace 136-7
freedom through 141-2
gospel of 114-15
see also gospel
prayer for.....................................360
reign of sin versus reign of grace
.... 124-5
standing under grace....... 102-3, 140
superabundance through Christ......
.... 123-5
greetings 21-30, 352-7, 360-1

Hagar...212
Havergal, Frances...........................146

heart
circumcision of the heart...61, 63, 65
darkening of the heart.............. 44-5
hardening of the heart..246-8, 258-9
Law of God in the heart 57-8
heaven...189
heirship.. 185-6
Hermas 355
Hermes..355
Herodion 355, 357
'higher life' teaching 129, 138-9
holiness
concerns of 'weak' Jewish Christians
...........................298-303, 305-14
holy sacrifice 270-1
second coming as motive for.. 293-4
see also sanctification
Holy Spirit
as bringer of hope 191-3
descent on Gentiles.....................306
as a downpayment................... 186-7
empowerment of Paul's apostleship
.... 334-5
as first fruits 192-3
and the flesh............................. 176-83
gift of a new heart 63, 108
inner presence of...... 104-5, 272, 293
as major concern of Romans.........14
as poured out Spirit of holiness ...27
pouring out the love of God 193
prayer of 193-4
and the resurrection of the body . 180-1
as the Spirit of sonship 179, 183-6
test for the presence of.................179
walking according to the Spirit ..169,
....293
homosexual practices 47-8
hope................... 94, 101, 104, 186-93, 329
brought by the Holy Spirit...... 191-3
of the glory of God.......................103
rejoicing in....................................280
through scripture 318-19
hospitality.............................281, 352
humanism....................................... 126-7
humility 33, 252, 274, 276, 282
of Christ....................................316, 360
hypocrisy.. 278-9
double standards in law-keeping ....
.... 58-61

Idolatry..........45, 54, 177, 181, 272, 364
Illyricum 337

image of God 78, 196
intercession 31, 109, 194, 200-1
Isaac...198, 212
Ishmael...212
Israel
    'all Israel' that is to be saved... 255-6
    calling as light to the nations............
    .... 59-60, 64
    the children of promise within.........
    ....211-12, 221, 243-5
    circumcision and 61-5, 234-5
    election of 211-13, 255, 256-9
    grafting of the Gentiles in to the tree
        of Israel 251-3
    hardening of...................246-8, 258-9
    historical blessings of 208-10
    jealousy of influx of Gentile
        believers.................................250
    New Israel 113
    remnant of................. 217, 221, 243-5
    ultimate salvation of 215, 249-51,
    ....254-6, 257-9
        see also Jews
Israel's rejection of the Messiah....16, 27,
    ....54, 65-8, 207
    as disobedience to the gospel ..237-40
    and God's acceptance of the
        Gentiles...215-16, 234-40, 249-50
    God's promises and 210-13, 243-5
    through a hardening of heart .. 246-8
    and the justice of God............ 213-16
    Paul's sorrow over.......207-10, 225-6
    as the rejection of the righteousness
        of God 225-7
    as stumbling over the 'Stone'...218-20
    as warning to the Gentiles 251-4

Jacob 212, 221
James, brother of Jesus 22-3, 346
Jason..361
Jericho 208
Jerusalem................. 8, 78, 337, 338, 342-7
    church in...............................279, 281
    Jerusalem Council 338
    New Jerusalem 329, 331
    Paul's collection for the church of....
    ....331-2, 342-4, 347
    Paul's plans to visit............ 340, 342-4
    temple culture of 270
Jesus Christ
    confession of Jesus as Lord 232-3
    contrasted with Adam... 114, 119-22

divinity of..........................210, 235-6
as the 'end of the law'............. 227-9
ethic of forgiveness 283
ethics and the teaching of Jesus ....
.... 267-9
faithfulness of 77-8
as foundation of the gospel 335-6
God's love and the death of Christ ..
.... 106-7
handed over to death...................96
humility of............................316, 360
importance in Romans of salvation
    through...................................13
justification through 122
    see also justification by faith
as 'Lamb of God' 270
lordship of............................... 232-6
mediatorship of ..31, 108-9, 200-1, 271
as Messiah see messiahship of Jesus
as minister to the weak.......... 316-17
obedience of 78, 114
as pre-eminent in God's family ..196
propitiatory death of 79-81
resurrection of ...27-8, 96-7, 134, 138
as second Man 92
as servant......................... 316-17, 327
as Son of God 25-8, 169, 184-5,
....231, 236
as son of man... 123, 186, 191, 210, 317
as the 'Stone' 218-20
as suffering servant............ 96, 122-3
teaching on defilement........307, 313
union with Christ in death and
    resurrection........................ 133-9
word of Christ...............................238
    see also gospel
Jews
    discharge of Jewish believers from
        Law.................................... 156-9
    evangelism of.......................238, 321
    expelled from Rome 9, 30, 34,
    ....288, 299
    Gentile Christians to welcome 'weak'
        Jewish Christians 297-321
    and Gentiles to receive one another
    325-9
    to glorify God together with the
        Gentiles....... 83, 302, 319-20, 343
    Jewish communities in Rome.... 8-9,
    ....30, 34
    Jewish disbelief and the faithfulness
        of God 65-7, 68
    Paul's addressing of Jewish
        believers..................................12

Paul's collection for the Jewish
   believers in Jerusalem...... 331-2,
   .... 342-4, 347
Paul's longing for the salvation of ...
   ....89, 207-10, 225-6, 319-20
and the re-defining of covenant
   membership................. 65, 234-5
re-entry to Rome after death of
   Claudius .. 8, 100, 299, 338-9, 354
reasons for God's judgment on the
   Jews.................................. 52-61
as recipients of the Law............ 56-7,
   .... 58-61, 65, 209
rejection of the Messiah
   see Israel's rejection of the Messiah
the true Jew 61-5
warnings to Gentile Christians
   against Jewish deceivers 358-60
zeal for God................................226
   see also zealots
   see also Israel
John the Baptist 62, 235
Jonah 363
Joppa 306
Joseph of Arimathea 25
Josephus, Flavius...............................150
Judaea 335, 342, 346
Judas.......................................96
Judea see Judaea
judgment
   according to the truth................. 52-6
   according to works 54-6, 221
   of brothers 304-5
   for double standards 58-61
   held back in anticipation of death of
      Christ 80-1
   on law-breakers.......................... 56-8
   reasons for God's judgment on the
      Jews.................................. 52-61
   revelation of God's verdict...38, 99-100
   revelation of God's wrath and ...42-51
   righteous judgment of God 66,
      ....80-1, 213-16
Julia 355
Junia 332, 355, 356-7
justice 213-16
   state authority and 285-90
justification by faith
   Abraham's justification ... 72, 88-9, 90-1
   Christ's resurrection as basis for ..97
   condemnation ruled out by..199-201
   confessed by the believer 231-4
   and denial of cheap grace 136-7

in the determination of God ..197-201
justification in Christ versus
   condemnation in Adam 122
nature of 38, 82
the New Perspective on.......... 16-17,
   .... 71-2, 222
as ongoing activity.......................79
peace with God through 100-2
reconciliation and.................... 107-9
standing under grace through...102-3

Kindness of God 53-4
kingdom of God 189, 309
knowledge of God........................... 43-6
understanding through the conscience..
   ....207, 289

Last Day ..38, 43, 46, 70, 99-100, 104-5
   see also end times; judgment;
      resurrection of the body
Law
   Christ as 'end of the law'......... 227-9
   Christian life not under Law . 140-1,
      170-2
   Christological faith versus works of
      the Law 219, 222, 227-31
   circumcision and 61-4
      see also circumcision
   concerns of 'weak' Jewish Christians
      ....298-303, 305-14
   deliverance from the Law of sin and
      death 166-72
   discharge of Jewish believers from..
      156-9
   double standards concerning...58-61
   end of era of 76, 156-9, 222, 227-9
   fulfilled by Christ.........................228
   fulfilled through life in the Spirit.....
      170-2
   God's wrath engendered by 92
   gospel as end of boasting in the
      Law.. 81-4
   impossibility of keeping the law 'in
      the flesh'........................... 162-5
   inability of Law to give victory over
      sin and death 162-5
   as instrument of condemnation ..63,
     229
   Jews as recipients of the Law .. 56-7,
      .... 58-61, 65, 209
   judgment on law-breakers........ 56-8

law-keeping slavery.....................184
legalism..........................172, 241, 278
    see also Pharisaism
love as fulfilling of the Law ... 170-2,
    ....267-9, 291-3
as major concern of Romans... 13-14
the New Perspective on.......... 15-16,
    .... 71-2, 222
and the promises of God........... 92-3
relationship to faith..................... 83-5
revealing universality of sin.. 69-71,
    75-6
righteousness of Law and
    righteousness of faith ..219, 222,
    227-31
sin provoked by........75-6, 92-3, 124,
    159-61
law-breaking
    covenant-breaking 76, 229
    judgment on law-breakers........ 56-8
       see also sin
legalism...................................172, 241, 278
    see also Law; Pharisaism
liberalism, theological.................242, 261
life
    the Christian life see Christian life
    eternal 39, 121, 148-9, 177
Loukios 361
love
    of Christ...................................... 201-2
    in the Church 279-82
    of enemies 283, 291
    exhortations to........................ 278-85
    of God 104, 105-7, 193, 197,
    ....198-9, 202-3
    Law fulfilled through ..170-2, 267-9,
    291-3
    for the outsider 282-5, 291
    transformation through........ 267-73,
    ....278-85, 291-3
    walking in love 305-31
Luther, Martin..... 15, 79n10, 82, 183, 241

Macedonia ..7, 29, 336, 337, 340, 342
marriage.. 48-9
Mary..355, 357
meat-eating 298-301, 305-9, 310-14
Melanchthon, Philipp..........................10
mercy 213, 215-17, 221
    on the Gentiles.............................216
    on a remnant of Israel...... 217, 243-5
    the triumph of mercy for Jew and
    Gentile 256-9, 260

mercy seat...........................79n10, 80n11
messiahship of Jesus . 26-7, 102, 123, 210
    Christ as the 'Stone' 218-20
    foretold in the Old Testament . 26-7,
   77
    and fulfillment of God's promises to
    Abraham...............................329
    Jewish rejection of
       see Israel's rejection of the Messiah
mind
    of the flesh 176-8
    renewal of................................272
    of the Spirit............111, 177, 186, 194
ministering 277
    see also service
miracles..334
Moo, D. 154-5n2, 255
Moses 76, 230-1
    Law of see Law
Munck, Johannes....................................15
mystery of salvation.....254, 258-9, 363-4

Nabataea 337
Narcissus 355
Nathan 26
Nereus..355
Nero 8, 48, 299
new creation............................. 189-92
New Israel 113
Nicene Creed 131n5

Obedience
    of Christ...........................78, 114, 122
    civil... 285-90
    of faith......... 28-9, 237, 330, 333, 336,
    ....347, 348
    fruit of....................................... 147-8
    to the gospel.................... 237-40, 333
    from the heart........................142, 143
    under the Law 231
    to the teaching 142-3
    see also slavery
observance of special days............. 301-3
'old man'..136
olive tree of Israel 205, 251-3, 265
Olympas 355
original sin.......................... 13, 78, 113-18
    effect on creation 188-9
    the sin of humanity in Adam....115-18
    transmission of 118
orphans..281

Patience....................103, 104, 193, 280
of God 43, 80, 215-16, 221, 260
Patrobas 355
Paul, Apostle
   as apostle to the Gentiles ... 28-9, 34-6,
   ....329-39, 340-9
   appeal for prayer to support his
     travels 344-7
   autobiography of Romans 7 .. 154-5,
   ....160-1, 162-5
   background to writing Romans.......
   ....7-8, 32-6
   collection for the Jewish believers in
     Jerusalem.........331-2, 342-4, 347
   conversion of............................29, 62
   greetings to people and groups in
     Rome 30, 352-7, 360-1
   the New Perspective on Paul in
     Romans..........14-17, 71-2, 221-2,
   ....233, 241
   plans to visit Rome 32-6, 337-8,
   .... 340-1, 346
   purpose of writing Romans.... 10-12
   self-description as slave and apostle
   22-3
   sketch of Paul's theology in Romans
   13-14
   thanksgiving and prayer for the
     saints in Rome 30-3
peace
   with God..................................... 100-2
   prayer for...347
   pursuance of 310-11
Pelagianism 126, 150
perfectionism 138-9
persecution........201-3, 248, 280-1, 282-5,
  342-3
Persis 355, 357
Peter, Apostle 9, 27, 306, 338-9
Pharaoh............................ 213-14, 247
Pharisaism............................82, 150, 278
Philippi 7, 336
Philo 59-60, 61
Philologus..355
Phlegon...355
Phoebe..................7, 276, 281, 351-2, 357
Pilate, Pontius 96, 287
praise see doxologies
prayer.................................. 30-3, 197, 335
   of the Holy Spirit...................... 193-4
   of Jesus as our advocate .. 109, 200-1
   for Paul and his ministry......... 344-7
   for peace 347
preaching...24
   see also evangelism
predestination............................. 194-201
pride 81-4, 276, 282
Priscilla (Prisca) .. 9, 10, 332, 355, 356, 357
promises of God
   to Abraham 64, 66-7, 91-5, 211-12,
   ....327, 329
   and Israel's rejection of the Messiah
   ....210-13, 243-5, 257-9
   and the keeping of the Law 92-3
   messianic..102
   Old Testament promises of the
     gospel.........24-5, 327-9, 343, 363
prophesying 276-7
propitiation 79-81
providence... 194-5
purity
   'everything is pure' 306, 311-14
   moral purity.....................................270
     see also holiness
   purity laws 16, 298, 364
   pursuit of...307

Quartus...361

Rebecca..212
rebellion... 44-5
reconciliation 107-9
   peace with God......................... 100-2
redemption........................79-81, 189-93
renewal
   of creation............................... 188-93
   of the mind.....................................272
repentance...54
resurrection of Christ ..27-8, 96-7, 134, 138
   sharing in.................................... 133-9
resurrection of the body 180-1, 189-93
revelation
   of God's verdict 38, 99-100
   of the long-hidden mystery of the
     gospel...364
   of the righteousness of God.... 75-81
   of the sons of God 188, 190-1
   of the wrath of God.................. 42-51
revenge 283-5
'right time' of God........................... 105-6
righteousness of God.................. 37-9, 66
   and Christian slavery to
     righteousness..................... 143-6

and the confession of faith...... 231-4
and the 'end of the law'........... 227-9
equated with salvation 233
eternal life through 121
as gift of being declared right
    see grace; justification by faith
imputed 88-91, 94, 97
    see also justification by faith
and Israel's rejection of the Messiah
    ....213-16, 225-7
through the obedience of Christ 122
reckoned to Abraham........ 88-91, 94
revelation of 75-81
righteousness of Law and
    righteousness of faith ..219, 222,
    227-31
for the true children of Abraham.....
    95-6
universal failure to be righteous... 68-9
    see also sin
ritual..............220, 222, 241, 242, 266, 364
Rome 7-8
    Christianity in.............................. 8-10
    expulsion of Jews from.......9, 30, 34,
        ....288, 299
    Paul's gospel strategy as a Roman
        citizen....................................337
    Paul's greetings to people and
        groups in 30, 352-7, 360-1
    Paul's ministry plans for 32-6,
        ....337-8, 340-1, 346
    return of Jews to .. 8, 100, 299, 338-9,
       354
    Roman rule.............................. 285-90
    Saints in 9-10, 30-6, 352-7
Rufus..355, 357

Sabbath-keeping...........12, 59, 71, 266,
    ....298, 301
    elevated above obedience to the
        Messiah...........................219, 246
sacrifice 269-71, 309
    Paul's priestly 'offering' of the
        Gentiles............................... 330-2
salvation
    through Christ 13, 79-81, 166-72
        see also gospel; Jesus Christ
    deliverance from the Law of sin and
        death 166-72
    equated with righteousness........233
        see also righteousness of God
    gospel of see gospel

hope of final redemption 186-93
of Israel 215, 249-51, 254-6, 257-9
justification by faith
    see justification by faith
mystery of 254, 258-9, 363-4
revelation of God's righteousness....
   75-81
    see also deliverance; propitiation;
        redemption
salvation history 221
sanctification 139-48
    through presentation of the body
       269-71
    putting to death the deeds of the flesh
       178-83
    through renewal of the mind 272
second coming as motive for......... 293-4
Sanders, E. P. 15, 71
Sarah 94
Saul of Tarsus see Paul, Apostle
Scripture
    Christian use of 317-19
    indivisibility of 257-8
    Old Testament promises of the
        gospel.........24-5, 327-9, 343, 363
    Old Testament witness to the
        righteousness of God.......... 76-7
    revisionism of 27-8
second blessing teaching....................129
second coming 293-4
self-centredness 117, 127
self-dedication 145-6, 178
self-effort see works
self-judgment.......................................312
self-justification 16, 144
    see also works
Seneca, Lucius Annaeus.................. 44n4
service
    to Christ 309
    of Christ 316-17, 327
    of evangelism see evangelism
    gifts for......................................276-7
        see also spiritual gifts
    as a living sacrifice 270-1, 309
    through love...........................273-85
sexuality..46-9
signs and wonders 334
Silas 23
Silvanus 23, 352
Simeon 25
sin
    from Adam to Moses 118-19

all sins stemming from Adam's sin 116, 125
body of sin................136
death to sin................132-9
deliverance from the Law of sin and death 166-72
as everything not of faith 313
as indwelling principle of the 'flesh' 161-5, 182-3
see also flesh
of the Jewish people..51-7, 60-1, 65-8
life of victory over................139-48
original *see* original sin
and post-enlightenment humanism 126-7
power of................79, 162-5
provoked by the Law.......75-6, 92-3, ...124, 159-61
reign of sin versus reign of grace..... 124-5
and the rejection of antinomianism 131-3
and the revelation of the wrath of God................42-51
rule of sin over Gentile and Jew..67, ...131-2, 136
slavery to................141-2
termination of sin's rule 136-9
transmission of 118
universality of human sin revealed by the Law................69-71, 75-6
universality of sin shown by universality of death............132
wages of................148-9
slavery
final deliverance from 190-1
to sin................141-2
Spirit of slavery versus Spirit of sonship................183-6
willing slavery to righteousness 143-6
Son of God.......25-8, 169, 184-5, 231, 236
conformity to 196-7
see also Jesus Christ
Son of Man 123, 186, 191, 210, 317
sonship................179, 183-6, 216
Sosipater................361
Spain................8, 33, 34, 332, 337, 341-2
spirit, human................180, 185
Spirit of God *see* Holy Spirit
spiritual blindness................45, 66-7
spiritual gifts................33, 276-7
apostolic signs and wonders 334

spiritual pride 81-4, 276, 282
Stachys................355
state authority................285-90
Stephen................29, 226
submission to the state 285-90
Suetonius................8
sufferings................187-8, 248, 335
Christian attitude to................282-5
hope in................280
inconsequential to the love of God in Christ................201-3
working together for good......194-6
see also afflictions
Syntyche................336
Syria-Cilicia................29, 250, 337

Tacitus................300
teaching ministry 277
Temple 16, 226, 246
Jesus' action in 287, 317
Paul's priestly serving in the Temple of God 330-1
Temple cultus................209, 219, 270-1
Temple hierarchy 219, 246
upkeep................343
Tertius................361
thanksgiving................31
Thessalonica................7, 336
Thielicke, Helmut................287
Timothy 23, 332, 337, 352, 360-1
Titus................332, 337, 352
truth
apostolic................360
of God................42, 43, 46, 66, 327
of the gospel................277, 298, 360
judgment according to the truth...... ....52-6, 58, 61
stifling of................43, 44, 46, 50
Tryphaena................355, 357
Tryphosa................355, 357
Tychicus................352

Unity in Christ............12, 282, 302-3
transformed living in a united church 273-7, 310-11, 325-9
worship in................12, 265, 320, 321
Urbanus................355

Vengeance 283-5

W ages of sin 148-9
Wesley, Charles 140
wickedness 13, 42-3, 46, 49-50, 51,
.... 52-3, 105
  and the righteousness of God .. 66-9
  triumph of grace over 115, 124
widows 281
will of God 273
word of God
  gospel as 24, 37
    see also gospel
  and Israel's rejection of the Messiah
    210-13
  obedience to 142
    see also obedience
  Scripture see Scripture
  word of Christ 238
    see also gospel
works
  Abraham and 88-9
  Christological faith versus works of
    the Law 219, 222, 227-31
  of darkness 294

God's impartial judgment,
  according to 54-6
legalism 172, 241, 278
  see also Law; Pharisaism
as manifold expressions of Judaism
  220
worship 32, 43, 309
  Gentiles' perversion of 44-5, 46-7,
  60-1
  as a gift to Israel 209, 257
  of a living sacrifice 271
  refusal to 42, 45
  unity in 12, 265, 320, 321
wrath of God 42-51
  engendered by the Law 92
  leaving vengeance to the wrath of
    God 284
  propitiated through death of Christ
    .... 79-81, 107
  the triumph of mercy over .. 258, 260
Wright, N. T. 15, 16-17, 71, 255

Z eal for God 226, 279-82, 317
zealots 29, 62, 226, 286n13

Scripture Index

Genesis
3:15...................................360
3:23-24.............................78
6:9......................................178
12:1-3..............................326
12:3...........................327, 363
15:5.........................94, 211
15:6.....72, 87, 88–92, 94–96
15:17-21.........................209
16:1-16...........................212
17:5....................................93
21:12..................................212
22:12.................................198
22:16.................................198
25:23.................................212
32:22-32..........................345

Exodus
4:22...................................209
7:3......................................334
9:16...................................213
19:5-6..............................209
24:16................................209
33:19.................................213
34:6.....................................53

Leviticus
18:5...................................229
19:18.................................291

Numbers
15:17-21..........................251

Deuteronomy
4:34...................................334
6:4.......................12, 83, 235
6:4-5.................................291
6:5......................................210
9:7-21................................76
10:16............................61, 63
29:4.........................247–248
30:6.....................................63

30:11-14...........................230
30:14.................................232
32:21b...............................250
32:35.................................284
32:43.................................328

Joshua
6:17...................................208

2 Samuel
7:11-16...............................26
22:50.................................328

1 Kings
19:18.................................244

Ezra
7:24...................................290

Psalms
2 26
14:3.....................................68
18:49.................................328
19:4...................................239
23:4...................................199
32:1.....................................89
34:8.....................................53
36:1.....................................69
44:22.................................201
56:9-11.............................199
69:8...................................248
69:9...................................317
69:22.................................248
100:5.................................362
110:1.................................200
117:1.................................328

Proverbs
25:21-22.................284–285

Ecclesiastes
7:19-20..............................68

Isaiah
1:9......................................217
8:14...................................218
9:7......................................102
10:22-23...........................217
11:10.................................328
27:9...................................255
28:16.........................218, 234
29:10.........................247–248
42:1-7.......................327, 333
45:23.................................305
49:1.....................................22
49:6.........................59, 363
52:5.....................................60
52:7...................................237
52:13–53:12....................339
53:11-12...........................123
53:12.........................96, 200
59:20-21...........................255
61:1...................................236
65:1-2.....................239–240
66:18-20...............331, 343
66:19.................................341

Jeremiah
1:5.......................................22
9:25-26...............................61
31:31-33.............................63
31:32.........................76, 229

Ezekiel
3:7.......................................63
11:19-20.............................63
36:26-7...............................63
37:1-14.............................180

Daniel
7:13-14.............................123

Hosea
1:10...................................216
2:23...................................216
11:1...................................209

Joel
2:32.................................235

Micah
5:2-5................................102

Habakkuk
2:4.....................................39

Zechariah
8:23.................................250

Malachi
1:2-3................................212

Matthew
3:9.....................................62
5:17-48............................267
7:12.................................268
10:16...............................359
22:37-40..........................268
25:37.................................38
27:43.................................78
28:18-20.....................29, 348

Mark
2:10.................................210
7:15-23.....................306, 313
8:29...................................27
8:38.................................186
9:50.................................268
10:6-9...............................49
10:45........................123, 317
10:48.................................27
12:17........................268, 290
13:8.................................191
13:35-37..........................293
13:36...............................268
14:36.................................78
14:36a.............................184
16:6...................................97

Luke
2:25...................................25
2:38...................................25
2:49.................................185
6:27.................................268
6:27-28............................283
6:28.................................268
18:9-14..............................82
21:28...............................268
22:27...............................317
23:51.................................25

John
1:1...................................210
2:17.................................317

3:16...................................35
5:18.................................184
5:23.................................169
7:49.................................184
19:11...............................287
19:30...............................138

Acts
1:12-26..............................22
2:10.....................8, 30, 338
2:22-4................................28
2:32...................................28
2:36...................................28
6:1...................................356
6:1-6................................277
6:7...................................346
6:11-14............................226
9:23.................................346
9:29.................................346
10:9-16............................306
10:28...............................300
14:14.................................23
15:1...................................65
15:5.................................346
15:10...............................184
18:1-3..............................356
18:2-3.................................9
18:26...............................356
19:10...............................337
19:21...............................340
19:38-40..........................288
20:2-4..............................342
26:17-18............................64
28:2.................................299
28:14-15............................29

1 Corinthians
1:10-17..............................34
1:12............................9, 338
1:14.................................361
1:18..........................37, 334
1:21...................................24
1:22...................................45
1:23-24............................334
2:4.......................24, 334
2:9...................................104
3:10-12............................336
3:11.................................315
3:21-23..............................92
3:22.................................338
4:4............................38, 79
4:17.................................352
6:9-11................................48
8:7-13..............................307
8:13.................................315
9:1...................................23
9:5.....................9, 23, 338

9:16...........................35, 36
9:21..........................267, 314
10:33–11:1........................336
11:22....................282, 315
11:23.................................96
12–14.................................33
12:28...............................277
13:10...............................273
13:11...............................164
14:3.................................276
14:24-25..........................276
14:31...............................276
14:33...............................347
15:1-4..............................135
15:1-7................................24
15:3-4..............................133
15:4...................................97
15:5...................................22
15:6-7................................23
15:7.................................356
15:11.................................24
15:12-31..........................275
15:14.................................24
15:26...............................114
15:26-27..........................137
15:49.................................78
15:52...............................190
16:1-3..............................342
16:10...............................352
16:15-18..........................357
16:21...............................361
16:22...............................210

2 Corinthians
1:3...................................210
1:7...................................283
1:8-11................................34
1:19.................................361
1:20...................................25
2:17...................................24
3:3-6..................................63
3:6...........................158, 229
3:6-9..................................76
3:6-11...............................237
3:7...........................65, 222
3:9...................................229
3:11-14...................65, 222
3:14.......................57, 360
3:18.................................196
4:16-18............................104
4:17.................................188
5:8...................................303
5:9...........................178, 309
5:10.........................55, 270
5:14.........................79, 116
5:18-20....................107, 108
5:20...................................22

5:21..........................80, 169
6:2...................................38
6:4.................................335
6:6.................................278
6:7.................................335
8:1-15 343
8:9........................282, 360
8:16-18 352
8:23.................................23
9:12-15 343
10:9-11 34
10:13-16 338
10:16.............................338
11:7...............................282
11:24-26 248
11:25-26 344
11:26.............................244
11:29....................282, 315
12:12.............................334
12:14.............................185
12:18.............................352
13:10...............................34
13:11-12 278
13:12.............................353

Galatians
1:4.................................193
1:5.................................362
1:14.................................64
1:15-16 29
1:19.................................23
2:7-8 338
2:7-9 ....9, 342
2:15......................218, 300
3:1-5 179
3:13.................................80
4:4.................................169
5:2...................................62
5:6.................................171
5:11.................................62
5:22...............................330
6:6.................................277
6:11...............................361

Ephesians
3:1-9 364
3:20...............................362
4:11...............................277
4:17–5:20......................294
5:9.................................330
5:10...............................309

6:7.................................280
6:21-22 352

Philippians
2:1-18 282
2:3.................................279
2:25.................................23
2:25-30 352
3:6.........................82, 226
3:9...................................38
4:7.................................101
4:20...............................362
4:21...............................353

Colossians
1:6.................................337
1:25...............................335
3:23...............................280
4:7-8 352
4:12...............................345
4:18...............................361

1 Thessalonians
1:8.................................336
1:9.................................280
2:7...................................23
2:14-15 ....248, 346
3:2.................................362
5:14-22 278
5:26...............................353

2 Thessalonians
3:17...............................361

1 Timothy
1:17...............................362
2:1-2 290
4:13...............................277
5:1-2 279
5:3-16 281
5:17-18 277

2 Timothy
3:16...............................318

Titus
3:1.................................285
3:3.................................294

Hebrews
1:8.................................210
6:12...............................281

10:32-39 281
11:35-38 202
12:4-13 281
13:1-17 278
13:20-21 362
13:21.............................309
13:24.............................353

James
1:22.................................57
1:27...............................281
2:8.................................267
5:8.................................362

1 Peter
1:5...................................37
1:9...................................37
1:14...............................294
1:17.................................56
1:18...............................294
1:22......................278, 279
2:13-14 285
2:13-17 290
2:14...............................288
2:21-23 283
2:22-23 285
3:9-17 283
4:3-5 294
5:10...............................362
5:12...............................352
5:13...................................9

2 Peter
1:21...............................318
3:10...............................189

1 John
2:1.................................201
2:1-2 109
5:12...............................149

Jude
24..................................362

Revelation
1:18...............................137
3:2.................................362
13:10.............................202
21:1-8 104

Christian Focus Publications
publishes books for all ages

Our mission statement –

STAYING FAITHFUL
In dependence upon God we seek to help make His infallible Word, the Bible, relevant. Our aim is to ensure that the Lord Jesus Christ is presented as the only hope to obtain forgiveness of sin, live a useful life and look forward to heaven with Him.

REACHING OUT
Christ's last command requires us to reach out to our world with His gospel. We seek to help fulfill that by publishing books that point people towards Jesus and help them develop a Christ-like maturity. We aim to equip all levels of readers for life, work, ministry and mission.

Books in our adult range are published in three imprints.
Christian Focus contains popular works including biographies, commentaries, basic doctrine and Christian living. Our children's books are also published in this imprint.
Mentor focuses on books written at a level suitable for Bible College and seminary students, pastors, and other serious readers. The imprint includes commentaries, doctrinal studies, examination of current issues and church history.
Christian Heritage contains classic writings from the past.

Christian Focus Publications, Ltd
Geanies House, Fearn, Ross-shire,
IV20 1TW, Scotland, United Kingdom
info@christianfocus.com

www.christianfocus.com

City Women Country Women
Crossing the Boundaries

Other books in the 'Women's Voices, Women's Lives' series:

City Women
Country Women
Crossing the Boundaries

Edited by Jocelynne A. Scutt

Artemis

Artemis Publishing Pty Ltd
PO Box 151
Market Street Post Office
Melbourne 8007 Victoria
Tel: (03) 614 3920
Fax: (03) 417 3588

First published 1995

National Library of Australia
Cataloguing-in-Publication entry:

City women, country women: crossing the boundaries

  Includes index
  ISBN 1 875658 07 6
  1. Urban-rural migration – Australia – Biography.
  2. Rural-urban migration – Australia – Biography.
  3. Urban women – Australia – Biography.
  4. Rural women – Australia – Biography.
  I. Scutt, Jocelynne A., 1947- .
  (Series: Women's voices, women's lives; no. 6.)

304.8082

Typeset in Janson by Lorna Hendry
Printed in Australia by McPherson's Printing Group

"The universe is made of stories,
not of atoms."

Muriel Rukeyser, *Breaking Open*, 1973

Acknowledgements

City Women Country Women – Crossing the Boundaries is, like all books, the result of combined efforts of many. Contributors who wrote and who made themselves available for interview have ensured that women's lives and women's words are coming to take their rightful place in Australia's history, political, social and cultural life. Trish O'Carroll did the bulk of the wordprocessing and deciphered difficult tapes; Myra Wood wordprocessed a tape; Melinda McPherson proofread the manuscript; Jocelyn Terry contributed with wordprocessing, proofreading and indexing; Lorna Hendry did design and typesetting; Lin Tobias' design and photographs grace the cover, and Dairmuid Piggott's photograph of 'The Five Lamps of Knowledge' provides the link between each of the books in the Artemis 'Women's Voices, Women's Lives' series. I appreciate all their work.

Permissions from Magabala Books and the University of New England Press to publish extracts from Glenyse Ward's *Wandering Girl* and Margaret-Ann Franklin, Leonie M. Short and Elizabeth K. Teather's *Country Women at the Crossroads* are gratefully acknowledged. Photographs of Nancy Cato (Southern Cross Newspapers/Penny Stephens), Susan Hawthorne (Ponch Hawkes), Andrea Lofthouse (Michael van Ewijk), Sharene Morrison (*Bairnsdale Advertiser*), Bev Roberts (Virginia Wallace-Crabbe), Jocelynne A. Scutt (Sunshine Coast Newspapers), Belinda Tate (Auspic), Marjorie Thorpe (*Age*), Victoria Whitelaw (Polixeni Papapetrou) are reproduced with thanks.

City Women Country Women is the sixth book in the 'Women's Voices, Women's Lives' series and the third resulting from my stay, in June 1992, at Eleanor Dark's cottage in Katoomba as a consequence of the award of a writer's fellowship from the New South Wales government; this enabled me to do preliminary planning and writing of the outline for the book, and I am grateful. I appreciate too the strong support of the Women's Movement which I have the good fortune to have had for so many years of political writing and activism. I am particularly appreciative of the support of Rosemary Miller, Ann L. Irwin, Yvonne Pilatowicz, Wendy Lobwein and Jo Salomone during the writing and editing of this book. The enthusiasm of too many others to name lifts my spirits.

Jocelynne A. Scutt
Melbourne, January 1995

Contents

INTRODUCTION

   Jocelynne A. Scutt *Good Women, Grand Women* 1

PART 1
Politics Across Borders
  1 Claire Lupton *Ghosts, God and Country Towns* 17
  2 Marjorie Thorpe *A Fair and Equitable Settlement* 26
  3 Andrea Lofthouse *Moonraker Farm* 39
  4 Jane Wilkinson *Not a Strange, Exotic Community* 52
  5 Bev Roberts *Urban Consciousness and the Extravaganzas of Nature* .. 64
  6 Kathy Davey *Up and Out of the Kitchen Sink* 72

PART 2
Same/Difference
  7 Victoria Whitelaw *A Kelpie in the Backyard* 91
  8 Janet Powell *The Daring to Be Different* 99
  9 Susan Hawthorne *Plotting Circles in the Mind* 107
 10 Gwen Baldini *A Whole World of Difference* 117

PART 3
Two Worlds
 11 Doris M.E. Leadbetter *A Brassy, Vociferous Yelp...* 135
 12 Janeece Richards *Demanding a Voice* 144
 13 Agi Racz *The Best of Times* 154
 14 Belinda D. Tate *Respecting Other Choices* 159
 15 Sarah Stegley *Gourmet Cycling* 165
 16 Nancy Cato *Everyone a Hero* 178

PART 4

Betwixt and Between

17 Lorraine Hunter *Desert Over Concrete Any Day* 193
18 Lara Finlayson *Keeping My Options Open* 208
19 Merryl Robson *Abiding in the Field* 216
20 Sharene Morrison *Bairnsdale to Melbourne and Back* 229

PART 5

Country Life, City Life

21 Alison Brown *The Uplifting Glory of Nature* 235
22 Robin Jackson *A City Person* 244
23 Jacqualine Hobbs *Another Country* 250
24 Jenni Mitchell *The Miles Between* 257
25 Barbara Silinger *Accustomed to Country Life* 266
26 Deborah Towns *A Lucky Life* 274
27 Pat Richardson *The Voyage of the Argonaut* 286

EPILOGUE

Jocelynne A. Scutt *Country Conversations, City Conversions* 297

INDEX 319

INTRODUCTION

Good Women, Grand Women

Jocelynne A. Scutt

Australian women are a peripatetic lot. On the land, in the outback, 'up north', 'over east', in the country, gone to the city: women are there. Women are there, whether with long-standing family ties, for short periods, leaving family and friends behind, moving to make new friends, new connections, looking for change, seeking a new way of life, wanting to leave old ways behind, looking for a return to ways known in the past.

Australian workers have had to exhibit a high degree of mobility, moving from state to state and region to region following labour shortages and higher rates of pay, or chasing after improved industrial conditions. Women as workers and women as family members are naturally affected by general socio-economic and political factors in the choice of where to live or changing locality in response to external pressures. Women may be (and no doubt are) geographically mobile for many, even most, of the reasons men are. At the same time women's ambitions may differ from men's, whether in choice of work, career paths, in family relations and accepting family responsibilities, and involvement in public life, and this will affect other issues, such as where to live. To assume that all factors influencing men operate, and operate identically, for women is to miss the ways in which women's motivations can be different due to socialisation, economics, influences, life patterns and family constellations.

Whenever the questions are asked, women's lives are replete with answers. Why do women move from city to country, country to city? What motivates the 15 per cent of Australian women who are 'country' to live away from the capital cities? Within the 85 per cent of women who are city dwellers, which of them have country origins and who amongst them will return to the country after a spell of city living? Which of the city born 85 per cent will choose at one time or another or, perhaps, 'forever', to become a country woman? Where does the sense of doggedness, the indomitable spirit that drives so many country

1

women, have its origins? And is there truly a 'great divide' between city and country, country women and city women? How do we cross the boundaries?

'The country' has always been significant to Australia and Australians. From a very young age, the notion that Australia survived, economically, 'on the sheep's back' was drummed into children at school. Wheat, wool and cattle were known as the staples that supported a population that lived, mainly, in cities on the coast. Coalfields opened up country areas, sometimes in places where gold had been mined earlier. The Australian goldrushes brought a different perspective to country living, and were the forerunners to the problematical development of a mineral industry all over Australia – including Roxby Downs uranium mining and Radium Hill in South Australia, Ranger in the north, iron ore, copper, bauxite and other minerals in Kunnanurra, the Pilbara, Cockatoo Island and other centres in north west Western Australia, developments in the Northern Territory and Queensland, such as Rum Jungle and Mary Kathleen, and the petroleum industry in Bass Strait, the North West Shelf, Weipa and elsewhere.

> ...the notion that Australia survived, economically, 'on the sheep's back' was drummed into children at school.

The movement of people into country areas to farm and mine brings with it a complementary movement of pub and shopowners and, later, those who run garages, petrol pumps and the video store. The building of telegraph lines and railways followed, sometimes rapidly, sometimes more slowly, the 'opening up' (in European terms) of the Australian countryside by those who went to make a living as squatters, small landholders, camel herders, miners and marketgardeners. Since 1788, women have gone to and grown up in the country in these capacities, and as midwives, nurses, hotel keepers, prostitutes, shopkeepers, postmistresses, newsagents, journalists, teachers, writers, doctors, lawyers, shop assistants, householders, housewives. Some Australians have a permanent tradition of country life: there is a 60 000 or 120 000 year history of Aboriginal women (and men) living throughout Australia, in regions now designated as 'country' as well as in what are now urban and suburban areas.

Colonisation or invasion of Australia led the formal agrarian and the industrial development of both city and country. The first industries were prisons and prison factories. In *Our Antipodes*, published in 1852 and extracted by Kay Daniels and Mary Murnane in *Uphill All the Way*, G. C. Mundy observed a phenomenon peculiar to colonisation:

In the towns of New South Wales, the first object upon which the stranger's eye falls, is some grand building devoted to the custody and coercion of convicts; – in civiler terms, to the accommodation of its original white population; or to their protection, when age and disease, mental and bodily, may have overtaken them, – gaols, in short, hospitals, lunatic asylums, and the like.

At Parramatta, then a New South Wales country town (although today it is the population centre of the capital, Sydney), 'the most prominent of these establishments – a handsome solid stone edifice, a "stone-jug" well calculated to contain the most ardent and effervescent spirits – [was] the Female Factory, where prisoners of that sex, sanely or insanely unruly, are incarcerated'.

The origins and manner of colonial settlement of Australia meant that country centres were often the site of political action. When miners demonstrated against the licensing system on the goldfields in the nineteenth century, it was not men alone who led the protest, nor men alone who supported it. Women were prominent in the most well known insurrection, at the Eureka Stockade in Ballarat. The political activism of country women was increasingly visible in the miners' strikes of the 1890s. It continues in the networking and lobbying of women in

Women were prominent in the most well known insurrection, at the Eureka Stockade in Ballarat.

the 1990s, with the fall in wool prices, the drought, the recession and depression.

Australia has earlier examples of the political activism of country dwellers. Aboriginal people, both in the city *and* the country, struggled against white invasion, dating it and their struggle from 1770 and Captain Cook's incursion and continuing it when 1788 brought further intrusion. Convicts in both city *and* country settings disobeyed their guards and masters, and rioted in prison. '…it is not many years ago', reports *Our Antipodes*, that the 'Amazonian inmates [of the Parramatta Female Factory], amounting to seven or eight hundred, and headed by a ferocious giantess (by all accounts, a regular she-Ajax), rose upon the guards and turnkeys, and made a desperate attempt at escape by burning the building'. A force of a hundred men was sent from the stockade, together with a subaltern, 'to drive the fair insurgents within one of the yards, in order to secure them'. The women charged furiously upon the gates, laughing at the soldiers, and 'one man was knocked over by a brickbat from Mrs Ajax'. The outcome? 'The military were reinforced; the magistrate made them load with ball-cartridge, and the desperadoes were eventually subdued.' The immediate cause of the outbreak was said to be the 'periodical close-cropping of the women's hair' (and what room for speculation as to the women's motive that explanation provides). The prison governor acceded to the women's demands, 'being diplomatic enough to relax the depilatory laws'.

Where Aboriginal women and men protested against invasion of their country by white explorers and the settlers who followed them, they were killed, raped, chased into the hinterland, or taken into slavery. As Janine Roberts says in her book, published in 1978, *From Massacres to Mining. The Colonisation of Aboriginal Australia:*

> The Aborigines resisted the invasion... As the whites attempted to take their lands, the inhabitants banded together to fight guerrilla campaigns... Despite having only spears to fight guns, this warfare lasted some 160 years from the first battles at Sydney to the last massacres in the Northern Territory around 1930.

In Van Diemen's Land Aboriginal women were taken captive and taught muttonbirding and other methods of survival to white men who, working as whalers, took over the land and sea of the Straits. On 10 October 1829, G. A. Robinson wrote in his *Journal*, a portion of which appears in Kay Daniel's and Mary Murnane's *Up Hill All the Way:*

> The aboriginal female Mary informed me that the sealers at the Straits carry on a complete system of slavery; that they barter in exchange for women flour and potatoes; that she herself was bought off the black men for a bag of flour and potatoes; that they took her away by force, tied her hands and feet, and put her in the boat; that white men beat black women with a rope. Fanny, who speaks English well and knows not a word of the Aboriginal tongue, said there were fifty women at the Straits and plenty of children; that the three women from Brune Island who were coercively taken away by Baker, a man of colour, were at Kangaroo Island. The aboriginal Fanny states that this slave traffic is very common in the straits, and that women so bartered or sold are subjected to every hardship which their merciless tyrants can think of and that from the time their slavery commences they are habituated to all the fatiguing drudgery which their profitable trade imposes.

Robinson acknowledged the parallels between what was happening in the Australian colonies and what was being protested against, by some, in the United States and Britain: 'Surely this is the African slave trade in miniature, and the voice of reason as well as humanity loudly calls for its abolition.' Sadly, colonial courts and legislatures were of little help to Aboriginal women raped and taken in slavery. Thus when the cook at Cherubim Station wrote to the Chief Protector (sic) of Aborigines in Western Australia on 4 June 1925, the response was unhelpful. In a memorandum dated 5 October 1925 the 'Chief Protector' wrote:

There is unfortunately nothing in the *Aborigines Act* which enables me to take proceedings against a man who chains up a native as in this case.

'This case'?

On or about the 27th of March the Manager of the Cherubim Pastoral Company chained an Aboriginal woman to a tree, the mode of chaining was with a pair of steel handcuffs on one wrist, then attached with a chain to a tree and padlocked. The woman was on the chain for five or six days, on about the 4th day that the woman was on the chain the Manager (Jno. J. [S——]) went away early in the day and did not return until the following evening. On the afternoon of the day of Jn. [S——'s] departure the woman beckoned me over and told me she wanted to evacuate. I told her that I had not the key of the lock but that as soon as the woman who is attached to Jno. [S——] returned that I would ask her if she had the key of the lock. When the woman returned I asked her if Jack [S——] had left the key with her. That same night the unfortunate woman was left by herself the other women who were supposed to sleep near her had gone to the other camp about 1/4 mile away. I went over to where she was, she told me the women had left her by herself and that she was frightened.

  The sequence to the above occurrence is so disgusting that I consider myself justified in reporting the whole matter to you and risk being called an informer. A few days after the chaining episode I was in the garden while the garden was being watered and the woman who had been on the chain (her native name is Yebellee) goes by the name of Kitty said to me that Jno. J. [S——] had sent her to Jack [S——'s] bedside on two consecutive nights, that also on another occasion Jack [S——] had sent her to a man named Jack [C——] who when she came to his bedside and touched him, had lashed out with either his hand or foot and that she fled...

The realities of country living belie the notion that multiculturalism began in the 1970s and 1980s, or with the influx of immigrants after the second world war. Chinese marketgardeners were prominent on the goldfields, and during this period 60 000 people on average migrated each year. Forty-two thousand Chinese (women and men) migrated to Australia at this time and, as Caroline Alcorso reports in *Australia's Italians – Culture and community in a changing society*, published in 1992, two thousand Italians arrived, 'fleeing agricultural depression and lured by gold':

Japanese, Malays and Filipinos (women and men) worked in many industries, in country and city, and particularly in Australia's north, at least from the time of colonisation.

5

Australia's first Swiss-Italian community, complete with pasta factory, began to form near the goldfields at Daylesford in Victoria...

Long before the goldrushes, Afghan camel herders were a part of many of the expeditions travelling from the colonial capitals into the outback, cutting across the country from south to north and east to west. Japanese, Malays and Filipinos (women and men) worked in many industries, in country and city, and particularly in Australia's north, at least from the time of colonisation. The pearling industry in Broome and Derby in Western Australia was highly dependent upon them: women worked as pearlers, diving alongside men. Pacific Islanders were a significant part of the population, particularly in Queensland, after having been abducted from their island homes they were forced to work in sugarcane plantations and the households of the plantation owners.

The idea that during the colonial period women were absent from outback and country Australia has had a firm hold in the male-dominated world of the traditional historian. Where women's presence has been acknowledged, their participation in outback and country life has generally been recorded one dimensionally. Both visions are blinkered, as numerous accounts from women (and some men) who were there readily show.

...she had taken up farming for herself, with 'four ewes and nine breeding goats, 3 wethers and seven young ones' as stock.

Both women and men were drowned, and women and men were saved, when in March 1806 the settlement on the Hawkesbury River in country New South Wales was flooded. Margaret Catchpole was one of the fortunate ones, writing an account of the disaster in a letter to her uncle. After working on the Rouse homestead at Richmond Hill, she had taken up farming for herself, with 'four ewes and nine breeding goats, 3 wethers and seven young ones' as stock. Her six pigs appear to have been lost in the floods. Later, she increased her holding, writing on 2 September 1811 that she rented a small farm of fifteen acres, which comprised half standing timber and half cleared ground. Like the men who were farmers, she farmed and hired farm labourers to work the land:

> I hire men to put in my corn and I work a great deal myself. I have got 30 sheep and forty goats and 30 pigs and 2 dogs they take care of me for I live all alone, not one in the house. There is a house within twenty 2 rood of me...

Elizabeth Macarthur is one of the better known farmers, although her role has only recently been properly valued, and even now traditional history books continue to regard her husband John as the farmer, and she as the 'wife' and helpmeet. The reality is that not only in his long absences did she run the farm, which was initially of 250 acres, expanding to four to five hundred, and was worked by convict labour. Her diaries and letters confirm that she was the farm manager, whether he was at home or away. In *Life Lines – Australian women's letters and diaries 1788 to 1840* Patricia Clarke and Dale Spender extract the records of a number of women who farmed in country New South Wales and Victoria through that period, including Margaret Catchpole, Elizabeth Macarthur, Mary McDonald, Eliza Walsh, Anne Drysdale and Caroline Newcomb.

In Hahndorf, in South Australia, John Bull saw women working as shearers. In his *Early Experience of South Australia* (published in 1884 and extracted in *Fresh Evidence, New Witnesses*, edited by Margaret Allen, Mary Hutchinson and Alison Mackinnon), he wrote:

The shearers were principally young women, who were waited on by men of the village, who, when called on, caught and carried the sheep to the shearer who was ready. The sheep was carefully laid on its side; the young woman, without shoes and stockings, had a piece of Thick soft string tied to one of her great toes, the other end was then tied to the hind foot of the sheep; The girl's leg was then stretched out to extend the legs of the sheep; her knee or left hand was pressed on the neck or shoulder of the animal which was then left to her charge, and she commenced her clipping work, most carefully avoiding any snips of the skin... The whole party worked with a will, and the amount they earned went towards the payment of their land.

Aboriginal women, like non-Aboriginal women, worked as farm labourers and riders on cattlestations. In evidence to the Select Committee on the Aborigines Bill, conducted by the South Australian Parliament in 1899, Donald Molan, a Queensland pastoralist, noted that similar work was done by women and men:

...if you employ a man you should employ his wife as well. The wife is just as good at herding cattle or sheep, and other work as the man, as a rule... Men and women ride out and do most work together, except cattle-yard work. We have large numbers of cattle, and while the women do not work in the yards they do mustering and that sort of thing with their husbands...

In the colonies women held victuallers licences, licences for the sale of various forms of alcohol and for public houses, whilst some produced and sold 'sly grog'. Monica Perrott in *A Tolerable Good Success – Economic opportunities for women in New South Wales 1788-1830* records many instances where women were granted liquor licences. She notes that in 1811 in the colony of New South Wales seven women of a total of 37 applicants were granted beer licenses, four of the seven being ex-convicts. Six women were granted liquor licences out of 40 applicants, two of the women being ex-convicts. From 1799 through to 1806, more women are recorded as having been issued wine and spirit licences, beer licences, liquor licences, spirit licences and public house licences. Most were for city locations, but a number were allocated to the country. For example, Elizabeth Powell was issued a 'country spirit licence' for Halfway House, Parramatta Road, in 1818. Sarah Ward was issued a Parramatta licence in 1811, as were Sarah Ward and Martha Brown in 1813.

Aboriginal women and non-Aboriginal women have worked as servants and slaves in the country, in farming households, houses in country towns, and in the households of cattlestations. Glenyse Ward, placed in orphanages from the time of her birth in Western Australia in 1949, writes in *Wandering Girl* of leaving the Wandering Mission at 16 years of age to become a servant to non-Aboriginal families. 'I didn't want to go – but I had no choice.' Not only is she to work as directed, with no recognition of industrial rights. She is denied everyday human respect. As a servant, there is no china for her to drink from; rather, hers is an old tin mug:

I politely asked [Mrs Bigelow] if I could have a cup and saucer to drink from, as I wasn't used to drinking out of tin mugs and never had done so in the mission.

The answer I received back was in a very irate and furious tone of voice. She stated to me that I was there as her dark servant, that I was to obey her orders, and do what she told me to do! I took the tin jug and drank my tea with a very confused mind.

Beverley Kingston in *My Wife, My Daughter, and Poor Mary Ann – Women and Work in Australia* relates the stories of women workers and their mistresses at an earlier time. Servants were 'necessary' not only in the city, and many were encouraged to travel into the country and outback. Life in a large country house in South Australia in the late nineteenth century continued to require 'help' as well as the work of the 'lady of the house', as Dorothy Gilbert describes:

Mother's first job after breakfast was to do the lamps. Our only lighting was kerosene lamps & candles, & if anyone but Mother tended the lamps, they always flickered & smoked & smelt, so she kept that job in her own hands except when there was a very new baby. There was a handsome wrought iron standard lamp in the drawing-room, pendant lamps in the Hall & over the diningroom table. Table lamps of all sorts & sizes, for kitchen, nursery & school-room, wall lamps in the back passages, hurricane lamps to light the men visitors out to their quarters in the garden. Every bedroom was furnished with candle-sticks on the dressing-table, and a row of low silver candle-sticks on the halltable were there to light you on you [sic] way thro' the rather dim passages & provide a safe bed-side light. Having dealt with lamps etc Mother then interviewed the cook & organised the meals for the day.

That women have 'always' lived and worked in the country towns and settlements of the Australian outback, that women have lived and worked on farms, on cattlestations, in dairying and in every other country and outback endeavour is clear from an abundance of evidence. It is clear, too, that there have always been women with a commitment from birth to country living, whilst others have come to country living from the city, whether through marriage, seeking personal independence, wanting a 'different' or 'better' life, moving with family, or following jobs, trades and professions. The mirror image of this movement to country and outback is a movement by country-born and outback-bred women to the city, following the demands of work, education, family commitments, desire for personal fulfilment.

As Koori activist Elizabeth Williams says, a move from Sydney to Wagga Wagga was for her 'the beginning of a whole new existence'. As she writes in *Different Lives – Reflections on the Women's Movement and Visions of Its Future*, in 'Aboriginal First, Woman Second':

In 1972 I was 18 years old, pregnant, and living in a housing commission flat in Sydney with my mother… I…decided to move to Wagga Wagga to improve my lifestyle and that of my child, particularly our housing.

Elizabeth Williams found that her opportunities for worthwhile employment increased with her move to the country, when she was appointed to the healthworker position at Griffith in New South Wales:

The job was with the Health Commission and I worked with the local Aborigines and those living in the outer-lying areas. Working with my own people gave me a sense of well-being and fulfilment I had not previously experienced.

From Wagga Wagga and Griffith, she moved to Queanbeyan, a country town which neighbours Canberra, and continued her work in health.

Elisabeth Kirkby, actor and star of *Number 96*, left a burgeoning television career in 1975 to devote more time to a small property in the Lower Hunter Region, 'to establish a garden and return to the theatre'. As she observes in 'When the Airforce Holds Cake Stalls' in *Different Lives*, when she became an active Democrat in 1977 'the theatre had to take second place, the garden became a hobby for leisure hours – not a full-time pursuit' – and Elisabeth Kirkby began 'the long tough road to gain parliamentary office' – back in Sydney. She succeeded.

City Women Country Women is a tribute to good and grand women like Elizabeth Williams and Elisabeth Kirkby and the many thousands of good and grand women like them who, born in the country, have now made their homes in the city and those who, born in the city, now live a country life. Some have moved back and forth, between city and country, feeling at home – and 'different'. Each has taken with her memories of her birthplace and incorporated them into her vitality for living.

...the many thousands of good and grand women who, born in the country, have now made their homes in the city and those who, born in the city, now live a country life.

Country women are infused with an indomitable spirit: this is so whether they were country born or have converted to farm or countrytown life. Perhaps the need to survive brings with it a certain firmness of bearing, a 'no nonsense' demeanour, although being bred in the country or becoming a country dweller does not mean a complete loss of romanticism. Country women, like city women, dream.

It is simply that living miles away from the major city centres and being thrown upon one's own resourcefulness and initiative means developing a pragmatic ability to cope under all odds – or to go down. Whatever the odds, country women stride on. When the need for support and comfort arises, as it inevitably does, women are there again, to support one another. Where language differences and minority ethnic origins intrude upon a woman's security and access to resources in country areas, women's groups can be quick at developing and establishing themselves as support networks. *Country Women at the Crossroads*, edited by Margaret-Ann Franklin, Leonie M. Short and Elizabeth K. Teather in 1994, provides a number of examples. In 'Wagga Wagga Immigrant Women's Support Group', Bernadette Kelly writes of a New South Wales country town where a group of around 60 women from some 15 different countries – the Philippines, Iran, Greece, Papua New Guinea, India, Pakistan, Bangladesh, Malaysia, Brunei, Korea, Indonesia, Poland, El Salvador, South Africa and Eritrea – enable each other to gain support, information and assistance. Carolyn Reeve, writing of 'Migrant Women in North Western Mining Towns of Western Australia', describes the way in which government funding has been sought in the hope of stimulating the phenomenon in the Pilbara mining region. She has observed first hand the difficulties faced by non-English speaking background women in remote areas, which may not so starkly confront their city counterparts:

> My experience of the problems for migrant women living in remote areas, as opposed to urban areas, indicates that there are serious difficulties involved in settling here. In the larger of two towns of Hedland and Karratha, there are more than 60 different nationalities, but not enough of any one particular group to enable strong support networks to evolve. It is often these informal ethnic networks in cities that help the settlement process for new migrants. In a city, there are usually enough immigrants of one's own ethnic and social background and language to enable one to find people with whom one is naturally compatible. This is not so in small towns...

What do women of all backgrounds, ages, ethnicity, race do when faced with street violence, criminal assault at home and other forms of domestic violence? In the country and the city there has been a reluctance to see, a denial, or fear in acknowledging the darknesses of family life. Yet in city and country women have made demands. Country women have stood up against entrenched power and parochialism. Women's refuges and rape crisis centres

Country women have stood up against entrenched power and parochialism.

or centres against sexual assault have been established in country towns by brave women prepared to stand out against the narrowness of the notion that 'marriage and family' means forever, and that women and children have no right to expectations, nor to live independently of a tormentor who is husband and father.

Like the women before them, many women have been and are engaged in political action in the country and, like the political activism of women living in the city, it takes many forms and relates to many issues – environmentalism, local government, education, women's health, violence against women, Aboriginal Land Rights, eco-tourism. Bev Roberts, poet, writer and consultant, Jane Wilkinson, educationalist and advisor, Andrea Lofthouse, farmer and teacher, Marjorie Thorpe, public speaker and Aboriginal activist, Claire Lupton, journalist and television cameraperson, Kath Davey, public servant and now Victorian director of Amnesty International, take their political action across the city-country divide. For them, politics is not only about 'being in parliament'; it is about those issues that touch deeply upon them and their cohort, them and the people and countryside around them. It does not end at the garden gate, at the beginning of the track winding up to the farmhouse door, nor on the road leading home from the school house, the director's office, or the committee meetingroom. Politics is central to the lives of these women, and they work to ensure that their lives and the lives of others have a central importance to it. They know the value of alliances between city women and country women, alliances between country woman and country woman, and the support of city woman to city woman, in recognising 'Politics Across Borders'.

Is living in the country 'the same' as living in the city, or 'different': 'Same/Difference'? Victoria Whitelaw knows that there is a world of difference between city and country, and her life then and now, yet she has found a security in the city, in the feel of the plants in her garden, the dog in the yard. Janet Powell and Susan Hawthorne have a strong sense of place, a sense of same/difference, about their lives in the country and its influence, and their present day lives in the city. For Gwen Baldini there is a whole world of difference between her life in the city and her growing up in country Western Australia. Then, there was differentiation and discrimination without strong external messages of hope; now she and the organisation and people she works with hold out for optimism and ways of healing hurt, whether experienced in the lives of those born in the country or those born in the city.

Doris M. E. Leadbetter knows 'Two Worlds': the world of the country, and the world of the city. Like Agi Racz, who was born and spent her childhood years in Hungary, she emigrated to Australia. Country Victoria was a world away from life in a large industrial centre in England, just as life in Hobart and Canberra is a world away from the north west coast of Tasmania, for Belinda Tate. Janeece Richards protests against the 'city bred' notions that see country women as less interested in the policy issues of the day, and the lack of understanding of the vast geographical distances travelled by country women who are involved in making and debating policy. Why are most of the meetings held in the city? Sarah Stegley is mindful of distance and the difference between city and country too. She has a strong sense of place – and home for her is well and truly the country, her home nowhere else. Nancy Cato is a 'real country girl' – with firm recollections of the country childhood which gave her a strong sense of country values and involvement, and a basis for living now, as a city woman.

'Betwixt and Between': Lorraine Hunter grew up in Broome and Derby, lived in Perth, returned to the north, travelled to Indonesia, then lived in Arnhem Land and Queensland, returned home to Broome, travelled to Perth ... The country, not the city, is for her, but like others she accepts there are necessary connections with 'the city' that cannot be overlooked. Like Lorraine Hunter, Lara Finlayson and Sharene

Morrison have lived in the city and in the country, going back and forth. Back in Bairnsdale, Sharene Morrison looks toward another opportunity for city living; back in Melbourne from Shepparton, Lara Finlayson has just embarked on her second major bout of city living. Born in country South Australia, Merryl Robson has lived in country Victoria, Broken Hill, Melbourne and now Sydney. Like many women, she has gone back and forth, savouring the advantages of city life when she's living it, and those of the country during the periods of country living. Being 'betwixt and between' has more than one essence: there are those who enjoy both lifestyles, whether the move is chosen or required by circumstance; there are those who choose one over the other without any prevarication, yet know, and accept, that there are times when the one not preeminent must be 'fitted in' because of what it offers.

There is 'Country Life, City Life'. Does one stand head and shoulders above the other? What *are* the differences, *what* are the similarities? Alison Brown, Robin Jackson, Jacqualine Hobbs, Jenni Mitchell, Barbara Silinger, Deborah Towns and Pat Richardson write of the differences and the similarities for them, the differences and the similarities they see for other women. They write of the advantages and disadvantages of both, and the way they have incorporated their experiences of country life and city life into their own lives, and their design for living.

What do country women and city women have in common? There are differences, conflicts and misunderstandings, and personal and political battles that have to be fought to overcome them. Yet there are strong links, too. There are the efforts of country women to bring new perspectives to the understanding of city women. There are the efforts of city women to appreciate the distances, the lack of essential services, travel time. And there is an essential willingness to recognise the differences arising through different experiences, the hopes for city women and country women to work together on issues of essential importance for us all, and an optimism for a future where barriers to understanding are insignificant, or are no more.

Note: In the quotation on page 5, the cook from Cherubim Station, 'woman' and 'women' have been substitued throughout for the words 'gin' and 'gins'.

References

Margaret Allen, Mary Hutchinson and Alison Mackinnon, *Fresh Evidence, New Witnesses – Finding Women's History*, 1989, South Australian Government Printer, Adelaide

Stephen Castles, Caroline Alcorso, Gaetano Rando and Ellie Vasta, editors, *Australia's Italians – Culture and community in a changing society*, 1992, Allen & Unwin, St Leonards

Patricia Clarke and Dale Spender, editors, *Life Lines – Australian women's letters and diaries 1788 to 1840*, 1992, Allen & Unwin, St Leonards

Caroline Alcorso, 'Early Italian migration and the construction of European Australia 1788-1939' in *Australia's Italians*, 1992, Castles, Alcorso, Rando and Vasta, editors, Allen & Unwin, St Leonards

Kay Daniels and Mary Murnane, editors, *Uphill All the Way – A Documentary History of Women in Australia*, 1980, University of Queensland Press

Margaret-Ann Franklin, Leonie M. Short and Elizabeth K. Teather, *Country Women at the Crossroads – Perspectives on the lives of rural Australian women in the 1990s*, 1994, University of New England Press, Armidale

Bernadette Kelly, 'Wagga Wagga Immigrant Women's Support Group' in *Country Women at the Crossroads*, 1994, Franklin, Short and Teather, editors, University of New England Press, Armidale

Beverley Kingston, *My Wife, My Daughter, and Poor Mary Ann – Women and Work in Australia*, 1977, Nelson, Melbourne

Elisabeth Kirkby, 'When the Airforce Holds Cake Stalls' in *Different Lives*, 1987, Scutt, editor, Penguin Books Australia, Ringwood

Monica Perrott, *A Tolerable Good Success – Economic opportunities for women in New South Wales 1788-1830*, 1983, Hale & Iremonger, Sydney

Adele Pring, *Women of the Centre*, 1990, Pascoe Publishing, Apollo Bay

Carolyn Reeve, 'Migrant Women in the North West Mining Towns of Western Australia' in *Country Women at the Crossroads*, 1994, Franklin, Short and Teather, editors, University of New England Press, Armidale

Janine Roberts, *From Massacres to Mining. The Colonisation of Aboriginal Australia*, 1978, CIMRA and War on Want, London

Jocelynne A. Scutt, editor, *Different Lives – Reflections on the Women's Movement and Visions of Its Future*, 1987, Penguin Books Australia Ltd, Ringwood

Glenyse Ward, *Wandering Girl*, 1987, Magabala Books, Broome

Elizabeth Williams, 'Aboriginal First, Woman Second' in *Different Lives*, 1987, Scutt, editor, Penguin Books Australia, Ringwood

PART 1

Politics Across Borders

Ghosts, God and Country Towns

Claire Lupton

Claire Lupton is a mother of four, a widow and a journalist at Bega on the far south coast of New South Wales. She lives in an area surrounded by the most beautiful beaches and forests in Australia but never sets foot in either unless work demands. Her idea of a perfect holiday is going from cinema to cinema to theatre in Sydney or Melbourne with the odd art gallery and bookshop thrown in. She is however an ardent conservationist, as long as she doesn't have to see what is being conserved.

Claire Lupton's worst vice is book-buying, mainly history, and she is also a television addict, with the excuse that she has to write a weekly television column.

City or country? Sheep grazed on the paddock next to our home. A dairy farm was just a bike ride away. Everyone knew everybody else, who everyone's father was, where he worked and, in many cases, how much money he earned. 'It's half the size of New York cemetery and twice as dead,' moaned a Yankee serviceman during the war.

This was Canberra. The city where I lived most of my childhood years. My father was minister of St Andrew's Presbyterian Church. Across the paddock and the sheep was the Lodge and we were invariably jokingly referred to by prime ministers as 'nextdoor neighbours'.

It was an unusual community in those war years. Most of the population were public servants forced from Melbourne and Sydney to live in this wind-swept valley. The rest of the population was made up from ambassadorial members, their staff and servants, shop people, builders, gardeners and, of course, politicians.

The latter were forced to remain in Canberra for longer than they wished because of the difficult travel arrangements in those times, but few set up homes, preferring to live in boardinghouses or hotels.

When most children were perfecting their please and thank you manners, the children of Canberra were learning when to curtsey and how to address everyone from the Archbishop of Canterbury to the American ambassador's wife.

The schools were well-staffed and well-built. Canberra High was then reputed to be the best equipped school in the Southern Hemisphere. Any advances in education were tried out there. In my first year at Canberra High we were offered a choice of four languages – French, German, Japanese and Latin. In my second year in first year (I repeated because I was too young), the school experimented with having every student taught every subject. I loathed metalwork, woodwork, cooking, cleaning and, most of all, sewing!

I didn't ever regard Canberra as a city. It was totally lacking in entertainment for the young, such as Luna Park, zoos, museums and, to an extent, theatre.

There were cinemas and the Saturday afternoon matinee was a highlight of my week. So bereft were we of entertainment that when I was 12 and 13 I cycled to parliament house each sitting night to listen to question time. I fell in love with a handsome Liberal member from Franklin, Tasmania, but my favourite politician was Joe Gullet, another Liberal, because he was so outrageous and funny. However it was Labor's concern for the ordinary person that convinced me I should become a Labor (ALP) supporter. My father told Menzies, whose only comment was: 'She'll grow out of it.'

So bereft were we of entertainment that when I was 12 and 13 I cycled to parliament house each sitting night to listen to question time.

The person who most influenced my life in those early years, apart from my father, was Mrs Whitlam. She was profoundly deaf so when her husband went overseas either my sister or myself would go to stay there to answer the doorbell, phone or whatever.

I was nine when I first stayed with Mrs Whitlam. I had led a very sheltered and watched life because everybody knew my father was a minister and watched their tongue and behaviour when I was around. The bell rang one day and it was the local Salvation Army officer looking for donations. I informed Mrs Whitlam who gave him what I regarded as a very generous donation indeed. She told him she commended the work of the Salvation Army and added: 'I don't believe in Heaven or Hell, though.'

I was astounded. An adult who believed that, and even more, one who would say it in front of me, knowing who my father was. That evening I asked her why she didn't believe in such Christian fundamentals. She was happy to explain and went on to say she also believed in ghosts. She was a totally fascinating raconteur and she, unlike all the adults of my acquaintance, spoke to me as she would to another adult. She was very proud of her children, Gough and Freda.

My second culture shock came when I burst in after school (Telopea Park Primary School) one day to find a Causeway girl, Helen, in the kitchen. The Causeway was regarded as Canberra's slum. It was a road behind the American embassy. Nowhere in Canberra was really a slum, but it certainly didn't have the trim and pristine appearance of the rest of Canberra. The Causeway children attended the same primaryschools as we did, but disappeared when it came to secondary education. Helen was about 15 and was removing a dish from the oven when I appeared. 'Helen's just made a lovely souffle,' said Mrs Whitlam. The girl looked at me with a superior smile. She knew that I had no idea what a souffle was, and she was understandably pleased at my ignorance.

She knew that I had no idea what a souffle was, and she was understandably pleased at my ignorance.

Later Mrs Whitlam told me that she was teaching a number of Causeway girls to cook, and the boys she taught gardening. She was an expert at both. As far as I know she was the only person in Canberra who helped these children.

It was Mrs Whitlam who taught me to think for myself on every issue.

As far as I remember, we didn't think in terms of city or country in Canberra and it never occurred to me to think of how people lived in either place. I was also not aware of any discrimination against women while living my childhood in Canberra. My mother had been a piano teacher, but gave that up when the first of her four children was born. Both my mother and father expected all of us (three girls and a boy) to go on to tertiary education when secondary school was finished. Not that this was ever said, it was just implied. At school girls and boys vied for the top places in every subject.

In my third highschool year I was sent to Presbyterian Ladies College (PLC) in Melbourne as a boarder. My sister had already been there a year. My youngest sister had been born when my mother was over 40 years old and I think we were probably sent away to relieve the pressure on the household with this demanding baby. Fees at school were considerably reduced for ministers' children, so it was hardly more expensive than keeping us at home.

Most boarders were from the country where their parents were either doctors, lawyers or teachers, or were graziers' daughters. Despite this the differences in country-city life were never discussed, but just accepted.

I hated all my schooling (that is, classes), because I was a naturally fast reader, very fast in fact, and also had, at that time, a photographic memory, so I was bored by school and the constant reiteration. However

19

I loved PLC for its tradition and spent my years there soaking in its very women's liberation history.

The most famous Old Collegians were Nellie Melba and Henry Handel Richardson, but among the many others who achieved recognition were Vida Goldstein, who stood for the senate in 1903, the year after the Commonwealth had granted women voting rights, and Marion Phillips, who was, I think, the first Australian woman to be elected to parliament, except the parliament was Westminster. She was a trade union official and secretary of the British Labour Party.

It was implied at PLC that a woman could be what she wanted and so I still hadn't realised that there was any discrimination.

Having absolutely no idea what I wanted to be on leaving school I did what most Canberra children did and joined the public service. I was among the first female clerks to be admitted and it did take some time for the men in the office to accept the influx of young girls. Up to then, the only women were those in the typing pool, the tea ladies and the cleaners. Having matriculated and doing a part-time course at the university (commerce), I was, after a year or so, in charge of two men who I expect were clerical assistants or lower. As I was then only 19 this caused quite a few problems and I had to be very diplomatic. I joined the department of overseas trade in Canberra but then transferred to Melbourne. It was there that I (probably illegally) took on a number of part-time jobs to raise money for what I really wanted to do, go overseas.

I achieved this in three years and, like so many other girls of my day, went to England on a one-class ship for an extended visit. I had exactly £7 left when I arrived in London so finding work was my first aim. I became a temp. for most of my two year stay, or an Australian Sunshine Girl, handing out Australian pineapple juice, cheese, fruit and so on at stores throughout the country and trade fairs. I also took hitchhiking trips through England, Scotland, Wales, Ireland, and the Continent.

After two years I left for Canada. There I gained a position in the film research department of the Canadian Broadcasting Corporation, only on the condition that I would learn to type and learn quickly. In Australia being a typist or secretary was regarded as the career you took if you were unable to do anything else (at least among my contemporaries that was the feeling), but the Canadians regarded me as just being ill-educated in not knowing how. Everybody, male and female, did their own typing. Canada, at that stage, was way ahead in women's rights. My boss was a woman, and she was one of many.

My return to Australia after four years brought home to me that women were treated quite differently in our country. I went to the Australian Broadcasting Commission (ABC) to see if it had a similar job as the one I had been doing in Canada. It didn't, but those interviewing me were interested in setting one up, and asked me what salary I'd been getting. There was a collective gasp when I told them, and one interviewer said: 'No woman in the ABC is ever paid that amount.'

To fill in the time while waiting for the research job, the ABC gave me a position in the television news department as a film coordinator. After a while I became bored with the job and asked the head of the department, Wally Hamilton, if I could start training as a journalist. He was horrified and told me that women journalists became hard and tough, and what would a nice girl like me think of wanting to be like that, etc. However, to keep me amused, he said I could go out with the camera crews and take down the questions for the reverses, if I wasn't needed in my shift to coordinate film.

...asked me what salary I'd been getting. There was a collective gasp when I told them, and one interviewer said: 'No woman in the ABC is ever paid that amount.'

While waiting for filmstars, politicians and others to arrive the cameramen taught me the tricks of their trade. One funny incident happened when we were covering a story on taxation. The crew consisted of a cameraman, a soundman and a male interviewer. As each shot was lined up the cameraman called me over to check what he was aiming at in the viewfinder. When we'd finished and packed up, I was the last to leave. The taxation manager, who had been present throughout the filming, called me aside and said: 'You're very young to be a director and in charge of a camera crew.' Did I tell the truth? Of course, not. I just smiled and left. I didn't tell the crew either.

Finally the cameramen felt I'd completed my apprenticeship and asked me to apply to do a camera test, something they'd all had to do before being appointed. It was then that the department realised what I'd been doing and were aghast. However it was agreed I could do a test and I presume they knew what they were setting me up for when they chose it.

It was a huge speedcar race at Warwick Farm with the likes of Stirling Moss and other international stars taking part. The day was boiling and when I arrived at the field most of the drivers were stripped to the waist staying as cool as possible before togging up in their protective gear. I was given *carte blanche* to shoot what I wanted so I started my story in and around the drivers' tents filming them relaxing, gossiping and lolling about and, finally, dressing. Then it was time for the race and I offered my press card to the person at the gate to get across the track where all the other cameramen and photographers were waiting for the start. He was adamant I couldn't go there. No woman was allowed in that area. This had nothing to do with safety by the way as it was as safe as the area where the public was awaiting the start.

Frustrated I decided on the only course possible. I knew I couldn't shoot over the heads of the crowd who had been patiently waiting for some hours, so I lay down in front of the first row and aimed my camera at the car wheels, which revved up and spat dust as the flag descended.

The race was long and tedious, but I was allowed into the pits to get the drivers coming in for wheel changes and other maintenance and took some interesting footage of those forced out by mechanical problems. I had little hope of getting the winner when he actually drove in as there was too much kicking and shoving among the male photographers and cameramen to even try, but I waited by the tent and got the victor bringing back the cup.

There had been a staff cameraman covering such a big event but the test was to see if any of my footage was used in the news. It was. First of all the drivers relaxing and dressing, and, unbelievably, my start. I'd passed!

The ABC now had a big problem. A woman had passed a cameraman's test. It solved it by giving me a job in Port Moresby that I'd applied for months before hand, and letting me be the ABC's camera stringer there.

I was in Moresby for four years. After 12 months I married an ABC announcer, David Lupton, and I had to resign as wives weren't allowed to work in the same department as their husbands. I was still the camera stringer and also was allowed to do book reviews and travel talks for the ABC on a casual basis.

My girl twins were born in Moresby and when they were 18 months old we returned to Australia where David had been appointed deputy manager of 2CO Albury. We lived right in the town and I was given a 10 minute spot on radio each week in what was referred to as a women's session. The topics I covered were books, theatre, cinema and interesting women who lived in Albury or who'd visited. I can't remember whether any of these women were farmers or who had farming interests. My main passion in Albury was theatre and I was very involved as assistant director or director in a number of amateur productions. I was therefore horrified when my first review as a director was mentioned in the *Border Morning Mail* and, although my name in the program was Claire Lupton, I was called Mrs David Lupton. Apropos of nothing, the local ABC station manager's wife also told me that I'd been seen down the main street in slacks and that wasn't the kind of dress she thought I should be seen in. Most of my friends in Albury were theatre people, artists or journalists. Three or four of these also happened to be farmers, but, as in Canberra or at PLC, there was no querying of comparable lifestyles.

The ABC now had a big problem. A woman had passed a cameraman's test.

About five years and one daughter later, David was appointed as manager of the ABC regional station in Bega. That was my first real taste of country life, and it came as a shock.

Bega, up until a few years before, had only gravel roads on the highways into town so it had been isolated from all but the hardiest tourists and travellers. I was dismayed by its distance from any major centre, but principally Sydney and Melbourne. It virtually took a whole day to go to either, and there were no trains, so it was take the bus or drive the car.

I met women through the mothers' club at the twins' infant school but I found I had little in common with them and they, who had been born, educated, married, and lived all their lives in the Valley, must have thought me an oddity too.

For the first few years, David and I kept very much to ourselves. We had a busy social life with a constant stream of handover dinners for Apex, Rotary, and Lions in the various towns, and other public functions, but we made friends only with other expatriates from the cities and hardly entertained at all. When the alternates started arriving we soon found that they were 'our kind of people' and our circle grew to include these writers, actors, playwrights, crafts people and poets. However we got to know very few locals.

I found that women who had been brought to the district by their husbands in public service moves, mostly, were desperately lonely...

When I was one of the few who started a playgroup (I had another child by then, a boy), I did get to meet country women at least once a week, but again, most were new locals: that is, they hadn't been born in the Valley, so they hadn't families to look after their children.

Through playgroup I found that women who had been brought to the district by their husbands in public service moves, mostly, were desperately lonely, particularly if their children were too young for school. It wasn't that the local women were unkind, but they didn't need new friends. Their circles had been established from childhood, and they were quite happy to keep them as they were.

Yet it was mainly the new women in town who became leaders, serving on executives on the Parents and Citizens organisation (P and C), welfare committees, and standing for council. It was these same women who were heading the environmental lobby, the call for child services, the committee to have a women's refuge. They supported Aboriginal rights, and pestered politicians for more women's health services.

A major fundraising effort in Bega for the Bega and District Nursing Home brought me into close contact with what can only be termed the old guard in town.

The nursing home auxiliary raised funds by catering, and when I joined the group I was called on at least once a week to help. I was usually cast in the role of waitress and washer-up, as I hadn't the skills or the inclination to take on the cooking. However doing these tasks I made friends with women I would probably not have known well otherwise. It was this same group which rallied to help me when my husband died of cancer.

It was after David was diagnosed with cancer that I had to make the decision to stay in Bega or move back to Canberra, Melbourne, Sydney, or even Albury.

Two years before I would have decided to be out like a shot, but I had lately grown to like the Valley and its people and I knew that it was a marvellous place to raise children. I was also aware that the children would leave as soon as they had matriculated, but at that time they were five, seven and 15, and I had committed myself to stay.

I was still a stringer cameraman with the ABC, also WIN TV, and when my son started school I applied for and obtained a Grade B journalist's position with *Bega District News*. I had, in the last four years, done a librarian's course and attained a bachelor of arts from the University of New England (correspondence).

In the more than 20 years I have lived in Bega I have noticed incredible changes in attitudes. Now newcomers are assimilated fairly quickly and easily into the community. The huge gulf between the alternates and the women who had lived in the valley all their lives gradually broke down over the years, partly because of the alternate society women's skills in craft, music and art, but also their willingness to be at the forefront when changes were needed.

The alternates also grew to conform in dress, to a certain extent. When they first came to the Valley they were still attired in the muslin and flowers of the 1960s, and the Sanyassins wore their yellow and orange robes. Now they may dress a little more colourfully than the locals, but not noticeably so.

Now it is the women who have lived in the Valley all their lives who are the most at risk, or at least the poorer ones. With the recession their problems, which were probably there all the time, have been highlighted. Many are poorly educated and, with most of the newcomers having one or more degrees, they are unlikely to get jobs in an area where unemployment is high. They also suffer from isolation, being left on farms with no means to come into town to shop or socialise. They have their babies when very young and so are housebound.

Statistics in the 1990s have pointed to the Bega Valley Shire as having one of the greatest incidences of domestic violence in New South Wales. Support systems are trying to help, but there are probably many women who are unable, or are prevented, from taking advantage of them. Efforts have been made to have information days in the smaller country towns and hamlets to let everyone know what is available in the way of social services and support, but to even know these information days are on the woman would have to read the local papers, listen to the ABC or be in the town to read a poster, so many needing the information may never know it is offered.

Although my children have now left home I am quite content to stay in Bega (as long as I can go to the capital cities every three months or so). In fact, once I've been to the city, seen my children, my relatives, my friends and lots of films and theatre, I'm happy to return to the relaxed lifestyle and unpolluted air of Bega.

It's not perfect, but I've never known a perfect town or city.

A Fair and Equitable Settlement

Marjorie Thorpe

Born in 1954 in Yallourn, Victoria, Marjorie Thorpe is the manager of the Lake Tyers Trust. She is currently on leave and studying at the Key Centre for Women's Health at the University of Melbourne, where she is writing a thesis on Aboriginal women's health. Her research is centred in the field of mental health, deinstitutionalisation, funding for Aboriginal women's health, and the family; she is concerned to look at health in an holistic context.

Prior to being appointed manager of the Lake Tyers Trust, Marjorie Thorpe worked for seven years at the Aboriginal Childcare Agency, after working with the Aboriginal Health Service. She was involved in the review of adoption laws that led, in Victoria, to the passing of the 1984 *Adoption Act,* which was in the forefront in Australia, particularly in incorporating into the law the principle of placement of Aboriginal children in their own culture.

I went to primaryschool in Yallourn, where I was born, and was raised there until I was 16. When I left Yallourn it was a small country town, although fairly modern because of the industry. It was also a model town, one of a number of towns which had been architecturally designed. It was built as an ideal community.

I am the eldest of seven children. It was a big family and my mother and father were both in paid employment. My father was a shift worker and is still very active. We were the only Aboriginal family in the town, although, at the time, I didn't think about it that way.

My father was born at Lake Tyers mission. Because of the 'half-caste' Act (the Victorian *Aborigines Act*) and because my grandmother died in childbirth at Lake Tyers when she was having my uncle, my grandfather took his children away from Lake Tyers to the Orbost area.

In the 1950s my father was a worker in Yallourn. Then, the Yallourn power station was an essential part of the electricity grid for the SEC (State Electricity Commission, Victoria). There have been changes in technology and now, as the town coal mines were open cut, the power station doesn't exist any more. But when my father took the job there, people were migrating in large numbers to that part of the country. It was a big work area at that time and they went to find jobs.

The Aboriginal community in Morwell was far bigger than the community in Yallourn. We had family in Morwell so were a part of that community as well. The Lionel Rose Centre was in Morwell – it's now called the Morwell Aboriginal Cooperative. It was the office of the minister for Aboriginal affairs. I was a child and young adolescent at the time, but I can remember the beginnings of the development of federal involvement in Aboriginal issues and the way the Aboriginal community developed as a consequence of this. This was when the Aboriginal organisations were set up that now are a significant part of our communities.

I can remember the beginnings of the development of federal involvement in Aboriginal issues and the way the Aboriginal community developed as a consequence...

My father met my mother in Fitzroy. She's from Sandringham Aboriginal community and when my parents married they lived in the Sandringham area. As part of the assimilation policy operating in Australia in the 1950s, the government selected people to go to various parts of the state. Yallourn was the place for my family, and my father was sent to work with the SEC.

My mother and my father reinforced our identity throughout our lives. There was never any question about being Aboriginal. We came under the *Aborigines Act* because we were Black. We were the only Black kids in the school. At the same time, we'd been born in Yallourn, so we were part of the local community as well.

The girls and women I came into contact with in the town were my own friends, as well as the mothers of my friends. I had lots of friends. My mother was very much typical although she worked in paid employment. She supported us, and my father worked too. I had the responsibility of being the eldest, so had the children to look after.

We were part of the local community as much as anybody else in the town. At the same time we maintained our Aboriginality. My father said to us often: 'When you grow up you have to fight for the Aboriginal people.' I had debates with my father over the policies of the Bolte government, as well as about the giving of pensions to unmarried mothers. This was in the 1960s and 1970s. My mother was always very very strong about her identity and her family. So we had that. We never knew any differently.

We were accepted generally speaking by the people we contacted day-by-day, going to school and through my parents' work in Yallourn. Nonetheless there were differences in the attitudes and behaviour of people in the town. There was racism. If there was anything stolen and my brothers were near, the police came to our place. That was 'just what happened'. It was automatic. With particular people, we weren't allowed into their houses. We couldn't figure out why. I remember an occasion where one family who had just recently moved into the area called us 'Abos' and told us to go back to the humpies on the river. We didn't know what they were talking about. We knew we were Aboriginals and we knew about Lake Tyers being an Aboriginal settlement. Our parents always made sure that we knew our family and where we'd come from. The statements made by this family puzzled us.

> *There was racism. If there was anything stolen and my brothers were near, the police came to our place.*

When I was ready for secondary schooling, I went to MLC (Methodist Ladies College) in Kew. I ended up walking out of there at 18. I'd had enough. I was a boarder. I was taken from my family and put in an upperclass set-up: most of the girls who went to that school were the daughters of fairly wealthy people. I was the poor little black girl who went to MLC and was made to stand up in the classroom and say I had a scholarship to attend the school.

I know now that the government paid for my schooling at MLC: it was a government scholarship, similar to Austudy. I also am now aware that this happened to a lot of Aboriginal children. As you get older you start talking with a lot more people, and the pattern becomes clear. This was another way of imposing assimilationist views and policies onto Aboriginal people.

The reinforcement of my values by my family is what carried me through. I'd always had my grandmother who lived in Melbourne and was part of the Fitzroy community, so I visited her every Saturday. This meant I didn't have any real difficulty in adhering to my strong sense of my Aboriginality, although I felt a strong conflict between the values that were a part of schools such as MLC, and myself as a person and an Aboriginal. It was then that I began questioning the way things were and came to the conclusion I didn't like it at the school.

I had no contact with my family in Yallourn when I was at MLC. The rules at boardingschool were that the only time anyone was allowed to go out was on Saturday between 8.00 am and 8.00 pm. The curfew was very strict and this made life extraordinarily difficult for me. If I hadn't had my Nan living in Fitzroy, I don't know what I would have done. Being at that school certainly changed my attitude towards a lot of issues.

I began running away, just to escape. I was locked up. I cried every Saturday when I had to go back. When I was with my Nan I followed her around. I was like a little puppy from the time I arrived at her home. Everywhere she went, I was right behind her. Probably I drove her crazy!

My Nan went to the pub, down to the Builders, every Saturday night. This was after 6 o'clock closing had been abolished, and Saturday night was her night to go down to the pub with the local community. We'd stay at home all day, Nan and I, doing various things around the house. Then at 6 o'clock she'd begin to get dressed up. This was the signal for me to start getting ready to return to school. Nan couldn't get rid of me and had to take me with her, then she had to take me back to school to make sure I arrived on time. The rule was that the girls of MLC had to wear their school uniform wherever they went. No one who was from MLC was allowed to be seen in the street, or anywhere outside the school, without the uniform. Well, there was no way I was going to miss out on being with my Nan up to the last minute. So I'd go to the pub in my school uniform. The first time I ever went to the Builders, it was in my MLC uniform, with my grandmother. I've been back – out of uniform – and can still remember the times she'd take me away, in time to go crying back to school.

My grandmother was the only person I wanted to go to see on those authorised once-a-week visits. I didn't want to have outings to visit anybody else. There were times MLC tried to arrange for an alternative – some women somewhere who wanted to invite me out for the day. But the only place I could accept going to was to my own people. I was lucky that I had family in Melbourne to support me, as well having the knowledge that my family was back home in Yallourn.

Aboriginal people stood up to the government and refused to move from the lawns in front of parliament house. Aboriginal people came from all around Australia to 'sit in' at the embassy.

The late 1960s were the hard years of struggle for the Aboriginal people in this country. There was the 1967 referendum. Aboriginal people fought strongly for that. Then there was the tent embassy in Canberra. Aboriginal people stood up to the government and refused to move from the lawns in front of parliament house. Aboriginal people came from all around Australia to 'sit in' at the embassy. A little before that, I was involved with the Black Panthers. I'd been fortunate to be with people like my mother and grandmother, because they were always proud and strong in the way they went about their lives. This rubbed off on me.

My mother separated from my father at this time. He stayed in Yallourn and retired there recently. My mother took her seven children and came to Melbourne, so this meant there was, once again, a strong and immediate reinforcement of my sense of myself. My grandmother and mother have been an enormous influence in my life.

At the time my mother and sisters and brothers moved back to the city, people like Bruce McGuiness and Gary Foley were important in the struggle for Aboriginal people in Melbourne. They were centred in Fitzroy, where the Aboriginal community was strong. I was fortunate as a young woman to be involved with the community and to have Aboriginal people around me who were active and not intimidated by government policies or racist attitudes.

I was only 17 or 18. I was only a kid. But just to see these people speak and to hear what they were saying, and thinking 'they're right' was powerful. 'What they're saying, this is really true.' Those were my thoughts – as well as: 'God! I wish I could speak like these people.' And I didn't even know what the word 'bureaucracy' was, or 'the system'! I recall thinking, I wonder what this word or that expression means. And never being too afraid to ask because you didn't want to look like a fool. A lot of people knew that what was happening to the Aboriginal people was wrong, and that we were being made to feel negative and bad about ourselves constantly. There was a continuous struggle against being made to feel as if you were a dirty lazy black fellow, and if you were a woman it was a lot worse.

...women were raped by the police in the holding cells. Nobody outside the Aboriginal community cared.

Seeing other people, when we moved to Melbourne, who had come through terrible situations, particularly those who had been removed from their family and the community, brought home sharply to us all how Aboriginal people had been treated. We felt the full brunt of oppression, what with being harassed by police in Fitzroy in those days. There were times the police simply came into houses and buildings where Aboriginal people lived, without any proper reason or excuse. I know women who were raped by the police in the holding cells. Nobody outside the Aboriginal community cared.

The people in our community who were sick, especially those who were mentally sick, were not recognised as having any legitimate problems. They were the people who ended up in gaol, because the broader community saw them as the problem. It was a constant struggle to keep them out of prison. There was also the struggle of trying to keep children with their mothers, fighting those battles without any organisations to support us. This was before the organisations that now exist were established. We hid babies in various places. We wanted to provide our own services to meet our needs. The services that were there weren't meeting any of our needs. We wanted to do it the way we wanted to do it.

That was a time of talking about taking pride in saying: 'I'm an Aboriginal woman.' There was a stigma at the time I grew up. People would say, as if it were a compliment: 'You don't look like an Aboriginal, you could pass for a white person.' That is the most offensive thing for anyone to say to an Aboriginal person. It is a denial of anything positive about Aboriginality. To be white – or able to pass for white, to be non-Aboriginal – that was to portray to us as 'positive' and was being reinforced by government policy. The media presented it as a goal for us at the time: if only we could 'become' white, or be 'accepted' as white! The history of the whole country supported it. Living under that regime, surviving it isn't done easily – it can be done only with a proper support network, basically a family to help an Aboriginal person survive.

My living pattern is in a sense the reverse of that of my parents. I came to Melbourne as a young woman and lived in Melbourne for 20 years. My three daughters were born in Melbourne. Then in about 1991 I decided to go back to the country. This had a lot to do with what was happening around the community in Melbourne. As a family, we had gone through a fairly difficult time. There are factions in the Aboriginal community and we were ousted from an organisation. We had gone through an enormous upheaval, with our integrity and our politics being questioned. My family and I accepted the community's decision. It was what was, and what had to be accepted.

I was disillusioned with the way politics operate. But it was at this time that I was given the opportunity to apply for the job of manager at the Lake Tyers Aboriginal Trust.

Lake Tyers is a family community. As general manager I was in charge. I learnt about making roads. I don't know how to make a road, but I learned how to get the road contractors in and to supervise the making of the roads. I had to know sufficient to gauge if the road contractor was making a mess of the job or ripping the community off. I had to have the confidence to sack the contractor if necessary.

When I went to Lake Tyers to work, the workforce was made up, mostly, of men. There were bets made as to how long I would last. I did not want to go in, bossing everyone around. It was a tough job, and I was responsible for the entire running of the operation – sewerage, health, cattle, roads. I had to learn about cattle, roads, sewerage. Lake Tyers is one of the best cattle districts. Our cattle farm was written up in the farming paper the *Weekly Times*. That was to our credit, the work of the people there, the Aboriginal community.

Lake Tyers is a community development employment program (CDEP) community: there is goldmining and fishing. Lake Tyers is a saltwater lake, a fish breeding lake – prawns and fish. So we're traditional fishermen. And I've learnt fishing.

I was the only Aboriginal woman permanently on the workforce. There were two transient women workers, and one training to be a receptionist, there were the men workers, and there was me. Respect came with recognition of me and my work over time.

My work as manager of the Lake Tyers Trust taught me a great deal about assimilation policies and the way Aboriginal people's autonomy has been taken from us. When I began as manager, the men would ask me: 'Can I do x, y or z?' Their oppression and constant subjection to government control meant that no one had ever asked what they thought about anything. They had been bludgeoned into believing that they had to 'ask' before they 'were allowed' to do anything!

In my time at Lake Tyers, there have been tremendous changes. Landscaping and fencing have been completed at a fast rate. There is work on CDEP, and women are coming to be employed, particularly in the last six months. I am pleased with these changes. At the same time I don't want to encourage mothers of young children out of their homes and into the paid workforce, as mothers play a most important role in the whole community and must be given respect for the work they do and the role they play. I want to see children playing at their mother's feet, whilst the mothers work at tasks they can do in the home setting. It is important also that elders look after the children, talk to the kids, talk to the husband about his role. If there is no support in the family or of the family, then where are we? What do we have? The elders are most important, particularly in this way. The aunties are vital, too: they are 'the bosses'! Men's respect for women in the community is an important facet of Aboriginal life.

At Lake Tyers, we want to create our own economic base and we have been working on that. We are looking toward sending our produce out to market. We have been concentrating on building up the CDEP so that all the Aboriginal people in the community will develop skills for ourselves and build up the resources necessary to create our own work. We are determined to do this according to the way we want to work. We want to create and conserve our economic base on our own terms. Contending with the outside economy is a cut throat business. If we want to fish, for us to enter that market, we will have to be able to do it without making too many mistakes. Indeed, we cannot afford to make any mistakes, because that would be detrimental in the long term. I can see that for us there will be a continual fight with us saying: 'Well, this is the way we think such and such should be done,' yet what we believe will have to be repeated over and over again. Our knowledge of the land and the lake,

I want to see children playing at their mother's feet, whilst the mothers work at tasks they can do in the home setting.

our long-time commitment and our long-time connection, give us an expertise that is not readily available to anyone else.

We are now being confronted with eco-tourism, so this is another aspect of the outside world to deal with. 'Eco-tourism' is a big buzz-word at the moment. This means that in addition to taking on the large outside markets we have consultants prowling about Lake Tyers wanting to know everything about the lake, about the community and about the Aboriginal people. Eco-tourism involves people going camping in the bush and looking at trees. They also look at indigenous foods and indigenous people. Who should have control? There should be no question but that indigenous people should have power over the industry and its development, yet we have been effectively denied control of eco-tourism.

The whole question of eco-tourism, its relevance to our community, needs to be seen in the context of social justice. This is particularly so for Aboriginal people, the indigenous people who are living as does the community in Lake Tyers. It needs to be channelled along with other social justice issues that are arising now, for the community, and in the broader context of the world outside the Lake Tyers community.

We have problems with our lake. We want to have it closed. There has been over-fishing by commercial fishermen on the lake. This has been an enormous political issue in itself. Because the lake is affected, people are affected. We attempted to have the lake closed so that an environmental impact study could take place. Now the state government does not want to become involved, because at present it is terrified of anything that comes close to an issue over land with Blacks. At Lake Tyers there are many matters the government wishes to avoid tackling: for example, those involving offshore or sea rights.

Many of the old people, in particular, at Lake Tyers want the lake closed. One of the old men came up when I was working in the office, and sent one of the young fellows in on his behalf to request that I type up a petition there and then to close the lake. There is also the question of Land Rights and a rumour that the state government intends to put a non-native title claim on the lake and surrounding land, to prevent us from declaring our interest. Under the law as it is at present, following the *Mabo* decision, the onus is on us, the original inhabitants of the land, to prove that we have native title holders living in the Lake Tyers area. We are a small community, and national issues are confronting us daily. We cannot avoid them.

I sense that there is a general expectation that we will put in a native title claim on Lake Tyers. That expectation is fine, but there are also a

Under the law as it is at present, following the Mabo *decision, the onus is on us, the original inhabitants of the land, to prove that we have native title holders living in the Lake Tyers area.*

lot of issues within the community: politics is embedded in the Aboriginal community as a consequence of the way our rights have been dealt with in the last 200 or so years, and the way the Aboriginal people have been treated.

We know how to deal with our own matters. We know how to solve our own problems. We do it in a way that is different from the non-Aboriginal community. But it is effective. And this is not being allowed to happen. The information we are given is selective. It is delivered in a way that is not appreciated by Aboriginal people: the language and terminology isn't ours. Government people and bureaucrats talk to a people whose tradition is based on an oral tradition, not a written one. This important factor is being ignored.

There are issues, also, relating to oral traditions that are not recognised. Oral traditions are looked at in a simplistic way by people who are non-Aboriginal. The tendency in the non-Aboriginal culture is to assert that Aboriginal culture consists of somebody sitting down and telling a story. This is not the way our culture operates; it is not continuing *our culture* to sit someone down to tell a story. This is cultural stereotyping. It is saying that the storytellers are the ones who had and have control of the traditions. What is essential in any analysis is to look at the complexities of Aboriginal families and the subtle ways that traditions are passed on. I knew, for example, from the time I was very small whom, within Aboriginal cultural traditions, I could marry and whom I should not.

...something an Aboriginal person 'knows' from inside rather than someone sitting down in the middle of a circle and imposing rules through a European-style storytelling mode.

Because this is instilled from the time we are children, when the time comes we know what is expected of us. It is not a case of someone saying: 'You can marry so-and-so,' or 'You cannot marry X, Y or Z.' It is a far more complex and subtle matter, related to which group is acceptable, so that a member of a particular group does not interfere with the patterns existing in Aboriginal culture. To do so is to break the law. But no one said to me as a child: 'You will break the law if you marry outside group P, Q, or R.' This is the same in relation to my Aboriginality as a whole: it is something an Aboriginal person 'knows' from inside rather than someone sitting down in the middle of a circle and imposing rules through a European-style storytelling mode.

The account of an event by one person – a 'storyteller' – is not an accurate portrayal of anything connected with Aboriginality or Aboriginal culture. If you look at one story told by one person, obviously it isn't the only account of the event. There will be as many stories of one happening as there are people involved. And even people who are not directly involved have ways of describing, according to what they have been told or have learned. We do not have the structured method of a 'storyteller' passing down tradition through sitting down and 'telling you a story today'. This approach to storytelling and oral tradition is one which was imposed on us in 1770 when Captain Cook first came to Australia's shores, and has been continued ever since. It doesn't happen like that in the traditional Aboriginal community.

Misconceptions and misunderstandings arise when non-Aboriginal people assert that Aboriginal culture is passed on through the non-Aboriginal ways. Yet we are constantly confronted with the dominant non-Aboriginal culture imposing its stereotype.

In the Aboriginal culture, we do not teach and we do not train. Everyone of us learns. We learn from our elders, and when they 'teach' they don't teach in the sense of telling someone something. They expect you to learn from them, through what they do and say. It is a very different way of thinking that is misunderstood by those who look on from outside.

I live an Aboriginal lifestyle. What is being put to us still, and put to the young people in particular, is the aspiration to be white, to fit in to this Westernised culture. That is all very well if a person is on a middle-class income. But for the majority of Aboriginal people, this is an aspiration that is not relevant: everything is stacked against them from the beginning. How are Aboriginal people to set up our businesses when our thinking doesn't fit with the individualistic style of materialism that is prevalent in non-Aboriginal culture? In our culture, there is more sharing, more concern about others in the group. If you are an Aboriginal person you cannot deny someone – your grandmother or your brother or your sister – because that has far more effect on you from a personal perspective. To do that, to be indifferent, will cause great conflict.

Of course there are Aboriginal people who are able to work within the Westernised system. There are some Aboriginal people who have run organisations and businesses and done so brilliantly. But to apply a western concept of business to all Aboriginal people, to all the indigenous people, simply will not work. We know there are ways we can deal with this issue, however. We can look at different approaches.

I am a member of the Aboriginal Provision Government (APG), which is a people's movement ensuring the struggle for rights continues. At its base is Aboriginal sovereignty, autonomy and indigenous rights, and the recognition of all of them. The aim is to reforge cultural values. Young people learn through their own culture, and the APG sees it as important to start with the obvious – for example, young fellows learning to play the didgeridoo and the young women learning to play the clapsticks. It is important to instil in boys and girls and young women and young men a sense of the importance of their roles as women and men. Language, spirituality and health are all important, and the APG teaches that we need to protect that at all costs as these are the basis of our whole being. We are struggling against the whole assimilation process, which is genocidal. If Aboriginal people are not successful in this struggle against assimilation and to retain and maintain our cultural values, then genocide will continue to have a physiological impact on our communities. We are vulnerable; assimilation policies of successive governments have made us so. In the field of health, as in other areas, programs and service delivery have been determined by others. We are working to change this, and this is one of the purposes of my being at the Key Centre for Women's Health and studying Aboriginal women's health.

Coming from the environment of Fitzroy – inner city Melbourne – and going to live in a traditional environment, which was not only 'the country' but an Aboriginal community, was a great change for me.

What I want for myself and my children is to maintain our rights as indigenous women but also for them to have the benefits of being able to have a job of their choosing. And a peaceful life. Aboriginal people do not have that. It is not about materialism, or rights based in materialism. Materialism doesn't bring anybody much at all – nothing that is really worthwhile, anyway, because people are working themselves to death to acquire things.

When I began my work at Lake Tyers I began to learn a new way of living. This experience taught me a great deal. Coming from the environment of Fitzroy – inner city Melbourne – and going to live in a traditional environment, which was not only 'the country' but an Aboriginal community, was a great change for me. I went, thinking I was taking my skills there. I was taught as much – in fact much, much more – than I was able to teach!

The workforce at Lake Tyers is still predominantly male. Working with Aboriginal men who have lived for many years, perhaps all their lives, in a situation like that was not easy. At the beginning it was difficult for me to be accepted in any sense. The base upon which I gained acceptance was that I am descended from a Lake Tyers family, and I had a family on Lake Tyers. Being a woman who had lived in the city and particularly living and working around Fitzroy it was difficult to go back to a very isolated area. When I first arrived as manager, the Aboriginal women of Lake Tyers found it difficult too, because basically they did not know me and I was in a role in which Aboriginal women are not accustomed to seeing Aboriginal women. At the start I didn't have an affinity with anybody except my own family. Thank goodness for them!

There was a real fear at first of an Aboriginal woman presenting as I do. That is something that certainly doesn't go down really well in an area like East Gippsland, where women are not in such roles and do not see a lot of women in such a role – first hand, anyway. Yet having lived there for three years, I can say that I found country women to be far more sensible. I know I am generalising, but there is a significant matter-of-factness about country women. They are practical and down to earth. With the women I got to know, I saw them as being basically honest and – basic! Both the Aboriginal and non-Aboriginal women I met were quietly intelligent and very strong – in a quiet way. That was something I envied in a sense. They had a sureness about themselves, even though some of them did not have an easy life.

Then there were the non-Aboriginal women who were accustomed to dealing with Aboriginal women on a very different basis from what they were confronted with in me. That was very difficult. It was like going to another planet, to begin with.

...there is a significant matter-of-factness about country women. They are practical and down to earth.

I have found the country to be more family-orientated than the city. As well, everyone was far more friendly than in the city. I've never waved to people in the street as I did in the country. A person feels a bit stupid doing that in the city, but down there you see people and around the area where I come from everybody waves to everyone else. It's just so friendly. That's the way it is with country people. There's that willingness to look out for each other although there is also a sense in which people have to come to be accepted, too, for this to apply.

The attitude of country women to people who come from the city is notable. Country women are sick and tired of people coming down – both Black and white – thinking they are so sophisticated and are going to put their country brothers and sisters 'right'. There is a tendency for some people to criticise the words people use in the country, and to assume that everyone in the country is 'laid back' and not as smart as other people. But country commonsense is what is missing in the city, and it's certainly missing with those people who come to the country to put us 'right'. I wanted commonsense and a comforting environment, and I found it in the country.

After the 1967 referendum which meant that the federal government took responsibility for laws relating to Aboriginal people and the wellbeing of Aboriginal people, there was an attempt to close down Lake Tyers. This happened about twenty years ago. People were forced to go to other places, such as Moe and Yallourn. The wife of the last white manager of Lake Tyers (she is still alive) told me how she took people to these other country towns and helped them to settle in, buy the furniture and secure homes for the people in the middle of towns. This again was another perspective on the assimilationist policy that governments continually foisted upon Aboriginal people. Talking with this woman means I have now learned something of the policy as it directly affected Aboriginal people, particularly my family, both from the point of view of my father and mother in their move to Yallourn, and from a non-Aboriginal, from someone who was directly involved in moving families and saw her involvement as helping them to 'fit in' to their 'new' life.

I am a very direct person. I do not believe in wheeling and dealing that keeps issues and decisions away from the community. If something cannot be said up front in a meeting, then what is its value? It is important to say what has to be said, and that's it! That is my philosophy, and I use it in my overt political work, and in my work as manager of the Trust. I am also using that approach in my research work into Aboriginal women's health.

I used it also in my work with others who were concerned about the use of adoption to take Aboriginal children out of their own culture in an attempt to have them 'fit in' to non-Aboriginal society. This pattern of non-Aboriginal people adopting Aboriginal children was a part of the policies and practices that led to the separation of families, the movement of Aboriginal families and children around the country because of government policies, and the removal of children from families. All have led to anxiety, depression and other psychological disorders. There is a high suicide rate for Aboriginal people, and the deaths in custody issue is just one stark example of this. The principle adopted in the Victorian *Adoption Act* in 1984 for the first time in Australia recognised the importance of ensuring that if Aboriginal children are to be adopted, then they must be adopted into families which are culturally sympathetic to them; Aboriginal children must not be placed outside the Aboriginal culture. They have the right to grow up in a family which can truly create a strong base for them, culturally and emotionally. For Aboriginal people, our emotions and psychological wellbeing are, naturally, bound up in our culture.

> *Aboriginal children must not be placed outside the Aboriginal culture. They have the right to grow up in a family which can truly create a strong base for them, culturally and emotionally.*

I have been seen by government authorities as radical and uncontrollable. Government people spend a lot of their time (and ours) telling us how we should talk and how we should act. I know how to act in the right situations. I've been around long enough to know that. This is what is not being recognised. We are tired of fighting. We have lost so many people. We don't know how much longer we are going to live, to exist as a people. The statistics are against us. We have struggled for so long and what we are looking for is a fair and equitable settlement. Something that protects our rights. We too have something to contribute.

Moonraker Farm

Andrea Lofthouse

Andrea Lofthouse compiled the first *Who's Who of Australian Women*, published by Methuen in 1982. Born in England in 1943, she attended Fort Street Girls High School and Sydney University, then worked for 20 years as an English and history teacher. With Kaye Johnston she established Moonraker Farm, a permaculture/organic demonstration farm in Kangaroo Valley, New South Wales. In April 1994 she won the regional (Illawarra) section of the New South Wales 'Rural Woman of the Year' award, a national competition run by the ABC (Australian Broadcasting Corporation) radio *Country Hour* program.

Since 1983, with Kaye Johnston, Andrea Lofthouse has been developing ideas of women's self-sufficiency, writing and performing feminist comedy, teaching in women's programs at the local TAFE (technical and further education) college, and looking forward to the day the second edition of the *Who's Who of Australian Women* becomes possible.

January 1994. In the first days of the new year, we faced two of the horrors country people dread most. We both escaped unscathed (physically) but these episodes forced us to consider our strengths and weaknesses, and our reasons for living in the country.

'Wake Up! Wake up Andrea! There's a guy with a machete outside! Wake up!'

A guy with a machete. In fact there were *two* young men, yelling, terrorising us and several neighbours. Our nextdoor neighbour, half a kilometre away, crouched in her little house while the one with the machete walked all around it, searching for someone. Another woman neighbour was verbally abused by the two, after they had pushed a young woman out of their car and then gone looking for her.

The police came quickly. A potentially violent situation was defused. We'll never know the whole story, but the machete was probably more a sign of the young men's fear of the bush and the neighbour's dogs, than a means to hurt us.

The bushfires touched everybody, the way a war does. Nobody felt safe. City people saw houses on fire, in the suburbs of Sydney. Suddenly, in those roaring westerlies and 40 degrees celsius days, the bush came to the city.

Fire was forced into our consciousness. There were such emotional scenes, scenes of devastation, incredible luck, humour, courage: all the 'Australian' qualities distilled in those days. We saw *women* fighting the fires, women police evacuating people.

Kangaroo Valley had never been so dry. Every day, the westerly wind worsened, promising annihilation. The fire would come from the west, funnelling up to a final conflagration at our end of the valley, the narrow, eastern side. This valley has seen many fires, but no really serious ones for over 20 years. Older locals have muttered darkly for years that we were overdue for a big fire.

Like greenies everywhere, we have allowed the trees to grow back on our steep, over-grazed hillside. Photographs of this area from the 1950s show bare hills. The house is now surrounded by wattles and eucalypts, with pockets of regrowth rainforest. The weatherboard and fibro house would explode in a fire. Our water tank is low; there's been no rain for weeks.

Kaye packed a bag and was ready to go. I couldn't bring myself to do that. Every day for weeks we watched the smoke haze, checked the temperature, dreaded the build-up of the westerly wind, measured the water tank, and followed the progress of the fires on radio and tv. Every day the temperature reached the high thirties. We made new New Year resolutions: our support of the local volunteer bushfire brigade was going to rapidly improve.

The chooks stood, wings out, beaks open, waiting for each hot day to end. As we reduced our water consumption, theirs increased.

The threat exposed many weaknesses: both the extent of the hazard and our lack of preparedness. Our house would simply have to be left – no amount of work now would change anything. What we saw on tv proved that: with the wind in charge, whether your house survived or burned was the luck of the draw.

But we argued about other questions, such as which animals could be saved, what we could take, should we cut the fences, do this or that? The heat and wind made it difficult to think clearly.

The animals were so hot, but they have amazing powers of endurance. The chooks stood, wings out, beaks open, waiting for each hot day to end. As we reduced our water consumption, theirs increased. What did we *do* in those awful hot days? I found cooking comforting. I made bread, jam, chutney: like a demented housewife, I was not intending to be caught with an empty larder! At night we slept poorly, because the wind rustled the dry leaves. (Dry leaves, in Kangaroo Valley!)

I was prompted to think again about the country and the city. What do they mean? Why do city folk often hanker for a place in the country? We fulfilled a dream when we came here, and most of the time I believe we live in paradise. But will we stay? Can a dream become reality? Is it different for *women* who move to the country?

What does 'the country' mean? Deeply embedded in our psyches, it's where most people lived until recently. It's where food is grown. We may have a collective memory of a 'Garden of Eden'. We love its 'natural' beauty.

Many of our most valued skills: agriculture, horticulture, textiles, ceramics, originated in the country, and have also long been associated with women. The country supplies us with a strong women's literature: in Australia, there are Mary Gilmore, Miles Franklin, Katharine Susannah Prichard, and so on. Women should feel 'at home' in the country.

In the Western European tradition, women feature prominently in the stories of country life (not always in positive terms: one aspect of the country woman is the 'witch'). Feminist lesbian women celebrate the achievements of such mentors as the Ladies of Llangollen and Vita Sackville-West. There have always been many women in the organic farming movement, such as Lady Balfour, who wrote *The Living Soil*.

But in Australia, the country is not seen as a woman's place. The bush tradition is strongly male, even though the successful conquering of inland Australia by white people depended very much on women's work. There *were* lonely stockmen and explorers, but they were soon followed by settlement: women and children. The women's task was even more formidable than the men's.

The men made a great mess: hunted the Aborigines, killed the animals, cut down the trees, and the women then had to make something out of it.

The men made a great mess: hunted the Aborigines, killed the animals, cut down the trees, and the women then had to make something out of it.

Here and there we find recognition of women's role – 'The Drover's Wife' – but even women writers such as 'Waif Wander' used mainly male characters in their stories of the bush. The actual 'bush' is a male bastion and women can't succeed in it on the same terms as men. The image of the Australian country woman is of a stoutly-built, motherly scone-maker, who does good works through the Country Women's Association (CWA). Our equivalent of 'Mom and apple pie'.

Conditions in the country are harsh, and the bush is seen in physical terms. Women are less strong physically than men, therefore they can't succeed. But the real test in the bush is likely to be psychological, and here women have always had an advantage. While the men were off chasing the sheep, the women kept things going at home, day after dreary day.

The fires brought this home to me: the men standing there, watching the fires devour houses, unable to fight them. This is extraordinary stress. No amount of equipment could beat that wind.

Most Australians live in the city, and the city is 'where it's at'. Ideas, fashions, inventions, emanate from the city. During the nineteenth century, the once-thriving bush literature faded and the bush came to be seen as old-fashioned, irrelevant, quaint, even bizarre.

On the other hand, the city can be seen as a 'black hole' which devours the products and people of the countryside. The city dominates the country, similarly to the way heterosexuals dominate homosexuals. Lots of unspoken animosity, envy, bitchiness on both sides. Country people have a famous disdain for 'city slickers'. Pub talk often centres on illustrating how stupid the city mob are. For hundreds of years the peasants hid their best corn from the landlord: now the sport is to hide knowledge. The relationship is the same.

City people are very ignorant of country life. If they knew how much cruelty is involved in the production of their food, they would be horrified. Dairying is very cruel. People never see the little calves, taken from their mothers soon after birth, standing shivering together, never to know their mother's care. The males will be killed or castrated. The females become milk machines. Breeding cows are called 'vehicles'. Meanwhile, the depiction of cows in advertising reaches new heights of cuteness and unreality.

Most people know that battery hens suffer horribly, but they still buy the cheapest eggs. The treatment of animals which go for slaughter... feed-lots...genetic engineering...growth promotants...the list is endless, and endlessly dreadful.

It is strange that city folk should be so ignorant, but modern industrial-style food production requires it. If the city is where it's at – where most of the resources are – people there should be the *least* ignorant, shouldn't they?

This situation derives from the industrial revolution of the eighteenth and nineteenth centuries. Technological inventions led to the mechanisation of the production of food and goods. The factory age began; the growth of towns accelerated. English country people were forced off the land by the *Enclosure Acts*, and went to the shocking city slums. Crime escalated, and some of the apprehended unfortunates found themselves transported to Botany Bay or Van Diemen's Land.

The development of modern agricultural techniques helped to devalue the old ways and further denigrated women's skills and the initiative needed in country life. The modern industrial process alienates people from the land and from the methods of production of all necessary items. People no longer know how to feed and clothe themselves. Far from being freed from the toil needed to produce most of their requirements, people are locked-in to the military-industrial complex, and have to earn lots of *money* in order to have a reasonable life. And fashion dictates that what they ate or wore yesterday is now *outré*.

The country, then, embodies the 'eternal verities' where nothing changes. The poor city person is a creature of whim and a slave to fashion. Country folk exhibit the values of persistence, thrift, kindness, simplicity. See City Sue in her Blundstones and Drizabone!

But worse: the bush has receded in the city folk's mind, and become an unreal fantasy land. It is thought of as if it is 50 years ago. It becomes a nostalgia trip, a way of visiting the past. As a way of coping with the new technology, city people visit the country and want to find a land where women make sausagerolls and blowaway sponges, where we milk cows by hand (in the tv commercials we do!) and where the original bush has somehow escaped the ravages of 200 years of white settlement.

City people in the country are escapees from the city. This is not a positive reason for being there. For most, it is brief respite care, where they can gaze on a calm, harmonious scene, green, with animals perhaps. Most important, it must be calm, to soothe frazzled city nerves.

Realities of life in the country are similar to the city: paying the bills, getting a job, with the added worries of distance (the price of petrol) and such threats as fire and flood.

This attitude imposes on the country and its people an impossible, false, unfair burden. Realities of life in the country are similar to the city: paying the bills, getting a job, and so on, with the added worries of distance (the price of petrol) and such threats as fire and flood.

There are class differences at work here too. In the upheavals of the industrial revolution, as the towns grew, so did the middle-class, and middle-class values gained the upper hand. Certain niceties interfere with the city person's appreciation of the country. There is a horror of blood, shit, mud and pain – the realities of life itself. These people like long, hot showers, they worry about salmonella, they wear really clean clothes, all the time. One telling difference between the treatment of women and men in the country is seen when you go into town in dirty work clothes. This is totally acceptable, even admirable for men. Quite threatening and alarming when women do it.

Money is the key to the power, and the values, of middle-class society. Before the industrial revolution, there was little money around: the entity of greatest value was land. Most people never thought much about it: you lived on, and from, the land, and it was always there.

The landlord may have technically 'owned' it, but he had no reason to change its use until the technological inventions demanded the formation of large, enclosed fields. Old rights of land usage disappeared; the small-scale ways of farming went. Agriculture and horticulture are now business. But we now know that these large-scale, monocultural systems of food production, which feed our cities, are detrimental to the health of the soil, and create huge pest and disease problems.

Ironically, in some areas (such as Kangaroo Valley), the land now has a highly inflated value as real estate. Local farmers give up farming and earn their living as contract workers, running the farms of rich city people. Some of the locals have kept going by subdividing and selling off some of their land, the 'last cash crop'.

The money economy did much to destroy the old sense of 'community'. The response to the fires showed that the meaning of life has much more to do with 'simple' values, like helping each other, than the pursuit of profit. One way of rebuilding community is to look again at those old methods of small-scale production, which require cooperation and friendship. City people, even though physically close, often live isolated from their neighbours. Modern transport and communication mean that a city street can comprise strangers, with each household relating to family and friends far away.

Breaking down the stereotypes of city/country is possible. Bill Mollison and David Holmgren pointed the way to a city/country alliance with *Permaculture One* (first published in 1978). Several later books further develop their ideas. Drawing on their experience of how traditional societies have used their resources, they show how the alienation of the concrete jungle can be undone, and how community can be built through the cooperative production of food. Street plantings of fruit trees, city backyards joined up to create big gardens, and vacant blocks made into community gardens, will all transform the city.

Most people won't want to go back to being 'peasants', grubbing in the ground for spuds.

As the plants grow, so does the sense of community and cooperation. Instead of the city sucking the goodies from the country, it develops its own sense of self-sufficiency. And, in the process, perhaps recovering something of that Garden of Eden, which we all need.

We can't turn back the clock. Food production is extremely labour intensive. Most people won't want to go back to being 'peasants', grubbing in the ground for spuds. But if everyone grew some food, even pots of herbs on their balcony (and composted their scraps), that total dependence on the market place would be broken. People begin to think about where their food comes from. Values change, and there is less dependence on the artificially created scarcities of the money economy. It costs very little *money* to grow food. When plants are grown organically, on a small scale, in balance with Nature, the health of the soil is maintained, and there is no need for the other great expenses of modern farming: pesticides, herbicides, costly machinery, petrol.

But city people would have to give up some of their wicked ways. For instance, we can buy tomatoes throughout the year, but there is only one kind: tasteless, with a tough skin. We apparently have lots of 'choice' at the vegetable counter. But there once were dozens of tomato varieties. If we ate tomatoes only when they are in season – in summer – they would be really delicious and special. Could city people do that?

How much choice do we really have? Why is most bread made from wheat? Why is wheat the staple, instead of oats or barley? Why are there so many dairy products on the shelves of the supermarket? Does 'value-added' (now also very big on supermarket shelves) mean 'value' or 'profit'? Do we have to have everything?

And dare we contemplate the forces which create starvation in so much of the world? If food is basically cheap to produce, why do we have so much, and they have so little? If we led simpler lives, would they get more?

Women need to think about these questions, because women have to take part in the running of the world. We have to change the way food is produced, and our attitudes to it, and the images of it. One good which could come from the bushfires is that the country is regarded more realistically. Women who have that dream of country will face it with clear-eyed knowledge, rather than a fuzzy feminist nostalgia.

...we made every sort of mistake when we came to the country, and we spent years unlearning our old ways.

I say this because we made every sort of mistake when we came to the country, and we spent years unlearning our old ways. I believe the country, the Australian country in particular, is by far the best place to live, but it is also extremely challenging and real. It tests us, and our relationship, all the time. At certain times, when overwhelmed by Nature (usually, in this neck of the woods, it's floods, and landslides) we have wanted to leave. But somewhere along the line we became country women, and would feel like fish out of water in the city.

Since late 1985 we have lived at Moonraker Farm, 37 acres (15 hectares) perched on a hillside in Kangaroo Valley. We have rainforests, pasture, lots of trees, great sunsets, views of the valley and the escarpment of Budderoo Plateau, creatures such as wallabies, bandicoots and wombats. A creek which is still clean enough for platypus. Giant trees, including the red cedar; bird's nest ferns, orchids, vines. Wild ducks, black cockatoos. Many birds visit our garden: wrens, king parrots, rosellas, finches, honeyeaters, thrushes, magpies, silvereyes, yellow robins. We live with birdsong and the sounds of insects and frogs. Skinks wander in and out of the house. The mopoke owl and the shy native dove. Thick green, blue haze, white mists. Classic Australian bush beauty, with the extra bounty of regular, high rainfall and very fertile soil.

We have developed a large organic garden utilising many permaculture principles. Over 100 fruit trees, including some unusual ones such as persimmon, tamarillo and lychee, which grow well here. Half of them are in a Tatura trellis system, where the trees are planted closely together and espaliered on either side of a wire support. This means that older, shorter women can reach the fruit, and it is easily protected from birds by netting.

Two horses, four cows, four sheep, geese, ducks, chooks, guinea fowl. A goat called Thomas, our weed eater. Bees.

We have designed our own system of growing vegetables, where small fenced areas, connected to the chook houses, are rotated, and the chooks become little workers, clearing the weeds and eating pests. Our labour – and time-saving methods add up to a women's way of organic growing.

We have lots of animals. Two horses, four cows, four sheep, geese, ducks, chooks, guinea fowl. A goat called Thomas, our weed eater. Bees. The first hour of every day is spent attending to these animals' needs. Then there are the regular chores required by them; arranging to have the sheep shorn, the horses' hooves trimmed, fresh straw in the chook house, and so on.

The flower garden has a great selection of plants: old, fragrant roses, various ornamental sages, fuchsias, portwine magnolia, buddleia, elderberry, and climbers like the snail vine. The design ensures that Vita Sackville-West would feel at home here, in spite of the grevillea, bottlebrush, indigo, and other natives which share the garden.

We've learned a great range of skills, mostly through necessity, such as plumbing, fencing, building. Caring for sick and wounded animals, both wild and our own. Removing diamond pythons from the chook shed every summer, and re-locating them in a safe, wilder area across the creek. Periodically, I kill and 'dress' the extra roosters we get every year. From our garden, we provide much of our own needs: vegetables and fruit of all kinds, chickens, eggs, honey, herbs, flowers and, one day, wine.

This all takes lots of energy. Plants and animals require constant attention. Fruit trees need heaps of feeding, mulching, and water at the right time, as well as the right companion plants to help protect them from pests. We often feel 'tied down' by the responsibility of it all, unable to flit off for a holiday, or even a weekend, together.

The farm is certified Organic A with NASAA (National Association for Sustainable Agriculture Australia). This was a long process and involved much hard work, including stringent testing and record-keeping.

We wanted to have our own place, and know the quality of the food we eat. Everything here is untouched by pesticides or modern farming methods. Women don't usually have this sort of power. We've been able to play 'God' on our own little patch. This has been as humbling and instructive as it has been pleasing and satisfying.

We tried to combine all our loves: feminism, reading and teaching, gardening and growing things, raising and caring for animals, enjoying the sheer beauty of the place. And we felt there would be other women with the same desire for 'grassroots' living, who would want to share in the production of healthy food. There is a strong movement in Australia away from mass production and pesticides. Organic produce began to appear in shops. Free-range eggs. Meat that is not treated with growth promotants.

And we had examples close at hand. Just down the road a subscription farm was established. Members pay a yearly subscription (about $460) and work on the farm for 'five person hours' per month. Each member/family is in a group with several from the same locality. Every week someone from the group works at the farm, and delivers the boxes of vegetables to the others in the group.

People joined from Sydney, Wollongong, Nowra, and the local area, and in the first two years of operation, the farm had 40 to 50 subscribers. As well as learning about organic growing, other good things happened. City children learned about the country. Members had to be responsible to the others in their group, so cooperation was built.

We liked the idea of people being involved in the production of their own food. Women, the ones who feed people, should know about food – and technology, how to make things, *how* to use tools. Parents, who put so much thought into their children's education, should know what goes into their mouths!

We planned a subscription farm just for women. As a first step, we started the LOOFAH scheme in 1990. LOOFAH stands for Lesbians on Organic Farms as Active Helpers and derives from the WWOOF scheme (Willing Workers on Organic Farms), a world-wide network for travellers. We advertised regularly in *Lesbian Network* magazine, and for a time in *Lesbian Connection* (USA) and the Sydney-based *Lesbians on the Loose*. The subscription farm was affected by petrol price rises and lost the more remote members. We would solve this problem by offering accommodation. We are near the town of Berry, which is two and a half hours by train from Sydney, so women didn't have to have a car to get here. We never quite worked out how they would reach home with their bulging bags of vegies on Sydney's public transport!

In return for accommodation in our backyard caravan, women give us three hours' labour per day for a few days, or a week. We expect them to bring some food to contribute to our basic store of eggs, vegies, and so on. Three hours per day is quite substantial help. This includes weeding, planting, mulching, and helping with the morning chores.

For three years we had a steady stream of LOOFAHs, mostly international backpackers, and we got to know some really wonderful women. We had great meals together. Most turned out to be excellent cooks, and we now have a store of LOOFAH recipes. We had long raves about politics; in particular, German women gave us chilling first hand accounts of the problems of the new Germany. We felt less isolated from the world in general, and more in tune with lesbian culture worldwide. Women came from Alaska, Canada, the United States of America, England, Holland, Belgium, Germany, Scotland, Japan, and New Zealand and Australia.

We had long and passionate discussions with many of them about the world economy, and how lesbians could help save the world!

During these years, the various systems we had established on the farms, mostly designed by Kaye, began to mature. So the women who came learned about organic gardening and the design of self-sustaining systems. We had long and passionate discussions with many of them about the world economy, and how lesbians could help save the world! They then went away with new knowledge and ideas, and we found that even when women came knowing little about gardening, we still learned a lot from the interaction.

They took a great load from our shoulders: the work is too much for us two. When LOOFAHs came, we could get stuck into a really big job: starting a new vegetable garden, putting the nets over the fruit trees, cleaning the litter out of the chook houses, or giving the chooks their quarterly pedicure (treatment for scaly-leg mites, which involves softening the leg scales with a massage of warm soapy water, then applying a paste of sulphur and petroleum jelly; this suffocates the mites, and the chooks quite enjoy it).

And we still have to go to work. Even though this is a full-scale farm, we realised long ago that we'd never be able to live solely by its production. We both work as part-time teachers at the local TAFE (technical and further education) college. This means we never have enough time to develop the farm on a larger scale. But this development is also limited by topography and availability of water. We could probably double the amount of vegetables produced, but no more.

We found other options limited too. The marketing of organic produce is a huge job in itself. We give away our surplus; Kaye's parents receive a steady supply. Some is turned into jams and chutney. We sell most of the eggs, for money and for 'roos', the 'currency' in the LETS scheme (Local Energy Transfer System). We have rejected other options, such as becoming a guest house, partly because of our ambivalent attitude to tourism and the amount of work involved.

The LOOFAH system, though it worked well, was not the whole answer. Most LOOFAHs came from the city and had to be taught everything from scratch. This led to a cumulative sense of exhaustion (common to teachers everywhere!). They came erratically. When we needed them most, they were not around. When holiday times came, they wanted to come, just when we needed a break!

We thought back to our original plan for a lesbian subscription farm and tried to design a new system, to be called FROMs (Friends of Moonraker). Women would commit themselves for a year, and they would agree to come to the farm for eight weekends in a year. Every month there would be a designated FROMs weekend. As well as working on the farm, the FROMs would receive tuition in organic gardening and permaculture principles. In the evening we'd show videos and discuss various aspects of country life, especially in relation to women. We expected to have more jolly good meals! And on Sunday we'd pick the vegetables and fruit for them to take home.

This would solve the problem of having to relate to, and teach, new women every time. We expected that some women would want to continue beyond a year, but also that many would go away and start their own gardens. So we'd have some continuity, and new women joining in. These women would have a place in the country to visit regularly, and cheaply, and we would get to meet new faces.

But it didn't happen. Some women came, but only once. Several stayed in touch for a while, and said they enjoyed the experience, but they did not return. One woman came regularly. She lived nearby, and soon had her own garden going and was busy with that.

We expected this system to be rather haphazard at first but we were shocked at the lack of interest. At the same time, the subscription farm was struggling to keep going. We puzzled over the reasons: was the idea wrong? were we too formidable? do women suspect something that is 'free'? does it sound like too much hard work?

But at the same time, as this idea fizzled, as we looked around, we saw that after eight years' work, the farm has reached a stage of maturity which is extremely heartening. The fruit trees produce fruit. The many trees we've planted tower over us. The systems work: no new construction needed, only maintenance. And no crowds of happy women rushing to join us!

We'll never know if it is the times we live in, or ourselves, which is the reason. Most lesbians live in the city, and they like the cafés, dance parties, movies...they're not exactly into country life. And we became somewhat tougher as a result of the challenges we'd faced. We used to accept any woman who wanted to come, even when it wasn't convenient. We began to question them more closely when they rang: were they really interested in organic gardening? or were they fleeing the city/a relationship/drugs/whatever?

While women were coming less often, we found we were showing the farm to more and more mixed groups. Kaye has regularly used the farm to teach her TAFE students, because she teaches horticulture, but we also showed it to groups of students doing permaculture courses held on other farms in Kangaroo Valley in recent years. Nearly 300 visitors came in 1993. We always point out to them that all the work here has been done by women.

I remind myself of this success whenever I go through a negative phase, thinking that a small 'hobby' farm like this is middle-class indulgence. Like Marie Antoinette dressing up as a shepherdess. To actually own productive land, and do so little with it is outrageous in a world of starving people. And if we are now exhausted, and see no way of continuing, aren't we just city slickers who stayed longer than most, but who can't hack it? What we've done is uneconomic – we can have the farm only while we have jobs – so aren't we kidding ourselves?

We were ambitious, and what makes this place unusual is that we've done it all within the context of lesbian politics. We went public. We tried to live our lesbian feminist politics and there are few available examples of this in the Australian countryside. The crystallisation of this every year has been the Moonraker Fair, held every December since 1989. The ingredients are live women's music (in 1993, this was the local women's rock band, *Which Witch*), stalls selling food, books, anything; women's sports, such as handbag-hurling; the display and sale of women's crafts, especially the ceramic art of Suzanne Bellamy, and the comprehensive garden tour, led by Kaye. The highlight of the day is the Grand Parade, an alternative version of all grand parades, and an excuse for spontaneous, mad, feminist theatre. Women come from all over for a pleasant day among friends.

A new phase is beginning for Moonraker Farm. However much we complain of being tied down here, the very success of what we've done so far keeps us going. Whenever we've been particularly battered by natural circumstance, such as a week of torrential rain, some other aspect asserts itself and pulls us back. Every winter, when it's cold and wet, we talk of leaving; then the blossom comes out, a fruit appears, the fog thins and brilliant sunshine strikes through...

And so many of our adventures have been shared by the women who've stayed here. Some of them write regularly, and if we ever do get that promised trip away, we know we have lesbian friends all over the world. We found there *are* women interested in getting 'back to basics' and I believe this trend will continue. In spite of our own ups and downs, we are part of a fluctuating, volatile, dynamic process.

We feel part of an important movement of social change: towards humanity and community, and away from greed and misery. Being human involves contact with the weather, green grass, animals, even dirt and mess. City people, hemmed in by asphalt and concrete, suffer 'country life deprivation' and need the country, and not just as escape. The country can come to the city in a positive way, and the city can be greened.

Women have to take their rightful place in the country. We belong to local organisations, and take part in community activities, often as a couple, even when this creates confusion. Kaye joined the town band and came home to tell me of the forthcoming Christmas party: wives to bring a plate! I'm happy to report there are several new *women* members of the band.

City people, hemmed in by asphalt and concrete, suffer 'country life deprivation' and need the country, and not just as escape.

Although our relationship has been tested here, we're still together and having fun. We've learned the discipline needed for the country, without, I hope, losing our sense of humour. The comedy scripts we write just get crazier. And we've done it all with ingenuity, rather than money.

It is different for women in the country. If you weren't born there, it's like beginning life all over again. We've learned so much: to build, design gardens, grow roses, care for animals, handle pythons, fix plumbing, mend fences, heal wounded birds, spin wool, discuss ideas, meet women of the world, put ideas into practice...

What more could anyone wish to do?

Not a Strange, Exotic Community

Jane Wilkinson

Born in Melbourne in 1958, Jane Wilkinson attended local government schools and completed an honours degree in English at Monash University. She then taught in rural Victoria for two years before returning to live in Melbourne for another four years. After gaining the degree of master of arts in English, she returned to rural Victoria in 1988 and married in 1991.

Jane Wilkinson worked with the Victorian Department of Education in various roles, first as a curriculum consultant, then gaining promotion to middle-management level. In 1994 she was acting associate principal of Horsham College, a secondary school of 1200 students. She moved to Wagga Wagga in New South Wales in late 1994 and simultaneously with sampling the delights of parenthood is completing a degree in Women's Studies. In June 1994 her and her husband's first child, Sarah was born.

I am a committed trade unionist and a member of the Australian Labor Party (ALP). I am a feminist. I come from an anglo saxon/celtic/eastern european background. I love theatre, films, music and literature and my idea of an ideal holiday is to spend a week by the beach, reading books, sleeping and socialising. I love the sea. So why am I living in inland Victoria, in a provincial town which until the 1993 federal election was the safest National Party seat in Australia? Where there are few women GP's and one woman lawyer and the local paper still advertises social 'do's' with the rider: 'Ladies, bring a plate.'

I was born in 1958 in the outer Melbourne suburb of Oakleigh. I was the third daughter. My mother was pleased to have three daughters. My father wanted a son.

My parents had bought a block of land in Clayton, a nearby suburb, in the early 1950s. My grandfather could not understand why his daughter and son-in-law had so foolishly invested their money in the 'bush'. Nowadays, Clayton is an ageing suburb, no longer outer suburban. Then, it had no footpaths, no macadamised roads, no sewerage and my mother had tremendous difficulty pushing the pram along. Years later, one of my mother's fellow workers reminisced about how he had spent his youth chasing rabbits over the area where our 1950s suburban weatherboard still stands.

My eldest sister kept her horse agisted in a nearby paddock and would go riding along the farmland where VFL (Victorian Football League) Park is now located.

...one of my mother's fellow workers reminisced about how he had spent his youth chasing rabbits over the area where our 1950s suburban weatherboard still stands.

I attended the local government primaryschool. It was what would now be called a 'multicultural' school. My friends were the children of the local Greek, Italian, Yugoslavian and Egyptian migrants. Many of their parents were, like my mother, process workers, although there were some anglo saxon children whose parents owned small businesses or had 'white collar' jobs.

I felt myself to be a peculiar hybrid, not really identifying with either the migrant or anglo saxon children. My mother had been born in Australia but her grandparents were Zionists who migrated from Hungary to Palestine and exchanged their Jewish name for the name of the village they had left behind. My grandparents were born in Palestine but emigrated to Australia a few years before my mother was born. Tragically, my grandmother died when my mother was still a baby and at the age of four my mother and her sister, along with my grandfather, returned to Palestine, where they lived until my mother was 20 years old. Thus English was not my mother's first language. Nonetheless, she retained a strong affinity for the country in which she had been born and returned to Australia with her sister as an adult.

My father was of anglo saxon and Irish background. His mother's parents had emigrated from England in the late nineteenth century. When he first arrived in Australia, his grandfather had worked as a strapper for an English lord who owned a stable of horses in Melbourne. My father's family were keen lovers of horse flesh and racing. The family home in Essendon which my great-grandfather built when he settled in Melbourne from England was full of trophies the family had won in England through horse and whippet racing. Thus from an early age Dad had a love of horses instilled in him. It was hardly surprising, then, that he joined the Victorian police force and became a mounted policeman.

I have vague but fond memories of going with my family to the mounted police stables in St Kilda Road, Melbourne and watching my father work his horse out, muck out its stable, saddle the horse, exercise it and brush it down. The smell of horse manure and straw, the sweat of the horses after they had been exercised, and the light filtering through the windows of what seemed to me, as a four-year-old, to be a huge indoor racecourse, left a strong impression.

When I was five, my parents separated. My father moved to inland New South Wales and eventually married the daughter of a farmer who kept a horse stud. My father bought the farm from his parents-in-law and achieved a long held dream. He had always wished to live in the country; my mother did not. The country was, for my mother, an alien land. The few family members she had, lived in Melbourne – it was her home.

We made one trip to the country prior to my parents' separation. I disliked it intensely – the soil was red and got into one's shoes and clothes. There was no sea a child could swim in to find relief from the intense, inland heat, only dams. As I sat on the wooden seat in the outside dunny, with my four year old legs swinging in the air, I could safely inspect strange, large insects crawling around the floor. I was terrified of crossing between the house and the toilet as there seemed to be bull ants all over the ground wherever I looked. I was convinced they would bite me.

...from a very young age, the country came to symbolise my father, and the city my mother.

No doubt my feelings about the trip were strongly coloured by the fact that I was picking up the unhappiness and strain between my parents. However, from a very young age it was a fact for me that the country came to symbolise my father, and the city my mother. When I first moved to the country as a young teacher I felt a great amount of guilt for I felt that, in a way, I was replicating my father's desertion of my mother. It took a long time for those feelings to go.

After that trip, we returned to Melbourne and I began school. My strongest memories of primaryschool are of intense boredom. I was six to ten months older than most students in my class (I turned six in July of the first year of my schooling), and prior to coming to school had been taught by my mother to read, write and do sums. I borrowed my older sisters' books and read anything I could get my hands on. I wondered if this was all that school was about.

I also resented the fact that the girls and boys were made to sit on the opposite side of the class and that it didn't seem to be acceptable for girls and boys to be friends without some implication that 'she/he had a crush on you'. At playtime this division remained. My best friend prior to starting school had been the boy across the road but he had gone to a different school. I thought that 'kiss chasey' and the other games many of the girls played were childish and I longed to be able to play with the boys. At home I played with my dolls and trucks. My great-aunt was a skilled tailor and her twin sister, my grandmother, an excellent handywoman who, in her seventies, had built a garage in her backyard and did all the household repairs. (She and my grandfather had separated when my father was small and Nana had reared Dad on her own.) I resented the artificial gap created between the boys and the girls and did not form any real friendships with boys again until senior highschool when it was acceptable for such friendships to occur.

In my highschool years I was fortunate enough to have a handful of teachers who challenged me intellectually. Huntingdale High in the early 1970s was staffed by a number of radical Monash University graduates. There were frequent strikes and I remember being bored with having to spend so many days at home. I don't recall a lot of resentment towards the teachers for their actions – although concern was expressed that the senior students' work was suffering. My mother by this time had worked in a factory for a number of years and I was conscious of how important the union was in her factory as a means of protecting workers from some of the bosses who attempted to ride roughshod over them. I was also conscious that my mother, as a single parent, was particularly vulnerable to being exploited. For example, some tradespeople assumed that, because she did not have a husband, they could quote exorbitantly high prices for repairs and get away with it. That my mother knew they were doing this and told them in no uncertain terms what she thought of them embarrassed me no end as a child, but now I look back and admire her courage.

I loved English and French at school but also enjoyed maths. I liked the fact that there was a logical pattern one could follow and that a clearcut answer could be found. However, I lacked confidence in my own abilities and, after having a couple of very poor teachers, dropped it at the end of Year 11. I don't recall getting any discouragement from teachers in maths and science, but nor do I recall any positive encouragement. In that way, despite the fact that it was a reasonable government school, Huntingdale High was fairly typical of most schools. Girls tended to do humanities, boys maths/science, and being a bright girl who liked to ask lots of questions was not the most comfortable position in which to find oneself. Thus university, with its intellectual challenges, opened up a new world to me. I found out that there were other people in the world who shared similar ideas about education. It was a boon to me.

I gained a teaching studentship which paid me a generous allowance (thus relieving my guilt feelings about my mother working to support me through university and which allowed me to complete an honours degree in arts). It tied me to the Victorian Education Department for three years, meaning that I could be sent anywhere in the state of Victoria.

'Anywhere' turned out to be Goroke, a small country town 370 kilometres west of Melbourne. It was a Prep to Year 10 college in a cropping and grazing area of Victoria. My dreams of teaching senior literature to eager Year 11 and 12 students were dashed. My dreams of teaching senior anything in fact, were gone. I had never heard of a consolidated school and where in the heck was Goroke, anyway? I have no doubt that the staffing officer who interrupted my holiday with the glad tidings had been asked this question a thousand times before. 'Oh, it's about three hours drive from Melbourne,' he assured me. It's four and a quarter hours. Try doing that every weekend for three years – mind you, some people did.

My first impressions of Goroke were of driving down the deserted main street one hot Sunday afternoon in January. At this time of the year, the countryside looks at its worst. There was no sign of life apart from a dog thumping its tail in the middle of the road. It didn't bother to get out of the way – really there was no need – we just drove around it.

There was no sign of life apart from a dog thumping its tail in the middle of the road. It didn't bother to get out of the way...

The teacher's house where I was to live had not been lived in for two years and was filthy. My mother, sister and I spent the afternoon cleaning it, removing spiders, cobwebs and dead flies from their mortuaries in the window ledges.

I was in culture shock for the first few weeks. There was no cinema, theatre, bookshop, butcher or supermarket. Many people drove in to the nearby provincial town to do their main grocery shopping. What did people do for entertainment? The hardest thing to get used to was the lack of anonymity – the fact that you were the teacher 24 hours a day, seven days a week. The only time I could escape from this reality was when I travelled back to Melbourne or spent a blissful few hours shopping in Horsham, which at least had 13 000 people, a reasonable number of shops, and where I was anonymous.

After two months of living in Goroke, I moved to Horsham and spent the next two years commuting in a car pool 140 kilometres a day to work. Since I had not played netball since I was 12 and had naively answered the persistent question of what sports did I play, with 'well, um, I like swimming and yoga', Horsham held out more social promise for me than Goroke. It allowed me to enjoy my teaching without feeling that I had to wear the label 'teacher' constantly. I grew fond of my students and struck a chord with one of my terrorist Year 9 boys through engaging him in in-depth conversations about possible repairs needed on my HR Holden. Though the students initially seemed alien and different from the kids with whom I had grown up (I never got used to some of the students' animated conversations about 'bunny bashing' on the weekends), I did discover that, oh cliché of clichés, they were very like kids all over the place. In general, they lacked the sophistication of city children but, on the other hand, they had a hard headed practicality and resourcefulness obtained from growing up in a geographically isolated environment which I, as a city person, lacked. I admired this quality.

I also discovered that Goroke had its fair share of interesting and diverse people. One of the best yoga teachers I have ever had lived there. I spent some enjoyable times at her house admiring how she and the friend who shared the house with her could stand on their heads for minutes at a time. She claimed this kept her fit and well and, since both women were incredibly fit and active in their late fifties, I could only agree.

I gained a transfer back to Melbourne two years later. The camaraderie amongst the school staff had been a great bonus. We were mainly a young staff and our social life tended to revolve around one another. The closeness and friendships we achieved at Goroke remain a bond today. I loved being back in the city, but missed this aspect of working life tremendously when I returned to Melbourne. I also realised that at Goroke I had had the opportunity to develop skills and experiences that I would not have had, had I begun teaching life in a large city school. At Goroke I was the only English and French teacher. I was in charge of a faculty budget (not a large one, admittedly, but that's not the point), and I had to make decisions about buying resources and writing curriculum. I taught all year levels and had a good deal of independence and freedom to teach as I chose. There were not the same opportunities for me in the city. I had to 'earn my stripes' as a teacher and there appeared to be a certain mystique surrounding the job of coordinating our large English faculty which I knew, from my limited experience at Goroke, was not deserved. Nonetheless I enjoyed teaching in a multicultural school where senior women teachers were a norm, not a rarity, and where coming from a background other than anglo saxon was common, not cause for racist comments.

...fulfilling the time honoured country tradition of bringing new blood to a town.

Four years later I took a deep breath and plunged back into country life. Having spent four years commuting up and down the Western Highway between Melbourne and Horsham, my boyfriend and I decided to give living together a try. Since he was a plant geneticist with little opportunity for a transfer and I was a teacher, with far more geographical mobility, the return to Horsham made sense. I was aware I was fulfilling the time honoured country tradition of bringing new blood to a town. It is a constant joke in the country (but also an important reality) that women teachers and nurses form a critically important role in providing partnerships for local country lads. It tends not to work the other way around much, although there are a handful of male teachers I know of who moved to a country town, married the local girl and stayed on. As a young female teacher, a woman is seen as fair game.

The women who marry into farming communities generally make a significant contribution to the community and often continue to bring in a very important second income which contributes significantly to off farm earnings. Yet this role is only slowly beginning to be recognised in the country and the women's earning capacity is still not valued in the way that income earned directly from a farm is. That is why the closure of the local hospital or school can be a disaster for a small town. The heart of the town is ripped out and those extra incomes are lost. Given the rural recession, this income may often be the only thing standing between a farm surviving and its being foreclosed.

Out of date attitudes towards women remain prevalent in country towns. I had a real concern about the effect of my move on my career. I was aware that in moving to Horsham I was restricting my career opportunities. Much to my surprise, this did not eventuate. I was offered a position as a curriculum consultant, working to develop what was then the new Victorian certificate of education (VCE). I was looking for new opportunities in my career; this was an ideal chance. I am conscious that had I been in Melbourne it would have been much more difficult for me to pick up such a job after only six years in teaching. The competition would have been much more fierce.

In 1992 I gained a promotion to a principal class position, and became one of two women in the subregion at a deputy principal level in the secondary system. There are no women principals in secondary schools in my area. That this is still the case is an indictment of our promotion system which until recently used seniority as the basis for promotion. Promotion through seniority is now abolished but old attitudes die hard. The discrimination against women in positions of power, particularly in the country, where there are far fewer senior women upon whom other women can look as role models, is now more subtle but just as pervasive. I was called 'ruthless' when I made a decision last year to appeal against initially not gaining promotion to a principal class position. I won my appeal, but I wondered at the time whether, had I been a man, I would have been so labelled. I doubt it.

In 1991 I made a decision to marry (and thus probably spend a good deal of my lifetime in the country). The decision was made from a position of financial independence – I had a flourishing career and so, in a sense, had choices that are not open to all women. My mother did not have the same level of choice. Having arrived in Australia at 20 with no English, my mother was deeply aware of the importance of a good education for her daughters and that it would give us the opportunities she had never had. I can never take for granted the opportunities I was given, and it has made me deeply conscious of and committed to ensuring, in my own small way, that those chances are there for all people, not just for those lucky enough to be born into a moneyed or privileged family.

Country life is tremendously different from life in the city. Neither is better than the other; they are simply different. Coming from the city, I felt the lack of access to resources, facilities and services deeply. Women in my town do not have access to a homebirthing unit. Their birthing choices are vastly curtailed. Until one or two years ago, we had to travel 200 kilometres to get a mammogram. On another level, we finally gained access to SBS (the Special Broadcasting Service) television a year or so ago. Given that my community is primarily monocultural, SBS often provides the only means by which country dwellers are exposed to the realities of our multicultural society. I found (and still find) the lack of ethnic diversity in my area one of the most difficult things to contend with. We have a small but strong Italian and Greek community, but not on the same scale as Melbourne. We also have a strong Koori community. Having grown up in an ethnically diverse area and coming from such a background myself, I miss the variety that living in the city provides.

Correlated to this lack of diversity is an intolerance of other ethnic groups that can be legitimised only by the fact that the people expressing these views have never lived anywhere else which would challenge such a viewpoint. I am grateful I grew up in the city and had the opportunity to mix with such a wide range of people. I have lived the reality of multiculturalism and believe that this has made me far more tolerant in my attitudes.

I am far more involved in the community here than I was in the city, and I have a far stronger sense of community than I did as an adult living in Melbourne.

Since neither my partner nor I have family in Horsham, our friends have become, in a sense, surrogate families. I rely on them in a way that I did not when I lived in Melbourne. There is also a large number of clubs and activities which are generally open to anyone, especially in a larger town. I am far more involved in the community here than I was in the city, and I have a far stronger sense of community than I did as an adult living in Melbourne. Since country people need to make their own entertainment, amateur theatre, sport, bookclubs and similar activities assume an importance that they do not have in the city. They are not 'add ons' but a critical means by which socialising occurs. Again, it is the resourcefulness of country people, the way in which the isolation of the location forces people to become more resourceful, that is one of the most admirable qualities of country living.

The Women's Movement is both similar and different. The issue of lack of access to resources and facilities is a general one for country dwellers, and would have to be one of the major issues facing country women. Resourcefulness can take a person only so far. A review of women's health services in our region revealed a critical difference between the women who lived in Ballarat (a major provincial town one and half hours drive from Melbourne) and those who lived further away. Whilst the women in Ballarat wanted more information about the services available to them, the women outside Ballarat complained about not having these services at all and were concerned about getting them. For women on farms who do not even have the 'luxury' of living close to basic services, the mode of delivery of such services is also particularly critical.

...stories of their husband keeping the keys to the family car, so they could not drive into the local town...

Tied to the lack of services is the issue of living in a country town where everybody knows everyone else, or living out on a farm where a female may go for days without seeing anyone else apart from her own family. A friend of mine, a journalist, ran a segment on the local radio several years ago on domestic violence in rural areas, particularly on farms. After the program she received a number of calls from women who refused to identify themselves but who lived on farms where such violence was occurring. They told stories of their husband keeping the keys to the family car, so they could not drive into the local town, or of being accompanied by their husband to the local town when they made their weekly shopping trips. They felt there was no one they could go to who would support them, even if they could manage to get out, as they lived in an area where the husband was a local identity and revealing his violence would disrupt the close knit farming community in which they lived. The attitude that 'those sorts of things don't happen in our community – they happen in the city or in bigger towns' is one that is commonly known to any socialworker who lives in a country town. It is a self-protective mechanism ensuring that the silence surrounding these issues is maintained and thus the denial of reality can continue.

In 1993 the Victorian government announced a 50 per cent cut in funding to family planning clinics. Where do young girls go when they want objective advice on contraception? To go to their local general practitioner who sees all the family, and where the receptionist is undoubtedly known to her, is hardly an attractive option. Travelling to a larger centre may mean a day off school and, given the lack of public transport in the country, may not be viable anyway. Hence, remoteness and lack of access to basic facilities are key issues facing country women. That is why the reduction of public services to country areas is particularly detrimental to country women.

Lack of prominent and diverse female role models in the country is another issue. That is not to say that there are not a large number of country women who have been successful, either on their own terms, or in the public's eyes. There are women who run successful businesses and farms. However, the reality is that in those areas that are seen as prominent in the public domain of country life, for example, law, medicine, business, the overwhelming majority are male. Though over 50 per cent of doctors and lawyers being trained are now female, this reality is not reflected in country areas, where it is far more difficult to attract such professionals. Despite the vast majority of our primaryschool teachers being female, our local town has no permanent female deputy principal or principal in the three main primaryschools. What message does that transmit to young people about where the real power in our society lies?

As for my own activism in relation to these issues, I was, until mid-1993, a member of the committee of management of a women's health information service in our area. The service was set up through federal funds to provide health services catering for women in every region in the nation. I established and coordinated a committee of women teachers in my area, which was responsible for organising professional development for women teachers. Our hope was to encourage more women to apply for promotion positions within the teaching service. I enjoy the solidarity that being a member of such groups gives me, as well as a sense that we are doing something positive for women, through breaking down the sense of isolation.

Two and a half years ago I was elected as a union representative to represent secondary teachers from my subregion at our state council. I followed in the footsteps of a male councillor who had represented us for over 20 years. I felt I was breaking new ground, as union representatives in my part of the country tend to be male. I was fortunate to have tremendous support and advice from the former councillor. This stood me in good stead, particularly in the early days when I wondered what I had taken on.

I ran for election as a union councillor as I saw it to be one of the few ways I could gain experience in the union movement while living in a rural area. I don't know that I would have been forced into such activism had I remained in the city where my beliefs were commonly shared. Being an active trade unionist in a very conservative country town is not easy. I suspect that being a woman and a prominent unionist is even less acceptable. Nonetheless, I know it is important to articulate my beliefs, particularly whilst living in an area where such beliefs are often not represented.

I joined the local branch of the ALP three years ago. Again, I don't know that I would have done this had I stayed in the city, but living in an electorate where at the 1992 state election the local National Party member achieved 76 per cent of the vote, I felt the need to meet with people who shared my political views. Handing out ALP how-to-vote cards in such an electorate really tests your political commitment! In Melbourne, I was surrounded by people who shared my political views. In the country, I am conscious that I am in a minority and that I must watch what I say and to whom I voice my opinions.

Handing out ALP how-to-vote cards in such an electorate really tests your political commitment!

Living in the country has forced me to become more active and resourceful in a way which I may not have achieved had I remained in the city. It has not radicalised my politics, but has given them a sharper edge and forced me to act on my beliefs. I can speak from self-knowledge about the negative impact that the cutting back of the public sector has on ordinary people. I know through personal experience the detrimental effects this has on rural communities and believe my voice is more powerful for having experienced this reality.

I am pleased I grew up in the city. It gave me a different experience of life that adds to my life in the country. At times it makes me feel like the alien and outsider I am. Far from narrowing my options, in a curious way living in the country has widened them. It has forced me to seek out experiences that I may never have tried otherwise. It has made me aware of the strength of community and the power of group action.

I have maintained strong links with family and friends in Melbourne. These links are important for me in both reminding me of who I am and where I have come from. Many of these people knew me before I moved to Horsham and provide a link back to life pre country. Also, I know that I have an 'escape route', when I need a 'fix' of city life. In that way I am fortunate, for many country people do not have access to experiencing life in the city in the way that I am able.

I have now reached a point after six years of country living where I feel I have adjusted to the very different lifestyle. I have enjoyed and been enriched by these past six years. It has given me a range of opportunities and experiences that I doubt I would have experienced had I remained in Melbourne. It has sharpened my political consciousness and provided me with the chance to work in solidarity with groups of women and the union movement in a way I had never envisaged. It has forced me to clarify, articulate and defend my values and, even more importantly, act upon them. I've discovered an inner resourcefulness I didn't know I had.

I now understand why a farmer's favourite topic is the weather and I see the knife edge on which rural communities live when what looks like being a bumper harvest turns into a disaster. I read the local paper with great interest. This is not some strange, exotic community I am reading about – it is the community I live in and will probably continue to live in for some time to come. I enjoy driving back from Melbourne to home and am discovering the delights and tedium of renovating our Edwardian house.

I will never be in my heart a country woman, but I enjoy and make the most of what country living has to offer. I feel that I have contributed something to the community which is different but valuable, and I look forward to continuing to do so.

Urban Consciousness and the Extravaganzas of Nature

Bev Roberts

Born in Adelaide, Bev Roberts has lived for most of her adult life in Melbourne. As a 'mature-age' student she studied history at the University of Melbourne and later tutored there. She has subsequently worked as assistant editor of *Meanjin,* as Victorian Literature Field Officer, and as coordinator of the Victorian Writers' Centre. She has published poetry, articles and reviews in many Australian literary and other magazines, and in anthologies. Two collections of her poems have been published: *The Transvestite Next Door* (Abalone Press, 1986) and *The Exorcism Trip* (Pariah Press, 1991).

For more than a decade Bev Roberts has been active in the community writing movement, working mostly with women's groups. She lives with her partner, two dogs and a cat in a small township on the south-west coast of Victoria.

Moving from the city to the country is more than a journey.

I told my mother I was leaving the city and going to live on a sand dune on the west coast. She said: 'Oh. But what about the snakes?'

I told my inner urban friends. They said: 'Oh. But won't you become isolated? Lose touch with reality? Won't your writing suffer?'

I told some women friends. They said: 'Oh. Won't you be afraid? Out there.'

Out there.

It might be when a howling wind is lashing through the trees, or when we see the world suddenly disappear behind the thick stripes of rain that rush towards us then batter our iron roof. It might be the nights when the sea roars and pounds itself on the sand, or when lightning rips up the darkness and the crash of thunder reverberates in our bones. These are the times when we are reminded that we are City Women, that we have not yet come to terms with the forces and elements that rampage out in the vast space of the countryside. Away from the protective nestling of city life, we feel vulnerable and exposed in that space. Some atavistic fear prickles...

But that's to speak of the extremes and extravaganzas of nature. In general, and in the ordinary, I have noted that here in the country we have lost some of the fears we carried with us. I see one measure of this in the different quality of our sleep. In the city we maintained an alertness within sleep: we slept like our dogs, with one ear up, waiting for the strange sound. Do all City Women sleep this way? I thought so in my poem 'Her Night Thoughts' -

In the mid-night
that time of deep quivering silence
when you think you could hear
the plants growing
outside the window,
she lies awake
anticipating other sounds:
the shuff of a foot,
of cloth rubbing,
a breath,
the slow turning of a knob,
a prising scrape of metal.

Gran taught her about dogs –
don't be afraid, they'll smell it.
She thinks of out there,
everywhere,
in the shadow moving darkness,
men's nostrils twitching
with the scent of women's fear

Now, after four years out of the city, we sleep undisturbed in noisy darkness, knowing the sounds of surf, wind, night-birds, and knowing that the rattle of door or window is only that.

City Woman. Country Woman. I wouldn't call myself either of these.
I think of the words Country Woman and of the connotations they have for me. Mostly literary, from Mary Grant Bruce to Barbara

Baynton: from the romantic to the realistic with nothing in between unless it's the archetype of a CWA member, proffering tea and scones. Country Woman as strong, capable, tireless, isolated, stoic. Country Woman as having a deep and strong sense of place, if not always a symbiotic relationship with the familiar place/land. At ease in and part of the natural world.

...a tiny coastal township which qualifies as 'country' despite being within 20 kilometres of a major provincial city and not much more than an hour's drive from Melbourne.

I'm not a Country Woman. For more than four years I've lived in a tiny coastal township which qualifies as 'country' despite being within 20 kilometres of a major provincial city and not much more than an hour's drive from Melbourne. I've changed a lot in those four and a bit years, but I couldn't call myself a Country Woman – and I know that I never can, even if I stay here for the rest of my life. The urban consciousness, the urban self, is inescapable, immutable.

I'm thinking of words like urban: urban and urbane, metropolis and metropolitan, cosmopolitan, city. Thinking of some of the connotations of City Woman... sharp, sophisticated, self-assured, commanding in her dealing with people. City Woman in expensive elegance, walking confidently through the vast atria of grey glass skyscrapers and taking the elevator to lofty office suites. City Woman at home and at ease in the city, her relationship with this place probably stronger than any other place.

I wouldn't call myself a City Woman though I've never lived anywhere other than cities until I came here. Three cities, to be precise: Adelaide, Melbourne and London. I don't call myself a City Woman because what I think of as city is the centre, the core or heart of large conurbations, and I've never fully established a relationship with those cores. I've lived close to them, in inner urban suburbs, but have always felt this as the periphery, living on the fringe.

I think I may have to call myself a Suburban Woman. Reflecting now, it seems that my formative years in suburbia were more truly formative than I'd realised: especially in shaping that particular meaning of 'city' as the core or heart, marking the distance and difference between it and the suburbs on the edge. The City as destination, a place to which journeys are often or sometimes made, a place where one goes to work, to shop, etc. The relationship with the city as one of familiarity but not feeling or knowing.

I grew up surrounded by the anxiety and repression of the middling classes in their suburban fortresses, their HOMES. The Home was a separate country – a small secessionist fragment from the surrounding city. The closest relationship with place was with the Home, where every room, every piece of furniture, every object was known, possessed, loved. Every part of the garden too. The Home was the territory of Suburban Woman.

(I write this in the past tense because it's my history, but I suspect it also talks about the present for others.)

Suburban woman was uneasy in The City. Her way of life was intensely, stiflingly privatised, focused in on the family in the home. She liked to go inside her house and shut the gate and doors and have everything to herself and as she wanted it – to have ORDER. Outside the home was DISORDER, especially in The City where there was a life, a kind of activity, which she did not understand. Outside there was uncleanliness, the danger of infection, and GERMS. A powerful and telling metaphor: The City is full of germs (in cinemas, in toilets, in cafes, in trains and trams). How often I heard this in my childhood!

In London I met an elderly Australian woman who was carrying on her world travels a bottle of disinfectant, a lavatory cleaning brush and a smaller brush for scrubbing baths and hand-basins.

In an Australian city, my friend's elderly aunt lapsed into dottiness which was marked by her attempts to catch city-bound trains, carrying a mop and a bucket.

Suburban Woman thought/thinks The Country is also extremely dirty and full of germs, but these are of a different order. They are associated with shit and blood and flies and maggots, part of the disorder of Nature which is out there beyond civilisation.

I'm not at all like my pictures of Suburban Woman. But that formative experience has left its impact; I am forever, in some small, deep part of my being, apprehensive and not at home in cities. More urbane and sophisticated than my mother, I know what goes on in cities; I have worked in cities; have spent years of days in cities; have eaten, drunk, danced, kissed and slept in cities. I have felt enormous enjoyment and happiness in cities. But I have always been happiest when I have gone into my house on the fringe and shut the gate and the doors and...

...shit and blood and flies and maggots, part of the disorder of Nature which is out there beyond civilisation.

Cities are shaped and made and ruled by men.

Since I became a country-dweller I have become squeamish, or do I mean more sensitive? Frequently driving to and from Melbourne on the busy highway I begin to see the road as a killing field, lined with the smashed bodies of rabbits, birds, foxes and the occasional lizard, snake or possum. (And, increasingly, chooks which have escaped from cages on city-bound trucks, suggestive of a host of other horrors.) On the roads closer to home there are always tragedies, many of them dogs and cats from farms and outlying houses. With time I do not become less sensitive, more accustomed to these sad little bodies. With time – and perhaps with the accumulating numbers – I become more sensitive, less able to look at the mess as I drive by.

Year after year I watch the generations of animals in the paddocks, delight in the crazy leaping of lambs and the serious-playground-stuff jostling of the brown and white calves. Now I look through these pictures at the butchers' windows and supermarket meat departments and walk quickly away.

Is anthropomorphism the problem, deeply ingrained in the urban consciousness? I was considering this when I wrote 'Swallows':

If this is last year's swallow pair
returned to nest again
on the front porch lamp
then it may be right to say
the magpie was grieving,
standing still at the road side
by the crushed bird
with the wing that moved
in a sad parody of flight
as my car passed.

The country is, as I'd always suspected, always been conditioned to believe, a place of violence and matter of fact death. I cannot be like Suburban Woman and hide from reality inside my happily-ever-after home, or encounter violence and death as distant abstractions on pages or screens.

As I write I can hear the sounds of not-so-distant gunfire. It's a beautiful morning, just past dawn. Autumn mists are already starting to rise and clear. Now the men by the lake can see the ducks so they lift their guns and shoot. All morning we hear the guns. There's nowhere to hide from the sound.

A strange thing is happening: I am becoming involved in local politics. The strangeness is not to do with the *politics* since I've always been an intensely political person, but with the *involvement*, because the expression of my political concern has rarely been in an organisational or public context. It might be said that I've moved from political passivity to political activity, and it might be asked what caused this transformation.

At one level I'd say that away from the city things have seemed sharper and clearer. This is certainly the case with local issues, which are smaller in scale and therefore easier to identify and understand. At the local or regional level it is easier not just to identify the issues but to see where the power lies, and to recognise the opportunities for involvement.

Away from the city I also seem to have acquired a new and clarifying perspective on the wider issues. I don't think I can work this out, except to say that there's something about the quiet and the uncluttered space around me now. In comparison, living in the city was being surrounded by white noise which fogged thought, and my mind seemed constrained by the cityscape – hemmed in by buildings.

At another level – that of gut feeling – I can see myself as a textbook case, a cliché of political behaviour, having been spurred into action by threats to my own interests. When my relatively untouched environment of coast, dunes and wetlands was threatened on all sides by various proposals for 'development', I became aware for the first time of the feeling I have for this place. I joined the local residents' association and was soon a member of the committee. I became more familiar with local government in the area and was appointed to council advisory committees.

There isn't one high profile woman in this regional city, and no more than a handful in any positions of influence. Men run everything – even the girls schools.

As I edge my way towards the centre of power I am discovering the crude reality of provincial politics: the total domination of men. There isn't one high profile woman in this regional city, and no more than a handful in any positions of influence. Men run everything – even the girls schools. I find there's a great and uncomfortable contrast between meetings I attend here and meetings in the city. The problems aren't just that suddenly and for the first time I'm so conspicuously one of the minority, so obviously tokenistic. The real problems are in the blatant ways the men assume and assert their dominance and control: running their bit of the world, advancing their own interests, looking after their mates – completely disregarding the existence of women.

The blatancy, and the discrimination, would be challenged (and, one hopes, defeated) in The City. Here there's no challenge. Most of the women I've met seem compliant or resigned, or frustrated and bitter. Some of them tell me I'm brave, trying to break into the men's world. Others think I'm just foolish. Depressing: it's like stepping into a time-warp, hearing the voices of my mother's generation speaking to their daughters 20 or 30 years ago.

If I want to continue with my involvement in local politics, whether brave, foolish or futile, I will have to learn to control my anger. Here, or 'out here', I cannot say what I think to these men.

An important regional committee was appointed here a few months ago. Of the sixteen members only three are women and they are to represent the areas of the arts, health and welfare. Of course – 'Woman's Issues'! So far, none of these areas has made it to the agenda of the committee's meetings.

Has feminism ever moved beyond cities?

Wildlife and the Wild Woman are both endangered species.

Clarissa Pinkola Estés

There is also the complementary or apparently contradictory desire for detachment, for disengagement.

Not City Woman or Country Woman or Suburban Woman, I am a woman who has become tired of city life and gone off to live in the country. 'City' means many things which all seem to begin with 'c' – confinement, crowding, complexity, conflict, confusion. 'Country' means space, isolation, simplicity, clarity, the absence of everything associated with city. I have found this on the dunes, with Bass Strait stretching to the horizon on one side of me and a long vista of wetlands, paddocks and trees on the other.

> *I am a woman who has become tired of city life and gone off to live in the country.*

'Country' means a place where I can be by myself and be myself. A place where the Wild Woman might be found – where it seems important that she would be found.

I am trying to rid myself of what now feels like the useless clutter, the detritus of a lifetime's urban experience. I have discovered in the middle of my life what Clarissa Pinkola Estés discovered at the beginning of hers –

Rather than chairs and tables, I preferred the ground, trees and caves...

I have a lot of work to do on detaching myself from my city ways and habits. I need to concentrate on bringing in the focus of my mind, gradually moving from the huge and general to the small and particular. I want to be able to see a blade of grass move, and to see the ant which has moved it. And to hear -

In this place
what I first took for silence
is now filled with sound.
I know the various voices of the waves, the cries by which I have named the birds.

There is always wind keening through dunes.
On still days the crabs click
under turned rocks.

I am learning how one becomes part of a place through the successive stages of naming. In the first stage, when we were strangers, we invented our own names for the houses, people, birds, trees, plants, dogs and points along the pathways of this township. This was a private language. In the second stage, when we began to meet and know people, we learnt the names used by the township people – the local language. With this knowledge we could become part of our little society and could have a closer understanding of our environment. In the third stage we learn the universal language: botanical names, classification of shells, species of birds.

In the city these things are abstractions. In the country they are lived and felt.

In the country I am intensely aware of living and feeling. And increasingly aware of the kinds and degrees of relationship which can be developed and experienced with all that is represented by and contained in 'place'.

And ultimately I think this is what's important. I've found the male construct of a City/Country dichotomy to be just that: a male construct. A metaphor for tension and conflict between the poles of engagement and disengagement – which I think really meant an either/or situation of choice between power over people in The City vs power over nature in The Country.

City/Country is about the possibility of harmony, about the diversity of broadening and balancing of experience.

I don't find it a matter of tension or conflict, or of polarities. City/Country is about the possibility of harmony, about the diversity of broadening and balancing of experience. There are, of course, many constants in women's lives, whether in urban or rural environments. But there are different ways of living and being in City and Country, and those who are able to know both are indeed fortunate.

A new perspective. At night I stand on my dune under the enormous dome of sky and see far away on the horizon a glowing smudge, a cinder smouldering in the darkness. The City.

Note: The poems 'Her Night Thoughts' and 'Swallows' are quoted from my book *The Exorcism Trip*, Pariah Press, 1991. The lines from Clarissa Pinkola Estés are from her *Women Who Run with the Wolves*, Rider, 1992.

Up and Out of the Kitchen Sink

Kath Davey

Kath Davey has worked in community development, personnel management, social planning, rural affairs and adult education. Born in 1945 in Kew, Victoria, she has lived and worked in Melbourne, Albury-Wodonga, Lake Blowering, Gippsland and the United Kingdom. She is currently completing a masters (sic!) degree (on rural feminist activism) in Women's Studies and holds a bachelor of arts and an associate diploma of administration, all completed part-time as a mature-age student whilst juggling paidwork, community activism and childrearing.

One of Kath Davey's main projects at present is to find a name for herself that is not part of the patriarchy. She has a daughter, a son and a granddaughter as well as horses and dogs.

My childhood was in suburban Melbourne in the 1940s and 1950s, youngest of five children in a crowded and fraught home where the parents fought continuously and bitterly. This was the time of the post-war baby boom and the encouragement of women to remain in the home and be efficient, proper housewives and mothers. My mother embraced the role of mother but seemed to struggle totally alone against the confines of marriage. She missed the supportive wave of the Women's Movements early or later in the century. The daughter of a country bank manager and a strong Presbyterian, she had come to the city in the early 1930s to become a nurse. She had not long been qualified when, at the age of 26, she married a young man a few years her senior and from a strong urban Irish/German Catholic background. Her freedom and independence seemed to disappear from that moment.

Their marriage of almost three decades was a battle-ground. No doubt it began with amity and affection, as most marriages do, but time, events and outside pressures combined to pit the partners against each other. My mother was a fighter and did not take easily to the dictates of the Catholic Church and my father's family. Five children in fairly rapid succession was the result of religious oppression. She loved us all dearly but told us she would have been happy to stop at one child, if she had been allowed or knew how to. Contraception was not easily available in the 1930s, 1940s or 1950s in Australia. Catholics were certainly not allowed to use it. In the early 1940s, my mother performed an abortion on herself in the bedroom – her third pregnancy in rapid succession but certainly not the last.

If she had been born in my generation, my mother would have been able to limit her number of children without her husband's permission, to work, use childcare, leave him if she wished, go to a refuge, get a divorce, a pension, in fact all the options women have struggled for and won in a few short decades. However, these things were out of her reach. Her only option was to stay. If she left, she would lose her children. She would have nowhere to go, no money, no pension, no maintenance. Such supports were available only to women whose husbands left them and he would not do that. So the battle raged through our childhood. When my mother's fighting spirit became too much for my father and for the neighbours in our eastern Melbourne suburb, he had her committed to a mental institution and declared insane. One of my earliest and most vivid memories is of the police coming to our home to take my mother forcibly away. I did not know her crime then but I do now – she refused to give in.

In the early 1940s, my mother performed an abortion on herself in the bedroom – her third pregnancy in rapid succession but certainly not the last.

Several bouts of some months in such institutions and unknown numbers of shock treatments did not break her spirit entirely – though it certainly did bruise it. She returned to the family home, set herself up in a separate room to my father (the verandah if there was no other option), and vowed she would stay until the last child had left home.

I (we) did not really believe her at the time but, true to her word, she left my father the day after I left home at age 20. I was the youngest and last to leave, the others having already dispersed to jobs and lives throughout Australia. My mother went to the hop fields of Eurobin in north east Victoria as a casual picker, a job she found through an advertisement in the *Weekly Times*. I realise only now how brave she was – 55, penniless, not having worked for 30 years, taking a couple of suitcases and heading off alone. Though I suspect she loved it and felt free for the first time in 30 years.

During our childhood, my mother was a great storyteller. The stories she told were of her childhood in rural Western Australia and Victoria. They sustained her and inspired me. Horses and dogs featured large and her love for her animal companions continued all her life. In great detail, over and over, she told us of the lifestyle of the country: visits to farms, horse-drawn vehicles, picnics, shows, entertaining visitors. One of my best loved stories was of her, at age 16, driving a Tin Lizzie (Ford) from Victoria to Queensland with her mother and father and how, when the car became bogged on a lonely mountainside, they thrilled to the sound of a bullocky's swearing and whip-cracking coming slowly up the hill till he reached them and hauled them out.

At 69 years of age, my mother returned to Rupanyup, the small rural town in Western Victoria where her father had been a bank manager and where she had lived during her highschool years. She stayed there until she died at 82 years old, obviously feeling she had returned home. Small towns being what they are, many of her old acquaintances were still there and welcomed her back.

These legacies from my mother, refusal to bow to any man, love of bush and animals, fierce belief in women's independence all compounded to give me a fierce sense of justice, of self-worth...

I gained my romantic notion of the bush not from my mother alone. My primaryschool education oozed patriotism, steeped us in Dorothea MacKellar, Henry Lawson and Banjo Paterson, sunburnt plains, heroism, horses and a fierce sense of justice. My mother reinforced this by reading us poems such as the 'Ballad of the Drover' (and somehow we came to feel sadder about the horse and dog that drowned than for the man) and giving us Mary Grant Bruce books for Christmas and birthdays. Norah of Billabong was an early heroine of mine.

These legacies from my mother, refusal to bow to any man, love of bush and animals, fierce belief in women's independence (though, contrarily, she didn't like women's libbers), all compounded to give me a fierce sense of justice, of self-worth and to focus my dreams on a life in the country. Ironically, my father also reinforced these views through his working-class Melbourne origins. However, his refusal to support any of his four daughters to undertake tertiary education proved to be the major conflict between him and me and taught me my biggest lesson in life – that you don't have to do what those in authority tell you, particularly if they are men. We were all talented students, perhaps gaining solace and identity from schoolwork achievements to make up for some of the lack of pleasantness at home. When I completed Year 11, leaving certificate, I was told by my father to go to work like all the other girls. My brother had just matriculated and was to be supported by my father to go to university – the common belief being that boys must be educated as they would have to support a family, girls would marry and be supported. My mother wished me to continue at school, believing girls should have an education too, but she had no money whatsoever.

I fought with my father and refused to leave school. He didn't throw me out of home but would not support my matriculation studies so I paid for them myself, working several part-time jobs as a housecleaner and shop assistant. Ironically, my brother never did complete his university education, chafing against the pressures of a course in chemical engineering which he hated because he really wanted to do politics or mathematics. In common with my sisters, all my tertiary studies were undertaken part-time in later life. Also ironically, the four girls of our family have all been fully or partly responsible for raising children whereas my brother has not.

In 1972 I gave birth to my first child, a daughter. I was 27 years old, living in Cheltenham in Melbourne, and a confirmed city dweller. After matriculating I had worked as a personnel management trainee with Massey-Ferguson, studied arts part-time at their sponsorship, married, travelled overseas for two years and worked for four years as personnel officer with Gillette (Australia), part of a multinational corporate empire. Life had been full and interesting. I felt in control until my baby daughter arrived and let me know who was the real boss in this household.

This was only a few short years before maternity leave became an accepted practice. I left the full-time paid workforce. Submerged in the suburbs, in love with my baby but without stimulating company or challenge, I fretted for excitement and adventure. This was the time of Rachel Carson, Germaine Greer and Ralph Nader. Also of Whitlam. Noisy, crowded, polluted cities seemed no way to live. If I was to be home with a baby, surely that would be better in the country. So in January 1974 we moved to Albury-Wodonga, the newly declared national growth centre, the city in the country as it was dubbed.

Once in the country, I discovered a number of things: particularly that a country suburb can be the same as a city one if you know no one and your self-confidence has slipped down the kitchen sink with the washing up water. The air might have been cleaner but I was just as lonely and just as isolated as I had been in Melbourne. This was just before playgroups blossomed as a way for new mothers and their children to meet and I was at a complete loss to know how to meet people. I walked the local streets with my toddler in the pusher, played solitary swing games with her in the local park, but never seemed to meet a single soul.

Although I did not wish to return to the full-time paid workforce, I was also extremely concerned that bright young men would be forging past me in the personnel management career stakes. It was the time of the Whitlam government's education reforms. Tertiary fees had been abolished and a scheme called the Married Women's Retraining Scheme (forerunner to National Employment and Training – NEAT) was established. This would give me a precious $12 per week to pay for books and other sundries to support study. My thinking in those days was as traditional as many and, although I intended to resume a career one day, I didn't see it as a priority to use precious housekeeping money for my own education. Buoyed by my $12 per week income, I returned to study for an associate diploma of administration at the then Riverina College of Advanced Education in Albury.

This had a number of side effects: it revitalised my flagging spirits, brought me into contact with a wider range of people than I had ever known, and introduced me to academic knowledge at a time when my life experience badly need a theoretical base. My original intention had been to upgrade my personnel management skills whilst out of the full-time workforce. However, part-way through studying politics and sociology I became involved in the establishment of playgroups and childcare centres, the Women's Movement and Labor Party (ALP) politics. My life exploded with people, ideas and I discovered activism. I realised that everything is connected to everything else and vowed never to return to private enterprise until I had worked for government, union and community. (I am still out.) I was nearly 30 and, for the first time in my life, friendships with women blossomed, interesting and interested women all becoming concerned about their role as mothers, wives, workers and citizens. Over morning coffee, lunches, at playgroup and the swimming pool we discussed life, our lot, politics and the world. Discussions became shared understandings, understandings developed into friendship, awareness of the world and our part in it, awareness developed into activism. Most of us were struggling to raise young children as well as our aspirations for life. Friendships grew, marriages stumbled, as we supported each other through our childrearing and our activism for the Labor Party, for women's refuges, family planning clinics, childcare centres, education access, and so on.

...for the first time in my life, friendships with women blossomed, interesting and interested women all becoming concerned about their role as mothers, wives, workers and citizens.

The strength and energy of our group of women was not only noticed by us. We were changing. A number of the husbands started to become very nervous, their security as dominant partners threatened. One took his wife off to Adelaide, another bought an outlying farm, and mine took a job as a forest ranger on an isolated ranger station on Lake Blowering, last dam in the Snowy Mountains Scheme. With a three-year-old and a five-week-old baby I left my new found activism and friends and headed off to the mountains, part of me looking forward to immersing myself in rural pursuits, the other terrified at the social isolation for which I was heading.

For the next two years I indulged in what I now call my 'stoneground, wholemeal' phase of life, as many of us did in the mid- to late-1970s.

I raised children, acquired a sheep and some cows, spun and dyed wool, grew vegies and flowers, baked bread and pies, bottled fruit and jam. I felt a long way from my confident, jet-setting days as a career woman in the city. I stood in my gumboots hanging out nappies against a backdrop of sky, mountains and forests. Overhead in the still air trailed the vapour of the jets flying between Melbourne and Sydney. A few years before I had been on those planes, flying from state to state as part of my daily work. How life changes I thought.

My sanity was my study: completing my associate diploma by correspondence in the splendid isolation of a forest ranger station surrounded by pine forest, mountains and lake, the only other humanbeing, apart from my family, being the caretaker at the camp. Many a rural woman has had to complete her studies in circumstances such as mine: 3.00 am, textbook on one arm, feeding baby on the other; trying to fathom the intricacies of computer studies without ever having seen one; fabricating assignments on organisational development that required research on a group of 12 people by using my husband, the caretaker and myself as four people each (my only other choice was to use kangaroos, wombats or emus).

I stood in my gumboots hanging out nappies against a backdrop of sky, mountains and forests. Overhead in the still air trailed the vapour of the jets flying between Melbourne and Sydney.

When I had announced to my friends in Albury that we were moving to the forest ranger station, one of my best friends (she is still) announced that she thought this would be the best thing that ever happened to my marriage. She was right, but not in the way she intended. After 18 months of isolation I had had plenty of time to consider the previous 10 years and the changes that had happened to my husband and myself. Being alone meant having to find myself in ways that I had never dared consider. Many an afternoon I sat in the big picture windows of the ranger's house, gazing at one of the most superb views of lake, mountain and sky you could wish for but feeling empty and deeply unhappy. Or I walked through the pine forests with my chattering three-year-old and my baby in a sling. Many women come to awareness of themselves through talking with others. They were triggers indeed, but I came to my own awareness through not being with others, through having to face things I had not wanted to face and had been able to shield through social activity and busyness. A little over two years after we had left Albury to go to the ranger station I was back, separated and working full-time, a sole parent with two small children to care for. My time in the forest had been well spent and, yes, it had been the best thing that ever happened to my marriage. I finally grew up and took control of my life at thirty-three.

Back in Albury as a sole parent, I discovered a whole new meaning to living outside cities. My women friends were there to welcome me back and to support me though the pain and turmoil of marriage breakup, returning to full-time work, settling children into new childcare arrangements. Some of them had been through the same mill. Living in a regional city had some really practical advantages for me. My work, my daughter's school, my son's family daycare, our home, the shops were all within a few minutes of each other, significantly decreasing the hassles of organising life for myself and my children. Had I been living in the city I am sure I would not have been able to cope – there would have been at least an hour extra at the end of each day for travel between work, childcare, school and so on that would not have enabled me to survive.

I had been fortunate that my studies enabled me to obtain a job in a new career in community development and I found myself in one of life's most fortunate positions: doing what you most want to do *and* being paid for it. Feminism and my women friends sustained and inspired me. When I really felt I couldn't cope with the emotional hassles of a marriage breakup, a friend took to coming around in the afternoon before I finished work, picking up the children, cleaning the house, lighting the fire and, most importantly, being there for a drink and a talk. Without her help and presence over those months I would never have survived. She, some time previously, had received the same sort of assistance from me. This became a pattern amongst us women as one by one the marriages disintegrated in pain and hurt. Over the years I have repaid the support of the women who helped me by opening my home to other women who would arrive on my doorstep at any hour of the day or night, in need of a bed, a drink, a listening ear. I cannot know if this would have happened in the city. I think our physical nearness to each other and the bonds that had been created by our struggles and shared oppression may have contributed to the situation. Perhaps in the city we would have turned to family. Perhaps not.

The 1980s became a vital and interesting time for me, focusing on women's issues. I was employed by the Albury-Wodonga Development Corporation to find ways of helping newcomers settle into the national growth centre, which Albury-Wodonga had become. Five thousand new people a year were coming to the town, most of them young, newly established families with husbands in work and mothers in the home with small children. My own experience of motherhood and isolation proved invaluable in finding ways to help settle newcomers, particularly women. Visiting housebound, socially isolated women fuelled my feminism as I came to realise how trapped they were by the modern day dream of a new home, children, husband and their own frustration and irritability at not being able to participate in life fully, their guilt at their anger. Betty Friedan walked with me.

In 1980, the mid-year of the United Nations Decade for Women, consultations were held around Australia to gauge women's views on the status of women. They were sponsored by the national and state women's consultative councils. I was asked by the New South Wales Women's Co-ordination Unit to help organise a consultation in the Albury area. This I did with the help of a handful of other women.

We were overwhelmed by the response – 200 women turning up when we had expected twenty. Energetic debate and discussion on every topic: work, education, childcare, and more. The key speaker sent to represent the New South Wales Women's Consultative Council was diminutive and dynamic as ever but truly inspirational to us all with her clarity of purpose, immense knowledge and commitment to women. Most importantly, she brought us news of the gains women were making in Sydney and Canberra, the campaigns being fought and won. This was our first meeting and our paths have crossed ever since.

The collective included all sorts of women: young, old, working, at home, students, local. One of its great strengths was the network we developed amongst ourselves.

The women at our consultation were fired with enthusiasm and awareness. They now knew they were not alone, there were women everywhere struggling for change including in their own town. They did not want to just leave it as a 'one-off'. So we formed the Albury-Wodonga Women's Collective with 100 women members. Our aim was to keep ourselves in touch with each other, with women's issues and with the Women's Movement. For the next six years we operated as a loose network, putting out a regular newsletter of local events and national/international news on the Women's Movement. We ran women's film nights, concerts with singers such as Judy Small and Margaret Roadknight, organised political lobbying on local issues, travelled to conferences and seminars that we now knew about as our names were added to mailing lists in Melbourne, Sydney and Canberra.

The collective included all sorts of women: young, old, working, at home, students, local. One of its great strengths was the network we developed amongst ourselves. This is one of the ways in which the often claustrophobic lack of anonymity of country areas can be put to good advantage. Just as the men had their networks formed through council, Rotary and used them, so too we women found that we had collective members everywhere: employed in government agencies, working with or on council, in education institutions, churches, the media, and the community generally. This was better than toiling alone, thinking you were the only woman in the area to despair over woman's lot.

By this time my children were in primaryschool. As a full-time working sole parent who also had night time meetings to attend, I had little time to go out socially. Much of our activism for women was planned and discussed around the dining table at our homes. We took our children and our food and wine to each others homes and shared our loves and hurts as well as our struggles for change. It was a time of great fun and energy.

And we had our enemies too. In rural areas, the personal really does become political in many ways not experienced by city women. If you struggle for childcare, everyone knows who is doing it and labels you accordingly, often as an unfit mother who wants to abandon her children. If you leave your husband, the whole town knows and takes an opinion. If your child is in trouble at school, the teacher will tell you it is because you are a sole parent and the child does not have appropriate male role models. You meet your enemies in the supermarket, at the school council meeting, the picture theatre or they can be your boss!

The results of our struggles included many improved conditions for women: childcare, neighbourhood houses, sexual assault services, family planning clinics, emergency services, access to technical and further education (TAFE), women's programs in adult education. We were greatly assisted in these struggles by women in Melbourne, Sydney and Canberra in the large bureaucracies and political parties who could hear our plea and make sure it was taken to the right quarters, or would give us advice on how next to proceed.

Two campaigns stand out in my memory as most controversial. These were the setting up of a family planning clinic in Wodonga (which we achieved) and our attempt to stop the New South Wales Labor government giving the publicly funded but Catholic controlled Sisters of the Mercy Hospital the responsibility in all obstetric and gynaecological care in Albury (in which we failed). Both issues strike at the heart of patriarchy and feminism as they are about the struggle of women to control their own bodies and reproduction. They were therefore the two issues that created the greatest furore in the town. Wherever we turned to try to achieve our aims we were confronted with men in positions of power: the health department, hospital boards, medical profession, newspaper, local councils, the Labor Party, the Liberal Party, the Catholic Church. All opposed our stance for women. In each organisation or group we found that the leading men were Catholic. Their networks were strong and their power considerable.

The priests denounced us from the pulpit on Sundays, the paper derided and condemned us almost every day, the council wrote to our employers requesting we be sacked, public officials silenced their women employees with threats of disciplinary action. If council or priest made derogatory statements about us they were headlines in the paper. If we made statements they usually went unreported or received a minor position in the paper or were distorted. The Australian

Broadcasting Commission (ABC) radio and metropolitan media were our only neutral sources.

Three of us involved in the Mercy Hospital campaign were also in the Albury-Lavington branch of the ALP and had assisted the branch to write a submission to the New South Wales Health Department on the branch's view that the women's health services should stay with the secular hospital. Unknown to us, some men in the branch took a copy of this submission, put our three names on it and 'leaked' it to the *Border Morning Mail*, the local paper. This began a particularly vicious public tirade against us three.

The *Border Morning Mail* had a field day. They took select pieces from the submission, distorted them, sought the views of the Catholic Church and denounced the three of us. We were portrayed as modern day witches intent on harming the good women the nuns. The local paper printed scores of letters, many defending us but most condemning us. Many letters supporting us were never printed, including some from local health professionals who hand-delivered them to ensure publication. The local ALP branch supported us but senior Labor party politicians flew in from Sydney to distance themselves from us. Liberal Party hacks flew in to make political mileage from the fracas. There were echoes of witch burning in the whole saga. The paper printed picture after picture of smiling nuns with babies and mothers, and denounced us for daring to call ourselves 'Ms'. Pitting women against women is a great strategy, one that works extra well in a rural community and one that serves to divert the public debate away from the real issue. We had to defend ourselves rather than push for the services we knew women had the right to in a free and secular society. Our jobs were threatened and our families suffered.

The paper printed picture after picture of smiling nuns with babies and mothers, and denounced us for daring to call ourselves 'Ms'.

It is at times like these that women's friendships become strongest. Locally we supported each other; every day the paper printed another diatribe against us, my phone rang hot with calls from supporters and my frontdoor was always open for the parade of visitors. Women from the city who knew us and of our struggle lent their help. Without such help the three of us would not have been able to stay afloat in what often felt like the eye of the storm. I recall at one point receiving a card from an old friend, Yoland Wadsworth, who lived in Melbourne and, as she hadn't heard from me for a while, was enquiring as to whether everything was alright. I replied by sending her copies of the front page of the *Border Morning Mail* for the previous ten days – all featuring some lurid representation of us three. By return mail I received the following poem:

A MATTER OF BREAKING SILENCE

1. These three women speak
   These three women speak for women
   with fettered tongues who:
   are counselled by nuns to be silent
   at the back-breaking load
   of the unexpected pregnancy.
   The husband who beats,
   or doesn't care.
   The son on drugs
   The dementing aged parent.
   The loss of self.
   Or who feel unease at having
   the figure of a dead man
   on a dead tree
   over their bed
   as they struggle to feel well.
   Or who feel guilt at complaining,
   amongst the saintly. Or at
   uttering the stray expletive.

2. And the women with fettered tongues
   Look silently at the photos
   of three strong women
   in the Border Morning Male.
   And know.
   Not immediately.
   But in the fullness of time
   they will Real-ise their Knowledge

3. It is not the woman who does not know
   her marital status.
   It is the men who cannot tell
   whether she is already possessed,
   or is available for them to possess.
   And the men with the loud mouths
   Look at the photos of the three
   strong women
   and clamour 'to kill...'
   the story.

4. These three women labour.
    These Labor women labour
    for labouring silent women
    and silent women in labour.
    Now Labor women in Melbourne
    Labour
    for these three women
    They don't burn witches anymore
    but the covens are still strong
    Feel our strength
    We are with you.
    Our hands are on your arms,
    as you break silence.

    Yoland Wadsworth

A few days later, I had a call from Marg, a friend in Canberra, to say that she had organised a plane ticket from Albury to Canberra for me to attend the Ronnie Gilbert and Judy Small Concert and that another mutual friend, Trisha, from Melbourne, had bought the concert ticket. I said I couldn't possibly go as I had an important meeting that night and I had no one to mind the children overnight. No problem, said Margie, Kay is minding your kids and Liz is going to your meeting for you. I flew out on a wet and miserable Albury winter's night and had a wonderful time at the concert, made all the more enjoyable by the sense of being surrounded in my life by the warmth of friends, in both city and country.

It wasn't all gloom and fear of course. We had some fun in the process. The same friend Marg from Canberra wrote a song that was first sung to me around a bonfire on Queen's birthday weekend 1986.

(TUNE: BATTLE HYMN (HER?) OF THE REPUBLIC)

The mail came the other day – a parcel was for me
The post mark was familiar, it was from Albury.
Enclosed there were some articles about Nuns and Maternity
They were from Kath Davey.

I read (chorus)

    Calls to sack the social planner
    Calls to sack the social planner
    Calls to sack the social planner
    Were printed every day.

The *Border Morning Mail*, it was, that needed news one day
To distort reports is policy – they know no other way
The Editor is right of right and he launched into the fray
His aim was very clear...

We need (chorus)

All the little babes in Albury should be born under the cross
And the watching eyes of Mercy Nuns who should always be your boss.
We are caring, glaring sisters who are like fairy floss
We want you young and old.

And don't mind (chorus)

There were letters to the editor saying – let the poor Nuns be,
They came from angry members of the wide community
Australia Post was noted for its sudden efficiency
As there was one from Tarrawingee...

It supported... (chorus)

It seems that hand delivered mail gets lost from time to time
The one side of the argument is altogether fine.
To confuse it with the women's views is against the line
Of white male Catholic slime.

We print (chorus)

The Labor Higher Echelons all wet themselves with fright
As marginal electorates are no place for women's rights
So keep all the health reports hidden away from sight
While we remain whiter than white.

And don't resist... (chorus)

We look around and see the many changes happening here –
For women are getting stronger and united need not fear.
We will win the struggles that we all hold most dear
To control our lives and say –

They will not win... (chorus)

I wasn't sacked but we didn't win. All women in Albury now must go to the Catholic controlled but publicly funded hospital to have their babies. The combined effect of the barrage from the local paper and the Catholic forces won on the day. We did, however, get the right for women to have abortions performed at a secular hospital, the Albury Base, which was a major gain as previously they had no option other than Melbourne or Sydney. Many people supported us privately but were not able to put a public position for fear of receiving the kind of treatment we had. It was a very effective method of social control. For quite some time after this, many women were reluctant to speak out on any issue that appeared to push for women's rights for fear they would arouse the ire of the male clerics and their powerbrokers throughout the community.

Many people supported us privately but were not able to put a public position for fear of receiving the kind of treatment we had.

Not long after the worst of this was over, I left Albury-Wodonga. In rural areas, one of the tradeoffs I had long been aware of was that your career prospects are often limited and changing jobs often means changing locations. I applied and got a job as senior rural affairs adviser for the Gippsland region of Victoria.

With two kids, a dog, cat and two horses, I upped stakes and moved across the state. Leaving my established network of women friends and colleagues in Albury-Wodonga was a great wrench – they had made it all worthwhile. We had some wonderful farewell parties before I left including one at which Margaret Roadknight sang all my favourites and we all sang 'Calls to Sack the Social Planner' with much delight. Two of my dearest friends, Linnette and Bev, wrote and recited the 'Ode to Kath':

Our sister, who art in transit
remembered by us women
the network grows
the friendship flows
in Albury as it will in Gippsland

You showed us fight
and shared your bread
and we talked of the strength
to repel those who trespass against us

Now our way is not of compromise
we see freedom from patriarchy
for *we are* the Goddess
and the Power, and the Story
forever, and ever Ah-Women

As an older woman told me when I was leaving Albury-Wodonga, you never lose your friends when you move, only your acquaintances. However, life never stands still, my children were older and I also wanted to return to some part-time studies. We settled in the rural hamlet of Tyers in the Latrobe Valley. The new job provided challenges that stretched my skills and knowledge. I was working with women, rural communities, Aborigines and political decision-makers. The purpose of my job in the office of rural affairs was to improve communication between these groups and government. Working across a range of issues and geographic areas: environment, transport, community services, education, from the eastern edge of Melbourne to the border of New South Wales and taking in areas as diverse as the dairying communities of South Gippsland, the industrial towns of the LaTrobe Valley, and the politically and environmentally sensitive forests of East Gippsland. I knew no one when I arrived but didn't have to wait long to tap into the local networks. I had been in my new office for only a few days when women began ringing me up, wanting to come to talk about some of the local issues. They had been told about my arrival from women they knew in the Albury-Wodonga area and were keen to enlist my aid on some of the local struggles. And I thought I had come to Gippsland for a quieter time!

I was told not to bother with greenies, townies, single parents, bring-ins, newcomers, hobby farmers and women whose husbands had not inherited their farms. Single parents came in for the greatest vitriol...

Gippsland is the strip of Australia in eastern Victoria bounded by sea and mountains, and is certainly diverse. I thought I was a seasoned operator but I still was shocked when I came across vicious prejudice within the established rural community sector. People who knew the area better than I suggested that a person moves backward in time as she moves east from Melbourne. It was like living in a timewarp in some ways. My role of working with women was controversial in certain quarters. At meetings I was told by Farmers' Federation representatives not to waste my taxpayer funded time in talking with other than 'real farm women'. When I questioned this definition I was told not to bother with greenies, townies, single parents, bring-ins, newcomers, hobby farmers and women whose husbands had not inherited their farms. Single parents came in for the greatest vitriol, being described by one male police officer as the scum of the earth and their kids as the dregs and by a male farmer as 'bloody good breeders' who waste taxpayers money. After that last epithet I was very tempted to follow through with the animal husbandry (sic) analogy and suggest that there was ample evidence within the room of the need for selective breeding within the human race and perhaps we could start with ringing the speaker (and I didn't mean calling him on the phone). I didn't; kept my cool and attempted to develop a more tolerant and meaningful discussion, with some success. They had no idea I was a sole parent as it never occurred to them that someone in my position of responsibility might be and besides, I seemed so nice.

One of the most outspoken of these misogynist farmers was eventually taken to the edge by his views. I was told by a colleague that some years after our first altercation, the farmer in question had dropped dead of a heart attack at a public meeting just after having delivered another blistering attack on bureaucrats. It was felt he went doing what he loved best, which may be so. However, I did note that the day he died was International Women's Day. I was also bemused to discover some weeks later that his heart attack was not without warning. He had evidently suffered a 'turn' some days previously at the farm and been cajoled by his wife to visit the doctor. As luck would have it, their doctor was not in so his wife talked him in to going to the hospital. Then the unthinkable happened, a woman doctor came to attend him. This farmer had very strong views about the things that women should do in life and being a doctor was not one of them. He was for buttoning up his shirt right there and then and leaving the hospital. They managed to convince him he should have a couple of tests but he would not let the woman doctor examine him properly or advise him. She sent the test results to his own doctor who rang him immediately and asked him to come in straight away. He had an appointment immediately following the bureaucratic meeting at which he died.

During the three years I was with the office of rural affairs I came to know another strength of rural women: the tenacity and courage of those involved in the environmental movement. Until I moved to Gippsland I had little knowledge of the superb physical environments in this corner of Australia: rainforest, national parks, coastal scrub, wildlife habitats, wetlands, still clear river and lakes, hundreds of miles of perfect beaches. When city dwellers hear of environmental clashes over logging or ocean outfalls, they have little knowledge that often these issues have been raised by a handful of environmental watchdogs in the rural areas, people who make no individual gain out of battling to protect what is left of our environment and who attract considerable bitter personal attack in their own communities for doing so. Most of them are women. City dwellers owe them a debt.

I saw some of this environmental activism coupled with the beauty of women's ways of organising on issues such as the very fast train (VFT), a multi-million dollar private enterprise project that threatened the social and environmental fabric of south eastern Australia. The full details of the battle is enough for another whole story. What I witnessed was the energy, intelligence and compassion of women who organised across hundreds of miles of difficult country to bring information to the people, to question the corporate giants and to prod governments into socially responsible actions. And as always with women, they did this on top of their jobs and family responsibilities. The feminism of many of them led them to observe with irony that they might just be cleaning up yet another mess after the boys, a type of global housekeeping, but they did it nonetheless as they saw no alternative.

Despite the struggles I still love living in the country. I have learned to ride a horse and ski cross-country. I have the opportunity to live where there is space and bush. I miss the vitality of the city, the intellectual stimulation and the instant access to activities and services. However, since I first came to live in the country, much has changed to make it better for women. It is not yet up to city standard but we are working on it. The major gain for me since moving to the country is the friendship of the women with whom I share the struggle. Because of the struggle and friendship of women, in both city and country, our lives are very different from that of my mother.

PART 2

Same/
Difference

A Kelpie in the Backyard

Victoria Whitelaw

Victoria Whitelaw conducts a law practice in Melbourne. In the 1970s she studied arts/law degrees at the University of Melbourne majoring in English literature and Middle Eastern studies. In the 1980s she was a comedian on Radio 3RRR's *Beauty and the Hedgehog,* a claims officer for the State Insurance Office, and a legal aid lawyer. In the latter capacity she specialised, first, as a duty solicitor and, later, in major crime. She has also done a lot of waitressing, selling sunglasses at the markets, and childcare.

Active in the past in her union, Victoria Whitelaw describes herself as 'feminist' with a personal interest in multiculturalism (her first son is half Greek). She finds extremist ideology restrictive and boring. She is married to a barrister, Jim Bessell. They have a one-year-old son and an eight-year-old son from her former marriage. Her current interests include going to the races (often with her mother-in-law), reading psychology books, swimming with her sons, and adding to her eclectic garden.

The country of my nightmares is the backyard to our farm house. It is the border territory between my mother's world – the combustion-stoved kitchen – and my father's world, the stables and horsepaddocks beyond. My psyche must have settled there as a compromise between the parents who tore me apart with their fighting.

I was active in my mother's world – dancing and playing the piano, particularly to entertain city visitors. Away from the house, which was stuffed closed with flywire and cottonwool (my mother had a mission to keep the flies out, and to get my father to take his dirty boots off outside and the men to wipe up their own piss from the toilet floor) I felt I could breathe a little easier. Whilst I liked to be with Mum, it was an anxious home in which Dad's raving interruptions were always expected.

Outside, there was real action – shooting the stupid sheep (to this day I love eating lamb) with my bow and arrow from astride my bare-back horse. But if Dad caught me for work, it was hard physical labour to which there was no end. Trudging back through the mud from feeding a horse in a back paddock I vowed that I would never romanticise country life. We are all prone to nostalgia, but I habitually rose early to 'ride work', and finished late, having either danced until the evening then ridden home, or worked with the stock, and although it did me no harm it is not my choice of lifestyle.

The backyard was littered with dogs, cats (most of which were drowned by my sister when they gave my baby nephew conjunctivitis), water tanks, a rotary clothes line, workmen's sleeping quarters and a little naked girl – me – wearing nothing but undies, lying away from the heat in the shade of the ute.

All was confusion, turmoil and mess on our farm. Even the name, 'Greenslopes', was a confusion because the place was as flat as a tack. Home life would have been the same wherever my parents had played out the last 20 years of their unhappy marriage. Perhaps there would have been more containment in Caulfield.

> All was confusion, turmoil and mess on our farm. Even the name, 'Greenslopes', was a confusion because the place was as flat as a tack.

A Jewish obstetrician and an experienced nurse delivered me in a private city hospital. My mother and I had a spontaneously thrombosed umbilical cord. In 1956, I was one of only two babies known to have survived the condition. In the country I would have been born dead.

We lived in Caulfield. My father was a State Savings Bank accountant. He had spent his childhood in Kerang, moving to Melbourne with his immediate family when his father became violent, unemployable and fatally ill with a brain tumour. The Depression set in and his mother raised the family by making and selling boiled lollies.

The legacy from the country and the Depression was that Dad rode trackwork, ran professionally, and trained footrunners in Caulfield Park after a day at the bank: he was always hungry for a quid.

My mother was born in country Victoria – Castlemaine – while her father was there to build the Thompson's foundry chimneys, but her experience was largely urban. Her education was interrupted by the Depression and her lack of application. She 'only' achieved a half scholarship and could not stay at Methodist Ladies College (MLC), Kew. She became a Burroughs machine operator, leaving her work at Kraft, Fishermans Bend, in the early years of the second world war in order to have her first child. Her parents had wanted her to be an architect.

We moved to Benalla when I was about three. My family were preoccupied with running a newsagency for a year and failed to notice my nanny was an alcoholic. We lived on the Hume Highway. I wandered the streets and ran up guineas worth of bills at the corner milkbar, buying Twisties. During the recent slump in the economy, a Benalla bank manager – of urban origin – confided in me that it was an unbreakable custom and an economic problem for local businesses that goods purchased be 'put on the account'.

My father went to the North East because the big gum tees indicated fertile, reliable land, unlike the Mallee of his youth. After a year he found a very wet and lush farm with a triple fronted brick veneer, including flushing toilet. That fixture persuaded Mum to embark on rural life. Dad then became a racehorse trainer for most of my life, but he was always called 'Jack the Banker' at the track. He also grazed cross-bred cattle and sheep.

I went to the local state school – number 31 – old and quaint like our little Church of England. Mum would take me out of school for excursions to the city. My feet hurt terribly at the end of such a day. Apart from that, there were no family holidays. May and September holidays were spent docking and branding lambs.

We were not considered locals, although I think our lack of social life was as much due to my parents' attitude as to our ambivalent social status – racing people fell into the demi-monde, mixing as we did with the poorest and the wealthiest. A judge and a knight figured amongst my father's mates but they largely remained in the city. Strangely, my father was a Rechabite (teetotaller) and a non-smoker so we didn't even fit into our own millieu. My day to day associates were alcoholics, compulsive gamblers and wizened apprentice jockeys who worked around the stables, usually for board alone. Their undernourished appearance seemed to have been with them since childhood.

My day to day associates were alcoholics, compulsive gamblers and wizened apprentice jockeys who worked around the stables, usually for board alone.

Our farm was not isolated but I still needed my horse if I was to escape the fighting. When I was still too little to reach Coongy's neck, one apprentice jockey would not bridle the horse without a sexual kiss. Mum was too naive or distracted to understand me when I sought protection. Lacking any sexual education I was easy prey for several more occasions of more severe sexual abuse by other apprentices, until I developed some cunning. I was dumb like a fox and never spoke of these matters with mother again, worrying – until I was 14 and my period came – that I might be pregnant. The Church of England literature about procreation and vocation, sent to me by my sister on the eve of boardingschool, was not illuminating.

I now find my reception very warm when I return to Benalla, but back in the 1960s my first kick in the teeth from the community came at the completion of primaryschool. The Mothers' Club refused me the scholarship raised annually for the top student, the excuse given (for the first time ever) that I was to continue on to a private school. The headmaster tried to articulate that the recipient was not, in fact, the top student, but I was never acknowledged personally for that achievement. A very lonely childhood as the school 'brain', with non-participating and eccentric parents who dressed me in mini-skirts before they had 'come in' in the country; my inexplicable inability to achieve the basketball team; and a seat alone on the schoolbus culminated in my rejection, as I saw it, on my last day of primaryschool. For a long time afterward I harboured a sour feeling about narrow country people.

I was 11 years old. In the photograph I look nine. I stand in classical ballet's first position but my knees are knocked forward. My mother says it doesn't matter what you do for children, they will always say you were wrong.

We took another photograph on the top of Pretty Sally when we were closer to Melbourne. Mum and I had spent weeks sewing on Cash's name tags to everything – the regulation undies, the regulation this, the regulation that. Away from the tearing, searing fighting of home, I hoped to achieve a kind of religious peace with the Sisters of the Church. It was shocking to find that boardingschool was a dumping ground for children from other dysfunctional and disintegrating families. There was plenty of bullying, violence and skulduggery.

My mother says it doesn't matter what you do for children, they will always say you were wrong.

My father took my cases up the curved front stairs at St Michael's and never returned to visit me. Those gracious stairs were used by the girls only on arrival day and by the seniors when they came down the staircase to go to The Ball, ogled by us littlies sitting outside Sister Scholastica's parlour and the chapel at the base of the stairs. Resplendent leaving and matriculation girls in long high-waisted velvet dresses, choker ribbons, hair piled in curls, a corsage here and there. Beautiful. Conservative. The more charismatic of them would be the 'crush' of a younger girl, who would be at the beck and call of the older girl, sending the older one love letters and generally soothing her ego and being a little confidante and protege. Always an annoying individualist, I did not participate in this repressed but institutionalised (and therefore acceptable) form of lesbianism. The logic of the arrangement escaped me and so I missed out on having a mentor with its associated protection and comfort.

My sister and Mum had made sure I went off with Tampax in my suitcase – no Modess: I was to be 'liberated!' The Tampax lay there for three years, unused, dry and dehydrating by the day, until the dreaded moment arrived and there was 'Charlie' or 'George' (as the period was called at St Michael's) sitting on my undies. How lonely I felt in the dunny, trying to shove what felt like a cardboard gun up my vagina.

During school hours I passed a note across to a mate: 'How do I get a tampon IN?' Amidst laughter, back came the reply: 'VASELINE.'

It worked. I've continued with lubrications of humour, sex, romantic love and other deceits to ease my loneliness, pain and anger.

My mother wrote to me every day – sometimes twice a day, in the early years when there were two daily mail deliveries. By my fifth year away (when I had changed schools) I would catch the envelopes flung down by prefects from a balcony at MLC, read cursorily, and then fling the letters into a bin. I now understand my anger. Intimacy and comfort were a secret craving. Mum kept me 'hooked in' with the letter writing – endless narrative about the doings of the family from which I was locked away. But pieces of paper could never substitute for the human contact. My mother threw out all my letters, too.

Many years later when I looked at the residue of the supposedly Great (male) Love of My Life, all I had left were some letters and an anxious disposition. The intimacy I longed for but missed in these teenage years is still a problem.

My mother said recently: 'Well you think they will get used to it.'

In my second year of boardingschool I came home for a term because I was so ill. Glandular fever had been misdiagnosed as appendicitis and post-operative infection set in. Again, I nearly died. But I had the undivided attention of mother, and I struggle with stress-related and psychosomatic-based illness to this day.

Upon substantial recovery, I was sent back to school and worked hard academically, but by third form I knew I was stuck. I was such a dag, winning the divinity prize every year. I let my mind begin to wander, became naughty, and became popular.

Near the close of my third year, I won scholarships to MLC, Kew. The change, occurring as it did just as I had achieved companionship, my first kiss (playing spin-the-bottle with the Haileybury boys) and my period, was devastating. Loneliness and the death wish set in again, until I met Rene Craig who turned out to be related by adoption. My great-great-grandfather, Samuel Rinder, adopted Rene's great-aunt Floss in Wedderburn. It's a small world for country girls.

An all-girls school has its advantages academically and would have been okay if we could have had a decent feed and returned to the bosom of our families frequently. I needed to see my brothers and interact socially and naturally with boys. My relationship with boys or men was ambivalent because (so far as I could see) my mother hated my father. There was no daily affection. Any physical closeness with other girls was strictly taboo and immediately labelled as being sexual. Our culture was a cold one, and the underbelly of it a dirty-mindedness born of repression, so my relationship with the male was also highly sexualised.

We wonder now at the history of Aboriginal children being torn from their mothers but, while it would be silly to compare their suffering with my privileged alienation, my experience tells me that anglo saxon culture believes that institutionalisation is the correct approach. The upper middle-class version of institutionalisation and assimilation of the 'other' is, to this day, boardingschool.

At a family conference from which I was excluded my family had identified their reasons for sending me away. My experience of the state education system was extremely positive and all my Benalla teachers were excellent – later I completed higher school certificate (HSC) at Benalla High and gained entry to the University of Melbourne's medical school. I changed to law/arts degrees and now practise as a lawyer. Nonetheless, it was generally perceived that a lower standard of education existed in the country. And so the family conference decided I would go. I had to leave the country if I wanted to study medicine or law, and had to leave the farm because my family didn't function properly.

Mrs Lorna Croxford from the dairy across the road told Mum: 'Grace, never learn to milk a cow.' And Mum didn't.

My siblings had been spectacular academic failures. Carole, the eldest, failed matriculation at MLC while we still lived in Caulfield. James did not weather the change from Melbourne High School well and at Benalla High School failed matriculation twice, the second year contracting hepatitis (probably from our open sewers). John, unbeknown to my parents, was chucked out of Dookie Agricultural College. They blamed their academic failure on the intrusions of my father's bad temper and, in the case of the three of us who went on to live on the farm (Carole went off to primary teachers college), his demands for farm work. It was considered better that I continue my preordained academic career away from our stormy family life.

Father agreed because of his longstanding sense of loss in the academic sphere. When offered a sporting scholarship to Scotch, lack of money for the uniform meant he could not be sent. He then assisted his younger sisters' and brother's academic careers through his less prestigious though lucrative work. Many of my cousins were academically brilliant and my father felt his offsprings' failures sorely. I was the last child and the last hope for a tertiary qualification. Ironically, Carole, James and John later achieved membership of state parliament and tertiary qualifications, respectively.

In the midst of all this, I had strong women role models. Mrs Lorna Croxford from the dairy across the road told Mum: 'Grace, never learn to milk a cow.' And Mum didn't. Yet Lorna Croxford's example, out in the dairy and excelling in the kitchen, taught me that women can do everything.

My music teachers, Mrs Erica Hoffrichter of Benalla and Miss Emily Taylor of St Michael's, taught me music, which has remained a great comfort and pleasure to me.

My ballet teacher, Adrienne Leitch, taught me that the endurance of the female body is almost limitless. She danced with the Borovansky company and turned up in Benalla because her husband was teaching there. Childbirth interrupted her litheness and beauty only for a day or two.

Until recently I was bitter about boardingschool interrupting my ballet lessons. But I now learn that the Alida, after whom Mrs Leitch named a little ballet she choreographed for me, suffered anorexia and a lost childhood. Perhaps the Sisters' social disapproval of dancers also had some basis in commonsense.

...she wanted me to be everything – 'good' girl, 'bad' (free) girl, career girl, family girl, Mum's girl (not Dad's), a doctor, a lawyer, a musician, a mother, not a mother.

My mother had the greatest influence on me but it has always been a confusing one, probably because she wanted me to be everything – 'good' girl, 'bad' (free) girl, career girl, family girl, Mum's girl (not Dad's), a doctor, a lawyer, a musician, a mother, not a mother. I do thank her for her assistance with and encouragement for my musical life, and making me return to school, after some communal living at the age of 16, to complete my HSC. She then drove me fortnightly to a suitably qualified piano teacher, Mrs Whittaker, in Wangaratta. The house was full of music – opera on the record player, singing with Mum at the piano. Television was never allowed to interfere with my piano practice.

Mum stopped living vicariously through me when, in her sixties, she returned to her own studies, eventually completing postgraduate work in literature.

The real relief and joy in my life have been my two children, whom I felt able, despite illness during pregnancy, to bring into the world without physical fear because I grew up caring for other little animals and birds – chooks, injured native birds, kittens, puppies and poddy calves, and delivering offspring. On both occasions I pushed my babies out, it was with a flood of relief and understanding that I took them to my breast.

Farm life at least gave me an ability to relate to animals, and in my adult life the cats I have had as pets in the city have helped me over a bridge from my own emotional prison to committed, responsible relationships of love with humanbeings.

The emotional frustration and confusion resulting from my family life overflowed for many years into my urban life at university. The city offers a host of distractions, mainly social, from one's inner turmoil; the quietness of the country does not. At one time, I returned to Benalla once a month but, for now, I have stopped the retreats because I found the unearthing of old traumas too distressing.

Eventually, the reasons for my father's paranoia and aggression were diagnosed when he began suffering strokes; he had hardening of the arteries to the brain. My father died in a cupboard into which he had wandered, in the geriatric wing of the Benalla hospital. It took a week to find the body.

About a decade later a relative by marriage shot himself dead as a result of police harassment over a crime his cousin, not he, had committed.

In the city it is possible to forget angst at a K-Mart nearby. Pain takes on some anonymity and is more palatable; joy is more subdued.

Messy events like this fill city Sunday newspapers, but in the country they stand out in the emotional landscape. Country towns are micro-societies of the wider culture; from time to time the good and the bad are delineated clearly. In the city it is possible to forget angst at a K-Mart nearby. Pain takes on some anonymity and is more palatable; joy is more subdued.

The country has changed. Women communicate more, particularly since the onset of the recession and depression of the 1980s and 1990s, when their roles on farms and in providing outside income have become more valued. Despite funding cutbacks, support services now exist and there is greater awareness of the battered and sexually abused.

My conclusion is that the responsibilities of family malaise and family secrets can be harboured by victim children whether they live in the country or the city.

To write about the Benalla I knew – its snobbery, its macho footy club, the way people looked at you oddly if you used long words – is not to write about the Benalla that now exists. The world has become a global village, the population more informed and broader minded. And I have grown away from my own family's paranoia. I find the Benallanese warmer and friendlier now.

I miss the smell of eucalypt and the song of magpies and the smell of horses. But I choose to live in the city. The suburb in which I live functions like a friendly country village, and my garden is dishevelled with trees and birds, a cat and a dog.

I feel safer here, and not just because I have a kelpie in the backyard.

The Daring to be Different

Janet Powell

Janet Powell first entered parliament as an Australian Democrat senator in September 1986 to fill Don Chipp's casual vacancy. She was elected senator for Victoria (six year term) in July 1987, was leader of the Australian Democrats from 1 July 1990 to 20 August 1991, and from 31 July 1992 until June 1993 was independent senator for Victoria. She held many shadow portfolios including primary industry, social security, consumer affairs, health, prime minister and cabinet, and women, and she was the first woman to gain passage of a private member's bill, which resulted in a ban on print advertising of tobacco products.

Janet Powell has had and continues her extensive involvement in a range of community based organisations and she is a member of the Australian Conservation Foundation (ACF); Greenpeace; Campaign for International Cooperation and Disarmament; Women's Electoral Lobby (WEL); Young Women's Christian Association (YWCA); and President of Friends of the ABC (Vic.). She is the mother of four – two women aged 27 and 26 and two boys aged 20 and 18.

Born in the local hospital in Nhill, a town of just over 2000 people in north western Victoria, together with my older brother and younger sister I was brought up on a farm 10 miles from town. There was not much between us in age – less than four years.

My parents were farmers. They spent most of their lives paying for the farm. We were not the wealthy property owners that the city people so often seem to see farmers as being.

Ours was almost a subsistence lifestyle. The farm was a mixed cereal (wheat and oats) and wool-producing property and we had a few cows, a couple of pigs and some poultry for cash-flow crops. We had a thriving vegetable garden and some fruit trees. Eggs, milk, meat and vegetables were always on hand. We often sat down to a meal and noted how much of what was before us had been produced on the farm.

We led an isolated and self-contained existence. The family travelled to town only every two weeks or so in my early years. The road was often impassable in winter. We were off the beaten track, in spite of not being a very long distance from town, because the branch railway lines had gone out from the town in different directions, followed by roads and other development, leaving us as a bit of a back-water.

But a rich community life surrounded us. I have vivid early memories of my life on the farm. There were many fund-raising events – particularly dances held in our shearing shed for wartime Red Cross Relief Fund. As I was born in 1942, these must be very early memories. It was fun making the floor of the barn slippery for the dancers by shaving candlewax, spreading it over the floor and rubbing it in. This was done most effectively by an adult pulling an old wheat bag around at a great speed with a small child clinging desperately to the bag to weigh it down. On the big night, I would be allowed two or three dances – whirled in the arms of Daddy or one of the other men – then back to the house to bed.

My brother and I would then creep out to the garden gate and watch the men in steady procession to and from the scrub behind the sheds – officially for a toilet break but actually because a beer barrel was strategically located there. The women would gather up at the house – to feed babies, to have a quiet break and a cuppa or just to have a private chat. We felt so daring spying on all this grown-up activity. And our parents never knew what we had been up to until we told them years later.

This is one of the earliest impressions I had of the separation between men and women which was so much a feature of the social pattern. They didn't seem to do things together. Was it the same in the city at that time – 1940s, 1950s and into the 1960s? I don't really know, but I suspect it was similar. As I grew older, I felt it even more strongly and innately disapproved. I enjoyed male company and in our family circle there seemed to be less of a gulf.

My brother had a group of male friends who socialised with us at our home – playing tennis, and staying to Sunday tea, then singing and dancing. In the privacy of our own loungeroom, my sister, mother and I taught many local lads to dance. As a result, we were able to have many natural and uncomplicated male friendships which might not have been possible otherwise.

There always seemed to be someone coming and going. We usually had a working man, living in a workman's hut on the farm and there was extra labour at busy times – especially shearing – and sometimes even someone to help my mother in the house. There were salesmen, agents, repair men and, very early in my life, an old Afghan hawker with an amazing truckful of goods.

The teacher boarded with us too. The school, Propodollah State School, was on our farm but (inconveniently I always felt, as I pedalled my small bike about a mile to get there) at the other end of the property. It was a little white timber one-room schoolhouse.

There were salesmen, agents, repair men and, very early in my life, an old Afghan hawker with an amazing truckful of goods.

I was delighted to be asked to unveil a commemorative stone on the school site in the 1988 bicentennial year. It was an extraordinary experience to join with about 300 people who gathered on a windswept paddock to be once again part of the community from which they had sprung – a community which never consisted of bricks and mortar, but rather of human bonds which clearly were strong and enduring. The human bonds were more enduring even than the two buildings the community (or settlement) boasted in my childhood – the church, since physically moved to another site, and the school we were commemorating. The school still stands – no longer white, the paint weathered off, with one side wall opened up as it serves as a storage shed for stock feed.

We began school at an early age because attendance was low and the school was under threat of closure. I was just over four years old when I began. I think there were seven of us that year. My father, president or secretary of the school committee, fought to keep the school open – writing letters, organising deputations and even flying to Melbourne to see 'very important people'. Seeing him off on a terrifyingly noisy aeroplane at the local aerodrome is another of my early memories.

When the school enrolment was down to five the year my sister joined us, it was closed. This event led to a succession of big changes in all our lives. Although, or perhaps because, neither of my parents was highly educated, they placed great importance on education for their children. There was no school bus, so the family moved to town, and a share-farmer came to live on the farm. For about five years we were townies. Then my parents and sister went back to the farm and my brother and I went to boardingschool – different schools in different cities. My sister, still in primaryschool, was saved from boardingschool because a neighbour was commuting to town daily – rare in those days – and drove her to school. But the next year she joined me in Ballarat. The unmade roads continued to make the trip to town a difficult one – especially in winter.

I became ill in my second year at boardingschool, and after months of unsuccessful tests and many absences, I was sent home to recuperate for the rest of the year. In Term 3, I enrolled in the correspondence school because I wanted to keep up with my studies.

The next year my brother left school to work on the farm and my sister and I took a seven mile journey in the opposite direction from town to catch a school bus which then took us nine more miles to the highschool, where I eventually matriculated.

Like my parents, I placed great importance on my schooling. I loved every minute of it – wherever I was – and had decided, very early on, that I would be a teacher. My mother could not even get to highschool because there was none in her town, and her widowed mother, with four children to support, could not afford to send her away. She was always very supportive of my ambition and shared my enjoyment of learning. She read avidly and I visited the town library with her regularly and from an early age.

When we moved to the town, my maternal grandmother came to live nextdoor to us and we lived as an extended family. Most family outings, even after we returned to the farm and later when I had my own family and lived in the town, included Nanny. When I later took my two small daughters to the United States of America to live for three years, I was pleased that we developed a close friendship with three older women in our apartment building because I did not want my girls to miss out on the perspective I gained in my life from my grandmother. She died while we were overseas.

I was pleased that we developed a close friendship with three older women in our apartment building because I did not want my girls to miss out on the perspective I gained in my life from my grandmother.

We did not always have an annual holiday when we were young, but on several occasions we visited my aunt, my father's younger sister, in 'the big smoke'. She lived, with her husband, in a southern bayside suburb. It took all day to get to Melbourne – about 250 miles – and then when we arrived we invariably lost our way because we had to cross through the city. Once we were there it was days at the beach and trips into the hills. One day during the visit, Aunty Jean would take us into the city by train. It was all such a whirl that few vivid memories remain. All those backyards whizzing past the train – so many people! And the shops! So much to buy.

No wonder Aunty Jean's Christmas presents were so imaginative. As my city Aunt she seemed quite different. She was young and pretty, without children, went out to work and seemed almost like an independent woman. She went back to the country eventually, brought up a family and is now retired in a small town like the one in which she grew up. This was the beginning of my impression that there were differences between city and country women.

When I went to university at the age of 17 in 1960, which meant moving to live in the city, with absolutely no idea of what to expect, I felt the difference keenly. The country kids could be spotted a mile off. We were in dirndl skirts and blouses – *they* were sleek and sophisticated by comparison. We soon shaped up, but these days mass media and other communication have ensured a greater homogeneity. As well, country children now seem to have many more opportunities for hands-on experience in the city – a trend which I applaud.

The country kids could be spotted a mile off. We were in dirndl skirts and blouses – they *were sleek and sophisticated by comparison. We soon shaped up…*

Many of the country girls who made the transition when I did found the culture shock more than they could cope with. Some failed exams, some fled back to peace and predicability, others met exotic new experiences full-on, one even ending up on the front page of *Truth*. But most of us survived and many headed back to the country as I did as soon as possible once we had graduated. There I stayed, living in country towns, for over 20 more years – except for three years in the United States while my then husband was studying.

I made the choice because I firmly believed in the value of country living. I found it, on balance, a positive experience and was particularly keen to bring up my family in the country. Though I had found my years at university fascinating, exciting and stimulating, I was not unhappy living a quieter existence in the country. I confess, however, to some frustration at the lack of mental stimulation, and a desire to continue to learn and have new experiences.

To some extent, my needs were met in a variety of ways. Early married life brought with it some travel to new parts of Australia; a new doctor's wife came to town and started a women's public speaking group – the Penguins – where we could be involved in self-improvement as opposed to the more pervasive female pursuits usually centred around community and family needs. A group of women and I began a CAE (Council of Adult Education) book club so that we could not only read, but could also *discuss* what we were reading. I also returned to some part-time teaching.

The three years spent in the United States of America, at the beginning of the 1970s, were full of new experiences, people and opportunities. After that experience, in hindsight I see that it was almost inevitable that I would eventually move to the city – even though we did settle in the country on our return and add two more children to the family. However, I was more unsettled, and felt the need for more challenges and stimulation. I would have liked to undertake further study, but we were 200 kilometres from the city in Echuca, and with four children it wasn't possible to organise.

103

The challenge and stimulation came in 1977 with the formation of the Australian Democrats in which I became very involved. My political and community involvement, and that of my husband in the politics of his chiropractic profession, were the twin pressures which saw us move, in 1982, to the rural fringe of Melbourne. We were still in the country – and I was back 'on the land' – 15 beautiful acres of hill country.

My appointment to the senate finally pushed us into the city – so the boys could be close to schools and friends, so we would have a more compact lifestyle.

So I have been a city woman – living and working in the city, for eight years. I did not put down any roots in the outer suburb where I lived for the first seven years. I was, of course, travelling to Canberra almost half of each year. The only real tie was the school attended by the younger children – a tie which has now been broken as they have both left the school.

Having been divorced during those years also gave me a real choice of where to go. I felt the pull of the inner city fringe, and indeed my life has now done a complete about-face – from isolated farm to inner city. In making this choice I do not reject or devalue my long rural experience – on the farm or in the country towns. When I reflect upon my life so far I am struck by the force with which I feel the influence of those years.

When we three small children were growing up on the farm it seemed that I was barely at all affected by my environment. I was the one who helped out in the house, I was the domesticated child, I was a bookworm. It was the others – my brother and our tomboy sister – who would be found outdoors, with the animals, clambering around the machinery, working with the stock and generally appearing to appreciate the outdoor farm life.

Nevertheless, I have no doubt that my decision to live for so long in the country came from a very full appreciation of the peaceful and clean rural atmosphere, the low stress and socially supportive community environment which surrounded me.

In a direct way I have drawn on my background in my political life, by being very involved in rural policy development, in representation for rural areas and in carrying the primary industry portfolio for the Democrats in the senate for four years. I have taken a particular interest in rural environmental issues and was successful in establishing a senate select committee on agricultural and veterinary chemicals and their alternatives. In the years since then, the concept of clean, green agriculture has become a mainstream approach and underpins a major export thrust, backed by industry and government.

While none of the three of us – my brother, my sister or me – stayed on the land, I probably more directly applied my farm experience in my later years via the political process. In another respect, too, my farm upbringing has had a marked influence on my perspective on life, and the way I practise my political activism.

The relative isolation of our farm meant that many of the more modern amenities were not part of my early life experience. There was no mains electricity – just a few lights in key areas like the kitchen, the bathroom, the cow-shed and the dairy, powered by a small generator. For the rest of the house we used candles and lamps. We were fortunate to be allocated a fridge towards the end of the war; we used a Coolgardie hessian cool-safe before then. There was no ice for an ice-chest. Bread was delivered three times a week, we saved the string and brown paper wrapping. The farm water supply was undrinkable hard bore water so the house relied on rain-water tanks which ran very low every summer. Water conservation was a fact of life.

...my farm upbringing has had a marked influence on my perspective on life, and the way I practise my political activism.

All this meant that my lifestyle was not typical of most of my contemporaries, and that I have shared experiences common to people older than I am, and of people who do not have access even now to all modern amenities, whether because of poverty or because they live in isolation or in a less developed society.

Rampant consumerism has never been attractive to me and I was quite repelled by many aspects of United States society when I lived there. That experience played a significant role in my politicisation.

At very stressful moments whenever I contemplated leaving politics, it was always the fact that I am a woman that was the deciding factor in my decision to continue. I was conscious of the opportunities I had been given and the responsibility I carried as a woman with a record of achievement in a non-traditional field. I was reluctant to stand aside because I understand the importance of female role models – for men and women alike. The only regret I had when I lost my parliamentary seat in 1993 was for the loss of a woman from politics.

I hope that the women who were part of my early country life will not be offended by my belief that the strong feeling I have about the need for non-traditional role models stems from their absence in my experience. There were many women whom I admired, and from whom I learnt a great deal – not least my own mother. They worked hard and achieved a great deal in traditional fields of women's endeavour.

A large part of my life has been spent pursuing the traditional female role, treading traditional female pathways. But there has always been a tendency to take a sidestep or leap forward, as the case may be. That tendency has accelerated as the years have gone on and as my life experiences have broadened my perspective.

For all women of my age, growing up in the 1940s and 1950s, wherever they lived, there were few females publicly breaking new ground – especially when compared with the 1970s, 1980s and 1990s. Most of the female 'firsts' of public note have occurred over the 1970s and 1980s, and even those women who did move outside the mainstream earlier did so without a great deal of public acknowledgment.

I would not want to speculate on whether it would have been better or worse for me had I had more influence from women outside the traditional mainstream at earlier stages of my life. It is what one does with one's life in the present that is important.

The recent trend, which was given considerable impetus in the bicentennial year, 1988, to acknowledge the extraordinary efforts of pioneer women – particularly women on the land and in isolated communities, is much to be welcomed. The unsung heroines are numerous and the generally unassuming nature of women as a group probably means they always will be. But women must strive for full acknowledgment of their contribution in the family, the community, the economy, in life in general. There is an essential inequity in lauding the roles and lives of males and taking the female contributions for granted.

It is easier to be different in the city than it is in the country. One contribution I am strongly committed to making is to ease the negative pressures on women who dare to be different – wherever they live, but particularly those in the country.

Plotting Circles in the Mind

Susan Hawthorne

The author of a novel, *The Falling Woman* (Spinifex Press, 1992), a collection of poems, *The Language in My Tongue,* published in the volume Four New Poets (Penguin Books, April 1993) and a feminist quiz book, *The Spinifex Quiz Book: A Book of Women's Answers* (Spinifex Press, 1991/93), Susan Hawthorne's work has been widely published in magazines and anthologies. She has coedited five anthologies, the most recent of which is *Australia for Women: Travel and Culture* (Spinfex Press, 1994, with Renate Klein), and two of her books were published in Germany in 1994.

In 1989 Susan Hawthorn received the Pandora Florence James Award for Outstanding Contribution to Women's Publishing. She lives in Melbourne, Victoria.

Take a girl of seven, put her in a landscape. Plot circles on a map and place her at the centre. Spreading out around her, like ripples on a dam, are images, transparent as film. The innermost circle is filled with flowers: roses, valerian, sweetpeas, forget-me-nots, stocks, phlox, and irises. Also in this circle are budgerigars, galahs, willy wagtails and a black labrador. The house itself contains remnants of an earlier time – a mangle, a cream separator, a meat safe on the eastern verandah.

It could be anywhere – a suburban garden, a country town.

The next circle locates our heroine. We pass through the privet hedge on to a flat wide landscape. From the tankstand that towers over the garden, you can see the bushland, the untouched scrub where callitris pines, with their soft blue-green needles, grow. Beyond the scrub a low blue hill rises from the plain. Turning in a clockwise direction your gaze passes over the wall of the dam, the only source of water for the garden. In the paddock between you and the dam, a jersey cow and her calf wander between dried-out cow pats, ambling around the woodheap towards the milking yard and the sheds.

Still turning, two old eucalypts next to the grain shed and the cow yard come into view. Beneath these trees she has stood and watched her father kill sheep, the carcasses winched from the branches of the eucalypt. Another roof rises behind the eucalypts – the only other visible house, inhabited by our heroine's father's cousin and his family. This is where the aunt who makes the best cakes in the district lives. Sometimes our small heroine walks the quarter mile distance after breakfast, goes round to the back entrance where the sun lies like a lazy dog, and walks through the screen door into a kitchen filled with smells of baking. She runs her fingers around the edge of the mixing bowl and licks them as an old corgi snuffles in her sleep under the table.

Turning another quarter circle your gaze settles once again on the garden. At the back is the chookyard with its ducks, bantams and hens, and the sheepdog in heat, temporarily locked into the fox proof, dog proof chicken coop. It's too soon for another litter of pups. An arbour of roses follows the path to the house alongside the orchard where she sits with her sister and brother eating oranges until their mother calls from the back step. Gazing across the roof top (which our heroine dreams of painting in rainbow colours) the land stretches and stretches, lying flat and yellow with heavy-headed wheat, barley and oats. In the far distance, Bungin Bill, the highest point in the area, is just visible.

At the back is the chookyard with its ducks, bantams and hens, and the sheepdog in heat, temporarily locked into the fox proof, dog proof chicken coop. It's too soon for another litter of pups.

Take another figure – similar, but larger, older, possibly no wiser – place her in a landscape, step back and look.

Around her are plants: a benjaminia fig, maidenhair fern, an iris, miniature roses; nearby basil, parsley, mint and rosemary in a terracotta pot. Behind her is a wall of books.

It could be anywhere – a country house, a weatherboard town house, a terrace in the inner city.

There is nowhere to climb, so you move out on to the balcony and look south towards the city. The skyline is like trees clustered near a creek, a waterhole, a depression in the land. Here the buildings follow the river down to the sea. Container ships hover in the bay then move towards the dock to the west which you cannot see. In fact, you cannot see any of the other horizons, even though your perch on this balcony is higher than that tankstand you climbed so long ago.

At night, instead of looking up and following the southern cross pointer to the south you look at the lights that glitter up and down the buildings. You shift your gaze from the yellow diamond of the

Commonwealth Bank sign to the red star of the National Australia Bank. The blue star of Nauru House is now hidden behind a newer, higher building. Sometimes, exploding fireworks shatter the night as they rise and fall over the river behind the buildings.

Our heroine is 38 and there are times when the memory of her country childhood shoves aside the things that surround her. She first visited the inner suburb she lives in when she was 17 – when she loitered between market stalls whose vendors sold carrots, sweet corn, tomatoes and herbs; or she bargained for cheaper cuts of meat among the men and carcasses.

In 20 years of city life she has learned other ways of being, her life spins faster each day and she wonders whether she will ever finish all the things she has to do. She contemplates a return to the country but too many things would have to change to make it possible. Although she dreams of it, she does not want to live in the country yet.

My life can be quite simply cut in two.

The first half filled with the smells, sounds and sights of rural Australia; the second with the bustle and variety of city life. It's never possible to say which is best. In moments of greed I want both, simultaneously! In reality I know I have made decisions about where and how to live. Each has had its role in forming me, and though my heart is on a piece of land in the Riverina, I know that even if I were to return to the country I would go somewhere different. And though my heart is in the country, my life is made up of city blocks, high buildings, books and potted plants.

...though my heart is in the country, my life is made up of city blocks, high buildings, books and potted plants.

I was born in Wagga Wagga, New South Wales, on one of the hottest days of a very hot summer. My mother tells me that some country hospitals placed infants temporarily in fridges during that summer so they wouldn't die of heat exhaustion. My father was engaged in fighting a grass fire on a neighbour's property the day I was born. It was a traumatic day for all of us, but the long term consequences only showed later. The doctor, an officious type, insisted that he be present at every birth. But when my birth was imminent the doctor had vanished – to lunch is the story I have heard. I don't know how late he was, but to my mother it seemed hours, as midwives attempted to slow the process under strict medical orders. As a result of this birth trauma my early days were less than perfect. I had infantile fits and my mother on a fairly isolated property dealt with this as best she could. It was some three years before I was diagnosed as having epilepsy. In the 1950s, especially in a small rural community, such things were not spoken about. I was not informed of this until I was around 14 years old. No one wanted a child's indiscretion to foster the inevitable prejudice that would result. Nowadays, even in the city, fear still prevents many people with epilepsy from discussing it openly, so it is hardly surprising that my parents took this course.

I hated my first day of school. All I remember was an overwhelming sense of loss and confusion, amidst a stream of tears. Ardlethan Central School was six miles from our farm and Mum drove us the three miles to the bus stop each day. We travelled on a red and white bus we all fondly called the Biscuit Tin. Boys sat on the long seat at the back and though we state school children and the Catholics mixed, I remember us calling the Catholic girls 'chocolate legs' for the thick brown stockings they wore during the winter months. No doubt they had names for us too, but I don't remember them. At that time all the roads in the region were hard dirt and so every trip on the bus, or in any vehicle, was a series of bumps from one pot hole to the next. Yo-yos would appear magically about every three years and the Coca-Cola yo-yos, the best balanced of the lot, were traded across seats on the Biscuit Tin.

Growing up on a farm has been a major influence in my life and in that of my brother and sister. Sometimes it was isolating, and I think the shock of my first day of school was, in part, due to fear of so many other children. We were protected, sometimes overly much, but we had the freedom to explore on our own as we grew older. Across the road was an area of scrub we called The Woods in which we built cubby houses, made bonfires each cracker night, climbed trees and generally tested ourselves in different ways. My brother and I seemed to spend half our life with our feet off the ground, whether it was trees, the creeper near the chookyard, the wooden supports of the rose arbour, the woodpile in the back paddock, the alluring height of the roof, or the railings of the woolshed. After school during winter we would go to the woolshed and throw ourselves from the rafters into the greasy wool. The activity of shearing was a great drawcard.

In different ways we all participated in the work of the farm, although I know other children who worked many more hours than we did. The farm grew wheat and oats and supported large flocks of sheep. The cycles of farm living were determined by the rhythms and growth patterns of these things. Sowing, shearing and harvesting were all times of intense activity and my father often fell asleep over the newspaper and sometimes over dinner during these periods. Sowing demanded little of us, but it wasn't unusual for my father or one of the men to work until well after dark driving round and round the paddock. Shearing meant the three of us droving sheep from one end of the farm to the other, controlling the dogs and not letting the sheep get away. Harvesting meant, once again, long hours driving in ever-decreasing circles around paddocks, the ubiquitous smell of wheat and oat dust, and the itch of oat straw. And our play focused on these rhythms too. While we were still small and light we would ride on the backs of sheep in the stockyards that surrounded the woolshed, and during harvest time we threw ourselves around inside the wheat bins in the same way we had with the wool. My brother and I dreamed of becoming acrobats in a circus.

The farm was the same farm my father had been born to; in fact, he'd been born in the house we lived in. The previous generation had divided the land between two brothers and it was subsequently divided in his generation between his cousin and brother who owned the adjoining land. My mother's forebears alternated generationally between country and city living. My mother had grown up in the city and was the daughter of a mother whose family had large tracts of land in South Australia, and who was fierce about financial independence for women. With this background my mother was determined to have her say in the running of the farm and she acquired some additional adjoining land which provided her with an independent income. She also had an endorsed truck licence and was a qualified wool classer. She was an important model for me as few other women in the area seemed to be so involved in the running of their farms (though I wonder now whether this was simply a front, put on to assuage the egos of their husbands). One thing was clear: that the women were essential to the community spirit, and their activities – milking the cow, producing eggs, chickens, pigs or sustaining vegetable gardens – were critical to the continuing existence of the farms. They also organised community events. The annual flower show was a high point of the year. At school we would grow seedlings on saucers covered with damp cottonwool and the intricate patterns that resulted would be judged. And at the agricultural show there were remarkable cakes, most of the prizes being awarded to my aunt. The show, along with sports days, golf tournaments, Anzac Day, cracker night, visiting circuses and a host of other regular events provided us with entertainment that saw us through the quieter times. My uncle ran the local picture theatre, aptly named The Globe, with films every Wednesday and Saturday. Here I saw all the latest of Hollywood or the British film studios, classics like *Bridge over the River Kwai*, *Ben Hur* as well as *Dad and Dave*, a black and white film that broke 18 times in a single showing! We were not culturally starved, certainly no more than any other Australian in the 1950s.

The town was not so important to me, except as a source of fish and chips, pies, icy poles and soft drink. The farm, the house and the land around us were central influences.

...during harvest time we threw ourselves around inside the wheat bins in the same way we had with the wool. My brother and I dreamed of becoming acrobats in a circus.

After the harvest, usually around mid-January, we would go away for a three weeks' holiday at the sea. For many years we went to Cronulla and stayed at the Cecil Hotel, until my sister, two years older than I, and fed up with children's games and with being treated as a child, said she wouldn't go. I enjoyed these holidays which meant long days by the ocean, surfing, staying up late, drinking red fizzy drink with every meal and learning to play billiards and poker. Not to mention the daily three-hour stint in front of the television set watching *Zorro*, *The Cisco Kid*, *The Three Stooges* and anything else that was on. Television didn't become the norm in Ardlethan until the mid-1960s, and we were one of the last families to get a set. Our trips to Cronulla also meant shopping trips into Sydney and my annual appointment with the neurologist. The latter made me feel special as I didn't understand what it was about, and it was fun to go shopping for new clothes and anything else that only the big city could supply. When my parents bought a second farm near Wagga, we spent days shopping for furniture and new crockery, curtains and bedspreads and a whole array of household goods.

By then I was at boardingschool where I quickly realised that a class of 35 was much more difficult to top than the five boys and three girls I'd been used to. My confidence fell to such a point that I failed, sometimes abysmally, subjects I'd previously been good at. Boardingschool was also infinitely distracting. No quiet room to escape to; no Woods to walk through; no long rides on my bicycle or on the horse. I spent the first four years of boardingschool doing very little schoolwork and it was only in the fifth year when there were only two or, at most, three of us sharing a room, that I began to settle to more concentrated work. I still failed at the end of my sixth year but scraped together enough marks to go to teachers college. This was when my city life really began.

After one more year of protected life in a hostel I moved into a flat in Carlton. This, I thought, was life. And so it was.

After one more year of protected life in a hostel I moved into a flat in Carlton. This, I thought, was life. And so it was. We lived in one another's pockets, dressed and acted like hippies, tried illicit substances and went to the movies at the Bug House (the Carlton Movie Theatre) once or twice a week. This change proved to be fairly short-lived, as a more profound change was entering my life. Feminism saw me throw away all my former friendships and I entered a circle that was more challenging, more political and more exciting than anything I'd previously known. It was 1973 and by then I was a student at LaTrobe University at the height of its radicalism. I became involved in student politics and most importantly in a CR (consciousness raising) group that had a profound effect on the direction of my life. I discovered that I wasn't alone and for the first time ever I found a group I trusted sufficiently to tell them about my epilepsy. And it was just as well since within a year I began to have regular seizures after a very long period without any. My commitment to women and to feminism became all encompassing as I joined successive voluntary groups: graffiti bandits, a women's centre roster, the first rape crisis centre and the first women's refuge in Melbourne.

Since then I have lived in about 15 houses in almost all of Melbourne's northern or western inner suburbs, and I have stayed anywhere from two weeks to four years. I have worked in a variety of jobs including teaching swimming, youth work, arts administrator, running a health food shop, teaching English as a second language (ESL), teaching in universities and adult education, working in publishing, and most recently co-founding Spinifex Press with Renate Klein. I have also had periods of study, unemployment or simply time out.

My city life is constructed of books. My country life had also been filled with books as I watched my mother devour at least five thick hardbacks a week from the local library. I can't help wondering whether the importance of books to country women's life may well have imprinted itself on my mind, but I also know that had I remained in the country, I'd have been a reader and not engaged in producing them as I now have. The opportunities of city life are undeniable, but the chances of failure are equally pressing.

I think I was fortunate to have a long transition period of moving to the city – six years of boardingschool gave me enough confidence and enough experience in finding my way around the city to make the final adjustment to city living easy. I hankered for country life sometimes, but loved the excitement and comparative open-mindedness of urban life. I did return to the country for two years about eight years after leaving school, but it was urban countryside only 40 minutes by motor bike from the city centre. It had none of the difficulties of rural life in a small community, but many of the advantages: fresh air, a vegetable garden, wood to chop, a nearby creek to walk along each morning and chooks and ducks.

City life has given me a great deal. An education that has not only sustained me, but taken me further than I imagined possible in my under-confident teenage years. It has given me a sense of meaning through the involvement in the Women's Movement and a sense of belonging sharply different from the sense of belonging I feel in a landscape. The two complement one another and I try to get away from the city once a year, if possible to the wide open deserts that are at the centre of this ancient land.

I know I could not lead the life I do in the country. There are too many reasons for me to become an outcast. I'd be regarded as a weirdo, although perhaps I'd be excused as a 'creative type' in my writer guise.

As a lesbian there would be little chance of community for me, although increasingly lesbians are found in country towns and on farms throughout the country. Although unlikely, if I were to have a seizure in a public place in a country town there would be none of the protection offered by the anonymity of urban life. The resulting exposure and my own sense of vulnerability would mean extra pressures to remain hidden in just the same way as happened in rural communities in the 1950s.

In my first years in the city I often felt estranged from those with city origins.

In my first years in the city I often felt estranged from those with city origins. Friendships during my school years helped to shed light on how city people lived. But I find it hard to imagine an urban childhood, hard to imagine a life without a backdrop of landscape, horizons, star-filled night skies and a sense of wide open spaces.

Recently, after a break of 20 years, I returned to the house and the farm on which I grew up. The land feels the same, familiar shapes of trees I have climbed or sat under are restamped firmly in my mind's eye, I recognise the smell, and the 40 degree heat caresses me like an old friend. I drive along the tracks through the paddocks as if I'd been here yesterday. The familiarity is in my bones and under my skin. There is no other place so redolent with memory and so replete with emotion that it seems almost primordial.

Approaching the house I see a series of mental film clips: that's where the horse fell from the truck, that's where the sheep got away from us, that's where my sister was put out of the car and had to walk home, that's where my brother and I rode our bicycles, that's the dam we swam in. The house looks just the same from the road, but one of the gates is blocked and I have to drive in what used to be the out gate. The hedge is mostly down and the grass has extended itself under the cedar tree where we did wheelies on our bicycles. I walk through the frontgate, now gateless, and am shocked by the disarray of the garden. The parallel beds along the front path have merged with everything else, there are no roses, no flowers, only gangly weeds. I walk along the verandah that used to be surrounded by climbing roses, past the invisible sandpit, swing and aviary. The path past the willow tree to the vegetable garden is blocked. I go back and around to the other side, find a way into the sleepout and through to the orchard at the back. The creeper that shaded the rear of the house has gone, but other creepers are taking over the entire area behind the house. A single red rose blooms where once there was an arbour and the wire and wooden supports have collapsed. Grapefruit lie beneath the trees and I pick some up as I walk towards the chookyard. The old dunny, in which chooks would lay clutches of eggs, has fallen on its side, the chicken coop has gone and only ghosts of chooks, ducks and bantams can be heard. Still standing is the huge eucalypt under which my father used to kill the sheep that were the staple of our diet. I return to the house and finding a way in I walk through rooms strewn with rubbish. The house seems so much smaller to my adult eyes, eyes not enlarged by child memory. I mentally refurnish all the rooms with dining table, piano, dressing tables, and a plethora of small objects. But this memory, too, will remain with me. I watch myself tally up the memories as they slide into place. I cannot catch the emotions that seem to flow through my bloodstream. Instead, I collect the grapefruit and drive to visit my aunt only to feel it wash over me again as I make my way through the garden to her backdoor.

Now two images battle for ascendancy in my mind. But what remains constant is the feel, the texture of the air and the deep silence. Two environments battle also. The country which sustains me psychically and to which I retreat for its regenerating effect; the city which drives me and keeps me mentally challenged and politically active. I wonder sometimes what it would be like to return to the country at this age, how would it change me again?

The country which sustains me psychically and to which I retreat for its regenerating effect; the city which drives me and keeps me mentally challenged and politically active.

I return to my city family, my work, my frenetic lifestyle. I know these images will always remain; how they have determined the shape of my life is harder to gauge. I would not be who I am without them, but nor would I be without the influence of feminism, so integrally connected with my experiences in the city, and no doubt with the country women around me during my childhood. I feel privileged to feel at home in two worlds, to draw as I need on one source or the other.

The mix has been there all along, as I heard stories of my mother's city upbringing, or my father's bullock dray days as a teenager. It was there in the culture of books and films during my childhood alongside the huge outdoor playground of a farm. The holidays in the city and during my teenage years, holidays at home during term breaks. In the mix of schools, a country school that could take its students into their fifteenth year, but no further, and the all-girls school that gave me a range of role models, even if the shock eroded my confidence. And it is present in my life now as I try to balance city existence with time in the country or with pot plants and a horizon that gives me a sense of green and space.

I look out the south window of the flat towards the city that is almost hidden by smog, though it's less than a mile distant. This year the pot plants have outdone themselves with constant cascades of flowers. Though I cannot see the city, there is at least a large space between where I sit and the nearest building. This is what the little girl longs for.

In my mind I can return to the cubby house beneath the callitris trees, or the willow tree with its platform and thick wide branches, I can run surefooted along the woodpile and slide down the creeper near the chookyard. The place in the mind doesn't change even if the external landscape does.

A Whole World of Difference

Gwen Baldini

Born in Katanning, in the south west of Western Australia, on 21 January 1935, Gwen Baldini now lives in Nollamara, a suburb of Perth. She runs Yorgum Aboriginal Family Counselling Service, an organisation designed to support and assist Aboriginal people. She studied at Perth College of Technical and Further Education (TAFE), completing a diploma of community welfare in 1989.

Gwen Baldini was a member of the Western Australian Chief Justice's Task Force on bias in the judiciary and the legal system, which reported in 1994.

A lot of my relatives were taken away from their families, under the Western Australian *Aborigines Act*. Many of them lived on reserves, native reserves. There were also people like my parents, for whom an exception was made so that they did not come under the Act's restrictions. My parents avoided the Act by managing to live according to 'the rules'. In Western Australia, some Aboriginal people were able to escape the operation of the Act because of the way they lived, where they lived, and the work they did. They had to prove themselves by working and 'doing the right thing' and being accepted.

That some Aboriginal people came under the Act and some didn't meant that we missed out on knowing members of our own family. I had a whole string of relatives, my grannies, sisters and brother, with whom we didn't mix; the law did not permit us to. Government policies and guidelines split families.

As I have grown older and become more radical, I have begun to look at these issues. I am an activist, which means I demand to know why people were treated in such a way. Why were Aboriginal people divided? Why? Why were Aboriginal people not allowed to keep their language?

117

Why were so many forced to live on reserves?

The principal reason was government policy: down south, and south west, in places like Katanning, Bunbury and Bussleton (as in other parts of Australia), many of us were 'assimilated' by government force, into white ways. The 1905 *Aborigines Act* was passed so that government authorities could take children away from their parents and exercise control over them. That was one of the methods used to impose 'white' ways on Aboriginals.

There is an enormous amount of Aboriginal pain out there in the community. I have read books and listened to people, and I've heard their stories and heard their pain. I am learning a great deal about the issues Aboriginal people have never ever been able to talk about. Some women stay drunk. Some men stay drunk. Then you hear people saying: 'Oh! Dirty black alcoholics,' or 'dirty women', and other such remarks. But if these women and men were to stop drinking, they'd have to start remembering that they were taken away from their parents. For many of them, their parents died before they could find them, or they passed their brothers and sisters in the street not knowing they were related. Or they stood by while their relatives walked past them in the street, ignoring them, because they were obliged to do so. Government policy said that Aboriginal people under the Act were not permitted to have any interaction whatsoever with Aboriginal people who were 'free' of the Act. There was a notion that if Aboriginal people who had been 'assimilated' got together with Aboriginal people who lived on reserves, this would 'contaminate' the ones who were being allowed to 'pass' in white society.

...if these women and men were to stop drinking, they'd have to start remembering that they were taken away from their parents.

Many women have been abused by non-Aboriginal men, with the rape and bashing being accepted by the non-Aboriginal community and the authorities doing nothing to stop it. This abusive conduct was accepted in the times I was growing up in Katanning, and for some time after. And that is not so long ago. It is only since the end of the 1960s that the federal government has had responsibility for Aboriginal people's rights and welfare. The 1967 referendum meant that state governments were no longer free to impose their policies and guidelines on Aboriginal people. Since then, we have been covered by federal government policies.

The history of white treatment of Aboriginal people is a shame that Australia and Australians have to carry. Aboriginal people need to talk about their past, however much this might discomfort non-Aboriginal Australia. For all Aboriginal people, the past is today, the past is their future, and the future is their past. Aboriginal people must be allowed to talk about the shame of white Australia's past. This is not a question of blame. It is about dealing with the pain and the shame.

Ironically, Aboriginal people talk about *their* shame, when it is not their shame, but the shame of those who pursued policies of assimilation and segregation of Aboriginal people. Ironically, too, the shame Aboriginal people talk about is not like the easy remarks non-Aboriginal people make. It is not in the order of: 'Oh, god! I'm too ashamed to go out today. I should be home doing my washing,' or 'I should be doing this or that – what a shame I can't go'. Or 'Isn't it a shame you didn't get that last bunch of flowers'. If you listen to an Aboriginal person talking about shame, and ask them what shame means to them, there's a whole world of difference.

For Aboriginal people, sometimes it's a very sad shame; sometimes it is a good shame. 'Shame' can mean a lot of different things. So I listen, and I've learnt a great deal from my Aboriginal relatives, my Aboriginal kin. I have enjoyed learning, but I have a lot of sorrow and a lot of pain for them. Many terrible happenings in the lives of Aboriginal people have gone unknown to anyone else. Today, more than two hundred years after the lives of Aboriginal people were totally disrupted, you would think that government policies and practices would have changed. Two hundred years ago they were taking children from their parents. Yet here we are in the 1990s, and they are still taking Aboriginal children away. Of course, it is done under a different auspice. It is done in a new guise. It is called something else. But in some cases the children are still being taken away. Some of the parents who have children taken away were taken away from their mothers, too. And so it goes. It is a cycle that goes around.

Yet some Aboriginal people have broken that cycle. They have had to fight, because there is always somebody watching to see if they are about to 'muck up' or let the 'protectors' down. So it is important to acknowledge that what has happened to Aboriginal people is horrific, and that it is still happening to some. It is important too, to recognise that what has happened to Aboriginal people has not applied in reverse: nothing like it has happened to non-Aboriginal people, other than what has been done to the indigenous people of other countries and to the Jewish people.

So much of what has happened in the past is repeated today. When I was a child and youth in Katanning, I and my family members spoke English, but we could understand the broken language that was used by many Aboriginal people. People lived in Katanning and other country centres who spoke Nyungar language. But it wasn't allowed to be spoken in schools. This meant that Aboriginal children *had* to learn English and a great deal of pressure was placed on them not to speak their own language.

Aboriginal children had to learn English and a great deal of pressure was placed on them not to speak their own language.

119

This ignorance of language continues today. In my work with the Chief Justice's Task Force on bias in the legal system I was outspoken about a number of issues, and in particular the prison system. The right to speak language and be understood should exist not only in the world outside the prison, but also when people are locked up. The people who work in the prisons hold the key to everything that occurs there. They hold the key literally, and they hold the key figuratively in terms of controlling the people who are required to live there. Those who are in the prison system because the legal system says they have to be have everything taken away from them. Aboriginal people, men and women, make up large numbers. Many studies have confirmed the bias that results in Aboriginal people 'ending up' in prison. Once there, they don't get a good deal. There is no provision for official Aboriginal visitors. There is no requirement that Aboriginal people have access to interpreters, or that they have visits from people who speak their own language. Or that they are entitled to use their own language and be understood by the prison authorities. It is this, amongst all the other issues that are important to Aboriginal people, that I am fighting for.

There have been important changes. At that time I was a child in the south west, anyone who was Aboriginal was put off the streets at five o'clock. There was a curfew, so that Nyungars had to be inside before dusk. Six o'clock was the very latest that anyone could be on the streets coming home. It was a rule: out of town you had to be! Aboriginal people weren't allowed in pubs at all. At the movies, Aboriginal people had to sit right down the front or right at the back of the theatre. The kids were all down the front, looking up and getting a crick in the neck, and they had to duck in when the lights were out. They weren't allowed to be seen coming in, at least not when the lights were up. Similarly in hospitals, the Aborigines were outside on the verandah or, if they were lucky, there was a separate ward for them, or they might have had a room close to the morgue.

South African apartheid had its legislative base in laws passed in Australia.

Yet generally, and more often today, the violence and destruction of Aboriginal culture and the attempts to undermine and destroy Aboriginal people is hidden. It is not out in the open, like apartheid was in South Africa. And it is important for all Australians to know that South African apartheid had its legislative base in laws passed in Australia. I have learned that the South African apartheid laws were based on the 1905 Western Australian Act.

In the West, non-Aboriginal people must take responsibility for their involvement in the control of Aboriginal people. No one wants to hold them up to ransom, but Aboriginal people do want non-Aboriginal people to accept some of the responsibility. That's what I am about in being radical. I don't see why I should hide behind doors if I have a pain for my own people and see them being badly treated, or if I see happenings that don't sit well with me. Of course I will go out to talk about it. Of course I will say there needs to be a recognition of what has happened. Of course I will demand that if there is to be a particular treatment of Aboriginal people, then there has to be some justification for it and a good reason.

I will also be involved in environmental and heritage issues, because when this continent was first created and Aboriginal people came to be, they took from the land only what they needed. Nowadays, the land is stripped bare. Non-Aboriginal ways have treated the land as if it is there to serve materialist wants. If these practices continue, the land will be laid barren, and laid to waste. There will be nothing there.

Trees have been cut down. They are not replaced. The native foliage and bushes are not replanted. Animals and birds have been forced off the land.

When I look around me, I can see that the land is not as good and plentiful as it was when I was young. Trees have been cut down. They are not replaced. The native foliage and bushes are not replanted. Animals and birds have been forced off the land. The environment has changed. And the change has not come because of anything birds and animals or plants have done. It is because humanbeings have done it, in the name of western culture.

It is vital that people in authority, people on the land, and the ordinary, everyday person in the street begin to start thinking clearly about what Aboriginal people are saying. In particular, the elders are saying, as they always have, that it is important to leave something for the land; that it is important to care for and look after the land more than people do at present. It is important to look after all aspects of the environment. Aboriginal people must be taken notice of. Is it so radical to ask for attention to be paid?

When I was growing up, we didn't have a lot of material possessions. We missed out on a lot because we were living in the country. But we often visited farms to buy a sheep to eat. We went kangaroo shooting and rabbiting, and ate kangaroo and rabbit. There was always something different to do each season: sometimes we went gum picking, picking gum. You eat it, and it is wonderful. Manna gum, it was called, and we picked bags of it. Dad took us out early in the gum season and we sold it to the lolly factory. They made sweets out of it. When my granny was alive, we'd go up to the bush and she would tell us about the different fruits, what you could eat and what you couldn't. She told us about the quandongs and showed them to us, so that we could recognise them. We had a tree nextdoor, and picked the fruit for Mum to make quandong jam. We made marbles with quandongs, too.

I was strongly influenced by my family. My granny was a lay nurse. She went around with the doctor and delivered people's babies. She lay out the bed, ready for the woman to lie on when the baby was being born. This knowledge of my granny's hospital work, observing her being a nurse, drew me into the field. I have a desire to do grief counselling, and this is connected with my granny and my present work with Aboriginal people. Grief is very close to the hearts of Aboriginal people, it is at the heart of their experience. Aboriginal people are going through their own grieving, centred in their own experience as Aborigines.

After leaving school I worked in a hospital. Just as I had discovered on other occasions, always, always it was necessary for Aboriginal people to prove our worth. We had to work hard the whole time, and Aboriginal people were continually on trial. This is how it was for me, in the hospital. If the authorities or the other nurses, or any one at all in your field, didn't want to have the Aboriginal person included in some activity, well, there it was. You couldn't do anything about it. It was a case of put your head down, and keep working – harder than anyone else, just to prove them wrong.

When we were young girls, my cousins and I went to the hotels. There was a constant stream of policewomen to our table, asking whether we were under age, whether we were Aboriginal or were we white. With constant harassment of that sort, all the time we had to be on our guard, defending ourselves.

I didn't stay in the country long enough to put up with it, but I know that some of my friends, my Aboriginal friends, had trouble. They were always on guard, proving they were just as good. If they were sent out of the pub, or the non-Aboriginals didn't mix with them, that was just something that had to be endured. If you wanted to get somewhere, you put up with it, so that you could achieve. Sometimes, working hard and doing just as well or even better than non-Aboriginals was not enough. Aborigines might study, but be denied the results; or they would be refused a certificate such as the non-Aboriginal people received. There was no acknowledgment for Aboriginal people of the study they had done and the completion of the course. You'd do just as well, and still you wouldn't get the certificate.

For me, living in the country meant a lot of fighting and standing up for your rights, and saying: 'I'm entitled to this, that and the other.' Then I moved from Katanning to live in Perth. I had many relatives living in the city, which made it easier for me, because everything was new, noisier and faster. I was also able to keep in contact with my family in Katanning. There was an old steam train running between Perth and

Albany. I often went on it, although it was an overnight trip and a day to travel to Katanning.

In the city, there were more people, and people smiled a bit more. There were more things to do. But it was frightening, too. It was a long way from home. Yet I had good friends, and many of them are still my friends today.

For many people, living in the country can be good because a person can get to know everyone in the town and the surrounding countryside, and find work easily. But if there is no work, it is necessary to move on to another area or town or a city. This makes for a lonely life for many, because they need to move away from their family and the places they are familiar with. I was never forced into this situation, because I married in Perth, and I could visit my own people because they then moved to Perth. I often went to visit them, staying with them overnight. My sister moved to Perth too, and before my parents came up from the country they often visited, staying with aunties who were Perth-based.

I would never return to the country, because I have very happy memories here, in Nollamara. That is why I am not selling my house: it has been home for 37 years. I am happy and comfortable, so why would I return to the country? I'd only go back to visit my family up on the hill: they are all buried up in the cemetery there, in Katanning, and I'd go back to see them. But it's not the same as if they were living there.

When my brother was alive, we often travelled down to visit, but my ties are cut, now. That is a sad aspect to that: I loved going there, and the kids loved being in the old family home, yarning with Pop and the brothers, but there's nothing there now. There are only memories, and no close relatives living in Katanning. They've moved on to other country towns, or to the city. And the country is not like it was. It's changed. We've grown older. Old! We've all made our own way in life, and have our roots elsewhere. I am a single person now, I'm happy with my lifestyle, I'm safe and secure. I have been such a long time away from the country that I feel like a suburban girl, a Nollamara person.

I expect I tried harder. I thought that to eliminate racism and discrimination, I had to grow away from the Aboriginal culture.

My husband was a taxi driver. He has been dead for 11 years now, and it seems like another life. He was always the one who came to pick up my friends and me when we were going out for the evening. We struck up a friendship, and it went on from there. He was a lovely man, the only boy in his family, with two sisters. I was not Italian. He was. That was not so bad – but me being an Aboriginal, a Black woman – that was terrible! At least, that was the view of his family. I felt so sorry for him, because he was a very loving man and was torn between his family and me. He didn't ever speak to me in anger about it. He was a gentle person.

I expect I tried harder. I thought that to eliminate racism and discrimination, I had to grow away from the Aboriginal culture. It was not a growing away from my family, but away from being an Aboriginal. My in-laws should have had more blasted sense, but they were racist. I tried to be a good mother, a good wife, and in doing so didn't have time for my own race, my own Aboriginality, my own identity. I was weighed down by trying to be 'Miss Perfect'. I had to bring the children up the 'right way'. They had to go to church. They had a lot of time to see their grandmother and grandfather and uncles and all their Aboriginal relatives, but the racism and discrimination from the in-laws couldn't help but affect them. This means that have to a large extent 'lost' their Aboriginal side, which is very sad. People should think before they speak, but unfortunately they don't always have the sense to do so. This means that racist and discriminatory ideas can be expressed before people think of the consequences for other humanbeings.

I was put on trial, and had to prove myself. It was bad timing for me: if I had met my husband in the present day, if he and I had been born at a different time, being 'on trial' and having to endure racism would never have occurred. Today, the world is a lot different. But at the time, I thought I was doing the right thing, trying to be 'best', trying to be 'good'. For an Aboriginal woman the world can be doubly painful it she is in a mixed marriage, because she is trying to be 'Miss Perfect' which means, too often, that she forgets about herself. Sometimes you can forget about the real person. That is what happened to me.

If I had my life to live over again, I think I would have told my in-laws of the pressures they placed on me and my husband. Yet there is nothing I can do about it now, because it is in the past. But I can thank them for my radicalism.

When we married, we lived with the in-laws in a big old house in York Street, Subiaco. There was a large empty block next to it, and at the back of the Victoria Hotel. People parked in our yard to go to the football. My relatives often did so, because they were great East Perth followers; sometimes, because of the conduct of my in-laws, I prayed to god they'd park the car and just go. Just go, not call in. But they'd call in. I really loved them and enjoyed them coming in to visit, but after they had left, there was abuse and a flow of racist remarks. One of the daughters (my sister-in-law) tried hard to support me, but the others in that family followed the lead of the parents. Fortunately I had an inner strength. My husband and I supported each other. We cared very deeply for one another, which meant that we endured a lot of things we shouldn't have had to put up with. Women, especially Black women, and indeed all women, should not have to weather abuse of any sort. Discrimination and racism are forms of abuse that should not have to be endured.

My husband owned his taxi, so we were comfortably off. The children went to Catholic schools, and we owned our own home. When we moved out of the family house in Subiaco, it was to live in Nollamara, where I have lived ever since. My husband and I worked hard. I went out to work when the children had grown up a bit and were old enough to look after themselves. The oldest one was about 14, and I took work that fitted in between seeing them off to school, then their coming home. Sometimes I worked in the middle of the night, taking night shift because it meant I could be with the children in the day time. I worked for Silver Chain – home help for the elderly – for five or six years. I could set the number of hours I wanted to work, or the houses I would visit: this meant it could fit in with my children and my work around the house. I worked at Bakewell pies, making crumpets. That was the most awful job out! When the electricity went off, it seemed that the crumpets kept coming, rolling on inexorably.

I stayed with my children a great deal of the time because I had my sister's kids to look after too, and also cared for other people's children. I often babysat at home, so that I could be with the kids. When we were at York Street in Subiaco, I became accustomed to taking on the responsibility for having meals on the table for all the family. In my family, we sat down to meals together always. We shared what we had to share, talking and exchanging ideas and opinions. I enjoyed that way of living.

I came to the conclusion that I was tired of being 'good'. I was tired of being 'acceptable'...

I recognised from a very young age that I was a political person. My political stand became stronger and stronger. Even though I was busy trying to be 'Miss Perfect' all those years with the in-laws, the experience was strengthening my political understanding. My in-laws had a great deal to do with me 'getting on'. I recognised racism and discrimination. I understood how Aboriginal people were put down. I saw that it didn't matter how hard you tried to be accepted, some fool would come along and say: 'Oh, you're alright, Gwen. You're an Aboriginal, but you're a good Aboriginal. You live in house. You're a decent Aboriginal. Your kids go to school and do the right thing.'

I sat down and thought about this. I came to the conclusion that I was tired of being 'good'. I was tired of being 'acceptable' – as they saw it. Then I began questioning *them*. I didn't get out so much to rallies or demonstrations, but I was very supportive of such political action. My brother came with the elderly to our home, and he came with his friends, visiting. He was in the native welfare department and worked with welfare groups and organisations. He brought a constant stream of Aboriginal visitors to me. And many members of my family came. It made me eventually come to see (although it took a long time) that it was important to think about my culture and to be proud of being Aboriginal. If a person keeps being hit on the head with a hammer, at the same time as statements being made such as: 'You're black,' or 'You're dirty', even though she is trying to do whatever she thinks will be positive in the eyes of those who are raising the hammer and making the statements, she gets tired. I got sick of it.

I got radical.

I thought, you take me as you find me.

There were always the 'little' shocks of life to reinforce the need for us to take pride in our heritage and our culture. One day as I was walking along the road a policeman drove up in his van. He passed me, parked the car and got out. Then as I came up, toward him, he said: 'Are you the nigger from down the road?' I was totally shocked. People do shock you – quite often. You think you're in your own safe little house, accepted, calm and happy. Then it comes, like a blow out of the blue, blue sky.

You think you're in your own safe little house, accepted, calm and happy. Then it comes, like a blow out of the blue, blue sky.

My neighbours from over the road were walking behind me, and all I could say was: 'Did you hear what he called me – a nigger!' I was so overwhelmed I didn't have the sense to take his number. We went to the commissioner of police and complained. The commissioner came out to my home, apologising, saying: 'There's only just so many rotten apples in the basket.' Yet if I'd had enough sense – like the young people do today – I'd have had pencil and paper out immediately. But back in those days, you didn't think about such activism – although it seems such a straightforward thing to do, nowadays.

After that experience, I thought about all the issues: being Black, my Aboriginality, my culture, my rights in this world, all the indigenous people of this country – and I thought, well, I'm an okay person. My kids go to school. I'm doing everything 'right'. And the thought went through my head – if they talk to me like that, how must they talk to the rest of my people?

Today I hear non-Aboriginal people saying: 'Oh, Aboriginals, if they wanted a job they could get one.' But there are a lot of Aboriginal people at 40, 47, 48, 50 who have no formal education, none at all. It is not because, like some youths nowadays, they don't go to school or have people chasing them to get them in to classes, or leave early to go home. It is because Aboriginals were not allowed in the schools: at a lot of places, Aboriginals were not accepted into the education system at all, or were not allowed to stay at school after they reached a certain age. Luckily for me, I was accepted, just as my family was accepted in

Katanning. But a lot of Aboriginal people were not. The response of the education system was similar to that which Aboriginal people met if they went to dances or to pubs or to parties: 'Oh, Aboriginal. You can't come in.' It was a case of 'the whites' always watching, keeping an eye on what was happening, to see if Aboriginal people played up.

Aboriginal people had to fight hard to get into universities. We had cases where Aboriginal people were refused entry into law, and had to go outside the state to study it. My family did not experience the same difficulty: my children have been to university. One is a socialworker, one was an economist and now has her own real estate business. My sons have good jobs; another daughter has worked 25 or 30 years in the one chemist shop.

The introduction of Abstudy has meant that education is far more accessible to Aboriginal people. The government has accepted the responsibility of Aboriginals not having been accepted into schools years ago, establishing a scheme designed to 'get them back' so that they can gain an education, even though for some of them it was a long time overdue. It makes me very sad to know that Aboriginal people have always had to push to be accepted.

Today, I find less discrimination because I simply won't countenance it. I am a loud, outspoken person and I demand that people justify their actions in treating Aboriginal people in the way they do. If anyone tried to discriminate against me, they'd have to justify it. And similarly if it happened to any of my friends; we'd make a good song and dance about it. This is what Aboriginal people are doing now, working hard (again!) to change people's thinking.

Yet it is still very difficult in our society. We have multi-culturalism, but where does the Aboriginal person fit in? Aboriginals don't fit in; we are still on the outside because multi-culturalism is about people coming from another country to Australia. Aboriginal people have never left this land, so we cannot be slotted into 'multi-culturalism'. Yet sometimes, governments have tried to do that to us! It's ridiculous! At the same time, there are many organisations and services established for multiculturalism – committees, groups, funding. But Aboriginal people are not included. Why aren't there advisory groups and Aboriginal clubrooms? Where do Aboriginal people have their own sporting grounds like other nationalities? What about other culturally specific services?

Then there is the example of Black people who come to Australia from other countries. Aboriginal people often find that such people are respected in Australia. Yet the indigenous Black people of this country are at the lowest end of the scale so far as 'respect' is concerned. Because I am articulate and speak out, people enter into conversation with me about my nationality. They say: 'We've been thinking about what nationality you are.' 'Well, what were your thoughts?' I'll ask. 'Oh, we thought you were Maori, we thought you were from the Asian countries.' And so on. They have thought of everything except the truth. I say: 'Well, why didn't you ask me? Do you want to know what I am? I'm Aboriginal.' Then they say: 'Oh, my god' You can see the distaste.

When my husband died, suddenly, in 1983 he and I had recently returned from a holiday in Singapore. We took care of him at home. There was no hospice care available at that time. My two youngest children cared for their father, the youngest son taking time off from work and my youngest daughter caring for her father when her brother needed time for himself. There was a lot of strain, because there is good and bad about nursing someone at home and coming to terms with death. It's very very hard. Either a person can deal with such a situation, or cannot. When you are looking after someone who is dying, there's not much time to grieve: to go through stages of acceptance and denial, and finally letting go. I put on the pretext that I was alright. But I couldn't sleep after my husband died. I took to walking up to sit in the park, with my dog, at four o'clock in the morning. Early daylight. And I'm sitting there with the dog. When I told my cousin, she was angry with me: 'Oh, how dare you, Gweny! You mustn't do that. Come and sleep up at my house.'

I couldn't sleep after my husband died. I took to walking up to sit in the park, with my dog, at four o'clock in the morning. Early daylight. And I'm sitting there with the dog.

My husband died six months after the Christmas of 1982. I didn't know what to do with my life. I had been very happily married, despite the goings on from my in-laws. I had put up a brick wall around me, so that the barbs and taunts didn't hurt me, or so I thought. But they did. My husband's death brought a lot of issues home to me. So I stayed with my cousin, for comfort. It stopped me being lonely. I'd go up and sit watching television: it was the company I wanted, just the knowledge that there was someone else there in the house with me. Finally, it led to my decision to take up formal studies, through Abstudy. I think my cousin became tired of having me sleeping in her house. She got talking, saying she was intending to study at the TAFE. 'Come to TAFE,' she said. I went up and enrolled. I began using brains that I had never used before. If you are happy being a housewife, you don't pay much attention to academic or professional opportunities. Sometimes you don't know that you are still able to study and that there can be so many possibilities out there in the world.

I did the group workers course and the counsellors course, and became a welfare officer. I became very attuned to study and learning. I met many people. They knew my husband had died, but didn't make me feel as if I should be at home mourning instead of out in the world learning and having new experiences. I had gone back to work immediately after my husband's death, to try to deal with the grief by not thinking about it. That didn't work. Using my brains and going in a new direction did.

I now do a lot of community work, and for three years – from 1988 to 1990 – I worked in the women's refuge at Marangaroo. A huge percentage of the women seeking shelter were Aboriginal. This was not new to me. When I was a child, we lived with domestic violence. My father was a violent and angry person. When he came back from the war there was nothing for him. Like other men who bash their wives, he was not made accountable. This needs to change, because the violence is so damaging to so many women.

In the Aboriginal community, we are finding it very difficult to deal with this issue. We want to walk with the men. We want to solve it. Yet there are so many issues for Aboriginal women, particularly around housing and income, and there is the added problem: so many Aboriginal men go to prison. Do we want to add to the numbers? We are looking at educational programs, particularly those which emphasise that it is the man's problem and that he has to deal with it. The men have to start banding together and helping each other, supporting each other. Women cannot do it all. But it is a very hard task, because Aboriginal men know non-Aboriginal men, who say that it is not *their* problem. Therefore, why should Aboriginal men recognise that violence against Aboriginal women, by them, is the Aboriginal *man's* problem? Men do not want to own their own violence, but it will never change unless they do. They have to take hold of their problem. They have to work it out. For too long they have said: 'Oh, I didn't mean to do it, I'm sorry.' Well, it's way past being sorry.

Men do not want to own their own violence, but it will never change unless they do. They have to take hold of their problem.

The women who are beaten are often so traumatised, down so low, that they need time out to think clearly about their situation. They need to be able to look carefully at their own lives and ask (and answer) questions such as: 'Is it safe for me?' 'Am I going to put up with continual bashings?' 'Does this relationship have to go on, or end?' Because there is a great deal of violence against women, and it is important to end it. A lot of women have had to come to terms with being bashed, and a lot of women haven't had the strength or encouragement to get out of a marriage where they've been bashed continually. Some of them die in that relationship because they don't know how to get out of it.

Yorgum Aboriginal Family Counselling Service, the organisation where I work, is named for the eucalyptus tree, a white gumtree. We counsel and support many, many Aboriginal people. Women who have been bashed and raped. Women and men who have been stolen from their families. Women who have had their children taken away. Women who were taken from their own mothers, and now are threatened with having their children removed from them. We have women and men who have relied on drink to take them out of their misery and shame, but it has only made their lives more complicated and unhappy. There are people who are suffering an identity crisis, trauma, change, grief and loss, who are seeking an understanding of why they were taken away from their parents. There are kids who don't understand why they have been put into homes. There are kids who don't understand why their mothers drank all the time. There are kids growing up in family violence and taking the violence along with them. We help them to deal with their pain. It is about cultural healing, and healing the culture. It is important for them to understand that they can to talk to someone, and to know that we share what they have been going through. We have an understanding of what they have suffered; they can talk about anything and everything.

People from minority groups need to be free to talk in a way that can be understood. They need to be heard by someone who connects with what they are saying.

For the people who come to us, no one has helped them through the traumas of being raped, through the pain and grief of incest. People out there are willing to talk to them, but do not talk on the same level; they use terms and language that the people cannot understand. People from minority groups need to be free to talk in a way that can be understood. They need to be heard by someone who connects with what they are saying. At Yorgum, we talk the same language. We don't profess to be any better or any worse than they are. We are of the same culture. There may be social workers and psychologists 'out there', but we are using our culture and are open to listen to the *whole* story, the wider picture. We listen to the pain that is back in the dark recesses, the pain that has come up to haunt them today. The pain is still with them, they haven't 'got over' it. We work though that pain and the sadness they feel.

I have been here at Yorgum, and the organisation has existed, only since the end of June 1994. Word of mouth is how most people come to us. They just want to talk. The timing's right for them, and they see that it is time now for them to heal. They come because they have a sense that it is good to be an Aboriginal person, and it's good to be what, who and where they are, despite the pain and the shame. It is this inner strength, this inner sense of self that is propelling Aboriginal people. People are sharing. We make appointments, but no one forces them to come. It is a case of when they're ready. And generally they come back!

When people contact Yorgum, I go out to assess the counselling needs. We sit down, yarning. A lot of the time I know the family, or they look at me and say: 'Oh, you must be related to this one or that one,' and they're right. Aboriginal people *do* know your kin, and further down the track they will generally have it that you are related to them! 'Oh, I know your relative so-and-so. She (or he)'s married to my relative such-and-such.'

The white gum has healing powers, and we wanted Aboriginal people to come to us, knowing that there will be a healing. We wanted to promote the idea of healing ourselves, through Yorgum. We have so much to come to terms with, so it seemed right to use that tree as the name and symbol of our organisation.

Recently the South African author, Fatima Dekay, visited Australia. I went to hear her speak. She is a wonderful person, and it was wonderful to listen to her. But she said: 'You Aboriginal people are the sweetest, gentlest people out. You're too sweet. That's why it was a pushover to subdue you. For South African people, it wasn't like that.'

And that's really true, isn't it.

Note: Yorgum Aboriginal family Counselling Service is located at 190 Treasure Road, Queens Park, Western Australia, 6061.

PART 3

Two Worlds

A Brassy, Vociferous Yelp...

Doris M.E. Leadbetter

Doris Leadbetter immigrated to Australia in 1963, as a 'ten-pound migrant' from England. She arrived with much optimism and no prejudices. And she liked what she found. She took up writing when she stopped 'real' work, using early retirement as her excuse. Now she writes every morning, either poetry (which usually gets published in the mainstream literary journals) or joyfully polishing off her latest novel. Being politically incorrect (her latest excuse), it will almost certainly not be published. Still, it's fun to try.

A recent career change for her husband has brought Doris Leadbetter back to city life. She now lives in Eltham on the fringe of Melbourne, Victoria, surrounded by arboriphiles, belled cats, and bellbirds which ping like monotoned windchimes. This is not city life as it used to be.

I am 65 years old. I came to Australia when I was 35 years old. For the last eight years I have lived in an Australian country town whose inhabitants number some 62 000 and call the town a city.

Before coming to live in the town, I lived in cities.

There were many advantages for Englishwomen born in cities at the turn of the century. My mother, who never had a paid job, went with her mother to visit the poor on a regular basis. Both saw this as a vocation that had more to do with being well off than with being religious. My family was moderately well off, and moderately religious.

My mother was born in London, and access to the deserving poor of the city was easy. One tram ride took them to the Jewish part of Southall, where my grandmother's and mother's clothes were made; another tram ride further down the line provided the opportunity to deliver the food they carried in a wicker hamper. If the journey were broken to allow a fitting, the tailor's wife would take the opportunity to add a bowl of soup or a homemade, spicy sausage to the basket.

My mother told me how well received she and her mother were by the women who expected the fortnightly visit. She told me how she would be directed to neighbours who were not well, or who were newly delivered of yet another child, or who had lost someone since the last visit. The neighbours cared. The women were aware of each other's needs.

The neighbours cared. The women were aware of each other's needs.

I was told many stories of the people my mother visited. There was a murderer's wife and three children; a suicidal son of a fallen woman; several fallen women (with whom my mother was not allowed to chat), and a redeemable drunk.

The food would be delivered, along with a homily or two, and my grandmother would retreat to the comfort of her home, confident of having done her duty and feeling good about it.

I grew up in an industrial city in Yorkshire, with a population of about half a million people. From an early age, I accompanied my mother on weekly visits to the old people who had retired from working in the family mill; they had retired because of old age, or ill health, or an accident. My mother had a list of those who needed her visits; the list was monitored by Mrs Hardaker, the senior clerk at the mill. She knew everybody and kept an eye on things.

Sometimes an old millhand would ask my mother to drop in on a neighbour who was not connected with the family, but who needed comfort or help.

The city, it seemed to me, was a slow-moving carrier of people, a machine which oiled its own wheels.

I was born in the family home, a few days after full ripeness, urged into existence by my mother scrubbing the floor. When our 'daily' arrived, she found my mother doing the daily's work and promptly woke my father who sent for the doctor. There was not, and I often asked my mother about this, a frantic race to boil water. Plenty of towels were available from the airing cupboard at the top of the stairs, but the boiling water seen in so many films was not needed.

My father took my older sister round to my grandpa's house and came back to find me already delivered and my mother swathed in lavender water and a fine wool bedjacket. He was disappointed, of course, that I was a girl. He had already enrolled me as a life member of the Yorkshire Cricket Club and my birth in the city ensured my eligibility to play for the county.

My home city was a leader in education in its day. The needs of schoolchildren were met by the local government, which provided scholarships for the bright children, and encouraged a variety of experimental schools to set up shop. I was three when I began at the Montessori school. I could read soon after, and write, if barely legibly, at four.

I went to the Montessori school because it was close by, not just through choice. The children came from both sides of 'Grange Road', the dividing line between rich and poor. Contiguity was the only criterion; if the parents couldn't pay the fees, the council did.

I had friends at a Rudolf Steiner school, at a community school where parents taught more extra-curricular subjects than the teachers taught formal subjects, and at a few religious schools which were open to other religions, or none at all, and were scrupulously monitored by the council to ensure that the curriculum was up to scratch and no actual nonsense was taught. Religion, yes. Nonsense, no. You could teach people to believe in God, in some form or another, but you couldn't teach them creationism which was obviously (to the council and most of the citizens) a nonsense.

Because we were well off, we spent three weeks a year on holiday. Our preference, my parents' preference, was for the quieter beaches on the Isle of Wight, or Scarborough. Bournemouth, maybe. Certainly not the working-class attractions of Blackpool, Morecambe, or Filey. Not that the expression 'working-class' was used much in my family. We knew exactly, with astonishing nicety, our location in society. We were expected to vote Labour, as my grandfather was a founding member of the Independent Labour Party, and his grandfather was the millowner who destroyed his own loom when the Luddite Rioters persuaded him that it was wrong to take away the jobs of workers by undue mechanisation of their work.

When she was twelve my sister burst into tears in a butcher shop and became a vegetarian.

We were well to do, left wing, barely religious, and I was being very well educated.

Mme Montessori devised her system of education to provide children from poor city homes with opportunities to see farm animals and have other experiences unlikely to happen by chance. I never went to a farm. When she was twelve my sister burst into tears in a butcher shop and became a vegetarian. It was deemed politic and sensible for me to avoid any such confrontations. I still tend to believe that steak, like tofu, is a product of a clever imagination and something vegetable.

It was assumed by my parents that my very pretty sister would marry well. She attended the Masonic balls, the Hunt balls, and the smartest of the county parties. I was fat and clever. My father was proud of me but my mother felt very sorry for me and thought I would miss out on the good things in life. She had, after all, been a flapper, a Bright Young Thing. She had not danced with, but she had met, the Duke of Windsor.

My parents gently steered me towards a career.

We always had a big black car. An Austin Princess. Every Sunday my father would drive the family up onto the moors, where we would stop and run about. There might be a few blackfaced sheep there, but they scattered as we arrived, like the rings spread away from a pebble dropped in a smooth pond. We inhaled the good fresh air, which lacked the tang of wool scouring and the gritty feel of mill chimney output. We played a little cricket. Then my father would drive us to a country pub, where my parents and my sister would eat good country cooking and I would stay in the car and read. I was embarrassed to eat with my family in public. They behaved perfectly well; it was something to do with my pubescence.

Once every few months my mother would take me to London to visit her relatives. I had to sleep in a dreadfully soft feather bed, to which I attribute my putative claustrophobia. We did nothing, as the relatives preferred to talk.

We inhaled the good fresh air, which lacked the tang of wool scouring and the gritty feel of mill chimney output.

After the Montessori school, I went to an upmarket, private, Anglican, all-girls school. I did well there, although my socialistic principles were considered something less than *de rigeur*. I read sociology at London University, acquired a post-graduate diploma of some standing, and was offered my first job: recruiting fifteen-year-old boys to work at Mars Bars. Not what I had in mind. In fact, I had written a strenuously researched thesis on the male homosexual in society, which was well enough received. Sadly, there were few jobs on offer for straight females who knew all about male homosexuals. Their closet firmly excluded me.

It also excluded my mother who never knew what topic my thesis had pursued. My one attempt to explain it had been waved away, like a persistent fly. Victorian lesbians escaped punitive sentence because the Queen did not believe women capable of such behaviour; my mother did not believe anyone capable of it, and chose to hear nothing to the contrary.

In London as a university student I discovered another benefit of living in a city; anonymity. The poor people kept an eye on each other's needs, but people living in the huge houses of Notting Hill Gate and Bayswater chose not to see their neighbours at all. The ceiling of your 'bed-sit' might obviously be a quarter of a whole ceiling, with two thin walls enclosing your space, but the people beyond those walls were only noises.

Many of the people I lived close to for five years were students like I was. I knew some, and I knew others by sight. I once knocked on the door of a neighbour one flight of stairs up and asked for help because I had fallen and a cut on my forehead was bleeding. I had seen his nameplate on the frontdoor: 'Dr Jeremy Snaith'. He offered me a sticking plaster and explained that he was a PhD, not a medical doctor. I never spoke to him again.

Some of my friends were country people. They talked about the simple pleasures of their childhood; reading by lamplight, going for long rambles over the moors of my own country, doing homework while watching over farm animals. All of them, as I recall, had been encouraged to 'better themselves', by getting a university education and then a job in a city. Only the oldest son was kept back to take over the farm in good time.

There was a woman living in the house in Notting Hill Gate who went out into the overgrown and otherwise unused back garden of the house every time there was a new moon. She danced in its light wearing a long white frock and, if it were chilly, a woollen scarf. You could set your lunar clock by her, if you cared to. I don't know her name, or whether she was all right in the head, or an early 'New Age' exponent. She was a neighbour, and had a right to total privacy.

Ten years after starting out in London, I went back to the industrial city where I was born and spent there the years that were left before I decided to migrate to Australia.

I did not in fact decide to come to Australia. My older sister, tired after an exhausting and just-resolved bad marriage, decided to come to Australia. A year after she arrived in Perth and discovered permanent sunshine, she said I should come to Australia, too, and bring our mother and my two children from a long-resolved bad marriage.

...my mother and I agreed that we would make up our minds after we had been interviewed by the Immigration people. We would interview them.

I sent in the application forms, and my mother and I agreed that we would make up our minds after we had been interviewed by the Immigration people. We would interview them.

Two months later, we received our tickets. There was no interview, no time for thinking twice about our decision (little enough time for thinking about it once) and we were on our way on the *SS Orion*, a large and terminal ship.

Perth was to be my home for 12 years. Perth was so isolated that the next nearest city is on another continent. At the time of my arrival there, it had little live theatre, few restaurants, and a lifestyle based on the beach. I had always been involved in the theatre (as a promising director, bad actor, useful backstage worker), I loved foreign food, and I hated heat. I spent the required hours on the beach – in winter – and watched the foreign ships coming and going from Fremantle harbour, sometimes wishing I could go with them.

I married again – happily. I married my present husband. Like me, he is a migrant. He came from Montana in search of sun and found me.

Very romantic. And happy.

There were some customs prevailing in Perth which astounded me. It was considered – this was 1963 – bad form not to wear a hat and gloves for a visit to town. Stockings were absolutely mandatory, summer or winter. Nobody walked around in their bathers, even at the beach, without a towel decently obscuring where their legs joined on. Bottoms were indecent, and remained concealed at all times. Breasts were a little more liberated, but that was more to do with their design than the design of the bathers.

I worked with scientists; many had come from Britain like I had, and shared my perceptions about Australia. The class distinctions which we perceived without comment among us dissipated in the egalitarian atmosphere. The only class distinctions left after a few years were those between British wives, who would not wear hats and gloves and stockings, and the Australian wives who did.

Like most of the British mothers, I asked permission from my daughter's school for her not to be so over-dressed in summer. I also asked for both my children to be excluded from parading on Anzac Day. I was told how wrong I was on both counts and reminded that my daughter, in particular, was being educated for her Rightful Place in Society. If she were to marry appropriately, she must first learn to behave – and dress – like a lady. This was a different Catholic school from the one my daughter had briefly attended in England. I had been a Catholic for three years; my conversion was to last only as long as my daughter's education. We then both behaved like women rather than ladies.

From Perth, we moved to Canberra and had eight years of pleasure, enjoying the politics, the gossip, the oddities of life in a miniature city.

And now I live in an Australian country town, whose inhabitants number some 62 000 and call the town a city.

I arrived here with a full bundle of certainties about myself, about my talents, about my capabilities and how all these would become a useful future. Within a short time, I dropped my bundle. I soon learned that I was not simply an experienced committee worker, I was a woman. I might have had a few useful experiences, but I was only a woman. A professional career had provided many opportunities to sharpen my skills, especially when the federal Labor government insisted that women should be more visible on committees, interviewing panels and the like; at the time this directive came around in Canberra, I was one of only three senior women in my workplace, so I was kept very busy learning how not to be a token woman.

When I offered this experience in the country, I was at first an embarrassment. Women who wish to be useful join useful clubs and groups. They do charitable work – almost invariably for no payment at all. They hold office in groups that foster the arts, or that foster their menfolk. They join school boards and hold what offices the men leave open for them.

What women in the country do not do is sit on development boards, hospital boards, building society boards, university councils. They can be local councillors, if the voters can be persuaded. But they rarely get appointed to places of influence and power. The few women who get past the gatekeepers do so by virtue of their own sympathies for tradition, or because they have highly specific and relevant qualifications, such as nursing.

I arrived in the town an 'early retiree'. I was an experienced committee hand, a tireless enthusiast for work, a creative and diligent person with a useful background. I was an able person. Now, for the first time in a long while, I had to recognise that I was also a woman, and thus suspect.

When I first raised the possibility of joining one of the boards, and pointed out how useful I could be, the chairman told me that I was too ambitious. He told me that I didn't know the place yet, nor how it worked. He told me that local knowledge was all-important. He suggested I join a group of women dedicated to raising funds. Recently, the local hospital board rejected for all time ('the matter is closed') the need to open an abortion clinic.

I became a writer, producing a weekly humorous column for the local newspaper. I write serious stuff, too; poetry, short stories. I poke fun at the traditions of the country, but with perceived affection. Irony is not a strong suit here.

Perhaps if I had moved to the country before the age of feminist activity I might have done better. Certainly my attempts to become a useful citizen have been thwarted because of my gender, which means that whenever I have mentioned this fact I have been labelled a 'rabid feminist', which gives the holders of power another excuse to exclude me and the likes of me.

Recently, the local hospital board rejected for all time ('the matter is closed') the need to open an abortion clinic.

Because I am 'famous' within the area of distribution of my newspaper, I am often asked to give talks to groups of people. Many of the groups operate in remote country towns where all the people who come to hear me are farmers. I meet country women who do all the backbreaking work on the farm; widowed farmers; women whose husbands have to work a long way away to bring in enough money to buy feed for their stock. I meet women as tough-minded as drought and poverty can make anyone. I meet very few younger people; most of the farmers I meet have sent their children away to make a living in the city.

At the meetings I go to as a guest speaker, the country people arrange 'trading tables', where they sell home grown vegetables, cakes, eggs, jams and pickles. They provide lunches served from casserole dishes brimful of delicious food made from generations-old recipes. They ask after each other's relatives, they coo over the new babies and share comfort when somebody has died.

But they all tell me the same thing: the country is a beautiful place to live, if you have money. You need money to eat, to support your animals and crops, to send your kids away for education, to maintain the farmhouse, to buy a few clothes. They don't leave because they can't. Hardly anyone expects their life to become easier; droughts break but broken hearts and backs don't mend.

The countrywomen I meet talk to me about their lives with a sense of describing something almost legendary. They are still pioneer women, and they still suffer from the same fears of isolation and poverty as their great-grandmothers.

They are still pioneer women, and they still suffer from the same fears of isolation and poverty as their great-grandmothers.

Back here, in the country town whose inhabitants number some 62 000 and call the town a city, I sometimes feel as if I am still living in my home town, just before the second world war. The newspaper, which was the vital source of information in my childhood, holds that same role here. Residents don't think of themselves so much as Australians, or as Victorians; they belong to the town. So television and radio, which reflect the more sophisticated views of the world seen from a major city, tend not to say very much of relevance here. We don't have rapists, we don't have important visitors, we don't have crime waves, and we certainly don't need an abortion clinic.

The local newspaper has several pages each week devoted to religious news. I remarked once in my column that the Second Coming would get only half a column on page six of a metropolitan newspaper, and someone sent me a letter accusing me of taking the Lord's name in vain, in coloured crayon letters. There are columns in the newspaper devoted to the activities of all the clubs, to wedding celebrations, and to the successes of local people in competitions.

There are competitions here. Each year, children from dancing classes strive to achieve the best they can in front of judges brought from Melbourne to ensure fairness. These children tap dance, they do ballet, they do what is euphemistically called 'modern' dancing. It is exactly the kind of thing I did myself when I was seven or eight years old; in my home city in England the last such competition was held a couple of years before the second world war. I have a photograph of me in a frilly frock holding a £1 note, a prize worth considerably more than is given these days.

That is where my country town feels to me to be isolated. It is 1937.

People have concerns for the future, especially with farming relatives. The world overseas is threatening again. The weather is always a problem. The cinema shows pleasant films and all children go to bed at a reasonable time. Whatever undercurrents there are of vice, of cruelty, of violence are subsumed in the respectability of white gloves and a belief in the continuing and actively benevolent presence of God.

Women have a role to play and, on the whole, we play it to the same old rules. All behaviour is covered in the patina of propriety.

Just occasionally the patina gets rubbed up the wrong way and a brassy, vociferous yelp can be heard.

Demanding a Voice

Janeece Richards

Janeece Richards is a multi-skilled woman. She is just as comfortable compering fashion parades and modelling as she is milking a 200 cow dairy herd, delivering a calf or driving a forage harvester. A workplace trainer and senior clerical officer, she often sits on selection panels and frequently flies to Sydney from her home in country New South Wales to attend meetings at the premier's department. She is a member of the Central Coordinating Committee for Spokeswomen, a program in that department.

A bachelor of social science, Janeece Richards is committed to learning and is presently undertaking research for a further degree. She sees herself as typical of the modern day country women.

I was born in the country, the third of a family of five children living in a semi-rural area. Being raised on possibly the first 'hobby farm' ever to exist I quickly learned how to milk a cow, kill and clean chickens, and chop wood. Our home consisted of both parents, four girls and one boy; there was no room for 'gender' jobs. Everyone needed to pitch in and my brother was equally adept at setting the table, washing up and making beds as he was in gardening or finding the cow to be milked. The girls were expected to assist with all outside work. My father ran a manufacturing plant and my mother played the role of sharer and supporter, wearing the hats of full-time housewife, mother, accountant, legal adviser, and mediator. Her skills were highly valued by husband and children as well as community members who came to her for assistance. As with most women, my mother was attuned to the needs of both family and community. The contribution made by my mother and other women of the same ilk in the family setting was never acknowledged and government and community need to recognise the status of these women, for the value of their contribution to the community.

Environmental issues were always part of our daily living. Everything was recycled where possible. We had a compost heap and recycled our clothes with me getting my sisters' and cousins' hand-me downs. Other clothes were cut down and made into shirts or shorts. The bath water was dished out each evening and placed on the garden so as to save the tank water. With the addition of a wire handle, paint cans became buckets. Cats were not allowed as they would frighten away the birds needed to protect the vegetable garden from pests.

At the age of six came my first lesson in gender power. My father's employee took us to the local pictures and whilst there I was sexually assaulted. My childhood was in need of redefinition with this loss of childhood innocence. I never bothered to tell my mother of this incident as I had already observed her lack of power when my father became annoyed. That her choices were restricted was readily apparent; I wonder if more choices would have existed had she lived in Sydney. As a country woman, my mother was very well educated but still bound to a situation over which she had little control, and her sense of inadequacy was evident. Yet it was through my mother that we children were encouraged to succeed at school and so be in a position to move to the city and make something of our lives. We were encouraged from an early age to become feminists.

My first visit to the city was at the age of 12. The train trip itself was an experience. Then, wide eyed, I beheld the city traffic and tall buildings as I alighted from the train at Central Station. The one experience that will remain with me always is my first visit to a Chinese restaurant where for the first time I tasted prawn omelette. At this time I also received my first culture shock. Whilst in a large shopping centre I watched in horror as a women dropped her groceries on the pavement. No one came to her assistance, not even my father. When I questioned him about this, his comment was: 'People don't get involved in the city, it's a lot different from the country.' In my own community, should I drop my groceries on the pavement I would receive assistance. I am reassured by the security of this knowledge. Because country towns were and are close knit, life surrounds the neighbourhood happenings and more often than not gossip becomes the 'norm'. No malice is intended and people are genuinely concerned for each other. It is true that country people know each other's business.

...wide eyed, I beheld the city traffic and tall buildings as I alighted from the train at Central Station.

Years later, when working for a local veterinarian, I was asked to organise a tuberculosis test run for local farms. Instead of telephoning each farm I phoned the local country telephone exchange and spoke with the telephonist, a valuable source of information. I told her what I needed and she reorganised my schedule with such comments as: 'Don't bother sending the vet to Mr Smith's at 10.00 am on Monday 'cause he'll still be milking, get the vet to pick him up on the way back.' And: 'It's easier to do Mr Schneider's farm before Mr Boothe's as the vet just has to slip through the back lane and will save doubling back.'

Often I would phone a local telephone exchange to be put through to a particular telephone number only to be told by the telephonist that the person had 'just gone to town and definitely won't be back until 4.00 pm after they've picked up the kids from school'.

...to be told by the telephonist that the person had 'just gone to town and definitely won't be back until 4.00 pm after they've picked up the kids from school'.

My schooling took place at a coed country primary-school with boys and girls totally segregated from Year 3 to Year 6, and from Year 7 to Year 12 segregated in the playground only, with classes mixed. It mattered not whether segregation existed in the school as the neighbourhood in which I grew up consisted mainly of boys and, through childhood games, fights and swimming together in the river, any gender barriers that school may have erected were broken down. This easy relationship with members of the opposite sex learned in childhood has continued to mature over time and today I feel equally comfortable in a group of men as with women. My husband, on the other hand, having attended a Catholic boys boardingschool has difficulty communicating with women and attributes this problem to his schooling.

The extended family within a country town is a priceless gift. I grew up surrounded by my parents, siblings, aunts and uncles, cousins and my grandmother. I loved walking to my grandmother's house and sitting in her rocking chair gazing out at the river and hills and dreaming about when I grew up. I saw my grandmother as a constant source of encouragement to go out to conquer the world.

Birthday parties were a major event. Cooking took place over three or four days with the women of the family supplying their *piece de resistance*. Aunt Nell would make the rainbow sponge, gran would make the trifle. Grandma's birthdays were always the best. My father made an annual statement from the time Gran reached 75 years that this could be her last year 'so let's make this birthday party the best yet', and of course it was. Gran lived to be 96 so we had some wonderful, unforgettable parties. The sad thing was that each year we would watch Gran open the gifts of bed socks, talc, soaps and slippers with her 'oohing' and 'aahing' only to discover, upon her death, drawers filled with unused soaps, talcs, and slippers. What a learning curve for me. For my mother's birthday I try not to give presents but instead organise a local limousine to pick her and her friends up from their homes to take them to a restaurant for lunch, or I give her an IOU for *Phantom of the Opera* or some other activity redeemable during the following three months.

On completing highschool I was deprived of my range of options. I should have received more informative advice from my careers officer as to my future pathways. Instead, I was advised by the careers adviser to become either a teacher or a nurse. As I wanted to do neither I moved from my family to live in Sydney, joining the public sector. I was to learn later that city female students were given much more information on career paths than were their country sisters.

There was, however, great excitement in making this move to the city as I had long considered that to live in the country was deprivation and exciting people lived in the city where public transport was a common occurrence rather than a bi-weekly event, and people didn't appear to have to wear their cousins' cast offs. I had no idea what life would be like without my family close by. I needed to adjust to my new lifestyle and its faster pace, different culture and change in focus. My real growing up was now to take place.

The city appeared huge to a 17-year-old and I experienced great difficulty in finding my way around. Many a time I would ask a passerby how to get to a particular place and which direction the train went to the city so that I knew which platform to stand on. On one occasion I asked a bus driver to let me know when we had arrived at my destination. He didn't, and I ended up totally lost. I was surrounded by so many people yet the loneliness and isolation was at times unbearable, and many nights I cried myself to sleep, drowning in a sea of self-pity and homesick nostalgia. It was difficult looking into the faces of strangers when I knew most of the faces in my home town. There was no one to talk to and the people with whom I worked were polite but unfriendly. As recently as 1993 I was attending a meeting of the premier's department and needed to go to the department of school education at Rozelle. I caught a taxi in the CBD (central business district) at 1.25 pm and arrived at my destination at 2.50 pm, having travelled via the harbour bridge as far as St Leonards before the driver realised we were going to Roseville and not Rozelle. We then turned around and again he stopped near Hunter's Hill admitting he was lost. I took his street directory from him and navigated back to our destination. No, I didn't report him but didn't pay him more than the appropriate fare. The past distress of being lost in the city as a teenager was, however, certainly revisited.

Many a time I would ask a passerby how to get to a particular place and which direction the train went to the city so that I knew which platform to stand on.

I often felt that as a country person I was treated as quaint and I struggled daily to fit in with the city culture. I would buy the same magazines as I saw my colleagues reading and study the pictures of the magazines to find out what they were interested in, and desperately tried to become 'one of them'. Over the years I have mentioned this to other country women who lived for a time in a city. All have agreed that they too were treated in a peculiar way and felt they had to work twice as hard within their work place to become accepted, not only by their peers but also by their supervisors.

I continued to miss the closeness of family life. I regularly took the country night train, sitting up for seven hours to arrive back in my home town around 4.30 am to spend the weekend with my parents. At this time I became the centre of attention. My clothes were the latest, my hair professionally styled and my country cousins openly admired the new me, together with my highly exaggerated and colourful lifestyle escapades. These were, in reality, totally drab and uninteresting. However, to country cousins, having to catch the 7.30 am electric train to the city and walk from Wynyard to Elizabeth Street daily was rather exciting, whilst eating at a city restaurant and listening to Don Burrows play at a coffee shop were the ultimate in sophistication.

As a country woman I was slowly accepted into the city community. I began to receive invitations to the theatre, barbeques, and beach parties. Boyfriends came and went as I learned that the type of friendship I had experienced in the country was not necessarily on their agenda. During this time in Sydney I made only one close female friend; the friendship has continued to flourish. Today, my friend Jenny lives in Queensland and is in constant contact. She now sees herself as a country woman.

Everyone living in the country knows that it takes at least 15 years to become accepted by the community.

I pursued my career path with diligence and vigour and after four years of city living I returned to the country to marry a 'local' boy who was a farmer. Once again I was to pass through one of life's unstable periods. Adjustment was required! My career path in insurance law had now turned into a cul d' sac and socially I was in limbo. By the time I had returned to the country all my school friends had moved to the city to work and I no longer had any friends close by. I was now looked upon by the rest of the community as a 'blow in' and no longer one of them. Everyone living in the country knows that it takes at least 15 years to become accepted by the community. So began the long haul to reestablish my country identity. I longed for the excitement of the city, the restaurants, theatres, coffee shop get-togethers and the stimulation of being part of the agenda-setting team. I threw myself into the role of wife and mother whilst teaching at the local TAFE (technical and further education) college.

Because we lived on a property, my children grew up believing that each Christmas day it was normal practice for all families to help bring in the hay and have a late Christmas day lunch. It took them a while to understand that other children didn't come home from school, then change into work clothes to help feed the cattle in the stalls and collect the eggs. Today I observe with interest that my children are choosing careers that will allow them to reside in the city.

I finally returned to university as an external student. It is difficult moving from the city to come to terms with the fact that one cannot access university other than through the external mode. If a TAFE college exists within the town it may not always offer the course a person is seeking. I became acutely aware of the socio-economic climate surrounding me and became involved in women's issues. I was invited to join the local QUOTA club and accepted, trying to find an answer to my needs and to fill the void of no career path. Had I continued to live in the city I know I would now be involved in law. Because my choice was to return to the country my future lies in the arena of human resources, my community and its people.

Because of my experience I possess a need to ensure that my sisters both country and city are not disadvantaged through making choices to put their careers on hold whilst attending to family and childraising. For country women, encouragement is needed to focus on the positives and not the negative of country isolation. The resources are ours to access but there is a need both to recognise this and to seek out the disseminator of the important information.

In 1991 I joined the Spokeswomen's Programme within the New South Wales Public Service and in 1993 was elected to the central coordinating committee of this program. The Spokeswomen's Programme was born in 1977 following Professor Peter Wilenski's report, the *Review of NSW Government Administration*. He identified the status of women within the New South Wales government sector as inappropriately low. The statistics showed women in employment as making up a large portion of the total workforce but with a small percentage only holding senior executive positions. Even now in the public sector only 12 per cent of persons employed in the senior executive service (SES) are women. Professor Wilenski also discovered that most women were congregated in the traditional 'female occupations with limited career paths'. His report stated:

• there was discrimination against women;
• although women occupied approximately 50 per cent of the paid workforce, they held only a small percentage of promotional positions and their labour was used mainly within the perceived female occupations.

The labour market is characterised by segregation according to sex and women are concentrated mainly in the lower paid jobs. Overwhelmingly, women make up the largest proportion filling clerical positions.

The premier of the day (Neville Wran) made a commitment to ensure that discrimination against women was removed from the public sector and this was followed by the Public Service Board seeking ways to ensure women were given equal opportunity. One area targeted was to provide a network for women and through this the Spokeswomen's Programme evolved.

The *Spokeswomen's Programme Manual* sets out the mission statement for the Spokeswomen's Programme. It is:

> To promote efficiency and effectiveness in the public sector by assisting women to develop their knowledge and skills to enable full participation on equal terms in a merit environment.

The program addresses the needs of all women regardless of where the women live. It is able to traverse the borders between city and country allowing women access to the program by arranging information days and regional conferences in both city and country towns so that no woman is disadvantaged through her need or desire to live in the country, and so women's lives are both enriched and empowered. The role of a spokeswoman is to give women 'encouragement, and access to information and skills which will allow them to speak and act for themselves': *Spokeswomen's Programme Manual*

Spokeswomen pursue the following aims:
- collection and dissemination of information to women on matters concerning equal opportunity in employment;
- active encouragement of women to reach optimum potential in the workforce;
- encouraging the development of career opportunities for women;
- acting as a reference point in matters of equal opportunity and career development;
- promoting general awareness of the problems relating to women's employment;
- developing an informal communication network;
- influencing policy relating to women;
- promoting the program as a management strategy: *Spokeswomen's Programme Manual*

It is not intended that spokeswomen replace management, staff personnel or unions. Their function is to complement and consolidate the activities of these groups whilst at the same time drawing attention to the needs of women both country and city, ensuring that women receive the same access to career opportunities as men through the provision of information, direction and support.

Ancillary staff in schools are seen as a group of woman in the traditional female occupation making up approximately 98 per cent of the workforce in this area. Recently I was involved in structuring a professional association for ancillary staff in schools so that through this avenue women both city and country will have access to further studies, and professional development, and will receive recognition for the contribution they make in the field of education. This association – the School Ancillary Staff Professional Association (NSW) – was born on Tuesday 24 January 1994 and has as its objectives to:

• provide recognition of the role of school ancillary staff;
• provide a corporate voice for school ancillary staff;
• increase contribution by school ancillary staff in the decision making processes;
• encourage and promote ongoing training and development;
• relate the changes in education and administrative issues to the role of school ancillary staff;
• provide networking opportunities for school ancillary staff;
• promote cooperation between organisations with similar interests.

Through living in both the country and the city, my experience has shown me that there is a difference between city and country women. I have discovered that city women are not as adaptable as country women. Maybe this is due to the lack of resources available to country women who automatically look for a solution wherever they can. If the car breaks down, they use the push bike. If one is unavailable, they walk.

If the car breaks down, they use the push bike. If one is unavailable, they walk.

Country women don't have access to much public transport but that doesn't stop them putting little Freddy on the front of the stroller and, with baby strapped in, walking the five kilometres to the shops – then sharing a taxi home with someone they have met down town and who lives in the same area. Country women have greater freedom to move around without the fear of street violence, allowing them more independence. As a consequence, they demonstrate great sensitivity to one another. They appear more friendly, prepared to give of themselves and possess the initiative to open a conversation with a smile or general comment.

Country women appear more resilient. Not having access to the counsellors and welfare projects their city sisters have, discussing the options country women make do, over a cup of tea with a neighbour. In the country the community spirit has not suffered from fragmentation to the same degree as in city communities. Country women are tough.

Many are not consciously aware of gender bias. They don't know of any option other than to stay on the land and work shoulder to shoulder with their husband fighting drought, flood, pestilence and the economy. They do not, however, appear to build up an immunity toward disasters. A country friend of mine refused to give to the 1994 bushfire appeal for city people. When I asked her about this, she told of an incident back in 1989 or thereabouts when huge fires ravaged the state's south west. Farmers lost not only their homes but also their livelihood and stock together with pastures, fences and barns. She was very aware of the lack of interest or concern shown by city people in the trauma experienced by their country colleagues. As I listened to her I came to understand that healing needs to take place between city and country women, just as we all need to develop a greater understanding that we must pull together as a total community.

...healing needs to take place between city and country women, just as we all need to develop a greater understanding that we must pull together as a total community.

Understanding across different perspectives particularly needs to occur in the role of farmers and country people in conservation. As they did when I was a child, environmental issues continue to play an important role with country women. However, the scene and focus now appears to have changed, with many country women appearing to be at loggerheads with the conservationists, greenies, animal liberation movement, and ecologists. In spite of this, country women regard themselves as dedicated to the protection of the environment.

Having experienced living in the city, I am frustrated by country isolation. Being removed by a distance requiring four hours travel to the city, I find it impossible as a career woman to attend meetings in Sydney such as breakfast meetings or early afternoon meetings that run for maybe one to two hours. This predicament forces me to refuse positions on sub committees and I am forced to take on roles requiring less meeting times and intensity.

At meetings I am identified as a country delegate. This immediately sets me apart and targets me as being different. It is true that country women do have different needs to be met, but we also have the same desired outcomes. When I speak I am given the courtesy of being listened to, but because I am often speaking on country women's issues my comments impact to a lesser degree than were I a city delegate. Other members can be condescending to the beliefs and values I express as a woman living in the country. This adds to my recognition that much work is needed to develop the profile of women living in rural Australia.

As a country woman I enjoy more quality time than many of my city sisters. On a recent trip to Sydney it was pointed out to me that it took the same length of time to travel from the sixteenth floor of my hotel to the lobby as it does from my frontdoor to my place of work. As I pondered this I also acknowledged that daily I have two or three extra hours which, were I living in the city, would be spent sitting behind the wheel of my car fighting traffic or commuting by train or bus in to the city to my place of work.

Having been brought up in the country, lived in the city, returned to the country and now residing in both city and rural areas allows me some insight into the position and aspirations of women of Australia. I see that all women, both country and city, are becoming empowered and seek enrichment through equality. Women are taking control of their own space. They have recognised their options and are prepared to exercise them. Women have access to information and information means power. Regardless of whether country or city, women are prepared to speak out and demand to have their voices heard.

Each one of us is a product of our environment and our childhood colours the rest of our lives. We need to see ourselves firstly as women and all other differences should be placed on the backburner so we can, as a corporate group working solidly together, resolve the issues that directly impact on us as women and together forge our future.

The Best of Times

Agi Racz

Born in Budapest on 13 August 1948, Agi Racz crossed the border in to Austria in 1956 and soon after landed in Fremantle on the Italian migrant ship *La Famiglia*. She attended Presentation Convent in Windsor, Victoria, and soon after joined the Australian Broadcasting Commission (ABC). After travelling and working for the British Broadcasting Corporation (BBC) in television, and for the Canadian Broadcasting Commission, producing radio documentaries, she attended Columbia College in Los Angeles, California. She studied film and television production, joined the CBS Network writing for various shows, including *Laugh In*, then returned to the ABC, joining 3LO Melbourne, later creating new program formats for 2CN in Canberra and 6WF in Perth, Western Australia.

In 1989 Agi Racz initiated an ABC regional network, targeting country audiences. More recently she visited the border regions of war-torn Yugoslavia and for eight weeks trained broadcasters in the English section of Radio Budapest which broadcasts to North and Central America and Europe. What little spare time she has left is spent sailing, cooking, reading and enjoying Mozart – activities which she shares with friends.

These were the best of times... My early formative years from the ages of three to seven spent in the country with my grandmother during the warm breezy summer months of July and August, on the mountain border region with Austria, now better known as Burganland. My grandmother's estate was on the Hungarian side of the border surrounded by medieval villages, mountains and fields which became my playground. It was a safe haven from the turbulence that was once again enveloping Central Europe. The rumblings of Russian tanks through the capital city of Budapest and imminent loss of thousands of lives was as fate decreed on a collision course. I was oblivious to the political machinations and spent most carefree days of my life picking berries, playing games with neighbourhood children and swimming in the cool mountain streams, then reading aloud to my grandmother late into the night. My intention was to read through her entire library, which lined the four walls. There were the greats of literature and philosophy, from Goethe and Schiller to Hans Christian Andersen. The vastness of knowledge was surpassed only by the mountains surrounding us, which contained other joys. Even now, there are moments when through a sense of smell I'm transported back to the tranquillity and beauty of those leather bound volumes which at such an early age satisfied my curiosity and stirred my imagination. I experienced an ongoing thirst for knowledge.

In comparison, my life in the city was frantic with activities of a different kind. From ballet lessons, piano tuition and gymnastics, these were my staple diet of self-development with a rather strict school regime specialising in languages. This was the bane of my life. My love of books continued to sustain me and I read everything I could, mainly under the bedcovers by the light of a torch. It was in this warm cocoon under the eiderdown that through books I first felt sorrow and love and understood that life was not always fair but that good does prevail though sometimes through a torturous road.

I read everything I could, mainly under the bedcovers by the light of a torch.

My own life was suddenly turned upside down when my grandmother's property was confiscated by the government some time before the 1956 revolution and the occupation by Russian forces. Food became scarce, particularly in the city, and those with a big enough backyard were allowed to keep livestock as long as it was for home consumption. We had a variety of animals which inevitably became pets for my brother and myself, before ending up on the dinner table. This was distressing for us and created endless scenes with my mother when we refused to eat the splendid array of rabbit and chicken dishes, but none of this compared to the day when our two pigs, Hansel and Gretel, were being weighed and prepared for the butcher's knife. This was an outrage. It was murder in the first degree as far as my brother and I, the feeders and caretakers of Hansel and Gretel, were concerned. I was in charge of Hansel and my brother nurtured Gretel, only to see the butcher driving two parallel steel rods into the hard snow covered ground that was our backyard. Instinctively we knew what was to follow, we pleaded for their lives and though treated sympathetically all our pleas fell on deaf ears, so the only course left to us was to lock ourselves in the bathroom and put our hands over our ears whilst the ugly deed was done. Our grief was not universal, as there was much merriment and celebration for friends and relatives and neighbours – all were to receive packages containing morsels of Hansel and Gretel. When we came outside, although fresh snow had fallen, the underlying sea of blood was still visible like a blanket of red rubies.

I retreated, not in weakness but in strength, and resolved never to be part of such cruelty again. It was a resolve I never had to break. The tanks rolled through the streets, the revolution had begun and we fled to Austria, leaving the torsos of Hansel and Gretel hanging in the smoke house in our backyard.

...although fresh snow had fallen, the underlying sea of blood was still visible like a blanket of red rubies.

Our first port of call in Australia as migrants was Fremantle where we spent some months before travelling to our final destination, Melbourne. Little did I imagine that the theme of country/city would once again play such an important part in my life. A new country, a new life and turbulence were the staple of our daily lives... The pressures of this new world split up our family and I was ensconced in boardingschool with the hope that at least there would be some stability and continuity along with a high standard of education, a theme in which both my parents placed a lot of faith. Presentation Convent in Dandenong Road, Windsor was run by the Irish order of presentation nuns, a fairly strict teaching order with high academic standards. Many of its past pupils have excelled in their chosen fields, Germaine Greer, Jana Wendt, Diana Trask being some of the high achievers. As a boarder I was one of only a few who did not come from country Victoria. I, too, excelled at creating diversions, amusements and havoc, wherever possible. For these acts I was rewarded by having to learn passages of literature, translating them to Latin, then reciting them. This suited me, for I was once again at home in a fine library and proceeded to make it my life's work to have as many books translated as possible. For my diligence in this quest I was allowed to stay with friends in the country during school holidays, where I proceeded to translate the more explicit description of the sexual act from Mary McCarthy's book *The Group* into Latin. Having distributed these in leaflet form, I persuaded my school chums that the reading of this in Latin would be a suitable topic for the confessional. The nuns in their wisdom decided that all my future energies were to be disposed of on the tennis and basketball courts. However, I was still allowed out and spent a good part of my holidays over a five year period in country Victoria. I was very much at home establishing my country links again enjoying the freedom and happiness reminiscent of my earlier childhood.

The carefree days were once again with me, as well as the responsibility of chores. Whereas my friends who spent all their lives on the land found going home rather an isolating experience after many months in the city and yearned to return to the bright city lights, I rejoiced in it and felt a knot in my stomach when we packed our bags into the stationwagon and headed back to Windsor.

Benjamin Franklin said: 'Happiness is produced not so much by great pieces of good fortune but by little advantages that occur every day.' I was by now a master of adapting to changed circumstances and making the most of the 'little advantages'. which led me to broadcasting, both overseas and on a national scale in Australia with the Australian Broadcasting Corporation (ABC). (I joined when it was still the 'Australian Broadcasting Commission'.)

One of my great challenges to date has been establishing the regional program unit for the ABC in Victoria. This entailed creating programs from a Melbourne base for country listeners. It was a major priority for ABC regional radio to broadcast a variety of current affairs and information programs specifically catering to audiences throughout the state. With over a million listeners the regional program unit has expanded not only its audience reach but the variety of its programs as well as its staff. By 1994, there were now four regional radio stations, Mildura, Albury, Bendigo and Sale, and four radio studio outposts: Horsham, Shepparton, Traralgon and Warrnambool. My present role is that of producer for the Bernard Lynch program which in 1993 was awarded the Victorian tourism electronic media prize for excellence. A strong component of my job is to organise outside broadcasts from various country locations. All in all, over the past six years there have been over thirty outside broadcasts and once again I have found myself linked with rural lifestyles. The tremendous loyalty of country listeners to the ABC, their hospitality, uncomplicated lifestyles and generosity are exemplary. As a female producer working mainly with male presenters there have been occasions, in the initial stages of travelling around, where there has been surprise that the female member of the crew is in fact the producer and not the coffee and tea lady, and being called 'girlie' even with the best of intentions was not acceptable. Often there was a sheepish apology for such errors. The job has been a mutual learning process, and a rewarding experience for me.

...surprise that the female member of the crew is in fact the producer and not the coffee and tea lady, and being called 'girlie' even with the best of intentions was not acceptable.

Excursions into the country highlight the strong community spirit even in the most recession affected areas. My association with country areas at these times is purely professional. It's now a routine of deadlines trying always to keep ahead of time... There is no time for past reflections or dwelling on my youthful sojourns. It's all in the present, for that's what goes to air. However there is a 'freeing up' from city disciplines: we take an active part in local activities such as motor gliding, or doing interviews on a paddle steamer in Echuca, and hot air ballooning. We also study the lifestyle and feel of a town. Even if on the surface the distress of unemployment and hardships are not totally visible, this is evident when we take talkback on air and the true picture emerges. Even at the worst of times everyone in the community seems to have their place, whether running the local tourism office, selling strawberries by the roadside or fishing bait, or perhaps sitting around watching us as we broadcast from the main street. The ebb and flow has an order to it and there is a sense of belonging, compared to the lost souls and dispossessed who roam our city streets. Though Melbourne has some magnificent parks, the natural country scenes (unlike city attractions), gum trees and abundant wild life fill me with a sense of well-being that involves all the senses.

People in the country still take time out to spin a yarn which highlights their acceptance of those who are different. There is almost a reverence for the eccentrics amongst us, contradicting the general belief that rural folk are in the main very conservative. I am continually impressed by the personal quality of caring for one another even in the larger towns. It is this personal quality that we try to convey through our programs, not so much in a welfare or official way but through the medium of one to one. This connection keeps people afloat at the worst of times. Radio is an intimate communicator and we are constantly aware that we are guests in people's homes, on their tractors, in their shops... We have the responsibility not to be intrusive or offensive, but like any good friend we must be supportive and as professionals bring some joy as well as useful information to our listeners. Clarifying the issues of the day also adds to our relevance as communicators.

Where will future journeys take me? This is speculation but I know it is rare for anyone to have the good fortune I have had. My life theme has been to discover and learn, and my obligation has been to pass it on.

Respecting Other Choices

Belinda D. Tate

Belinda D. Tate was born in Hobart on 12 March 1971. She lived in Triabunna, on the East Coast of Tasmania, and attended Triabunna District High School until 1986 when she finished Year 10. She then moved to Hobart and completed her higher schools certificate (HSC) at Elizabeth College in 1987 and 1988. For the next five years she studied at the University of Tasmania and graduated with a combined arts and law degree with honours in May 1994.

At the end of 1993, Belinda Tate was employed by the Commonwealth Attorney General's Department in Canberra and moved to the Australian Capital Territory (ACT) to assume that position in February 1994. She was admitted to practice as a barrister and solicitor of the Supreme Court of the ACT and the High Court of Australia in 1994, and is currently seconded as assistant advisor to the minister for justice in Canberra, dealing with copyright law and policy issues. When not at work, she swims, as well as enjoying keeping up with current affairs. In the future she intends to travel or study overseas for an extended period.

I spent the first 15 years of my life in Triabunna, Tasmania – it was 'home', and probably always will be. A town of less than a thousand people on the east coast of Australia's island state, about 90 kilometres north of Hobart, it is a mixture of old rural based families and new immigrants in search of a livelihood courtesy of the Wood Chip Mill which was established in the year of my birth, 1971.

My family are the first kind: I am a sixth generation east coast girl; my maternal grandfather's family came from Scotland in the nineteenth century and have maintained a continuous tie with the area.

Despite the influx of workers and their families since the opening of the mill, Triabunna remains a close-knit community. There is a continual surveillance of comings and goings, and anyone new is the talk of the town. My grandmother, fresh from the Women's Land Army in the second world war, came to Triabunna in search of sea air for her bronchitis. She found it, and my grandfather. She often speaks of dark figures peering out from behind curtains and jokes that she has only just been accorded 'local' status after almost 50 years.

There is also a tacit and subtle division between the older rural families and newer arrivals to the area. Kids from farms were sent to private schools in 'town' (Hobart), while the mill's workers' children of my generation attended the local district highschool, which catered for all from Kindergarten to Grade 10. The influx of people since the early 1970s has forced change, and the mill families and their offspring provide the backbone of the community. Traditional livelihoods such as farming, fishing, and orcharding have all but disappeared. The mill families have remained, bringing with them a variety of new services for the community: a bank, a pharmacy, an upgrading of the hospital, and the school, and service stations.

Traditional livelihoods such as farming, fishing, and orcharding have all but disappeared.

I'm not sure why I was born in a maternity hospital in Hobart rather than the local district nursing centre. It had 10 staff, led by a legendary 'go anywhere do anything' sister, and saw many of my friends come into the world. My baby book records that my first trip was 'home from the hospital' with my Grandfather McNeill nursing me.

My mother attended highschool and completed teacher training in Hobart, and taught at the local school. My father left when I was very young, so doesn't enter the equation. Until his death on my fourteenth birthday in 1985, my grandfather became the father I had never known. He was a TPI pensioner, and had a lot of ill health during my life, but before I was born had been an orchard hand for Jones and Co., as well as a soldier and joint owner of the local hardware store with his brother-in-law. My grandmother is an exceptional woman, and has led her life performing a variety of jobs trying to make ends meet. A meagre pension forced her to split scallops, cook for shearers, pick apricots, cook in hotels, take in sewing and ironing, and even paint houses. This was on top of her own ill health, and the pressure of educating three children and caring for a sick husband. And all without one single complaint, and very little thanks. I think it was her determination that rubbed off on me, and gave me an inclination that if I were successful in some way, I could do more than survive.

Kindergarten to Grade 10, for me, was spent at Triabunna District High School (TDHS). There was never any real question of my being packed off to a private school in Hobart at a young age. The idea was mooted as I progressed through upper primaryschool, as there was always the assumption that 'town schools' were better for the smarter kids, and offered more subjects and better opportunities. However, when it came to the crunch, financial and emotional constraints prevailed. I couldn't bear to leave home, and it probably would have killed my grandfather to see me go. So TDHS it was to be.

I couldn't wait to go to school, and from a very young age would sit at the end of the kitchen table copying writing from the breakfast cereal box or whatever else was around. However, having a parent teaching at my school meant that the other kids resented me as a pet, and my mum attempted to overcompensate for this, which meant I got the rough end of the proverbial stick. My early years at school were a bit traumatic and I became a loner. I was always a perfectionist with whatever I did. Unfortunately this was misinterpreted as slow, even lazy, so I never really excelled in infant and primaryschool.

My grandfather's health deteriorated as I entered highschool, and I threw myself into my study. It seemed that the better I did at school, the more I was resented by my peers. It was just not 'cool' to do well at school, be quiet and polite, and to respect the teachers. I was guilty of all of these. I think it was at this time that I made a crucial connection between academic success and getting out of Triabunna. It was a sphere I could excel in, even a way of 'sticking it' to the rest of the class. I wanted to show them that I could make something of my life, and was unhappy and wanted to get out. It had a spiral effect – the more I achieved, the more interest the teachers took in me. The better I got along with the teachers the more the other kids resented me, and I didn't ever feel like I was accepted into cliques and friendship groups.

It was just not 'cool' to do well at school, be quiet and polite, and to respect the teachers. I was guilty of all of these.

My teachers were always encouraging, but with a lack of resources and a community of people oriented towards life survival education (not English literature or philosophy) I was never really pushed hard. Because there were never any more than 40 kids in my year at school, advanced maths and other subjects for the bright ones were limited. We did have all the basics though, plus German, art, cooking, sewing, typing, woodwork, metalwork and technical drawing. Few girls did the latter three. I was particularly impressed by a lot of the younger teachers – first year teachers tend to be dumped in the country schools. Having come from the city to teach in Triabunna they seemed so worldly and different, and spoke of their days at university, and travel, and careers.

For eight years, every Friday, my grandmother drove me to Hobart for classical ballet lessons. I was dying to be a city girl – they seemed so much prettier than I, dressed as if they belonged in the latest clothes catalogues, and spoke of rushing off to the pictures, the pool, shopping and whatever else city girls did. It all seemed so exciting to me, as we had to plan weeks in advance to do any of those things. We also went to Hobart for grocery shopping. I had what can only be described as an obsession with elevators and escalators, and made any excuse (usually the need to go to the toilet) to use them. This provided me with a taste of city living – I knew it was for me.

Triabunna women habitually assumed support roles. The local doctor, pharmacist, bank manager, school principal, town clerk, policeman and foresters were always, and still are, men. Triabunna nurses are women, as are most of the infant and primaryschool teachers and the secretaries. On the land, women also assume support roles. I frequently visited cousins on their farm just out of Triabunna, and the men undertook the day to day running of the farm whilst the women assisted cooking for shearers and keeping the household running. There was certainly a perception that the men did all the 'real' work.

To continue to study was to break the mould, and was not understood by many.

By the end of highschool, I had outgrown Triabunna. I thought that there must be more to life than this. I was frustrated with the way everyone knew what everyone else was doing, the stifling of individuality, and the pressure to follow in the previous generation's footsteps and leave school at Grade 10, work for a few years, then marry. To continue to study was to break the mould, and was not understood by many.

I loved Year 11 and 12 in Hobart. Elizabeth College provided me with 1200 other people to meet and learn from. My learning curve skyrocketed, and I was shocked, but then stimulated, by the diversity of people I encountered. I saw punks and hippies and, God forbid, mature-age students, and learnt tolerance. This cocktail of people taught me not to be so quick to dismiss the new and unknown, and to demonstrate a greater level of tolerance for alternative culture. As a mechanism of survival, Triabunna had rejected what was new and challenging. If something challenged, it disturbed and threatened.

University further broadened my horizons. A teacher in Year 12 was the first to seriously discuss tertiary studies with me. I had previously viewed university as an abstract concept, where rich kids from private schools went to prepare to follow in their father's footsteps. For the first time I was told that I could do it too and that I would be good at it. The teacher was right – I did well and my five year combined arts/law degree has transformed me into a person with opinions and passion. I loved the uni student lifestyle, and in the early years largely cut myself off from Triabunna. I liked the anonymity of it all – I could pursue intellectual discussions or nightclub all night if I wanted to. Through uni I took with me the 'stick it to them' motivation, carrying a chip on my shoulder about being a country girl and not having a privileged background. To me, success equated with acceptance this time, not rejection.

Women's issues have become important to me only in the last few years. While I was at uni, I became involved in actively encouraging country women to continue their education, visiting isolated areas of Tasmania, speaking to schoolgirls about uni and sharing my experiences with them. Most of them just needed to be reassured that they had the ability to do it. The main issue is one of awareness – I have been asked several times if girls can do bachelors degrees, or are they just for boys? This doesn't seem to be such an issue for city women, who at least know where the university is, and perhaps have older siblings at uni.

That I have had to struggle and fight a bit harder than most has made me a determined and single minded individual. I have virtually had to turn my back on my childhood existence, which had vastly different priorities. I had put a lot of pressure on myself, and am still struggling with the 'stick it to them' factor in my self-motivation, which I realise now is destructive. I feel pangs of guilt as I cringe at the Australian attachment to the rural idea I longed to escape. I still have a huge complex about not being as sophisticated and as world-wise as city women. This is probably the only thing inhibiting me now – I find myself making excuses for my country upbringing, rather than focusing on the positive aspects of having a safe and secure environment in which to spend my formative years.

My grandmother and a lot of my school friends still live in Triabunna. My grandmother is extremely supportive, and I am constantly flattered by the way she informs everyone of my progress and, if she doesn't, they ask. My school friends could never really understand what I was all about – there was very little common ground, and I was always worried I would say something to offend their priorities and life ambitions. It got better over the last few years – with new levels of maturity, we learnt to respect one another's choices and went from there.

I think the experience of a country upbringing has clarified a lot of questions for me, and put my own existence into perspective. Triabunna has ever been a constant for me – a point of reference that didn't change much, and a measure of how much I was changing. It means I can look back now and say: 'Well, haven't I done a lot of things in 22 years?' And it also means I can form an insight into how it all happened – what motivated me, for example. Nonetheless it also means I am very critical of others – I resent and reject those who have had everything handed to them on a platter all their lives, and view them as extremely narrow people who don't think too much. My problem is that I think too much.

My city life is an intricate network of friends, associates and acquaintances; a Triabunna within a larger city. When I first moved to Hobart, I befriended other women from the country. We were all instant friends, with similar education and life experiences. Gradually I branched out and met a diversity of people. I am certain this was a substitute for not having a family around. I am told by my friends that I am an amazing 'people person' – instantly very friendly, open and humorous. This is almost certainly derived from my fear of rejection and the need to feel comfortable and accepted by those around me.

In March 1994 I had been in Canberra four weeks, and was waiting to begin as a solicitor with the Commonwealth Attorney-General's Department. It was a natural progression, really. Just as Triabunna had got too small, after two years of HSC (higher schools certificate) and a five year degree, I also outgrew Hobart. I was bored, it got too comfortable, and I am now the kind of person who needs constant change and challenge. Does Canberra have that to offer me? I'm once more embarking on that process of making friends and establishing a support network. Only this time it's in a largely political sphere, and I can't go running home if it all gets too much for me.

Gourmet Cycling

Sarah Stegley

Sarah Stegley was born in Brighton, a seaside suburb of Melbourne, on 16 October 1951. She holds a degree in agricultural science from Massey University in New Zealand and is a partner in the gourmet retreat Howqua Dale, situated between Jamieson and Mansfield, in country Victoria.

A director of the Stegley Foundation, a philanthropic trust based in Melbourne, Sarah Stegley's pastimes include horse riding, kyaking and cycling.

Ever since I was a little kid all I wanted to be was a farmer. My first memory is of wanting to be out on the land, farming. In those days if I watched television I concentrated on series such as *Hopalong Cassidy* and *The Texas Rangers*, and any other programs where horses and being outside was the theme. I'd watch Westerns forever, not because they were 'Westerns' but because of the horses and the countryside and the fact that all the action took place in the outdoors.

My father was a Melbourne person and had always been city-based, but he also had a profound hankering to be on the land. My longing for a rural life may therefore have been inherited. All I know is that I have had the desire for an outdoor life for as long as I can remember.

Our family history is not very well known to us, but what we do know indicates there is no heritage of country living. My father's father was a Danish immigrant. He was a jockey, so the love of horses may have come from that line, but all my relatives have been city people, and the tradition in our family is one of city living. However nothing remains static, and we are now developing a new tradition with a strong attachment to the country. My father bought a number of properties in the country, one of 3500 acres at Howqua Dale. I now live on that property, and my siblings live on the other properties. Of six children, three of us are in the country and a fourth is a landscape gardener in Melbourne. Thus four out of the six of us are involved in plants and animals, and three of us live in the country.

In the 1960s I studied agricultural science at Massey University in New Zealand. In those days women were not allowed to study at Dookie Agricultural College in Victoria, even though it was government owned and funded. I applied to Dookie, and saw a man in the department of agriculture at the state government offices in Melbourne. He advised me that no women could go to Dookie: it was a facility for men only. I asked why. He responded that it was presumed that women would marry and, if they did, it was a waste of money to educate them to be farmers. I replied that even if women did get married, then presumably one with my interests would marry a farmer. Therefore, both of us would be educated for farming. He then suggested that nothing but problems would be created if there was all that knowledge in the one family! That was his last word. It didn't stop me from doing what I wanted, but I had to change countries to do it.

At Massey, agricultural science was a three year course with a lot of practical work involved. This persuaded me to do that particular course. I was the only woman in a class of 100: there were 99 men and I was the hundredth. So I worked very hard in order to come first, which I did.

For the first three months none of the men would talk to me. They referred to me as 'Mary-Lou', a reference to sexist jokes going around at the time, where the female of the duo – a figment of their imaginations – was Mary-Lou. Because I was in their eyes the 'token woman', I was given that name. A few women had gone through the course before I did. I have no idea what the other students called them. Most of the men called me Mary-Lou right through the entire course. None of them ever called me by my name, Sarah.

He began every lecture with the words: 'Welcome lady and gentlemen.'

The teachers appreciated the fact that I worked so hard – in the way most teachers do. One lecturer – and one only – was clearly embarrassed to have me in the class. He began every lecture with the words: 'Welcome lady and gentlemen.' Any time he mentioned the mammary gland of the cow he became red-faced and began shuffling behind the podium. My presence obviously had an enormous effect – there could be no doubt he knew I was in the class.

At Massey I lived in one of the women's colleges. An argument the man at the department of agriculture in Melbourne had used when I challenged him about my right to be a student at Dookie was that there were no facilities for women. This now has changed, and women are able to study at Dookie College. There are other agricultural colleges where women are students, Longranong and Glenormiston, for example. They were developed after I was excluded from Dookie. There are also several private colleges. At the time I applied, there was one at Geelong where restrictions were even more extreme than at Dookie. There, the authorities disallowed anyone from attending unless they were the sons of Protestants.

For my primary and secondary education I went to Sacre Coeur, an all-girls Catholic school in Glen Iris. There was no encouragement for the girls to take up farming. At the same time, there was no discouragement or disincentive to do so. Many of the boarders at the school came from farms. There was an understanding of the farming community and farming life, and a perception of what it meant to be on the land. Sacre Coeur had many boarders, and predominant among them were farmers' daughters. Everyone was aware that at the end of school term these kids would get on trains and head off to the bush. We also knew that their experience on the farms and in the bush over the holidays was quite different from what we experienced as city kids. I made sure I made friends with girls whose fathers had farms, because I was particularly interested in getting out into the country over the vacations. Through befriending the daughters of farmers I went to Echuca and also up around the Alexandra area in Victoria, which is north east of Melbourne, half way between Melbourne and Mansfield.

...at the end of school term these kids would get on trains and head off to the bush.

I had no role models at school, probably because I was in the wrong context. I was extremely bored and knew it wasn't the right school for me. I would have much preferred being at a technical college, doing practical subjects. Studying history and French, particularly languages, I thought a complete waste of time. I didn't expect to be speaking French to the cows! I wouldn't concentrate in class and, when asked why, that was the answer I would give. I suspect I was a bit of a nuisance to the teachers.

At school we studied very little Australian history; school would have been much more interesting to me if we had. Mostly, we did European history. This meant I had no opportunity to learn about great women farmers such as Elizabeth Macarthur. I did, however, learn in a practical way about women farmers. I spent some time with one of the boarders at school whose family had a farm near Mansfield. Because our farm was nearby, our families spent time together. The mother of that family was really the farmer: the husband was a war veteran, so she did most of the farming. When the girls were home from boardingschool, she and her daughters rode around on the farm every minute of the time they had available. It was they who got the work done.

This meant I was very aware that women contributed on farms and that they often did a lot or most of the farming. It was never my view that living on a farm or wanting to be a farmer was unusual or that I would have any trouble in reaching my goal. The first time it came home to me that there may be a problem was when I was confronted by the Victorian government's response to my wanting to go to one of their agricultural institutions. The realisation came with a sudden shock that there could be barriers placed in the way of my gaining necessary knowledge and learning about farming. I knew that knowledge and education were essential. Farming was becoming professionalised. I was determined that my desires would not be interfered with or barred, and the denial of my right to study agricultural science in my home state spurred me on. I didn't intend letting bureaucratic nonsense stand in my way.

Learning never stops. Care for the environment is an important aspect of farming, and the emphasis on this, for farmers, is relatively new. Landcare is one of the most profoundly important programmes that has come into being in agricultural communities. It is an environmental program directed specifically at the farming community, and farmers are directly involved in the form and content of the Landcare program.

Landcare is one of the most profoundly important programmes that has come into being in agricultural communities.

In Mansfield the work done in the Landcare program led to the writing and staging of the educative and celebratory play *Hanrahan Be Damned*. It contains humour and rap dancing alongside the serious message of Landcare: that the wellbeing of the land is vital to agriculture and the continuing existence of farms and farmers, and that it is important for farmers to nurture the soil, rotate crops, plant trees, keep the trees that are already there, and ensure that the land is not denuded and left without proper nutrients.

Environmental awareness is a recent development in traditional farming. It came about after I completed my agricultural studies. The Landcare program has brought home the message that we all need to remain aware of new developments in agriculture and new perspectives on the way we have always carried out our work. In Mansfield a committee was set up to promote Landcare and determine how Mansfield could be involved, with Marieke Brugman as the chairperson. Both women and men are members of the committee. The development of *Hanrahan Be Damned* was one of the byproducts of Project Mansfield's work. The show looks at a whole range of agricultural issues, particularly the endless cycle of drought and flood. The title 'Hanrahan' refers to the poem 'We'll all be ruined, said Hanrahan' – where no matter what the farmers did, something always went wrong. When there was no rain, the message was 'doom' – there would be drought; when it did rain, Hanrahan was not happy, because there would be floods, so again – 'doom'. In Mansfield the people were determined that there would be a comprehensive response to the need to protect the environment. *Hanrahan Be Damned* is an innovative social and theatrical response to the problems being confronted in rural areas. The play has travelled to many country centres, been performed at conferences and country gatherings, and was staged at the Victorian parliament so that the town politicians as well as those from the country could see what was happening in the rural community.

My degree in New Zealand was completed in three years. After returning home I worked in Australia for a short time, on a farm near Busselton and Bunbury in the south west of Western Australia. It was in the Margaret River area, before the wineries were established there. Today when I go back, visiting Margaret River in my role as partner in the Howqua Dale gourmet retreat, and it is interesting to see the developments. It was very different when I worked there.

I went to Perth looking for a job. Wesfarmers acted as a broker for farmers needing workers. I applied. I had no idea where Busselton or Bunbury were, but the job was offered, I got on the train, and went there. The farmer was at the station to meet me.

I was about 20 years old. The farmer took me to the farm, and I had never seen a greater wreck of a place in my life. There were years and years of rubbish accumulating around the house, thongs, old clothing, tyres, bits of machinery...

It was a potato and wheat farm. There was another woman worker, a New Zealand lass who was pregnant and housekeeping for the farmer. One day she told the story of how she became pregnant by a fellow who worked at an hotel in Perth. I felt very sorry for her. But she was off to the nuns when it came closer to the time of the birth, and I do not know what became of her.

The other worker was an Aboriginal man, the first with whom I had ever worked closely. He worked the machinery alongside me. One of the jobs involved sorting potatoes on a machine that is pulled along behind the tractor and digs up the potatoes. It was hard work, but I enjoyed it.

Then I got the travel bug and took off overseas. It was at this time I wished I had studied more when I had the opportunity of learning French and German at school! I travelled the way lots of young Australians did at that time: a backpack on my back, hitchhiking. And I saw the world. I didn't make any deliberate excursions into rural areas, spending time in museums, galleries, camping grounds.

I hitchhiked through Africa and it was then I fell in love with Lesotho. It is a small independent nation state surrounded by the Republic of South Africa. The men leave to go to work in the mines, while the farming is done by the women. I had hitchhiked through Africa, from Cairo to Cape Town then back up again to Kenya, most of the time by myself. Rather than choosing Lesotho as the place I wanted to be, the country picked me.

I loved Lesotho, everything about it, the high, high mountains, the starkness of the environment: it is completely denuded; there are no trees. This is where the Senqu River rises, which as it flows along becomes known as the Orange River. The diamonds ending up on the beach in South West Africa come from the mountains of Lesotho. The Drakensberg Mountains are incredibly beautiful. I just had to live there, and the only way I could was to marry a Basotho or work for one of the United Nations organisations. I decided that the latter was probably more achievable.

I was the only expatriate on the entire project who bothered to learn the language.

I returned to Australia for a short while, filling in time after travelling in the United States of America and completing the necessary application forms. The United Nations dealt with the paperwork, and I returned to Lesotho, working for the Food and Agricultural Organisation (FAO) for two years.

I worked with the women farmers. It was fascinating work, and it didn't take me long to determine that the concept of the project on which we were working was wrong: it was both misconceived and misguided. Given my previous disenchantment with language, I concentrated hard and learned sufficient Sesotho to be able to make my way about. I was the only expatriate on the entire project who bothered to learn the language.

I went around telling the women not to involve themselves in the project. Effectively, I suppose, I was blackballing it. That was dangerous because the person behind the project was the deputy prime minister – who had his hand in the till, so to speak. The times were interesting, but the project wasn't working.

The rationale of the project was that Lesotho would export crops to other countries. The African women would stop growing sustainable crops like maize and sorghum. They were told they had to plant cash crops that they could sell, the idea being that this would increase Lesotho's independence from South Africa. The misconception was that the only place to sell the crops was South Africa, so they were in fact increasing their dependence on that country. The project was misguided because in giving up the sustainable crops, the women were robbing themselves of the crops on which they and the rest of the community lived. They then had to buy food, whereas they had been self-sustaining before.

I left Lesotho and returned to Australia in 1976. From 1971 to 1974 I had spent my time travelling around the world. From 1974 to 1976 I lived and farmed in Lesotho. In 1976, upon my return to Australia, I had to work out how I would fulfil my original desire of farming in the Australian countryside.

My father had died, and my mother was dying. I had intended to go to work in South America in agriculture, but when I realised my mother was unwell I stayed at home, getting on with helping the family to deal with what was happening. That was when I went back to the Howqua Dale property. I decided I would do everything I could to retain the property, even though it was not 'making its way' and the intention was to sell it off.

When I returned to Australia, I found that because I had left school at 17, then left the country to study, then been away travelling and working for so long, I had no friends. I was 25. I had to begin cultivating friendships and the way I chose was to contact girls I had known at school. Several of us began a women's culinary group. Patricia O'Donnel, sister of Mietta O'Donnel of Mietta's, was in the group. We had all attended Sacre Coeur. It was then that I became interested in food.

The idea of going to the country to eat well was unheard of...

When the problem of how to retain Howqua Dale arose, I immediately thought of Marieke Brugman, with whom I had gone to school, who was in the culinary group, and whom I had identified as a very good cook. She was not a professional cook at the time. Rather, she was an artist and art history lecturer. We decided that we should open up the house at Howqua Dale and attempt to attract into the country city people who love food and wine.

This was an astonishing notion in those days. The idea of going to the country to eat well was unheard of, and it was slow at the beginning. Had we opened a similar place just out of Sydney as opposed to just out of Melbourne, it would, I think, have taken off a lot faster. But the love of the property meant that it was necessary to come up with a means of making a living without actually farming.

Howqua Dale had never succeeded as a farm. However the gourmet retreat has become a means of making a living, together with the cooking school we began a few years later.

We put an advertisement in the paper, saying we were open for business. Magazines became interested in the venture because we were new. *Vogue Entertaining* wrote a huge article about the gourmet retreat. There were other news stories and features in magazines. The first weekend we opened, we had put an advertisement in the newspaper. I went off skiing at Hotham, then received a frantic telephone call from Marieke who said I'd better get back quick smart because a magazine called *Pol* had booked in. *Pol* was a bright new magazine, part of the new trend in publishing in the 1970s, and Don Dunstan had been the editor for several years.

For some ridiculous reason (as I think back on it) in those early days we didn't want to look like the new girls on the block. We decided we should pretend we had been in business for some time, and that we had a varied range of guests. We invited family, friends and others to make up the numbers.

I proved to be a particularly bad liar, when as the hostess I talked with guests whilst posing as if I had never previously met them. I developed a bad habit of turning to guests of whom I supposedly knew absolutely nothing apart from their names, and asking such questions as: 'How's Simon?' Simon is my younger brother, just as he is the brother of Kristin, who was the guest I was addressing on that occasion. Kristin was far more clever than I, responding by looking at me with questioning eyes: 'Who?' It was ridiculous, and I think the 'real' guests thought we were completely mad. Yet I don't think they ever guessed that they were the only strangers, whilst everyone else *knew* everyone else and had for a long time!

Pol gave us a wonderful spread, about six pages. Yet it was such new days for this concept that I don't think we had one booking out of it. Everybody we have met, even to this day, tells us they saw the *Pol* story – but it didn't make them instantly book in to Howqua Dale. It was important, however, simply to have people reading about places in the country where they could spend a weekend and have fabulous food and wine. It was necessary to generate stories in magazines and the feature pages of newspapers to bring people to accept that there was a genre of food and wine culture in rural Australia.

We use local produce at Howqua Dale as much as is possible, but the best seafood and vegetables are transported from Melbourne. We use only the best, and there always seems to be only one place where the best is. There are some very good vineyards around us, Delatite being the most famous, with a woman winemaker by the name of Rosalyn Ritchie. She is a little younger than I, and went to Roseworthy. The mother of two children as well as a winemaker, she's very busy, and makes magnificent wine.

An important offshoot of the gourmet retreat is the notion of gourmet cycling. The peripatetic side of my personality has reared its head once more: we've hit the road regularly with cycling tours. These are predominantly gourmet tours; the cycling side of it is for exercise. We go to both wineries and restaurants, as well as the special events that we make happen for inclusion in the tours. This means exercise opportunities are vital.

Eight years ago Marieke Brugman and I put a lot of money and time into producing *Gourmet Tours of Australia*. There were no bikes involved. The tours were chauffeur driven, designed for the United States market – a deluxe American market – and the reason we dreamt it up was that we were very aware Australia has a fantastic food and wine culture and countryside unknown to the rest of the world. The only way to ensure these delights are known, is to run tours. We intended to target the United States market, encouraging gourmets to come to Australia to tour around the wine areas and restaurants of country Australia – the

Barossa Valley in South Australia, Margaret River in Western Australia, the Hunter Valley in New South Wales, the wineries and restaurants of rural Victoria. Unfortunately, our plan didn't work because we didn't have the millions of dollars necessary to market it overseas.

Here we are, eight years later, concentrating on marketing to Australians, and doing it with bicycles. It is a lot cheaper than the original concept. We go to places like the Hunter and Mudgee in New South Wales; we're going to Margaret River and the Swan Valley in Western Australia in September; and there's South Australia, and parts of Victoria. These tours are a wonderful way of staying in touch with the best developments in Australia in the countryside, in relation to both wine and food.

I took up cycling about ten years ago, to keep fit and to do something about the results of a constant diet of gourmet food. It is ironic that my cycling now is particularly bound up in getting to places where yet more gourmet food is available!

The tours are coach supported, so participants don't have to get on a bicycle at all if they don't want to. Folk who can cycle 40 kilometres may do so if they feel they want to do that. If they want to cycle 20 kilometres, they can, then put the bicycle and themselves on board the coach. We have fabulous dinners and lunches and meet the winemakers. We go only to the best wineries, and they show us their best wines. It is a very selective process, which means that people are not wasting time with wines in which they have no interest.

The cycle tours are becoming well known, and more and more people are participating. Just as with the guests coming to Howqua Dale, we have a wide range of people coming on the tours. We've had people in their seventies come, and there are those who are in their forties and fifties. The tours are well supported by all sorts of food and wine lovers. Couples come, and singles come. No one needs to have a partner: it's good to have single people along, because everyone is having fun and the time is taken up with the activities, eating, drinking, touring, within a big group. People dine together in a big group, and because everyone dines together, it is not like being isolated at a function or feeling alone during meals.

We supply everything – the bikes, the coach, reservations at restaurants, accommodation, wine tours. The bicycles are rented en masse from somewhere in the city at the start of each tour. We make it clear at the beginning of each tour that people can do as much or as little of whatever they like, so long as they are happy. The last thing we would wish to do is turn gourmet cycling into a commandant operation: 'You WILL be on your bike!!' Initially some people are a little nervous as to whether they will be able to do the cycling, and half way through the day they decide they've had enough, so they put the bike on the bus, and sit back to enjoy the countryside streaming past!

Howqua Dale is somewhere between Jamieson, a really tiny town, and Mansfield, with a population of about 5000 in the district. The size of the community has a big effect on a person's place in it and how effective anyone can be in the community. Mansfield is a good size for community involvement, and in Jamieson everyone has a place and a sense of themselves. In towns that are much bigger, though still in the country, like Shepparton, it is necessary to make a place for yourself. There is a difference to the psyche, I am sure, connected with the size of the population of the town or area in which a person lives.

I am sure that if I lived in the city, I wouldn't have much idea about the whereabouts, the interests and so on of anyone else. Because the city is so large, everyone has a place in a much tinier part of the community. This means, ironically, that in a small country town everyone knows a lot more people, their activities, what are their interests, than do people in the city, where there are so many more people.

Jamieson has a population of about 150, and everyone of them is on the same or different committees. They keep re-forming in different interest groups: there are about seven such groups. There is the sports group, the Parent and Teachers organisation, the town hall group, the fire brigade group and so on. They all know each other and care about each other. They don't necessarily *like* each other, but there is a sense of looking out for one another. This is what the country is about. It is very different from what occurs in the city.

> They don't necessarily like *each other, but there is a sense of looking out for one another.*

Women participate in the various groups. When the organisation is 'grassroots', when it has come from within the community itself, then women are very much a part of the group. Often women are the ones who initiate the organisation. When the organisation is 'top down' or has been in existence for a long time, men are more entrenched. These groups have been male dominated for a long time, and there is a different expectation of the role women will play on the committees, if they are on the committees at all.

Yet even this has changed a lot in the last few years. When I first became a member of the hospital board, for example, I was the only woman on it. By the time I had completed my term, women made up half the committee.

I am happy to make the statement publicly in my communities that I am a feminist. I don't hear too many other people in Mansfield or Jamieson going about making that statement. Yet I don't think it matters, because it doesn't mean that they're not, or that they despise me because I am. People are real individuals in the country, which means that if I pass a group of people they won't say: 'There's Sarah, the feminist from Howqua Dale.' In the country they tend to describe who you are by what you do. This goes for women and men.

In Mansfield I believe there is a strong understanding about women's role and participation in the community. That is, women are not pushed into a box that ignores their work as farmers and the importance of their contribution. People feel comfortable in their own communities. The reason they feel comfortable is that they are a part of the community. People recognise each other as they walk down the street. You can stop and talk with anyone: they know who you are, and you know who they are. There are points of connection that are instantly recognisable. No one feels out of place or lost and lonely.

In addition to all this, living in the country has a significant impact on my ability to do work which is city-based: in particular, with the Stegley Foundation. The foundation makes grants for projects which can be city-based or country-based. Proper consideration of applications would be impossible without an appreciation of what is important out in the country, and of rural needs. A close familiarity with rural culture and values assists in the sympathetic assessment of projects involving rural issues. As a member of the board of the foundation, I can call on my knowledge and experience of country life. We want to be sure that the foundation can usefully support the promotion of meaningful communication between the city and the country, and promote an insightful understanding of rural concerns. A collective past experience of sitting on local and regional boards of TAFE, Mansfield Hospital, Project Mansfield, and the Alpine Advisory Committee is invaluable to me in this work.

Many city people see the country only as the place you stay when you're on holiday, or where the holiday house is.

I don't think city people understand the country at all. Many city people see the country only as the place you stay when you're on holiday, or where the holiday house is. There is little understanding of the expense of living in the country. Someone on holidays, up from the city for Christmas, might exclaim that the general store at Jamieson is expensive: 'We can't believe that it is so many dollars an item more than in Melbourne.' Or they might remark that the petrol is 'terribly expensive up there'. They don't recognise that the cost of petrol and everyday items is the same all the year around for the people who live in Mansfield and Jamieson: the prices aren't 'put up' just for the Christmas holidaymakers! People in Mansfield pay the same price for petrol every day of the year. Every time someone picks up the telephone, the cost is STD outside the local area.

There are other disadvantages. People have to send their children further away for education. Distances travelled are enormous. Driving to

Melbourne takes two and a half hours. I have to travel to the city every three weeks or so, for meetings and other business. I can't come on the train: the train hasn't run for about 25 years. They do have a V-Line bus, which I take, occasionally – if I'm really exhausted. I stay over for at least a night, then go back. People might telephone at, say, 10.00 am to talk about some of the issues to be raised at a meeting later that day. 'Will I be seeing you at the meeting?' they say. 'Not unless I'm Superwoman, you won't,' I reply. The meeting is set for 11.30 am. There is no way I can physically get to the meeting by that time – yet the city callers appear to have no conception of travel, time, distance! Then there is surprise expressed at the fact that I might not be at every meeting: yet all the meetings take place in the city, two and a half hours from where I live.

Australians tend to think of 'the country' and 'the bush' as what makes them Australian.

If a country person were to say: 'Let's hold all the meetings at x, where I live, from now on,' there would be outrage expressed by city people. 'Why should we travel two and a half hours?' 'Why on earth should we go out to the sticks?' Yet there is no compunction about setting meeting places in the city, as if travel time for everyone is the same, or the convenience factor is identical for all!

On the other hand, the benefits of country living include peace and quiet and some isolation. They're worth the travel time and the expense of petrol and other items. We who live in the country are fortunate, because most Australians don't have the pleasures of rural life. Australia is the most urban country on earth: more Australians (about 85 per cent of the 17 million) live in the cities. Nonetheless Australians tend to think of 'the country' and 'the bush' as what makes them Australian. The media, art, history, poetry, Banjo Paterson and Henry Lawson, and films like *The Man From Snowy River* as well as television programs emphasise the bucolic aspects of Australian society. The country village or country town is the centre of so many television programs. Why? Because in a small community everyone knows everyone, and everyone knows what everyone else is up to, people can keep an eye on each other. No one would believe it if a television series were made about the comings and goings of people in, say, Brighton, with everyone knowing the affairs of everyone else. It would be totally unrealistic.

Why do we keep promoting the picture of Australians as the great outdoorsmen? Perhaps it's associated with the same impetus that persuades Americans that they are all boys from the Wild West. Yet it is true that Australians do like to get out into the country, and a huge proportion of the population drive a four-wheeldrive. Sometimes this can be for pretentious reasons, but often it is because the drivers do go into the country and need a vehicle that can cope with the terrain.

That I grew up in the city has made a difference to the way I am, and to the way I live my life in the country. Had I not grown up in the city, I don't think I would have thought of setting up a gourmet retreat at Howqua Dale. Probably, I would have drifted, kept plugging away, trying to run the property as a farm. It is because I knew city people and their expectations and interests that I knew there was a chance to make Howqua Dale work in the bush. The confidence to do it sprang from my city roots. I may not have had the confidence had I been born in the country.

Anyone coming to a new community is regarded with suspicion at first. This was the same for me. I overcame it by persistence – staying around long enough. One of the local farmers begrudgingly said to me recently that Marieke and I were the only people who had ever made a profit out of Howqua Dale. In other words, it had been a farm in existence for 70 or 80 years, had been bought and sold and bought and sold and bought and sold, and we are the only ones ever to have settled down to make it work. That backhanded compliment was about as good as it gets in Mansfield. It means we've made it!

I haven't lived in the city since I was 17, and I know I never will again. It's filthy and there is a very real fear of losing your sense of place. My place is in the country, and if I were moved to the city, I'd be unhappy, profoundly unhappy. I'd rather be dead.

A love of place is fundamental to me, and it is the overriding point of Howqua Dale. When people say, why are you here, why are you running the business – my response is that the business is a means to an end, and the end is to live in this one particular place. After all that travelling around the world, I realise I have a very strong sense of place, and Howqua Dale is that place.

Everyone a Hero

Nancy Cato

Nancy Cato was born in Swan Hill, Victoria on 3 December 1939, to Leslie and Margaret Cato. With what seemed like a distinct disadvantage at the time, she was born both lefthanded and suffering hearing-loss, two factors which led her one way and another to an intensive involvement with the theatre from an early age. She became a professional actor and entered country television for which she wrote, scripted and directed; her involvement with the famous television series for children, *Magic Circle Club* and *Adventure Island,* is well documented.

Quite apart from handling projects in the Mallee desert and Alice Springs, Nancy Cato has overcome paraplegia after a studio accident, has four children, and is currently helping to launch a new Arts Centre in Prahran, Melbourne.

Had I been a Bear of Small Brain like my friend Pooh, rather than a child of considerable curiosity, it probably wouldn't have mattered where I was born. And it must be admitted that Swan Hill, Victoria is neither the most exotic nor pecunious location to have splashed on anyone's birth certificate. But I am prepared to swear that being a country kid in Swan Hill had a profound effect on the rest of my life.

I mean if you were a stickybeak and happened to be a fish, where would you choose to live? A pond where you're safe and secure and can experience an entire lifecycle? Or the ocean? Head out the frontdoor and Snap, you're gone!!

Not that I *chose* Swan Hill, mind you. My father went there as a dentist in the early 1930s and, as my mother was there too, that's where I landed.

I shall always be grateful to Swan Hill. I doubt that I could ever have picked a more perfect spot to launch my mission in life – to find out WHAT WENT ON!

Presumably things 'went on' in the City too, but in Swan Hill I knew everybody – well nearly everybody, and because I could take in the entire length and breadth of the town while mucking around on my bike on a Saturday 'arvo', I saw most things that could possibly be ascribed to human behaviour. (And some things that couldn't!!!)

What a Paradise for a child of considerable curiosity – one long play with a cast of thousands; some of them quite weird.

There was Mr Singh, the Indian hawker, whose skin you would swear was 'Genuine Australian Made Aluminium', so hung about was he with his pots and pans. He plonked a saucepan on my head whenever he saw me, which can't have been too hygienic, and squealed with laughter at such a high pitch that all the local dogs would come running into our garden. I hid if I got half a warning, but even with all his metallic encumbrances he was a remarkably quick fellow.

And then there was Old Fred, the Metho Man, who always tried to convince me he needed methylated spirits from my father's surgery in order to start his car. Even I knew he didn't have a car!

In those early days of my life, my friends were: kids, the Murray River, shopkeepers, farmers – men and women who paid for my father's dental services with oranges, potatoes, grapes or anything healthier than their bank accounts, and old Danny Marks, the Aborigine who lived in an old garage around the corner from our house.

...shopkeepers, farmers – men and women who paid for my father's dental services with oranges, potatoes, grapes or anything healthier than their bank accounts...

I also liked Mr H the milkman who came in the screech-owl hours and poured a quart of milk out of his huge can into our billy. He was ethereal – like Santa Claus – you were never really sure he existed. I remember one day creeping out really early to check on a fairy ring my mother had made out of rose petals. I wanted to see the fairies delivering the shiny new penny which miraculously appeared there from time to time. Instead I saw Mr H delivering his milk and wondered why he never woke up anyone, such was his whistling and billy clattering.

Mr S the baker didn't fare so well with my affections however. Each morning he would bring the bread to our door in a large square wicker basket. I'm sure the variety he offered had far more to do with his mood than the bread he actually carried in his old bread truck.

On a good day his basket would be brim full of high-tin technology so recently removed from the oven you could smell it from the very depths of your latest Biggles novel at the tree-house (who needed tv?). He would chat to himself and pat our cockerspaniel who after eight years still didn't want to recognise him as a daily visitor. But on a bad day – oh dear! I could never smell him coming. There'd be a miserable sandwich loaf rolling around on its own and the spaniel more often than not

...in the days of the famous Mallee Duststorms, it was the only way you could find your way home – crawling on all fours along the gutter by the side of the road.

received a wicker bump on his head for his greeting. I should be grateful, as I rattled off my protest in essay form to the RSPCA and won a statewide competition which happened to be on at the time.

It was during these early formative years that I first learnt to grovel. Not out of a sense of obsequious necessity mind you, but in the days of the famous Mallee Duststorms, it was the only way you could find your way home – crawling on all fours along the gutter by the side of the road.

You could see these duststorms coming from miles away to the west, where the Mallee farmers had cleared the land of its scrub so successfully that every so often the top soil would rise up in protest, face the wind and take off – mostly into my face on the way home from school. People who didn't go through it don't believe how frightening it was. The sun would be entirely blocked out, a dust eclipse, street lights would come on and you could barely see your hand in front of your face. Sometimes we'd sleep through a duststorm, but next morning our pillows would be dark brown except for white circles where our heads had been.

It was a paradise to grow up in though – this country town of 7000 people. A microcosm of life where almost anyone could be a hero at something and more likely than not have not much more than a MAA (mere average ability) in the larger scheme of things.

I certainly didn't feel deprived not growing up in the city although there were times when my Sunday School teacher's effort failed and I did sink to the depths of coveting some city kids' experiences like trips to Myers and the escalators, the beach, traffic lights and the Tivoli. I comforted myself that Dad packed us into the old Buick, complete with runningboard, every January and made what I now know to be a three and a half hour trip in eight hours of familial chaos to sample some of these delights. I also knew that I could ride almost anywhere in town on my bike, was known by all the local traders and therefore likely to score a bonus lolly or biscuit (especially from Moran and Cato, the latter of which bore the same family name as mine), had access to every sport imaginable, and was bound to land a place in the local amateur theatre company production, especially at Shakespearean Festival Time when every poor sod in town who looked half decent in seventeenth century pantaloons was dragged in.

Marjorie McLeod ran the Shakespearean Festival. A truly remarkable woman, Marjorie, and one of my childhood mentors. She was a playwright, speech-training teacher and theatre director but her undoubted first talent was in getting people involved. I'll never forget Mr J the plumber telling me: 'Gawd! that Marjorie McLeod – she asked me if

I'd be in Shakespeare and I thought she meant putting a bet on the horse by that name in the seventh! "Too right," I said. In five minutes she had me in tights and a wig reading Snug from *A Midsummer Night's Dream.*'

I admired Marjorie's fortitude and cunning, and most of all her ability to make a low-budget amateur production look like something from the West End!

I don't think I'd ever heard the word 'feminism' in those days. Playing doctors and nurses with the boy next door notwithstanding, I think the first time I realised I was a girl was when my attempts at the age of six to become the mascot of the Swan Hill Football Club were foiled, knocked back, humiliated. Even worse, my successful rival was the same boy next door, that same baggy-panted smart alec who, on seeing through a gap in our fence my inclination to emulate, nay, to be Hopalong Cassidy, screamed rather pathetically 'penis envy!' before bobbing out of sight and out of range of my locally famous shanghai arm.

I think the first time I realised I was a girl was when my attempts at the age of six to become the mascot of the Swan Hill Football Club were foiled, knocked back, humiliated.

I was incensed, enraged, choking with the realisation of the unfairness of it all; what were the football authorities thinking of! Didn't they know I knew everything about the team? Height, weight, drinking habits...? Didn't they care that I could wipe the floor with that snotty nosed kid at marbles; was it of no concern that when I kicked his miserable football it sailed out of sight sending him snivelling and breathless to fetch it while I sat and smirked, but then when he kicked it back I had to run so far forward to get it I forgot what sport we were playing.

'Appeal,' I said to myself. And appeal I did straight to the president.

'I'm perfect for the job,' I said, master of the self-promotion bred by the country town confidence of having a reasonable chance by sheer dint of numbers to be better than everyone else at *something*.

'I'm perfect for it,' I repeated. 'Got the outfit and Dougy Morpeth's number nine on my back.'

The shake of his head panicked me.

'But I can kick and run further and faster than he can,' I wailed. And then it came. The phrase. A rumbling, ominous roll of thunder.

'But you're a girl!'

I was dumbstruck. Never in all my six years had it occurred to me that in this country paradise I could ever be penalised for being a girl! A slow, malicious thought took over my entire consciousness.

'Just wait till he wants to play doctors and nurses again!'

Although I hadn't heard of the word 'feminism', I accepted that women worked on their farms seemingly as hard as their men. It didn't occur to me that they were also doing the cooking, washing, cleaning and child supervision. Women seemed to go to work as much as they wanted to. It was only a couple of isolated instances that alerted me to the insidious nature of discrimination against girls in a country town. Girls were rarely sent away to boardingschool even if the family could afford it. There was no question that my brother (who was not the slightest bit interested in things academic) would be sent to boardingschool to continue the tradition of his father. It was never an option considered for me or my sister in spite of obvious academic potential.

Perhaps it was a good thing not being sent away to boardingschool. For one thing, I adored the free, happy lifestyle afforded an outrageous tomboy who would do almost anything to increase the pleasures of life – including riding on the open tray of our neighbour's truck to the cemetery on Sunday afternoons knowing full well they stopped for a penny ice-block on the way back. Having no personal experience of death I could never understand why anyone would want to spend Sunday afternoons emptying smelly vases of dead flowers only to fill them up with fresh ones, when it was perfectly obvious that they were just going to die again! Such was the lure of the penny ice-block!

You could start at the age of three and high on the curriculum priorities were languages, religious studies and speed reading!

More importantly, had I gone to boardingschool I would have missed what I now see as an extraordinary education. Donnington Girls Grammar School. I think it was probably light years ahead of its time. A small institution started in the thirties by two single women, Misses H and B. It was quite extraordinary. You could start at the age of three and high on the curriculum priorities were languages, religious studies and speed reading! The only snag in starting off in a progressive and unusual system such as this is what happens if the doors have to close prematurely as happened in my case aged 12. Battling conventional lessons in the local highschool as well as BOYS was quite a challenge!

But what really rang alarm bells for me was my rather hysterical interview with the careers advisor when I was all of 16, head prefect of the highschool and about to sit for my matriculation as it was known in those days. Her naturally rather grave face turned apoplectic when I told her I fancied becoming a professional actor or writer. Within five minutes she deployed my cherished notions into the pigeon hole – 'childhood fantasy' and gave me some 'serious options' to contemplate: nursing, banking, retail, teaching or marriage (I swear she went into a cataclysm of ecstasy when she uttered the last). No mention of university or further education of any kind. I went home and nursed my indignation – but it did make me think. It made me think about how people treat other people and the influence they wield. I suppose that was the start of my serious formulation of ideas about humanrights. I was suddenly conscious of incidents over the years which may have gone unnoticed in the city. I suppose the price you paid for the free and easy lifestyle in a country town was the lack of the anonymity enjoyed by your city sisters. Everyone knew what everyone else was up to in my town!

I must have been 12 years old when a baby was left on our doorstep. There she was in a basket I'd tripped over on my way out to school. She was cute, six weeks old and had cerebal palsy. They must have known my Mum would take her in, which she did. 'They say she'll just be a vegetable for the rest of her life,' said Mum with that look in her eye. 'We'll see about that!' We looked after her as our own for years and years which is probably why I became so aware of the marginalisation of those with disabilities. It wasn't at all that people were cruel or unkind – there was just a huge uncertainty about how to relate to a wheel-chaired body whose arms waved about alarmingly. 'What does it eat?' they would ask me ingenuously in front of her. 'Why don't you ask her yourself?' I always replied, knowing full well how intelligent and alert she was, but somehow fear or embarrassment took over and the question was rarely asked.

Of course I didn't realise it then, but the seeds of understanding the enormity and power of love were sown. Watching my mother shape this so-called vegetable into a lovely adult humanbeing was one of the real inspirations of my childhood.

I was about the same age when I noticed something else rather strange 'going on'. After school, one of the delights was a huge chocolate milkshake served in a heavy tall glass at the local Paragon Cafe. On the way, a group of us would walk along the street hailing the local traders in the hope of a mouth-watering handout. One day it dawned on me that I was receiving preferential treatment. Had I always? I thought back; with a sickening feeling I realised that I probably always had.

He told me wonderful Aboriginal myths and legends and stories of his tribal boyhood.

I asked my mother about it. 'It's because you're the dentist's daughter,' she said. 'It's wrong, but that's the way it is.'

I was getting preferential treatment because my father was a dentist? This was crazy. 'Is there a class-system in country towns?' I asked. Mum thought about it for a while. 'When I came here as a new bride,' she said, 'I used to have to leave calling cards when I visited. If the wives thought I was worth knowing, for whatever reason, they would ring and invite me to return!'

Going to see old Danny Marks was a great leveller for me. He sat on the postoffice steps when he was well enough. There was not too much left to show what a marvellous athlete he had once been. He was stooped and frail and obviously malnourished. He told me wonderful Aboriginal myths and legends and stories of his tribal boyhood. With great sadness he took me over the river to the New South Wales bank where most of his people were barely subsisting in old tin shanties. I vowed then to always remember his startling dignity and the respect he had given me for his race.

But for me life was good in Swan Hill – hectic in fact! I studied, played sport, went to Church, ran messages, attended every film and concert that came our way and forever learnt lines for my beloved stage productions. Such was the opportunity in the country! 'I'll probably be here for the rest of my life,' I thought. But at the same time I was restless. There were no demands on me. I needed an answer for the little voice that kept questioning: 'What should I do?'

The answer came in the shape of an ABC (Australian Broadcasting Commission) regional radio program. A series of radio plays was to be recorded in regional centres starring Patricia Kennedy and Wynn Roberts. Local thespians were encouraged to audition and to my joy I was accepted for the Swan Hill production. Not only that, Patricia suggested I might like to go down to Melbourne to audition for the ABC and stay with her. Might like to ??? She is probably still recovering from the hug I gave her.

My professional career was born!

Life in the city! To say the very least it was different! There were escalators, trams, trains and buses to ride, pollution to inhale, crowds to dodge, shop windows to ogle at, Coles cafeteria to eat in and rehearsals to attend. I began to doubt that the country had prepared me for anything at all. I was miserable and lonely. Everyone seemed to rush everywhere with no real involvement in anything – not as I knew involvement. It was really interesting to stand back and watch my unfoldment as a city dweller – to witness my dawning realisation that city people were indeed involved in many things – they just had to rush like mad and travel distances to take part.

Acting training with Professor Wal Cherry at the Emerald Hill Theatre Company was the real eye-opener. Here indeed was involvement – commitment to the hilt. People were as potty about the stage as I was. Professor Cherry used to laugh and tease me – knowing me from his days as an adjudicator at the Swan Hill Shakespearean Festival. 'You don't know how lucky you were, living in the country and getting to play every Shakespearean heroine before you were twenty!' How right he was.

Radio, tv and stage productions completely absorbed my time and energy in the early 1960s until someone alerted me to the fact that television stations were opening up in country centres. The chance to go back to the country.

I immediately wrote to Ballarat, Traralgon, Bendigo and Shepparton – stressing that I was a country girl. I was granted an interview with the general manager in Shepparton a few weeks later. I will never know if I got there on my own merits or because of a quirky accident, but on my way to the interview by taxi we were involved in a collision. My head went straight into the windscreen and I ended up looking like something out of the *Munsters*. Two very black eyes and a bulging forehead are not the usual tricks to take to an audition. Somehow I convinced the GM I was who I said I was. 'Well,' he said rather wearily after an hour of my enthusiasm: 'If you've got the gall to come here looking like that for an audition as station hostess you've got the job!'

My television career was born!

Where else but in the country could you get the depth of experience I enjoyed at GMV-6, Shepparton. I was the station hostess, compered and wrote scripts for the live-to-air children's session, anchored the women's session, was called upon to do 'voice-overs' and commercials and occasionally read the news! How I loved those days. I felt completely at home behind the camera because I was talking to people I knew – country people. These were some of the happiest times of my life.

I did go back to the city two or three years later, but this time I was ready. And this time I was to be station hostess of ATV-0 (as it was then) and compere of the *Magic Circle Club*.

I now had a clear purpose. Everything I'd learnt in my drama training could be put to good use to help overcome some of the inequities I'd observed from my 'childhood pond'. 'Marginalisation of the different' was the name of the game whether that difference was skin, disability, intellect or social standing. I was at last in a position to do something about it.

Some children appeared not to have the most basic of humanrights.

Getting the health authorities to allow me to include children with disabilities in my drama classes was a major challenge. 'It will restrict opportunities for *normal* children,' I was told. Or worse: 'The *normal* children will be frightened!'

Nevertheless children with disabilities were invariably included in my workshops for disadvantaged children. I know, and the children knew, it enriched everyone. There were disadvantaged children from every suburb – the word 'disadvantaged' covering a multitude of sins; children who, through no fault of their own, were deprived of parents or love or financial security or physical wellbeing or all of those things. Some children appeared not to have the most basic of humanrights.

I had two approaches in the workshops. One was to use drama as a teaching method – where, through an exciting adventure, relevant historical or geographical or mathematical information could be imparted. The other was to stimulate through various games and activities the children's natural creativity and then let them loose in a roomful of materials from which they could choose – pens, paper, paint, clay, costumes, glue – how the fingers would fly – and how the faces would glow, all in an atmosphere of equality, joy and fulfilment.

But whichever approach I took, I found it necessary to play a game of 'taking our labels off'. We piled our labels of 'clumsy', 'silly', 'shy', 'hopeless' *et al* in a corner and then jumped on them, metaphorically smashing them to pieces. What a relief!

There are hundreds of stories from that period. Heart warming stories of children from vastly different backgrounds with a multitude of challenges, all working together harmoniously and achieving a sense of 'personal best'. Like Billy who had a severe hearing impairment. He came from an inner city suburb and his mother had never heard him speak. Billy did his best to join in all the activities, feeling the vibrations of feet and hands, eyes watching sharper than a bald eagle. In one of those wonderful moments of inspiration I picked up a tambourine and gave it to him, mouthing clearly that he was in charge. The others were instructed to follow his beat – rat-a-tat-tat, ta-rum ta-rum. He became more and more excited and the more excited he became, the faster he made the beat. For the first time in his life – Billy was in charge! At the height of his exhilaration, when the poor kids in the group had dropped from exhaustion and laughter, in walked his mum. 'Billy, what have you been doing,' she exclaimed, alarmed at his high colour. He rushed to her, flung his tiny arms around her neck and bellowed: 'Mmm-u-m!' I don't need to tell you how much we laughed and cried together, Billy's mum and I.

It was at the height of all this activity that something happened to me which was to change the entire course of my life. Or at least how I perceived things.

It happened in a rehearsal of the *Magic Circle Club*. A set collapsed when I was right at the top of it. I landed on my back and I couldn't move a muscle! After days grew into weeks and tests became exhaustive it was clear that I was a paraplegic. I had to try to accept at the ripe old age of 25 that I would never walk again.

I moved in with my parents – back to Swan Hill.

Days were spent reading, drawing, writing, thinking and hanging by the armpits from a set of parallel bars my Dad had made for me while electric currents were sent up my body.

This particular day I had just spent an hour hanging from the bars and as I lay on my bed I reached for a book from my mother's bookcase at the end of the bed. I never cared what the book was as long as it was readable, but a particular sentence from the foreword caught my eye immediately. 'To those leaning on the sustaining infinite, today is big with blessings.'

My first reaction was to the word 'leaning'. Hadn't I just been leaning for an hour? Where were my blessings? A small voice that only I could hear answered me. 'No you haven't.' 'Haven't what?' I argued with myself. 'Haven't leaned, not totally, and *not* on the sustaining infinite,' said the voice. 'Yes I have,' I said defiantly. 'I've prayed for forgiveness for everything bad that I've done. Of course I've leaned.' 'No, you haven't,' said the voice. And at that moment I stopped struggling and arguing with what I think now was the Truth. Probably for the first time in my life I felt genuine humility. No, I hadn't leaned. At that exact moment, when that thought was occupying my consciousness to the exclusion of all else, my mother screamed. She was shaking and pointing at something and my father ran in wanting to know what was wrong. We looked where she pointed and a minute later my big toe flickered. That was precisely what she had seen. The book, *Science and Health*, by Mary Baker Eddy, was still lying open on the bed. I got up off the bed and took my first steps in 13 months.

And at that moment I stopped struggling and arguing with what I think now was the Truth.

I think that that was the point in my life when I decided to reject a sense of limitation about anyone. To add to my early lessons in the power of Love, I now had a very clear one about the power of Truth.

It was only a year or two after that experience and a stint overseas studying child drama that I met my husband of 23 years, Jonah Jones. We had four babies in five years, so for a while I didn't need to run any drama sessions for anyone. I had plenty of my own!

Inevitably we found ourselves back in the country. Even though Jonah had spent six years in Milan, Italy, he too was a country kid at heart and, after a short spell on a cattle station, we bought our own pig farm on Pental Island near Swan Hill. It was wonderful to get back to the country, particularly as we ran an arts and drama program for disadvantaged schools in the Mallee for the Schools Commission at the same time. Jonah was the administrator and I ran the drama program. It was great fun and rather confusing for people who asked us what we did – invariably one of us would say 'arts administrators' and the other 'pig-farmers'. We also had a van completely fitted out as a radio studio. We recorded programs with isolated children and bought time to air the programs on the local radio station.

But all good things must come to an end. We said: 'Goodbye' to our beloved pigs and took off for Alice Springs where Jonah was to be the inaugural director of the first arts centre in the Northern Territory.

How glad I was for my country upbringing and my city experience when we got to Alice. It was like no place I'd ever been in before, and Alice is a very special lady!

Environmentally the place was awesome – wild and rugged, magnificent with gaps and gorges that towered over you. Strange perspectives and stranger colours – bright orange earth, pink and purple rocks, red and white sands.

On the surface, Alice is a very tough town. A man's town they used to say, but one polarised not so much by the sexes but by race. The first thing most people wanted to know was how you felt about the Aborigines.

It was certainly isolated. Jonah used to enjoy saying in 1980 that we were 1500 kilometres from the nearest traffic lights. There was certainly no running home to mother on the first bus.

I found it hard watching the displaced urban Aborigines succumb to boredom and alcohol, and lie abandoned in the dry Todd riverbed. I found it hard to see little Aboriginal toddlers sniffing glue. I found it hard to understand the depth of racism from certain white quarters, and the level of violence suffered by women both Black and white. It seemed to me at the time that extreme isolation tended to lift the lid on any moral code of human behaviour for some people.

> *I found it hard to understand the depth of racism from certain white quarters, and the level of violence suffered by women both Black and white.*

But at the same time there was much to be celebrated in Alice and much work to be done. There was a wonderfully diverse, ever-changing population of interesting, talented and versatile people. There were tribal friends and trips to the bush. It was a place where children were automatically included in everything and diverse interests were assured of being catered for in a town which had the initiative to start a club for the most frivolous hobby.

And the women – ah! those bush women. What incredible strength and tenacity they showed, constitutions of steel, an indomitable spirit and yet a heart that would melt a hole in a cast-iron pot.

Yes, those years in Alice were very special, and the Araluen Arts Centre was duly built. How eerie it was to have the Albert Namatjira retrospective art exhibition opened by the nephew of the great man himself – our dear friend Gus who looks remarkably like his uncle. We learnt much in and from Alice and left wonderful friends behind – both Black and white. Like Swan Hill it will always be one of the special places in my heart.

We're back in Melbourne now. The wheel has turned full circle. My projects are very clear: children with disabilities are not represented in picture books unless they are the centre of a discussion about a disability; older women are still being replaced by younger models and need lots of confidence, love and guidance to see their own worth and creativity; homelessness and unemployment are making our young feel useless and hopeless when they are our major resource; and our own indigenous people are still battling for equality.

Writing this made my heart ache to see Swan Hill again and such is the quirky way of nature that our old friend, sculptor John Davis invited us to his exhibition at the Swan Hill Regional Art Gallery in early March 1994. John was also a student of the Swan Hill High School and wanted to give something back to the town. On reaching Lake Boga just 16 kilometres from Swan Hill my heart was pumping 19 to the dozen in anticipation. And no wonder. As soon as we entered the gallery we were engulfed in affection, laughter and 'do-you-remembers'.

I too want to give something back to the town that taught me so much and I wouldn't bet on my seeing out the rest of my days in the city.

I'm a country girl, dontcha know!

PART 4

Betwixt and Between

Desert Over Concrete Any Day

Lorraine Hunter

Born on 21 June 1967, Lorraine Hunter is a student-resident of St Catherine's College in the University of Western Australia where she is studying. Born in Derby, in the north of Western Australia, she has lived in Perth, Broome, the Northern Territory, Brisbane, and on the Atherton Tablelands in north Queensland, as well as Walpole and Albany in the south west of Western Australia. She is of the Myul Myul and the Narogin people.

Having had a long-time interest in journalism, Lorraine Hunter intends to be a writer when she completes her university studies.

I am a Gemini, and was born on the cusp. I did most of my schooling in Derby, Western Australia, where I was born. I attended the district school for my primary education, then Derby District High. I left school at 16.

Dad was a diver in his early days in Broome. He'd travelled to Thursday Island, Cairns, New Guinea, everywhere, diving. When he came back, he worked out on stations. He worked as a builder, building houses and fencing. Mum was a cleaner, washer, and ironer.

My schooling at Derby District High was completed when I was 15. After Year 10, all the Aboriginal students were sent to Perth to do further studies. If my Dad had had his way, I wouldn't have gone anywhere. This was the only time he let me out of his sight.

At home my father was very strict. I was not allowed to go visiting; we were very much kept to the house. So my time at school was the best time for me and I made the most of it. I even went to school if I had the chicken pox. I simply had to go. My father was afraid I would end up being used and abused like other young people if I was neglected, and didn't want me to fall in with any neglected youngsters. He was being protective, and was very old fashioned as well, extremely old fashioned.

193

One day at school in Derby the teachers lined up all the Aboriginal kids. I was very, very confused. Abruptly we were taken down to a room where we were lined up again, waiting to go into smaller rooms. My cousin, Maureen, and I were put together and taken into a tiny room. The man asked us what we wanted to do, now we had completed our schooling at Derby High. I was interested in taking up nursing but I was very shy, so didn't speak up. My cousin was also very shy, so she didn't speak up either. The man must have looked at our reports, because he abruptly said: 'You look as if you'd be good to go to do business studies.' I'd never heard of this subject or vocation before in my life. Then, suddenly, because he said so, we were to be taken off to do a commercial course in Perth! This place called Perth! Where was it? What was it?

Then, suddenly, because he said so, we were to be taken off to do a commercial course in Perth! This place called Perth! Where was it?

So, that was how it was – just like that. Instant advice. An immediate change to our lives. We walked out thinking it wasn't real. As we went out, a thought went through our minds, rather like: 'Oh, yeah, good meeting.' Then we were off to play.

Now that I think back, I realise it must have been government policy. For us it was just what happened to the Aboriginal children in the school. We thought nothing of it, and didn't even think that we should think about it. We didn't consider issues such as our right to ask questions, or to query what was happening. We simply went with it. Shortly after, we were off to Perth!

My cousin Maureen and I lived at one of the hostels in the city. There were a number of hostels and we didn't know in advance which we were going to. It was 1981, and we were in a hostel in a place called Perth. The suburb was Bentley, across from Curtin University. We did classes at Kent Street, at the highschool. Some girls went to Kent Street Senior High School. Some girls went to Carmalite Convent (the Roman Catholic girls in particular went there), and some to Kewdale High. My cousin and I learnt typing and shorthand.

There were about 20 girls from up north in that one hostel. Some were from Fitzroy Crossing, in the same region as Derby and Broome. Unlike myself and my cousin, some of them were enrolled in Years 11 and 12, studying for their higher school certificate (HSC). Somehow they had received the advice that this is what they should do. They were fortunate. We weren't given that choice. It could be that our grades were not good enough, but I was good at my school studies. At school I enjoyed writing and drama, I liked maths, I liked English, science, social studies. I loved doing project work and art. So basically I enjoyed all my subjects. But we were simply given no options. We were to do typing and shorthand, and that was it.

Life in Perth was a shock. It was exciting as well. Maureen and I didn't feel lonely and lost at all because we had each other, and the trip was exciting. We were like kids on a special adventure, so there was nothing sad about it, like parting from our parents and sisters and brothers, or 'missing home'. We travelled down by plane. I'd been on a plane before, but it was the first time I had been up in the air without my Mum and Dad. It was a little eerie. Mum and Dad were upset, and Dad felt a bit sad. But Maureen and I were off on an adventure!

Once in Perth, one of the first differences I noticed was the traffic. I wondered what all the 'things' rushing along the road were. My cousin and I were fascinated. What the hell is it, what is that thing? we asked each other. We didn't know about buses and how they operate so when on our first day at school our housemother dropped us off and told us we had to catch the bus to go back, we didn't know what she meant. She left us at school, in our wrap-around skirts, our thongs and T-shirts. This was the middle of winter, but it was all the clothing we had. We were cold. When we went into the classroom the teacher said: 'Girls, you can't come to school like that.' She was angry with us and told us so. We responded by saying: 'Excuse us, miss, but our uniforms are still coming.' She replied: 'Well, you can't come in like that. You're better off staying home!' We remained to be introduced to all our classmates, then finally went off home. It was then that we remembered we had to fathom what the 'bus thing' was! What was it? We simply didn't know. So we walked all the way from Kent Street to home. It was miles, and we didn't know where it was, but we found it. We asked an old lady whom we met which way we should go. She said: 'That way,' and pointed. So we just kept going that way. It took a very long time. Still, we were intrigued by everything around us, so the walk didn't seem so bad. It was all new, and it was fascinating to us.

The houses in Perth were different from those in Derby. We had never seen a house without a fan. Now, there was no house *with* a fan! We found this impossible to believe. It was extraordinary to us that people lived in houses without any fans. We were also overwhelmed by the beauty of the flowers that grew in the gardens, particularly roses. We had never seen such flowers. As we walked along we exclaimed to each other over them. 'Oh, that's so pretty.' And it was.

We had never seen a house without a fan. Now, there was no house with a fan!

We did learn how to travel on the bus. Our housemother, Mrs Coomb, who was from England originally and spent most of her time looking after students and young people staying in hostels, gave us very good directions the next time we went out. I had never travelled on a bus before, and had no idea of the procedure – having to pay money to the driver and take a ticket, having to pull the cord or press a button to let the driver know when we wanted to get off. Our housemother gave us step by step directions, and later in the year we travelled by train as well, by following her advice. Train travel was a real adventure. We went to the city, the first time, and were very excited. It was a change from bus travel and we thought it was great.

Thank goodness we'd seen typewriters before, back home. I would have been really worried otherwise! We studied typing and shorthand for eight months, and the school authorities told us we were training to be secretaries. Until I attended that course, I had never had anyone from the education system tell me anything about employment. There was no clear indication to us of where we'd get jobs, or that we'd get jobs at all, when we were at school in Derby. There was no advice about job seeking. A job was not even spoken about. But at Kent Street High Mrs Wilson drummed the message into us: 'You're going to become secretaries and work hard. You'll do well. There's a big wide world out there,' she said. 'Go get 'em.' Almost every day she said that to us.

There were about 30 girls in the class. Maureen and I were the only two who were from up north. The rest were from Perth and its suburbs. They responded to us in a funny way at first. Very odd. They were extremely reserved. It took a while, but later on they opened up, and so did we. I don't know if it was because we were shy that they didn't know how to approach us. I expect that they had a number of reasons for their reserve and that was one of them. Some time down the track everyone was friendly and we got on like a house on fire. There was a lot of vibrant fun and Maureen and I enjoyed ourselves in the class, and at the school.

At the end of that year, 1981, I returned to Broome where my Mum and Dad were living. They had moved there while I was at school in Perth. When the course at Kent Street High School ended, we were given various options. One was to go to business college. Maureen and I agreed that we would go to the business college that was situated right in the city of Perth, so the following year it was back to the city for the two of us. I had thought the old lady at Kent Street was a dear old principal, but the one at the business college was even older and even more staid. It was comical. We felt as if we were in a movie: you see characters in films, then you meet them and – wow! She was strict. *Was* she strict! We did more typing and shorthand. Yet we felt very isolated and lost there. All our friends from the hostel had gone to Olympia Business College which we thought was a far more modern establishment. The one we were attending was very old English style, dark and dismal. We weren't allowed to go outside for lunch: we had to stay in the corridor, a long, dark hallway, sitting there to eat at lunchtime. It was as if we were locked away in the dark and the damp, although we were in Hay Street, right in the middle of Perth. It was horrible. Perhaps they thought we would play truant, rushing off to the pictures, or wandering about in the shops and the streets, if we were allowed out. Probably we would have!

At business college we did typing and shorthand and accounts. It was a matter of studying everything all over again, the very same subjects we had done at Kent Street High. We told our hostel mother that we were unhappy, so she telephoned whoever was in charge and it was arranged that we would change. So the semester after the holidays, upon our return we went to Olympia. I stayed for a term. My cousin Maureen continued on and finished her course. I went home after that term and didn't go back to business college. I was extremely bored with the classes. It was drills, constantly; the same old thing. We'd heard all that before. I was young, and I wanted to learn more, to have new experiences.

At home I gained a job anyway, a clerical job with the Commonwealth Employment Service (CES).

At that time I decided I preferred to live at home, in the north. It was me. I was more comfortable. My family was there, too, and that had a lot to do with my decision. I didn't like the noise of the traffic, and all that speed and concrete in Perth. For me, concrete is the major drawback in the city: the look of it. I am very much a country person, because I have always been with nature. That is where I feel at home, it suits me. If I look at something concrete, it doesn't have anything for me. It's just – concrete.

I decided I preferred to live at home, in the north. It was me. I was more comfortable.

Now that I have returned (more than ten years later) to live in Perth to study at the University of Western Australia, it is far more difficult for me. I am not as naive as I was at 15. Now, I know what to expect. The same excitement and sense of adventure in seeing and experiencing new things is not there. This means that the impact of the city, its greyness, the concrete and its distance from nature is not tempered by my being wide-eyed about Perth.

When I left the CES job I found a job as a teaching assistant in Broome. I was encouraged to apply, so I did. It was at the Catholic school, St Mary's. The nuns knew my mother, so when I began working there it was like being welcomed back into the family again. My work involved being a teaching assistant for the little ones, aged about four to five. The teaching assistants helped the teacher, handing out the sheets of paper and working with the children on their numbers. We had no role in the 'thinking' side, the side where initiative was necessary and allowed to develop. We concentrated on the domestic matters, the practical aspects. We showed the pupils what to do. I was anxious to be more involved, but because I had had no formal training, I had to pull back. Not having been taught to teach meant I was diffident about my skills. I didn't ask the school about the possibility of learning to teach, and all of us were simply told to do a general education course, which is relevant to becoming a teaching assistant. I did that course with the nuns on campus. We had one day a week to do some maths, some English, general education. It was basic. Each student did it at her own pace. I stayed there for two years.

I left the position because I was bored. My mind was not being challenged. Some of the teachers had said: 'Oh, you should become a teacher.' But it was just a flying remark. There was no formal encouragement at all, no telling me or the other teaching assistants how to go about it. At the same time, I was at an age where there was a great attraction in socialising. There was a lot of partying, and I was becoming distracted by it. I went to work, but social activities became an important part of my life. Partying was more exciting than what I was doing at work. It was new. It was stimulating. But if the school had had a concrete proposal for teaching me to become a teacher, I would have taken it up at once.

I wasn't getting anywhere in Broome. I could feel myself getting too involved in social life. I needed to get out of the social scene. I did. After leaving St Mary's I went to Derby and took a position working in a hospital in the kitchen. I was a domestic. I wanted to get on my feet, and I did. I had decided to go travelling and needed to make some quick money. I had begun to make some money and was getting ready to go. Then my niece decided she'd come too. We intended to go right around Australia and suddenly, one day, began the trip. We got as far as Perth. Perth, of all places!

This time, Perth was not a good experience. I had very little money. We spent most of it along the way and the partying side began taking over once more. It was a bad time for me. I lived in Armadale, a Perth suburb. My parents weren't happy about my going travelling. I was 17 or 18 at the time, and came up against the authorities. When they discovered I was from the country they said the city wasn't the place for me, and that I'd be better going back home. I totally agreed. I wanted to go home. So I went.

Back home in Derby once more I decided I would be a health worker. I thought that this work would be stimulating and would get me going. It was at that time that I met someone with whom I became friendly, and he asked me to return to live in Perth with him. I asked my father's permission. Tom, my friend, was a dentist, successful and very stable. My father said yes. He gave me that permission. So life went from one extreme to the other. I was back in Perth. Tommy had already returned there when I arrived. He showed me an entirely different way of life. It was interesting. It was challenging. I saw people drinking in moderation, which I had not previously experienced: people sitting down to drink and laugh, having a good time without any fighting erupting. We travelled to Indonesia, too, where we lived for six months. I saw a totally new world, and I lived as part of it.

Going to Indonesia was Tommy's decision. One day I was in Perth. The next, I was off to Indonesia. When he came home and said: 'We're going to Indonesia,' I said: 'Where is that?' At the time, I had a job at Ikea, working in the cafeteria. But Tommy had made some money and off we went. He's very much like that, he's that sort of person: working for so long, then wanting to go off to have a holiday. Our time in Indonesia was a holiday. Tommy didn't work, and we moved around. He opened up a whole new culture to me.

One day I was in Perth. The next, I was off to Indonesia.

At the end of six months we returned to Australia and I went back up north. I had had enough. I wanted to go home. And the last place I wanted to see was Perth. I was craving for home, yearning to be with my people.

After four or five months I decided it was time to do my Year 11 and 12 certificate. I wanted to get it done and out of the way. I wanted to do *something* but I didn't know what it was. I had found out by this time that completing Years 11 and 12 was what a person needed to do to get into further education. It was the only way. So whether I wanted to become a nurse or a teacher, I had to get that certificate. I resolved that I would.

I went for a test and was accepted into Curtin University. I was ecstatic. I didn't care that this would mean *Perth* all over again. All I knew was: 'I'm going for that certificate.' Then Tom rang and said we were off somewhere again. This time it was a place called Arnhem Land. 'Oh, where's that?' I knew that this would interfere with my plans for Curtin University and the precious certificate. Tommy said I would be able to do the studies externally. 'Can I,' I said. 'Yeah.' 'Oh,' I said. Having done the general education course at St Mary's, I knew what it was like to study externally, so I wasn't particularly keen on the idea. But I thought it might be different, doing the certificate exams externally, from what it was doing the general education course. Maybe I can do this, I thought. So I said: 'Okay. Righteo. We're going to this place called Arnhem Land.' So, off we went.

I didn't finish my course. I did start it, and was doing really well. It was not like the one at St Mary's. The tutor was present a lot more, and she was in tune with the courses and accustomed to external studies and tutoring. She was extremely enthusiastic. And she did get me going. I was very happy with the course and the study at the same time as doing domestic jobs. Then Tom brought home the *Gazette* and pointed out one of the advertisements. It was for the position of Aboriginal community worker in the department of health and community services. I said: 'I can't do that.' He said: 'Yes, you can.' I said: 'No way.' I repeated that I couldn't do it.

Weeks and weeks went by. For weeks and weeks Tom talked to me, saying I could do the job. 'You've got the clerical skills,' he said. 'You've got the education.' 'No,' I repeated. 'I can't do that you know.' Anyway, at last I said I'd go for the interview. I went, and ended up with the job.

I was under the wing of Joyce Thompson, Jenny Morris, Robert Wintal and Peter. They taught me so much. If I did anything wrong, they did not scold me, but went through whatever it was with me. And they were really good teachers. They nurtured me through the process, because I did not only need to learn how to do the job, but I also had to learn a language. Yolmumattha is the Aboriginal language from that part of Arnhem Land. And it was the most difficult language I'd ever come across.

I learnt Yolmumattha with the people, on the job. Some of the people in the community could speak English but, for most, Yolmumattha was their only language. I had to learn it quickly. Really quickly. Because I was Aboriginal, I was expected to know it better than the non-Aboriginal person sitting next to them. I had to learn it better than the non-Aboriginal people, too. And oh, my goodness, the people in the community asked me all sorts of questions: 'Where you from?' 'What family are you?' I was pulled from this way to that, to this family from that family. I was given a name. I was given a totem. I was given a family. I was given everything.

I was Yomur. It was the most unbelievable experience I had ever had. I had seen nothing like it before. It was like being in a foreign land.

As Aboriginal community worker I was working with families, looking after family welfare. My areas were education in health, abuse, food and nutrition, budgeting – home budgeting, housekeeping. Everything relevant to living in the community. I went into the people's homes. And once I began the job, I found there were no resources. I had to make my own as I went along. I had a ball doing it. I made all sorts of games and posters and other educational aids. Tom was director of dentistry in Arnhem Land. He was the head man and was doing on-hand dentistry as well as managing the service. We travelled out on little planes to the communities, flying by tiny twin engine planes or the Nomad aeroplane. We went to Ramingining, Elcho Island, Milingimbi, Galiwinku, Gapuwiyak, Rabuma Island. Everywhere.

It was a very difficult job, particularly so because when I was involved with a family and there was progress, suddenly I had to go off to the next

We travelled out on little planes to the communities, flying by tiny twin engine planes or the Nomad aeroplane.

community to plan for the needs of another family. It was like juggling constantly, and it was too big a job for one person. But it was a great job. If you like a challenge.

I remained in the job for two and a half years. Then the position of women's issues officer came up. Again, everyone encouraged me to do it. Again, I was saying: 'No!' 'No.' Backing off once more. I had no confidence. My esteem was so very low. But the others were saying: 'Yes. Yes, you can.' 'No, no,' I said. 'I can't.' Fortunately my old boss from welfare had moved over into that area, and he was encouraging me even more than anyone else. 'I've got all these applications,' he'd say. 'But I haven't seen yours yet.' He said that to me often. 'Greg,' I would reply, 'I don't think so.' He came back with: 'I don't know so much…' He was persistent. Eventually I began talking to him about the job. What would it entail? 'You know how you started at that job in welfare,' he said. 'You know how you began with it being an open book, and it progressed as you made it? Well, that's how this job will be.' 'True?' 'Yeah.' 'Really?' 'Yeah.'

There was some unhappiness in the department with the way previous women's issues officer jobs had operated. Greg had seen the way I worked, and he wanted that input into the women's issues job. He wanted a clear practical sense of what was needed, instead of the bureaucratic approach.

Tom told me it was more money. I was furious when he made that comment, because I believe that that is not the way to look at anything, particularly work. I don't look at a job for the money. I look at it for the morals of it. I was angry with Tom, and this made me reluctant again to take the position. Still, I kept thinking about it. I had begun to see that there might be more power in the job to obtain more funding for the women. It is always such a struggle with health and community services. The authorities are always so stingy. That was why I had to make my own resources.

I don't look at a job for the money. I look at it for the morals of it.

Eventually I came to see that the funding possibilities and the power that went with the position were important, or at least they could be. So I spoke to Greg and I said: 'You promise?' wanting him to confirm that all he had told me about the job was true, that I could work out the needs of the job and determine its direction as I had with the community officer position. And he said: 'I promise.' 'Are you sure?' 'I'm sure.' So he made the promise of what the job would be like, and I took the plunge. And I got the job. I got it. And then I had to do the bloody thing, mate!

Well, it was *hard*. It was the most difficult job I have ever had to do.

One of the major obstacles was the male chauvinism within the department. It wasn't cruel chauvinism. They were just joking, and I didn't know how to judge what they were saying and doing. I was very sensitive. It was a new environment for me, and it was different from any environment I had ever been in. It wasn't as supportive as where I had come from. The other workers did try to look out for me, and guide me. But they wanted to guide me too much. They didn't give me sufficient freedom to get on and do the job in the way it had to be done. I was the one selected for the position, and I was selected for my expertise, my way of working, and my understanding of the issues and the community. Yet once I was in the job, this seemed to be forgotten by those with whom I was working, and instead of my being able to design the position and determine on the priorities, others set out to 'put me right'.

I realise now that a part of this was the workers attempting to acclimatise me to the department, so they were doing me a favour. Had I gone their way, it would have saved me a great deal of confusion. But because I was so accustomed to my own freedom, I wanted to exercise it straight away. I didn't want to take the time to learn how to read and speak their way. I didn't want to have to learn what went on in the office, or where various equipment and other items were found. I didn't want to take time up with learning the basic cultural aspects of the bureaucracy, the way the department operated. That was where I went wrong.

At the time, I blamed the others. They did counselling sessions with me. They went out of their way, holding extra meetings with me, and they gave me a supervisor – a man! One of my friends, Fiona Smith, a freelance socialworker who came from Queensland, did some straight talking to me. She was a 'Midland' – the slang word for a grazier from Queensland. She said: 'So, you're a Murri.' I said: 'Oh, am I?' She made me laugh. She said to me: 'A *man* supervising a *woman?* You've got a *male* supervisor?' She was outraged. She was f-u-r-i-o-u-s. 'Is that wrong?' I said. 'Yep!' she goes. '*YEP.*' 'Oh.' No one had ever told *me* that. 'Of course they're not going to tell you that,' she roared. '*I'm* telling you that!'

> '*A* man *supervising a* woman? You've got a* male *supervisor?' She was outraged.*

I had not been able to see clearly what was happening. I was never sure if it was me that was the problem, or them. Just as I had not worked with them before, they had not worked with me. Fiona was right in there with me, and she gave them back as much as they gave me. She had dealt with that sort of treatment in the past, in her own career, and she was able to give as much back as they gave me.

Greg was attempting to find a balance between the two aspects of the job: between my connection to the grassroots, and its vital importance to the position I held, and his duty in the bureaucratic sense. He found it very, very difficult. In the end, he told me, he left because he couldn't deal with the difficulties any more. He told me I should stay with the department, but take study leave, do some further education, then return to the job at a later date. My supervisor, Old Dave, Uncle Dave I called him for respect, took me back to his home one day and said: 'Here, have a beer. Sit down and I'm gonna have a yarn with you. Sit down.' So he gave me a beer and said: 'You girl, get your things together and go out and do what you want and learn about it more before you put yourself into something like this job again.'

My other boss told me the same thing. He said I should leave and get more experience. So there was encouragement in one sense, but in another way there was a barrier to my aspirations. They were not prepared to let me go through the whole system, learning as I went along and using my expertise and the experience and skills I had. They didn't think I was ready for it.

Ultimately they were right, because I wasn't ready for the system as it was. By that stage I was hating the job. I had to force myself to go to work each day and began drinking as a result. My Dad died. My relationship with Tom was falling to pieces. Everything was coming to an end and I felt as if I were falling apart. It was the worst experience I have ever been through. I felt I was in the middle of a nightmare and couldn't wake up.

Eventually I decided to resign. Then my German father, Papa, came to visit me. He decided that he should help me out. He recalled I had told him at one time that I was interested in journalism. As a birthday present he gave me a ticket to go to Brisbane to do a journalism course at the University of Queensland. It was an introductory course, and Papa said that if I found I enjoyed it and was good at it, I should apply to do the long course in journalism. After five years of good memories (because there *were* good times, and I had learnt a great deal and gained a lot of experience, enjoyed life and improved my skills) I left Arnhem Land. I couldn't believe I was leaving, but I did. I had my whole life with me in K-Mart bags. Huge ones, dragging them around the university. Through the huge city of Brisbane. I didn't even know where I was! Eventually, I arrived at the campus, finally found the room I was allocated and the keys to it. I completed the course, then Papa discovered that a conference was taking place in the hills of Atherton. 'Where the hell's that?' I'll go. I'll go.

I had my whole life with me in K-Mart bags. Huge ones, dragging them around the university. Through the huge city of Brisbane.

Off I went to Atherton. The conference was being held on a farm where an old man, Uncle Jess, and Aunty Norma, were looking after kids who had come off the street. They were neglected children, and youths released from reform school or prison. I began working with the kids and they were the best you'd ever find. Yes, they were arrogant. They were wicked as tyrants. They were unreal. But it was an interesting experience, and I stayed for five or six months.

But I was still a bit lost. I was drinking still. I decided I wanted to go home. That was where I wanted to be. I managed to find a ride with someone in an old Holden. It took us six months to travel from Queensland to Broome.

The old Holden carried us right around Darwin and all the way back to the north of Western Australia. The trip was a nightmare. The car was unregistered, and the driver unlicensed. It was chaotic. We lived on pancakes and tea. We had no money. Whenever we could find one, we lived in an old humpy. It was as if we were living the life of hippies. When I could get a casual job, I took it. Then I would think about my job in the department, and all the security I had had. I had come from the highs of life to the lowest of lows. But finally I made it home.

I managed to find a ride with someone in an old Holden. It took us six months to travel from Queensland to Broome.

Then I set off for Walpole, south of Albany. Papa had moved there from Germany. I was brought up by my foster family, my uncle and aunt, while Papa spent time living between Australia and Germany, going back and forth. My aunt and uncle had only one child, and looked after all of us. I had known nothing of Papa, my biological father, until my Mum told me about him one day when I was playing in the sand. I was about ten years of age and didn't think about it at the time. Suddenly, when I was 23 years old and living in Gove, I received a lettergram. The name that my mother had told me all those years ago was at the end of the paper. I remembered who the man was immediately, and thought: 'Well, I'll be damned.' It spun me right out. He had come looking for me, and had found my sister. My sister told him where he could find me, and that was how we met. I flew back to Derby and met him. Our relationship just went on from there.

It was at about this time that Dad died. I went through a confusing stage. My Dad who had raised me was dead. Another man had come into my life who was my father, and seemed to be blocking out my Dad. It was difficult to accept, and I felt the need to blame and to neglect my Papa as well as to go to see him in Walpole, where he had decided to settle down.

I travelled as far as Mandurah, then ended in hospital. I was there for a month, or maybe longer. It was in many ways the best thing that had happened to me, because it meant I gave up alcohol. I will never touch it again. I know now how bad alcohol is for anyone. And once you have given it up, you don't miss it. You know you are better off without it. A person doesn't need to drink to have fun.

When I arrived in Mandurah I felt a sickness coming on and told the nurses: 'You've got to put me in hospital.' They kept sending me away. I told them I didn't know what it was I was suffering from, but I was having some bad attacks. I was hyperventilating and suffering from severe anxiety attacks. I forced them to put me in hospital – but it took me making many, many telephone calls and eventually going to the police.

When I arrived in Walpole, Papa and Susie (Papa's wife) were shocked at what had happened. They were good to me, and cared for me during a horrible time. I spent nights standing up, afraid to lie down and go to sleep. Other nights I tossed and turned until all hours. Eventually Papa made me do work around the property, and this helped me come to my senses.

Papa told me to work in the back storage area of the business. I began doing odd jobs. I started to get on my feet. I ate healthier food, whereas before, particularly when travelling, I had eaten junk food and my nutrition was really bad. I began to think again about trying to do the certificate. I was still determined to do it; it was there, at the back of my mind, always. It was all I could think about at that time. So I decided. 'Papa, I want to go to Albany.'

Off I went, booking myself into a backpackers hotel. I got a job. I began making enquiries. I was ready to apply. Then something pulled me back. I decided no, that's not what I want to do just yet. I was indecisive. I did not want to put myself into a situation where I might be insulted. I still had doubts about my ability, and I realised that I couldn't subject myself to any more humiliation. I backed off doing the certificate and allowed my itchy feet to take me travelling again.

I knew that if I wanted to study, then I would have to stay in one place. If I wanted to travel, then I had to get that over and done with first. So I planned my life: I decided to travel first, then study. I had my priorities worked out – but Papa was furious. He was m-a-d.

I met up with Roz, Mickey, Gary and Biggles, took a train to town, and that was it. We were off. We spent about eight months travelling from Albany, back up north. They wanted to see the north and I said I would show them. I showed them alright. They hadn't seen bush like it in their lives. Roz is from Ireland, Mickey from Japan, and Gary and Biggles are from England. They were rapt – until we reached the hot desert area. They couldn't handle the flies and the heat. But if that is what you want to see, then it's the real thing. If you've seen the Australian desert up north, you've seen it all. They saw it.

At one stage, Gary was driving and the four of them were saying: 'This is like driving through snow.' Suddenly we came over a hill, facing into a huge hole. The van nose-dived. We had collected my Mum in Broome, so she was in the Kombi, and she went flying. The van was bogged. With determination and lots of pulling, shoving and shouting (not to mention a little swearing) we dragged it out.

As we drove on, we speculated on what the 'flap, flap' was that kept sounding on the road. We were at least 250 kms away from Broome, and carried on driving. Gary's explanation was that the noise was the flap under the wheel dragging on the asphalt. Then the radiator broke. My niece, being a real bushwoman, was shouting: 'Eggs, eggs, eggs.' As they were handed to her, one by one, she put them down the radiator to stop it from leaking. She is a real bush mechanic. So when Gary kept on asserting that the 'flap, flap' was the rubber flap hanging off the mudguard, she told him smartly that it wasn't, it was something far more serious. 'No, no, no,' declared Gary. My niece was getting wild, and her anger was directed at him! 'He's not from the bush, he's from England,' she said. What would he know? Earlier, he had driven right over a pile of wood lying in the road. My niece had sat looking red in the face, her arms folded, saying: 'He's definitely not from Australia. No Australian would go over that.'

Then the radiator broke. My niece, being a real bushwoman, was shouting: 'Eggs, eggs, eggs.'

Anyway, she was right. The 'flap, flap' wasn't the mudflaps. When we pulled up to have it checked, Gary and Roz, who were both fiery, were arguing with each other. Gary was saying: 'See, it is the mudflap.' Roz was fighting back: 'No, it's not.' 'Yes, it is.' 'No it isn't.' 'How do you know,' said Gary. And Roz says: 'I know, because *I cut the bloody thing off!*'

The entire tread of the tyre was ripped. We could have had an extremely serious accident, yet we didn't. Someone was looking after us.

So, I was back home. Sitting there one day, I began to think once more about the studying business. Maybe I'll give travelling a miss, I thought. Maybe I'll go and get that certificate. So I applied for entry at the beginning of 1994.

I learnt about the course at the University of Western Australia when I read about it on an old piece of paper someone had sent me. I don't know where it came from. It must have been someone who remembered me, I don't know how. I rang to see if testing was still available. Everything was organised from the University of Western Australia Aboriginal Programme Centre. I travelled back to Perth for testing, and stayed at St Catherine's College, just across from the university. When they told me I was admitted to the course, they asked where I would like to live, on Abstudy. I decided to apply to St Catherine's College, because I was familiar with it and had enjoyed my earlier stay. I met Madonna, one of my friends, now, at college. To find someone who was mature-age and going through the same sort of experiences as I was a boon. We were both wanting to qualify to study further, and being from the same country, up north, was important. It meant I have someone to relate to.

So here I am again, in the big city. I cannot believe I have almost finished the course. My subjects are anthropology, social science, sociology, psychology and some history. We studied foundations of university studies as a compulsory unit in the second semester, and another compulsory unit was 'Aboriginal perspectives'.

I intend to be a writer, but what sort of writing I have not yet decided. I'd like to try a bit of everything. As my Papa remembered, I had an interest in journalism at one time. That is a skill I would like to learn. I am very involved in creative writing as well.

I return to Broome for the holidays. That makes it easier in some ways and more difficult in others. Although I am now quite experienced in living in the city, because I have had a number of spells here, I prefer living in the north, in Broome and Derby. That is where I feel at home. That is my country.

Keeping My Options Open

Lara Finlayson

Lara Finlayson spent 1993 working as a teacher in London and travelling extensively around Europe and parts of Africa and Asia. Currently working full-time as a secondary science teacher at Wantirna Secondary College, Lara Finlayson is studying law part-time and enjoying spending time at the theatre, seeing plenty of movies and attempting to balance work, study and socialising.

Born in Shepparton, Victoria, in 1968, Lara Finlayson lived there until she became a boarder at Methodist Ladies College (MLC) in Kew for her final three years of school. Following completion of her secondary schooling, she spent four years at university in Melbourne to complete a bachelor of education (secondary science) after which she moved back to Shepparton where she taught science at North Shepparton Secondary College for three years. During this time she completed an honours degree in Women's Studies through Deakin University.

Many of the issues addressed by the Women's Movement impact differently upon country women and city women. Isolation, lack of education, lack of public transport and access to women's health services are problems faced by country women to a greater extent than city women. Although housing is slightly cheaper, almost everything else costs more! Access to education, particularly tertiary, is also a problem for country women. Violence is of as much concern to women in the country as it is to women in the city! It is a myth that people are safer in the country. The Women's Movement has an active presence in Shepparton, the country town I know best, but many attitudes that are deeply ingrained into country people are difficult to change. As a gross generalisation, I have found country people more conservative than those in the city. This means that many of the problems country women face are not openly recognised, or are not considered to be problems.

In 1968, when I was born in country Victoria, Shepparton was a large country town, rapidly expanding in size and population. I was my parent's first child, and entered the world after a fairly routine, if long, birth. My parents took me home from the local base hospital to deposit me in the same bedroom I inhabit today.

My parents lived just out of town, in a new estate. This meant we had no fences or town services, and our kitchen window overlooked paddocks full of long grass and the occasional cow. My early years were spent playing in self-constructed cubby houses out in the garden, climbing trees and riding my bike down the bike track which clung to the bank of the creek that flowed at the end of the road. I also spent a great deal of time reading, or playing Barbie dolls with neighbouring kids. My father went to work early and returned in the late afternoon, while my mother spent her days at home with me and my younger brother. As we grew older, and began school, my mother became heavily involved in the school mothers' club and in voluntary community work.

...we had no fences or town services, and our kitchen window overlooked paddocks full of long grass and the occasional cow.

A new primaryschool opened in Shepparton the year I began school, and I was in the first grade to go right through the school from Prep to Grade 6. I did not particularly enjoy primaryschool. I was a small child, the youngest in my grade, intelligent and I always received good school reports. However, I was not pretty or good at sport, and never felt that I fitted in well socially. I rode my bike to school most days. My memories of primaryschool are now extremely dim; I remember the feelings that I had more than events that occurred.

My brother and I spent holidays at our cousins' farm. It was a novelty to collect the eggs from the chookhouse, or tag along as sheep were checked during lambing season. My aunt worked alongside my uncle on the farm, as did my cousins, and I considered everyone in the family a farmer. On other family holidays we met kids from the city whose automatic assumption was that we were farmers once we said that we didn't live in Melbourne. It often seemed to them a shock that not all country people lived on farms!

Occasionally we would take a trip to Melbourne, usually to visit the orthodontist for my brother's braces or to visit some of my parents' friends. We dressed up in our good clothes, and bugged my parents all the way there in the car with 'are we there yet?' Once we had arrived in Melbourne we would beg my parents for a tram ride. It was also a great thrill to see the Christmas windows at Myer. Melbourne was very much 'the big smoke'; it was a place of wonder and excitement but full of potential hazards. For many country people it still is. I continue to be amazed at hearing country people (particularly women) say that they would be scared to drive in Melbourne, when I know they are competent behind the wheel and in many other areas! The city is still perceived as a challenge.

I began highschool in 1980 at one of the four state secondary schools in Shepparton. Originally it was a girls school, and although it had been coeducational for a number of years it still had more girls attending than boys. My Year 7 form was all-female. I achieved the same high grades at highschool as I had at primaryschool. When I was in Year 8 my mother approached me about going to boardingschool in Melbourne, starting from Year 10. I agreed, and can't recall considering this a difficult decision. Although I had found a group of friends in the school choir and band, the prospect of leaving did not particularly bother me.

Early in 1983 my parents and I loaded up the car and took what was to be the first of many trips to Kew, as I began Year 10 at Methodist Ladies College (MLC). The size of the school astounded me. Although I had been there for interviews and admission tests, the sheer number of girls, all dressed in green, was incredible. I had gone from a coeducational country highschool of approximately 600 students to a huge city school of 2000 girls. There were 100 girls in the boardinghouse, from country Victoria and New South Wales as well as places as distant as New Guinea, Thailand and Hong Kong. I also suffered the profound shock of going from the top of the class to being another average student. Already insecure, I was no longer able to sustain myself through social and sporting ineptitude with the thought that at least I was the smartest.

It took me all of that first year to settle in to boardingschool. I became friends with a group of day girls, but did not feel comfortable with most of the other boarders. I spent much of my time in the boardinghouse studying (in order to get the grades I had been used to) or reading second hand Mills and Boon novels, bought from the local opportunity shop. I joined the school choir, and involved myself in house drama and chorals. Over the three years that I attended MLC I began to learn more social skills and to make more and more friends. There were no boys around to worry about, or in front of whom to appear stupid or awkward. I became more outspoken about my own thoughts and opinions and I began to relax and be myself. It didn't matter as much if I wasn't pretty and couldn't play sport. I had a host of marvellous, intelligent and strong women teaching me (as well as the occasional marvellous and intelligent man!), many potential friends to choose from and a huge variety of activities in which I could participate. It was easy to find a niche in which I could feel comfortable once I overcame my initial reticence.

Why did my parents send me to boardingschool? My highschool in Shepparton was certainly adequate, and I was succeeding there. I was sent to MLC more for the boarding experience than the fact that it was a private school, although that fact was a contributing factor. Mum and Dad thought that boardingschool would give me the opportunity to come out of my shell and extend my confidence and social skills. They also thought that educationally it would possibly be more challenging and ensure that I made the most of my abilities, particularly because it was all girls. They definitely thought that a private school education would open more doors to me than the state system. I had the choice to stay in Shepparton if I wished; my brother decided not to go to boardingschool in Melbourne but instead stayed at one of the local technical schools. With the benefit of hindsight, I think that my HSC (higher school certificate) results would possibly have been better had I stayed at home in the country, since at MLC my social skills did blossom and I spent more of my final years socialising and involving myself in extra-curricular activities than studying! This has not affected my eventual career plan however, and the personal growth I experienced at MLC was worth the drop in marks. I am now a staunch supporter of single-sex schooling for girls. After my own experiences in both coeducation and all-female schools, as well as the numerous studies I have read on the issue, I believe that girls do have many more educational opportunities in a girls school.

Mum and Dad thought that boardingschool would give me the opportunity to come out of my shell and extend my confidence and social skills.

Once I reached senior school (Years 11 and 12) at MLC I was actively encouraged to continue studying science. Although I was achieving in most subjects across the curriculum, science was my strong point, so I enrolled in straight science subjects, as did many of the other students. The careers teacher encouraged me to take up engineering upon leaving school, but I never really understood quite what it was! I didn't particularly know what I wanted to do, but I did want to keep my 'options open'. I applied for medicine and science at university, but ended up getting into applied biology at RMIT (Royal Melbourne Institute of Technology).

I had not seriously thought about what I would do after school other than go to university. I didn't know exactly what I would do there; I would just go. I hated my course at RMIT (although I relished the social life and freedom I experienced living in a residential college) and by half way through the first year, I realised I would have to get out. I wanted to continue my tertiary education, although still for no clear reason, and so began to look around for other courses. Some of my friends were doing teaching and enjoying it, so I thought 'why not me?' In 1987 I went into the second year of a bachelor of education in secondary science at Melbourne College of Advanced Education (MCAE). During this time I lived in North Melbourne and worked in a casual job in the city. I loved living in Melbourne; it presented me with so many different opportunities. The pace was ideal for a woman in her late teens and early twenties. I went to the theatre, movies, concerts, restaurants, and spent many hours with much-loved friends.

I moved back to my home town of Shepparton to take up a teaching position when I graduated in 1990. There were several reasons behind my wish to return home, the first being to live with my parents again and save money. This I have certainly been able to do! The second reason was that I thought that the love and support of my parents would be invaluable as I began teaching secondary students, at an age of only 21 myself. This proved to be true. The support proved to be invaluable when my three-year relationship ended soon after I returned home.

In late 1992 I had been living with my parents and working in Shepparton for three years, and was about to leave to travel overseas. My original goal of saving money held true. I also completed another degree part-time: a bachelor of letters (honours) in Women's Studies, through Deakin University. Once I had completed my BEd I thought that I would never study again, but after a year off I discovered I was craving to learn especially for my own personal growth. I then enrolled at Deakin. The Women's Studies course was stimulating. Once again, it is thanks to the generosity of my parents that I have been able to work full-time and study part-time successfully; I doubt that I could have done it if I had been looking after my own house, with the many hours of work associated with doing so.

I thought that I would never study again, but after a year off I discovered I was craving to learn...

Living in the country after my years in the city was a mixed bag. Shepparton is a large country centre, and only two hours drive from Melbourne, so in some aspects I could have the best of both worlds. In many ways I love being in Shepparton; the air is cleaner, and many of the people more straightforward and less pretentious. My parents have been fantastic, and I have met some great people. However, the lack of cultural activities, and the limited social circles, are a real handicap. Most people in their early to mid-twenties have lived in Shepparton for most, if not all, of their lives, and have friendship circles going back to their schooldays. Many of the younger people I met were very conservative and saw the world in a very restricted way. There is much more conformity, and less tolerance of people seen as 'different'. I am sure that the same people exist in the city, but in the city there are so many more young people to meet that it is easier to find like-minded, more compatible friends.

My life became far more structured and regimented than it was in the city; it is harder to do things on the spur of the moment as many activities simply aren't available for long hours. You can't buy a cappuccino at two in the morning on a Wednesday! I do like to have structure in my life, but I also like to have options. As a schoolteacher in a country town I have found that I always have to make sure that I am acting as an appropriate role model. Someone always knows who you are, and you never know when a student is watching! Hopefully there are more places to hide in the city. I enjoy the clean air, open countryside and lack of crowds in Shepparton, and the way that it takes only 15 minutes to drive from one end of town to the other. I have more time available to pursue different activities, although in the city I had more choice of activities to pursue. Much of my life in the country and city is the same however: I still go to work, study, eat, drink, sleep, socialise, travel, and try to pay the bills!

My involvement in the Women's Movement has also germinated and grown as I returned to the country, although the seed was planted while I was in the city. I can clearly recall the shock I felt when I left MLC and entered the broader world of university. At MLC I believed that women could do anything they wished; we were actively encouraged to do so. Before I left school I hadn't really recognised that sexism and misogyny did exist in a broad and pervasive sense. I knew that people sometimes told sexist jokes, but I thought that was about as far as it went. How naive! There was no specific incident that alerted me to the fact; just a growing awareness that things that happened in the world around me were often unjust, and that women were usually on the receiving end simply because they were women. However, I didn't really try to do anything about it, other than protest against what directly affected me. Even through this simple action my friends began to regard me as a bit of a 'women's libber'.

The harassment directed at me did not last very long, as I am fairly vocal and complained loudly.

Once I returned to the country and began working, I discovered that sexism was certainly alive and kicking. The population of the school in which I taught was predominantly male. I was a target of sexist and sexual comments by students on yard duty, and in class. The harassment directed at me did not last very long, as I am fairly vocal and complained loudly. I was eventually backed up by the remainder of the staff (although many of the men thought I was taking it all far too seriously and that it wasn't really a problem!) and a sexual harassment policy was devised. This has helped to eliminate blatant harassment, but to some extent more subtle forms continue. I am now sure that harassment is commonplace in most, if not all, schools, but is often so ingrained that it is not always recognised!

The main causes behind the problems being experienced at work were the attitudes held by many members of the school community, and the community in general. This fuelled my interest in women's issues and the Women's Movement. I also began to attend the semi-regular functions held by the newly formed 'Goulburn Valley Loose Women's Group'. The name of the group caused a few giggles, but the aim was to provide informal functions that covered issues of specific interest to women. It was through this group that I listened to inspiring women including Valerie McDougall (one of the mainstays of the group) and, later, Renate Klein. They fuelled and strengthened my conviction that women are a group who have been oppressed but also possess numerous qualities and abilities, and are actively utilising them to fight and overcome discrimination in all its forms.

I had also begun Women's Studies, and voraciously consumed books by women about women, particularly feminist discussions. This degree also brought me into contact with Robyn Rowland and Renate Klein on a regular basis. Both these women, particularly Renate, helped me to solidify my commitment to the Women's Movement, and to further marvel at the sheer number of activities that women manage to successfully fit into their lives. Although at this time I was working for the movement mainly within the circles I am part of, I hoped to extend upon my commitment to women upon returning from overseas. The Goulburn Valley Loose Women's Group has been an important forum in which up to 100 local women have been able to support and appreciate one another.

I now openly identify myself as feminist, almost as much to breakdown stereotypes of what a feminist is like as to declare my beliefs and the importance I attach to them. Through discussion, reading, experiencing and thinking, I have gradually become aware of the vital importance of the Women's Movement for all women, whether they live in the country or the city. MLC nurtured my belief in what women could do, and the many women I have met since leaving school have confirmed it and further increased my awareness of women's oppression. I still find it difficult to believe that more women have not come to this conclusion by my age. My parents, particularly my mother, have been key influences in my identification with the Women's Movement. My mother's strength, commonsense and competence, as she has moved from bringing up her children while carrying out voluntary community work to a senior position in the full-time workforce, has been inspirational. Both my parents have a strong sense of injustice, and have instilled this in me.

I live quite happily in the country, and live quite happily in the city. My return to Melbourne upon arriving back from overseas was planned. In many ways, I think that I make the most of whatever place I live in, but when living in the country I feel I am a city girl, and in the city I find the reverse: that I am from the country. Most of my closest friends also come from this dual background, and have never lived exclusively in one or the other. My friendship circles encompass both city and country people. Valuable experiences can be gained from either environment, and can combine to give a wider picture of what living in Australia (or Victoria in my case!) is really like. It is easy to become narrow in your thinking when your experiences are limited, or not to consider that many issues affecting our community have differing impacts depending on where you live. Living in both has made me a better person. Living and teaching in the country has also increased my awareness of social inequality in Victoria, and that some people are born luckier than others. It was something I never thought about when a private-school pupil and later a university student! I strive to remember that not everybody experiences life in the way I do, nor do they think in the same way. I think that it is important to recognise that 'different' does not necessarily mean 'wrong', and that in many cases difference should be valued far more than it is.

Living and teaching in the country has increased my awareness of social inequality in Victoria, and that some people are born luckier than others.

I am not sure of what my future holds. At present I have thought only as far as my travels overseas and returning to live in Melbourne; whether I wish to return to teaching is another matter. I have thoroughly enjoyed teaching, and find the contact with kids the best part of it. However it was never a lifetime commitment for me. I hope to go back to university at some stage and continue my formal education: this is one thing that cannot easily be done in the country. I have had many ideas of what I would like to study and then enter as a career: law, business, psychology, journalism. Today, I don't really know for sure. I do know I want to do something that in some way will help women. I want to do something important with my life. In years to come I want to be proud of what I have achieved both up to now and in the future as both a city woman and a country woman.

Abiding in the Field

Merryl Robson

Graduating BSc from the University of Adelaide in 1962, Merryl Kay Robson completed her honours year in 1963, and gained the degree of master of science from the University of Melbourne in 1965. Some 30 years later (with periods of study in between) she returned to formal study, graduating from the University of Ballarat in 1994 with a graduate diploma in business management. She was born and grew up in Adelaide and has lived or holidayed in Port Pirie, Melbourne, Broken Hill, Mildura, Hamilton and Sydney, amongst other places, and has worked in many occupations, including as rural affairs advisor, biologist, lecturer and consultant.

Merryl Robson has organised many festivals, colloquiums and seminars on a wide range of issues, including chemical, salinity, and bandicoot awareness. She organised festivals on 'Celebrating the Bandicoot in Hamilton' in 1991, the 1986 National Organic Gardening and Farming Festival, and Wood Craft workshops at the Melbourne Meat Market Craft Centre in 1988. She initiated Aboriginal Keeping Place, Hamilton; Aussie Wool Art Cooperative; the Bandicoot Information Centre and the Wool and Rural Industries Skills Training Centre.

I was born to devoted parents in a small Adelaide suburban hospital at the beginning of the second world war. I was their first born, and they continually reminded me of this. My mother, Alice Laura Burley, was of Cornish decent and father, Conrad Wilfred Mader, was very German. He had spoken little English until leaving his home and family in the Barossa Valley and going to Adelaide High School. It is a great disappointment to me that I am not able to speak any German. However, the German genes and influence persist. This sense of German identity has been strengthened in recent years by initiating, and then coordinating, two 'Kulturfests' in the small Victorian town of Tarrington, which had been called 'Hochkirch' until 1917.

Life in suburban Adelaide in the 1940s and 1950s was easy and fun. We were a very contained middle-class family. My mother and father lived lives bound together by us three children (Beverly is 18 months younger and Lyndon five years younger than I), their garden and their church. Our life, apart from the local primaryschool, was circumscribed by my father's school, my mother's piano pupils, and Holder Memorial Methodist Church. I cannot remember attending any night activity or weekend activity that was not organised by this church. All my sport (basketball in winter, tennis in summer and table-tennis throughout the year) was in church teams. All picnics were church organised. It was a structured, happy life that appeared to be fundamentally similar to the hundred or so other families in the congregation.

The local Lockleys Primary School, which we children attended, was a short bus distance away. It had a beautiful big peppermint tree in the yard. In an art class, with instructions to draw some aspect of this tree, it was the first time that I was struck by the intricacies of living objects, their smell, and an intriguing world that I was made to examine closely. The school was cold in winter. It was also overcrowded, even in those days. So we trudged down the street to the local church hall for some classes, and it was even colder. My best friend was Lilliana Casablanca, an Italian girl from a nearby market garden. She was lively, gifted, beautifully dark-skinned with dark shining eyes.

...it was the first time that I was struck by the intricacies of living objects, their smell, and an intriguing world that I was made to examine closely.

Holidays were ordered. Every May holiday the family went by car to the South Australian industrial country town of Port Pirie to stay with cousins Brian and Ian Bayly. Mum's sister, Mabel, had married a schoolteacher too. But he was different altogether from my father. He was dark and smoked and swore and delighted in his boys being rough. Climbing the pine trees was 'in', but I got blisters. Playing in the church yard nextdoor was 'in', but I fell in the gravel. Eating boiled eggs was expected, but I choked. However, mushrooming in nearby Germein Gorge was fun; climbing through fences for the choicest ones seemed outrageously adventurous. September holidays were 'Adelaide Show' time. Then our lives revolved around the flower pavilion. Our immense garden was a treasure trove to be harnessed each spring for the show and at other times for local shows. It was a big production. Everyone helped from morning to late at night for days in preparation for the large displays that Mum did with us (kids and Dad) helping. We carried pots and put them ready for Mum to arrange 10' by 8' displays making sure that all pots were covered with moss which we had gathered from McLaren Vale the previous week. As we grew older we were allowed to compete ourselves. There were some successes: Merryl Mader – first prize for best decorated saucer, under eight years. This was often spoiled when we heard outwardly friendly people bickering behind backs about small details of awards and judging. Each day, after watering duties, we could scamper off to play around the sideshows and mooch around other pavilions. Days had a strange double existence. The order and quiet of the flower pavilion became chaos and noise in sideshow alley.

Highschool was Adelaide High School. It was another world. It was an all-girls school where I found that I was hopeless at history, to my chagrin and Miss Miztelfeldt's consternation, but excelled at science with Mr Doug Anders (the only male teacher in the whole school) and singing madrigals with Mrs Elizabeth Silsbury. The 100 per cent science, 40 per cent history streamed me early into science subjects with music as a balance. This balance of art and science has generally been the norm for me since that time. Our teachers were a mixed lot but always in control. We were there to learn their wisdom. We knew our place. Only a few times did I buck the system, and then only in minor ways. Any misdemeanours, even after school hours, seemed to be noticed. Hats and gloves and uniform had to be correct, and there were lines if found wanting at gate inspections. It was a strong teaching and discipline school, and was most supportive of students in many ways. I ended my days by being a prefect for two years, and school vice-captain and law house captain. I still have my white prefect's hat inscribed with all who were at Ziggy's for a 'shake' on the last day of school. My law house, the blue and gold, won the house choir but came last in house sports and the other house captains gave me a sympathy card. It was a school where country girls came for leaving and honours years. They were strong, robust girls and several became best friends. They stayed at Miethke house and played hockey. Most went on to teachers college. The Boys High was down the road. I went there for leaving honours physics. It was noisy, jocular. For the first time I failed physics, but enjoyed the distractions.

> Our teachers were a mixed lot but always in control. We were there to learn their wisdom. We knew our place.

Holder Memorial Methodist Church still dominated my life out of school. It was a structured, cohesive, conforming way of life; church and Sunday School three times on Sunday, Billy Graham revivals, church sport clubs all Saturday, church camps in the country, and playing the piano for sing-songs after church on Sunday nights.

An influence remaining with me to this day comes from my music education. Barbara Hanrahan talked of this time, and our common teacher, Miss Dorothy McGregor, in her book *The Scent of the Eucalypt*. Miss McGregor got me through my turbulent teen years. 'Relax Merryl, you need to relax to make a beautiful sound,' she continually instructed me, waving my arms in mid air. It seemed that I did sometimes make a beautiful sound since I was asked to play in many concerts at the Theosophical Society, the organ at church, the piano at Sunday School Anniversaries with a full orchestra and my father conducting in a packed Thebarton Town Hall. I even earned some money playing at nationalisation ceremonies at Thebarton Town Hall and passed, generally with honours, eight piano grades, even playing in a concert for the best of that year's students at the Elder Conservatorium.

Boys were another dimension taking much time and energy when discovered. Thank heavens for Miss McGregor. She was, and still is, different. When she became engaged to her great love they saved for those three years to amass all the 'necessities' needed for their new life together. But he died. She still wears the engagement ring, some 70 years later, and continually fondles it and talks of how beautiful it was, dear. She floats around in chiffon and smiles with arms outstretched to embrace. And still lives in her immaculate house and garden at 1 Devon Street, Mile End with its prickly roses and a bench on the verandah where you waited until the previous pupil had finished their lesson. You could hear them together as you waited, her and the pupil. We would hear if there had been sufficient work done during the week by the student for it to be a love lesson, or otherwise. She was much in demand and did not tolerate laxness in preparation for long. We played Ravel, Schostakovich, Miriam Hyde, Bach, Beethoven, Mozart and Debussey. And scales, arpeggios, exercises. We learned untold joy and discipline. Her mother has died now, but had lived there too. We write at Christmas and other times. Her letters I keep nearby. They are so full of love for 'Dear One Merryl' from 'Heart's love, Best Wishes, and joy too, Dorothy M (X)'. They show a wonderful disregard for moderation that still suggests to me that the bountiful rather than the meek inherit the earth. She is the epitome of conservative thought and deed in herself, but delights in the unexpected, the gifted, the different in others and supports them.

...a wonderful disregard for moderation that still suggests to me that the bountiful rather than the meek inherit the earth.

The end of secondary school heralded great decisions. What should I do? I had managed to pass leaving honours with straight science – English, two maths, physics and chemistry. I rebelled against doing what everyone expected – go to teachers college. Medicine would have been my choice, but it took five years, as a start, and it seemed unfair for a girl to inflict such a cost on parents. It was a time when it was not hard to get jobs. I went to a number of possibilities, but they seemed so inane and boring. Then I learnt that one of Miss McGregor's students held a cadetship at

Adelaide University, and on enquiry found there was one in genetics. It seemed too good to be true – I could study and work at the same time, and be paid a little. I applied and frantically tried to find out, from a dictionary, something about this mysterious concept. The interview I will always remember. Professor Bennett looked and seemed the epitome of an absentminded professor, but kind. It was the start of a new era. I looked after all the different mice stocks; was their marriage guidance counsellor, midwife and burial supervisor; and had nineteen hours off during term for attending lectures.

Five years later I completed the ordinary degree, the first person to do so at Adelaide Uni as a cadet throughout, said my professor. The time had not been uneventful. Young people were able to get a car licence at 16 years in South Australia. My mother had a wonderful little pale green Fiat 600 which was a dream to get around in. In my third year, great interest in an honours organic chemistry fellow led to ordinary results – and prof's reprove. The following year, he called me in to his office and made me list my outside interests and subsequently gained my commitment to drop tennis so that the previous year's results would not be repeated. They were not, but I was miserable. Thankfully I was still learning piano from Miss McGregor. I attribute getting through this troubled teen period to her love and endurance. I repeated the extra curriculum activities in my last year and earned a 'supp' for my final subject, biochem II. My parents had begun an insurance policy when I and my sister were born. This matured when we were 21, and we had planned a trip by sea to Fiji and Noumea for three weeks after Christmas. Trauma. We decided to go when I found that we got back four days before the supp. I worked with little break for those days – and passed. It confirmed for me that I am capable of working hard, and that I work best when pushed, when a goal is in sight.

It was then another time of decisions and change. The main alternatives were a position at Saskatchewan University in Canada, or a Rockefeller scholarship with Dr Peter Parsons at Melbourne University to do an honours year in genetics (this subject was part of the zoology department). I decided on the latter for several reasons, not the least the need for a break from the organic chemist. Mother lined up a position at Women's College where, although I was a 'fresher', I had my own key. It was the first time I had been away from home and I was terribly homesick. Although Women's College was exciting, with new friends from many disciplines, and there was 'triggle' with the Ormond 'gentlemen', I yearned for the familiar, loving, structured yet carefree, existence that I had known with my family in Adelaide. Thankfully I had beautiful 'Aunty' Kaye, after whom I was named because she was my mother's best friend. She had no children and lived in Melbourne with her charming husband. A number of times she collected me for a treat of afternoon tea at Georges. It was very special.

My honours topics were an analysis of some data collected over many years at the Royal Women's Hospital on women who had aborted spontaneously, and a small survey of the dermatoglyphics (quantifying the number of ridges in various fingerprint patterns) of central Australian Aboriginal people. Both were interesting and statistical. I managed a first class honours, the first for ten years Professor M.J.D. White said. It led to a masters degree analysing data collected on an eight week field trip around central Australia funded by the fledgling Institute of Aboriginal Studies with Peter Parsons, Mary Connor (a southern American on a Fulbright scholarship also staying at Women's College), and another honours student, Doug Hatt, who was an avid mountain-climber and died climbing Mount Cook in New Zealand the following summer. The country was stark, surreal, stunning and wonderful. I found the sparseness almost unbearable in its beauty, and the Aboriginal people so dark and shy, and yet openly giving. It was the time of the 'blue streak' rocket launch, so at Yeundumu, a government settlement well west of Alice Springs, some men were hurriedly put into trousers for our 'benefit'. What could not be hidden was the dignified faces with long black hair pulled back with hair woven into a ribbon and dyed red with ochre. The sombre looks would, however, often break out into giggles. A breakdown of our landrover at Ernabella allowed a more leisurely time to learn some of the Pitjantjatjara language, to spin hair on my thigh, to draw some of those intricate patterns that they had already begun to do on silk scarves and slippers for the 'tourist trade', to play 'football' their style, or to just scuff in the dust in quiet companionship as we gesticulated some desires that were more easily physically transcribed. At the time the stop was considered a disaster, but to me it was the highlight. Back in Melbourne, it was the hard slog of analysing the fingerprints, eventually using canonical variates to differentiate the four tribal groups on which we had gained most information, the central Aranda and Wailbri, in comparison with the desert Pitjantjatjara and Pintubi people. These were then compared with blood group information to see if there were historical differences (dermatoglyphics are laid down in the first four foetal months and then do not change, whereas blood groups are known to be influenced in the evolutionary sense by environmental factors).

Just before finishing my masters degree I married David Morris Robson with Presbyterian formalities in my mother's full floral splendour at my old Holder Memorial Methodist Church. It is a

The country was stark, surreal, stunning and wonderful.

221

marriage that has lasted nearly 30 years. He was a pharmacist studying medicine at Melbourne University and one of the Ormond gentlemen. We lived in a three bedroom flat belonging to his mother in North Melbourne while I finished my degree and then worked at Kew Cottages as a biologist, and he finished medicine. Then we went to live in Broken Hill while he did his 'residency' and I accepted a lecturing position at the Macquarie University outpost. This position did not eventuate as I became very ill with my first pregnancy. To help me adjust to becoming a mother, a psychiatrist friend gave me a beautiful golden retriever puppy when I emerged from hospital . The puppy was called 'Speculum' (Spec for short) because she was into everything.

Fiona Kay Robson was born with little trouble while I did my breathing exercises with my physio friend, Margi Calder, and David intermittently saw me, patients and a hospital party. It rained dust a few days later. The dust blotted out the sun at midday and completely covered the flowery carpet in the hospital house in Bromide Street where we were living. It was bizarre and gave you an eerie feeling of not being on planet Earth. There was no way anyone could be 'house-proud'. Fiona and I lived an idyllic existence. It was too hot to do much other than go to the local pool most of the day, after watering the tin roof and tin sides of the house.

The only thing we came to crave was green grass, and a trip along the Darling to Mildura cured that.

One time I did not water, and the candles inside were melted when we returned. Pro Hart became a friend and we would often go to his Saturday night parties. Broken Hill was a party place. Friends were easy to make and many remain to this day. We had a ball. The town seemed to have everything that we enjoyed. The scenery was amazing; the colours can never be exaggerated. Picnics were often expeditions to find unusual earth metals. There were Australian Broadcasting Commission (ABC) concerts and regular local theatre productions, and artists all around. The only thing we came to crave was green grass, and a trip along the Darling to Mildura cured that. There was a strong bond that was not just among us newcomers from 'away', but also the 'been there for years people'. Religion was not part of this scene and has not been much since.

After a year of country living David decided to return to the Children's Hospital in Melbourne. He was given a roll of notes as he left. All pay was in cash as though banks were not to be trusted. We gave a big party and Pro said thanks with a dust storm painting, and we bought one of his insect paintings. It was the start of a passion for buying art.

We returned to city life with Fiona on my lap, Spec around my shoulders and our old Falcon filled with all our possessions. We went back into David's mother's flat and Spec went to the Guide Dog home to breed. I went to work part-time with Dr Margaret Garson at St Vincent's Department of Medicine on a research grant while a kindly neighbour looked after Fiona. It was great work. We grew and analysed chromosomes from leukaemia cells. Analysis of chromosomes from people who had been given regular and known doses of LSD by a psychiatrist led to a paper which *Time* magazine considered to be one of the best four to have been published that year, 1968. We spent what little time David had off playing golf with old medical friends.

Scott Davis Robson was born at 7.30 am on Christmas morning (my research grant finished on Christmas eve). There was great joy to all, except the anaesthetist who had to be dragged from Christmas dinner to pull out Scott's stuck placenta. Scott is still often unpredictable. And our family Christmas has since always finished after Christmas dinner, when Scott's birthday starts.

A few weeks after Scott was born we moved to Hamilton, the Western Victorian country town where David had grown up, for David to practice his medicine as a 'kids only' doctor. It was an isolating experience for me. I knew very few people, and the children were then 14 months and a few weeks old, and not very sociable. Some 15 years before, David had left Hamilton High School at 13 years of age to go to Geelong College. He was back for a year after finishing pharmacy to work in his father's shop. All his old friends were married and it is generally the wives who invite people for dinner, the main means of entertaining in a cold country town. After we moved there as a family, Nana sometimes took me to ABC and gallery meetings and these became my saviour, as was her flat in South Yarra. Sometimes I would walk down the main Gray Street just hoping to meet someone I would know or who might say hello. We were not yet part of any community group. It was such a far cry from my previous lives that I became depressed and took on matric English literature to do something constructive and use what seemed to be my dwindling brain.

My Hamilton country life was in many ways the antithesis of my Broken Hill country life. On reflection it seems that climate played some part. The clear blue skies and velvety evenings in Broken Hill meant that people were easy going and partied. True we did not have any children to limit our going out, and when Fiona was born she could easily fit in to this scene as it was not at all structured. In contrast, Hamilton is cold, wet and windy. It is also the prototype conservative town. Although babysitters were not a problem (reliable phone sitters were often more troublesome to find), there were few spontaneous 'gatherings'. Also David's position, I guess, limited previous acquaintances. He had come back as a doctor. And I found that country people put newcomers into a little box, and mine was labelled 'doctor's wife', and I was sometimes called Mrs Dr Robson. (One of the remarks I remember most when an article in the Melbourne *Herald* included me, was one person saying: 'You are a person in your own right!') Most of the people with whom David had gone to highschool had stayed in Hamilton, married the girl down the road, and become skilled workers. Those who, like David, had left to go to a boardingschool, were generally on properties, their social lives centred around dinner parties, tennis and golf, neither of which David played. This was the 1970s, and although times were good, it was soon noticed that most farms had a considerable input by both partners. This was often understated, so that sometimes it would be quaintly put by women that they were 'abiding in the field', or 'helping Chris', but it was very evident that they were an integral part of the farm management, both physically and in budgeting and buying.

...it would be quaintly put by women that they were 'abiding in the field', but it was very evident that they were an integral part of the farm management...

For me, it seemed that the best option was to be biologically creative again. And to build a home. Katriona Anne was due to be born the day we moved into our Graeme Gunn designed, and Noel and Murray Gunn built, house that was so different for Hamilton that some thought it was a factory. The windows faced the back, those on the street were high up. The angles were 37 degrees. It was different and I loved it. Katriona was late, allowing me some nest building before she arrived on Easter Monday. I went to hospital after my sister and her husband had left to return to Melbourne. She was 'showing' when I arrived at the hospital and was born before they got home four hours later. I will always be grateful that my doctor, Clyde Scaife, allowed me to do my exercises just as I had done with my other babies, and not have any anaesthetics. However, Katriona was immediately taken to be weighed: a hospital statistic that was most important, but which I cannot remember.

With three children under four years, my life became one long reaction to their needs, and to David's. The telephone took priority, whatever else was going on, in case somebody in the community needed a doctor. The children were a handful. Each was very different, and a challenge. There were few quiet times. They were rarely good, but always interesting. The country life allows space and considerable freedom of movement, and we generally thrived. However, when the local catholic girls school asked me to teach their matric biology classes, I was pleased. It was an association that was to last intermittently for the next 10 years. Country schools had a great need for science, maths and biology teachers, and they were immensely grateful to have me, even without teaching qualifications. To entice me after the girls school was taken over by the larger boys school, they provided a creche for my by then four little children under six years. Alistair Morris was born two years after Katriona, and in the middle of the school year. I took three weeks off to have him, and to have my tubes tied. He would sometimes be the subject for a biology lesson when there had not been time for adequate preparation. For the children it was a good arrangement. Monivae College provided a Brother for them and extended the males they knew, since being a committed country practitioner restricts hours available to children. And I enjoyed teaching.

Then disaster struck. My parents-in-law were due to return from several months holidaying overseas. They had retired to a lovely property at the edge of Hamilton and I went with Katriona (then three years) and Alistair (17 months) to clean windows and put casseroles in the fridge before going to a luncheon with my friend Lyn Shilliday. I was not travelling fast nor turning to see how the children in the back were faring. As I came over a small rise on a back road into Hamilton I saw the dark green Melbourne-to-Hamilton train emerge from behind a clump of pine trees. There was no time to stop. I hit the train at its front left side and derailed it. Alistair was jolted through the back window into the water-filled culvert, from where he climbed out suffering only bruises and cuts. Katriona jumped out the back 'like a rabbit' she said, and had only a broken collar-bone. I had no blood on my good dress, only a compound Potts fracture of my right ankle, and some cuts. We were unusual statistics. To me, it was really a miracle.

I saw the dark green Melbourne-to-Hamilton train emerge from behind a clump of pine trees. There was no time to stop.

The accident taught me many things. First, life is tenuous. It can change dramatically in just a few seconds. One moment everything is wonderful, the next disaster strikes without warning. Secondly, there is a cohesive tribal quality of country people when one of them suffers a crisis. They were amazing. People whom I did not know rallied around us with not just kind words, but kind deeds. The legendary 'pulling together' of country people when there is a need is not a myth. This was again shown some 15 years later when Fiona suddenly had a stroke during her last year of science just as she was about to drive back to Melbourne University and Ormond College. We were fortunate that there was an air ambulance in the area to take Fiona and me to the Royal Melbourne to meet Scott who was doing science at Monash. David travelled by car with Katriona and Alistair and met us before Fiona had brain surgery to remove the blood clot and mend the ruptures. Thirdly, the family comes together in such times. My mother immediately came to help with the children, and my father as soon as he could. Fourthly, children are resilient. Although I blame the accident for Katriona being emotionally fragile for years after and Alistair not speaking for years, they have each grown out of these troubles. And fifthly, I have a phobia about driving Holdens. David had got rid of my beautiful big black old Wolseley with leather inside just before the accident, and replaced it with a Holden which needed a different way of driving. Whether this was a contributing factor I will never know. But I do know that when the local Holden salesman came around a few days after we came home from hospital I was aghast and superstitiously vowed never to trust myself to a Holden again. It seemed best not to knowingly tempt fate twice!

We all more-or-less mended physically and mentally and emotionally and went on with our country lives. The country controlled many options. For me, it meant that I could not work at what I had been trained to do – genetics. Teaching was an enjoyable alternative but I sometimes envied my contemporaries who had the academic options at their backdoor. I tried to compromise several times. For a number of years I returned to St Vincent's Department of Medicine and Margaret Garson very part-time until it got too much for me and the four small children. Then later, I began a PhD at LaTrobe with a scholarship to study the genetic and social interactions of a stable rural community, but that was again difficult from such a long way away, and there were other distractions. The major distraction was agreeing to coordinate the 1984 Hamilton Heritage Festival. This was a fantastic learning experience and would not have been possible had I been living in a city – there would have been 'professionals'. I am proud of the result. And some of the outcomes have been lasting. I initiated the Aboriginal Keeping Place with LaTrobe University. Great local Aboriginal women such as Lynette Austin and Rita Ellis now manage it under the Yangennanock Women's Group. Much energy went into organising the funding for a large wool tapestry designed by Les Kossatz which hangs in the Hamilton Art Gallery. This was a time I learnt the value of networking, of surrounding myself with like-minded activists. That it is the people who count. This philosophy was reinforced when I became a rural advisor to the Victorian government. One of the publications we researched and printed was on how some towns achieve. All towns have the bureaucracy to counter, but some managed to overcome the hurdles. Those that did were the excellent networkers; they worked with people to make things happen.

One of the most positive aspects of a provincial rural city is that you can immediately contribute to the life around you. We wanted Musica Viva concerts, so we organised them. We wanted to preserve the Hamilton bandicoot and some rare native grasslands, so we worked hard to do just that. Things seem to be more possible in the country; it is more 'grassroots'. It seems that when I have lived in Melbourne and Sydney, although not in Adelaide, the projects are done by professionals.

This importance of the people factor in country communities was again demonstrated in Hamilton Region 2000. I was contracted to write its story for the federal department of local government. It achieved much through its slogan of 'people helping people'. The report highlighted the stories of various projects undertaken. Generally these projects were with small amounts of capital funding. Ventures were not picked. Instead people with energy and commitment were helped to exploit resources to achieve tangible benefits for the community. The initial notion was the Potter Farmland Plan which was based on the concept that the land needed to be managed as a whole, that individual farmers were themselves able to address the acutely serious environmental and production threats of land degradation and ecological imbalance. Hamilton Region 2000 grew from this beginning to breathe life into a complacent country community by supporting its doers. It empowered many to find inspiration for starting new ventures such as the Wool & Rural Industries Skills Training Centre, the Hamilton Environmental Awareness & Learning (HEAL) project, the Knitting Industry Research Project, Ultrafine Ltd, Hamilton District Tour Guides, Cassette Tours, Hamilton Proteas, to name a few. It was a time of significant cultural change in country Victoria, especially in such a conservative wool-dependent region as that centred on Hamilton. A very homogeneous stable region it was settled in the 1850s by the Scottish, English, Irish and German people in approximately equal numbers. There are still the same groups in the same proportion now with even the same families five generations later. Hamilton Region 2000 allowed a process of understanding of this culture and new perspectives to be evolved. This sort of community process is not nearly so easy in a city, especially one as large as Sydney. There are so many more variables and impinging values and experiences. Thus the importance of the people factor is lessened.

This year, I have returned to academic life at Sydney University with a friend from Adelaide University days, John Sved, and his wife Marianne Frommer. Sydney is a far cry from the cares and tribulations of country Victoria. Here, everything is abundant and easily accessed. At any time there is a myriad of possible events, galleries, theatre, opera, orchestra, chamber music, films, tv channels, lectures, experiences, restaurants, gardens and more, that one can go to often with little money. All are at the end of a walk or public transport. And I am able to completely enjoy them with no nagging responsibility to make sure that they happen, that they are well attended, that they break even, or even make a profit. I have no responsibility to clean up the venue afterwards, write the thank you letters and the reports. It is extraordinarily hedonistic, and I have thoroughly enjoyed the experience. In Hamilton six months of doing lunches, golf, bridge and tennis, and I was bored and needed to find a vacuum to fill, a project, a job. In Sydney, the jobs (associate lecturer and research assistant both half-time) have been so immensely time consuming in their preparation, and emotionally draining, that I have needed the compensations of the weather and the entertainment.

Survival in the new jobs was paramount. It has been the antithesis of my previous Hamilton life. The Sydney plurality and professionalism, and sheer numbers of people, cars, transport, houses – everything is mindblowing to a country person. Sometimes the sheer volume of possibilities makes me unable to make a decision. It is all too much. I have not joined a single society, not contributed in any way as I had done for two decades in Hamilton. It is a very different life in Sydney city. There may be communities, there may be environmental issues, but I am not involved. It is strange. I ring to hear how the bandicoots are going, and glory in their survival knowing that I contributed. I go back, and hear how the Aboriginal community is working things out and delight in their self-assurance knowing that I have been involved. Throughout 1993 I was on the steering committee for a national 'Images of Women' conference at the National Museum and remembered I was very involved in women's issues in Hamilton.

The Sydney plurality and professionalism, and sheer numbers of people, cars, transport, houses – everything is mindblowing to a country person.

Yes, there is a difference between country and city, and between different country towns. I have enjoyed each for different reasons. Adelaide was very much like a country town, especially the cohesive church community I was part of. Then Melbourne, at various times, provided new opportunities, both academic and social. Broken Hill was a 'blue-sky' country town that had its advantages and disadvantages. Hamilton, although initially isolating for me, became special. I committed much time and energy into disparate arts, environment and women's projects. It was where our four children grew up. Sydney now is the antithesis of that life, and again a different set of opportunities are there for the taking. Vive la difference!

Bairnsdale to Melbourne and Back

Sharene Morrison

Sharene Morrison was born on 9 August 1973 in country Victoria. In 1990, at 17, she completed highschool in Bairnsdale and commenced studying dressmaking and design in Melbourne.

On finishing her course, Sharene Morrison returned to Bairnsdale, where she now runs her own fashion design and dressmaking business, *Creme*. She anticipates returning to live in the city at some time in the future.

When I was born in the country town of Bairnsdale, in Victoria, at Bairnsdale Hospital, Bairnsdale had a population of 10 000 people. It is now a city of 15 000. Apart from the year I had in Melbourne after I completed highschool, I have lived on a 30 acre farmlet, three kilometres from Bairnsdale, all my life.

As it is only a small property, there are not many farm duties. Occasionally, chasing cows is on the list of chores. This is one activity I have not had to do as one time I was charged by a steer (former bull) and became scared of this breed of animal.

My father is a builder who has his own business and my mother manages the canteen at Bairnsdale High School. At the age of 17, I was accepted into the McCabe Academy of Dressmaking and Design. My sister Julie was at that time 21 years old and working as a word processor operator at the department of conservation and environment. The whole family was in a trail riding club that met once a month.

My acceptance into the McCabe Academy was the start of fulfilling a childhood ambition of becoming a dressmaker and fashion designer. To fulfil this ambition, it was necessary for me to move to the city of Melbourne. This evoked feelings of both excitement and anxiety.

However, I had always wanted to live in the city at some stage in my life and I felt the need to explore outside Bairnsdale.

At the age of 17, moving from Bairnsdale, from the security of my family, was a major step. Melbourne was quite foreign to me as my family did not visit the city often. My earliest memory of the city is driving away from the zoo and getting completely lost, then having to seek assistance from a policeman.

My major concern with the shift to Melbourne was that the girls from the city would have a much higher level of education than I did. No one actually said anything to make me think this. It was just an idea I had always had. I later found out city educated people are not really advanced compared to country people. Natural ability counts for a lot.

> *I found out city educated people are not really advanced compared to country people.*

I confirmed arrangements with McCabe Academy to begin my 11 month course in January 1991. I found a flat in West Brunswick that was close to public transport, and moved in on 12 January that year. I found it much easier not to have a driver's licence in Melbourne – although not always reliable, public transport was great.

The change in my lifestyle and my new feelings of independence were certainly an experience. One of my most memorable encounters at the Academy was with the ethnic women in my class. They came from many countries, including Turkey, Germany, Italy and Greece, and there were a number of Australian-born women whose families had come to Australia from other countries. This meant the classes were very different from those I was used to at Bairnsdale High School. I felt like a stranger in my own country. I learnt what it was 'not to speak the language'. I have never felt so alienated and alone.

The common perception of a country person was a 'hillbilly'. As the teacher was taking my measurements for a garment, he commented: 'Girls from the country tend to have hunchbacks from carrying pails of milk,' and 'country girls have very loud voices from conducting conversations across the street' – my answer being: 'You wouldn't be able to hear over the traffic.'

I could not believe these ludicrous images. It was as if everyone believed everything they saw on television, as if they thought we all came from *A Country Practice*.

It took six long months for the girls in my class to be friendly with me. One of my main problems was becoming ill and desperately trying to communicate with clinics, wanting a female doctor. I had feelings of insecurity and vulnerability, as at home I had always consulted my family doctor. Yet the city taught me to stand up for what was right and not allow anyone to walk over me. Learning to use my elbows in the markets, for example! City people were different from country people in that they were more aggressive and verbal. Needless to say, I did increase (not improve) my vocabulary in more than one different language.

Growing up in the country gives you patience and time to appreciate the world and life around you. However, these qualities seemed to have no place in the city. I had to learn to be as aggressive as the rest of them if I was to survive. One day I was on the tram home (via zoo) and a lady said: 'Look at the beautiful countryside.' Another time a man commented on the fresh air in the same area! I wonder if these people have ever seen the real country.

Living in the city taught me how to be independent and that I have the ability to look after myself without someone looking over my shoulder all the time. I had the support of my parents and my elder sister, but essentially I was alone. At night I would go outside and look at the sky – the sky looks the same no matter where you are. On some occasions, the country came into the lounge room! I was really excited when I saw the Patties Bakery advertisement on a Melbourne channel; the company originated in Lakes Entrance/Bairnsdale. This was a welcome symbol that country people could succeed, as well as the Patties Factory being almost visible from our house. The advertisement was like a special message, just to me.

One day I was on the tram home (via zoo) and a lady said: 'Look at the beautiful countryside.'

Throughout the period I lived in Melbourne, I received a letter from Mum every Friday, and a phone call from Mum, Dad and Julie every Sunday. I was really annoyed if they didn't ring right on 6.00 pm. Now, I am back in the country where I have a successful dressmaking business – *Creme* – and I work at a local nightclub to earn some extra money. I look forward to the day I can move back to the city. I would like to return, as I enjoyed the challenge and the feeling of independence.

PART 5

Country Life, City Life

The Uplifting Glory of Nature

Alison Brown

An artist, wife and mother, Alison Brown has had the advantage of living in many different areas of Australia. Rarely has she been bored, although at times she would enjoy a little boredom. Friendship has been one of the treasures of her life and she echoes her father's thoughts when he said: 'There are times I am almost afraid of life, but then comes stealing on the air the soft strains of the harmony of life's most beautiful friendships and I realise just how rich are the real and lasting treasures of life.'

People are important to her, and Alison Brown has used her art to investigate the relationships of people and their interaction with their environments. Two of her paintings in a series done in conjunction with women in the oncology department of Royal Women's Hospital in Melbourne appear as covers on books in the Artemis 'Women's Voices, Women's Lives' series, *Sisters – Sibling Rivalry, Sisterly Love* and *Living Generously – Women Mentoring Women.*

I turn off the main road and drive up into the foothills of the Jeeralangs. The hills are navy as always, flashes of greens, reds and purples. Five minutes later I turn in to the drive to be greeted by our crazy, black, one-eyed dog.

I am home.

Renmark, South Australia, 1940, and the fear of war in the air. It was one of those February heatwaves, 114 degrees fahrenheit. In the little country hospital my mother gave birth to me. Two weeks later, my father enlisted.

But my first memories are not of Renmark but of Kadina, a town on Yorke Peninsula near my maternal grandparents' farm, where my mother, older brother and I moved when my father went overseas two years later. He was a Congregational minister and was to spend the next four years in the Pacific as a padré in the army, not returning until the end of 1946.

Those first few years were magical for me. Was there really a war going on? In my secure and loving environment war had little meaning, except that that was where my dad was. Often dad's mother came and stayed with us. How we loved each other! When I was three, she bought me a little wicker pram. Soon after, early one night, the town siren sounded. An attack! We all knew what to do. My mother and grandmother gathered up two sleepy children, blankets, pillows and, at my insistence, my new pram, and we all spent the night most uncomfortably under the kitchen table. No attack, it was only the fire siren going off: the local bakery had caught on fire.

In our backyard, among the violets and mosses, were fairies. Real ones, I was sure. My mother had often told me about them: they danced in the moonlight, slid down a moonbeam and sprinkled stardust with their wands. My mother had a wonderful imagination, thanks to her Cornish heritage, and before I started school she spent many hours telling her two children stories, playing games with us, and gently guiding us. Mind you, sometimes not so gently as my brother and I could be very mischievous, filling hollow bamboo with rotten wood and smoking it, or collecting tadpoles in a dangerous pond, setting fire to the woodshed or climbing into the culvert under the railway line to see if the steamtrain really did empty its ashes there.

In our backyard, among the violets and mosses, were fairies. Real ones, I was sure.

We loved to go out to our grandparents' farm. Petrol was rationed and few people had cars, so we often went in grandpa's horse and buggy. This method of transport leaves a lot to be desired for today's hectic lifestyle, but it did allow little girls to see all the exciting play places along the roadside. The mallee scrub has its own beauty and I loved to play with my cousins and our dolls under the trees among the wildflowers and creepers, and make daisy chains. Even now, when I'm driving in this area, I have a great urge to be a part of this scrub; sometimes I give in, stop the car, get out and wander for a few minutes and become a child again, all cares and responsibilities gone, caught up in this little world of our Australian mallee scrub. This memory was the inspiration for one of my paintings, 'Dolls and Daisy Chains'.

My country grandma was a giant of a woman, tall, strong and so capable. Grandpa was a sheep and wheat farmer, so Grandma carried out all the tasks that many women on farms still do. She could make the most mouth-watering Cornish pasties, and her pot of stew never seemed to empty. She had had seven children in 10 years, and her hair had turned snow-white long before I remember her. Grandma was so clever, she could crochet and as a little girl I watched the crochet hook twirling in and out while her fingers hardly moved and a beautiful pattern began to emerge. Grandma taught me to crochet, and I thank her for the pleasure this craft has given me. Grandma crocheted a special piece for each of her granddaughters. Mine was a beautiful shell-patterned stole, which I later used for my baby daughter's shawl; she in turn used it for her daughter.

My city grandmother could not crochet but she could knit, so another skill was added to my fingers. This grandma knitted warm woollen socks, a skill almost lost today. My dad told me later of an incident when he was at war. They were fighting their way through the jungle; his feet were in a very bad way, socks worn through and his feet bleeding badly. He knew he would not be able to walk much further like that and to fall behind was probably death. There was a mail drop from a plane and in the mail was a parcel from his mother, containing two pairs of her hand knitted socks. He was able to go on.

During the war years, we did have some trips to the city. It was a major excursion then, usually by train, and seemed to me to take all day. We stayed with our city grandma and could catch the train in to the city of Adelaide to visit the museum and art gallery with all the most peculiar, interesting treasures they held. We had nothing like this in the country! Another treat was to be able to go to a restaurant and have a pink meringue with ice cream. John Martins at Christmas time was a store full of wonder. It was a special treat to see the decorations and walk through the animated story made especially for Christmas. To ride on the big wooden rocking horses, Nipper and Nimble, was best of all. Even better than a ride on grandpa's horses on the farm.

To ride on the big wooden rocking horses, Nipper and Nimble, was best of all. Even better than a ride on grandpa's horses on the farm.

Through these years my mother had been the centre of my world. My father was a distant, shadowy figure in a uniform, who occasionally came home for a few days, then went away again. I thought mum to be the most beautiful lady; she spent a lot of time with us, told us stories, read to us for hours, and made us feel secure in a very insecure time. She continues to be our family's inspiration, strength and guiding light.

When dad returned from the war we went back to Renmark where he was the minister of the Congregational Church. Here my brother and I spent the best three and a half years of our childhood. Renmark in those years must have been one of the best places in Australia to bring up children: a small country town where everyone knew nearly everybody else, and where we all felt safe.

Two women had a special influence in shaping my life at this time. One was a middle-aged spinster (as single women were termed then), whom we all called Aunty Marj. She had thick, greying hair, a severe stutter and soon after our arrival back in Renmark came to ask Dad if she could take afternoon Sunday School. Dad said yes, a decision he never regretted. We children loved Sunday School. Aunty Marj made it so much fun, so exciting; we sang, dressed up and acted stories, put on plays and concerts and Sunday School anniversaries. Rather incidentally we learnt of Christianity, good moral values and life in many overseas countries.

The other woman by whom I was influenced was a farmer's wife who lived some distance out of Renmark on the banks of the Murray River. Grace had an appreciation of beauty, her garden was beautiful, her house was beautiful and she was a beautiful person. This beauty came not from wealth or good looks particularly, but from her ability to see beauty in the most commonplace object and to give it meaning through her own beautiful personality. She could make a meal of chops and mashed potato look like a piece of art, just by the way she placed the food on the plate. Her love of the beauty of simple things has remained with me. Grace was a great conservationist. She never left the tap running while cleaning her teeth: rainwater was precious and still is. Grace's husband died tragically at a fairly young age. She then showed what a truly remarkable woman she was by managing their sheep and wheat property for many years. She was often to be found in overalls, boots and hat, working with sheep and lambs, doing what was considered a man's work. Yet she never lost her femininity, she was always a lady.

She could make a meal of chops and mashed potato look like a piece of art...

Soon after settling back into life at Renmark our family were to go on the first of many visits to a very special place in my life, one which has become my second home, my anchor, my stable haven. My father's cousin lived on a farm near a tiny country town 30 kilometres east of Tailem Bend. They had been the greatest of mates from childhood and remained so all their lives. Uncle's wife was a tiny woman not quite five feet. She reminded us of a little sparrow, busy doing all those chores which need to be done on a farm, and loving to chat as she went along. Her heart was huge. She had time for everyone, and the door was always open, to friends and strangers alike. As a child and teenager I loved going there, I took my husband there on our honeymoon, our children loved going there, our youngest daughter lived with them for a year and now our eldest daughter is planning to take her two young children there. Each generation on both sides of the family have kept this very close friendship. The women of this farm have been 'nothing special' but 'very special'. They have provided their farming husbands with the support which has kept them going in desperate times, worked physically on the farm or followed their own career, as well as bringing up a family.

I have seen the current young teenage daughters ring the lambs and inject the pigs when their father has been harvesting. What a shock this would be to most city teenage girls, but quite everyday for many farmers' daughters. I'm pleased to see that this generation is able to have a wider experience than past generations. Improved transport now means they can go to the nearby large country town, or occasionally to Adelaide for whatever is not available at home. They are able to join gymnastic or ballet classes and to attend concerts and theatre without having to make a major excursion as I did when young.

In April of 1950, dad was asked to go to Queensland to look at a boys' home with the view to becoming superintendent there. I can still picture him coming home, throwing his hat off and saying: 'I hope to God I never see that place again!' Well, God had different plans and in mid-May we sadly left our happy days at Renmark and set off in our old Buick with a trailer behind, and a dog on the runningboard, for Queensland. That trip, with rain and floods all the way from Canberra, is another story.

I was 10 years old at the time and was to spend the next 12 years sharing my parents and my life with the boys of Marsden Home. It was extremely Dickensian when we arrived, but soon became one big family with my parents becoming mum and pop to the boys, many of whom still retain very close contact. Kallangur, the town where the home was situated, was about 25 kilometres from Brisbane, but in the 1950s it seemed much further. We went to a small three teacher school, and I found the attitude in this country town very different from that of Renmark. Here I first came across 'discrimination', not against women but against the boys from the home.

In the early 1950s the boys were very much looked down on. There was a minor escapade in which several local boys as well as some boys from Marsden – and me – were involved. (We took a stick of chalk from our school to mark numbers on footy jumpers!) Later, one of the teachers came into our classroom venting her spleen about the incident and putting the blame on 'the Home boys' and saying what she thought of such low examples of humanity! I sat there seething at the injustice until I could take it no longer, so stood up and had my say. In stunned silence I told her how bigoted and unjust she was just because these boys were in a home, and that they were just as good as, if not better than, any other boy in the district. The teacher turned on her heel and in silence walked out. I sat down rather shocked at myself, and our extremely wise headmaster quietly went on with the lesson. He never said a word to me about my outburst, but the teacher never forgave me.

I know that my teenage years were far different from those of other girls, but I would not change them. My parents had the wisdom to send me to an all-girls highschool, to balance my home life, as I was starting to find it difficult to communicate with girls.

For the next four years I had the benefit of a group of women teachers at Brisbane Girls Grammar. I was a tomboy, a bit of a rebel and certainly not ladylike. How these teachers put up with me at times, I sometimes wonder. However with the exception of one, who really gave me a bad time (and I probably reciprocated), I loved those teachers and owe them such a lot, not only for teaching me, but for the patience and care they took with my rather wild character. I was directed in my life, but my spirit was never broken.

From the time I was 11 years, one of the boys and I had become extra good friends. Through our teenage years this friendship deepened and in our early twenties we married. About three years later, with a baby daughter, we were to begin many years of city living. My husband was transferred to Sydney in 1965.

The real estate agents would take me to old, crumbling, mouldy, brick shanties and tell me what a great bargain they were...

This was culture shock! After living all my life in small country towns, to be thrown in at the deep end of city life at the age of 24 was as though I was on another planet. We had been living in a small, attractive, three bedroom, timber home when we first married and on moving sold it for, what was to us, a reasonable profit. It was a laughable amount to buy a home in Sydney. The real estate agents would take me to old, crumbling, mouldy, brick shanties and tell me what a great bargain they were – and I would go back to our rented house in despair. What was this place we had come to? So many people, so much traffic, but I knew no one and no one wanted to know me. How lonely a housewife can be, as a stranger in a big city!

Three months later, we moved into an old, brick, three bedroom house where we lived for the next six years. We had three more children, the last two of whom were twins. It was extremely hard to get to know people. Everyone kept to themselves in the streets around us and, as I had always been very outgoing and a chatterbox, this did not suit me at all. I made a point of talking to everyone I saw, and introduced our side neighbours to our back neighbours, who had all lived there for over 20 years, but had never met.

City life introduced me to fear, something I really had not known before. When our oldest son was about two, a little Sydney boy was abducted and found murdered. This was the first time I had been aware of such horrific happenings and I would hardly let the children out of my sight for months afterwards. In the country I seemed to know everyone and the local town drunk wouldn't hurt a fly. But the city was quite different, I hardly knew a soul and people were hurt by other people.

Rearing four little children was exhausting. The only help I had was from my husband who hung out the nappies before he went to work each morning, vacuumed the floors on Saturdays and let me sleep in on Sundays while he gave the children breakfast, always cereal, toast and boiled eggs! He was working full-time as an engineer and studying at college at night so he didn't have many spare moments.

I began what was to become my future career: oil painting. Over the next 20 years painting became far more than 'a nice hobby dear', and I spent many years studying art, beginning in Sydney and later completing a degree and graduate diploma in visual arts at the Gippsland Institute of Advanced Education. I used the family on the farm as the subject for a series of screen prints in my art studies. I compared and contrasted their love for and dependence on the land with that of a small group who had a community garden in Fitzroy, Melbourne.

Our family was to leave Sydney and spend six happy years in Perth, returning to Sydney for another four years, before moving to our home in the foothills of the Jeeralang Ranges on the southern side of the Latrobe Valley.

Each time we were transferred, I found that I had to start my life afresh. I had to leave behind the friends I had made, the home where all was familiar, my art colleagues and the clientele I had built up. In a new area, once we had bought or built a house, I would first see that the children were settled into school, cubs, guides, Sunday School or other activities in which they were interested, then set about making a life for myself.

In a new area, I was not known as an artist, so I would have to start anew to make a name for myself. In a city where there are many established, well known names, this could take a long time, even if your work was equal to if not better than that of the well known names. In a country area, becoming known and established as an artist was relatively easy by comparison. I soon came to know people and, by exhibiting my work in local art shows, it was not too long before people knew my work. I became one of a small group of Gippsland artists who have successfully exhibited throughout Victorian country towns.

We were told that this was a city gallery and as we were country artists we really were not good enough!

Realising that we should take the plunge and exhibit in Melbourne, we made enquires as to holding an exhibition at a gallery on the outskirts of Melbourne. We were told that this was a city gallery and as we were country artists we really were not good enough! We have since held several successful exhibitions in other suburban galleries.

When my children were growing up, one of my many occupations was that of 'taxi driver'! In the city I often drove my children to and from their various activities because I did not consider it safe for them to use public transport or walk to many places in the city and suburbs. Living in the country I drove them as there was no public transport at all, so I was usually 'the taxi' until they were 18 years of age and passed their driver's licence test – then I stayed awake until the small hours and worried until they came home!

I shop in a town 20 kilometres from home, not far in comparison to many country women, but oh! my petrol bill. My little car averages 22 000 kilometres a year and I do envy city people the price of petrol. After all, they have the choice of using a car or public transport. We in the country don't and often pay 10 cents a litre more.

Water is a commodity many city women take for granted, with two showers a day, dishwashers, automatic washing machines and wasteful garden sprinklers. I have learnt to value the 'preciousness' of water. We rely completely on rainwater tanks and, in summer, these can run dry.

One of the joys of my life has been the friendships that I have made with women I have met. The first of these is a girl with whom I went to school at Renmark. Sometimes we don't see or hear from each other for a few years, as we both lead busy lives, but when we meet again, we seem to pick up the conversation and the friendship just where we left off, and we feel very relaxed, no obligations.

Two of my best women friends live in Perth. We were all young mums together and often helped each other out, minding each other's children, discussing sickness, problems and remedies over a cuppa, and so developing a deep and lasting friendship.

I've also made some very close country women friends, one in particular was a great support when my children were going through their rebellious teenage years. She was never shocked by anything they did, but helped me to see beyond their defiance to the great young adults that they have all become. My country farm relatives are far more than just relatives. These women are friends and their doors are always open. Friendship is one characteristic city women and country women share.

On the whole I think my preference must be for country life. I know it is far more difficult to attend concerts, theatre and exhibitions, and the petrol is dearer, but none of that really makes up for what I have now, my home in the bush. I love my space, my personal space and my geographical space. I am thankful to my husband and children who have allowed me this space. We are all a very close, loving family, even though now geographically scattered from Perth to Cairns.

Late one morning in 1993 a good friend and I drove up into the hills to Leongatha. The sun was shining, the sky a beautiful blue with a few clouds drifting by. The hills were a vibrant green and the day sparkled. We both felt so uplifted by the beauty of this countryside that the drive was a better tonic than any available in a bottle. This is what I treasure about living in the country, the uplifting glory of nature that surrounds me. The city woman does not have this on her doorstep. She has noise, hustle and bustle. Yes, I have noise too, it is not quiet in the bush. But my noise is made by the wind blowing through the trees, the bell birds tinkling, kookaburras laughing and the raucous call of the rosellas and gang gang cockatoos.

I stand at my kitchen window and look out at the tall trees. Behind are the hills, folding and rising. It is late afternoon and the setting sun casts a rosy glow over the scene. I lift my eyes up to the hills...

I am at peace.

A City Person

Robin Jackson

Robin Jackson was born in Daylesford, Victoria on 28 April 1948. She moved to Melbourne when she was one, to Leopold when she was 11, and back to Melbourne when she was 17. She worked as a cytotechnologist at the Royal Women's Hospital for two years, then for the department of social security for over 20 years which included a two-year secondment to the Law Reform Commission of Victoria.

After six years of part-time study whilst working full-time, Robin Jackson obtained a bachelor of arts (majoring in sociology and media studies) at Swinburne Institute of Technology. She completed post-graduate studies in librarianship at the University of Melbourne in 1993, and is now working as librarian at the Toorak campus of Deakin University. She has become totally immersed in the local history of Richmond and is writing a history of her street.

I have lived in both the city and the country twice. My family moved to Melbourne from Daylesford on my first birthday then, in December 1959, we went to Leopold to live. I left school in December 1965, and returned to Melbourne to live in February 1966. The country/city dichotomy was important in shaping my life and making me the person I am today.

I don't remember anything about living in Daylesford, and my earliest recollection of life in Melbourne was going to the Middle Brighton sea baths. I came from a large family, and mum and dad made sure that all of us could swim at a very early age. I still love swimming today, and go to either the beach or a swimming pool as often as I can. Other memories of this time are school, which I loved, reading and playing with our cockerspaniel and a million cats. At the time, whether I lived in the country or the city wasn't very important, because I was one child in a large family and we usually made our own entertainment. We were encouraged to be independent from an early age and rode our bikes everywhere. We lived a free and unsupervised existence compared with children nowadays.

In 1953, my parents bought a dairy farm in Leopold, which is eight miles from Geelong on the way to Queenscliff. Dad continued to work at the felt and textile woollen mill in Bentleigh for five or six years.

The farm was looked after by a share-farmer, Les Willis and his family. They lived in half the farmhouse. The Jackson family went down for long weekends and holidays, and stayed in the other half of the house. The farm was about 200 acres, and was set on the shore of Lake Connewarre. Part of the house was quite old – the original four rooms were built in 1862 – and it was an idyllic place to spend holidays as a child. I loved the farm, particularly curled up reading books in front of an open fire in the evening, and longed to live there permanently. My bedroom in the old part of the house had a window with a pair of half doors underneath, through which I could sneak out early in the morning without waking up my parents. I was crazy about my horse ('Nugget') and there were always dogs and cats.

...every now and then after heavy rain, we would find a dead sheep tangled in the branches.

A lagoon ran between two hills into the lake. It was bordered with dead trees and, every now and then after heavy rain, we would find a dead sheep tangled in the branches. Once a crow was eating out the sheep's eyes. I was absolutely horrified, and yet fascinated at the same time. I also remember sticking my hands down old tree stumps to find bird eggs for my collection.

Well, my wish came true. Mum and dad told the family that they were selling the Melbourne home and we were going to Leopold to live on the farm. I was to go to 'The Hermitage' – Church of England Girls Grammar School, Geelong. Mum took my sister Pam and me to Geelong to be inspected by the then headmistress Miss Krome. The Hermitage was a magnificent old two-storey house (once owned by the Armitage family of 'Como'), set in lovely grounds and surrounded by a modern library and science building, along with various other buildings.

Only when I came to leave my friends in Melbourne did I begin to have second thoughts about living in the country. But the decision had been taken and I had no choice. My two oldest sisters were working and remained in Melbourne. My other sister, two brothers and I were still at school and had to go with our parents.

I hated school at The Hermitage that first year. I had completed Form 1 at my previous school, and so I was placed in Form 2 but, after a day, it was decided that I had better repeat Form 1. So I was told to go to a new class, no one introduced me to anyone else, and I was stuck in a corner where I was too scared to speak. The teacher finally snapped at me, and I was so nervous I forgot her name. It took me a while to settle in. However, I soon came to realise that The Hermitage was an excellent school and I was extremely fortunate to have gone to school there. First Miss Krome and later on Mrs Coggin expected high standards from all the girls. The assumption there was that we would all go on to university. (I had decided long ago that I wanted to be a doctor.) I am one of those people who strongly believe that single-sex schools for girls are far superior to mixed ones, academically at least. In leaving and matriculation, I went to Geelong College for physics, and the boys from Geelong College came to our school for biology. I and most of the other girls would pay attention to the boys rather than the work, because of the novelty. I was too scared to put up my hand to ask a question, because some guy was bound to mutter: 'What sort of a dumb question is that?' Most of the girls were similarly affected, so hardly any of the girls asked questions. With this exception, the boys were reasonably well behaved, mainly because our biology teacher, Miss Featherstone, was fairly strict, and she would not stand for any nonsense from the boys.

My mother trained as a physiotherapist and immediately after she graduated from the University of Melbourne went to the country, to Sale, to care for victims of the polio epidemic in 1938. My father worked at the Gippsland woollen mill there, and met mum when he went to the hospital for a minor ailment (rumour was that he had heard that there was a new young attractive physio at the hospital). They immediately clicked and decided very quickly to become engaged. They were married on 24 December 1938, because Christmas was the only time that they could get holidays. Dad told me he had carefully booked the wedding night at an hotel, but when he and mum went there later that night, the room had been given to someone else: dad had never stayed at an hotel before and had not realised that he should have sent a deposit to confirm the booking. So he and mum spent their wedding night stuck in a tiny room right over the band which played on late into the night! Dad often chuckled over that story.

Having been to university Mum thought her children should go as well. She and dad had given up a great deal to send six children to private schools. But not one of us did go to university straight after school. Years later, when I studied for my arts degree at Swinburne Institute of Technology (now Swinburne University), mum was delighted and very proud of me. One of my biggest regrets was that she died before I graduated.

Whilst it seemed that my parents had a fairly conventional marriage – that is, dad working full-time first in the woollen mill and then on the farm, and mum the dependent wife – the reality was quite different. Dad, for instance, insisted that all of us, both boys and girls, help him milk the cows once a week, otherwise we received no pocket money. It wasn't only milking; we had to muck out the yard, drive the tractor, help with the hay, and learn how machinery worked. He would show me how to change fuses and light globes, do simple mechanical repairs and, later, look after my car. In fact, he would not allow me to drive my car until I had taken off each tyre and replaced it in turn. He said: 'You're not going to be one of those women who stand by their car looking helpless when they get a flat tyre'! I loved learning about practical and mechanical matters and he was delighted I was interested. Even though he

...my father regularly did the washing up after the evening meal with one of us kids to help.

considered himself very much a man's man, my father regularly did the washing up after the evening meal with one of us kids to help. His view was that mum had cooked the meal so it was up to someone else to clean up after her. He washed the floors and, later on, when mum became sick, he would wash the clothes and do most of the other household tasks.

Mum, on the other hand, was quite an independent woman for those times. In Melbourne, she had a housekeeper to help her look after the house and six boisterous children. In Leopold, she was involved in the Red Cross and the Australian-Asian Society. She had her own car and drove herself around, often at night.

Although I was quite happy at school after an initial settling-in period, I kept waiting for the day I would be able to go back to Melbourne. From my earliest memories I had wanted to be a doctor – it was accepted by mum and dad that I would go to university in Melbourne. However, I failed matriculation miserably, and then had no idea at all of what I wanted to do. I thought that I would still like to work in a hospital, but knew that I did not want to be a nurse. All I could find which was suitable was either a laboratory assistant or technologist. I tried (not very hard) to get a job in Geelong but they had no vacancies, so there was really no choice and I was allowed to return to Melbourne to live.

I loved life in Melbourne. I got a job at the Royal Women's Hospital as a cyto-technologist (examining Pap smears). Three of us young girls (all of 17 years of age) started work on the same day, and soon became close friends. We went to dances, parties, pictures, anywhere for a good time. It was the swinging '60s and the world was at our feet. I went to discos such as the Thumping Tum, Sebastian's, 431 and Powerhouse where I had the most wonderful time. I loved dancing and went out several times a week, dancing until three or four in the morning, till the band begged us to go home so they could close up and leave.

I had no desire to return to Leopold and my family. For years and years I was the odd one out. All my brothers and sisters were married, had children, and lived in the country. I was constantly being asked why I wasn't married, and I was the last person to ask – after all, at that time I would have loved to get married. It did not occur to me for many years that I actually might not get married; that was never considered a valid option.

In 1968, I joined the Commonwealth Public Service. It was about this time that women were allowed to stay in the public service after they married – before this they had to resign. I didn't even have equal pay. Females received about 75 per cent of the male wage. In those days promotion was based strictly on seniority – that is, the day on which a person joined the public service. When a staff member was absent, the next senior person did the vacant job and got paid higher duties, even for just a day. But that system had long term implications. My first boss asked me, after I had worked there for a few months, if I would mind a bloke who started work the day after me taking the acting higher duties, because he was a married man and he needed the money more than I! I was so dumb that I said yes. Of course, this set a precedent: it meant that as this had happened once and I had not objected, the man would now have all the higher duties in the future. Luckily (but in tune with the practice of the time!), he left a few months later to go to a higher paying job.

> *I didn't even have equal pay. Females received about 75 per cent of the male wage.*

Much has been said about the inequity of the seniority system in the public service. In hindsight, it does seem ridiculous and totally unfair to give someone a promotion only because they have been in the place longer than another person. And yet, another point of view is that this system assisted many women to reach fairly high levels in the public service. It meant that women such as myself and most of my friends, who had never sat down and thought about a career path, ended up after many years in well-paid secure positions. We didn't have to make decisions about jobs, we were just pulled up the ladder as the positions above us became vacant. I have never seen analysis of the way this aspect of the public service actually helped women. Now the system has been modernised and is based on merit. But the old way enabled many of my female friends in the service, who were single, to buy their own homes and often travel extensively overseas.

I like living in a big city – I would choose Melbourne over any other city in the world to live in. I have lived in Richmond, an inner suburb, for 17 years and love its being so central to everything. I go regularly to the cinema and the theatre, concerts and opera. I can go to a performance at the State Theatre in the arts precinct, make a swift exit from a show which ends at 10.30 pm, to my car in the car park below, and be home by 10.45 pm. I cycle everywhere during the day, but at night I want my car to feel secure. I love being able to go to alternative theatre and opera at places like Theaterworks, La Mama, Anthill and others. I would find it difficult to live without the choice that city living gives me. I like the fact that in my street the neighbours are friendly without being nosy. I like it so much that I am writing a history of my street.

To me, living in the country has a down side as well as an up side. People may be more friendly to you, but you also lose a lot of privacy as everyone knows you and is aware of what you are doing. I enjoy visiting the country, seeing some open space and breathing the fresh air, but that is all I want – a visit. I am a city person and I like it that way.

Another Country

Jacqualine Hobbs

Jacquie Hobbs was born on 16 October 1966 in Port Augusta, South Australia. She attended Quorn Area School from 1971 to 1980, completing Year 10 at Annesley College in Adelaide in 1981. Her current position is community based trainer with the South Australian Family Violence Intervention Program, although she has had no formal training in family violence intervention, gaining insight, knowledge and training on this issue through personal experience and past and current employment. She has studied at TAFE Port Augusta, gaining certificates in Aboriginal childcare and community management. She has worked as trainee custodial officer at Port Augusta Prison and administrative service officer in the Aboriginal and Torres Strait Islander Commission, Port Augusta.

Jacquie Hobbs loves walking on the beach, gardening, family gatherings and listening to all types of music. Her family and cultural ties are vitally important to her, as is the support of her husband, Don, who is a non-Aboriginal man, and her children.

I was delivered by natural childbirth at the Port Augusta hospital and spent my first years growing up in a small country town called Quorn, in the Flinders Ranges. I was the only girl in the family, having two younger brothers. My father worked in the highways department (now called the department of road transport) at Leigh Creek. His work involved being away from the family for long periods of time, coming home at intervals for time off from work. At one time my father jointly owned a truck with my uncle and undertook contract work for the highways department. Later, the truck was sold and Dad returned to the highways department as a grader operator. He worked on the road maintenance patrol, consisting of the grader operator and truck driver, patrolling an area for 19 days maintaining the roads.

My mother remained at home, doing household duties, and was also given the task of being legal guardian to my three cousins. With Dad away, Mum had the role of bringing up six young children, with me the only girl. I had the job of helping her.

I attended the local area school, Quorn area school, with students from reception through to highschool. It was there that I completed my education until Year 9, secondary school. I was then given the opportunity to attend school in Adelaide, where I was enrolled into Annesley College (formerly the Methodist Ladies College (MLC)). As I was not doing very well at school in my home town, my parents thought it better for me to attend a private school in the city where it was hoped I would get higher and better education. I attended as a day student, while living with my mother's sister and her husband.

Annesley College was an all-girls school. I did not like the idea of an all-girls school at first, as I missed the coed school and my friends and family. The school had an effect on the way I grew up, as a lot of the studies were orientated towards female issues, and I was used to doing subjects that included technical and male-orientated studies. Through the students at the college I gained a wide insight into the many issues affecting girls, as many of the students were from rural and country areas as well as from the city. This schooling and the interaction with the other girls turned my whole way of thinking. Through interaction with the other students and involvement in the studies undertaken in the college, I was exposed to ideas that had not been expressed during my earlier years in the country.

This schooling experience meant it became difficult for me to interact with male family members and friends. I had grown accustomed to being in an all-female environment.

As a country girl I had wanted to see the city, and often visited and stayed with my Aunty for weekends. However living in the city and studying there was a different matter. I longed to stay in the country as I felt comfortable in the surroundings and particularly the loving environment of my family. This all changed for me when I went to the city to go to school.

The city did not appeal to me. I had spent holidays in the city, staying only for a short while. The year I spent at MLC, in Adelaide, placed me under strict house rules. I did not have much time to spend with friends my own age when I was not at school. Rather, I spent time with friends of my Aunty and Uncle. The household was torn by domestic violence and I was often involved both directly and indirectly. Consequently I was not able to have friends home, nor to go out with them. I believed that this rule was applied because I may have had a 'good time' out, with friends, and this would have upset my Aunty and Uncle.

Upon completing Year 10 at the college I returned to the country to live with my family. Nonetheless I kept in contact with a lot of my city friends and visited them whenever I went to Adelaide.

Often the chance to travel to Adelaide arose when my mother had to take one of my cousins to the Children's Hospital. There was not much time for shopping or sight seeing, however I can remember Mum hanging onto our hands as we transferred off the bus onto the train halfway during the trip to take us into the city, and on the return trip, too. Mum made sure that on each trip we had a change of clothes, a blanket and a pillow in case we became sleepy. She always had plenty of snacks for us to eat on the long journey.

I had many role models to follow when growing up in the country and their influence remains with me. The main one was my mother, who would often tell me stories of her growing up in the bush and of how she and her older brothers had to start work at an early age to help out the family. She emphasised that the family had to help each other out, and that to get along we had to work hard to make things happen.

My grandmothers had an impact on my childhood, too. My father's mother was a half-blood Aboriginal. From her I learnt a lot about her lifestyle, of her growing up in a European/Aboriginal family in the outback, and of how she struggled through her teenage years, through marriage, and then the struggle to raise her four children on her own. My mother's mother, a full-blood Aboriginal woman, taught me the traditional ways. *She taught me what was passed on down to her while she was growing up in the outback bush* and then in country towns. Grandma, as we all called her, came from a big family and her stories of the family growing up full of caring and sharing, and of the struggles endured as an Aboriginal family, helped me to understand and appreciate what I had. I learnt that I should not take anything for granted.

My mother and two grandmothers are the role models I have chosen to follow. Although my grandmothers are both deceased, I remember what they taught me and often think back, remembering. My mother still lives in the country and will do so for the remainder of her life. Now she is a grandmother, my children, a boy called Matthew, and twin girls Donna and Jainee, are gaining the knowledge from their grandmother and the precious stories and memories are being passed on to them. This is especially so for the two girls.

Apart from my mother and grandmothers, the women who most inspired me, who captured my admiration, in growing up in the country and living in the city for the time I was at school, and are the unseen women who have had to endure deprivation, isolation and all that the history of Australia has meant to them. These women are the women of the outback, the women on stations, those living at railway sidings and on Aboriginal reserves and in Aboriginal communities, the women who have struggled through to this day and have not gained recognition for their efforts.

As a child growing up in a country town, I was raised amongst children who came from farming backgrounds. Their mothers helped their fathers on the farm and when the kids were not at school they, too, helped on the farms. Many, if not all, the women worked at the daily tasks of cooking for the shearers, rounding up the sheep, fencing, and all facets of farm work or what was commonly known as the 'station jobs'. Nevertheless from the stories told to me as a child from the people I knew who worked on the farms and stations, I grew up understanding that on most farms and stations, most of the hard work was done by the men, with the women doing the light duties.

I have found it very different, living in the city, in comparison to the country. Being in the city means there are more restrictions placed on children, and more care has to be taken. In the country, children can walk around more freely. Everyone knows one another, so there is a greater trust. In the city, however, there are a lot more activities for children to participate in and there are more opportunities. The ideas and expectations I have for myself and my family are higher than if we were still living in a country town.

Women growing up in the country often have farming backgrounds, which means they strive for employment in agricultural positions. Yet the options for women in the country are not so great, and opportunities that there are, are less accessible. In order to gain equal status in employment, often women are forced to move to the city. Employment is the big difference between the country and the city for women and men, but particularly for women.

Work meant that I returned to the city. Because I am employed in a statewide program dealing with the incidence of family violence in Aboriginal and Torres Strait Islander communities, and the intervention in the communities this brings about, I am living in the city of Adelaide. This means I am able to see issues concerning women throughout the entire state. In July 1993 the program was transferred to the Adelaide metropolitan area so that the necessary state resources would be available.

Living in the city is a challenge to me as an Aboriginal woman, because of the rush-and-hurry lifestyle.

Living in the city is a challenge to me as an Aboriginal woman, because of the rush-and-hurry lifestyle. I am not as in touch with my spiritual and ancestral teachings, ways and beliefs, nor with my natural surroundings. I am living in a 'concrete jungle'. Nature revolves around an area covered with man-made buildings and monuments. In the country, everything seems to proceed at a slow to moderate pace, but I have found, in coming to live in the city, that it is necessary to allow time for everything that is to be done.

Growing up in the country has given me a greater insight into the lives of women, the way the world works, and how I am able to be active in Women's Movement issues. Moving to the city has not made me more of an activist, but I am able to contribute particular insights because of my background. Country women have to make do with what is available in the way of resources, basic necessities and general commodities. Country women face more challenges than do city women. They have to put everything into fighting for issues that are focused on women. What are 'women's issues' are, in fact, issues that concern the whole community. But it is difficult to get this message across. All women should be given a fair go and have the opportunity to voice their opinions. This is not always easy, particularly for women living in the country.

I do not take services and resources for granted in the city. Knowing the country, where resources and services are scarce, makes me mindful of the need to conserve what there is. On the other hand, material resources are not the only source of support. In moving from the country to the city, the biggest adjustment I had to make was leaving my family back in the country. When I was living in the country, if I needed help or had any problems my family was only a short drive away. There was always respect for elders where I grew up. This is one of the aspects of growing up in an Aboriginal family which is central. There is discipline, and a respect too for the teachings of the cultural ways to the younger members of the family. Everyone within the Aboriginal family has her and his place and responsibilities. Families help each other when needed. In the city, I have found that amongst my friends a lot of the learning, and the respect for elders, had been lost and replaced by less important issues. I have come to adjust slowly, knowing that living in the city is a short term plan and that I will return to the country. I will go back to my family and to where I grew up, continuing to work and to overcome each challenge as it appears.

There was always respect for elders where I grew up.

I feel different from the women who have grown up in the city. In talking with my friends I find that while there are some similarities, the differences are considerable. One of the major differences is that, growing up in a small country town, everyone knows who you are and families are very close. When something happens to a community member, everyone knows about it. Often everyone wants to help out. In the city everyone lives in their 'own world', each contending with their own little everyday tasks. Many of the issues and problems are masked. They are discovered only when the problem explodes and becomes known to everyone.

I have also had to adjust to living in a place where there are few Aboriginal faces. The town of Port Augusta has Aboriginal groups from all over the state as well as interstate, making it a great place to find different Aboriginal cultures and families. It is that part of life I miss the most, of having that kinship system present and close all the time. The city seems like another country.

Our youngest son died in June 1993, in a tragic accident. Not having family close by makes the bereavement more painful. We cannot share so closely the hurt and loss we feel. But we meet with my family when visiting our son's resting place, and my parents write letters to their grandchildren as well as to me and my husband, to maintain what closeness we can, despite the miles separating us. Keeping in contact with my family (even if it can be only by letters and telephone calls at present) is the most important thing to me and, without their support, my ability to face each problem as it comes would be so much more difficult. Although we are miles apart, I have not moved away from my family in the 'emotional' or 'understanding' sense. Because of the tragic loss we have shared, the accident which led to my son's death has brought our families closer together emotionally. Although we are separated geographically, the family bond remains great.

I have formed familiar links with some people in the city, too. I have a friend who lives in Adelaide, and whom I have known since we were both quite young. Along with her family, she is very close to me. She and her family, and my family, are there when I need them. I have formed a close friendship with the coordinator of the program for which I work, as well. She and her family have become close friends of my family. If I need to talk with someone and am unable to contact my family in the country I know I can turn to the people that I consider to be my 'city family'.

I have maintained contact with women in the country, as well as my family. My employment as a community based trainer with the South Australian Family Violence Intervention program means I am able to travel throughout the state visiting urban, rural and remote communities. Through my work, we deal with both women and men on issues relating to family violence and those that tie in with family violence. As a training and resource centre, we deal with a broad range of issues, and are dealing with the specific issues of family violence in a broad way.

Growing up in the country, from childhood, with a lot of room to play, to move and to grow, and having to grow up facing everyday issues concerning Aboriginal people, has affected my working life. All these factors helped me to decide upon the career path I have chosen. My country upbringing relates to the work I am doing in family violence, in that it involves travelling to the rural and remote parts of South Australia. In many of the communities we visit or with which the program has links, there are my family and family relatives. I am able to keep contact with them all through my work, and that they are a part of the communities assists me in the job.

My parents, grandparents and older relatives always told me that it is necessary to help others less fortunate. When, as a child and young woman, I saw what was happening to Aboriginal people I decided to work in Aboriginal organisations so that I could work for Aboriginal people and give back what I have learned. This is more important to me than Women's Movement activities as such, but I keep up with the issues that are important to all women by attending seminars and conferences, workshops and training programs on family violence and related issues.

...the women's struggle and fight for equal status in the workforce, family violence issues, judicial issues, and the right to have a say in questions affecting both women and men.

Growing up in the country, and now living in the city, has given me an advantage in understanding the issues that concern women of the country. The woman I have become is to a large degree due to the upbringing I had as a country girl. The beliefs and ideas with which I grew up are important to me. My cultural background and upbringing has been significant in making me the person I am today.

City women and country women do share similar issues through the past, as history shows: the women's struggle and fight for equal status in the workforce, family violence issues, judicial issues, and the right to have a say in questions affecting both women and men. The right to be heard and the right to have equal status are directly relevant to city women and country women, Aboriginal women and non-Aboriginal women. Women are speaking out about what they want and what changes need to happen. In the past, most men have been given the power to influence and control, but slowly over the years women have the opportunity to have the same benefits and equal status in society. Women are becoming more powerful through the Women's Movement and are making changes. Women are becoming involved in decision-making within government, affecting policies. Women are coming to the point of having a say in anything that affects women today, and in the future, in everyday living.

The Miles Between

Jenni Mitchell

Jenni Mitchell has called many diverse places home, from Poowong in South Gippsland and Mildura in the Mallee, to Mount Waverley, a south east suburb of Melbourne, to Williamstown in the western suburbs. She trained as a primaryschool teacher, worked with children from non-English speaking (NESB) backgrounds then, as her children grew she grew, along with the Neighbourhood Centre Movement in Victoria from the early 1970s until 1985. Jenni Mitchell then took up a position with the Victorian government's office of rural affairs and helped establish the Rural Women's Network.

Jenni Mitchell currently works with the Melbourne YWCA (Young Women's Christian Association) coordinating the Designs by Wise Women Shop. This is a project which provides a retail outlet for craftswomen, as well as giving unemployed women some experience and training in the retail trade.

Whenever I tell people that I was born in a dairying district of South Gippsland, they nod their heads and say something like: 'That explains the complexion. All that country air, fresh milk and cream.' I'm never too sure how to take such a remark. I have lived for nearly 30 years now in suburban Melbourne and have spent the last seven years working with and for rural women. Did my growing up in the hills of South Gippsland give me a good start to understanding rural women, or was it the suburban street, so isolating and so different to the small town where practically everyone took an interest in your growing up? City and country – the great divide or the great equaliser? To me the experiences are so different, yet they bring out the same words of description: isolation, intimidation, lack of access to choices and information.

I was born in a small town just six miles from my home. I don't know what the place – building – was called though I have always believed it to be like a doctor's rooms, a place where the doctor visited once a week. Maybe I was there because that was where the doctor was that day. There were several beds for patients in this place, however our regular bush nursing hospital was 12 miles from home. (Knowing the distance and the time it took to go to the different towns was like knowing your own name.)

My father owned a butter factory. The small town where I grew up had two garages, two general stores – one that was part of the butter factory business, two milk bars, butcher and baker, postoffice, and a public hall which I remember being used for Friday night pictures and Saturday night dances (once a month). The hall had a small library in it and the librarian sent ten books or so home for my father each fortnight. I don't think he ever had to choose his own; it was just another country service. My father signed his initials in the back, and the librarian kept a record of which books he had already read.

The small town where I grew up had two garages, two general stores – one that was part of the butter factory business, two milk bars, butcher and baker, postoffice, and a public hall

The countryside around our town was all rolling green hills and valleys. Years later, whenever I travelled around this part of Victoria as part of my work in the 1980s and early 1990s, the green hills of Gippsland brought back a yearning that is hard to contain.

'Of course you can! No one will bite you!' My mother's words still ring in my ears. 'Of course you can' was the answer to anything that held a fear for me, the fear of other-than-family people. I was protected, most of my growing-up years, by a brother and three sisters older than I, and three more younger sisters. I was seldom the eldest and therefore the responsible one, yet I was 'old enough' to go out and do what the big kids did, or be the eldest of the 'kids' (that is those younger than I was). My mum never understood my anxiety about doing things in front of other people and away from the others. It made me a good team player, with a job in the chorus, a good fill-in person, never feeling confident that I could do the right thing but always knowing that if I really had to, then I could fill-in. Consequently I have always seen myself as the emergency, in the family, in sport, in school, only taking on something until the right person came along.

This attitude has made my life one of opportunity and freshness. I have always been able to be part of a new idea and a new beginning because the permanency of my responsibility was never apparent to me. My only brother, the eldest in the family and the only son (a bit of a hero really, at least in my growing up mind), was a very different person from the rest of us. He was successful academically, which in hindsight, and with the information we now have about the expectations of girls in schools, I think had as much to do with his being male and his position in the family as his ability to achieve and gain scholarship. On the other hand my eldest sister spent a lot of her growing up time caring for the rest of us and when the family business was threatened it was she who was called home to supply the much needed extra brain to get the organisation back on track again.

My brother was always a mystery to me – older and male, he didn't feature in my emotional world. My sisters, on the other hand, were my life. Still today, though we have grown independent of each other, the bond is as strong as ever. Love mixed with instant frustration, needing to know about each other, keeping distance but keeping concerned. We are tarred with the same brush; our children could almost come from the same households. Our homes, our language, our mannerisms all keep us as one. Our loves, our lives, and our passions differ in appearance and politics, but not in presentation. I 'create' sisters wherever I am. I replace my family with other woman and maintain my security.

As a child I was quite shy so, when I was away from home, I always found a friend who could hold a conversation. I would simply smile a lot and she would talk – just like my sister. I watched and learnt from my sisters. When one of them was being taught to ride a bike and receiving the full brunt of my mother's frustration, I quickly got on another bike and rode it immediately without the lessons. No point in receiving the same attention.

...I quickly got on another bike and rode it immediately without the lessons.

My memory is that although my mother had eight children, she was still a partner with my father in the family business. My father was called by many of the locals 'the boss'. Being manager-owner of the major business in town – the butter factory and general store – made him so! He was a fairly quiet man, except while he was playing with us, and was a strong public figure in the church, the local hall committee, and later the school. Yet in terms of impact on people's lives, my memory would have my mother as the pivotal support for many people, especially those employed in the factory or the store.

At Christmas 1992 one of my sisters prepared a slide show for the family based on a stash of slides found in an old cupboard. What memories it brought back! There was my mother's beautiful garden. She went into the garden in the early afternoon; I think it was her escape. She had flowers growing everywhere. Then there was the slide of the new milk tanker being delivered to the factory, a big day as previously the milk was collected twice a day and in cans. We, the kids, were often employed in the general store during the school holidays. We did the 'orders', the grocery orders from farm families that were then taken out on the milk truck. The orders were phoned in or brought in by the truck drivers on the last milk run. This new refrigerated bulk tanker meant that once a day collection of milk from the farm's own cooled tank would take over, and some of the other personalised services would have to cease. A tanker cannot carry a dozen boxes of groceries on the back!

The slides of my youngest sister in her ballet costumes brought groans from all sides. As in most families, the youngest always gets away with everything and always does the best things! More memories as family jokes and responses were back for the airing again.

My favourite of all slides, and the one that brought tears, is one of my mother half way up a tree trying to pick a banksia flower from the branch. All her fun, her sense of humour, her energy, her love of flowers, her joy in life, her cheekiness is in that photo. She was about the age I am now when the photo was taken and just before her health started to deteriorate. During the last 15 or so years of her life she lost a lot of the vitality and compassion I had grown up with; my children's Nanna was not the same person who had given me an extra dose of understanding and the meaning of justice.

My favourite of all slides, and the one that brought tears, is one of my mother half way up a tree trying to pick a banksia flower from the branch.

I learnt most from my next oldest sister whom I followed through school. One lunchtime she arrived home with a spelling list pinned to the back of her jumper. A note on it from the teacher said: 'This is all your daughter has done all morning!' My mother just wrote on the back of the note: 'That doesn't say much for your teaching, does it!' and sent it back. Teaching was for teachers; her job was to be our Mum although she did hear our spelling every morning as she brushed our hair, and mistakes meant the back of the hairbrush on our buttocks!

My mother ruled all her eight children, and any friends or cousins who happened to be around, with a rough hand. Discipline using straps, twigs from trees, her hand, was used to let us know when we had breached her idea of fair play. Yet what I remember of her is her love, and her warmth, her care of all people who formed part of the extended family. In his memoirs, my father included a story that encapsulates her no nonsense approach to people. My father and one of the factory foremen were backed up against a wall and being threatened by a big local man with a gun. The man believed that his dog had been wrongly shot by someone from the factory for savaging the sheep on the factory property. My mother, who was just five foot two inches tall, arrived on the scene and quickly dismissed all three men with the words... 'Jimmy (man with the gun)! What are you doing? Your mother would be ashamed of you! Archie (my dad)! Where have you been? Your dinner is on the table!' All three men scattered.

We had our Christmas school holidays at the beach – Frankston, McCrae, Chelsea, and then the house at Carrum which was bought when the factory was sold in the early 1960s. I can still sit in my mother's chair in this house and appreciate everything that was done to keep us together and enjoy being surrounded by family and friends. Apart from all 'us kids' there were always, it seemed to me, other people in our house. Friends staying for holidays, cousins having a break from their own families, and schoolteachers who needed a place to board in the small town. My education and schooling was varied and mostly wonderful. I began school mid-year at the age of four. Six months in the 'bubs', and then another five years at the state primaryschool which was a mile away at the opposite end of the town. We would ride our bikes to school, then home and back again at lunchtime. Tough sometimes, especially in winter. Mum would bring or send hot soup to us at school to save us the cold and very often wet ride home at lunchtime. While I was at the school, many of the surrounding smaller schools were closed, the buildings were moved onto our school land, and the pupils were bussed in every day. Teachers were part of the community and we often had a teacher boarding with us. One teacher lived with us for six years.

I began my secondary schooling in a higher elementary school (Years 7 to Year 10) 13 miles away. I travelled on a school bus there and back every day, often 'accidentally-on-purpose' forgetting my lunch, so that I could borrow 'two bob' from the chemist, who put it on the account, and then buy myself a pie and a hot milk shake 'down the street' for lunch. I loved this school and started my real growing up there. Boys, sport, singing and, for one glorious year, I was the only one of my family at the school. However, like all my sisters and my brother, I was sent to boardingschool in my third year of secondary schooling. I was devastated and incredibly homesick.

My mother did not allow homesickness any more than she allowed fear at the dentist...

My mother did not allow homesickness any more than she allowed fear at the dentist; same thing, really, 'a lot of nonsense'. What I was being offered was available to very few country kids, a good education! I should be grateful, not homesick. But homesick I was, quietly, and it had a bad effect on my ability to continue to do well. I failed miserably at school work, regressed socially, and totally lost my sense of self in the huge school population. The boardinghouse where I lived had one hundred students, as did the other boardinghouse. I have no idea how many day-students attended the school. I tried to find the centre of the group and secure my foothold, but I found none, only rules, tradition, and classwork that I did not understand or follow.

For reasons I probably will never know, I was moved to another boardingschool the following year. This school was only just opening up to boarders and to classes beyond the intermediate certificate (Year 9). I was one of the initial 20 boarders and also in the only group of students, about 25 of us, 'doing our intermediate'. I loved the new school and I blossomed, but my school work never really recovered. I had to repeat my leaving certificate (Year 11) and then went on to a new teachers college in Burwood. Teaching was then considered an excellent career for a female because, if anything happened to your future husband, you would always be able to get a job!

So my growing up and my schooling was mostly around girls, and my teachers were nearly always female. My father's obvious authority as 'the boss' and his strong leadership in church and the local community were my only male role models of any significance. Yet it was always apparent to me then that male thought and male knowing were more significant 'in the world order' than that of females, and that in the end we females needed to bow to the correct authority, male, at least in public.

Having been seen as a clever child (schoolwise) till my boardingschool experience, I then drifted into lower expectations. I do not recall any questions about why I had begun to fail, except some accusations that I was just being lazy. My father put great store on 'a good education', but the girls of the family never quite achieved the academic qualifications of our brother. Judging by what we have all managed to do with the rest of our lives, this seems extraordinary. It has given me a healthy scepticism about academic achievement which is not surrounded by an equal amount of personal and person knowledge.

My overriding sense of my mother's mothering is that of fairness and justice. She is the first feminist I have known – a title with which I am sure neither she nor some of my sisters would agree, but she did demand her place and her rights. She used instinct and learning side by side and, above all, she treated all people equally with compassion and dignity. No one was better because they had money or education or position. They were better if they treated others better. I remember a student minister who moved to our country parish with his wife and small children while still studying at the University of Melbourne. This meant that each week he travelled to the city to attend lectures and returned at the weekend to 'his' parish and his family. He tells a story of one particular Friday night returning home to a family who had all been sick and had received some help from my mother. My mother greeted him at the door, and in his words 'gave him the rounds of the kitchen'. He was told in no uncertain terms that the world's work, and God's work for that matter, could wait until the family were well and no longer needed him.

I find this story of particular significance. Here was my mother, who had left school at 11, spent most of her growing-up on her family's dairy farm, challenging the church, the male authority, the head of the household, challenging the accepted position of mother as carer-no-matter-what, and academia at its most powerful. A man studying to serve

'God' against the needs of a woman and a few children who happen to have the 'flu'! On the other hand, she would be teaching us that although we had each other, there were much more needy people and a world of work and care that had to be attended to. I carry this image of my mother as the image of country women, and see this as the practical application they have to their lives and loves.

Sundays meant Sunday School and church. My father was the superintendent of the Sunday School and an elder in the church. Sunday was the day of dusting, tidying, and changing the flowers in the house ready for the new week. This was all done before we went to church along with the roast going in the oven and the vegies being prepared for our Sunday dinner when we returned home. I can still see my mother in the kitchen in her petticoat, turning over the roast. She would rush in from the church service, take off her good dress, and attend to the meat all before most of us were in the door. She was caught doing this one day by the new teacher-boarder arriving with her family for dinner before moving in with us!

She would rush in from the church service, take off her good dress, and attend to the meat all before most of us were in the door.

On Sunday afternoons I often walked with my dad to the factory reservoir to check the pump. To get the water supply for the factory, we had to go down the lane, past 'Mary Minuses house' (she was the town witch and very scary), cut across the paddock, before the abattoirs, watch that the old red bull is not about, then down to the very large dam at the corner of the two small creeks. The little corrugated iron shed housed the pump and motor, smelling of grease and oil. Dad would check this out but I am not sure if the purpose of the visit was to start up the motor or not. The reservoir was still and surrounded by tall reeds. I felt very safe with my Dad, especially when he showed me the 'old joe blake' (snake) on the fence that he had killed. He was definitely a hero! One day I actually saw my Mum kill a snake with the spade she had been using in the garden. She was always much more comfortable with the outside world than was my father.

Sometimes on Sunday afternoons we would buy the bread as it came out of the oven at the bakery, bread for tea to eat with the cold, left-over roast dinner. The joy of eating the hot, doughy, fresh bread from the middle of the loaf! The half mile walk back home from the baker was sufficient to ruin nearly a whole loaf, and trying to spread what was left of the inside of the bread to cover the hole was a complicated business. I do not remember ever being in trouble for doing this, and I do not know why.

On other occasions, shopping for Mum was difficult, especially meat shopping: she was very fussy about her meat. It had to be properly hung and very tender, or it would go back. The butcher was always careful with the meat for 'Mrs B'.

Going for a drive was another Sunday treat. We all had our own places in the car – four across the back seat, one on Mum's knee, another in the middle of the front seat – always for my eldest sister because she got car sick! and then two little stools between the back and front seats against the doors. My seat was one of these, directly behind Mum. The drives had special features. Dad would try all sorts of back roads and invariably get lost, Mum would want to stop and pick the heath and egg 'n' bacon plant, and we would all sing most of the way.

As I moved into my teenage years and went off to boardingschool, my mother began taking on more responsibility in the business. She frequently shopped up and down Flinders Lane, in the city, to buy for the clothing shop that had become part of the business. She shopped often with specific customer needs in mind. Always there was a choice of two for the mother-of-the-bride – the unchosen dress going back into stock. A special outfit for the twenty-first birthday or engagement party were all part of the service. In earlier years trips to 'the city' were probably only once or twice a year for me. The Myer mural hall and Milady's lounge have strong memories for me.

Every Sunday my father used to write a letter to those of us who were away from home at the time. Sometimes, eight copies were needed, meaning that the person who was sent the bottom copy could hardly read it. He never started with 'dear' and he never signed off. I think he was really writing a journal – a pity we did not keep them all.

I married a 'city man' and my first few years of marriage were spent in a large country town. That is where I wanted to stay. Often, I hanker for the open space and the clear night sky. Nowadays, the family beach house (which we still maintain) and the small rural property belonging to some very close friends provide me with sustenance.

Often, I hanker for the open space and the clear night sky.

It seems that for one half of my life my home was in the country. When I was 23, my partner's job meant a shift to Melbourne and suburbia. I was disappointed and certainly didn't think I would still be in Melbourne 28 years later! My early years of marriage were spent in an outer eastern suburb of Melbourne with four children and the shopping and I walked almost everywhere. There was a bus service between our home and the train station but for some reason my partner needed the car. He was away from the house from 7.30 in the morning until 6.30 in the evening, every day. I spent a lot of my day 'across the road' with my friend talking endlessly about how we should get all the women together, without the children, to tackle the problems of the world. It was the 1960s and we were ripe for the messages of change, love, and peace. The children kept us at home being good 'mums', but as soon as my youngest child was three I began the search for work in the world and for my own identity. I ended up working for 12 years in one of the first neighbourhood houses in Victoria and on a crusade for education for women. We set out to claim women's education that did not require the formal constraints of the classroom exams, and someone else's authority. Looking back I can see the impact of growing up in a small community, and I compared that to the loneliness and isolation of suburbia: all women and kids and nowhere to go for relief and broader horizons. I compared my life as a young mum to the community life of my own mother. I compared the life of my children (who had only two adults and a teacher as they grew, to interact with on a daily basis), to my own life where the staff of the factory, the people in the town, neighbours and friends all played a part in my development until I was 11 years old. I thought the life that my children and I had in the city was much more disadvantaged than the country life I knew and understood.

As my career took a new turn I was once again in the country for a lot of the time, working on the development of a rural women's network, and working to change some of the isolation that is experienced by women everywhere. I know that who my mother was and what she taught me were crucial to my ability to do this job. But so, too, was my understanding of isolation as a product of my own suburban experience and the neighbourhood house work. The isolation women feel is caused as much by the needs of dependants (including partners and parents) as it is by the miles between them. Women on farming properties are usually closer and more dependent in the business and practical sense to the (usually) male partner than are their suburban or small town counterparts. That, however, creates a distance which adds to the miles: the distance from the next woman who can share the familiar and similar experience. Because the experiences are often denied, or at the least seen to be unimportant to a world view, these obvious situations of dependency, distance, domination, and isolation are not taken into account or considered very important...

Accustomed to Country Life

Barbara Silinger

Born in Dunedin, New Zealand on 5 September 1947, Barbara Silinger moved, together with her family, to live in Western Australia when she was five years old. She grew up in Perth, attended Hollywood Senior High School, studied at the University of Western Australia, and qualified as a teacher, graduating from Claremont Teachers College in 1966.

Barbara Silinger has lived and worked as a teacher in a number of Western Australian country towns including Wagin, Wundowie, Narrogin, Kojonup, Collie, Gelorup and Bunbury. After taking some time off for childrearing, she is now back teaching full-time and living in Bunbury, in the southern part of Western Australia.

As children, my mother and my father lived in country areas in New Zealand. My paternal grandfather was an engineer on a hydro-electricity plant in the Southern Alps and his family lived in Lake Coleridge for the first six years of my father's life. My maternal grandfather worked with the New Zealand railways until his death when my mother was nine years old. She spent those early years in country towns in the south of the South Island. When her father died, her mother took the three children to live in Dunedin. Although my parents spent those formative years in the country, most of their lives have been spent in cities and they consider themselves well and truly to be city people.

In 1947, when I was born, the population of Dunedin was approximately 85 000. Dunedin was the main business and educational centre for the southern part of the South Island of New Zealand.

I was born at Iona Private Maternity Hospital and my first five years were spent in the suburbs of Dunedin. Two weeks before I was born my father, who was the director of music at King Edward Technical College, left Dunedin to take up a scholarship entailing post-graduate study in music and music education in the United Kingdom and the United States of America. My mother, my older sister, June, then aged three and a half, and I remained in New Zealand, living with my maternal grandmother who had been widowed at the age of 30.

The scholarship meant that my father was overseas for two years; he did not see me, or I him, for the first two years of my life. I lived in an entirely female household. Money was scarce. My mother was a full-time homemaker and we lived on my father's half-salary, a grant from a university trust, and money raised from two benefit concerts held before my father went abroad. This money had to cover my father's expenses overseas and my mother's expenses looking after her children.

...my father was overseas for two years; he did not see me, or I him, for the first two years of my life.

In September 1952 at the age of five I commenced primaryschool in Dunedin at Musselborough State School. In March 1953 my whole family, to which two sons had been added, moved to Perth, Western Australia, where my father had been appointed reader in music at the University of Western Australia. In March, I began primaryschool in Standard 1 at Nedlands State School.

Over the next few months I briefly attended Eric Street State School, Cottesloe, Floreat Park State School and, by September, had returned to Nedlands State School. The moves were prompted by the difficulty we had in securing the university house which should have been allocated to my family as soon as we arrived in Western Australia. Finally, we moved into a university house in September of that year. I remained at Nedlands State School until 1957 when we purchased our home and I attended Hollywood State School. From there I continued on to Hollywood High School.

Both schools were within walking distance of my home. My parents had no qualms about sending me to the local state schools and I received an excellent education from dedicated and genuine teachers, both male and female. The schools were coeducational, and this gave me a balanced perception of the world. Having two younger brothers and a number of male friends in the neighbourhood meant I grew up mixing equally with boys and girls.

Sometimes at primaryschool I played cricket and football with the boys at recess time. One teacher in particular encouraged us to play together at physical education lessons, and teams were made up of both boys and girls. This engendered a mutual respect. A change came at highschool, where all physical education lessons and sport sessions were segregated.

In primaryschool, girls did sewing for two sessions a week while boys did manual training. I considered this was unfair: I would much rather have made purses out of leather or a matchstick kettle stand than sew a doll's petticoat or handkerchiefs. Often at the end of the year, when we had completed all our sewing 'models', the girls who wanted to were allowed to make something out of leather and thonging. We enjoyed the opportunity.

The division of domestic science lessons for girls and manual arts lessons for boys continued for the first three years of highschool, where domestic science (sewing, cooking and laundry) was compulsory for girls whilst boys had to study manual arts (woodwork, metal work and technical drawing). Nowadays everything is different, with boys and girls able to study the subjects of their choice, a great improvement.

When I was at school, apart from the domestic science-manual arts distinction and the 'commercial studies course', all other subjects were studied by both girls and boys. At the end of first year, some girls opted to study a commercial course of typewriting, shorthand and office procedures. This course spanned one year, then the girls were able to leave school and take a job. No boys ever did this course. In upper school, where we prepared for university or tertiary college entrance, I studied English, French, geography, biology, maths A, maths B, and music. The classes consisted of fairly even numbers of boys and girls. Students were encouraged to do any subject they wished; whether a subject was boy or girl orientated was never a factor.

As a girl growing up in the city, I had no thoughts of living in the country. My only country sojourn was a two week stay on a small property a few miles outside Collie (210 kilometres south west of Perth) in 1958. One of my father's students, who was also our babysitter, owned the property and took my sister, two brothers and myself there for a holiday. The property was a few acres in size, but had no animals or crops. The only true country aspect of it was that it was not in the city! All I knew of country life was from my reading – and I had no way of testing its accuracy. Although I probably would have enjoyed the open spaces and carefree life I imagined living in the country would have provided, the prospect had no relevance to me. My family had always lived in the city. All my friends lived in the city and were in a similar situation to myself.

All I knew of country life was from my reading – and I had no way of testing its accuracy.

My perception of country women was one of women working in a large farmhouse kitchen cooking meals and cakes for the men working on the farm. So far as I saw it, the only farmwork women performed was feeding the hens and collecting the eggs. At school, particularly primaryschool, so far as I can recall we did not learn about women in history, let alone country women. We learnt all about the world explorers and Australia being 'opened up' by men, but women played no role so far as history lessons went.

I grew up with the notion that men did all the farmwork, while women did all the domestic chores in the house. My views were, in retrospect, unrealistic; they were gleaned only from reading fiction books about children growing up on farms.

In 1967 I moved to the country to begin my career as a schoolteacher. My first appointment was to Wagin, a farming community of approximately 2000 people, situated 230 kilometres south of Perth. In 1970 I married Peter Silinger, also a schoolteacher, whom I had met at university. Since then we have lived in Wundowie, Narrogin, Kojonup, Collie and for the last 15 years have resided in Gelorup, approximately 10 kilometres south of Bunbury. Bunbury is the major port and city in the south west of Western Australia.

Living only 200 kilometres away from Perth means that we can visit often, even for a day. I have managed to keep very close links with my family through telephone calls, mail and visits. For me it is important to keep in touch with family. As a child I was brought up with no extended family living in Australia. I never really knew my cousins, aunts and uncles, or grandparents, having known them only until I was five years old and seeing them again for a brief visit when I was 17. My own children see their relatives regularly: always at Christmas, several times during the year, and at any family celebrations or get-togethers.

Comparing the lifestyle of my city-living family to my own, there is no great difference in our perspectives. Yet because the rest of my family sees much more of each other and goes out together socially more often, they have more shared experiences. This means they can discuss and relate to one another around these issues and activities: they often attend concerts together, or visit old family friends who are able to stay in touch more easily. My family would not be able to relate to my experiences in the country, or perhaps they would not understand how important they are to me.

I am able to look at issues from a different point of view, living in the country and having lived in the city. I know, for example, how country women react to various political decisions compared with city women's reactions. When I went to Wagin to begin my teaching career, the only organisation I joined was the church youth group. At 19 I did not feel qualified to join community groups such as the Country Women's Association (CWA). As the main reason for my living in the country is as a professional person, I did not really fit in to country women's groups which I consider to be mainly for farmers' wives and women who are farmers. However my awareness of country women's political perspectives has grown over the years.

The main debates in the country revolve around wheat and wool prices, and the struggle to ensure farmers receive a fair price for their produce. Country women are prepared to fight for the rights of country producers, to stand up for what they consider a 'fair' deal. Country women often feel city people don't understand how they live and the difficulties they experience in just making a living. That many country women work hard alongside their husbands means they are prepared to fight hard for what they consider to be their rights. The real picture of country women is very different from what I understood it to be when I was growing up.

Country women are prepared to fight for the rights of country producers, to stand up for what they consider a 'fair' deal.

The country lifestyle is definitely more relaxed and 'laid back' than that of the city. The pace of life is much slower and there are less hassles in everyday life. Being able to go from place to place in a short space of time without being held up in the traffic is a considerable bonus. People are friendly. If anyone is in trouble or needs help, others are readily willing to lend a hand. There is a support network in the community.

When I lived in the city, life was lived at a hectic pace, with people too involved in the busy day to day necessities to have time to really care about others. Living in the country, I found that it didn't matter if the tea was not served at 5.30 pm exactly, but whenever everybody was ready. If visitors dropped in around meal time, they were invited to stay and somehow there was always plenty of food to go around.

Country children have a carefree, safe environment in which to play. In the country they are able to grow at a pace suitable to their age, rather than having various sophisticated material goods and entertainments to occupy them. In Gelorup, we have one acre of land which provides us with lots of space for recreational pursuits. When my children were growing up, there was plenty of room for football and cricket games, swimming and tennis. The area is quiet, and cycling and walking could be done in perfect safety, even when the children were quite small. City children grow up quickly. Country children still have old fashioned ideals and notions, which I find refreshing.

Nonetheless as people become more mobile, with communications and travel improving, country people are able to enjoy more facilities which in the past were available only in the city. Yet I still enjoy visiting Perth to take advantage of larger shops with more variety of merchandise and to attend the theatre and concerts. But I am relieved and happy to return to the easy-paced life of home, to which I have become accustomed.

When I first moved to the country, I had to get used to being a little bit out of touch with what was going on in the world. There was no television, and every newspaper was an early edition, without the latest developments in world affairs. This has improved dramatically over the years. Yet I found and still find that country people are far more interested in what is going on in their local community. Almost everyone buys the local newspaper, fewer people buy the West Australian.

Shopping in the country is a very different experience. In the country, it is not only the lack of variety which is significant. Particularly in my earlier years of teaching, major items such as washing machines had to be bought in the city or ordered to be delivered to the country. However day to day shopping at the local stores has always been a far more pleasant experience than city commerce. Shopkeepers and assistants are friendly and keen to stop and chat; it does not take long to become known to them. In Bunbury today, many of the shop assistants are former or current students of mine. We are able to keep in touch in a way that would not be possible in a busy metropolis.

...major items such as washing machines had to be bought in the city or ordered to be delivered to the country.

Yet I find it difficult to be anonymous in a country town. I found it disconcerting when I first moved to the country to find that many people already knew about me. I was the new schoolteacher. They knew where I lived, when I went out and what I said. I had to be careful of what I did, where I went and with whom. Now I am used to the fact that my family and I mix socially with parents of my students and sometimes even with the students themselves. This seldom occurs in the city.

When I went to school as a student, I rarely saw any of my teachers out of school. In my first three years of teaching (which were also my first three years of living in the country) I found myself babysitting some of my pupils as they lived across the road. The mother of one of my students made my wedding dress. I spent many enjoyable outings with the families of my pupils. The students themselves seemed to accept all this as quite natural and we managed to maintain a wonderful rapport.

We were able to be friendly out of school and to have dinner together in a family situation and participate in other activities. Once school was on it became a student/teacher relationship once more. My own three children attended the school in which my husband and I teach. At one time my husband taught two of our children. The children's friends were at the school. This meant we often had our students visit our home and join in our family activities. It seemed perfectly natural. This aspect of country life was very different. I am sure it does not occur in the city. It added to the quality of life in the country and was a pleasant adjustment from city life.

In the great scheme of things, these adjustments may be viewed as relatively minor. Nonetheless I feel I have succeeded in making the necessary changes to accommodate a country lifestyle. I know I feel much more comfortable and 'at home' living in the country than in the city. It is wonderful to visit Perth to see family and friends, or to attend the theatre or a sporting event, but it is nice to return home to the security and easy pace of country life.

I was brought up in the city. I have lived more than half my life in the country. This gives me a balance of life experiences. Living in Bunbury is somewhere between city and rural life, as Bunbury has many features of a city while still being small enough to have the friendly, neighbourly feel of a country town. The experiences I have had beyond the country, my education and travelling overseas, are of benefit to me in my work as a schoolteacher. I can relate to my students what it was like for me to be educated in a large city school, having access to large libraries, theatres, concert halls and sports grounds, and being able to mix with students from a wide variety of backgrounds. I can relate these experiences to my own children, too. They have been brought up exclusively in the country, but have now commenced tertiary studies in Perth. I have been able to prepare them for city life, recalling my own experiences of city living. They have the added advantage of having grandparents, aunts, uncles and cousins in Perth.

When I first left the city, I met people who had no conception of university life and studies. When people learned that my father was a university professor and had been knighted, they seemed to think I must be really different from them. When I lived in the city, particularly during my school and tertiary studies days, it was nothing out of the ordinary. I attended school with the children of doctors, university professors, a former premier, lawyers. So at first I felt different from the people in the country. Yet I found after a short time that people are far more interested in you as a person and not in your background or upbringing. People like to accept people for what they are.

...gone to the theatre whenever I wanted, been to concerts, travelled abroad, taken large department stores and shopping centres for granted, been able to buy what I wanted on the spot.

The only way in which I feel different from people who grew up in the country is that perhaps I have shared in a greater variety of experiences. I have met people from all walks of life, gone to the theatre whenever I wanted, been to concerts, travelled abroad, taken large department stores and shopping centres for granted, been able to buy what I wanted on the spot. In the country, I found that the people I lived with and generally mixed with had stayed at school until the age of 14 or 15. They had no idea of what university life and studies entailed. I was 19 when I left Perth to live in Wagin. In those 19 years I enjoyed all the benefits that living in the city can bring – a good education in an affluent school with all facilities and plenty of choice of subjects. I was able to attend university and teachers training college without having to leave home, so I had the support of my parents and family as I completed my education. I enjoyed a full social life in the city with plenty of opportunities and choices. Having experienced all that, I was happy to slip into country life and enjoy what it had to offer. I recognised that I had an advantage over country people my age, in that I had experienced many more situations in my life – education, travel, meeting a variety of people – which my counterparts in the country had had no opportunity to do.

People who move away from their family in the city, to make their lives in the country, develop a kind of substitute family. I was fortunate to live with an ex-farming family who were very homely and provided me with a home away from home on my first teaching job. They made my adjustment to living away from home easy. After I married, our social group of friends was usually other young couples in a similar situation to ourselves, living away from their families. We set up a support group, especially when we began having children. We used one another as babysitters and were there for each other in an emergency, just as my family would have been there for me had they been close by. Friends are more like family, particularly friends who do not have their family nearby. When my first child was born I received a great deal of help from my neighbour who was always ready to help out, and was there if I ran into difficulties, just as my mother would have been there for me. I knew I could call on her at any time of the day or night. When our subsequent children arrived, she was there to look after the older ones when I went to hospital in the middle of the night. Later on, other friends and I shared childminding as we had part-time jobs. In a way these friends have been like a family to me, as I have been to them.

Having lived in the country for 27 years, I feel I have adjusted to country life completely.

A Lucky Life

Deborah Towns

Deborah Towns grew up in Corio, near Geelong, in Victoria, after she and her family migrated to Australia from Europe in 1950. Her parents met during the second world war and following the war went first to Indonesia, then to Holland, where Deborah Towns was born. After graduating in arts and education from the Universities of Monash and LaTrobe in the 1970s, she worked as a teacher, then as a government educational advisor, as a political advisor and more recently with the agribusiness company ICM.

Currently working on her PhD at the University of Melbourne, Deborah Towns has a long abiding interest in Egypt and trades in Egyptian art and artefacts, and has learnt to belly-dance.

I was born in 1949 in the city of Den Haag, the Netherlands. I had a hospital birth, which took place with my father in attendance, as was the custom in Holland in those days. We emigrated to Australia in 1950, when I was a year old. For the first 20 years of my life, we lived in the country.

My mother began paidwork when I was 12 years old. She qualified for entry to Geelong Teachers College but decided to work as a medical secretary because she would receive immediate remuneration. Before marriage my mother worked at the CSIRO (Commonwealth Scientific and Industrial Research Organisation) as a laboratory assistant and studied science at RMIT (Royal Melbourne Institute of Technology). My father worked at the newly established Shell Oil Refinery, a Dutch owned company. He became a schoolteacher later. Now aged in his seventies, my father still tutors in Indonesian, Dutch and German. He attended Leyden University in Holland when I was a baby because he was training to become a district officer in Indonesia but, before he was able to take up the post, Indonesia became a republic.

Growing up in the country I had a healthy, outdoors life. I ran around a lot because I savoured the feeling of freedom. I had lots of exercise. In later years I roamed around the countryside, taking my dog on long walks through the paddocks. There were picnics in the bush with my family and friends.

I was a member of the Gould League of Birdlovers and took my membership seriously. I climbed trees at the You Yangs and watched birds for hours. Zebra finches, fire tail finches, silver eyes and spotted pardalotes were birds I particularly looked out for; there were all sorts of parrots, cockatoos and magpies. We had lots of pets, including a baby magpie which we raised until she flew away, happily. I roamed everywhere, learned how to ride horses, and had a job strapping race horses. I bred dogs and budgerigars and ran a little business clipping dogs.

I watched ground larks for hours and was thrilled when I located their nests, which I left undisturbed. Often, I lay on my back in the paddock 'over the road' watching caterpillars slowly climb up ladders of long grass, with the clouds fluffy white overhead. 'Over the road' was the Geelong Road, which is now the multi-laned Princes Highway. When I was growing up, hardly a car went past.

I roamed around the countryside, taking my dog on long walks through the paddocks.

One day my father took me to see the film, *The Ten Commandments*. After returning home I immediately made my own bricks out of dried grass and mud, because Moses was employed in this way. I dried grass myself and created a large mud puddle and hopped in; I loved the feeling of the mud between my toes. I made a wall for my guinea pig 'farm' from those bricks.

In the 1950s I attended the local coeducational country primaryschool, and still can recall the school's registered number – Corio Number 124. I had one year in the original bluestone school room with separate entrances for girls and boys. The most serious punishment was to be made to sit next to the school dunce. A big boy of 13 years of age, he was bound to repeat Grade 6 until he was old enough to leave school altogether. I was often to be found perched precariously on the very edge of the desk seat as far away from him as possible without falling off! Because I was forever talking I was also threatened with the paper guillotine, and the teacher even forced me to put my tongue on the guillotine. Fortunately, his hand didn't slip and I didn't knock the machine or dislodge the blade.

The school celebrated its centenary in 1959. We learnt that we were virtually on the path that Matthew Flinders took when he walked from Corio Bay to the You Yangs in order to survey the area.

I read whatever I could, especially books about history, famous people, and animals. I was first to finish any book or exercise or lesson we were set; then I annoyed everybody else, particularly the teacher. Perhaps that was the incentive to be finished first!

Miss Verity, my Grade 3 teacher, impressed me and I wanted to please and impress her. In the school holidays I was chosen to mind the class goldfish, and the teacher drove me home in her car, together with the fish. I was very proud. In the Girl Guides, I looked up to the guide leaders, and tried hard to impress them. As a patrol leader I worked with my patrol to do the best to win every competition in bushcraft and in other activities. We often went bushwalking or hiking in the You Yangs and surrounding countryside. My hard work must have paid off because I was asked to lead the guides in prayer one Commonwealth Youth Sunday in Geelong when I read the speech the Queen made when she was 18 years old, and which began: 'I declare before you all, etc, etc.'

The Grade 6 teacher was considered by the girls to be a 'dirty old man'. We said amongst ourselves that he picked up papers under the steps so that he could look up our dresses. One day, in a social studies lesson, he referred to my olive skin, saying that if I took all my clothes off I would be the same colour all over. What he said was not true, but I was too embarrassed to say anything about it to anyone.

Perhaps the school did not consider it appropriate to have a girl as dux of the school.

I attended a coeducational school for my secondary education. We travelled there by bus. It was the closest highschool and had been established not long before in temporary buildings which are still standing 30 years later. The year I began, 1962, the school was only four years old. We were surrounded by paddocks and farms. There was plenty of space in which to roam around.

I was always very clever in primaryschool, although in hindsight I believe I would have achieved better as a student in a single-sex environment. A voracious reader, I read and re-read every book available in primaryschool. I excelled at the daily general knowledge tests and mental arithmetic tests, and received 100 per cent for all mathematics tests, and was runner up to the dux of the primaryschool. Even at the age of 12 I was suspicious of this result. I wondered why the boy who was awarded the honour became dux of Corio Primary School when I had higher marks than he did, in every test. I received the 'most improved' prize because, I suspect, the school knew I deserved a prize, but I was really embarrassed about going onto the stage to receive it. I thought anybody could get this prize. It was as though I was not so clever and I had recently improved, yet I was consistently receiving the highest marks in every subject throughout the year. Perhaps the school did not consider it appropriate to have a girl as dux of the school.

I loved school. In primaryschool I enjoyed playing cowboys and Indians and horses because I loved running. I was the scout in one game and the stallion, Thunderhead, in the other. As well as having plenty of room for running around, our school had lots of trees to climb. Throughout most of my primary years I was the fastest runner in the school and generally a very competitive person. I preferred individual sports to team games and was timid in basketball. But softball was a favourite sport for me, mainly because a player could really slog the ball and run for her life around the bases, then when fielding it meant running after the ball. I loved to run and to feel free.

Living in the country as a child and young woman enabled me to have a lot of physical freedom, lots of practical experience and plenty of time to think. We did not have television until I was 12 years old.

At highschool I continued to do well in every subject, as well as excelling in athletics and swimming sports. In Form 1 I worked at lunchtime in the library as a library monitor. I enjoyed hockey because it meant I was running and slogging the ball. I hated needlework and cookery, because these subjects were irrelevant to me: I would be a professional woman, a vet. I did not find domestic subjects interesting, but I loved animals. My cousin lived on a dairy farm. She was studying to be a vet, and this probably influenced me.

I went to bed every night sleeping in agony, with rollers in my hair so that my hair would be perfect the next day.

By Form 3 I began to do badly in mathematics. I was in the 'professional' stream in the school rather than the secretarial – a stream for girls. In Form 2 I achieved a mark in the nineties for maths. By the end of Form 3 I scored less than 50 per cent. For every other subject my marks were in the eighties and nineties. In Form 4 my marks continued to deteriorate. History and English were still in the eighties and nineties, but most other subjects had low scores.

I was motivated by the presence of boys and some male teachers. I went to bed every night sleeping in agony, with rollers in my hair so that my hair would be perfect the next day. I worried about what height my socks should be and every pimple was a major catastrophe. The classroom experience became, in the main, just an interlude between getting back into the corridors as classes changed rooms, so that I could see particular boys again. Lunchtime and recess were also important 'spotting' times. My girlfriend, Susanne, and I chose to do bin duty every day so we could pick up papers in the 'boys yard'. I studied the timetable religiously so that I knew exactly where particular boys and teachers were at any time of the day.

I saw the maths and science subjects as the superior areas in which to do well, because I wanted to become a vet. The 'sciences' were the most esteemed subjects in the school. But these were the very subjects where my work began to deteriorate.

Was it 'fear of success'? The Form 2 maths teacher was a kind elderly man. He was encouraging and motivated me to do well. I loved his classes and my Form 2 maths book. The Form 3 maths teacher was a cold and aggressive man who favoured the boys and had his pets among them. I was sensitive to this atmosphere and it worried me. I became nervous in his classes and was so stressed in the exams that perspiration, rubbing out and smudging made a mess of my answer sheet, and he refused to mark my paper. In Form 4 our teacher was similar. I ended up at the end of Form 4 passing a special arithmetic test rather than continuing with the professional maths course. The names of the Form 3 and Form 4 teachers are clearly imprinted on my memory.

Fortunately, my Form 5 English teacher was a young, enthusiastic woman teacher. Reading and writing had always come easily to me. Now, she taught me the skills of literature appreciation, and poetry became an important part of my life. I learnt how to be disciplined in my writing, and I learnt different styles of writing.

Nonetheless in Form 5 I became a humanities student with lots of boyfriends and no hope of becoming a vet. Now, I do not regret not becoming a vet. I found pleasure in studying the humanities subjects and the social sciences, and continue to do so. At the same time I regret that under different conditions I could have mastered mathematics. Numbers fascinate me and I like to use arithmetic and statistics, which I do in my work, and I use numbers in my interest in astrology and numerology. Both are dependent upon an understanding of the patterns and calculations with numbers.

I have been divorced and a single parent for 10 years, so I know a lot about the romantic myth from first hand experience.

I incorporate these lifetime interests in my current occupations. One of my areas of earning money is as a bankteller which is now a woman dominated job. At my bank we have a woman bank manager as well. All our staff are women. I enjoy working in this environment, and I remember meeting the first woman bankteller in Geelong in the early 1960s, and how impressed I was!

As well as working as a bankteller, I am a PhD student at Melbourne University researching in the history of policy development in education and women's affairs. Research is finding that some of the cleverest girls at around the age of 14 begin to put their extraordinary drive for achievement, combined with a new need for love and belonging, into the pursuit of love and relationships rather than into self-esteem and achievement. The agenda is a 'romantic agenda' and what is valued for females is romantic success. Girls realise this and put all their energy into it. I was one of those girls. Much later, I was married for ten years. I have been divorced and a single parent for 10 years, so I know a lot about the romantic myth from first hand experience.

When I was in my twenties, working in the area of the elimination of sexism, my grandmother told me that I was encouraging girls to be independent, just as her mother had brought her up to be. In her family, all the girls had a 'trade'. Her mother told her: 'You must be independent' because 'you cannot trust men. They might not marry you, they frequently die on you, or they leave you'!

Now, although I believe I would have done better at a single-sex school, I do not regret having attended a coeducational highschool. On reflection it was better preparation for the 'coeducational world', with all its faults and challenges, joys and experiences. My older son, Sam, who has attended a single-sex school and a coed school prefers coed. But he is a boy! In my education philosophy there is a place for coed and a place for single-sex in every child's educational experience. Both single-sex and coeducational schools are necessary until the educational environment can be non-sexist in every sense, and all children can achieve their maximum potential.

In the country I was surrounded by women who were 'farmers' wives' and 'farmers' daughters'. They worked on farms and handled all sorts of animals. Still, as I saw it, women and men both worked, but they did different jobs. I saw it as being unusual for women to be farmers, despite knowing women who did jobs on the farm with their husbands, such as driving trucks of wheat, driving tractors, and rounding up sheep. I saw the man as the farmer.

I wanted to be a city girl. I enjoyed staying with relatives in the city, and being able to look at the shops, visit the museum, and watch all the people going about their business. The city was a lot more interesting than the country. I loved the clothes shops and the bookshops. I loved swimming in baths, because in Geelong it was possible only to swim in the sea and often the sea was too choppy for me to enjoy swimming. Today, I prefer the sea to chlorine.

I had no desire to have children from the city come to stay with me in the country. I wanted to stay with people in the city. We regularly made the long drive to Melbourne, before the freeway was built and modern cars, with their added comfort and extra speed, came onto the market. We often stopped along the way in Werribee or somewhere along the side of the road so that the car could cool down. My sister Louise and my brother Michael and I saw it as part of the adventure. We visited the zoo and the museum, which in the 1950s and 1960s was also the art gallery. We travelled to the city to see *The King and I* and *The Sound of Music* and *My Fair Lady* on stage, and because I learnt ballet I visited Melbourne to see some professional ballet productions. We visited my grandparents, who lived in Surrey Hills, and I enjoyed travelling on the trams.

As I grew older I insisted that we visit Melbourne to buy clothes so that I could have 'the latest' – which was not available in the country. When I completed my schooling and began university, I moved to the city to live. Life in the city was very different from life in the country. There is more choice about everything. People are more broadminded about issues. People are more adventurous and engage in more varied activities. People use their time in a more diverse way. There are more cultural pursuits. A person can be more independent in the city because people do not know her.

I found that the country was cliquish where friendships and groups of friends was concerned. People were very critical of anyone whom they thought did not fit in. They were most concerned about whether a person went to the 'right' school. 'New Australians' had a particularly difficult time.

Nevertheless I love the Australian countryside and have many friends who live in country towns and rural areas, and I enjoy their friendship and lifestyle. I appreciate the importance of the rural sector to the economy and know how hard country people work. Growing up in the country gave me an added insight into the lives of women because I have shared their experiences and I know about the way all sorts of woman live their lives from first hand experience. Many women, especially on farms, have the responsibility of running the home and caring for the children. But farm women can also jump in and do all the jobs on the farm as well. For many couples this means teamwork is rewarding – but does the woman get the same support with 'her' work?

> *A person can be more independent in the city because people do not know her.*

I have worked with farm animals and horses, and I enjoyed it. I have driven tractors and worked with other farm machinery, and picked up hay bales and worked in the paddocks. Once, I thought I would be very happy married to a farmer, and was almost engaged to a most attractive fellow. But other adventures led me to university and the city.

I attended Geelong Teachers College, but in the late 1960s stayed with university friends who lived in Carlton. I became part of their life at weekends and attended lectures in all sorts of subjects during my holidays. On one occasion I attended a lecture with a friend in sixth year medicine. As I took notes I thought, I can do this. I gained an extended studentship which enabled me to go on to university. Subsequently I gained a bachelor of arts, a bachelor of education and a master of education.

The weekend before university began, in March 1970, I moved into college and took up the hems of all my skirts, so that they were very short. I had to make new friends because my Melbourne friends were at other universities. I had often stayed away from home, so didn't have to adjust in any remarkable way. The previous summer I had spent six weeks working at the Retta Dixon Children's Home for Aboriginal children in Darwin, so for me, moving to the city and going to university was just another experience.

I liked to be surrounded by people who are involved in many areas, so that I can be involved with politics and with issues. This was not so readily available to me in the country. I feel closer to international affairs and future issues in the city. Growing up in the country has not, however, made me feel any different from city women. Every now and then I may meet someone new, who is over familiar and comments about the way I speak: I am considered to have a 'country' accent; sometimes people think I come from Northern Queensland because I have a broad Australian accent. Such a response upset me in the past.

My family do not speak with the same accent as I. My father, who was raised in the Dutch East Indies (now Indonesia) speaks fluently in five Asian and European languages, and speaks English with a slight accent. My mother, born in Australia, speaks with an almost British accent – probably because she attended an independent Anglican girls school in Melbourne.

Now, I think I probably developed my accent because I hated being considered a New Australian in the Geelong area in the 1950s. It was not a very pleasant time for migrants in Australia. Our family name was difficult to pronounce and spell, so we anglicised it in 1962 when I was 12 years old and began secondary school. I wanted to be as Australian as possible. At school I did not want to be considered a drip or bookish or a 'professor' as they were called in those days. I did not want to be considered cultured in any way. I wanted to be accepted by my peers.

I was the only woman who was not working as a secretary or administrative assistant.

In 1977 I began working as 'Coordinator for the Elimination of Sexism in Schools', a position in the office of the director general of education. This was where the minister and most senior education department people worked. In an office of approximately 20 people, I was the only woman who was not working as a secretary or administrative assistant. One of the senior men who met me when I first began in the office rudely commented: 'I can tell by your voice that you are not a college girl.' I constantly battled prejudice because the men and women in the office could not place me in a position which they could accept. Women typists would not type for me, but they would happily type for younger, junior men. I had to be resourceful and enterprising so that I could do my job.

When I first moved to the city I became involved in the anti-Viet Nam war movement. I learnt to work in the political process. This helped me when I began to be active in the Women's Movement. As a secondary teacher I joined the Australian Women's Education Coalition

(AWEC). I do not think I brought any new issues to the organisation when I joined in 1976, but in my paidwork as coordinator for the elimination of sexism I was prepared to travel anywhere in Victoria to organise inservice days for teachers, and to talk to students throughout rural Victoria. Driving alone hundreds of kilometres over the years reminded me of when I roamed all over the local countryside as a young woman. As I drove around in various government cars I often saw men working in road gangs or in pairs, and this made me even more conscious of what a lonely job mine was. When I stayed overnight in hotels and motels, mostly I was the only woman in the communal breakfast, surrounded by men in crisp white business shirts. I would think to myself about who had produced the immaculate shirt. When travelling interstate by plane I was one of the very few women on the early morning flights. The flight attendants brightly greeted the passengers: 'Good morning, sir.' But they didn't seem to know what to say to me. They happily handed out newspapers to men, and offered me a *Women's Weekly*. It was not that I minded looking at the magazines, but it made me feel out of things. The plane was like a male breakfast club.

When travelling interstate by plane I was one of the very few women on the early morning flights. The flight attendants brightly greeted the passengers: 'Good morning, sir.'

My years of wandering around the countryside and dropping in on people enabled me to cope with the hours of working and travelling I had to undertake on the job. I have always had a vivid imagination and a positive nature so I could entertain myself on long country trips as well. Most of the country women were happy to see me because they were a lone voice in their school or local community. I seemed to have some authority because I was employed by the central administration of the education department, but many males in rural areas and country schools were not so happy to see me. On a number of occasions male principals seemed to disappear from the school when I arrived, or would suddenly find that marking out the football oval in a far away paddock was imperative. If a male had driven hundreds of kilometres from 2 Treasury Place he would not have been treated so rudely.

The Country Women's Association (CWA) was invariably supportive of me and my work. One of the first speaking engagements I undertook in 1977 was at the invitation of the Country Women's Association. The topic was sexism in the curriculum. Parents and Citizens organisations in rural areas were also supportive of my work. In some country towns I was invited to stay with families or teachers, which added pleasure to the job.

I fitted in wherever I was. I had had many experiences in common with many of the other women. Having lived in the country and in the city, and having had a migrant background, made me aware of how women lived and worked. I had also experienced discrimination as a woman and as a migrant. It was a good background for advising on education generally, and particularly in sexism in education.

Knowing both country and city life, I know that the issues for the Women's Movement are, politically, the same in the country and the city. The patriarchal system is organised so that the decision-makers are mainly men, whether in the country or the city. Women lack access to decision-making positions in education, and there is a dearth of women in politics. Women in the country and the city find it equally difficult to make an input into the day to day concerns of life, let alone how Australia is run. However in the city there are more activities that a woman can be part of which make her feel that women are making our presence felt. There are more issues to be active about and more women being active on behalf of women.

Historically, in the country young women have stayed longer at school than boys, but this is because there is more work for boys and local training programs are more likely to be for boys than for girls. This may be partly responsible for my activism in the Women's Movement having been centred around educational issues that are relevant to both city woman and country women: women's access to education and training throughout their lives. There are more avenues for education and training in the city, but it can be just as difficult for a city woman to have access to them, because of a lack of confidence, through being unaware of what is available, and as a consequence of the responsibility of a young family or other caring responsibilities. Educational facilities are so institutionalised, even now, that they find it very difficult to be flexible in regard to the typical woman's needs.

My country background gave me a good rapport with the rural community. This was an advantage in the employment market. In the city I obtained a job with an agribusiness company, ICM, which was the umbrella company to Uncle Tobys. The job involved establishing a foundation with the aim of encouraging a greater appreciation of agricultural and agribusiness careers for young people. We also ran a student exchange program, exchanging secondary students between rural and city areas throughout Australia. Special emphasis was placed on encouraging girls to consider agricultural and agribusiness careers, which are dominated by men.

The job also involved pioneering work and travelling into rural areas throughout Australia. I travelled to nine overseas countries to investigate agricultural education, so met country people in Europe, the United States of America, Israel and New Zealand. I helped to establish the ICM Pacific Agribusiness Marketing Award, a prize for tertiary students presenting a marketing plan for an agribusiness product.

I have been disappointed, but not surprised, that at conferences concerning rural and farming matters and rural industry affairs there are relatively few women. In my four years with ICM, women's representation was less than one per cent. Whatever the paucity of city women in politics, country women are not as involved in politics and the important decision-making areas. However rare women are as members of parliament, there are far fewer who represent country areas or rural issues. Notably, male farmers complain about how difficult it is for *them* to attend conferences. Their wives, left behind, run the farm and mind the children at these times.

> *...male farmers complain about how difficult it is for them to attend conferences. Their wives, left behind, run the farm and mind the children at these times.*

The CWA is an important service for women, and particularly women in the country. Living on a farm is isolating for many women. I have met dynamic women members of the CWA and in other rural organisations, but few seem to want to have a more public party political role on behalf of rural women, or the rural sector. This may be because rural women find it even more difficult than do city women to find the necessary support.

Yet the city has its drawbacks, conditions that do not apply so readily to the country. In the city there are more physical attacks on women, an increasing problem for women living and travelling alone. Single parent families headed by women are more prevalent in the city, where the cost of living is higher than in the country, despite high transport costs for goods going from city to country.

The city demonstrates more of the 'masculinity' stereotype, particularly in the aggressiveness of advertising and marketing, not only in relation to its sexism. The city lifestyle is overtly greedy with waste and exploitation that is blatant. Life appears to be short-term: products have a built in obsolescence; fashions and entertainments change over night. Pollution swirls around us. The car is significant in the culture of the city: is driving fast in a big, noisy, thrusting car a phallic right?

The country demonstrates the 'feminine', paganism, the goddess, because mother nature is preeminent. The seasons are part of the work pattern in the country. People have to be patient, allowing nature to take its course. The dependence of human beings on the earth is immediately apparent. In the absence of city lights, the stars are thickly studded in rural night skies. Being in the country makes people appreciative of the ancient peoples' understanding of the importance of caring for nature and respecting the natural life cycles. It is also clear why the sun, moon and stars played such an important part in the organisation of their lives, and in decision-making. In the city people can forget all about nature through living and working in artificial environments.

My family still lives in the country but have moved to a suburb of Geelong, close to the beach. My parents comment on the city traffic and how difficult it is to get around in the city because of the cars and the numbers of people. Nonetheless they come to the city because they need to – for business, to visit family, to travel, for exhibitions at the gallery and other cultural activities that do not exist in the country. Often, they come to buy items that are not available in the country (although most basic products are cheaper in the country than the city, which means a more economical lifestyle). Because goods and activities are less readily available, it is necessary to be practical and resourceful. This training stands me in good stead.

Although I have been a 'city person' for over 20 years I continue to enjoy visiting the Geelong area because of its history, and particularly the place it has in the founding of Victoria. (My mother's ancestors landed at Point Henry in the nineteenth century.) Football also plays an important part: I am still a staunch Geelong supporter.

I keep up links with my family and am closer to my parents in the emotional sense since I have moved away. I make more of an effort to be friends with them because it is important to me to appreciate their lives. I do not see them as often as I would like to, so this is an incentive to grow closer. My parents are not 'just' my parents any more. They are individuals in whom I am interested and about whom I care very much. They have made an effort to appreciate me as an individual with interests and needs different from theirs. My mother often makes arrangements to meet with me socially: she comes to the city to see me more than I go to the country.

It is important for me to retain these links not only for myself, but so that my two sons, Sam and Max, have a lot of contact with their grandparents. This is not easy, as city life is exciting for them and their sporting responsibilities take up a lot of weekend time. However as my parents are interesting people, my sons enjoy visiting them when we can organise the time. The telephone is vital, but std calls are expensive, making communication difficult.

I have been lucky to have lived in the countryside of Australia. Dorothea Mackellar's poem 'My Country', which I had to learn by heart from my primaryschool reader, is always there, in the recesses of my mind: '… A land of sweeping plains… I love her far horizons… The wide brown land for me…'

So, too, are the words of Jean Jacques Rousseau, and Mary Wollstonecraft's response. 'Educate women like men,' says Rousseau, 'and the more they resemble our sex the less power will they have over us.' But as Mary Wollstonecraft said: 'This is the very point I aim at. I do not wish them to have power over men; but over themselves.'

We need to go beyond 'equal opportunity'.

The Voyage of the Argonaut

Pat Richardson

Pat Richardson, aka 'Belle the Bushie' began to read her 'Belle the Bushie' stories over 2SER-FM each week on the *New Horizons* program for the over-fifty-fives in November 1989. Her first book of 60 stories and poems, *Belle the Bushie*, was self-published in 1991 under the Gumleaf Press imprint and won the New South Wales Women Writers Society, Hilarie Lindsay Award. Her second book of 45 stories, *Belle on a Broomstick,* published in 1992, was highly commended in the Xerox-Fastbooks Award for self-published books in 1992. Her poem, 'Women Alone', was written in 1989, and has been published in many feminist and mental health journals and in the *Weekend Australian* on 4 September 1993.

In September 1992, Pat Richardson moved back to Nambucca Heads on the mid-north coast of New South Wales. She still writes a story each week for the Sydney program, sending it down by cassette for broadcast, and calls herself the 'Scheherazade of the Airwaves'!

THE ARGONAUT'S PLEDGE

Before the sun and the night
and the blue sea,
I vow to stand faithfully by all
that is brave and beautiful.
To seek adventure
and having discovered aught of wonder
or delight,
of merriment or loveliness,
To share it freely with my comrades,
The Band of Happy Rowers.

I rang my old mate, 'Belle the Bushie', last Sunday as per usual. (Cheaper rates, long distance, and all that.) I asked her whether she'd got around to writing that piece yet...

She began with a list of excuses. You know what writers are like, prevaricators from way back.

'Jack,' she replied. 'How am I supposed to write anything? Life back here in the bush is so full and busy, what with playing Social Tennis on Monday and Thursday mornings and Ladies mid-week Comp on Tuesdays.' (This physical activity of hers amazes me more than anything. Maureen at Rozelle Post Office couldn't believe it when I showed her a photo of Belle in her tennis outfit, all tanned and fit and about a stone lighter.) She continued: 'You remember, I swore that when I moved back here, I'd live a quiet life. But somehow I've "scored" being the publicity officer for the busiest Red Cross branch in the state, I'm newsletter "putter-outer" for the Arts Council and also its Minutes Secretary and now, believe it or not, they've made me a Rotarian and I've "scored" doing the weekly newsletter for them as well!!... I've rejoined the VIEW Club and on top of all this, I'm being pressed into service as a guest speaker at various groups around the place... I even spoke at the old people's home the other day,... you can see I'm not getting much writing done!'

> '...everyone is so busy with their own affairs in Sydney. Nearly all women in the city these days are at work.'

'Well,' I answered. 'I'm glad you're getting out and about. You sound very happy. I was worried about you down here in Sydney. You weren't getting any exercise and you were very lonely.'

Belle agreed. 'Yes, everyone is so busy with their own affairs in Sydney. Nearly all women in the city these days are at work. Where I lived down there in Leichhardt Street, only two women were home during the day out of 57 units. And even though Minnie Mouse lived around the corner, I saw her only when she'd pop in with the two bubs late on Friday afternoons, after she'd picked them up from daycare. Her schedule would frighten the horses, with a full-time job as mistress of "Modern Technologies" at a selective highschool, two small tots and a husband. Makes me feel tired even thinking about it.

'And, of course, you were away so often those last 18 months. First in New Zealand and then back at work again... Well, I thought to myself, what am I doing here? Why aren't I back in Banksia? After all, I still know practically everyone here. JR and I moved here in 1974 and ended up building half the new houses in the valley over the next ten years.

'As well as this, while I was away in Sydney, I always had the local paper sent to me. Plus over those eight years, I came up at least twice a year to stay with Yvonne and I used to give her a hand with the Art Show. I always volunteered to sell the raffle tickets at the Arts Council soirees and that kept me *au fait* with the names of the new "movers and shakers" in town.

'I don't know why it took me so long to make up my mind to come back. After all, the reasons I left here in the first place no longer applied. When I left here eight years ago to go to Sydney, I thought there would be more help for Meggie in Sydney for her schizophrenia, but found with all the government cut-backs, there was nothing at all. Then she "buggered-off" back here to live and that meant I had to keep two places going. All very expensive!

'Back in 1984 though, I thought everything exciting was happening in Sydney. But I didn't realise that the women I'd met at the various conferences were still working and lived all over the place... AND the married ones had more than enough to do on the weekends.

'Those women who were unattached, didn't always have the money to come with me to the opera or the theatre. I might add, I lived in Sydney for eight years, and never once even sighted a "straight" male who might be looking for a lively 55-year-old. Yvonne Preston said that a woman's chances of being asked out on a date over the age of 40 in Sydney were just as likely as being hit with an Exocet missile.

'...a woman's chances of being asked out on a date over the age of 40 in Sydney were just as likely as being hit with an Exocet missile.'

'Actually, Jack, like you, all the nice good looking men I know are gay! But, even you wouldn't come with me, even though I offered to pay for the tickets, because you said you didn't want to be a "hag-fag"!'

I laughed at this. Belle and I met when we were talked into standing for the local council elections on a ticket for the Australian Democrats in September 1987. She was just completing her BA in communications at the University of Technology, Sydney (UTS) as a full-time student, the most 'mature-aged' student in Sydney. I'd just come down to live in Rozelle from Brisbane. I was recovering from a serious brush with cancer and I was still very weak from all the chemotherapy I'd undergone.

While our campaign was underway, she'd pop in with my mail from my postoffice box and do any errands for me. We'd have morning tea together and the habit continued for the next four years.

I was the campaign manager for the council election. (I organised Senator Macklin's campaigns in North Queensland years ago.) Neither Belle nor I had a clue about any of the local issues. But leave it to Belle to think of something. Years ago, she'd been on council up in Banksia, so she trotted off to have a consultation with the municipal engineer and he filled her in about all the major projects in the area. Following this, she didn't do too badly answering questions from the audience at the mandatory public meeting for candidates to face the voters.

Belle was away when the branch voted to support the Rozelle Bay marina project. She wasn't in favour of it herself, but it was too late for her to distance herself from the decision. (Australian Democrats' parliamentary representatives are free to vote their conscience on issues, although then they have to explain their actions to the members!)

Our campaign was sunk when it was found the 'bottom of the harbour' was toxic in Rozelle Bay! If they began to dredge it for a marina, all the fish in the harbour would cark it! Even so, we still nearly pulled off getting her elected. Not bad with only a $500 budget and a three week campaign. If we could have had all the polling booths and the pre-poll covered, she would have walked it in. Even so, she got to within 100 votes of getting up. No one was more amazed than she was. As she said, 'no one knew her from a bar of soap'! The count went on for 10 days and she was almost asking for a 'try-out' of the mayoral robes.

She began to write to fill in the days. Except for visiting me each day for morning tea, I don't think she saw anybody else, except her Avon Lady.

It was as well she didn't make it, because her younger daughter, Meggie, had just been hospitalised in Morisset Hospital.

Belle spent the next five years motoring up to visit Meggie once a week at the hospital. It's 60 miles from Sydney, so she spent the rest of the week recovering from the journey. Throughout this time, she was very lonely and very depressed. She began to write to fill in the days. Except for visiting me each day for morning tea, I don't think she saw anybody else, except her Avon Lady.

This is the poem she wrote at the time. It's been published in lots of mental health journals, and the lovely layout was done by the editors of *Woman-Church* magazine in spring 1989.

WOMAN ALONE

A woman sits alone every night
watching TV,
In a house, high above Manly.
She is eighty-two,
Widowed seventeen years,
Drives her yellow Mini
to Lawn Bowls twice a week,
Reads the *Daily Telegraph*, and
Murder Mysteries, books with a red dot,

from Manly Library.
Once a week, on Sunday, the family
arrives for lunch,
for the baked leg of lamb, and
Grandchildren fight on the floor.

Her daughter sits alone every night
watching TV,
In a Unit, at Glebe Point.
She is fifty-six,
Divorced eight years,
Drives an old Holden,
Attends Poetry classes,
Reads the *Sydney Morning Herald*,
Is writing a book, loves bookshops,
Listens to 2BL all day,
Babysits grandson,
Lived in the country,
Drives to Morisset every Saturday,
Across Sydney for lunch on Sunday.

Her daughter sits every night
Watching TV,
In Hospital, at Morisset.
She is thirty,
Never married,
Doesn't drive,
rarely reads, has schizophrenia,
Each day is allowed one packet
of cigs, and one bottle of Coke.
The nurses are kind to her,
Sometimes she writes poetry,
She is tired from dancing on
Television every night,
Her mother visits her every Saturday,
No one else lives in her world.

They all watch TV every night,
Alone in different suburbs, towns and
houses,
They cannot live together,
They have not been raised to live together,
It is too late now to try.

Belle and I are both keen gardeners. She's considered quite an expert on gardening on a balcony, especially using the *Sydney Morning Herald* under the pots. She always says she can't guarantee results with the *Telegraph Mirror!* She had only a courtyard garden here in Glebe.

These days, she has a massive old garden to practice on. It has huge azaleas, camellias and even rhododendrons, although it's only over the sand dune from the beach. It's very sheltered, of course. She reckons the wisteria is so rampant that passersby are lucky not to be caught and strangled by the roving tendrils. Actually, the wisteria grows right up the huge trees and hangs in great pink and purple drifts in September.

She asked me had I seen *Burke's Backyard* on Friday night. We always talk plants, we both used to listen to Valerie Swane on 2BL every Saturday morning (before she died) and discuss her advice for the rest of the week over cups of tea. I asked her if her tv reception had improved.

'No! I spent $500 getting the aerial upgraded, but I still get Don Burke "Thru a glass darkly". Mind you, NBN Newcastle is 250 miles away, but in any other spot in town I wouldn't need an aerial at all. You know how high and steep the town is but, unfortunately, this house is tucked down behind the cemetery and the State Forest AND beside the sea, behind masses of trees, well... I get Prime a bit better from Tamworth, but the tv man says my set is so old, and not the right make for the edge of a reception area. He says I'll get both these stations one-third better when I get a new set. NR-TV comes in okay from Coffs, though.

'Even when I was a little girl I lived for five o'clock to hear The Argonauts, *the children's program on the ABC. I can even remember my rowing number, I was Terpander 9!'*

'Thank Heavens, I get the ABC clearly. I'd die if I couldn't get Peter Ross on Sunday afternoons. And I couldn't live here if I didn't get Radio National, which luckily has its tentacles spread all over Australia now. It comes in on the FM band here. I couldn't live without Geraldine, Prue, Julie, and dear Phillip. I'm even getting used to Ramona Koval. The radio has always been a lifeline to me. Even when I was a little girl I lived for five o'clock to hear *The Argonauts*, the children's program on the ABC. I can even remember my rowing number, I was Terpander 9!

'Mind you, I sometimes think I'm listening to 2SER-FM. All the young people I remember from the University of Technology are now on Radio National. Karen Snowdon is on *The Country Hour*, and there's Brent Clough (I'm sure he was in one of my radio classes), and Joe Gelonisi.

'As long as I can garden on a Saturday afternoon, with my Walkman tucked in my apron, listening to *The Science Show* and John Cargher's *Singers of Renown*. I tell you, I wouldn't be dead for quids!

'The only thing I do miss on tv though is SBS. Not that I used to watch it that much, but I liked *The Bookshow* and the *News*. I think there's a committee in Coffs agitating for it to be extended into this area, so it might come soon. Here's hoping anyway.

'One big drawback here is that Telecom doesn't itemise the phone bill. I like to keep track of my trunk calls. The bill was supposed to be itemised by now, but it hasn't happened yet. Even a phone call to Coffs, 30 miles away, is a trunk line call. I'll bet Optus isn't interested in us here either, although it's the fastest growing area in Australia.

'I call the mid-north coast of New South Wales, the retirement capital of the world. The biggest industry here is "old age"! I reckon I don't have to move to a retirement village, I'm living in an "open" one already! And I reckon it's the last bastion of the anglo saxons as well!

'I don't think there are too many areas where you could field 36 good tennis players, men and women, twice a week, on four courts for social tennis. And lovely old players they are too! I tell you, the legs may be slower, but the hands are trickier.

'I think the other thing I like here is that if I go to any meetings or functions up at the local Hall, I only have to drive up there a few minutes beforehand, park anywhere in the street, and still get there in good time.' Belle suddenly changed the subject. 'How's your job going?'

I was caught a bit by surprise. 'Oh, good! I'm getting 30 hours work a week now.'

'Don't you go doing too much, you're not that well you know,' she admonished.

...five of my friends have died this year of HIV/AIDS. I've lost count of the number of my friends who've died. It's going to be a lonely old age for us survivors!

I assured her I would watch it. I drive brain-damaged men (damaged from strokes and Alzheimers), out to daycare for the home care service. I also bathe and feed old gentlemen. If I work on weekends, I get quite good money. Actually, I'm glad to be earning a decent wage again. I was on the sickness benefit for years. Belle said I should be on the invalid pension, but then they transferred me to job search. Belle was horrified, she thought it was disgraceful for me to have to find work again at 56.

Anyway, I enjoy my work, although I sometimes find it a strain. Also, five of my friends have died this year of HIV/AIDS. I don't know how much longer this is going to go on. I've lost count of the number of my friends who've died. It's going to be a lonely old age for us survivors!

'How's your social life?' I asked her.

'Absolutely wonderful. I've been here 10 months and I've been to countless picnics, dinners and luncheon parties, plus two recitals up at "The Promised Land" to hear the pianist, David Helfgott, plus many touring concerts from the New South Wales Arts Council. The Australian Chamber Orchestra is the next big attraction here in October. Not that I'm that high-brow,' she concluded.

I thought to myself: 'You can say that again!' Her idea of a good opera is one that ends up with dead bodies all over the stage!

She chatted on: 'I went to hear a group from the Conservatorium perform in a private home the other night, with supper thrown in for $10. Very sociable. I tell you, I didn't go to anything like this in Sydney. I used to read the *Metro* every week and stay home too confused to attempt to go anywhere. Besides which, I would have had to go on my own. It doesn't matter where I go here, I always know someone to sit with. I went to see the local players put on *The Removalists* the other night. They did a great job too! Plus, there was "Champers" and supper laid on for $10.

'I sat in the window of "The Troppo" in Glebe, year after year, and I can remember only one person ever seeing me and sitting down with me.'

'Here, if I go to Gloria's cafe for lunch, someone always sees me and joins me for a cuppa and a chat. I sat in the window of "The Troppo" in Glebe, year after year, and I can remember only one person ever seeing me and sitting down with me.

'I guess I'm a small town girl at heart. After all, I spent the first seven years of my life in Kempsey before the war. Dad was third officer in the Commonwealth Bank there. Our six years in Sydney during the war were depressing. Dad was working long hours in the bank and Mum was ill all the time. Then, when Dad was transferred after the war to Tweed Heads on the far North Coast, to his own Branch, I can still remember the elation I felt as the train left Central Station, heading north.

'I was 13 when we moved to Tweed Heads and I lived there for 10 years. I did the intermediate, and then, like lots of girls of my generation, I went into the bank, the Bank of Australasia actually, as a clerk.

'I married at 20 and had my first two kids, Dickie and Minnie Mouse, in Murwillumbah Hospital. I thought at the time it might become an annual event!

'I accidentally landed back in the city, when I was widowed a couple of years later (caught between towns, and minus a house). Dad had been transferred back to Sydney and they were living in a bank residence in the Western suburbs of Sydney. I joined them out there. What a hellhole! All I could think of was: "How am I going to escape back to the country?"

'Even though I was only just 24, I knew I most probably wouldn't be able to get work in the country. I'd lived there half my life and I knew you had to have money to survive there, otherwise you were just a shitshoveller and at the mercy of a handful of bosses. In the city, I was able to get work in a neighbouring branch of the Commonwealth Bank. The kids were both under three at the time. I left them at a childminding place all day, although it was not a proper place like they have these days.

'Some people have very romanticised ideas of life in the country, but I always say, "don't underestimate the locals". If they've survived there for a few generations, they're very tough indeed. If any jobs are going, they give them to their mates and "rellies" first. The only exceptions to this are footballers from the big Sydney clubs, who are always found jobs on the council to fortify the local teams! Anyway,' she ran on: 'You know all this, you grew up in a small coastal town in New Zealand.'

...I had to leave New Zealand in those days because it was illegal to be "gay". I moved to Melbourne, in cities you can be more anonymous! Perhaps I'll go back to New Zealand to die, like an old elephant!

I got a word in here and said: 'Yes, I'd like to go back there one day myself. But I had to leave New Zealand in those days (even though I was in a promotions position as a teacher), because it was illegal to be "gay". I moved to Melbourne, in cities you can be more anonymous! Perhaps I'll go back to New Zealand to die, like an old elephant!'

'That's a cheery thought!' she replied. 'I won't have that far to go when I die. The cemetery here is just up the hill behind me! But I'll bet it won't make it any cheaper!'

She rattled on: 'Are you still bringing your sister here to stay while I'm away in England? I'm looking forward to seeing Haworth and Bath. I can't wait to see Sissinghurst and the White Garden. Although it will be nearly winter when I'm there. I might call a chapter in my next book, 'Around the World with Margaret and Gough'!

'Gough's going to take us to see the Old Bailey and the Houses of Parliament. I think the tour will be tax deductible because it's a literary tour. And there's only one person in Australia who has to be convinced I'm a writer, and that's the Income Tax Commissioner!'

I asked: 'Have you begun to use your computer properly yet?'

She laughed: 'I still haven't learnt to right-justify on it! You wouldn't think I earned my living for eight years as a senior computer programmer would you? My brains seem to have gone into neutral with electronics these days. I use my computer as an electric typewriter and it's very handy even to do that.

'Have I sent you my new long poem? It's called "The Woman's Ten Commandments"! It's an ironic look at the original lot from a woman's perspective. Would you like me to read a little bit of it?'

I said I would.

She rustled her papers at the other end of the line: 'I'll do the seventh commandment.' A pause.
'Adultery!' she said.
'Adultery,' she repeated.

A foolish exercise the human race indulges
A woman ventures more than men, No matter what some say.
A home to lose, and children too.
Judgement's still severe today.

However, 'boys will still be boys',
You've often heard it said.
Times haven't changed that much, my dear,
When it comes to games in bed,
Men only value when they pay,
Beauty vanishes with age,
Remember your retirement fund,
Say 'No' to freebies, ask a wage!

Twixt cup and lip, there's oft a slip!
Safe sex there's never been,
When condoms burst,
Before all's lost,
Fall back on Delfin Cream!

A further word before I go,
Please read my lips, my dears,
Just never mess with married men,
There's no future there you see,
They always go back home to Mum,
for chops and pies and peas.

If this advice you will ignore,
My dears, do be discreet!
Feeling randy?
If penetration's still your scene,
Be on The Pill and have some condoms handy.
With men, alas, no matter what they say,
You can't be certain where *'it's'* been today!

But bear in mind and practice when you may,
Solitary passion is all the rage today!

She paused expectantly at this point.

I laughed.

'My!' I said. 'The Argonaut is certainly speaking from experience there, methinks.'

'Alas!' replied Belle ruefully. 'I should have taken my own advice more often!'

EPILOGUE

Country Conversations, City Conversions

Jocelynne A. Scutt

Born in Perth, Western Australia on 8 June 1947, Jocelynne A. Scutt's childhood was lived in Gooseberry Hill and Perth, with six years spent in the wheatbelt towns of York and Meckering. After graduating in law from the University of Western Australia she studied at the University of Sydney and Michigan, as well as Cambridge, the University of New South Wales and Melbourne, and has also lived in Canberra and Freiburg in Breisgau, Germany.

An impressed participant in the 1994 Women and Farms Gathering at Glenormiston in country Victoria, Jocelynne Scutt presented a keynote speech and a workshop on the value of women's work as farmers, particularly on marital breakdown, in personal injuries cases, and in relation to family testators maintenance and inheritance.

The power of fantasy to pose as reality is nowhere stronger than in denying the real lives of women. The history of Australia since colonisation or invasion is replete with tales of men as pioneers 'opening up' the countryside. It is as if women were not there or, if there, were ever 'the drover's wife' – not the drover; 'the farmer's wife' – not the farmer; 'the miner's wife' – not the miner. And for the women who were in the 'wife role', there is an implication that their contribution to farming and country life was insignificant or secondary.

'Agriculture,' say Cheris Kramarae and Paula A. Treichler in *A Feminist Dictionary*, is the 'planting, harvesting and management of food, accomplishments of many women in ancient times and today'. A farmer's wife, they add, is 'a hard worker', quoting Elizabeth Akers:

297

The farmer and his men came in at noon,
full of the open air's fresh vigorous life,
and had an hour of rest:
a blessed boon
denied the farmer's wife.

Surrounded by the realities of women's country lives, girls growing up in the country have too often reached adulthood imbued with the false picture of women as not working equally hard as men, whether the work is alongside men in the paddocks and shearing shed; complementary work raising chickens, milking cows, cultivating vegetable gardens for family eating and the markets; or farming alone as single women or in women partnerships, whether by reason of widowhood or never having married. Girls growing up in the city have imbibed the same message through books, films and television.

As Andrea Lofthouse observes, in Australia 'the country' is seen as foreign to women: not a 'woman's place'. The acknowledged bush tradition is strongly male. The stories of Barbara Baynton, where women inhabit the bush, are seen as painting a false picture. Henry Lawson's vision of the 'drover's wife' is remarkable for its acceptance as a true depiction of country women and country life: women can be identified only through their connection with a man, rather than as individuals of significance leading their own lives. It is remarkable also for its companion piece, 'the drover's dog' – a wife and a dog hold a place of equal importance in the recognised life of the Australian drover. Even then, the dog may be the more lasting in the contemporary memory.

> *The acknowledged bush tradition is strongly male.*

Jacqualine Hobbs was raised in Quorn, in the South Australian Flinders Ranges, among children from farming backgrounds. Children and their mothers worked on the farms, women doing the daily task of cooking for the shearers in the shearing season, rounding up the sheep, fencing and all facets of farm work or 'station jobs'. Yet she grew up with stories of the hard work being done by men, whilst women did 'light duties'. Barbara Silinger was raised in Perth and knew nothing of the country apart from what she read in books. Her perception was of country women working in large farmhouses cooking meals and cakes for men doing the work. Women fed hens and collected eggs. Men did all the 'farm' work, women the 'domestic' chores. In Geelong, Victoria, Deborah Towns knew women farmers: she was surrounded by women working as farmers and handling all sorts of animals, yet was inculcated with the notion that it was unusual for women to be farmers. Alison Brown, experiencing country life in Kadina on the Yorke Peninsula and

Renmark in South Australia in the 1940s had, as one of her role models, a woman (a gardener and staunch conservationist) who managed the sheep and wheat property she had originally run with her husband who had died at a young age. The woman who in truth was the farmer was still seen as a 'farmer's wife'. Growing up in Triabunna, Tasmania, twenty years later, Belinda Tate's perception was that men were doing the 'real' work. Women in the town were in 'support' roles: the doctor, pharmacist, bank manager, school principal, town clerk, policeofficer, foresters were always (and still are) men. Women were the nurses, infant and primaryschool teachers, the secretaries. On the land, women were ever in 'support' roles, cooking for the shearers, keeping the household running.

Some, like Jenni Mitchell, understood the roles of country women to be 'joint and equal': this impression she gained through the direct experience of her mother and father working as partners in the family business, a butter factory. For others, like Kath Davey, the dominant male ethos of the bush did not deter them from dreams focused on the country, with them playing a central role.

...the dominant male ethos of the bush did not deter them from dreams focused on the country, with them playing a central role.

Lara Finlayson, born in Shepparton in country Victoria, spent her holidays at her cousins' farm, collecting eggs from the chookhouse, checking the sheep in the lambing season and doing other chores. Her aunt worked alongside her uncle, as did her cousins. She experienced first hand another country fantasy: the idea that everyone from the country is from a farm. Once people knew she did not live in Melbourne, the realisation that not all country people live on farms was slow in dawning.

What is 'the country' and what 'the city'? The country can range from tiny population centres of several hundreds or a few thousand, to large provincial cities of tens of thousands. Janet Powell was born in Nhill, in Victoria, population 2000, on a farm 10 miles from town. Jane Wilkinson's first experience of country living, as a 'just out' teacher, was in the even smaller town of Goroke. Like Jane Wilkinson, Barbara Silinger was a first year teacher when she moved from city to country, and Wagin, in the south west of Western Australia and 230 kilometres from Perth, was a small community of 2000 people. Born in the city, Sarah Stegley now lives between Jamieson, a town of 150, and Mansfield, area population 5000, while Triabunna, 'home' for Belinda Tate, is populated by less than 1000 people.

Then there are the slightly bigger farming centres. In the 20 or so years since Sharene Morrison's birth, her home town of Bairnsdale had grown from a population of 10 000 to 15 000, the same number as

Horsham when Jane Wilkinson moved there to live for several years, commuting to Goroke. And there are the large centres of population. After immigrating from England (where she lived in an industrial city in Yorkshire with a population of 500 000), then living in Perth, Western Australia, Doris Leadbetter spent eight years in an Australian country town, Bendigo, population 62 000. Like the smaller country centres, these towns can be a day's or several days' travel by car from the capital cities, as Kath Davey found when she moved to Albury-Wodonga, targeted by the Whitlam government as a 'growth centre'. Or they can be an hour or several hours away, like Geelong, nearby where Robin Jackson and Deborah Towns spent some of their growing years, and not far from where Bev Roberts now makes her home.

Like the smaller country centres, these towns can be a day's or several days' travel by car from the capital cities

As for city living, Claire Lupton grew up in Canberra when it was a 'country town', with the prime minister's residence, the Lodge, across a paddock of grazing sheep and roaming cows, and no Luna Park, no zoos, no museums and no theatre. When Jane Wilkinson grew up in an outer suburb of Melbourne her grandparents expressed surprise at her parents' move into the wilderness – there were no paved roads, no sewerage, and no footpaths; today the ageing suburb is unremarkable for its proximity to the city centre, whilst homes standing on quarter acre blocks stretch for miles beyond it, and houses on larger suburban acreages are way beyond those.

Unlike the conventional picture of country life, country towns and provincial centres are not solely associated with wheat and sheep farming, or even cattle and other cereal crops. Coffs Harbour, where Pat Richardson now lives, plays vigorous tennis, and writes, Kiwi fruit and plantains are the farming-base of the economy. In other communities, like Morwell where Marjorie Thorpe spent her childhood, secondary industry is far more important. For yet others, like Belinda Tate's Triabunna, farming has declined in importance and milling and wood chipping, of secondary importance during her childhood, are now seen as keeping the town economy alive, although wood chipping is not accepted as unproblematic where survival is in issue. In Derby and Broome, where Lorraine Hunter has her roots and her heritage, pearling and other fishing have been the mainstays, with mining dominating the economy in the Kimberley, as it does Broken Hill, where Merryl Robson spent the early years of her married life.

By no means do those who live in the country, or who grow up in the country then make their lives elsewhere, exclusively have 'country connections'. Agi Racz has a country tradition in her family: she spent time at her grandmother's home in the country of the border region between

Hungary and Austria, yet she had the experience of 'frantic city life' as well. When she went to boardingschool in Melbourne after living for some months in Fremantle, in Western Australia, she was one of the few students who did not come from country Victoria, but it meant that she was able to renew her country connections over the five years of her schooling by staying with fellow pupils during school holidays. Merryl Robson's experience outside suburban Adelaide was limited to Port Pirie, a provincial industrial centre, and a field trip to Central Australia. Marriage then meant that she spent her adult life in the country centres of Broken Hill and Hamilton, and it is only recently that she has returned to city living – in Sydney. Barbara Silinger had no thoughts of living in the country; her only country sojourn as a child was a two week stay on a small property a few miles outside Collie, 210 kilometres south west of Perth, when she was 11 years old: it was a plot of a few acres, with no animals and no crops. Since going to the country as a teacher at 19, she has lived all her adult in the country and now sees herself as 'a country person'. Jane Wilkinson, now living in Wagga Wagga, retains her city identity but like Barbara Silinger has, through her experience as a country teacher, developed a strong affinity for rural life.

...a plot of a few acres, with no animals and no crops.

Many children who grow up in the country do so as a consequence of their father's career or their mother's background. Nancy Cato was born in Swan Hill because her father moved there, as a dentist, in the 1930s, and met her mother. Pat Richardson's 'Belle the Bushie' tells a commonplace tale in uncommonplace prose – of the daughter of a banking official, spending the first seven years of her life in the New South Wales country centre of Kempsey, then back to Sydney, then back to the country on the north coast, at Tweed Heads. Kath Davey's mother was the daughter of a country bank manager, spending her childhood in rural Western Australia and Victoria, then moving in the early 1930s to the city to take up nursing. In her fifties, with her children grown, she returned to country living and to a welcome from the many old acquaintances who remained. Kath Davey experienced this 'welcoming back' when she, a confirmed city dweller in the early 1970s, became a country woman in Albury-Wodonga, left to go further into the country and into greater isolation with her husband, a forest ranger, then returned to the country growth centre upon the breakdown of her marriage and to the welcoming support of old friends. Victoria Whitelaw had a banking connection, too: born and spending her first three years in Caulfield, suburban Melbourne, her father was in banking and ever after was known as 'Jack the Banker' although when the family moved to Benalla, in country Victoria, the family ran a newsagency, then a farm, and he took up horse training.

Many women who move to the country from the suburbs, or from a rural centre to the city, do so because their own career or a husband's takes them there. Bev Roberts has gone from being a suburban dweller to an aficionado of country living because she wanted to write. A poet, she has found the country to be conducive to her creativity: the white noise of the city fogged her thought; the buildings hemmed her in. Country life has helped to clarify wider issues. Family responsibilities meant Pat Richardson moved from country to city. Her writing was, at least partly, an impetus to her returning to country life. For Andrea Lofthouse, the chance to put into practice conservationist ideals of gardening and farming propelled her into setting up Moonraker Farm with her partner, Kaye Johnston. This has also provided an opportunity for sharing skills, knowledge and rural air, rural work, with other women. Politics propelled Marjorie Thorpe away from the city, and her career and desire for Aboriginal autonomy led her back into the country – not the country of her childhood, but that of her father's childhood, at Lake Tyers. She has learnt fishing, negotiating and supervisory skills, and has managed cattle and roadmaking. Sharene Morrison wanted to explore the world outside her home town of Bairnsdale. Acceptance into a dress design course in Melbourne enabled her to do so, taking with her combined feelings of excitement and anxiety. Merryl Robson moved from Melbourne to Broken Hill when her husband's medical practice took the family there, as was so with her move to Hamilton; her move to Sydney is entirely for herself. Gwen Baldini's desire to follow her grandmother's example and take up nursing meant a move from Katanning to Perth; Jenni Mitchell married a 'city man', spent the first years of marriage in a large country town and wanted to stay, then moved to the city where she, like Barbara Silinger and Jane Wilkinson in reverse, has spent half her life. Lara Finlayson and Lorraine Hunter, like Susan Hawthorne and Deborah Towns some 20 years before them, moved from country to city to pursue tertiary studies. Nancy Cato's moves to Melbourne, then to Shepparton, came in pursuit of a career in television. Her moves to Alice Springs and back to Swan Hill came through her own and her husband's involvement in the arts: in Swan Hill, setting up as pig farmers and arts administrators; in Alice Springs, the establishment of Araleun, the arts centre. For Sarah Stegley, the country was where, she remembers, she always wanted to be. School holidays were arranged with this in mind; she studied agricultural science to provide her with skills essential for a country life; and she made a career opportunity happen at an old country property that had never previously thrived. Gourmet country eating was unheard

…the white noise of the city fogged her thought; the buildings hemmed her in. Country life has helped to clarify wider issues.

of in Victoria (or almost anywhere else) at the time Sarah Stegley and partner Marieke Brugman established Howqua Dale. Now, the gourmet retreat enables her to live the bucolic life she dreamed of as a child and young woman.

My parents' buying a cottage in Gooseberry Hill, some 15 miles from Perth, meant my early years were spent (like Alison Brown) amongst the glories of wild flowers, trees, bush tracks and bush animals. The bush came right up to the backdoor, and to the frontdoor. Bobtail goannas roved around the tankstands. The proudly erect head of a racehorse goanna was a common sight. The voices of cicadas singing in choruses of thousands provided the soprano and contralto to the dull baritone croaking of frogs in waterholes and creeks. Spider orchids, donkey orchids, hovea and sundews grew at the feet of banksias, eucalypts and wattle trees. The miles from the city stretched interminably on trips to and from my grandmothers' homes. Looking back with an adult comprehension of time it is difficult to believe it seemed to take s-o-o-o l-o-n-g from Swanbourne, the Perth suburb where my maternal grandmother, Maud Helen Needham, lived, through the city, up Greenmount, then along the bitumised roads to claysurface roads, to Aboyne Road and home to Rillawood. (Alison Brown had this experience too: Kallangu was 25 kilometres from Brisbane, but in the 1950s to a child just going into her early teens, 'it seemed much further'.) For a child of three, four and five years old this left lasting reminders of 'the bush', the sounds, the smells, the great open skies and every star set against the black velvet of the night, a truly idyllic childhood.

Our moves to York, 60 miles from Perth, and Meckering, 80 miles from the city, came (as for so many others) as a consequence of my father's work as an accountant and manager with Wesfarmers, the conglomerate that ran department stores in country towns and sold farm machinery and wheat silos. Like Janet Powell, I remember the country dances – 'barn' dances, although they were held in the local town hall, and no longer in barns – where children were drawn, shrieking in fun, across the floors, perched on wheatbags to weight them down as the men of the town 'spat and polished' for a good dancing surface. Like Janet Powell and Nancy Cato, too, I remember the itinerants and hawkers coming to the door with goods to sell and offers of chopping wood and doing other odd jobs. Just as Jenni Mitchell recalls the deliveries made by her parents' milkcart, I remember bread and milk deliveries arriving at our home in Gooseberry Hill, and the mail being delivered to a RMB (road mail box) at the turn off where a cluster of mail boxes served instead of individual deliveries to each household. Like Jenni Mitchell, I recall the times of fetching loaves of bread (in our case, from the mail box), and for me there was the excitement of scoring the half loaf with the convex rather than the concave end: this meant that eating the freshly cooked bread made less of an inroad into the loaf. And again like Jenni Mitchell, nor do I remember any chastisement for bringing home a depleted sandwich loaf which had suffered the removal of layer after layer of warm dough from the exposed end.

Education plays a central role in the life of any child, whether she or he enjoys school or doesn't. Many women growing up in the country have boardingschool experiences. There is no universal like or dislike of this form of education. Marjorie Thorpe was dragooned into attending Methodist Ladies College (MLC) in Melbourne through government assimilation policies. She survived only through being able to use her 'weekend pass' to visit her grandmother who lived in Fitzroy. Jacqualine Hobbs, in South Australia, had a similar experience, although she was a day-girl, living with relatives whilst attending school. Claire Lupton went from Canberra to board at Presbyterian Ladies College (PLC) in Melbourne to (as she now reflects) relieve pressure on a household where the youngest child had been born to a mother over 40 years of age. Alison Brown went from a small country town to boardingschool in Brisbane. Victoria Whitelaw's boardingschool experience was isolating, a consequence (as she remembers) of a family meeting which she did not attend, and family dysfunction. Jenni Mitchell was 'devastated and incredibly homesick' when at boardingschool: a good education was what was needed, vowed her family. Neither did Robin Jackson enjoy her boardingschool experience but now, looking back, she is appreciative of the learning she gained. Lara Finlayson was at first overwhelmed by the sheer numbers: she went from a country highschool of some 600 boys and girls to MLC, Kew, and 2000 girls, with 100 in the boardinghouse. Janet Powell's boardingschool life was lived in the large country centre of Ballarat: she went from a town of 2000 to one of some 50 000. For Susan Hawthorne, six years of boardingschool provide a transition for her from country to city living, making her introduction to city life as a tertiary student easier than it may have been, had she gone straight from a country school to a city teachers college. Belinda Tate had the major part of her schooling in her home town, then enjoyed the final two years of highschool at boardingschool in 'the big smoke' of Hobart. Similarly to Agi Racz, Sarah Stegley's boardingschool life meant she was presented with abiding friendships and opportunities for excursions into the country and country holidays: city born, she longed for the life of a farmer, and boardingschool provided her with opportunities she took up with alacrity.

She survived only through being able to use her 'weekend pass' to visit her grandmother who lived in Fitzroy.

A continuing theme with education for rural children is the lack of opportunity available at country schools. Victoria Whitelaw and Deborah Towns are, like others, convinced of their good fortune in attending the schools they did in their country centres. Victoria Whitelaw's family thought otherwise: this was one of the reasons for her becoming a boarder at a city school. Jacqualine Hobbs' parents believed their daughter would be advantaged by a city education and that there would be better discipline and incentive to academic achievement away from the country. So too with Belinda Tate's family: there was an assumption that 'town schools' were 'better', with more subjects and opportunities. Nonetheless she attended highschool in Triabunna where her teachers encouraged her academic aspirations, and it was not until her final years of schooling, then university, that she moved to Hobart.

Doris Leadbetter's experience indicates that there may be some universality of the notion of the inferiority of a country school education and the limits it may set on life experience and opportunity, at least so far as anglo-culture is concerned. At university in London she discovered amongst her friends from the country that a university education was seen as a way of encouraging the children to 'better themselves' away from the narrow limits of rural living, with only the oldest son being 'kept back' to take over the farm.

…a government official who decided typing and shorthand in Perth was the 'proper' educational experience for her…

Lorraine Hunter's Perth education was a consequence of government policy: 20 years before, Marjorie Thorpe and many other young Aborigines were taken from their families in a relatively less blatant way than those Aboriginal children removed without any continuing links and who make up so many of the numbers Gwen Baldini and others counsel and support. Lorraine Hunter's experience, 20 years on from Marjorie Thorpe, was nonetheless one where there was no choice: an interview, unannounced so far as she recalls, with a government official who decided typing and shorthand in Perth was the 'proper' educational experience for her and her cousin Maureen. It took her many years to gain access to higher school certificate (HSC) studies, an opportunity denied to her when it would have been far easier for her to complete her highschool education with this necessary entry qualification for university. Because of the notion held by a bureaucrat that business studies were what she was capable of, or what she 'should' do, rather than going straight on to HSC as a natural progression, she had to set out with determination, struggling against social, monetary and work pressures to complete HSC as an adult who had been away for some years from the everyday rigours of study. Gwen Baldini's experience of schooling, and her understanding developed over years of counselling fellow Aborigines, is that many of the difficulties now suffered by Aboriginal people have arisen because of policies (effected in both city and country) denying education to them, or depriving them of formal recognition for educational studies they had completed. Janeece Richards compares her school careers advice with that of her city sisters, and finds it wanting, whilst Nancy Cato's careers advisor had an apoplectic reaction to her expressed desire to become a professional writer or actor, and provided no information or encouragement for 'going on' to university.

Janet Powell's family moved into a larger neighbouring town, away from the smaller community of Nhill, when a drop in numbers to below six pupils meant the local school was closed. Her family was determined that education would be accessible to the children and this desire led to boardingschool later, then to highschool in a large country centre, and to a period of correspondence school. For Claire Lupton, although Canberra in her childhood was in many ways 'country', the education system was not: money was available for well-staffed and well-built schools. French, German, Japanese and Latin were part of the first year curriculum in highschool. There was an early recognition of the need for all subjects to be non-sex-specific: metalwork, woodwork, cooking, cleaning, sewing for all.

Primaryschool education in the country did have special qualities which I and so many others, as adults looking back, appreciate. My memories of York include Mrs Negus and Mrs Nottle thriving in a setting which afforded them the opportunity of organising grand spectaculars for the end-of-year celebration. Always, there was the Grand Ball, with the Grand March. Every class was involved, the children going through their paces with many rehearsals. Lines of children wove intricate patterns throughout the breadth and depth of the large town hall. A magnificent edifice, it towered in a town where there were grand old pubs on every street corner and grand old houses built with the coming of the pioneers. On one occasion Mrs Negus choreographed 'The Dance of the Sugarplum Fairy' from *The Nutcracker Suite*, and we wore costumes which, today (although the tops were in multi-coloured hues, and the whole in a shiny, satin-like material), would be recognised as 'Mao suits', at least in design. That was not, I am sure, Mrs Negus' intention.

I took this training with me to Meckering, initiating the local school children into the glories of 'the Grand March' which we did, endlessly, to the tune of Strauss waltzes on the enormous lawned area at the side of our home. It was in Meckering, too, that I had the good fortune to be taught by one of the best teachers I ever had: Mr Williams. A bachelor, he had devoted his life to his teaching – at least this sense of dedication came across to me, powerfully. He encouraged writing and speaking, all manner of verbal expression. This reinforced the encouragement my sisters and I received at home from a father whom we all recognised as 'good' at art, and a mother who wrote stories and plays which we retold to our school friends and acted at concerts and benefits we held raising funds for the Red Cross.

What is it about the Red Cross and rural fundraising? When at school at Gooseberry Hill my concerns for 'the less fortunate' were centred in a major way around support for people suffering from leprosy. At Mary's Mount, the all-boys convent I attended with my elder sister (girls were in fact allowed to attend until they reached eight years – this must have been the 'danger age' so far as the nuns were concerned), my teacher – a nun, as they all were – spoke often of the sufferings of leprosy and the need to support leper colonies. I took this very much to heart. For some reason, in Meckering leprosy lost priority and my fundraising efforts were directed towards the Red Cross.

How or why this change came about, I do not know. (Perhaps, after all, the Red Cross gave support to medical programs for those suffering from leprosy? Or had my field of concern and compassion simply expanded?) Yet it is remarkable that many women with country antecedents observe the central role the Red Cross played as a focus for fundraising efforts. Janet Powell remarks upon shearing shed dances and other fundraising events being held in Nhill for the Red Cross Relief Fund (during wartime). Robin Jackson observes that the Red Cross was one of her mother's major areas of fundraising interest. My sisters and I organised endless barbeques, concerts, dramatic performances and quiz-days, sending off regular amounts to the Red Cross in Perth. The spelling competition was ever my downfall: too gentle to rule any contestant out for a wrong spelling, I noted the error then gave each one a further chance with yet another word. This event invariably ended with my mother, concerned that the participants should be able to return home before nightfall, advising me that the matter should be resolved between the contestants by the simple expedient of 'eeny, meeny, miny, mo'. This seemed to please everyone, and overcame the problem I had of having to choose between people on the basis of intellect, and ruling anyone out as 'stupid'.

Gooseberry Hill was the place of the bushfire: flames raging, the crackle and burnt smell of bushes and trees...

Somehow the wind and rain, hail and sleet, heat and sun, and the dust, are more pronounced in the country than the city. Bev Roberts has learned this today, as an adult. For me, memories of bushfires, floods and cyclones are etched strongly in my psyche. Gooseberry Hill was the place of the bushfire: flames raging, the crackle and burnt smell of bushes and trees, my father going out in a utility with a waterpack on his back, together with others, spraying the flames and the undergrowth. When the banksias went up at the bottom of the valley it was like the Aurora Borealis, the flames red, orange and yellow in a hugh half-circle stretching across the horizon. Over on the other side of the continent, fires threatened Susan Hawthorne and her family. And 30 or 40 years later, Andrea Lofthouse remembers the bushfires, too. No rain for weeks. The earth is dry. There have been no fires for 20 years. Meanwhile at Moonraker Farm, her friend packs a bag, while the progress of the fires is traced on television and radio. She recalls her concern for the animals and plants, the fear of having 'home' burnt out from under, and the way the women fought the fires and evacuations were carried out under the wise supervision of women police.

In York it was floods. The Avon river burst its banks, the water coming right up to our backdoor. This time, my father was out with the others salvaging huge oil drums that had escaped from the storeyard. The drums floated down the river, past the tops of trees that were almost drowning in the flood. Then, almost as suddenly as it had come, the water retreated until only the last defiant tide slowly trickled back into the rightful place between the banks. And just as suddenly, the seasons had changed and the river seemed almost empty in places, the riverbed parched at the edges.

Bev Roberts listens to the howling wind lashing the trees, hears the broad thud of rain on the tin roof, sees the jagged thrust of lightening ripping the dark sky of the tiny coastal town of Breamlea, near Geelong. In Swan Hill, dust storms came from miles away to the west, and Nancy Cato woke to mornings where pillows were dark brown with particles of earth, except for the white circles where heads had lain. I recall the time the cyclone came to York, lifting the floor coverings to the ceiling as the wind surged into the house, whooping through the spaces between the doors and the floor. Forked lightening came in regular flashes, followed by the crash of thunder. My sisters and I knew all about conduction, and that rubber was an antidote to electrocution, so we stood in awe at the large bedroom windows gazing out at the spectacle, secure in our protection against being struck by lightening: as many elastic bands as we could find were wound securely around our wrists and ankles.

In Meckering, it was the earthquake. By the time it came, my family was no longer living in the country, and I was at university in Perth. Seven plus on the Richter scale, it tore the earth, destroyed one of the oldest homesteads in the district, and left behind the jagged rifts children learn of in physical geography as creating block mountains. Waiting for the bus to take me in to town and away from a family law lecture, I saw the road snake vigorously and a huge tree shudder as if to fall. In the true anglo Australian habit of the stiff upperlip and ignoring the embarrassing, I and the other woman who stood at the bus stop looked carefully out of the side of our eyes at one another, surreptitiously attempting to gauge whether we were hallucinating or the road really had moved in a defiant snake-like wriggle, tearing itself from one side to the other, as if being wrenched by giant hands. We didn't speak. When the bus arrived the passengers and driver maintained the same rigorous silence. Not for any of us the embarrassment of admitting anything untoward had occurred!

Distances mean both more *and* less in the country than the city. At a city conference a colleague reminds Janeece Richards that it takes longer to travel from the sixteenth floor of her hotel to the lobby than it does from home to Janeece's place of work. Janeece Richards is taken aback for a moment; the rest of the audience is stunned, uncomprehending. Pat Richardson is five minutes away from the tennis club, the local hall, meeting places, whatever she needs. Nancy Cato, like Robin Jackson, could cycle the length of the town and back in a trice. Claire Lupton could (and did) cycle across to parliamentary question time. For Lara Finlayson, it is 15 minutes drive from one end of her home town, Shepparton, to the other, and the bike track from home to town is well utilised. Lorraine Hunter had never experienced public transport before she moved to Perth to study; like Janeece Richards 20 years earlier and 3000 miles away, she had to learn the techniques of hailing the bus, paying the fare, and pulling the cord to ensure the bus would stop at the appropriate place. Like Sharene Morrison, she had to ask directions. In Broome and Derby, the local facilities were within walking distance, so no public transport system was needed.

Yet distances are great for country people, too, and can be dangerous. Travelling from Broome and Derby to anywhere requires a four-wheel drive or access to an airline. Experience has taught Lorraine Hunter the need for a 'bush mechanic' as a passenger or co-driver to advise on mishaps such as leaking fuel, punctured petrol tanks and tattered tyres. Merryl Robson has learned first hand of the dangers of railway crossings and the trauma of car accidents and collisions on single-lane highways and deserted country roads.

...she had to learn the techniques of hailing the bus, paying the fare, and pulling the cord to ensure the bus would stop...

Jane Wilkinson was told Goroke was 'about three hours drive from Melbourne' when she was first appointed to teach there; it was four and a quarter hours distant. Jenni Mitchell remembers the long drives from country to city and the carsickness that accompanied them. Marjorie Thorpe spent weekends away from MLC with her grandmother in Fitzroy: she was unable to visit her family in distant Morwell once

COUNTRY CONVERSATIONS, CITY CONVERSIONS

during the long years at boardingschool. Claire Lupton experienced the shock of gravel roads that served as the highways leading into Bega. The town was distant from any major centre: it took almost an entire day to get to either Sydney or Melbourne, and the town was isolated from all but the most hardy of tourists and travellers. When Victoria Whitelaw and her mother went on excursions to the city from Benalla, time and distance meant she had to be taken out of school for the day.

Like so many other women, Janet Powell had to move from the country to the city to go to university; later, she had to move from the country to the outer suburbs, as it was impossible to live 200 kilometres from Melbourne, in Echuca, as a senator travelling regularly to Canberra, and with offices in Melbourne. Janeece Richards and Sarah Stegley are acutely aware of the time it takes to travel to the city for meetings, and the lack of understanding city people have of the hours country dwellers commit to participating on committees and boards – all held at city locations. 'Will you be at the meeting,' a caller says. The time? 10.00 am. The time set for the meeting? 11.30 am. Travelling time from home to meeting place? Two and a half hours. Impossible, as Sarah Stegley says. Unless a country dweller is Wonder Woman!

Distances mean women and girls may rarely see the city. Susan Hawthorne didn't go to Melbourne until she was in her teens. I knew school students at York who had never been to Perth, 60 miles distant.

...the smashed bodies of rabbits, birds and foxes, together with the occasional lizard, snake or possums.

And extensive driving from country to city, farms to local towns, and from country town to provincial centre brings home to the traveller the danger not only to humans but for animals and birds in the expansion of highways and high-speed vehicles hurtling along rural roads. Bev Roberts, like all of us, has seen the smashed bodies of rabbits, birds and foxes, together with the occasional lizard, snake or possums. Even domestic animals don't escape: chickens escape from cages set in lorries and other trucks, only to die in the thrashing of wings against windscreens or under the tyres of passing cars. Closer to farming areas, the bodies of cats and dogs lie abandoned, stark against the gravel edges of the highways.

Local country schooling and travel are often linked with memories of bus rides. For Susan Hawthorne, it was regular trips in the 'Biscuit Tin', as the children named the local school bus. Deborah Towns had the school bus experience as well, while Janet Powell and Jenni Mitchell could walk to their local schools until each was closed when the numbers went below the set quota. When she attended her local school, Jenni Mitchell was able to cycle home for lunch each day. When the school closed, it was the school bus for her and others. It was a bus to connect with the school bus, then a nine mile ride with other students to school for Janet Powell, when she attended highschool in the country.

Doris Leadbetter has a vast experience of travelling around to country towns as guest speaker in her role as newspaper columnist, poet and writer. Speaking engagements are arranged to coincide with trading of local produce through 'trading tables' of eggs, cakes, vegetables, jams, pickles: distance makes country women organise their travel time wisely, to combine the fun of entertainment and the practical demands of rural commerce. Similarly, Deborah Towns, Jenni Mitchell, Kath Davey and Jacqualine Hobbs have been able to use their acclimatisation to long distances and driving. Each has had jobs entailing trips into the country, and from one country centre to

Speaking engagements are arranged to coincide with trading of local produce through 'trading tables' of eggs, cakes, vegetables, jams, pickles: distance makes country women organise their travel time wisely...

another. Deborah Towns drove all over Victoria, meeting with a positive reception from the Country Women's Association (CWA), parents' groups, and women teachers, in her work in equal opportunity in education. Sadly, some male principals were less interested in this groundbreaking work, their reception of her into their schools blending a lack of professionalism with misogyny. As she observed, her approach coincided with a desperate need on the part of some school principals to mark out the footy field in a far distant paddock. Kath Davey's work took her all over Gippsland and up to the New South Wales border. Jenni Mitchell's work in the department of agriculture means she and her colleagues have established a strong network of women living in the country. The *Rural Women's Newsletter* is a central feature of Victorian country women's communication with one another, and it provides city women with insights into rural women's lives. Other states are now seeking to emulate this Victorian initiative. And today, Jacqualine Hobbs drives long distances throughout South Australia, carrying out her brief on violence against women. Country communities cannot be educated about criminal assault at home and other forms of domestic violence if there is no one to do the job, to take resources and opportunities to women in country areas, and to support women working in country areas in refuges, shelters, or whatever other facilities might be available or proposed. This need to ensure country women have some equivalence of the facilities available to urban dwellers requires continuing input and support from city women. Too many women suffer and are at risk from violence in city homes. Yet women living in rural communities run a far greater risk of being killed by husband or partner than do city women. Women who are wives form a significantly higher proportion of unlawful killings in the country than in urban and suburban areas.

Women engaging in political action in the country receive a mixed reception. The Country Women's Association (CWA) is deemed 'respectable', no doubt in part at least to its longevity (although any woman's organisation can be the subject of ridicule and misrepresentation, and the demands of any women be regarded as radical). At the same time, the CWA engages in political debate, generally centred around the need for resources, improved roads, public safety, support for women, and by no means a backing limited always to women in traditional women's roles. The encouragement Deborah Towns received from the CWA in her 'equal opportunity for girls' role is a ready example of this. More explicitly feminist organisations do establish themselves in country areas, one of the most lively being the Goulburn Valley Loose Women's Group, joined by Lara Finlayson and a source of role models and intellectual and practical stimulation for her. Andrea Lofthouse and her partner have established a feminist haven in country New South Wales, providing a means for like-minded women, and particularly lesbians, to experience farm living in a practical way, through participating in planting, harvesting and other farming work. And as Sarah Stegley says, not every woman has to explicitly announce herself as a feminist to be an adherent to feminist principles both in theory and practice. Some of the most practical, everyday country women live their lives working in non-traditional roles in ways that are supported and applauded by feminists whether of the city or the country. Nonetheless the political act of identifying as a feminist is both brave and important, and country women do do it, often in the face of personal attack and possible ostracism.

...the political act of identifying as a feminist is both brave and important, and country women do do it, often in the face of personal attack and possible ostracism.

Travelling out into the country and talking with country women about their goals and aspirations, about the issues concerning them, and about the way they live their lives provides insights that need to be taken into account. Often the traveller finds that country women have the same goals and aspirations as city women, and that the issues they confront and seek to deal with are the same or similar to those addressed by city women. As Jacqualine Hobbs points out, many issues are the same for the country and the city: the struggle and fight for equal status in the workforce, the struggle and fight against family violence, judicial controversies, and the right to have a say! Distance and expense, lack of facilities and resources, makes the needs greater or more pronounced. But they are the same needs, and the facilities and resources that are lacking are the very same facilities and resources city women have struggled to gain.

As a member of the New South Wales Women's Advisory Council from 1978 to 1981, I travelled with other members to many country centres in New South Wales: south coast towns including Merrimbula, Eden, Bega, towns in the Snowy Mountains, Queanbeyan, Lismore, Grafton, Coffs Harbour, Newcastle and more. Hundreds of women attended meetings where the work of the council was outlined and the participants spoke out about their demands for themselves, their children, their towns. As Kath Davey experienced in Albury-Wodonga, an expectation in calling such a meeting that a score or so of women will attend quickly proves false. Hundreds of women attended the meeting in Albury, as they did the meetings in other centres. At Queanbeyan, Lesley Norris put the strong view that resources should be made available for the setting up of a women's centre. One of the outcomes of that proposal was the establishment of Louisa, the Queanbeyan women's refuge (named after Louisa Lawson).

Environmental activism is a strong strand of women's politics in the country.

Environmental activism is a strong strand of women's politics in the country. The Landcare program, where farmers are dedicated to entrenching notions of the need for nurturance and care of the land, is firmly on the women's agenda in country towns and rural areas. At the fifth Women and Farms Gathering, held at Glenormiston in mid 1994, Landcare and the environment were topics high on the list. Gwen Baldini observes the need for non-Aboriginal Australia to learn from Aboriginal elders, and to once again inculcate the importance of replenishing the land rather than denuding it, and looking longterm at the consequences of land ravishment or land conservation. When Bev Roberts saw the environment threatened in Breamlea she joined the local residents' association. Eco-tourism is an essential issue so far as Marjorie Thorpe and the Lake Tyers Trust is concerned. With overfishing in Lake Tyers, who has control? Who has control over eco-tourism? These are issues for Janet Powell, who is concerned that so few women have a direct input into rural policy development, and so few women exercise political control in the field. Her country background meant that when she was in federal parliament she took up rural environmental issues, proposed the establishment of the senate select committee on agricultural and veterinary chemicals and alternatives. As Andrea Lofthouse says, the 'big' questions of agriculture are questions for women: land, the environment and agriculture are linked with how the world is run, how food is produced, why Western countries have so much, why some countries have so little, why there is famine. Organic gardening with permaculture principles can work. Unfortunately, politics can divide women, and care of the environment has triggered differences. The ecology movement has many strands that sometimes are seen, incongruously, in conflict. Thus despite the deep and growing commitment of so many country women to Landcare and associated environmental policies, Kath Davey found there was a divide between the 'country women' and the 'greenies'. The divide can arise, too, between ecologists and environmentalists, and loggers and the families of loggers and those working in the woodchip industry. Women are caught up in both sides of the argument.

In rural Australia (as elsewhere) life can be made difficult for women who identify clearly as feminist, and who dedicate their energy to achieving feminist goals. Doris Leadbetter notes that once the local council had pronounced there would be no abortion service available in her community – that was the end of it. NO ABORTION. Kath Davey and friends waged an enormous struggle in Albury-Wodonga for the right of women to have access to abortion in the local area, without having to travel the long distances to Melbourne or Sydney. She and her colleagues were vilified by the local press and both major political parties became involved.

Doris Leadbetter's expectation that she would participate in the business life of Bendigo was met with a swift denial: as she says, she quickly discovered that she was a *woman*, not simply an experienced committee worker. Business men and men in local government appeared to be embarrassed when she offered her experience. Development boards, hospital boards, building society boards and the university council were reserved for men only. *Women* should join 'useful' clubs and groups, do charitable work for no payment at all, and take office in groups fostering the arts or their menfolk, or so the men in power decreed. (Bev Roberts discovered this, too.) Sarah Stegley was the first woman ever, in her area, appointed to a hospital board, and her appointment was followed by appointments of more women. Bev Roberts finds that local politics in the country run on the basis of *involvement* rather than 'politics'. Local issues are sharper, clearer, smaller in scale and easier to identify and understand, so that a woman can take time to see where the power lies and assess the opportunities for involvement, then make a move. In Geelong she has found a total domination of men running everything, even girls schools, with less challenging of this inequity than would be so in the city. Lorraine Hunter's sense of being free is curtailed by the feeling of concrete underfoot, whilst as a lesbian feminist, Susan Hawthorne fears her life of relative freedom in Melbourne would be hampered were she to fulfil a sometime hankering for a return to country life.

Ironically, there may be greater job opportunities for women in the country. Jane Wilkinson found she was promoted up the teaching ladder with greater alacrity, handling budgets for her subjects, and developing skills and enjoying experiences that she would not have had had she begun her teaching life in a large city school. In acting and the arts,

Nancy Cato and Alison Brown met with this. Establishing herself as an artist was, for Alison Brown, hard work but relatively easy in the country: she participated in local artshows, and people quickly came to know her work. She exhibited throughout the country, which added to her confidence and to outside appreciation of her talent. (Although initial attempts to exhibit in the city were met with a rebuff – soon overcome – directly related to 'coming from the country'. Nothing is ever simple; is everything dual edged?) As for the aspiring actor, where else would one have the opportunity of playing all the major female Shakespearean roles before reaching the age of 20, asked one of Nancy Cato's mentors! As manager of the Lake Tyers Trust, Marjorie Thorpe has taken a job held only by men until her appointment, and has learned all sorts of skills and now knows the ins and outs of fishing, supervising road making, cattle breeding...

Yet opportunities can be curtailed, too, for women just as they can be for girls in schooling in rural areas. Janet Powell, Janeece Richards and Kath Davey each experienced difficulties in doing tertiary education from a long distance, particularly in having to juggle other responsibilities – of children, work, family and so on, as did Merryl Robson. Lara Finlayson, on the other hand, completed her Women's Studies degree with Deakin University without undue problems arising from her working in Shepparton at the time. Some educational institutions may be more attuned to the needs of long distance students, and mindful of setting assignments requiring 12 or 20 or 100 participants when the student lives in a 'community' of three or four, as did Kath Davey when she was doing a degree and living the live of a wife-of-a-forester somewhere in the Snowy Mountains scheme.

Women talk of the isolation of living in the country: this happened for Merryl Robson when she moved, with her husband, to Hamilton. Yet she had experienced a strong sense of community in Broken Hill, a country centre where she and her husband had lived immediately before their second country move. The children began to grow up, she joined local arts and community groups, and gradually found the community spirit she had thought was lacking – so much so, that she now, living in Sydney, misses that closeness and supportiveness that living in a country town can bring.

Women talk also of the isolation city living can bring with it: Pat Richardson saw 'no one but the Avon lady' from day to day. Jenni Mitchell, transferring from country to city, was precipitated into becoming involved in the neighbourhood house movement. This was a direct result of her own isolation in the suburbs in the midst of a teeming metropolis, and an appreciation and awareness of the 'separateness' experienced by other women living, particularly with young children, in suburban Melbourne. Claire Lupton noted 'the desperate loneliness' of women transferring to the country with husbands in public service moves, particularly where their children were too young for school. The local women needed no new friends, as their circles had been established from childhood.

...'the desperate loneliness' of women transferring to the country with husbands in public service moves, particularly where their children were too young for school.

Nonetheless country-dwelling women are very aware of the support that comes with rural living: everyone knows everyone, everyone 'chips in' to help in times of trouble, as Merryl Robson learned when she and her children were involved in a serious car accident, and Claire Lupton discovered when her husband was diagnosed with cancer. There is a strong sense of 'belonging', as Sarah Stegley, Bev Roberts and others know. Living in London, Adelaide and Melbourne does not enable a person to establish fully a relationship with the core or heart of the community, writes Bev Roberts. In her work with Australian Broadcasting Corporation (ABC) regional radio Agi Racz has experienced the strong loyalty of country listeners to the ABC and the depth of the hospitality that exists in the country. In her work in the country she has a sense of belonging, which she contrasts starkly with displaced humanity roaming city streets. There is a strong caring for one another, even in the larger towns, and people, she writes, are readily accepted into other's homes. The ABC is important to rural dwellers, accepted as a 'friend' and the producers and announcers hailed when they travel to the country communities. Their voices are welcomed on radio, into homes, on the tractors, and in the shops.

In moving from city to country, women may initially be seen as the 'city slickers' knowing nothing, yet eventually become accepted as an integral part of the local community, as happened for Andrea Lofthouse. Sharene Morrison settled back in, but acceptance can take time: Janeece Richards discovered this on returning to her home town to marry a local boy after 15 years away. An advantage for Marjorie Thorpe in becoming a part of her country community was her family connections with Lake Tyers. Belinda Tate's grandmother jokes that she's perhaps becoming a 'local' after 50 years in her neighbourhood!

Despite the greater ease with which community spirit exists in country communities, caring between neighbours can be fostered in the city. Victoria Whitelaw experiences this in her local community of Brunswick, inner-city Melbourne. Gwen Baldini has a strong attachment to the community that surrounds her home of 37 years in Nollamara, a Perth suburb.

And at the same time as being part of a community when living in the country, constant exposure to a culture where everyone *does* know everyone can be stifling. Knowledge of Barbara Silinger, who she was, where she was to stay, swept before her when she went, as a 19-year-old, to live in Wagin, her first school appointment. Living in Goroke as the school teacher meant Jane Wilkinson, although finding many positive aspects of 'everyone knowing everyone', had to 'escape' at times to the larger nearby town of Horsham to be 'anonymous'. For Gwen Baldini, leaving the country was essential to her wellbeing: as part of the Aboriginal community, she and her friends were singled out for harassment in hotels and at dances. She was deprived of the right to socialise with members of her family who were not exempt from the provisions of the *Aborigines Act*. Kath Davey found that political activism in a small country community can be extremely exposing: if one engages in a struggle for childcare, *everyone* knows who it is doing the agitating, and the label of 'abandoned or abandoning mother' is attached.

...constant exposure to a culture where everyone does know everyone can be stifling.

If someone's child creates trouble at school – it's no secret. If a woman leaves her husband, everyone knows. If a woman needs to escape from a brutal marriage or a child from familial abuse and exploitation, as Jacqualine Hobbs, Victoria Whitelaw and others know from their work in the field and their experience of living in the country, it is doubly difficult when rural attitudes, small communities, and local social censure are the penalties.

Rural communities are often depicted as conservative because they lack the racial and ethnic mix of cosmopolitan cities. In York, one of the earliest Western Australian settlements, Aboriginal people were certainly there, but did not take their rightful place in the local community: racist behaviour, backed by racist laws and attitudes, dictated otherwise. Forced to live as 'fringe dwellers', their experience was no doubt akin to that of Gwen Baldini in Katanning, an experience she escaped by leaving and going to Perth. There were marketgardens run by women and men of Italian descent, and like so many Australian country towns, in the 1950s and 1960s the Chinese restaurant was one of the few 'eating out' venues or places to buy takeaway food.

Jane Wilkinson's ethnic heritage includes a mother born in Australia who returned to Palestine as a baby, then back to Australia where she married a man whose family came from England. Doris Leadbetter settled in Bendigo after emigrating from England. Agi Racz brings to her work in regional radio her Hungarian heritage and memories of a country occupied by foreign forces. Merryl Robson has a Cornish and German heritage, and Alison Brown takes memories of a mother born in Cornwall with her on her travels in the country exhibiting her art, whilst Barbara Silinger, now 'completely a country person' was born in a New Zealand city; Deborah Towns, a committed city woman, emigrated to Australia as a one-year-old – she, like her father, was born in another country.

What shines through the stories of city women who were born in the country and country women born in the city is their appreciation of the dual experience of city and rural living. Determined not to romanticise the country or their lives outside Australia's capital cities, they cannot disguise the strength that has become a part of them. Lara Finlayson and Sharene Morrison know they are fortunate to have lived both in the city and the country. Agi Racz thrives on the strong sense of community her work in rural Victoria provides. Alison Brown glories in the beauty of nature. Nancy Cato, Janet Powell, Jenni Mitchell, Doris Leadbetter and others go back and forth, whether for 'permanent' stays or in taking day and week-long trips for work that is based in the city but country-orientated.

Determined not to romanticise the country or their lives outside Australia's capital cities, they cannot disguise the strength that has become a part of them.

Yet no one who has lived in the country can romanticise it. Gwen Baldini's memories of country life are tinged with recollections of racism. This experience can never be shut out, but Gwen Baldini invests her work with her understanding. Marjorie Thorpe experienced instances of racism that stand out against a childhood lived with strong family support for her Aboriginal cultural heritage and positive community friendships. Jacqualine Hobbs and Lorraine Hunter have strong cultural ties to support them through their country and city lives, too. As they say, the wisdom of elders can create a vision for us all.

Only those who have had no real connection with life in a rural community can invest it with foolish romanticism. Agi Racz, Jenni Mitchell, Robin Jackson, Victoria Whitelaw, Susan Hawthorne and others remember, in the midst of the bucolic splendours of the country, the death of loved pet pigs to replenish a larder starved through war, or the bloody slaying of sheep as a regular ritual of rural life. I remember with horror the brutality of kangaroo shooting at Wandering, near Pingelly, in the south west of Western Australia where my aunt had a farm and the nextdoor neighbours swept about the paddocks in a utility, spotlight blazing, careless of a poor aim, and taking multiple shots to kill. Death, blood, unnecessary brutality and an essential starkness are a part of country life, too.

Yet whether new or old converts to country life, or recent or long ago converts to the life of the city, *City Women Country Women* know they have been blessed. The smells and the sounds of the country can never be lost to women who have spent time on the land and in rural and mining towns. There is something very special about the Australian bush. *City Women Country Women* know this, without any shadow of doubt.

Index

Aborigines, Pacific and Torres Strait
    Islanders 2, 9, 23, 26-38 *passim*,
    59, 86, 117-131 *passim*, 169, 179,
    183-4, 188, 193-207 *passim*, 221,
    228, 250-6 *passim*, 302, 318
    and *Aborigines Act* 1905 (WA) 117,
    118, 120, 317
    and *Aborigines Act* 1910 (Vic.) 26
    and *Aborigines Act* 1928 (Vic.) 27
    and *Aborigines Bill* (SA) 7
    and Abstudy 127, 128, 206
    and adoption/*Adoption Act* (Vic.) 26,
    38
    alienation from own culture 124
    and assimilation/assimilationist
    policies 26, 28, 37-8, 117, 118,
    193-4
    and business/business methods 32-
    3, 35, 36-7, 38
    and bushtucker 121
    captured as slaves 4-5, 6
    and Community Employment
    Development Program (CEDP)
    31-3 *passim*
    and cultural stereotyping 34-5
    and curfew 120
    discrimination against/racism 12,
    26, 28, 117-131, 188, 305-6, 317,
    318
    and education 127, 128-9, 305-6
    and Land Rights 11, 33-4
    and language 117, 119-20, 200, 221
    and *Mabo* decision 33
    and need for autonomous services
    30, 127, 129-31
    and need for grief counselling 122
    and 1967 federal referendum 29, 37,
    118
    and oral traditions 34-5
    and police harassment 30, 122, 317
    and prison system 30, 120
    as servants 8
    and 'shame' 118-9, 120, 130

    and South African apartheid 120
    and taking of children 96, 117, 119,
    306
    violence against (particularly
    Aboriginal women) 4, 5, 30, 41,
    118
Aboriginal *see also* Lake Tyers
    Aboriginal Trust, Land Rights,
    political action
    Childcare Agency (Vic.) 26
    culture 34-6, 38
    Embassy (Canberra) 29
    health (particularly women's health)
    26, 30, 36, 38, 120, 122
    Health Service (Vic.) 26
    Keeping Place, Hamilton 226
    identity 27, 28, 31, 38, 252
    Lionel Rose Centre 27
    Cooperative, Morwell 27
    Provisional Government (APG) 35-6
Aboriginal and Torres Strait Islander
    Commission 250
abortion 73, 80-5 *passim*, 141, 142,
    314 *see also* family planning/
    contraception
Adams, Phillip 291
Adventure Island (television program)
    178
AIDS *see* HIV/AIDS
Akers, Elizabeth 297-8
Alcorso, Caroline 5-6, 13, 14
Albury-Wodonga Development
    Corporation 78
Albury-Wodonga Women's
    Collective 79
Amnesty International 11
Anders, Doug 218
Andersen, Hans Christian 155
Anthill Theatre 249
Araluen Arts Centre 188
Aranda (Arrente) 221 *see also*
    Aborigines, Pacific and Torres
    Strait Islanders

Argonauts, The (radio program) 291
'Argonaut's Pledge, The' 286
Aussie Wool Art Cooperative 216
Austin, Lynette 226
Australia for Women: Travel and Culture (Hawthorne and Klein) 107
Australia's Italians – Culture and community in a changing society (Castles, Alcorso, Rando and Vasta) 5, 13
Australian-Asian Society 247
Australian Broadcasting Commission/ Australian Broadcasting Corporation (ABC) 20, 20-22 *passim*, 24, 25, 39, 80-1, 154, 157-8, 184, 222, 223, 291, 316
    Friends of 99
    Regional Networks 154, 157-8, 316
Australian bush 41, 42, 43, 46, 53, 74, 88, 107, 167, 176, 235, 237, 243, 298, 299, 303, 318
Australian character 1-13 *passim*, 31, 41-2, 52, 58, 59, 66, 74, 111, 140, 143, 151-2, 176, 183, 188, 222, 230, 235, 252-3, 294, 297-8, 299, 309
Australian Conservation Foundation 99
Australian Democrats 10, 99, 104-5, 288-9
Australian desert/outback 113, 188, 205-6, 253, 318
Australian Farmers' Federation 86
Australian Labor government (federal) 140
Australian Labor Party (ALP) 18, 52, 62, 76, 80, 81, 84, 140
Australian Women's Education Coalition (AWEC) 281-2

Bach, Johan Sebastian 219
Baldini, Gwen 12, 117-131, 302, 305, 313, 316, 317, 318
'Ballad of the Drover, The'/'the drover's wife' (H. Lawson) 41, 74, 298
Bandicoot Information Centre 216

Bayly, Brian 217
Bayly, Ian 217
Bayly, Mabel (nee Burley) 217
Baynton, Barbara 65-6, 298
Beethoven, Ludwig von 219
Beauty and the Hedgehog (radio program) 91
Bellamy, Suzanne 50
Belle the Bushie 286-96 *passim*, 301
    see also Richardson, Pat
Belle on a Broomstick (Richardson) 286
Belle the Bushie (Richardson) 286
Ben Hur (film) 111
Bennett, Professor 220
Bessell, Jim 91
Biggles (W.E. Johns character) 179
Black Panthers 29
boardingschool 19-20, 28-9, 93, 94-7, 101-2, 112, 113, 146, 156, 167, 182, 210-11, 240, 261-2, 264, 304, 305, 310
Bolte government (Victoria) 27
Book Show, The (television program) 292
Bridge over the River Kwai, The (film) 111
British Broadcasting Corporation (BBC) 154
British Labour Party 20, 137
broadcasting *see* radio/radio stations, television/television stations
Brown, Alison 13, 235-43, 298, 303, 304, 315, 317, 318
Brown, Martha 8
Bruce, Mary Grant 65, 74
Brugman, Marieke 168, 171-4 *passim*, 176-7, 303
Bull, John 7
Burke's Backyard (television program) 291
Burley, Alice Laura 216-7

Calder, Margi 222
Campaign for International Cooperation and Disarmament 99

Canadian Broadcasting
    Commission/Corporation 20, 154
capital cities 318
    Adelaide, SA 66, 76, 217-9, 216,
        226, 228, 237, 239, 250, 251, 252,
        316
    Brisbane, Qld 193, 203, 239, 240,
        288, 303, 304
    Canberra, ACT 9, 12, 17-20 *passim*,
        79, 80, 140, 164, 239, 297, 300,
        304, 306, 310
    Hobart, Tas. 12, 159, 160, 161-2,
        304
    Melbourne, Vic. 13, 17, 19, 20, 27-
        8, 30-1, 52, 53, 56, 57, 59, 60-6
        passim, 72, 73, 74, 75, 79, 80, 85,
        86, 92, 94, 102, 104, 107, 108-9
        passim, 117-8, 135, 156, 165, 166,
        171, 188, 197, 198-9, 209-10,
        211, 212, 214-5, 216, 220-1, 223,
        224, 226, 228, 229, 230, 241-2,
        244, 245, 247, 248-9, 257, 264,
        279, 299, 300, 301, 302, 304, 309,
        310, 314, 316
    Perth, WA 12, 122, 123-4, 139-40,
        169, 194, 195-7, 206-7, 241, 242,
        266, 267, 269, 270, 271-2, 297,
        298, 299, 300, 301, 302, 303, 305,
        306, 307, 308, 310, 316, 317
    Sydney, NSW 10, 13, 17, 47, 79,
        80, 85, 86, 112, 144, 147, 148,
        171, 226, 227-8, 240, 241, 287,
        288, 290, 293, 301, 302, 310, 314
Captain Cook 3, 35
careers advice 147, 182, 194, 196, 211,
    305, 306 *see also* education
Cargher, John 291
Carlton Movie Theatre ('the Bug
    House') 112
Carson, Rachel 75
Casablanca, Lilliana 217
Catchpole, Margaret 6, 7
Cato, Leslie 178
Cato, Margaret 178,
Cato, Nancy 12, 178-89, 301, 302,
    303, 306, 308, 309, 314-5, 318
Cherry, Wal 184

Chief Justice's Task Force on Bias in
    the Judiciary, WA 117, 120
childcare *see* playgroups
Children's Hospital, Adelaide 252
Children's Hospital, Melbourne 222
Chipp, Don 99
Cisco Kid, The (television series) 112
city-country antagonism *see* country-
    city antagonism
city/urban life *see also* capital cities,
    country-city antagonism,
    distance/isolation
    advantages/disadvantages of 13, 23,
        46, 57, 62, 64-71 *passim*, 88, 97-8,
        113-4, 123, 138, 148, 161-2, 197,
        209-10, 212-3, 226-7, 228, 230,
        231, 237, 239, 240, 241-2, 247,
        248-9, 251, 253-4, 257, 264-5, 270,
        271-2, 273, 279, 280, 281, 284-5,
        287-94 *passim*, 302, 315, 316, 318
    reasons for moving from/to 1, 2, 9,
        10, 20, 28, 29-30, 64-71 *passim*,
        122, 147, 104, 209, 211, 220, 222,
        229, 240, 241, 245, 247, 252, 253,
        267, 280, 293, 302
Clough, Brent 291
coalfields 2, 27 *see also* industry
Coggin, Mrs 246
Commonwealth Employment Service
    (CES) 197
Commonwealth Public Service 248
Commonwealth Scientific and
    Industrial Research Organisation
    (CSIRO) 274
Commonwealth Youth Sunday 276
Connor, Mary 221
conservation *see* environmentalism,
    Landcare
contraception *see* family planning/
    contraception
Coomb, Mrs 195-6
Country Hour, The (radio program) 39,
    291
country-city antagonism 42, 71, 152
country/rural life *see also* country-city
    antagonism, country/provincial
    towns, distance/isolation

advantages/disadvantages of 9, 13,
23-6 *passim*, 37, 38, 41, 46, 51, 57,
59-60, 62-3, 64-71 *passim*, 86-7,
88, 98, 104, 115, 138, 145-6, 156-
8 *passim*, 163, 174, 175, 176, 208-
9, 212-3, 223-4, 225, 226, 228,
231, 236, 237, 240, 241-3 *passim*,
245, 249, 251, 253, 254, 255-6,
257, 265, 270, 271, 272, 275,
276-7, 279, 280, 281, 284-5, 287-
94 *passim*, 299-300, 309, 314, 315,
316-7, 318
reasons for moving from/to 1, 2, 9,
10, 22, 27, 31, 37, 43, 47, 50, 51,
54, 55-6, 57-8, 64-71 *passim*, 70,
75, 93, 148, 167, 171, 176-7, 212,
221, 222, 223, 229, 269, 287-94
passim, 299, 301, 302, 316
Country Practice, A (television series)
230
country towns/provincial cities
Albany, WA 123, 193, 204, 205
Albury-Wodonga, NSW/Vic. 22,
24, 72, 75-85 *passim*, 157-8
passim, 300, 301, 313, 314
Alice Springs, NT 187-8, 221, 302
Ardlethan, NSW 112
Ballarat, Vic. 60, 101, 185, 304
Bairnsdale, Vic. 229, 231, 299, 302
Bega, Vic. 17, 22-5 *passim*, 313
Benalla, Vic. 91-98 *passim*, 301, 310
Bendigo, Vic. 157-8 *passim*, 185,
300, 314, 317
Berry, NSW 47-8
Breamlea, Vic. 64-71 *passim*, 308, 313
Broken Hill, NSW 13, 216, 222,
223, 228, 300, 302, 315
Broome, WA 6, 12, 193, 194, 196,
197-8, 204, 205, 207, 300, 309
Bunbury, WA 118, 169, 266, 269,
271, 272
Bussleton, WA 118, 169
Cairns, Qld 193, 242
Castlemaine, Vic. 92
Coffs Harbour, NSW 291, 292,
300, 313
Collie, WA 266, 268, 269, 301

Darwin, NT 204
Daylesford, Vic. 6, 244
Derby, WA 6, 12, 193-4, 196, 198,
204, 207, 300, 309
Echuca, Vic. 103, 310-5 *passim*, 313
Ernabella, NT 221
Eurobin, Vic. 73
Fishermans Bend, Vic. 92
Fitzroy Crossing, WA 194
Galiwinku, NT 200
Gapuwiyak, NT 200
Geelong, Vic. 245, 247, 275, 276,
278, 285, 298, 300, 314
Gelorup, WA 266, 269, 270
Glenormiston, Vic. 312
Goroke, Vic. 56, 57, 299, 300, 309,
317
Grafton, NSW 313
Griffith, NSW 9
Hamilton, Vic. 216, 222, 223-7,
228, 302, 315
Hahndorf, SA 7
Hedland, WA 11
Horsham, Vic. 57, 59, 62, 157-8
passim, 300, 317
Hotham, Vic. 171
Jamieson, Vic. 165, 174-5, 299
Kadina, SA 235-7, 298
Kallangur 239, 303
Karratha, WA 11
Katanning, WA 117-23, 126-7, 302,
317
Kempsey, NSW 293, 301
Kerang, Vic. 92
Kojonup, WA 266, 269
Lake Tyers, Vic. 26, 28, 31-8
passim, 85-8, 302, 313
Lakes Entrance, Vic. 231
Leigh Creek, SA 250
Leongatha, Vic. 242
Leopold, Vic. 244, 244, 247
Lismore, NSW 313
Mandurah, WA 204-5
Mansfield, Vic. 165, 168-9, 174-5, 299
Margaret River, WA 169, 173
Meckering, WA 297, 303, 306, 307,
308

Mildura, Vic. 157-8 *passim*, 216, 222, 257
Milingimbi, NT 200
Moe, Vic. 37
Morriset, NSW 290
Morwell, Vic. 27, 300, 309
Mudgee, NSW 173
Murwillumbah, NSW 293
Nambucca Heads, NSW 286
Narrogin, WA 266, 269
Newcastle, NSW 313
Nhill, Vic. 99-101 *passim*, 299, 306, 307
Nowra, NSW 47
Parramatta (18/19th century), NSW 8
Pingelly, WA 318
Point Henry, Vic. 285
Poowong, Vic. 257
Port Augusta, SA 250, 255
Port Pirie, SA 216, 217
Quorn, SA 250, 251, 298
Queanbeyan, NSW 9, 313
Ramingining, NT 200
Renmark, SA 235, 237-9, 242, 298
Rupanyup, Vic. 74
Sale, Vic. 157-8 *passim*
Shepparton, Vic. 12, 157-8 *passim*, 174, 185, 208, 209, 211, 212-3, 299, 302, 309, 315
Swan Hill, Vic. 178-84, 186-7, 188, 189, 301, 302, 308
Tailem Bend, SA 238
Tamworth, NSW 291
Taree, NSW 144-58 *passim*
Tarrawingee, NSW 84
Tarrington (formerly Hochkirch), SA 216
Traralgon, Vic. 157-8 *passim*, 185
Triabunna, Tas. 159-64 *passim*, 299, 300
Tweed Heads, NSW 293, 301
Wagga Wagga, NSW 9, 10, 14, 52, 109, 112, 301
Wagin, WA 266, 269, 299, 317
Walpole, WA 193, 204, 205
Wandering, WA 8, 318
Wangaratta, Vic. 97

Warnambool, Vic. 157-8 *passim*
Wattamolla, NSW 39-51 *passim*
Wedderburn, Vic. 95
Wollongong, NSW 47
Wundowie, WA 266, 269
Yallourn, Vic. 26-9, 37-8 *passim*
Yeundumu, NT 221
York, WA 297, 298, 303, 306, 308, 310
Country Women at the Crossroads – Perspectives on the lives of rural Australian women in the 1990s (Franklin, Short and Teather) 10-1, 14
Country Women's Association (CWA) 41, 66, 269, 282, 284, 311, 312
Craig, Rene 95
Craig (Rinder), Floss 95
Creme (fashion design/dressmaking) 229, 231
criminal assault at home *see* violence against women
Croxford, Lorna 96-7

Dad and Dave (film) 111
Davey, Kath 11-12, 72-88, 299, 300, 301, 311, 313, 314, 315, 317
Davis, John 189
Debussy 219
Dekay, Fatima 131
department stores/supermarkets 56, 80, 162, 270, 272
  Coles 184
  Georges 221
  Ikea 199
  John Martins 237
  K-Mart 98, 203
  Moran and Cato 180
  Myer 180, 209, 264
Different Lives – Reflections on the Women's Movement and Visions of Its Future (Scutt) 9, 10, 14
disabilities *see* impairments
distance/isolation 12, 13, 23, 24, 36, 39, 43, 44, 56, 57, 59-60, 64, 66, 70, 75, 76, 77, 78, 87-8, 93, 100,

102, 104, 105, 109, 113, 123-4, 142, 147, 149, 152-3, 175-6, 184, 188, 195, 197, 212, 217, 223, 237, 239, 240, 242, 248, 257, 262, 264-5, 268, 269, 270-1, 279, 282, 284, 289, 290, 292, 300, 303, 309-11, 312, 314, 315-6
'Dolls and Daisy Chains' (painting, Brown) 236
Doogue, Geraldine 291
Drysdale, Anne 7
Dunstan, Don 172

Early Experience of South Australia (Bull) 7
eco-tourism 33, 313 *see also* environmentalism/conservation, Landcare
education 11, 18, 76, 79, 80, 119, 122, 136-7, 138, 142, 144, 151, 160, 175, 224-5, 230, 245-6, 251, 260, 261, 262, 265, 278, 279, 283, 285, 310, 315
    see also boardingschool, careers advice, schools, tertiary education/institutions
    Council of Adult Education book club 103
    primary 26, 53, 54-5, 74, 93-4, 101, 110, 136-7, 146, 160-1, 167, 182, 209, 210, 217, 267-8, 275, 276-8, 304-6, 307
    Dora Montessori school 137, 138
    Rudolf Steiner school 137
    secondary 18, 19-20, 28-9, 55, 94-5, 101-2, 138, 147, 161-2, 167, 182, 194, 195, 199, 210, 210, 213, 218, 229, 239, 240, 261, 267-8, 272, 276, 283, 305, 306-7
Ellis, Rita 226
Emerald Hill Theatre Company 184
Enclosure Acts (UK) 42
entertainment 29, 52, 56, 59, 91, 100, 110, 111, 172-4, 178, 222, 224, 227, 228, 237, 242, 245, 249, 258, 270, 279, 285, 287, 288, 292, 303

see also department stores/supermarkets, festivals/agricultural shows, radio/radio stations, television/television stations, transport
art galleries/concerts 17, 103, 169, 183, 219, 226, 227, 237, 239, 241, 242, 270, 272, 279, 292-3
books/bookshops/libraries 17, 56, 59, 91, 103, 113, 155, 156, 188, 209, 245, 258, 272, 275, 277, 289, 290, 298
theatre, film 17, 18, 25, 29, 52, 56, 59, 67, 80, 111, 120, 143, 148, 162, 180-1, 183, 222, 227, 239, 242, 248-9, 258, 270, 272, 288, 298
environmentalism 11, 33, 39-51 *passim*, 87-8, 104, 105, 121, 145, 152, 168-9, 228, 229, 238, 242, 313-4 *see also* Landcare
and political differences between women 87, 152, 313-4
Estes, Clarissa Pinkola 70, 71
Exorcism Trip, The (Roberts) 64, 71

Falling Woman, The (Hawthorne) 107
family planning/contraception 60-1, 73, 76, 80-5 *passim*, 93 *see also* abortion
Featherstone, Miss 246
Female Factory, The 3
feminism *see* Women's Movement
Feminist Dictionary, A (Kramarae and Treichler) 297-8
festivals/agricultural shows 111, 216
    Adelaide Agricultural Show 217-8
    Celebrating the Bandicoot in Hamilton 216
    Hamilton Heritage 226
    Moonraker Farm 55
    National Organic Gardening and Farming 216
    Shakespearean, Swan Hill 180-1, 184
Finlayson, Lara 12-13, 208-15, 299, 302, 304, 309, 312, 315, 318
Flinders, Matthew 275

flora and fauna
  domesticated 6, 12, 40-1, 44, 46, 53,
    56, 65, 67-8, 72, 77, 85, 93, 97,
    98, 107-8, 110, 114-5, 121, 144,
    145, 160, 169, 195, 209, 217, 222,
    229, 235, 236, 237, 244, 245, 260,
    275, 280, 291, 298, 299, 300, 310
  killing of 42, 57, 67-8, 92, 108, 115,
    121, 144, 155-6, 318
  native 45-6, 54, 51, 65, 67, 68, 71,
    77, 97, 98, 107-8, 114-5, 121,
    129-30, 135, 195, 217, 226, 227,
    236, 243, 245, 260, 263, 275, 284,
    291, 298, 303, 310, 318
Florence James Award (Pandora) 107
Foley, Gary 30
Food and Agricultural Organisation
    (FAO, UN) 170
431 (discotheque) 247
Franklin, Benjamin 157
Franklin, Miles 41
Fresh Evidence, New Witnesses (Allen,
    Hutchison and Mackinnon) 7, 13
Friedan, Betty 78
*From Massacres to Mining. The
    Colonisation of Aboriginal Australia*
    (Roberts) 4, 14
Frommer, Marianne 227

Garson, Margaret 223, 226
Gelonisi, Joe 291
Gilbert, Dorothy 8-9
Gilbert, Ronnie 83
Gilmore, Mary 41
Girl Guides 276
Goethe, Wolfgang 155
goldrushes 2
Goldstein, Vida 20
Goulburn Valley Loose Women's
    Group 214, 312
Gould League of Birdlovers 275
gourmet cycling tours 173-4
Gourmet Tours of Australia (Brugman
    and Stegley) 172-3
Goward, Prue 291
Graham, Billy 218

Greenpeace 99
Greer, Germaine 74, 156
Group, The (McCarthy) 156
Gullet, Joe 18
Gunn, Graeme 224
Gunn, Murray 224
Gunn, Noel 224

Hamilton Art Gallery 226
Hamilton Region 2000 227
Hamilton, Wally 21
Hanrahan, Barbara 218
Hanrahan Be Damned (play) 168-9
Hapsburg, Marie Antoinette 50
Hart, Pro 222
Hatt, Doug 221
Hawthorne, Susan 12, 107-16, 302,
    304, 308, 310, 314, 318
Helfgott, David 292
'Her Night Thoughts' (Roberts) 65
Hilarie Lindsay Award (NSW
    Women Writers Society) 286
HIV/AIDS 292
Hobbs, Don 250, 255 *passim*
Hobbs, Donna 252, 255 *passim*
Hobbs, Jacqueline 13, 250-6, 298,
    304, 305, 311, 312, 318
Hobbs, Jainee 252, 255 *passim*
Hobbs, Matthew 252, 255 *passim*
Hoffrichter, Erica 97
Hopalong Cassidy (television series) 165
Howqua Dale (gourmet retreat) 165,
    171-2, 174, 175, 176-7, 303
Hunter, Lorraine 12-3, 193-207, 300,
    302, 305, 309, 314, 318
Hyde, Miriam 219

impairments 114, 178
  activities involving children with
    183, 185-6
  children with 18, 109-10, 112, 183, 188
  community attitudes towards 112-3
  recovery from 178, 186-7
incest *see* violence against women
Independent Labour Party (UK) 137

industry 2-3, 6, 31-4, 42, 44-7, 53, 55,
     104, 159-60, 300, 314
  dairy 17, 42, 258
  farm 6-7, 31-4 *passim*, 42-50 *passim*,
     99-100, 160
  hotel/boardinghouse 7-8
  horse racing/training 53-4, 92, 93,
     165, 275, 280, 301
  mineral 2
  prison industry 2-3
  secondary, in country centres 27,
     159-60
International Women's Day 87

Jackson, Robin 13, 244-9, 300, 304,
     307, 309, 318
Johnston, Kaye 39-51 *passim*, 302
Jones, Jonah 187-9 *passim*
Journal (Robinson) 4
judicial bias 256, 312
  Chief Justice's Task Force on (WA)
     117, 120

Kelly, Bernadette 10, 14
Kennedy, Patricia 184
Key Centre for Women's Health 26, 36
King and I, The (musical) 279
Kirkby, Elisabeth 10, 14
Klein, Renate 107, 113, 214
Koori/s *see* Aborigines, Pacific and
     Torres Strait Islanders,
     Aboriginal
Kossatz, Les 226
Koval, Ramona 291
Krome, Miss 245, 246
Kyle, Louise 279
Kyle, Michael 279

La Mama 249
Ladies of Llangollen 41
Lake Tyers Aboriginal Trust 26, 31-8
     passim, 313, 315
Land Rights 11, 33-4, 168-9
Landcare 168-9 *passim*, 313, 314

  see also environmentalism,
     eco-tourism
Language in My Tongue, The
     (Hawthorne) 107
Laugh In (television series) 154
Law Reform Commission, Victoria 244
Lawson, Henry 74, 176
Lawson, Louisa 313
Leadbetter, Doris M. E. 12, 135-43,
     300, 305, 311, 314, 317, 318
Leitch, Adrienne 97
lesbians/lesbianism 47-51, 94, 114,
     138, 312
Lesbians On Organic Farms as Active
     Helpers (LOOFAH) 47-9
Liberal Party of Australia 80, 81
*Life Lines – Australian women's letters
     and diaries 1788 to 1840* (Clarke
     and Spender) 7, 14
*Living Generously – Women Mentoring
     Women* (Scutt) 235
Living Soil, The (Balfour) 41
Local Energy Transfer System
     (LETS) 49
Lofthouse, Andrea 11-2, 39-51, 298,
     302, 308, 312, 313, 316
Louisa Women's Refuge, Queanbeyan
     313
Lupton, Claire 11-2, 17-25, 300, 304,
     306, 309, 310, 316
Lupton, David 22-4 *passim*
Lynch, Bernard 157

Macarthur, Elizabeth 6-7, 167
McLeod, Marjorie 180-1
McDonald, Mary 7
McDougall, Valerie 214
McGregor, Dorothy 218-20
McGuiness, Bruce 30
MacKellar, Dorothea 74, 285
Macklin, Senator 288
Mader, Conrad Wilfred 216
Mader, Merryl *see* Merryl Robson
Magic Circle Club (television program)
     178, 184, 186
Man from Snowy River, The (film) 176

Marangaroo Women's Refuge 129
Marks, Danny 179, 183-4
Married Women's Retraining Scheme/National Employment and Training (NEAT) 75-6
Marsden Home 239
'Matter of Breaking Silence, A' (Wadsworth) 82-3
Melba, Nellie 20
Melbourne Meat Market Craft Centre 216
Menzies, Robert 18
Middle Brighton sea baths 245
Midsummer Night's Dream, A (William Shakespeare) 181
migration/migrant experience 5-6, 10-11, 12, 53, 135, 139, 154, 156, 159, 216, 267, 274, 280, 281, 282-3, 284, 314, 317-8
    of Chinese 5, 317
    of Italians 5-6, 123, 317
    by ship
        SS Orion 139
        La Famiglia 154
Minus, Mary 264
Mitchell, Jenni 13, 257-65, 299, 303, 304, 309, 310, 311, 315, 318
Mitzelfeldt, Miss 218
Molan, Donald 7
Moonraker Farm 39-51 *passim*, 302, 308 *see also* festivals
    Friends of Moonraker (FROMS) 49-50
    Moonraker Fair 50
Morpeth, Doug (Dougy) 181
Morris, Jenny 200
Morriset Hospital 289
Morrison, Sharene 12-3, 229-31, 299-300, 309, 316, 318
Morrison, Julie 229
Moses 275
Moss, Stirling 21
Mozart, Wolfgang Amadeus 219
multiculturalism 5-6, 53, 57, 58, 72, 91, 123-4, 127-8, 179, 216, 227, 230, 235, 236, 257, 274, 281, 292, 317

Munsters, The (television series) 185
Murri/s 202 *see also* Aborigines, Pacific and Torres Strait Islanders, Aboriginal
Myul Myul 193 *see also* Aborigines, Pacific and Torres Strait Islanders, Aboriginal
'My Country' (MacKellar) 285
My Fair Lady (musical) 279
My Wife, My Daughter, and Poor Mary Ann – Women and Work in Australia (Kingston) 8-9, 14

Nader, Ralph 75
Namatjira, Albert 188
Namatjira, Gus 188
Narogin people 193 *see also* Aborigines, Pacific and Torres Strait Islanders, Aboriginal
National Association for Sustainable Agriculture Australia (NASAA) 47
National Museum of Australia 228
National Party 52, 62
natural elements/disasters 63, 64-71 *passim*, 152, 239, 284, 307
    bushfires 40-1, 43, 44, 109, 152, 307-8
    cyclones/duststorms 180, 222, 307, 308
    droughts 142, 152
    earthquakes/landslides 45, 308
    famine/food shortage 155-6
    floods 6, 43, 45, 152, 239, 307, 308
    weather 63, 64-5, 143, 223, 228
Needham, Maud Helen 303
Negus, Mrs 306
New Horizons (radio program) 286
New South Wales Health Commission/Department 9, 81
Newcomb, Caroline 7
Neighbourhood Centre/House Movement 80, 257, 265, 315
newspapers/journals/magazines 52, 98, 99, 141, 142, 270-1
    Australian Women's Weekly 282
    Bega District News 24

Border Morning Mail
(Albury/Wodonga) 22, 81-83, 84
Daily Telegraph 289
Government Gazette 199
Lesbian Connection (USA) 47
Lesbian Network 47
Lesbians on the Loose 47
Meanjin 64
Metro (*SMH* insert) 293
Pol 171-2
Rural Women's Newsletter 311
Sydney Morning Herald (SMH) 290,
291
Telegraph Mirror 291
Time 223
Truth 103
Vogue Entertaining 171
Weekend Australian 286
Weekly Times (Gippsland) 31, 73
Woman-Church 289
Norah of the Billabong 74
Norris, Lesley 313
Nottle, Mrs 306
Number 96 (television program) 10
Nutcracker Suite, The (Tchaikowski)
306
Nyungar/s, Nyungar language 119,
120 *see also* Aborigines, Pacific and
Torres Strait Islanders, Aboriginal

O'Donnel, Mietta 171
O'Donnel, Patricia 171
Our Antipodes (Mundy) 2-3

Pacific Agribusiness Marketing Award
(ICM) 283
Paragon Cafe, Swan Hill 183
Parents and Citizens (P & C)
association/organisation 23, 174,
282
Parsons, Peter 220, 221
Paterson, Banjo 74
patriarchal
attitudes/behaviour/influences 54,
55, 67, 69, 70, 71, 72, 74-5, 80-5,
86-7, 98, 100, 141, 145, 146, 152,
157, 166-7, 174, 181, 277, 282,
283, 284, 297-9
Patties Bakery 231
Penguins (speakers' club) 103
Permaculture One (Mollison and
Holmgren) 44
Phantom of the Opera, The (musical)
147
Phillips, Marion 20
Pintubi 221 *see also* Aborigines, Pacific
and Torres Strait Islanders,
Aboriginal
Pitjantjatjara 221 *see also* Aborigines,
Pacific and Torres Strait
Islanders, Aboriginal
playgroups/childcare 23, 75, 76, 80
see also services/resources, support
networks
political action/activism 3-4, 11-12,
18, 23, 27, 38, 50, 52, 55, 61, 62,
68-70, 76, 79-88 *passim*, 101,
103-5 *passim*, 117, 125-8, 137,
140, 141, 153, 174-5, 269-70,
281-2, 283, 284, 288-9, 312, 317,
314 *see also* abortion,
environmentalism/conservation,
Land Rights, trade unionism,
violence against women
Aboriginal activism 4, 27, 29-31,
32-3, 35-6, 37-8, 117-8, 120-2,
125-6, 127-31 *passim*, 200-1, 250,
252, 256
Eureka Stockade 3
on goldfields 3
miners strikes 3
1956 Hungarian revolution/
uprising 155
prison riots 3
anti-Viet Nam war 281
Port Augusta Prison 250
Potter Farmland Plan 227
Powell, Elizabeth 8
Powell, Janet 12, 99-106, 299, 303,
304, 306, 307, 310, 311, 313, 315,
318
Power House 247

Preston, Yvonne 288
Prichard, Katharine Susannah 41

QUOTA Clubs 149

Racz, Agi 12, 154-8, 300-1, 304, 316, 317, 318
radio/radio stations 40, 60, 142, 286
    see also Australian Broadcasting Commission/Corporation, Canadian Broadcasting Corporation, women in television/radio industry
  Radio Budapest 154
  Radio National 291
  Radio 3RRR 91
  6WF Perth 154
  3LO Melbourne 154
  2BL Sydney 290, 291
  2CN Canberra 154
  2CO Albury 22
  2SER FM 286, 291
rape see violence against women
rape crisis centres see services/resources
Ravel 219
Red Cross/Red Cross Relief Fund 100, 247, 287, 307
Reeve, Carolyn 10-1, 14
regions/islands/mountains
  Arnhem Land, NT 12, 199, 200-3
  Atherton Tablelands, Qld 193, 203
  Barrossa Valley, SA 216
  Bass Strait, Tas./Vic. 4, 70
  Brune Island, Tas. 4
  Budderoo Plateau, NSW 45
  Bungin Bill, NSW 108
  Central Australia, NT/SA 301
  Cherubim Station/Pastoral Co., WA 4-5
  Cockatoo Island, WA 2
  Corio Bay, Vic. 275
  Darling, NSW/Vic. 222
  East Coast, Tas. 159
  Elcho Island, NT 201

Flinders Ranges, SA 250, 298
Germein Gorge, SA 217
Gippsland, Vic. 72, 85-8 passim, 241, 246, 257, 258, 311
Gove, NT 204
Hawkesbury River, NSW 6
Hunter/Lower Hunter, NSW 10, 173
Jeeralang Ranges, Vic. 235, 241
Kangaroo Island, Tas. 4
Kangaroo Valley, NSW 41-57 passim
Kimberley, WA 300
Lake Blowering, Vic. 72, 76
Lake Connewarre, Vic. 245
Latrobe Valley, Vic. 241
McLaren Vale, SA 217
Mallee, Vic. 93, 178, 180, 187, 257
Murray River, NSW/SA/Vic. 179, 238
North West Coast, Tas. 12
North West Shelf, WA 2
Pental Island, Vic.187
Pilbara, WA 2
Queenscliff, Vic. 245
Rabuma Island, NT 201
Radium Hill, SA 2
Richmond Hill, NSW 6
Riverina, NSW 109
Roxby Downs, SA 2
Snowy Mountains/Snowy Mountains Scheme 76, 313
Swan Valley, WA 173
Thursday Island, TS 193
Yorke Peninsula, SA 235
You Yangs, Vic. 275, 276
wheatbelt, WA 297
Removalists, The (play) 293
Retta Dixon Children's Home 280-1
Review of Government Administration (NSW, Wilenski)
Richards, Janeece 12, 144-153, 309, 310, 315, 316
Richardson, Henry Handel 20
Richardson, Pat 13, 286-96, 300, 301, 302, 309, 315 see also Belle the Bushie
Rigg, Julie 291
Rinder, Samuel 95

Ritchie, Rosalyn 172
Roadknight, Margaret 79, 85
Roberts, Bev 11-2, 64-71, 300, 302, 307, 308, 310, 313, 314, 316
Roberts, Janine 4, 14
Roberts, Wynn 184
Robson, Alistair Morris 225-6
Robson, David Morris 221-6 *passim*
Robson, Fiona 222-3, 225
Robson, Katriona Anne 224, 225-6
Robson, Merryl 13, 216-28, 300, 301, 302, 309, 315, 316, 317
Robson, Scott Davis 223, 225
role models 32, 54-5, 58, 61, 96-7, 102, 105, 115, 167, 180-1, 210, 213, 214, 218-9, 237-8, 252, 253-4, 299, 312
    Aboriginal elders as 32, 121, 254, 313, 318
    grandmothers/grandfathers as 29-30, 55, 102, 160, 236-7, 252
    mothers/fathers as 27, 29-30, 58, 73-4, 97, 106, 111, 214, 236, 237, 252, 258-64 *passim*, 307
    need for 105-6
Ross, Peter 291
Rousseau, Jean Jacques 285
Rowland, Robyn 214
Royal Society for the Prevention of Cruelty to Animals (RSPCA) 180
Royal Women's Hospital 221, 222, 235, 247
Rural Woman of the Year Award (ABC) 39
Rural Women's Network 257

Sackville-West, Vita 41, 46
SBS News (television program) 292
Scaife, Clyde 224
Scent of the Eucalypt, The (Hanrahan) 218
Schiller 155
schools *see also* boardingschool, education
    Adelaide High School (SA) 216, 218
    Annesley College (SA) 250, 251-2
    Ardlethan Central School (NSW) 110
    Bairnsdale High School (Vic.) 229, 230
    Benalla High School (Vic.) 96
    Brisbane Girls Grammar (Qld) 240
    Canberra High (ACT) 18
    Carmalite Convent (WA) 194
    Church of England Girls Grammar School ('The Hermitage')(Vic.) 245-6
    Corio Primary School (Vic.) 275, 276
    Derby District High School (WA) 193, 194
    Donnington Girls Grammar School (Vic.) 182
    Elizabeth College (Tas.) 162
    Eric Street State School (WA) 267
    Floreat Park State School (WA) 267
    Fort Street Girls High School (NSW) 39
    Geelong College (Vic.) 223, 246
    Haileybury College (Vic.) 95
    Hamilton High School (Vic.) 223
    Hollywood Senior High School (WA) 266, 267
    Hollywood State School (WA) 267
    Horsham College (Vic.) 52
    Huntingdale High (Vic.) 55
    Kent Street High School (WA) 194, 195, 196, 197
    Kewdale High School (WA) 194
    Mary's Mount (WA) 307
    Melbourne High School (Vic.) 96
    Methodist Ladies College (MLC)(Vic./SA) 28-9, 92, 95, 208, 210-1, 213, 214, 251, 304, 309-110
    Monivae College (Vic.) 225
    Musselborough State School (NZ) 267
    Nedlands State School (WA) 267
    North Shepparton Secondary College (Vic.) 208
    Presbyterian Ladies College (PLC)(Vic.) 19, 20, 305

Presentation Convent (Vic.) 154, 156

Propodollah State School (Vic.) 101

Quorn Area School (SA) 250, 251

Sacre Coeur (Vic.) 167, 171

St Mary's (WA) 197-8, 199

St Michaels (Vic.) 94-5

Scotch College (Vic.) 96

Swan Hill High School (Vic.) 182-3, 189

Telopea Park Primary School (ACT) 19

Triabunna District High School (Tas.) 159, 160-61

Wantirna Secondary College (Vic.) 208

Science and Health (Baker Eddy) 187

Science Show, The (radio program) 291

Schostakovich 219

Scutt, Jocelynne A. 1-14, 297-318

Sebastians 247

services/resources 10, 11, 13, 24-5, 32, 53, 58, 59, 73, 73, 76, 80, 98, 105, 151, 152, 200, 201, 208, 254, 300, 311, 312, 313 *see also* support networks, violence against women

bread/milk/grocery deliveries 179, 259-60, 303

mail deliveries 303

service clubs 23

Rotary, Apex, Lions 23, 79, 287

sexual/sexist harassment *see* violence against women

Shilliday, Lyn 225

Silinger, Barbara 13, 266-73, 298, 299, 301, 302, 317

Silinger, Peter 269

Silsbury, Elizabeth 218

Silver Chain (help for the elderly) 125

Singers of Renown (radio program) 291

Sisters – Sibling Rivalry, Sisterly Love (Scutt) 235

Small, Judy 79, 83

Smith, Fiona 202

Snowdon, Karen 291

Sound of Music, The (musical) 279

South Australian Family Violence Intervention Program 250, 255

Special Broadcasting Service (SBS) 58, 292

Spokeswomen's Programme, NSW Public Service 149-51

Central Coordinating Committee of 144

Spokeswomen's Programme Manual (NSW) 150-1

Spinifex Quiz Book: A Book of Women's Answers, The (Hawthorne) 107

St Vincent's Hospital 223, 226

State Theatre 248

Stegley Foundation 165, 175

Stegley, Kristin 172

Stegley, Sarah 12, 165-77, 302-3, 304, 310, 312, 314, 316

Stegley, Simon 172

Strauss, Johan 306

support networks 10-11, 32, 47-51 *passim*, 57, 62, 73, 76, 78, 81, 88, 98, 101, 104, 112-3, 130-1, 135-6, 146, 150, 158, 159-60, 164, 174, 214, 231, 242, 250, 254-5, 259, 269, 270, 271, 273, 283, 284, 311, 312, 315, 316

Sved, John 227

'Swallows' (Roberts) 68

Swan Hill Football Club 181

Swan Hill Regional Art Gallery 189

Swane, Valerie 291

Tate, Belinda D. 12, 159-64, 299, 300, 304, 305, 316

Taylor, Emily 97

television/television stations 17, 40, 97, 142, 176, 227, 277, 290, 291, 298 *see also* Australian Broadcasting Commission/ Corporation, Canadian Broadcasting Commission, Special Broadcasting Service, women in television/radio industry

ATV-O/Channel 10 185

CBS Network (USA) 154

GMV-6 Shepparton 185
NBN Newcastle 291
NR-TV 291
Prime TV 291
WIN TV 24
tertiary education/institutions 19, 36,
    55, 74, 75, 76, 77, 103, 112, 128,
    138, 148, 149, 162-3, 166, 169,
    208, 211-2, 215, 220, 226, 230,
    241, 246, 247, 262, 266-7, 272,
    279, 280, 305, 315
    Aboriginal Program Centre (UWA)
        (WA) 207
    Bega College of Technical and
        Further Education (TAFE)(NSW)
        39, 48
    Burwood Teachers College (Vic.) 262
    Claremont Teachers College (WA)
        266
    Columbia College, Los Angeles
        (USA) 154
    Council for Adult Education (CAE)
        (Vic.) 103
    Curtin University (WA) 194, 199
    Deakin University (Vic.) 208, 212,
        244, 315
    Dookie Agricultural College (Vic.)
        96, 166, 167
    Geelong Teachers College (Vic.)
        274, 280
    Glenormiston College (Vic.) 166,
        297, 313
    Gippsland Institute of Advanced
        Education (Vic.) 241
    King Edward Technical College
        (NZ) 266
    LaTrobe University (Vic.) 112-3,
        226, 274
    Leyden University (Netherlands)
        274
    London University (UK) 138, 305
    Longranong Agricultural College
        (Vic.) 166
    McCabe Academy of Dressmaking
        and Design (Vic.) 229, 230
    Macquarie University (NSW) 222
    Massey University (NZ) 165, 166

    Melbourne College of Advanced
        Education (MCAE)(Vic.) 212
    Monash University (Vic.) 52, 55,
        225, 274
    Olympia Business College (WA)
        196, 197
    Ormond College (Melb. Univ.)(Vic.)
        220, 222, 225
    Perth College of Technical and
        Further Education (TAFE)(WA)
        117, 128-9
    Port Augusta College of Technical
        and Further Education (TAFE)
        (SA) 250
    Riverina College of Advanced
        Education (CAE)(NSW) 76
    Royal Melbourne Institute of
        Technology (RMIT)(Vic.) 211,
        274
    St Catherine's College (UWA)(WA)
        193, 206
    Swinburne Institute of Technology/
        Swinburne University (Vic.) 244,
        246
    University of Adelaide (SA) 216,
        220, 227
    University of Ballarat (Vic.) 216
    University of Cambridge (UK) 297
    University of Melbourne (Vic.) 64,
        91, 216, 220, 222, 225, 244, 246,
        262, 274, 278, 297
    University of Michigan (USA) 297
    University of New England (NSW)
        24
    University of New South Wales
        (NSW) 297
    University of Queensland (Qld) 203
    University of Saskatchewan
        (Canada) 220
    University of Sydney (NSW) 297
    University of Tasmania (Tas.) 159,
        162-3
    University of Technology, Sydney
        (NSW) 288, 291
    University of Western Australia
        (WA) 193, 197, 206-7, 266, 267,
        269, 297, 308

Women's College (Melbourne Univ.)(Vic.) 220, 221

Texas Rangers, The (television series) 165

Theatre Works 249

Thebarton Town Hall 219

Thompson, Joyce 200

Thorpe, Marjorie 11-12, 26-38, 300, 302, 304, 305, 309-10, 313, 316, 318

Three Stooges, The (television series) 112

Thumping Tum 247

Tivoli 180

Tolerable Good Success – Economic opportunities for women in New South Wales 1788-1830, A (Perrott) 7-8, 14

Towns, Deborah 13, 274-85, 298, 300, 302, 305, 310, 311, 312, 317-8

Towns, Max 285

Towns, Sam 279, 285

trade unionism 52, 55, 61-2, 91

transport/transport systems 44, 67, 147, 151, 208, 228, 230, 236, 239, 242, 248-9, 264, 266, 284,

  by bicycle 17, 18, 101, 151, 172-4 *passim*, 179, 209, 248, 259, 261, 270, 309, 310

  by bus/train/tram 67, 102, 122-3, 135-6, 145, 147, 162, 167, 195-6, 209, 237, 257, 279, 293, 308-9

  horse and buggy 74, 236

  by plane 195

  by school bus 94, 102, 110, 276, 310-11

Transvestite Next Door, The (Roberts) 64

Trask, Diana 156

Uncle Tobys 283

United Nations Decade for Women 79

University of Melbourne 96, *see also* Key Centre for Women's Health

Uphill All the Way (Daniels and Murnane) 2, 4-5, 14

Verity, Miss 276

Victorian Department of Education 52, 55

Victorian Writers Centre 64

VIEW Club (Voice, Interests and Education of Women) 287

violence against women 4, 5, 11, 23, 24-5, 30, 39, 60, 73, 93, 98, 112, 118, 129, 130, 145, 151, 208, 213, 250, 251, 253, 312, 37

Wadsworth, Yoland 81-3

Wagga Wagga Immigrant Women's Support Group 10

Waif Wander 41

Wailbri (Walpiri) 121 *see also* Aborigines, Pacific and Torres Strait Islanders, Aboriginal

Walsh, Eliza 7

Wandering Girl (Ward) 8, 14

Ward, Sarah 8

Ward, Glenyse 8, 14

weather *see* natural elements/disasters

Wendt, Jana 156

Wesfarmers 169, 303

Wintal, Robert 200

Women's Electoral Lobby (WEL) 99

Which Witch (women's rock band) 50

White, M.J.D. 221

Whitelaw, Victoria 12, 91-8, 301, 304, 310, 316, 317, 318

Whitlam, Freda 19

Whitlam, Gough 19, 75, 294

Whitlam government 75, 300

Whitlam, Margaret 294

Whitlam, Mrs (snr) 18-9

Whittaker, Mrs 97

Who's Who of Australian Women (Lofthouse) 39

Wilenski, Peter 149-50

Wilkinson, Jane 11-2, 52-63, 299, 300, 301, 302, 309, 314, 317
Wilkinson, Sarah 52
Williams, Elizabeth 9, 10, 14
Williams, Stanley 306-7
Willing Workers On Organic Farms (WWOOF) 47
Wilson, Mrs 196
Winnie the Pooh 178
Wollstonecraft, Mary 285
'Woman Alone' (Richardson) 289-90
women
  as actors/acrobats/artists 41, 111, 178, 184-6, 187, 235, 241-2, 315
  and cattle farming 31, 302, 315
  as cattlehands/sheep herders 7, 110, 229, 279, 298
  in dairy industry 9, 299
  discrimination against 19, 20-2, 58, 69, 106, 149-51, 166-7, 168, 181-2, 188, 201-3, 248, 282, 283, 314
  and (un)equal pay 248
  as family members/support 2, 32, 58-9, 72-3, 75, 77, 91, 105, 106, 135-6, 144-5, 148, 160, 163, 170-1, 217, 224, 236, 237, 251, 259, 267, 280, 297-8, 315
  as farmers/farm labourers 5-6, 7, 110-1, 141-2, 144, 165, 167-8, 169, 170, 209, 224, 236, 238-9, 253, 279, 280, 297-8, 311, 312
  and fear of success 277-8
  and fishing industry 31-2, 302, 315
  and fundraising 23, 100, 141, 307, 314
  and gardening/as gardeners 2, 5, 41, 46-51 passim, 91, 217, 238, 259, 291, 294, 298, 299, 313, 317
  and health 9, 11, 23, 26, 36, 59, 61, 67, 80-85 passim, 92, 95, 97, 101-2, 109-10, 136, 186-7, 204-5, 208, 223, 260
  representation in media 80-5 passim, 314
  and seniority system 58, 248
  and sense of place 12, 66, 177
  and sexism/sexist 'jokes' 166, 213-4, 246, 278, 276, 311
  as slaves/servants 4-5, 8-9
  as shearers 7
  in television/radio/media industry 17, 20-2, 24, 79, 157-8, 178, 184-6, 286
  as travellers 1, 20, 22, 26, 75, 154, 159, 160-1, 165, 169-70, 199, 200, 204-6, 208, 212, 220, 221, 248, 272, 282, 283, 309
  as victuallers/hotel licensees 7
  as workers 1, 2, 5, 20, 27, 31, 36-7, 39-51 passim, 55, 57-8, 78, 87, 91, 92, 98, 122, 140-1, 144-5, 162, 170, 171-2, 175, 181-2, 193, 197-8, 199-203 passim, 212, 213, 214, 215, 226, 246, 247, 248, 250, 256, 268, 269, 273, 274, 278, 281, 282, 283, 287, 294, 298, 299, 301, 302, 312, 314, 315
Women of the Centre (Pring) 14
Women and Farms Gathering 313
Women's Advisory Council (NSW)/ Women's Coordination Unit 79, 313
Women's Land Army 160
Women's Movement/feminism 60, 70, 72, 78, 88, 112-3, 115, 141, 145, 174-5, 181-2, 208, 213, 214, 256, 262-3 passim, 281-2, 283, 294, 312, 313, 314
Women's presses/publishing *see also* newspapers/journals/magazines
  Artemis Publishing 235
  Gumleaf Press 286
  Pandora Press 107
  Spinifex Press 107, 113
women's refuges *see* services/resources
Women's Studies 52, 208, 212, 214
'Women's Ten Commandments, The' (Richardson) 294-5
Wool and Rural Industries Skills Training Centre 216
Wran, Neville 150

Xerox Fastbooks Award 286

Yangennanock Women's Group 226
Yorgum Aboriginal Family
    Counselling Service 117, 129-31
Yorkshire Cricket Club 136
Young Women's Christian
    Association (YWCA) 99, 257
  Designs by Wise Women Shop 257

Zorro (television series) 112

About Artemis Publishing

Artemis Publishing is a feminist publishing house established to publish and promote women's writing. Artemis specialises in biography and autobiography, publishing the series 'Women's Voices, Women's Lives', series editor Jocelynne A. Scutt. Books in the series include *Breaking Through – Women, Work and Careers, As a Woman – Writing Women's Lives, Glorious Age – Growing Older Gloriously, No Fear of Flying – Women at Home and Abroad, Taking a Stand – Women in Politics and Society*, and *City Women Country Women – Crossing the Boundaries*.

Forthcoming books in the 'Women's Voices, Women's Lives' series include *Singular Women – Reclaiming Spinsterhood, Sisters – Sibling Rivalry, Sisterly Love, Living Generously – Women Mentoring Women, My Mother, My Daughter, Different Lives – Reflections on the Women's Movement and Visions of its Future, Growing Up Feminist – The New Generation of Australian Women, Growing Up Feminist Too – Raising Women, Raising Consciousness*, and *Force of Circumstance*.

Artemis also publishes feminist crime fiction, detection and mystery writing. Melissa Chan's *One Too Many* and Sue Neacy's *Murder in Northbridge* head the list, together with Melissa Chan's short stories, *More On Getting Your Man*. The Artemis crime anthologies include *A Modern Woman and other crimes, Calling Up The Devil and associated misdemeanours* and *Don't Go Near the Water and additional warnings*, edited by Melissa Chan and J. Terry.

Breaking Through
Women, Work and Careers

compiled & edited by Jocelynne A. Scutt

'If you go about saying you want and like to be a Worker, you'll be considered dangerous,' Elizabeth Hawes wrote in 1948.

The 22 contributors to *Breaking Through* are women who enjoy being Workers – their work and careers are central to their lives. Their lives are filled also with the pleasures and support of friends, mothers, children, partners; memories of impressive maiden aunts and grandmothers; recognition from fathers or school principals; 'cheering on' from colleagues or acquaintances.

With an introduction and epilogue by Jocelynne A. Scutt, *Breaking Through – Women, Work and Careers* tells the stories of women who are gloriously, admirably, wonderfully dangerous.

Contributors: Lisa Bellear, Greta Bird, Patricia Brennan, Jane Cafarella, Jennifer Coate, Gay Davidson, Irina Dunn, Diane Fingleton, Lariane Fonseca, Janine Haines, Jackie Huggins, Louise Liddy-Corpus, Melba Marginson, Irene Moss, Dawn Rowan, Sue Schmolke, Gracelyn Smallwood, Shirley Stott Despoja, Fiona Tito, Irene Watson, Carolyn Watts, Beth Wilson.

ISBN 1 875658 00 9
RRP $19.95

As a Woman
Writing Women's Lives

compiled & edited by Jocelynne A. Scutt

In her book, *Silences*, the United States feminist Tillie Olsen writes of the 'unnatural silences' of those who have never been able to write, or have never been able to find the time to do so. In Australia in 1888, some eighty years earlier, Louise Lawson determined that women should have a 'printing ink champion' to ensure women's voices should not only be heard, but be projected through the printed word.

In Australia in the 1990s, the silences that abound about women's lives and in women's lives must continue to be broken.

With an introduction and epilogue by Jocelynne A. Scutt, *As A Woman – Writing Women's Lives* brings into the broader public arena the words and voices of 22 women. These women have stepped out, into the world, as political and social beings. They are 'ordinary' and 'extraordinary' women.

Contributors: Patmalar Ambikapathy, Marie Andrews, Katie Ball, Faith Bandler, Pamela Ditton, Irene Greenwood, Edith Hall, Merrin Hartrick, Robin Joyce, Renate Klein, Lenore Manderson, Rebecca Maxwell, Betty Olle, Moira Rayner, Julie Reiter, Michelle Schwarz, Kay Setches, Sandra Shotlander, Judy Small, Lynne Spender, Anne Thacker, Gail Warman.

ISBN 1 875658 02 5
RRP $19.95

Glorious Age
Growing Older Gloriously

compiled & edited by Jocelynne A. Scutt

'Fifty to sixty is a great decade. You've developed your confidence,' says Thea Astley. 'You're brash in your teens, timorous in your twenties, and perhaps into your thirties. Confidence starts developing at about 40.' The contributors to *Glorious Age – Growing Older Gloriously* talk about their experience of 'growing older' – gloriously.

The arrival of that first grey hair, that first wrinkle, is matched in these 22 women by a developing sense of being anchored firmly in the world. Added years bring added wisdom. Whether engaged in political action or personal contemplation, the women have found that ageing can be joyous, creative, powerful. 'The most creative force in the world is the menopausal woman with zest.' Margaret Mead's words are echoed in *Glorious Age*.

Contributors: Kath Balfour, Fran Bladell, Val Buswell, Joyce Clague, Joan Coxsedge, Heather Crosby, Susan Duffy, Lella Fazzalori, Ellie Gaffney, Jill Gallagher, Margaret Henry, Thelma Hunter, Ethel Kirsop, Meme McDonald, Thea Mendelsohn, Margaret Reynolds, Giovanna Salomone, Phil Slattery, Joyce Stevens, Jean Tom, Joan Tompsett, Edith A. Webb.

ISBN 1 875658 03 3
RRP $19.95

No Fear of Flying
Women at Home and Abroad

compiled & edited by Jocelynne A. Scutt

'I should like to go back to Australia,' wrote Australian writer Christina Stead to a compatriot in 1950, 'but the fare there and back is so much!' Distance and the cost of travel did not, however, prevent her from going to Europe nor, later, returning home.

What leads women to travel thousands of miles to make new lives for themselves, whether at home or away from home? *No Fear of Flying – Women at Home and Abroad* recounts the lives of 25 women and their courage in leaving Australia for life abroad, or leaving home and making 'home' in Australia. *No Fear of Flying* is a tribute to the humour and initiative of all women who have travelled and who plan to do so.

Contributors: Penelope A. Andrews, Vivien M. Altman, Mary Ann Bin-Sallik, Vivienne Correa, Janice Farrell, Gisela Gardener, Gillian Hanscombe, Sylvia Hennessy, Kristin Henry, Anne Hickling Hudson, Kathy Kituai, Janet Labatut, Gloria Lee, Ofelia Lopez, Sandra McCallum, Dorota Malchevski, Jan Mock, Susan Ogier, Marlies Puentener, Jennifer Simon, Tui Taurua, Lynne Wenig, Ania Wilczynski, Janet Wilczynski, Mickey Zhu.

ISBN 1 875658 04 1
RRP $19.95

Taking a Stand
Women in Politics and Society

compiled & edited by Jocelynne A. Scutt

There is nothing more political than a political woman! In May 1889, the first anniversary of the publication of the *Dawn*, Louisa Lawson observed that over the year, 'scores of women' with similar aims and hopes came forward to support the journal. Almost one hundred years later, Pat Eatock, a Koori activist dividing her time between New South Wales and Canberra, noted the strong role Aboriginal women play in the fight against racism and for recognition: 'The Land Rights Movement would not have survived had it not been for the role of Aboriginal women...'

Taking a Stand looks, through women's eyes, at the many ways in which women individually and as members of organisations stand up for the rights of women, and of themselves.

Contributors: Jean Arnot, Melanie Eagle, Sabina Erika, Marlene Goldsmith, Peg Hewett, Donna Jackson, Judy Jackson, Sheila Jeffreys, Eva Johnson, Rhondda Johnson, Barbara Lewis, Edith McNeill, Annie Ngyina Milgin, Chris Momot, Carmelle Pavan, Nancy Rehfeldt, Lee Rhiannon, Misha Schubert, Daisy Serong, Moira Shannon, Joan Taggart, Jo Vallentine, Dawn Wilson.

ISBN 1 875658 12 2
RRP $19.95

Singular Women
Reclaiming Spinsterhood

The seventh book in the 'Women's Voices, Women's Lives' series

Spinsters unite! Revel in the splendours of the singularity of life, determined to make choices independently, while fortunate enough to have strong support from friends and family – and other 'singular women'.

I have made my way 'without aid from any man's arm,' Alice Henry declared, reviewing Cicely Hamilton's book, *Marriage as Trade*.

Australia has a great spinster tradition. Catherine Helen Spence, Vida Goldstein, Stella Miles Franklin and Alice Henry, amongst many others, built on the lives of single women before them, and established a clear lead for singular women today. They wrote, argued, travelled, politicked, debated, fought for the vote in Australia and internationally, spoke from public platforms, lobbied in the labour movement, worked in the suffrage movement, and added to the foundations of the past to create the Women's Movement of today.

Economic independence, the right to say and do what one wants, to live an autonomous life – these are important aims for women. In *Singular Women – Reclaiming Spinsterhood* women who have never married write of the pleasure in singularity that comes with being 'your own person' – and the multiplicity of ways in which the world regards singular women – and singular women regard it.

Contributors include: Yvonne Allen, Veronica Brady, Beverley Broadbent, Jan Dillow, Edwina Doe, Margaret Doyle, Kym Druitt, Janet Hunt, Jeanette Knox, Louise Lavarack, Kathryn Mill, Julie Morgan, Kathy Mueller, Sue Neacy, Gayle Poppi, Ruth Ross, Bernadette Selfe, Jean Skuse, Mary Stainesby, Leonie V. Still.

ISBN 1 875658 11 4
Forthcoming April/May 1995

Living Generously
Women Mentoring Women

The eighth book in the 'Women's Voices, Women's Lives' series

'It's the people around me, the people I know, who impress me and are my role models,' writes Marie Andrews, anthropologist and lawyer. 'My grandmother, mother and sisters I have admired and looked up to.'

Role models and mentors: women *do* have them – all around. Far from being bereft of models to emulate, supporters to encourage and advise, women's lives are replete with modelling and mentoring. Then, having appreciated the support and encouragement of others, these women have an opportunity themselves to become and to be role models and mentors to others.

So many women recognise the importance of other women in their lives: the supports of grandmothers, mothers, sisters, great aunts, the woman down the road, the nextdoor neighbour, the school principal. And many women, having taken advantage of that advice, the wit and wisdom, seek to return this gift by handling on their own friendship and support to others.

Living Generously – Women Mentoring Women tells through the voices of women the ways in which women support women and reciprocate in kind, living lives of generosity and so creating generous lives.

Contributors: Val Ahern, June Benson, Edna Chamberlain, Jan Chapman-Davis, Lenore Coltheart, Carmel Guerra, Susan Kelly, Joan Kirner, Ruth E. Letche, Audrey McDonald, Melinda McPherson, Val Marsden, Edith Morgan, Joyce Nicholson, Marj Oke, Mary Owen, Kay Saunders, Evelyn Scott, Natasha Stott Despoja, Maureen Watson, Wendy Weeks.

ISBN 1 875658 09 2
Forthcoming April/May 1995